The Development of the Criminal Law of Evidence in the Netherlands, France and Germany between 1750 and 1870

Legal History Library

VOLUME 32

Series Editors

C.H. (Remco) van Rhee, *Maastricht University*
Dirk Heirbaut, *Ghent University*
Matthew C. Mirow, *Florida International University*

Editorial Board

Hamilton Bryson, *University of Richmond*
Thomas P. Gallanis, *University of Iowa*
James Gordley, *Tulane University*
Richard Helmholz, *University of Chicago*
Michael Hoeflich, *University of Kansas*
Neil Jones, *University of Cambridge*
Hector MacQueen, *University of Edinburgh*
Paul Oberhammer, *University of Vienna*
Marko Petrak, *University of Zagreb*
Jacques du Plessis, *University of Stellenbosch*
Mathias Reimann, *University of Michigan*
Jan M. Smits, *Maastricht University*
Alain Wijffels, *Université Catholique de Louvain, Leiden University*, CNRS
Reinhard Zimmermann, *Max-Planck-Institut für ausländisches und internationales Privatrecht, Hamburg*

The titles published in this series are listed at *brill.com/lhl*

The Development of the Criminal Law of Evidence in the Netherlands, France and Germany between 1750 and 1870

From the System of Legal Proofs to the Free Evaluation of the Evidence

By

Ronnie Bloemberg

BRILL
NIJHOFF

LEIDEN | BOSTON

Cover illustration: Execution of J.B.F. van Gogh, on Saturday the 4th of April, 1778. Engraving by Dirk Schuurman. Collectie Atlas Dreesmann, Stadsarchief Amsterdam.

Library of Congress Cataloging-in-Publication Data

Names: Bloemberg, Ronnie, author.
Title: The development of the criminal law of evidence in the Netherlands, France, and Germany between 1750 and 1870 : from the system of legal proofs to the free evaluation of the evidence / Ronnie Bloemberg.
Description: Leiden ; Boston : Brill | Nijhoff, 2020. | Includes bibliographical references and index.
Identifiers: LCCN 2019044688 (print) | LCCN 2019044689 (ebook) | ISBN 9789004415010 (hardback) | ISBN 9789004415027 (ebook)
Subjects: LCSH: Evidence, Criminal--Europe--History. | Burden of proof--Europe--History. | Evidence, Criminal--Netherlands--History. | Evidence, Criminal--France--History. | Evidence, Criminal--Germany--History.c | Evidence (Law)--Europe--History.
Classification: LCC KJC9597 .B56 2020 (print) | LCC KJC9597 (ebook) | DDC 345.4/0609034--dc23
LC record available at https://lccn.loc.gov/2019044688
LC ebook record available at https://lccn.loc.gov/2019044689

Typeface for the Latin, Greek, and Cyrillic scripts: "Brill". See and download: brill.com/brill-typeface.

ISSN 1874-1793
ISBN 978-90-04-41501-0 (hardback)
ISBN 978-90-04-41502-7 (e-book)

Copyright 2020 by Koninklijke Brill NV, Leiden, The Netherlands.
Koninklijke Brill NV incorporates the imprints Brill, Brill Hes & De Graaf, Brill Nijhoff, Brill Rodopi, Brill Sense, Hotei Publishing, mentis Verlag, Verlag Ferdinand Schöningh and Wilhelm Fink Verlag.
All rights reserved. No part of this publication may be reproduced, translated, stored in a retrieval system, or transmitted in any form or by any means, electronic, mechanical, photocopying, recording or otherwise, without prior written permission from the publisher.
Authorization to photocopy items for internal or personal use is granted by Koninklijke Brill NV provided that the appropriate fees are paid directly to The Copyright Clearance Center, 222 Rosewood Drive, Suite 910, Danvers, MA 01923, USA. Fees are subject to change.

This book is printed on acid-free paper and produced in a sustainable manner.

Contents

Acknowledgements   IX

1 Introduction   1
   1.1 The Connection with the Criminal Justice System as a Whole   5
   1.2 The Theoretical Framework   10
   1.3 The Approach and Limitations   12
   1.4 The Periodization   15
   1.5 The Structure and Content of the Chapters   18

PART 1
The Theoretical Framework and the Development of the Criminal Law of Evidence in France and Germany

2 The Characteristics of the System of Legal Proofs   27
   2.1 Introduction   27
   2.2 The Abandonment of the Ordeal and the Development of the Inquisitorial Procedure   27
   2.3 The Central Characteristics of the System of Legal Proofs   38
   2.4 The Thesis of Langbein   55
   2.5 Conclusion   62

3 The Theoretical Framework   66
   3.1 Introduction   66
   3.2 The Political-constitutional Discourse   67
   3.3 The Epistemological Discourse   88
   3.4 Conclusion   115

4 The Reform of the Criminal Law of Evidence in France 1750–1870   118
   4.1 Introduction   118
   4.2 The Regulation of the Criminal Law of Evidence in France until 1789   120
   4.3 The Reform Discussion on the Criminal Law of Evidence between 1750 and 1789   124
   4.4 The Discussions in the Constitutional Assembly (1789–1791)   145

4.5 The Development of the Criminal Law of Evidence between 1791 and 1814   159
4.6 The Criminal Law of Evidence between 1815 and 1848   168
4.7 Conclusion   174

5 **The Development of the German Criminal Law of Evidence 1750–1870**   177
5.1 Introduction   177
5.2 1750–1812: The Abolition of Judicial Torture and the Start of the Reform Debate   181
5.3 The German Discussion between 1812 and 1848   196
5.4 The Discussion on the Criminal Law of Evidence between 1848 and the 1870s   239
5.5 Conclusion   242

PART 2
The Development of the Criminal Law of Evidence in the Netherlands 1750–1870

6 **The Criminal Law of Evidence in the Dutch Republic between 1600 and 1795**   247
6.1 Introduction   247
6.2 The Regulation of the Criminal Law of Evidence in the Juridical Literature   251
6.3 The Practice of the Criminal Law of Evidence in the Dutch Republic   278
6.4 Conclusion   285

7 **The Criminal Law of Evidence under Discussion: 1750–1795**   288
7.1 Introduction   288
7.2 Criticisms on the Use of Judicial Torture 1600–1750   290
7.3 The Reform-literature between 1750 and 1795   297
7.4 Reforms of (criminal) Ordinances in the Second Half of the Eighteenth Century   319
7.5 Conclusion   325

8 **The Criminal Law of Evidence in the Franco-Batavian Period 1795–1813**   328
8.1 Introduction   328
8.2 The Reform of the Criminal Law of Evidence in National Legislation 1795–1810   330

CONTENTS VII

    8.3   The Juridical Literature between 1795 and 1810   367
    8.4   The Incorporation of the Netherlands into the French Empire 1810–1813   378
    8.5   Conclusion   381

9   The Criminal Law of Evidence in the United Kingdom of the Netherlands 1813–1830   385
    9.1   Introduction   385
    9.2   The Development of the Discussion in the Juridical Literature between 1813 and 1830   387
    9.3   The Attempts to Create New Substantive and Procedural Criminal Codes 1813–1830   421
    9.4   The Consequences of the Belgian Separation from the Netherlands   444
    9.5   Conclusion   445

10   The Criminal Law of Evidence in the Netherlands between 1838 and 1870   452
    10.1   Introduction   452
    10.2   The Discussion on the Criminal Law of Evidence between 1838 and 1860   453
    10.3   The Discussion Regarding the Abolition of the Negative System of Legal Proofs in the 1860s   466
    10.4   Changes in the Criminal Law of Evidence after 1870   481
    10.5   Conclusion   485

11   Conclusion   488
    11.1   Introduction   488
    11.2   The Theoretical Framework   489
    11.3   The Connection with the Criminal Justice System as a Whole   500
    11.4   A Comparison between the Netherlands, France and Germany   506
    11.5   Developments in the Late Nineteenth and Twentieth Centuries   514

Bibliography   521
Subject Index   542
Author Index   543

Acknowledgements

Foremost I would like to express my sincere gratitude to the supervisors of my thesis: Prof. mr. dr. A.R. Mackor, Prof. mr. dr. G. Knigge and dr. B.S. Hellemans for their continuous support of my Ph.D study and research, and for their patience, motivation and enthusiasm throughout the process of writing this work.

Furthermore, I would like to thank my parents. Their continuous patience, encouragement and, support helped me throughout the process of writing this work.

CHAPTER 1

Introduction

> The proof that the accused has committed the crime for which he has been indicted can only be accepted by the judge if he has acquired the conviction [of the guilt of the accused] on the basis of lawful means of evidence presented during the investigation on trial.
> Article 338 of the Dutch Code of Criminal Procedural Law.[1]

This article contains one of the central rules of the Dutch criminal law of evidence: the judge needs to be convinced (*overtuigd*) of the guilt of the accused before he can convict him. The Dutch criminal law of evidence is characterized by the fact that the judge is almost entirely free in the evaluation of the evidence. Although nominally the Dutch criminal law of evidence can be described as a 'negative' system of legal proofs, there are virtually no rules which predetermine how the judge should evaluate the evidence. The Dutch system is sometimes characterized as a 'negative system of legal proofs' because the Dutch criminal procedural code contains several 'negative' rules or minimum standards which prescribe when a sufficient proof cannot be established. The most important rules are that the judge cannot convict someone solely on the basis of the testimony of one witness or on the basis of a bare confession without any other form of evidence. Although the legislator initially intended to partially limit the judiciary freedom of evaluation 'negatively' through these prescriptions, they soon lost almost all practical significance through a very restrictive interpretation by the Supreme Court of the Netherlands. What remained was an almost completely free evaluation of the evidence by the judge.[2]

The essential prerequisite to convict someone in the Dutch criminal law of evidence is that the judge needs to be convinced of the guilt of the accused. There is a consensus, furthermore, that it has to be a reasoned conviction based on grounds for which the judge has to account in the motivation of his verdict.

---

1 All the translations from Dutch into English have been made by the author.
2 For this reason, Dreissen, for example, states that the Dutch criminal law of evidence contains simply a variant of a system of a free evaluation of the evidence by the judge. See W.H.B. Dreissen, *Bewijsmotivering in Strafzaken,* pp. 99–101. See in a similar sense Nijboer in J.F. Nijboer, "Legaliteit en het strafrechtelijke bewijsrecht; uitholling van het wettelijk bewijsstelsel in strafzaken?", *Ars Aequi*, 2004, vol. 53, pp. 492–503.

It is also often stated that the conviction of the judge needs to be based on a very high probability of guilt.[3] The Dutch criminal law of evidence is similar, in this respect, to most continental European legal systems where the free evaluation of the evidence is considered one of the central principles of the modern criminal law of evidence. In France, for example, Article 353 of the *Code de procedure pénale* states that the jurors are free in the evaluation of the evidence and that they only have to ask themselves if they are internally convinced of the guilt of the accused. Similarly, Article 261 of the German *Strafprozessordnung* prescribes that the judge has to freely evaluate the evidence: "Über das Ergebnis der Beweisaufnahme entscheidet das Gericht nach seiner freien, aus dem Inbegriff der Verhandlung geschöpften Überzeugung".

However, the (largely) free evaluation of evidence has not always been an important part of the criminal law of evidence in continental European countries.[4] In fact, it has emerged only relatively recently and it is the fruit of a complex historical development. Before the freedom of evaluation was introduced, an evidentiary system existed in continental Europe which is generally known as 'the system of legal proofs'.[5] The system of legal proofs consisted of a relatively strict set of evidentiary rules that had developed in the late Middle Ages and which predetermined when sufficient evidence existed for a conviction. In general, only the confession of the defendant or the testimony of two reliable eyewitnesses could create a 'full proof' sufficient to convict someone to a severe corporal or capital punishment. A further important characteristic of the system of legal proofs was that it contained the possibility of judicial

---

3   See in this sense, for example, M.J. Dubelaar, "Nullius in verba: waarheidsvinding en getuigenverklaringen in het strafproces", pp. 95–120, and J.H. Crijns, "Een kroniek van de strafrechtelijke waarheidsvinding", p. 103. Some authors argue that this standard of a high probability of guilt is very similar to the Anglo-American 'beyond a reasonable doubt standard'. See, for example, J.F. Nijboer, *Strafrechtelijk bewijsrecht*, pp. 71–74.

4   The term 'continental European countries' will be used in this study as a short indication for the parts on the continent where the Roman-canonical *ius commune* was received. Although the general term continental Europe will be frequently used, the focus lies overwhelmingly on the French, German and Dutch territories.

5   As Carbasse observed, however, the term 'system of legal proofs' is somewhat misleading. The term seems to imply that the rules were prescribed by law while they were at first developed in the legal science and only later adopted in legal ordinances. Carbasse for this reason suggests that it might be better to speak of a "theory of objective proofs". In this study, nevertheless, the term 'system of legal proofs' will be used because this is the term which is normally used in the literature. Although the term is somewhat awkward, it would be, as Pihlajamäki stated, an exaggeration of the problem to try and invent a completely new terminology for this subject. See J-M. Carbasse, *Histoire du droit pénal et de la justice criminelle*, p. 194 and H. Pihlajamaki, *Evidence, Crime and the Legal Profession*, pp. 15–17.

torture. Judicial torture played a crucial role in the system of legal proofs because it provided an instrument to obtain a confession in those hard cases where strong evidence existed short of a full proof.

In the period between roughly 1750 and 1870 the system of legal proofs was abolished in most continental European countries and replaced by a system based on the free evaluation of the evidence by either professional judges or lay jurors. The central question in this study is how the criminal law of evidence was reformed in the Netherlands, France and Germany between 1750 and 1870 and how this transformation can be understood. Why was the system of legal proofs, which had functioned in continental Europe for almost six centuries, replaced, in a relatively short period of time, by a system based on the (largely) free evaluation of the evidence? The question becomes even more pressing when it is taken into consideration that the transition to the free evaluation of the evidence appears to be in contradiction to the ideals for which the reformers of the enlightenment and the early nineteenth century are known. Their goal was to limit the possibility of judicial arbitrariness by creating a comprehensive codification of the criminal law. Through a clear description of the criminal offences and the binding prescription of the corresponding punishments, the judge would ideally only have to mechanically apply the law. However, within the criminal law of evidence, the development went in the opposite direction. Why did the system of legal proofs quite suddenly seem to lose its plausibility and why did the reformers leave judges or jurors free in the evaluation of the evidence while they otherwise strove to bind the judge to the law as strictly as possible?

The focus in this study lies on a description of the development of the criminal law of evidence in the Netherlands. Unlike, for example, France and Germany, so far almost no historical research has been dedicated to describing and explaining the transition from a system of evidentiary rules to a system based on the largely free evaluation of the evidence that took place in the Netherlands between 1750 and 1870. Nevertheless, there have been several studies which touched upon aspects of this question. Bossers has, for example, dedicated a study to the discussion in the Netherlands from the late eighteenth century until the twentieth century on the question whether a jury system should be introduced. Bossers describes an important part of the discussion on the reform of the criminal law of evidence, but he focusses almost exclusively on the question why the jury system was not adopted here. Another work which has shed some light on the discussion regarding the criminal law of evidence was written by Dreissen. In her study on the development of the obligation to motivate the verdict she gives a summary description of some of the most important points of discussion concerning the criminal law of evidence in the nineteenth and twentieth centuries. However, she pays virtually no attention to what existed before the nineteenth century and how the transition from the system of legal proofs to the largely free evaluation of the evidence can be understood.[6] In short, there has been almost no research on the question how the criminal law of evidence changed between 1750 and 1870 in the Netherlands and it is still unclear why and how the system of legal proofs was abandoned for the largely free evaluation of the evidence.

Even though the focus lies on the development of the criminal law of evidence in the Netherlands, the study will not be limited to the Netherlands. The transition from the system of legal proofs to the free evaluation of the evidence was a continental-European-wide phenomenon and the reforms in the Netherlands can only be understood against this background. The changes in the Netherlands were often directly inspired by ideas of authors from other countries and by the example of reforms in other countries. Particular attention will be paid to the discussions in France and Germany because these countries provided by far the most influential role-models for the development of the criminal law of evidence in the Netherlands between 1750 and 1870.[7] The influence of France was particularly strong in the late eighteenth century and the first decades of the nineteenth century. It was in France, during the French Revolution, that the system of legal proofs was for the first time completely abolished and that a jury system was introduced in combination with the free evaluation of the evidence in 1791. After this important moment in the history of the criminal law of evidence, the dynamic and complex discussion in Germany became the most influential source of inspiration in the Netherlands during the nineteenth century. The comparative approach makes it possible to describe and analyse to what extent the reforms in the Netherlands followed a more general continental European pattern of reform, and to what extent the Netherlands diverged from its neighbouring countries.

---

6 See G.F.M. Bossers, *"Welk eene natie die de jurij gehad heeft, en ze weder afschaft!"*, and W.H.B. Dreissen, *Bewijsmotivering in Strafzaken*.
7 Although Belgium, for example, could also have been chosen for further comparison, some choices had to be made to keep the study feasible. The reason that Belgium has been left out lies predominantly in the fact that, despite the geographically close proximity, the Dutch discussion was not strongly influenced by the discussion in Belgium between 1750 and 1870. The obvious exception to this lack of influence was the period between 1815 and 1830 when the Belgian territories and the Netherlands were united in one kingdom. This period will be discussed in detail in Chapter nine.

1.1 The Connection with the Criminal Justice System as a Whole

Throughout this study it will become apparent that the reform of the criminal law of evidence between 1750 and 1870 was closely connected to changes in the criminal procedural law, the forms of punishments that were used and the substantive criminal law. Changes in the criminal law of evidence were part and parcel of an encompassing reform of the criminal justice system as a whole and they should be understood against this background. It will, therefore, be attempted to describe how the development of the criminal law of evidence was connected to the broader transformation of the criminal justice system. At least this will be done as much as is possible and necessary to better understand the developments in the criminal law of evidence.

In his work on the history of the criminal procedural law in Germany, Ignor came to the interesting conclusion that the transformation of the criminal justice system, roughly between 1750 and 1850, could be compared to Kuhn's idea of a paradigm shift. As Kuhn described, a paradigm shift does not so much occur through a continuous and progressive growth of knowledge within a certain scientific field, but is often decisively influenced by different economic, social, political and personal circumstances. Furthermore, a revolutionary shift occurs when the old paradigm seems to have lost its explanatory and problem-solving value and another promising paradigm is available. Ignor remarks that this was largely what happened to the criminal justice system. The ideas on the nature of crimes, the criminal procedural law and the purpose of punishing changed entirely.[8] Kuhn's idea of a paradigm shift can, in short, serve well as a general analogy to the momentous reforms of the criminal justice system in the period between 1750 and 1870.

The fact that the criminal justice system changed in virtually every respect in this period is the reason why it is difficult to explain the reform of the criminal law of evidence in isolation. The reforms of the different aspects of the criminal justice system often worked mutually reinforcing and the changes were, at least partially, dependent on each other. Three important connections can be distinguished: connections with the criminal procedural law, penology and with substantive criminal law. Firstly, this can be seen in the close connection between the reform of the criminal law of evidence and the reform of the overarching procedural framework. The system of legal proofs generally

---

8   A.M. Ignor, *Geschichte des Strafprozess in Deutschland*, pp. 288–290. Instead of, for example, seeing crimes as a breach of a divinely ordained order which needed to be avenged, crimes started to be seen as a breach of the social contract and only needed to be punished in so far as necessary to deter people from committing them.

formed part of an inquisitorial procedure, which was written, secret and granted the defendant few defensive rights.[9] The accused was very much an object of investigation. Furthermore, the inquisitorial procedure was strongly geared towards obtaining the confession of the accused. Within this procedural context, the system of legal proofs provided a check on the extensive powers of the judge and protected the accused against light-hearted convictions. In the reform discussions in France, Germany and the Netherlands between 1750 and 1870, many authors thought that it was too dangerous to allow the judge to freely evaluate the evidence within the context of the existing inquisitorial framework. The freedom of evaluation was only considered acceptable if new guarantees for the accused were created at the same time. These guarantees included larger defensive rights for the accused, a public and oral trial, the motivation of the verdict and often the introduction of a jury system.[10] The introduction of the free evaluation of the evidence, therefore, consistently formed part of a broader reform of the criminal procedural edifice.

Secondly, there was also an important relationship between the changes in the criminal law of evidence and the changes in penology. The system of legal proofs was closely connected with a scale of decision types and with the kinds of punishments that could be used. The strict criterion of a confession or the testimony of two eyewitnesses was only required for the application of a severe corporal or capital punishment. If strong evidence short of a full proof existed, however, the judge could either apply judicial torture to obtain a confession or he could convict the accused to a less severe or so-called 'extraordinary punishment', such as a banishment or confinement in a workhouse. If the evidence was even weaker, the judge could pronounce an *absolutio ab instantia*, which meant that although the accused was provisionally acquitted, the procedure could be restarted when new evidence turned up. In his decision on the question whether sufficient evidence existed for a more lenient punishment, the judge was left largely free. Briefly summarized, the judge was only bound by the strict criteria for a full proof if he wanted to pronounce a severe

---

9   The old inquisitorial procedure is generally described as 'secret' because it did not take place in public and because the accused was given very little information of the charge against him. The procedure is also characterized as 'written', because the testimony of witnesses and the accused was often presented to the judges in written statements that were recorded by the investigative judge. However, the extent to which the procedure was written differed between the various regions.
10 In the Netherlands, for example, when judicial torture was abolished in 1798 and the freedom to evaluate the evidence was enlarged, this reform went hand in hand with a significant strengthening of the defensive rights of the accused.

corporal or capital punishment, whereas he was left largely free to decide whether the evidence was sufficiently strong to pronounce an extraordinary punishment or an *absolutio ab instantia*.

It is important to emphasize that the old criminal justice system was not necessarily as severe and cruel as is often thought. The exemplary capital and severe corporal punishments were only intended for particularly heinous crimes and were pronounced only if a full proof had been obtained. The early modern criminal procedure offered various ways to circumvent the potential rigidity of the system of legal proofs and the severe punishments that were 'legally' prescribed. The large discretionary powers of the judge in applying punishments were not seen as particularly problematic under the *ancien régime*, because it was thought that they provided the judge with the necessary freedom to moderate the punishment to the specific circumstances of the case and to the strength of the evidence, thus giving him the possibility to be lenient and show clemency.

However, the penological system changed significantly between 1750 and 1870 and this had important repercussions for the criminal law of evidence. The broad judicial discretion in imposing punishments was no longer considered unproblematic and an attempt was made to regulate the punishments more strictly. For many enlightened reformers punishments should ideally be clearly and rigidly prescribed in a criminal codification so that the citizens could know exactly what punishment would follow on what sort of crime. Presuming a rationally calculating citizen, the reformers argued that the punishments should not be cruel, but merely so severe that they outweighed the potential benefits of the crime. Reformers such as Beccaria stressed time and again that the threat of a lenient but certain punishment was far more efficacious than the threat of a severe but uncertain punishment.[11] The codification of the (more lenient) punishments, therefore, served three purposes. Strictly prescribed punishments would be more effective as a deterrent, they would be more humane, while at the same time they would curtail the arbitrary powers of the judge considerably.[12] This new nexus around which modern penology

---

11 It is also for this reason that many of the reform-minded authors argued that the possibility for the king to use the royal pardon and annul punishments, should be abolished. This arbitrary power of the king undermined the deterrence of the criminal sanctions. On Beccaria's argumentation for certain but more lenient punishments and against the royal pardon, see J.M. Michiels, *Cesare Beccaria. Over misdaden en straffen*, pp. 101–136.

12 The decreased use of severe corporal and capital punishments in the eighteenth and nineteenth centuries was also, as Spierenburg has argued, influenced by a change in sensibilities. There was a growing antipathy in this period against gruesome physical punishments. This change in sensibility inspired a reform of the modes of punishment and, for

was built, made the broad discretionary powers of the judge in determining the punishment seem undesirable. Furthermore, the possibility to apply extraordinary punishments on less than a full proof appeared to give a dangerous and unjustifiable power to the criminal judge. Unjustifiable, because someone whose guilt had not yet been fully established could be convicted and punished.

Because of the close connection between the system of legal proofs and the possible forms of punishments, the change in penology between roughly 1750 and 1870 had a major impact on the criminal law of evidence. The decreasing use of severe corporal and capital punishments must have made the free evaluation of the evidence more acceptable in this period since a relatively free evaluation of the evidence had always been acceptable for less severe punishments. Conversely, the emergence of the free evaluation of the evidence may also have made it undesirable to maintain severe corporal and capital punishments for which previously the strict requirement of the confession or two eyewitnesses had applied. There was, therefore, clearly a confluence between the developments in the criminal law of evidence and the developments in penology, which mutually reinforced each other. However, to what precise extent the development in penology influenced the emergence of the free evaluation is a difficult question which can only be partially answered in this study. On this relationship further and more detailed research is required.

Langbein in particular, in his *Torture and the Law of Proof*, has famously defended the thesis that the emergence of the free evaluation of the evidence was merely a consequence of a change in penology. He argued that the free evaluation of the evidence was already used to pronounce less severe extraordinary punishments and that the increased use of these less severe punishments between the sixteenth and nineteenth centuries led to the *de facto* adoption of the free evaluation of the evidence. He thought that the legislative abolition of the system of legal proofs and the introduction of the free evaluation of the evidence between 1750 and 1870, therefore merely formed a ratification of a change that had already taken place in practice. Although Langbein was undeniably right in stressing the important link between the criminal law of evidence and penology, his attempt to reduce the reform of the criminal law of evidence to a change in penology is a too monocausal explanation, which does not do justice to the complexity of the developments. The emergence of the free evaluation of the evidence was also influenced by changes in

---

example, also made the use of judicial torture less acceptable. See P. Spierenburg, *The spectacle of suffering*, pp. 66–67 and 200–207.

the criminal procedural law and – as will be further described below – by changes in the underlying epistemological and political-constitutional ideas.[13]

Third and lastly, a significant connection existed between the transformation of the substantive criminal law and the criminal law of evidence between 1750 and 1870. In this period a stronger emphasis was placed, within the substantive criminal law, on the idea that the punishment needed to be proportioned to the degree of criminal intent. Consequently, it became more important that the criminal intent could actually be proven and that it was not just presumed – or derived from a forced confession – as had frequently been the case before the late eighteenth century. To adequately prove the criminal intent of the accused, however, the judge had to be able to infer this intent from the circumstances of the case, which was not altogether easy within the rigid confines of the system of legal proofs.[14] In the eighteenth and nineteenth centuries, many authors argued that it was particularly difficult to create evidentiary rules for the question whether the accused had the required criminal intent and that it was for this reason necessary to let the judge freely evaluate the evidence. There was, therefore, also an important confluence between the development of the criminal law of evidence and the development of the substantive criminal law. Whereas the necessity to prove the criminal intent was used as an argument for the introduction of the free evaluation of the evidence, the free evaluation of the evidence at the same time, formed an essential prerequisite for the judge to be able to moderate the punishment in accordance with the precise criminal intent of the accused. As Pihlajamäki stated: "Without the freedom of judgment ... the sophisticated categories of guilt provided by the latter [substantive criminal law] would have been impossible to put into practice".[15]

---

[13] A more detailed discussion and refutation of the thesis of Langbein will be given in Section four of Chapter two.

[14] The system of legal proofs was inadequate because the precise criminal intent is not something that is directly and outwardly visible to, for example, eyewitnesses. It is something that normally has to be inferred from the actions of the accused and the circumstances of the case and which is particularly difficult to regulate in general evidentiary rules.

[15] H. Pihlajamäki, *Evidence, Crime, and the legal profession*, pp. 5–6, 128–131 and 256. The thesis of Pihlajamäki that the increased need to prove the criminal intent of the accused formed one of the most important reasons for the introduction of the free evaluation of the evidence is, however, not supported by this study. Although the argument that it was impossible to create evidentiary rules to determine the criminal intent of the accused was often used by Dutch, German and French authors – especially from the 1830s onwards –, this idea does not appear to have been decisive for the introduction of the free evaluation

1.2 The Theoretical Framework

The main question in this study is how and why the transition occurred from the system of legal proofs to the free evaluation of the evidence between 1750 and 1870. The focus lies especially on describing and elucidating the ideas underlying this reform. Although there are many factors which led to or at least influenced the reform of the criminal law of evidence, it is the contention in this study that there were two developments which – at least on the level of the ideas underlying the reforms – were of central importance for the emergence of the free evaluation of the evidence. In this study these developments are characterized as the changed 'political-constitutional discourse' and the changed 'epistemological discourse'. In both discourses a significant transformation occurred between the seventeenth and nineteenth centuries. Moreover, these developments were closely intertwined and in their combination delivered the ideological foundation for the 'modern' criminal law of evidence. The changes in both discourses and their impact on the criminal law of evidence are discussed in more detail in Chapter three. Here only a brief overview will be given of the most important changes in both discourses.

The change in the epistemological discourse consisted of the adoption of a probabilistic approach to the criminal law of evidence in the seventeenth and eighteenth centuries, which formed part of the emergence of a more general probabilistic approach to knowledge in this period. In the late Middle Ages, the intellectual roots of the system of legal proofs can be found in the combination of Aristotelian philosophy and the scholastic method of categorization. A more 'absolute' idea existed of the certainty which needed to be attained in criminal cases. What could constitute this certainty was laid down in rules which determined *a priori* when sufficient evidence was present to convict someone. It was generally thought that sufficient certainty only existed when there were two eyewitnesses or a confession. The judge essentially needed to work in a deductive way, starting from the general rules, to establish whether the criteria were met and whether there was, therefore, a 'full proof'. The seventeenth and eighteenth centuries, however, saw the rise of a probabilistic approach to the criminal law of evidence and it became commonly accepted that only a high probability of guilt was required for a conviction. It was acknowledged, first of all, that the various kinds of evidence could not create certainty but only different degrees of probability dependent on the circumstances of

---

of the evidence. It was used predominantly as an important additional argument for the free evaluation of the evidence.

the case and, secondly, that the required high probability of guilt could principally be established by any kind of evidence. From the new probabilistic conception, it seemed impossible to predetermine, in general rules, at what point sufficiently strong evidence existed for a conviction in the concrete case. Instead it was argued that this should be left to the free evaluation of the judge. The central criterion for the question whether there was sufficient evidence to convict someone now became the (internal) conviction of the judge or jurors. The change of the epistemological discourse, in short, had an important impact on the reform of the criminal law of evidence.

The change in the political-constitutional discourse is very broadly understood in this study to mean the process of rethinking the relationship between the state and its citizens, which had its roots in a significant change in natural law and social contract theories in the seventeenth and eighteenth centuries. In the changed natural law and social contract theories it was stressed that people were naturally free and equal individuals and only later made a social contract to establish an authority. The legitimacy of (royal) authority and the existing social divisions were no longer taken for granted as part of an immutable and divinely ordained order. Instead the stress on an originally free and equal people from whom the sovereignty derived through a social contract, created a vantage point from which the exercise of power could be critically evaluated. Two important ideas in particular, which had an important bearing on the criminal law of evidence, were derived from the changed natural law and social contract theories.

Firstly, the changed natural law and social contract theories in the seventeenth and eighteenth centuries provided an important stimulus to the development of the 'modern' *nemo tenetur* principle (i.e. the principle that no one should be obliged to contribute to his own conviction) and the defensive rights of the accused. It was taken as a first principle that man's most important urge was to preserve himself and that it was against natural law to force someone to contribute to his own demise. From this idea arguments were derived against judicial torture and the inquisitorial procedure in which everything was geared towards obtaining the confession of the accused. It was argued that by natural law an accused should have the right not to incriminate himself and the right to freely defend himself with the help of legal counsel. These criticisms had a significant impact on the criminal law of evidence because they delegitimized the use of judicial torture and appeared to necessitate a fundamental change of the inquisitorial procedure and, therefore, the criminal law of evidence.

Secondly, from the changed political-constitutional discourse important arguments were derived in favour of the introduction of a jury system. A general tenet of social contract theories had been to argue that the sovereignty lay originally with the people who then transferred it through a social contract to the government. The idea that the sovereignty lay with the people and that it should also find an expression in the judicial branch – where 'the people would be judged by the people' – formed an influential argument in favour of the introduction of a jury system in the late eighteenth and early nineteenth centuries. Another important reason for the introduction of the jury system lay in the fact that there was a distrust in the professional judges. Particularly among the French revolutionaries there was a strong distrust against the possible arbitrariness and abuses of power by the criminal judges, while there was far more trust in the impartiality and disinterestedness of 'the people'. The introduction of a jury system functioned as an important catalyst for the abolition of the system of legal proofs in the period between 1750 and 1870, because the reformers agreed that lay jurors should freely evaluate the evidence and could not apply a complex and learned system of evidentiary rules.

Summarizing, it is the contention in this study that the transition from the system of legal proofs to the free evaluation of the evidence has to be understood in light of the changes in the underlying epistemological and political-constitutional discourses which will be discussed in more detail in Chapter three.

1.3 The Approach and Limitations

This work is primarily meant as a study of the juridical-dogmatic history of the criminal law of evidence. On the basis of juridical treatises and legislative discussions, an attempt is made to describe how and why the system of legal proofs was replaced by a system based on the free evaluation of the evidence. Furthermore, this study will focus on the description and explanation of the ideas underlying the reform of the criminal law of evidence, mainly by looking at how the jurists changed their understanding of what they were doing and how they expressed themselves. There are significant limitations to this approach. Most importantly, this study does not claim that the reforms in the criminal law of evidence can be explained exclusively in terms of the ideas underlying these changes or even that these ideas were the most important driving force behind them. The description of the ideas underlying the reform of the criminal law of evidence is only meant to provide one, albeit important, perspective from which the developments in the criminal law of evidence can be understood.

The claim of this study, therefore, is not that social, political, cultural and economic developments did not have an important impact on the changes in

INTRODUCTION

the criminal law of evidence. These factors indirectly and often directly shaped the way the criminal law of evidence was reformed. An important example of how these factors influenced the criminal law of evidence, is that the system of legal proofs and a top-down inquisitorial procedure could never have developed in the late Middle Ages without the large economic, demographic and societal changes between the eleventh and thirteenth centuries, which enabled the rise of stronger and more centralized forms of authority (such as in the church and the city states in Italy). The stronger forms of authority that emerged and began to actively uphold the public peace and punish certain forms of undesirable behaviour created the necessary preconditions under which the system of legal proofs could emerge in the first place. Similarly, the introduction of a jury system and the free evaluation of the evidence in revolutionary France can be explained from the perspective of social and economic changes. From this perspective, for example, it could be argued that first the rise of the middle classes led to the demand to abolish the privileges of the aristocracy, and secondly, that the demand for a jury system was largely founded on the distrust of these middle classes towards the aristocratic professional magistrates (the so-called *noblesse de robe*).

The usefulness of studying the development of the criminal law from these different perspectives is demonstrated by the large amount of literature that focuses on explaining the developments in penology in the eighteenth and nineteenth centuries. There are many studies which attempt to explain the changes in penology from a socio-economic perspective, from the perspective of cultural change and changes in sensibility and – following Foucault – from the perspective of changing 'technologies of power'. In his *Punishment and modern society* Garland has for example presented an excellent synthesis of the different perspectives from which the changes in penology can be understood. In this study he shows that these different perspectives are for the most part not mutually exclusive but on the contrary offer valuable and complementary insights to understand and explain the emergence of modern penology. The prosecution and punishment of crimes is a practice which is shaped not only by an internal juridical logic, but also by pervasive cultural attitudes, social and economic structures and the way that power and control are exercised. Any satisfactory explanation of the changes in penology and of the criminal justice system as a whole, therefore, has to be a multi-layered approach in which these different perspectives are integrated.[16] Importantly, in as far as the changes in the criminal law of evidence between 1750 and 1870 were induced

---

16   D. Garland, *Punishment and modern society*. See also T.A. Green, *Verdict According to Conscience*, p. xiv. On the important connection between economic developments and the

by a change in penology, the different explanations that have been given for the latter also have a significant (indirect) bearing on the developments in the criminal law of evidence.

Unfortunately, unlike the developments in penology, the development of the criminal procedural law and the criminal law of evidence between 1750 and 1870 has received far less attention. Because of the relative dearth of studies on this subject, an integration of different perspectives on the development of the criminal law of evidence is not yet possible. Instead the more modest and limited goal of this study is to describe how the criminal law of evidence was reformed and how the political-constitutional and epistemological ideas influenced the reforms. This study, therefore, does not give an exhaustive explanation of the emergence of the free evaluation of the evidence, but offers only one important perspective from which this change can be understood.

Finally, the approach of this study is also limited regarding the sources which have been used. The chapters on France and Germany are based predominantly on secondary sources and on a selection of the most important juridical treatises published between 1750 and 1870. As far as the chapters on the Netherlands are concerned, this study has been based, almost exclusively, on the original legal treatises and on the legislative discussions. Because almost no research has been carried out on the development of the criminal law (of evidence) in the Netherlands between 1750 and 1870, for this study many sources have been used that have so far received little attention. For any historian interested in the history of the criminal law (of evidence) in the Netherlands in the eighteenth and nineteenth centuries, this work gives a useful oversight of the most important juridical treatises and legislative discussions regarding this subject.

Nevertheless, an important limitation of this work is that no study of the case law has been performed to establish to what extent the changes in the juridical literature and legislation were accompanied or preceded by a change in juridical practice. The reason for this limitation is exclusively that additional archival research would have made the study unfeasible in terms of time. For the question to what extent the changes in juridical practice corresponded to – and perhaps even preceded – the changes in the juridical theory and legislation, this study principally relies on secondary sources. As far as the Netherlands is concerned, it is as yet particularly difficult to assess the precise relationship

---

changes in penology, see in particular M. Ignatieff, *A Just Measure of Pain: The Penitentiary in the Industrial Revolution, 1750–1870*.

between the developments in legal theory and legal practice because little research has been done regarding the practice of the criminal law (of evidence) in the eighteenth and nineteenth centuries.

1.4 The Periodization

Pihlajamäki, who has investigated the emergence of the free evaluation of the evidence in the nineteenth century in Finland, rightfully points out that an explanation of the reasons for the introduction of the free evaluation of the evidence unavoidably requires a long-term perspective of the history of the criminal law of evidence.[17] The system of legal proofs was created in the late Middle Ages and remained in force well into the eighteenth and nineteenth centuries. To explain the introduction of the free evaluation of the evidence and how it differed from the system of legal proofs, an understanding of the ideas and circumstances underlying the creation of the system of legal proofs is required. Only with an understanding of how and why the system of legal proofs was introduced in the first place, can it be explained what changed and why the free evaluation of the evidence came to be seen as a preferable option. A long-term perspective is, therefore, to a certain extent unavoidable.

Nevertheless, the focus in this work lies on the period between 1750 and 1870. This periodization for the large area of the Netherlands, France and Germany is intended as a rough demarcation of the timeframe in which the free evaluation of the evidence became accepted. The start of this periodization could have been placed earlier. As will become apparent in Chapter three, the change in the epistemological and political-constitutional discourses had already started in the seventeenth century and influenced the attitudes of jurist from the late seventeenth century onwards. Furthermore, the criticism of judicial torture had already intensified from the middle of the seventeenth century onwards and Frederick the Great, for example, made a first important attempt to strongly limit the use of judicial torture in Prussia in 1740.[18] These were still, however, relatively minor changes within the confines of the system of legal proofs compared to the reforms that would later occur.

---

17   H. Pihlajamaki, *Evidence, Crime and the Legal* Profession, p. 3.
18   On the attempt of Frederick the Great to limit the use of judicial torture see M. Schmoeckel, *Humanität und Staatsraison*, pp. 19–50.

The year 1750 is chosen as the starting point because it was during the second half of the eighteenth century that a dynamic and innovative discussion started on how to reform the criminal justice system. In this period a quite sudden and strong general interest emerged in reforming the criminal justice system which is reflected in the large number of publications and prize questions on this subject all over continental Europe. While the free evaluation of the evidence was only introduced for the first time in 1791, the idea to abolish the system of legal proofs and replace it with the free evaluation by lay jurors had already been discussed and developed in the literature in France during the second half of the eighteenth century. Although the discussion was as yet less radical in the Netherlands and Germany than it was in France, these countries also showed a new and more intensified interest in the reform of the criminal law of evidence during the second half of the eighteenth century.

It is not possible to pinpoint one moment in time when the free evaluation of the evidence became accepted in the Netherlands, France and Germany, as the time and pace of this development varied. In France, for example, the system of legal proofs was abolished and the free evaluation of the evidence was introduced in combination with a jury system in 1791. This reform was preserved in the criminal code of 1795 and in the *Code d'Instruction Criminelle* of 1808. It is demonstrated by the discussions leading up to the creation of the *Code d'Instruction Criminelle* of 1808 and in the discussions after 1814 that there was no strong desire to reinstate the system of legal proofs anymore during or after the nineteenth century. As far as France is concerned, therefore, the free evaluation of the evidence can be said to have become firmly established already in the first decade of the nineteenth century. The formulation of the Article in the *Code d'Instruction Criminelle* of 1808, which prescribed the jurors to freely evaluate the evidence, remained virtually unchanged into the twentieth century.

In the German territories and the Netherlands, abandoning the system of legal proofs and replacing it with a system based on the free evaluation of the evidence took longer and occurred more gradually. From the late eighteenth century until the 1840s, the discussion in the Netherlands and Germany was divided predominantly in two sides. One side was in favour of a negative system of legal proofs in combination with professional judges. This meant that the evidentiary rules would only determine certain minimum evidentiary standards while at the same time the internal conviction of the judge was always required to convict someone. The other side was in favour of the free evaluation of the evidence by lay jurors. The free evaluation of the evidence was still largely considered as something that was only acceptable in combination with a jury system, because supposedly only lay jurors could be trusted enough to decide without evidentiary rules. In many German states, the free evaluation of the evidence was for the first time introduced in combination with a jury system in the wake of the revolutionary year of 1848. In the Netherlands, on the other hand, a negative system of legal proofs was created in combination with professional judges in the criminal procedural code of 1838.

In the period from roughly the 1840s until the 1870s the discussion changed in the Netherlands and in the German states. It is during these decades that a majority of the authors in the juridical literature started to argue that even negative evidentiary rules were principally useless and logically untenable. The free evaluation of the evidence was no longer seen as something that could only be entrusted to lay jurors. It was now argued that it could function just as well with professional judges. By the 1860s, for example, almost all the publications in the Netherlands which reflected on the criminal law of evidence were in favour of the free evaluation of the evidence by professional judges. In the German literature as well, the free evaluation of the evidence by either professional judges or lay jurors was generally considered to be one of the essential characteristics of the German criminal procedural law by the 1860s.

The year 1870 has not been chosen as an end point in the periodization because it demarcates any significant legislative event regarding the criminal law of evidence; it has been chosen as the terminus because by the end of the 1860s the 'modern' approach to the criminal law of evidence had become established in France, Germany and the Netherlands, and because the principle of the free evaluation of the evidence had become generally accepted. Although there was still a minority of authors in the Netherlands who after the 1860s pleaded to retain some minimum evidentiary standards, they thought that only a very limited role could and should be played by these negative rules. Almost everyone by now agreed that in the end the decision had to depend on the (largely) free evaluation of the evidence by the judge in the concrete case. The idea that it was possible to determine *a priori* when a full proof existed was something that had become entirely superseded and was regarded as a thing of the past.[19]

---

19   Incidentally, for the Netherlands the period could also have been extended until 1926 when the criminal procedural code of 1838 was finally replaced by a new code. In this new code the important legislative change took place in which the negative evidentiary system was further hollowed out and the judge was left almost entirely free in the evaluation of the evidence. Nevertheless, the year 1870 can still be considered an appropriate terminus for the Netherlands as well because the arguments and the ideas which had led to the legislative change in 1926 had already been developed and had become commonly accepted by the 1860s. The discussion regarding the criminal law of evidence between 1870 and 1926, to an important extent, continued to be waged between those who desired a

Finally, the year 1870 is also a useful terminus because it marks the start of the period which contained the second great change in the modern criminal law of evidence. The period since the 1870s witnessed the rise of the forensic sciences which had a profound influence on penology and on the criminal law of evidence. In addition to the classical juridical approach of the nineteenth century, a sociological, psychological and bio-anthropological perspective was applied to analyze 'the criminal'. The ideas and claims from the forensic sciences had a significant impact on the criminal law of evidence. It led to a different understanding of criminal behavior, new investigative instruments – such as the study of fingerprints, footprints and the use of the polygraph – and to the increasing importance of the testimony of expert witnesses. The year 1870 can, therefore, also be used to demarcate the period in which the principle of the free evaluation had become accepted from the period in which the forensic sciences started to develop and play a far more important role.

1.5 The Structure and Content of the Chapters

This book essentially consists of two parts. The first part consists of Chapters two until five. In the first part a description is given of the most important characteristics of the system of legal proofs (Chapter two) and a more detailed explanation is given of the theoretical framework (Chapter three). The first part also contains a description of the development of the criminal law of evidence in France (Chapter four) and in the German territories (Chapter five) between 1750 and 1870. The second part is devoted to the development of the criminal law of evidence in the Netherlands between 1750 and 1870 and is divided into five chapters (Chapters six until ten).

The first two chapters of the first part are intended to provide the background information for the analysis of the development of the criminal law of evidence in the France, Germany and Netherlands. The chapters on France and Germany are intended to show how the free evaluation of the evidence

---

completely free evaluation of the evidence and those who wanted to retain some negative evidentiary rules. At least concerning the question whether the free evaluation of the evidence should be introduced, no fundamental changes occurred in the Dutch discussion between 1870 and 1926.

developed there and to provide a comparative framework for the developments in the Netherlands. The first part is, therefore, intended predominantly to provide both the theoretical framework and the comparative perspective with which the development of the Dutch criminal law of evidence can be understood and analysed.

The first part starts with Chapter two which gives a general description of the most important characteristics of the system of legal proofs. In this chapter attention will also be paid to the historiographical discussion regarding the question whether a system based on the free evaluation of the evidence had already emerged in the juridical practice before the end of the eighteenth century. This question will be discussed on the basis of Langbein's influential work *Torture and the law of proof* in which he defended the thesis that the free evaluation of the evidence had in fact developed in the juridical practice between the sixteenth and eighteenth centuries.

Chapter three contains the theoretical framework. In this chapter a more detailed description is given of how the political-constitutional discourse and the epistemological discourse changed from the seventeenth century onwards, and how these changes affected the criminal law of evidence.

Chapter four describes the reform of the criminal law of evidence in France. The emphasis in this chapter lies on the developments between the second half of the eighteenth century and the first decade of the nineteenth century, in which a complete reform of the criminal procedural law and the criminal law of evidence took shape. It was in France in the second half of the eighteenth century that for the first time a fundamental critique of the existing criminal law of evidence developed and that radical options for reform were discussed. Many French authors had become sceptical about the possibility to create evidentiary rules which predetermined when sufficient evidence existed to convict someone and they severely criticized the use of judicial torture. Inspired by the Anglo-Saxon procedural model, they proposed to create a public, oral trial in which jurors would decide on the basis of their freely formed *conviction intime* (internal conviction). This reform was realized early in the French revolution between 1789 and 1791 and – with some changes – was retained in the *Code d'Instruction Criminelle* of 1808. Thus, for the first time in continental Europe the system of legal proofs was explicitly abolished and the freedom of evaluation introduced in combination with a jury system.

Subsequently, Chapter five describes the reform of the criminal law of evidence in the German territories between 1750 and 1870. Here the emphasis lies on the development of the discussion in the nineteenth century. Unlike in France, in the German territories the system of legal proofs and the criminal procedural law were not yet criticized in a radical fashion during the second half of the eighteenth century. Although a more critical attitude is clearly discernible in this period – particularly regarding judicial torture –, there was as yet only a willingness to introduce relatively minor reforms to the system of legal proofs. This changed in the nineteenth century. The French reforms and their underlying ideas proved to be a significant role-model and catalyst for the discussion in the German territories. This did not lead to a simple reception of the French reforms, but to a complex debate in which several models for reform were critically discussed.

Eventually three views can be discerned in the German discussion in the nineteenth century. One group essentially followed the French ideas and argued for the introduction of a jury system. The second group wanted to create a 'negative' system of legal proofs. This meant that the evidentiary rules would only determine certain minimum evidentiary standards while at the same time the internal conviction of the judge was always required to convict someone. Finally, a third group pleaded for the possibility to let professional judges decide on the basis of their freely formed internal conviction. In contrast with the French idea of the *conviction intime*, however, the German authors argued that it needed to be a reasoned conviction based on grounds for which the judge needed to account in the motivation of his verdict.

The second part of this study focuses on the Netherlands. Chapter six describes how the criminal law of evidence functioned in the Dutch Republic in the seventeenth and eighteenth centuries. The aim of this chapter is to give an analysis of how the criminal law of evidence was regulated in the juridical handbooks and criminal legislation in this period. The analysis will show that the system of legal proofs was received and largely followed in the Dutch juridical literature, but that there was one important deviation from the common doctrine in the province of Holland. While normally it was the rule within the system of legal proofs that a a severe corporal or capital punishment could only be pronounced on the basis of a confession or the testimony of two reliable eyewitnesses, in the province of Holland the rule was that this was solely possible on the basis of a confession. Unsurprisingly, for this reason the inquisitorial procedure in Holland was strongly geared towards the acquisition of a confession.

Chapter seven describes the period between roughly 1750 and 1795 in which an increasing number of treatises appeared that criticized the existing criminal law of evidence. Like the discussions in the German territories in this period, the criticisms were still of a relatively moderate nature. The most important point of discussion in this period was whether judicial torture should be abolished. Between 1750 and 1795 the opinions were still divided on this subject and it cannot be said that there was a consensus on the desirability of abolishing judicial torture. Many authors argued for the retention of at least a limited use of judicial torture because they deemed that the criminal procedure would otherwise become ineffective. The opponents of judicial torture were also well aware that a significant change in the criminal law of evidence would become necessary if judicial torture was abolished. They accepted this consequence and often pleaded for an extension of the possibility to convict on the basis of other forms of evidence when judicial torture would be abolished. However, notwithstanding the increased criticisms of judicial torture, no meaningful (legislative) reforms were achieved between 1750 and 1795 in the Netherlands.

The situation changed significantly in the period between 1795 and 1813, which is the subject of Chapter eight. In the revolutionary year of 1795 the Batavian Republic was created and a national assembly was elected to create a constitution. A first important milestone was achieved with the concept constitution of 1798 which abolished judicial torture for the entire Dutch Republic. Secondly, between 1798 and 1804 a committee started to work on a codification of the criminal law of evidence. Without judicial torture, the concept codification essentially contained a negative system of legal proofs (although this term was not yet used). The concept codification contained a large number of rules which prescribed minimum evidentiary standards that the judge had to comply with, while at the same time the conviction of the judge was necessary to convict someone. Even though the concept ordinance of 1804 was never accepted, the first national codification of the criminal law that was later promulgated under king Louis Napoleon in 1809, essentially contained a summary version of the negative system of legal proofs that was proposed in the design of 1804. The lifespan of the new code of Louis Napoleon was, nevertheless, very short. After the incorporation of the Netherlands into the French empire, the French criminal legislation – which entailed the introduction of a public, oral trial with a jury system – was introduced in the Netherlands.

The period between 1815 and 1830, in which the Belgian provinces and the Dutch provinces were unified in the United Kingdom of the Netherlands, is described in Chapter nine. This period started with the decision by the Dutch government to provisionally retain the French criminal legislation until new national codifications would be created Nevertheless, several modifications to this legislation were made, the most significant of which was the abolition of the jury system. Because the regulation of the *Code d'Instruction Criminelle* otherwise remained the same, the consequence was that now professional judges had to decide solely on the basis of their *conviction intime*. Between 1815 and 1830 this was not yet seen as a desirable solution because most authors in the Netherlands did not trust professional judges enough to allow them complete freedom in the evaluation of the evidence. In this period a clear divergence emerged between the southern and the northern provinces which dominated the discussion on the criminal law of evidence.

In the southern provinces, a vast majority was in favour of reintroducing a jury system predominantly on the basis of political-constitutional grounds. Professional judges were distrusted and they were considered to be influenced too strongly by the central government while the judgement by the people was expected to be far more impartial. In the northern provinces, on the other hand, the trust in the professional judges was higher and the introduction of a jury system was generally considered undesirable because it was thought that skill and training were necessary to decide in criminal cases. In the north, a majority was in favour of reintroducing a negative system of legal proofs which would at least bind the judge to some minimum evidentiary standards. A negative system of legal proofs – very similar to that which existed in the criminal ordinance of 1809 – was also what was proposed by the legislator in the new concept criminal procedural ordinance in the late 1820s. Although the ordinance was accepted in parliament, it never acquired force of law due to the Belgian revolution of 1830. After Belgium became independent from the Netherlands, it was quickly decided there that the jury system would be reintroduced. In the Netherlands a revised concept criminal ordinance was eventually approved in 1838. This criminal ordinance left much intact of the French *Code d'Instruction Criminelle*, but regarding the criminal law of evidence a negative system of legal proofs was introduced in combination with professional judges.

In Chapter ten the final period from 1830 until 1870 is treated. In this period, the debate once again changed. Between 1815 and 1830 the discussion was divided between those who wanted to introduce the jury system in combination with the free evaluation of the evidence, and those who were in favour of a negative system of legal proofs with professional judges. In the final period, the two main sides consisted of those who were in favour of retaining a negative system of legal proofs and those who wanted a completely free evaluation of the evidence by professional judges. The latter group was particularly inspired by the developments in the German discussion where the principle of the free evaluation of the evidence gained increasing support. By the 1860s, a majority of the authors in the Netherlands appeared to be in favour of the introduction of the free evaluation of the evidence by professional judges. Almost all the publications in the 1860s pleaded for this option and in a revised criminal procedural ordinance in 1863 it was proposed to entirely abolish the negative system of legal proofs (although in the end this procedural ordinance never acquired force of law).

Summarizing, a large and significant development in the criminal law of evidence occurred between 1750 and 1870 in the Netherlands. While during the eighteenth century many authors still supported the system of legal proofs and it was thought that judicial torture was indispensable for an effective criminal procedure, by the 1860's a majority had grown in favour of completely abolishing the evidentiary rules and to let the judge decide after his freely formed conviction. Even those in favour of a negative system of legal proofs agreed that legal rules should only play a very limited role, while the judge should otherwise be left free in the evaluation of the evidence.

Finally, Chapter eleven contains the conclusion. In this chapter a final analysis is given of the development from the system of legal proofs to the free evaluation of the evidence In this chapter particular attention will also be paid to the question how the development of the criminal law of evidence between 1750 and 1870 related to the further developments of the criminal law of evidence in the late nineteenth and early twentieth centuries.

PART 1

The Theoretical Framework and the Development of the Criminal Law of Evidence in France and Germany

CHAPTER 2

The Characteristics of the System of Legal Proofs

2.1 Introduction

In this chapter a description is given of the most important characteristics of the system of legal proofs as it functioned in continental Europe from roughly the thirteenth until the nineteenth centuries. Naturally this can only be a summary description in which many of the complexities and historiographical issues surrounding the system of legal proofs cannot be discussed. Nevertheless, knowledge of the origins and effects of the system of legal proofs is vital to delineate the differences between the 'modern' criminal law of evidence and what existed before. Before the characteristics of the system of legal proofs are discussed, Section two will first describe how the ordeal was abolished and how the inquisitorial procedure developed between roughly the twelfth and fourteenth centuries. This section shortly explains what evidentiary system existed before the system of legal proofs.

Subsequently, the most important characteristics of the system of legal proofs are described in Section three. Finally, in Section four the important historiographical question will be discussed if and to what extent the judicial discretion under the system of legal proofs differed from the free evaluation of the evidence which was introduced from the end of the eighteenth century onwards. This question will be treated on the basis of the important work of Langbein who has stated that the free evaluation of the evidence had already developed in practice between the sixteenth and eighteenth centuries within the context of the system of legal proofs. In Section four it will be argued that this was not the case and that the 'modern' free evaluation of the evidence was only introduced in the eighteenth and nineteenth centuries.

2.2 The Abandonment of the Ordeal and the Development of the Inquisitorial Procedure

From the twelfth century onwards a new inquisitorial procedural law developed which formed the overarching framework of the system of legal proofs. However, from roughly the disappearance of the Roman empire until the twelfth century a completely different procedural law had existed. In this period a (clear) distinction between civil and criminal cases was not yet made. One common procedure existed. It was conducted in public and was accusatorial, meaning that a trial could normally only start on the basis of an accusation. The purpose of the trial was essentially conciliatory in nature. Nevertheless, the risk always existed that a conflict between two families might escalate into a violent feud. For example, if one member of a family killed the member of another family, this family had the right and to an extent even the moral obligation to exact vengeance (which in its turn could lead to the necessity for the other family to exact vengeance).[1]

Ties of kinship were of central importance and acts such as a murder or theft were normally not treated as something for which an individual was criminally responsible. Furthermore, no strong authority existed above the parties which could investigate and punish 'crimes' of individuals. The purpose of the accusatorial trial was to oblige a family to reach a peace settlement by paying a composition for a certain form of damage which had been inflicted. Naturally, the families could also conclude a private peace settlement in the form of a composition in which the family of, for example, the murderer paid a certain amount to prevent the exaction of vengeance. The aim of preventing the escalation of violence through feuds by obliging the families to reach a peaceful composition can be seen clearly in the Germanic laws of the sixth, seventh and eight centuries. The Germanic laws such as the *lex salica* or the *lex wisigothorum* contained long lists which prescribed composition amounts that varied according to the severity of the damage that had been inflicted and the status of the person who had been harmed.[2]

The law of evidence practised in this period differed markedly from the system of legal proofs which developed from the twelfth century onwards. When the accused party confessed before the tribunal or when the culprit was caught red-handed there was no evidentiary problem and the accusing party won. The use of written documents was rare and mostly applied to disputes over ownership of land. The extent to which witness testimony was used in criminal cases remains unclear.[3] Two important forms of evidence existed which were used when the claim of the accuser remained uncertain: the swearing of a purgatory oath and the use of the ordeal (*judicium Dei*). Someone who was accused of having committed, for example, a theft or a murder could establish his

---

1 J-M. Carbasse, *Histoire du droit pénal et de la justice criminelle*, pp. 87–89.
2 Ibidem, pp. 89–92.
3 Ibidem, pp. 193–194. Carbasse, for example, states that witness testimony remained a form of evidence of mere subsidiary importance before the twelfth century because a witness could at any time be contradicted by the accused. This contradiction could lead to the use of an ordeal against the witness which shows that testifying could be a risky affair.

innocence by swearing a purgatory oath. It was normally not sufficient that only the accused swore this oath. His oath needed to be supported by a certain number of oath helpers (*cojuratores* or *compurgatores*) depending on the severity of the crime and the social status of the accused. The *cojuratores* were a sort of character witnesses who swore an oath that supported the oath of the accused and his good character. They were not witnesses in a 'modern' sense who testified on something they had actually seen. The fear of divine punishment was supposed to prevent someone from making a false oath. Through the purgatory oath, supported by a certain number of *cojuratores*, the accused could 'prove' his innocence. Subsequently, the accuser could present a similar number of *cojuratores* supporting his accusation, after which the evidentiary situation remained unresolved.[4]

As Bartlett observed, the ordeal was used predominantly as a last resort when no other means were available. Common forms of the ordeal were the ordeal of fire, the ordeal of water, the ordeal of the cross and trial by combat. The ordeal of fire could consist of the fact that the accused had to pick up a hot piece of iron or of putting his hand in a pot of boiling water to pick up a ring or a small stone. Subsequently the hand was bound in a leather sack for three days after which it was inspected whether the wound was 'clean' (i.e. if it had healed properly without suppuration or discoloration). If the wound had healed properly this vindicated the innocence of the accused. The ordeal of water consisted of submerging someone in, for example, a pond or a stream. If the person sank he was accepted by the water and passed the ordeal. If, however, he remained afloat he was 'rejected' by the water and was considered guilty. Lastly, a more benign ordeal consisted of the ordeal of the cross. In this situation the accusing party and the accused placed their hands on a cross and whoever took his hand of the cross first lost the ordeal.[5]

The idea behind the ordeals was that God showed through this test who was right. While the ordeal of fire or water was applied to the accused alone, the ordeal of trial by combat was a bilateral ordeal which required both parties to participate. The accuser and the accused – or champions selected to fight for them – held a duel, often to the death. Although trial by combat differed in form from the other ordeals, the underlying idea was essentially the same. God would protect the one who was right and would let him win. Trial by combat would eventually be the ordeal that survived the longest because it came to be seen as a privilege of the nobility. Whereas people of the lower classes were

---

[4] Ibidem, pp. 92–94.
[5] R. Bartlett, *Trial by fire and water*, pp. 1–30.

often subjected to the unilateral ordeals of fire and water, the nobility had the privilege to ask for trial by combat in similar situations.[6]

2.2.1 The Abolition of the Ordeal

From the twelfth century onwards a transformation occurred in the continental legal systems which eventually led to the abolition of the ordeals and the creation of the system of legal proofs. This change was part and parcel of the large cultural, demographic and economic changes which are often designated as the Renaissance of the twelfth century. Prior to the twelfth century, law had remained largely un-systematized and no professional legal corps existed. This changed in the twelfth century with the emergence of universities and the 'rediscovery' of Roman law which started to be taught and studied at the universities. The developments in legal science went hand in hand with the development of stronger forms of centralized authority in the form of the city-governments the princes and particularly the church. A leading role in this development was performed by the church and the Italian city-states.[7]

The study of Roman law and the emergence of a corps of trained jurists led, first of all, to a more systematized and complex accusatorial procedure modeled on the Roman procedural law. This procedural law was reflected on, described and standardized in the juridical handbooks (the *ordines iudiciarii*). The accusatorial procedure was improved and strengthened under the ecclesiastical and communal authorities as an important instrument of pacification. Just like the older accusatorial trial, it was a means of channeling and resolving conflicts that otherwise might turn into violent feuds.[8] Besides the fact that the accusatorial procedure was strengthened, a new inquisitorial procedure developed which was applied to forms of behavior that started to be distinguished as 'criminal'. The church performed a leading role in the creation of the inquisitorial procedure and in the abolition of the ordeal. A highly important moment in this development was formed by the fourth Lateran Council of 1215 that attempted to abolish the judicial ordeal (or at least to forbid ecclesiastical involvement in ordeals) and which regulated an inquisitorial procedural form.

Much scholarly debate has been dedicated to the question to what extent the decisions in the fourth Lateran Council constituted an innovation or merely a confirmation of changes that had already occurred in the eleventh and twelfth centuries. This discussion will not be addressed here. Instead the focus

---

6 J-M. Carbasse, *Histoire du droit pénal et de la justice criminelle*, pp. 96–97.
7 See, for example, H.J. Berman, *Law and* Revolution, pp. 85–88.
8 On the transformation of the accusatorial procedure see M. Vallerani, *Medieval public justice*, pp. 12–31.

will lie on the effects of these changes. The development of the inquisitorial procedure in canon law was the result of the desire of a more centralized and hierarchized church to effectively discipline the clergy. Since the Gregorian revolution the church had attempted with new vigor to prohibit forbidden forms of behavior such as simony and concubinage (the selling of ecclesiastical offices and living with women by the clergy). The church wanted to improve its moral standing and to prevent scandalous behavior of the clergy that could discredit the reputation of the church. The accusatorial procedure was unsuited for this purpose for three reasons. First of all, the possibility of a punishment depended on the willingness of someone to present an accusation and to conduct a trial with all the risks and costs involved. Often this did not happen. It particularly did not happen when the culprit was a powerful person or when it concerned 'occult offences' that did not have a clear victim (such as simony, concubinage or heresy). Secondly, the judge was passive in the accusatorial procedure and was bound by the evidence that was presented to him by the accuser and the accused. Thirdly, the accusatorial procedure was public while the aim of the church was to prevent public scandals.[9]

Two procedural alternatives for the accusatorial procedure were presented in the fourth Lateran Council to prosecute 'crimes'. The first and most important alternative entitled an ecclesiastical judge to initiate proceedings *ex officio* on the basis of a public rumor (*publica fama*) that a crime had been committed. The reason why this procedure was created was precisely that the church wanted to have the possibility to quickly act when a public scandal was created by offenses of the clergy. The procedure was inquisitorial because there was no private accuser and the judge conducted the investigation and gathered the evidence himself. Instead of two parties who presented and discussed the evidence in front of a passive judge who was bound by their presentation of the evidence, the judge had to investigate and prove the crime himself and punish the accused accordingly. The procedure was, furthermore, conducted in secret to protect the reputation of the accused and of the church. The second option that was introduced was the procedure on the basis of a denunciation. This meant that a trial could be initiated by the denunciation of a crime after which the judge could investigate and punish the potential criminal. The innovative part of this procedural type was that the denouncer did not acquire the burdens and risks that would normally lie on the accuser in an accusatorial procedure.[10]

---

9   F. McAuley, "Canon Law and the End of the Ordeal", pp. 473–513.
10 The innovations which led to the creation of the inquisitorial procedure on the basis of *fama publica* were not created *ex vacuo* during the fourth Lateran Council. They were

The creation of the inquisitorial procedure, often called the 'extraordinary' procedure, formed an innovation which sat uneasily with the 'ordinary' accusatorial procedure. It was an acquisition of power which demanded a justification. The inquisitorial procedure was initially justified by the fiction that the public rumor of a crime (*publica fama*) constituted a complaint from an accuser on the basis of which the procedure could be started. More importantly, Fraher has demonstrated that Innocent III used a new vocabulary in which he tried to justify the inquisitorial procedure by stressing the necessity of effectively punishing crimes. This punitive vocabulary was particularly striking in the phrase "rei publicae interest, ne crimina remaneant impunita" (public interest requires that no crime remains unpunished) which was used time and again as an argument to justify the inquisitorial procedural innovations. The phrase was later also often used to further curb defensive rights that the accused would normally have in an accusatorial procedure and was, among other things, also used to justify judicial torture. The new punitive vocabulary which Innocent III used, not only justified the inquisitorial procedure but at the same time delineated an embryonic 'criminal law' and postulated as an axiom that it is in the public interest that 'crimes' are punished. In this manner 'crimes' were defined as an offense against the public interest on the basis of which 'the state' had a right to prosecute and punish them (similar to a private party whose interest had been offended and who could, therefore, start an accusatorial procedure).[11]

A complicated question is why the church became increasingly critical of the ordeal during the twelfth century and why it decided to abolish the ordeal during the fourth Lateran Council. As Bartlett has shown, the main theological arguments against the ordeal were not new in the twelfth century, but had already been expressed and developed as early as the ninth century. There were two main arguments why the ordeal was canonically unsound. Firstly, it was almost completely devoid of any Scriptural sanction. Except for one passage in the Book of Numbers, there were no examples which appeared to support the use of ordeals in the Bible. Secondly, it was argued that the ordeal was an unwarranted temptation of God. While miracles and the intervention of God in the temporal realm were certainly not questioned, it was, however, highly dubious if man could actively 'invoke' or force God to take a decision through

---

developed by Innocent III in a series of decretals issued in 1198, 1206 and 1212 and consolidated in the fourth Lateran Council. See F. McAuley, "Canon Law and the End of the Ordeal", pp. 489–491.

11 R. Fraher, "The theoretical justification for the new criminal law of the high middle ages: "Rei publicae interest, ne criminal remaneant impunita"", pp. 577–595.

the use of the ordeal. These two arguments against the ordeal had already been expressed in various sporadic texts from the ninth century onwards and were voiced with increased frequency and vehemence during the twelfth century. Nevertheless, before the twelfth century these criticisms had not led to any general movement to reform or abolish the judicial ordeal.[12] The question is why precisely during the twelfth century and the fourth Lateran Council the momentum did exist to abolish the ordeal.

There were three factors in particular which help explain the abolition of the judicial ordeal during the fourth Lateran Council. The first factor consisted of the old argument that the ordeal did not have a solid basis in canonical law. During the intensified theological discussion of the twelfth century the criticism was repeated frequently that there was no example in the Bible and that it formed an unwarranted temptation of God. The second factor was that the ordeal formed an ineffective and uncertain instrument in the attempts to discipline the clergy. The fourth Lateran Council shows that there was a clear desire to create a more effective apparatus to discipline offences by the clergy and for this the ordeal – but also the possibility to swear a purgatory oath – were unwieldy instruments. For this reason the Lateran Council attempted to abolish or limit their use and replace them by an inquest. Underlying the second factor was the process in which the power of the church was strengthened and centralized. The transformation into a stronger and more centralized form of authority was a *conditio sine qua non* for the possibility to create a procedural apparatus to discipline the clergy.[13] Third and lastly, the increased knowledge of Roman law in the twelfth century undoubtedly played an important role. Roman law provided a constant role model of a highly complex and developed legal and evidentiary system which did not use the ordeal. Roman law, in other words, presented an alternative procedural model which made it easier to imagine a law of evidence devoid of the ordeal and purgatory oaths.

The decision of the fourth Lateran Council to forbid the use of the ordeal and clerical participation in the ordeal had a strong influence on the disappearance of the ordeal from the thirteenth century onwards. Priests performed a central and necessary role in the ordeals by, for example, blessing the iron or

---

12 R. Bartlett, *Trial by fire and water*, pp. 70–90. On the theological criticisms see also F. McAuley, "Canon Law and the End of the Ordeal", pp. 477–484.

13 Pihlajamaki summarized this point neatly in the following remark: "From the point of view of a hierarchical administrative organization aiming at increased efficacy, ordeals involved serious setbacks. For one thing, ordeals did not provide for material truth, nor were they intended to do so. Put simply, ordeals belonged to a world with no central authority strong or capable enough to declare the truth in a judicial matter". See H. Pihlajamaki, *Evidence, Crime and the Legal* Profession, pp. 20–21.

water. The speed and thoroughness with which the prohibition of the Lateran Council was implemented varied according to local conditions. The earliest attempts to prohibit the ordeal occurred in smaller precociously centralized kingdoms such as Denmark and England which had a close relation with the papacy. The abolition of the ordeal was recognized in Denmark in a royal ordinance in 1216 and in England in 1219. Other kingdoms and principalities followed suit more slowly. In the German territories, for example, the prohibition of the ordeal appears to have taken place relatively late. In practice, there are numerous examples that the ordeal continued to be used until the end of the Middle Ages. Nevertheless, it is clear that from the thirteenth century onwards the ordeal started to disappear.[14] Similarly, the possibility for the accused to prove his innocence through a purgatory oath was increasingly restricted. Instead, two new evidentiary systems developed which replaced the old evidentiary system: the jury system in England and the system of legal proofs in continental Europe.

2.2.2 *The Spread of the Inquisitorial Procedure*

The secular authorities – the princes and the cities – underwent a similar development of centralization and hierarchisation as the church in the twelfth and thirteenth centuries. A reinvigorated interest is visible in maintaining the public peace and punishing behaviour that disturbed this peace. The renewed interest can be seen well in the peace- and truce of God movement. While the peace- and truce of god movement started as an attempt under the heading of local bishops to force nobleman and knights not to harass the weaker groups in society, in the eleventh and twelfth centuries the truce of God was increasingly put under the protection of secular authorities.[15] The peace- and truce of God were at first attempts to create a situation of 'peace' to forbid and curb the unbridled use of violence. Eventually, however, more elaborate lists of infractions of the peace were formulated and threatened with punishments. Particularly in the German territories a transition is visible wherein the *Landfrieden* started to function as the foundation on the basis of which certain 'crimes' were defined and threatened with a punishment.[16] In short, the increased

---

14   R. Bartlett, *Trial by fire and water*, pp. 127–135.
15   H.E.J. Cowdrey, "The Peace and Truce of God in the Eleventh Century", pp. 42–67.
16   E. Wadle, "Zur Delegitimierung der Fehde", pp. 19–28, H-W. Goetz, "Die Gottesfriedensbewegung im Licht neuerer Forschungen" pp. 31–54, and M.L. Klementowski, "Die entstehung der Grundsätze der strafrechtlichen Verantwortlichkeit und der öffentlichen Strafe im deutschen Reich bis zum 14. Jahrhundert", pp. 240–241. A good example of this development is given by Van Caenegem for Flanders. He described well how the count of Flanders increasingly started to uphold the *pax comitatis* (the ducal peace) with punitive

concern to protect the peace by the cities and the princes created a 'public interest' which was used as a justification to punish certain infractions and forms of behaviour that threatened the peace. It helped create an embryonic criminal *iurisdictio*.

The emergence of stronger authorities that desired to punish offences such as murder, rape and theft was accompanied by the creation of an inquisitorial procedure. In the period from the twelfth until the fifteenth century an inquisitorial procedure was established and became regularly practiced throughout continental Europe. In the Italian peninsula the inquisitorial procedure was developed by the ecclesiastical authorities and the city states on the basis of the combination of Roman and canonical law. The inquisitorial procedure in the Italian city-states, therefore, resembled and co-developed with the ecclesiastical inquisitorial procedure from its inception. The Roman-canonical inquisitorial procedure also spread in an early stage to the south of France (the *pays de droit écrit*). For the north of France, the Low Countries and the German territories the reception of the Roman-canonical law started later and for these territories it is more difficult to determine to what extent an inquisitorial procedure already developed 'domestically' out of the existing customary law, and to what extent the Roman-canonical model was followed in the creation of an inquisitorial procedure.

Schmidt has, for example, attempted to demonstrate that an inquisitorial procedure had already developed in the late Middle Ages in the German territories (autonomously from the Roman-canonical model), and that it was only later adapted to the learned law when this started to be received in the fifteenth and sixteenth centuries.[17] Similarly, Van Caenegem has described in detail how an inquisitorial procedure had developed largely 'autonomously' in Flanders between the twelfth and fourteenth centuries.[18] Jerouschek, on the other hand, argued that it is very likely that the Roman-canonical procedure performed the function of a role model even during this early period and that it was known through its practice in ecclesiastical courts in Germany.[19] Although it is difficult to assess to what extent the inquisitorial procedure in transalpine Europe developed 'domestically' and to what extent it was influenced from an early

measures in a more regularized judicial procedure in the course of the twelfth and thirteenth centuries. See R.C. van Caenegem, *Gechiedenis van het strafprocesrecht in Vlaanderen van de XIe tot de XIVe eeuw*, pp. 9–13.

17 E. Schmidt, *Einführung in die Geschichte der deutschen Strafrechtspflege*, pp. 86–107.
18 R.C. van Caenegem, *Gechiedenis van het strafprocesrecht in Vlaanderen van de XIe tot de XIVe eeuw*, pp. 56–63 and 237–238.
19 G. Jerouschek, "Die herausbildung des peinlichen Inquisitionsprozess im Spätmittelalter und in der frühen Neuzeit", pp. 347–360.

stage by the Roman-canonical procedural model, it is clear that it was adopted because there was a growing desire for a procedural form which could be used to punish certain crimes (and because forms of authority had developed which could actually apply an inquisitorial procedure).[20] Furthermore, although the path might be disputed the result is relatively clear. At least by the sixteenth century – and in some regions far earlier – the inquisitorial or 'extraordinary' procedure was commonly used as a judicial procedure in a by now clearly distinguished practice of 'criminal law'.

So far, for the sake of brevity, a rather summary and schematic description has been given of the emergence of the inquisitorial procedure and a distinct practice of criminal law. It however, needs to be stressed that the emergence of the inquisitorial procedure and a punitive practice in the late Middle Ages was far from a linear development whereby stronger forms of authority monopolized violence and attempted increasingly to apply a top-down punishment for any kind of offence. Recent research in particular has shown that the situation was far more complicated and that the inquisitorial procedure was but one instrument in a broader range of judicial and extra-judicial instruments that were used to deal with 'crimes' or (potentially) violent conflicts. Vallerani has, for example, described how the inquisitorial procedure developed in Bologna and Perugia in the thirteenth and fourteenth centuries and was how it used alongside a variety of other possible responses to 'crimes'. In fact a punitive approach through the use of the inquisitorial procedure remained relatively rare. Particularly for the established inhabitants of a city or the country-side, who enjoyed a good reputation, the emphasis lay on finding a reconciliation between the culprit and the victim through a monetary composition or other informal sanctions. This could be achieved by the use of an accusatorial procedure but also in an extrajudicial manner. It is important to realize that the full severity of the inquisitorial procedure and corporal or capital punishments were only used on established citizens in the relatively rare cases where the crime was deemed particularly heinous and where the culprit was considered incorrigible.[21] The emphasis on preventing the escalation of violent

---

20   As Schmoeckel, for example, remarked: "die Entstehung des Inquisitionsprozesses zeigt jedenfalls die Existenz eines öffentlichen Strafbedürfnisses". M. Schmoeckel, *Humanität und Staatsraison*, p. 245.

21   M. Vallerani, *Medieval Public Justice*, pp. 114–271. It is in this respect unsurprising that the full severity of the criminal law was used especially against vagabonds and strangers who were often poor and who were not part of the close mutual relations of a small community. It was particularly difficult to use traditional informal communal sanctions against an accused who was not inhabitant of the locality and who normally did not have the money to reach a negotiated settlement. Further important recent research which has

feuds – and generally to prevent significant disruptions of normal social relationships within communities – by establishing a reconciliation in the form of a monetary composition remained highly important throughout the late Middle Ages and the early modern period.[22]

Finally, it is important to note that the abolition of the ordeal and the emergence of the inquisitorial procedure had several important consequences for the criminal law of evidence. In the old accusatorial procedure the burden of proof lay, to a certain extent, with the accused. The accused was obliged to perform a purgatory oath or undergo the ordeal of fire or water. After the abolition of the ordeal and the reception of Roman law this situation changed. The rule in Roman law was *actori incumbit probatio*, meaning that the burden of proof lay with the accuser. After the abolition of the ordeal this entailed that in the accusatorial procedure the burden of proof now came to lie more strictly with the accusing party. In the inquisitorial procedure, however, it meant that the burden of proof came to lie with the investigating judge.[23]

There was, furthermore, an important difference between the accusatorial procedure and the inquisitorial procedure. In the accusatorial procedure the evidence was presented and discussed by the accuser and the accused. In this procedure the judge was relatively passive. He did not conduct an investigation *ex officio* and he was bound by the evidence as it was presented to him by the parties.[24] In the inquisitorial procedure, on the other hand, the judge had to actively investigate the truth and could convict the accused only if he had found sufficient evidence. In the accusatorial procedure the judge had to contend himself with a – what we would nowadays call – more 'procedural truth' which depended on the evidence presented by the parties. For the inquisitorial procedure the pretention was at least that the judge had to find the 'substantive truth'. As Vallerani observes, already in the reforms of Innocent III a strong

---

aimed at demonstrating the complexity of the development of a punitive criminal law can be found in D. Willoweit, *Die Entstehung des öffentlichen strafrechts*, and H. Schlosser, R. Sprandel and D. Willoweit, *Herrschaftliches Strafen seit dem Hochmittelalter*.

22   This can, for example, be seen particularly well in the provinces of Flanders and Brabant where a specialized court of *paysierders* ('peacemakers') continued to perform a central role in settling violent conflicts well into the sixteenth century. On the important role of the courts of *paysierders* and the settling of conflicts through a composition in the late Middle Ages in Flanders, see D.M. Nicholas, "Crime and punishment in fourteenth-century Ghent", pp. 297–314, G. Dupont, "Les temps des compositions. Pratiques judiciaires à Bruges et à Gand du XIVe au XVIe siècle", pp. 20–35 and W.P. Blockmans, "Vete, partijstrijd en staatsmacht", pp. 28–29.

23   J-M. Carbasse, *Histoire du droit pénal et de la justice criminelle*, p. 194.

24   K.W. Nörr, *Zur Stellung des Richters im gelehrten Prozess der Frühzeit: Iudex secundum allegata non secundum conscientiam iudicat*, pp. 40–43.

emphasis was placed on the fact that the inquisitorial procedure was directed at establishing the *veritas* (the truth).[25] The evidentiary logic and the purpose of the two procedural types, therefore, differed significantly.

Lastly, the different evidentiary standard in the inquisitorial procedure was strongly influenced by the possible outcome the procedure could have. Because the inquisitorial procedure could have the far-reaching effect of a capital or severe corporal punishment, it was continuously emphasized that in criminal affairs the evidence needed to be clearer than the light of the noonday sun (*in criminalibus, debent esse probationes luce meridiani clariores*).[26] In the emerging inquisitorial procedure the question whether there was sufficient evidence for a severe punishment was not left to the free evaluation of the evidence by the judge. Instead, from the twelfth century onwards a relatively strict and complex system of rules developed which predetermined when a 'full proof' existed on the basis of which a conviction could be pronounced. This system of rules came to be known as the system of legal proofs.

2.3 The Central Characteristics of the System of Legal Proofs

The aim here can only be to give a summary description of some of the most important characteristics of the system of legal proofs as it existed for almost six centuries in the large and diffuse area of continental Europe. In this long period significant developments took place within the function and organization of the criminal justice system as a whole, and within the criminal law of evidence. Furthermore, there were important regional differences in how and when the system of legal proofs was adopted and how it was applied in practice. Nevertheless, the form and the theory of the system of legal proofs remained a relatively coherent whole throughout this long period in continental Europe. Five characteristics can be discerned which were central to the system of legal proofs.

---

25   M. Vallerani, *Medieval Public Justice*, pp. 35–38. Naturally, the fact that in the inquisitorial procedure juridical rules existed which predetermined what forms of evidence were admissible and when there was sufficient proof, automatically meant that here as well a procedural truth reigned. Nevertheless, the pretention was at least that, unlike in the civil procedure, the accused could only be punished in the inquisitorial procedure on the basis of what had really happened. In contrast to the civil procedure, furthermore, the judge in criminal cases was not limited to the evidence that was presented by the parties.
26   J-M. Carbasse, *Histoire du droit pénal et de la justice criminelle*, p. 194.

A first characteristic of the system of legal proofs was that it was a product of juristic writing and existed first and foremost in the discussions and treatises of legal scholars. These legal scholars constructed a new juridical edifice by commenting on and reasoning from especially canon and Roman law. There was not one central authority which created and clearly prescribed the legal evidentiary rules, but it was the product of the discussions among legal scholars. As a consequence, the system of legal proofs can best be seen as a common core of rules and ideas on which consensus existed in the juridical literature and a grey area of questions which were permanently under dispute. At a later time city statutes and royal ordinances also explicitly referred to the system of legal proofs. Sometimes these ordinances merely acknowledged the validity of the system of legal proofs and left its regulation entirely to the common opinion in the juridical literature, and sometimes the ordinances presented a more detailed regulation of the system of legal proofs.

A second characteristic of the system of legal proofs was that it clearly had the function of a guarantee against judicial arbitrariness and against light-hearted convictions.[27] The possibility to convict an accused to a severe corporal or capital punishment was a redoubtable power which was from the start circumscribed by rules and the demand for a high standard of proof. The criminal procedure was far-reaching in its potential consequences not only for the accused but also for the judge who, as a Christian, might have to pronounce a death sentence. It was not deemed acceptable to let a decision with these consequences depend solely on the unregulated judgement of the judge. Out of the desire to create a guarantee against wrongful convictions the system of evidentiary rules was developed which prescribed under which circumstances the judge had sufficient proof for a conviction. If the judge did not follow these rules his judgment could be annulled and he could even be liable to be prosecuted himself.[28] Although the judge was bound by the legal evidentiary rules,

---

27   Some authors might say that the 'guarantistic' function was the primary and maybe even sole purpose of the system of legal proofs. Although it is obvious that the strict evidentiary rules were intended as a guarantee against light-hearted convictions, this still begs the question why the guarantee was given shape in this way in the late Middle Ages. In the eighteenth and nineteenth centuries guarantees were also sought against light-hearted convictions but it did no longer seem plausible or desirable to do this through a system of strict evidentiary rules (which even allowed judicial torture to obtain a confession). Instead guarantees were sought in, for example, the motivation of the verdict, the jury system and the publicity of the trial. The question, in short, is why the guarantees were given shape in such different ways in these different periods.

28   The 'guarantistic' function of the evidentiary rules can, for example be seen in the 'syndicate-procedure' which was used in the Italian city-states in the thirteenth and fourteenth centuries. In most city-states a team of judges was appointed for the term of a

it is important to stress that he was never expected to function as a sort of automaton who only had to mechanically apply the evidentiary rules to the concrete case. Instead, the judge had to substantively evaluate the reliability of the testimony of witnesses and of the accused, and many aspects of the evaluation of the evidence were explicitly left to the discretion of the judge.

The third characteristic consists of the fact that there were significant theological concerns underlying the function of judging in criminal cases. In this respect, Whitman has convincingly argued that there most likely existed an important element of moral anxiety in judging in criminal cases after the abolition of the ordeal. Whitman observes that criminal judges feared to make themselves into murderers by potentially unjustly administering capital punishments. The system of legal proofs on the continent and the jury system in England at least partially functioned to shift the responsibility of the decision away from the judges. On the continent it appeared to be the abstract rules of the law instead of the criminal judge which convicted the accused.[29] Apart from epistemological considerations, this moral anxiety of judging in capital cases may also have had an important impact on the reluctance to decide on the basis of indicia. While with witness testimony and the confession the moral responsibility for the conviction appeared to lie primarily on the witnesses and the accused who provided the evidence, indicia were dependent on

---

half year. These judges had the capacity to use the far-reaching powers of the inquisitorial procedure on the citizens of the city-state and a desire existed to circumscribe their powers as closely as possible. After their term as a judge, a 'syndicate-procedure' was always held to see whether the judges had abided by the legal rules. In this context the evidentiary rules had the function of a constraint on the basis of which the decisions of the judges could be evaluated. On the syndicate-procedure see, for example, M. Isenmann, *Legalität und Herrschaftskontrolle (1200–1600). Eine vergleichende Studie zum Syndikatsprozess: Florenz, Kastilien und Valencia.*

29 J.Q. Whitman, *The origins of reasonable doubt*, pp. 93–123. Similar to Whitman, Decock has argued that there was a certain moral anxiety underlying judgments in criminal cases and that there was an intense theological discussion on this topic throughout the late Middle Ages and the early modern period. A particularly difficult question in this respect concerned the potential sinfulness of judgements on suspicion. It is, therefore, clear that there were also important theological ideas underlying the system of legal proofs and the way it was expected that the judge would decide in criminal cases. Because of the focus in this study on the changing epistemological and political-constitutional ideas, the theological aspect will often not receive its due attention in this study. It is nevertheless, not the intention to deny the pervasive impact of theological considerations on the criminal law of evidence and the perception of how a good judge should conduct himself. See W. Decock, "The Judge's Conscience and the Protection of the Criminal Defendant: Moral Safeguards against Judicial Arbitrariness", pp. 69–94.

conclusions drawn by the judge and the moral responsibility for drawing the right conclusions rested on his shoulders. Conversely, it is likely that with a more secularized approach to the criminal procedure in the eighteenth and nineteenth centuries and a decreasing use of capital punishments, this moral anxiety lessened and made it more acceptable to decide on the basis of indicia.

Fourthly, the system of legal proofs was inspired by Aristotelian philosophy and was created with the 'scholastic' method in which the different possible forms of evidence were distinguished from each other and placed within a hierarchy which predetermined their value. Within late-medieval Aristotelian philosophy there was a relatively absolute ideal of what constituted *scientia* or 'knowledge'. For a proposition to be the object of *scientia* it needed to be necessary and universal, known on the basis of an affirmative demonstration. The epistemic ideal of *scientia* had the function of a role-model in how the certainty was conceived that needed to be acquired in criminal cases. The judge could not convict on the basis of a mere opinion or subjective feeling, he needed to have a form of knowledge which more resembled *scientia*. A relatively absolute standard was, therefore, created for criminal cases which was subject to general rules. Only when these rules were complied with – i.e. when there was a confession or the testimony of two irreproachable eyewitnesses –, was it deemed that the judge had a sufficient certainty.[30] The epistemological foundations of the system of legal proofs are discussed in more detail in the following chapter.

The fifth characteristic – which has often received too little attention – is the fact that the evidentiary requirements were strongly tied to a scale of decision types. The high standard of a full proof was normally required only for a capital or severe corporal punishment. A less severe or so-called 'extraordinary' punishment – such as a banishment or a fine – could be pronounced when there was strong evidence short of a full proof.[31] In fact, the criminal judge had two possibilities when he had strong evidence against the accused short of a full proof. He could either apply judicial torture to obtain a confession and thereby acquire a full proof to convict to the ordinary punishment, or he could choose to convict the accused to a lesser (extraordinary) punishment. The choice between these two possibilities was left largely to the discretion of the judge. They both formed important 'remedies' within the system of legal proofs against the strict requirements of a full proof which would otherwise

---

[30] On *Scientia* see R. Pasnau, "Medieval social epistemology: *Scientia* for mere mortals", pp. 23–41 and R. Pasnau, "Science and Certainty", pp. 357–368.
[31] M. Schmoeckel, *Humanität und Staatsraison*, pp. 295–296.

have meant that many crimes would go unpunished. When there was even weaker evidence the judge could pronounce an *absolutio ab instantia* (i.e. a provisional acquittal under which the investigation could be reopened at any time). Lastly, when the evidence was very weak the judge could pronounce a complete or unconditional acquittal.

There was, therefore, a far less absolute distinction between guilty and not-guilty under the system of legal proofs than that which would exist after the eighteenth century. Foucault has eloquently described the logic underlying the scale of decision types:

> The reason is to be found in the way in which criminal justice, in the classical period, operated in the production of truth. The different pieces of evidence did not constitute so many neutral elements, until such time as they could be gathered together into a single body of evidence that would bring the final certainty of guilt. Each piece of evidence aroused a particular degree of abomination. Guilt did not begin when all the evidence was gathered together; piece by piece, it was constituted by each of the elements that made it possible to recognize a guilty person. Thus a semi-proof did not leave the suspect innocent until such time as it was completed; it made him semi-guilty; slight evidence of a serious crime marked someone as slightly criminal. In short, penal demonstration did not obey a dualistic system: true or false; but a principle of continuous gradation; a degree reached in the demonstration already formed a degree of guilt and consequently involved a degree of punishment.[32]

2.3.1 The Regulation of the Different Forms of Evidence in the System of Legal Proofs

From the start a strong emphasis was placed in the juridical literature on the fact that a high level of certainty was required for a severe punishment. Very often the phrase, derived from Roman law, was repeated that in criminal cases the evidence needed to be clearer than the light of the noonday sun. Another important phrase that was repeated many times came from a rescript of the emperor Trajan which stated that someone could not be punished on the basis of a mere suspicion. This high standard of proof was differentiated from the standard of proof in civil cases which was lower. The reason for the more demanding standard of proof in criminal cases lay in the far-reaching

---

[32] M. Foucault, *Discipline and Punish*, p. 42.

consequences which could result from a criminal procedure.[33] In general only the confession and the testimony of two irreproachable eyewitnesses sufficed to pronounce the ordinary punishment. The question whether (undoubtable) indicia could form a full proof and justify the ordinary punishment was a point of constant discussion.

2.3.1.1   The Confession and 'notoriety'

The confession played a central and rather complex role within the system of legal proofs. Lévy remarked that the system of legal proofs can be considered as constituting an evidentiary pyramid. The top of this pyramid was formed by the fact that a crime could be *notorious*. Just below notoriety was the category of the full proof or *probatio plena*. Both sufficed for the ordinary punishment. The difference was that when a crime was notorious, the situation was considered to be so evident that a more summary procedure could be used in which the accused could be convicted almost directly. Notoriety stood above proof proper and made a fact so incontestable that no counterevidence could be produced against it. With a regular full proof there still needed to be a normal procedure. Notoriety was an original invention of canon law and its main purpose was to create the possibility to act quickly to avoid scandals and maintain ecclesiastical discipline effectively. Although several forms of notoriety were distinguished, two were by far the most important: *notorium facti* and *notorium iuris*. The former existed when the crime had been committed in front of a large crowd or, for example, in front of the court itself. The most important form of *notorium iuris* was formed by the voluntary confession of the accused in front of the court. Lévy mentions that a preliminary procedure was used to decide whether the crime was notorious and, when this was the case, subsequently only a summary procedure was held.[34]

Particularly in the formative centuries of the system of legal proofs the confession had a special standing which put it above a normal full proof. Several passages in Roman law were used to explain this special effect. There was for

---

33   M. Schmoeckel, *Humanität und Staatsraison*, pp. 193–199. In fact, the criminal procedure was at first differentiated from the civil procedure predominantly because of the more far-reaching consequences that the procedure could have. As Schmoeckel stated "Das gemeine Recht bestimmte das Verfahren auch nicht vom Verbrechensgegenstand bzw. dem öffentlichen Strafbedürfnis im Fall eines Verbrechens her, sondern nach der zu erwartenden Rechtsfolge".

34   J. PH. Lévy, *La hiérarchie des preuves dans le droit savant du Moyen-Age*, pp. 32–58, and P. Marchetti, *Testis Contra Se*, pp. 27–63. A too extensive use of notoriety was criticized because it was well understood that it formed a dangerous way of bypassing the normal procedure. Quite soon there was a tendency to restrict the use of notoriety.

example a remark by the jurist Paul which stated that with a confession the defendant convicted himself (*Confessus pro iudicato est, qui qoudammodo sua sententia damnatur*). By confessing the accused forfeited his right to a further procedure and more or less convicted himself. Although this view was never entirely accepted, it does reveal the tendency to see the confession as more than a normal form of evidence. The special standing of the confession was also reflected in its procedural effects. With a confession only a summary procedure was held. This meant that the production of counterevidence was no longer possible and that appeal was prohibited (*confessus non appellat*).[35] The idea of the high standing of the confession and its special procedural effects would remain important throughout the time that the system of legal proofs existed.[36] The persistence of this role of the confession is particularly striking in the province of Holland (which will be further discussed in Chapter six). Until the end of the eighteenth century in Holland the practice was retained that a severe corporal or capital punishment could only be applied on the basis of a confession, and that the confession made appeal impossible. For this reason, the criminal procedure in Holland remained strongly geared towards obtaining a confession.

Nevertheless, not every confession was sufficient. The confession had to be made in court and voluntarily. Furthermore, the accused needed to be of a certain age and the confession had to be credible. The fact that the confession needed to be voluntary appeared to be in conflict with the possibility to extract confessions under judicial torture, but the consensus in the juridical literature was that a voluntary confession was achieved when the accused later repeated his confession before the court after judicial torture had been applied. If the accused refused to repeat his confession he could be tortured again. It was also important that the confession was credible. In the juridical literature there are many admonitions to the judge that he needed to investigate whether the confession was actually true and that the confession needed to be supported by some other circumstances which verified it. Because the confession had to be made in court and the judges needed to evaluate its veracity, the judgement on the basis of the confession was in fact very similar to the judgement on the basis of a normal full proof (apart from the special procedural effects of the confession). As Lévy concluded: "Au fond peu de différences apparaissent

---

[35] Ibidem, pp. 54–61.
[36] Kleinheyer has, furthermore, argued that the central importance and special status of the confession also had roots in the development of German customary law. See G. von Kleinheyer, "Zur Rolle des Geständnisses im Strafverfahren des späten Mittelalters und der frühen Neuzeit", pp. 367–384.

entre l'aveu en justice et les preuves ordinaires, puisque son autorité n'est pas irréfragable".[37] Furthermore, as Rosoni observed, from around the sixteenth century onwards the evidentiary situation was simplified. The concept of notoriety became less important and the confession was treated increasingly as a normal, albeit the best, form of proof.[38]

2.3.1.2 Witness Testimony

In the Old and the New Testament and in Roman law many passages could be found which were used to support the rule that at least two or three witnesses were necessary for a conviction. A strong consensus existed in the juridical literature that at least two or three eyewitnesses were required to create a full proof. There was, furthermore, an extensive regulation of the criteria which needed to be met by the witnesses. First of all they needed to be witnesses *de visu*. Hearsay testimony was not allowed; the witnesses could only testify to what they had actually seen. Secondly, the witnesses needed to be 'irreproachable'. The capacity to testify was seen as a *dignitas*. One needed to be of such a social stature and reputation that one was literally worthy of trust. Especially in the formative centuries of the system of legal proofs a detailed categorization was made that prescribed when a witness was irreproachable. These categorizations predetermined what kind of witnesses were reliable and whose testimony could, therefore, create a full proof. Apart from the question whether the witness was irreproachable, the judge also needed to evaluate whether the testimony of the accused was credible and to what extent it concurred with the testimony of other witnesses.[39] The last aspect in particular was left to the evaluation of the judge and shows that he had to substantively evaluate their testimony.

Generally two aspects were distinguished which could make a witness reproachable. He could be reproachable because of his relation to the accused or because of personal qualities. Examples of the former were the lawyer of the accused, co-perpetrators of the crime and certain family members and servants of the accused. Examples of the latter were that the witness needed to have reached a certain age – twenty in criminal affairs and fourteen in civil affairs – and that the witness could not be infamous by law (which he would be if he was ever convicted of a crime). There was, in short, an extensive regulation

---

37   J-P. Lévy, *La hiérarchie des preuves dans le droit savant du Moyen-Age*, pp. 55–61.
38   I. Rosoni, *Quae singula non prosunt collecta iuvant*, pp. 74–75. Schmoeckel remarks in a similar way that the concept of notoriety became less important after the late middle ages. See Schmoeckel, *Humanität und Staatsraison*, p. 440.
39   J. PH. Lévy, *La hiérarchie des preuves dans le droit savant du Moyen-Age*, pp. 68–72.

of circumstances which too a large extent predetermined whether an accused was irreproachable and could therefore give credible testimony. The important practical consequence was that only a restricted number of people could give a 'trustworthy' testimony which could constitute a full proof. It was, nevertheless, not the case that the testimony of reproachable witnesses was completely without effect. They could still be used by the judge as an *indicium* of which the precise value was not easy to specify and left largely to the discretion of the judge. Finally, Schnapper observed an important change in the juridical doctrine concerning witness testimony from particularly the sixteenth century onwards. He found that the relatively rigid theory of the middle ages concerning witnesses was increasingly loosened. The judge was left more room to decide whether a witness was reproachable and it became possible to make more extensive use of the testimony of reproachable witnesses. Schnapper explains the change predominantly from the fact that a stronger emphasis was placed on effectively prosecuting crimes.[40]

2.3.1.3 Written Documents

The evidentiary value of written documents in criminal cases was relatively unclear. They could, for example, be used as important forms of evidence to prove the *corpus delicti* in crimes such as falsification. An often discussed question was, furthermore, whether the content of written documents should be trusted more than the testimony of witnesses. Many authors argued that witness testimony should be trusted because it was unnatural to place more faith in the skin of a dead animal than in a living witness, while some deemed written documents more reliable than witnesses. The question if and to what extent written documents could be used to contribute to a full proof remains uncertain and Schmoeckel remarks that no clear rule could be given regarding written documents in the middle ages.[41] Nevertheless, in any case written documents played only a very limited role in criminal cases between the thirteenth and eighteenth centuries, when a large majority of the population was still analphabetic.

2.3.1.4 Indicia and Probationes Semiplenae

Apart from describing what constituted a full proof on the basis of which the ordinary punishment could be pronounced, a difficult question was how to categorize the lesser forms of evidence and what their effect could be. Two

---

40 B. Schnapper, "Testes inhabiles. Les temoins reprochables dans l'ancien droit pénal", pp. 575–616.
41 M. Schmoeckel, *Humanität und Staatsraison*, pp. 207–209.

important concepts in this respect were *probatio semiplena* (half proof) and *indicium*. The term half proof derived from the idea that while two irreproachable eyewitnesses formed a full proof, one irreproachable eyewitness would thereby form a half proof. The term half proof has later often mistakenly been taken to imply that within the system of legal proofs there was a tendency to treat the different forms of evidence arithmetically. This was not the case. The term was used merely to express that a full proof was not achieved, and the term of *probatio semiplena* could and was often used interchangeably with the term *probatio imperfecta*. The idea that it was characteristic of the system of legal proof to work arithmetically with different fractions of proof (such as half and quarter proofs) was largely a polemical invention developed in the eighteenth century to discredit the system of legal proofs.[42]

Thus, the term half proof was merely meant to describe a relatively strong form of evidence. Below a half proof stood the term *indicium* which generally designated a less strong form of evidence. In the juridical treatises further elaborations on these terms can also be found, such as 'more than a half proof' and gradations within the concept of indicia, which were intended to express varying degrees of strength of the evidence. The terminology was quite vague and differed among authors. The categories were used as a sort of conceptual grid under which the different forms of evidence and their relative strength could be subsumed. Their significance lay in the fact that they were used in the juridical treatises to express what forms of evidence were necessary for different investigative measures and when, for example, judicial torture or an extraordinary punishment could be applied.[43]

The regulation of indicia was perhaps the most complex subject-matter within the system of legal proofs. Particularly because of the large variety of possible circumstances which were covered by this concept and the unclarity of its definition and legal consequences. The most clear and specific definition was that indicia were described as the conclusion of a known (circumstantial) fact to an unknown fact concerning the crime. This meant that indicia could be formed by any fact or circumstance from which a conclusion could be drawn regarding the crime, and that the number and variety of possible indicia was in theory endless.[44] Furthermore, because an indicium essentially consisted of the drawing of a conclusion, its existence was dependent on the

---

42 Ibidem, pp. 211–214.
43 H. Pihlajamaki, *Evidence, Crime and the Legal* Profession, pp. 26–29.
44 The term indicium was used to indicate the inference that was drawn as well as the fact from which the inference was made. To add to the vagueness of the terminology, the term indicium was sometimes also used to designate everything less than a full proof, meaning that an extrajudicial confession or the testimony of one witness were also subsumed

person judging. This particularly appeared to give indicia an element of subjectivity and uncertainty which the confession and witness testimony did not seem to have. The confession and witness testimony were thought to prove the crime 'directly' while indicia could only prove the crime 'indirectly'.

One important point of debate within the juridical literature was whether indicia could, through their cumulation, constitute a full proof sufficient for a conviction to the ordinary punishment. Generally the authors were very circumspect about this possibility and many argued decidedly that indicia could not create the certainty necessary for a full proof.[45] There were, nevertheless, also authors who deemed that in relatively exceptional cases the cumulative effect of indicia could be so strong that they created a full proof. One of the first to defend this possibility, which he called *indicia indubitata* (undoubtable indicia), was Thomas de Piperata from Bologna in a treatise written at the end of the thirteenth century. He described several situations in which he deemed that undoubtable indicia existed. For example, when someone was seen who was very pale and left a room with a bloody sword where someone was found dead while nobody else was in the room. De Piperata principally deemed it possible to convict someone on the basis of indicia.[46]

Soon after the creation of Thomas's work, Gandinus argued in his treatise that he and the doctors of Bologna were all opposed to this possibility and deemed it in conflict with the demand that the proof needed to be clearer than the light of the noonday sun. Gandinus did find that a pecuniary sanction was admissible under the circumstances discussed by De Piperata, but not the ordinary punishment. The examples discussed by De Piperata and the term *indicia indubitata* became widely known and would be very often discussed in later treatises on the criminal law of evidence. Importantly, those authors who argued that a conviction to the ordinary punishment was possible on the basis of *indicia indubitata* deemed this to be possible only under very exceptional circumstances. Many authors, however, found it safer when there were strong indicia against the accused to proceed either to judicial torture or to pronounce an extraordinary punishment. Summarizing, indicia were considered with suspicion and generally it was held that they could not form a sufficient proof for

---

under this category. Normally, however, the more specific definition of indicium was used. See M. Schmoeckel, *Humanität und Staatsraison*, pp. 216–220.

45 P. Marchetti, *Testis Contra Se*, pp. 100–103. An extraordinary punishment was possible on the basis of indicia. Marchetti also mentions the comment of Farinicius that indicia could not justify a corporal punishment, not even if there were a thousand indicia.

46 M. Schmoeckel, *Humanität und Staatsraison*, pp. 216–224.

a conviction to the ordinary punishment.[47] Instead, the importance of indicia lay predominantly in the investigative measures, such as judicial torture, and the lesser punishments that they could justify.

Many different categorizations can be found of indicia in the juridical treatises. The indicia were mostly classified in terms of the effect within the criminal procedure they could have. One often used division was that between close and remote indicia, in which close indicia were very strong and remote indicia far weaker. Indicia were further categorized in indicia sufficient to commence inquisitorial proceedings, indicia sufficient to arrest the accused and indicia sufficient to allow judicial torture. Another division was that between general indicia which could be found for any sort of crime, and indicia specific to certain sorts of crimes. Especially the question when indicia could be sufficient to justify judicial torture was a controversial question which was given a lot of attention in the juridical literature. In fact, indicia were at first almost always treated in connection with the subject of judicial torture.[48]

Normally the juridical treatises extensively treated a number of commonly found indicia in a casuistic way and described under which circumstances they could justify judicial torture or a less invasive investigative measure. Typical indicia that were treated in the juridical treatises were the social reputation of the accused, the flight of the accused, his animosity towards the victim and the possession of stolen goods or the murder weapon. It is, however, important to note that there was a clear awareness among the jurists that the subject of indicia could not be treated exhaustively and that in the end much needed to be left to the discretion of the judge. The treatment and classification of the indicia were meant as important examples which could help guide the judgement of the judge.[49]

2.3.1.5   The Social Reputation of the Accused

Lastly, the social standing or reputation of the accused was a factor of great importance within the system of legal proofs. The social reputation of the accused (also called the *infamia iuris*, in French the *renommée* and in German *Leumund*) influenced almost every aspect of the criminal procedure.[50] The

---

47   G. Alessi Palazzolo, *Prova legale e pena*, pp. 55–88. See also R. Fraher, "Conviction according to conscience: The medieval jurists' debate concerning judicial discretion and the law of proof", pp. 23–64, and I. Rosoni, *Quae singula non prosunt collecta iuvant*, pp. 135–149.
48   I. Rosoni, *Quae singula non prosunt collecta iuvant*, pp. 77–78.
49   M. Schmoeckel, *Humanität und Staatsraison*, pp. 220–228.
50   A distinction was generally made between the *infamia facti* and the *infamia iuris*. The *infamia facti* referred to the general *fama publica* or public rumour that a crime had been committed. It was the *infamia facti* which was required to start an inquisitorial procedure.

question how strong the evidence needed to be before judicial torture could be used and even if an inquisitorial procedure could be started at all, were all strongly influenced by the social reputation of the accused. The full force of the inquisitorial apparatus was used predominantly and far more easily against the lower classes, foreigners and vagabonds, while on the other hand the evidentiary requirements against persons of a better social reputation and who had the right of citizenship were far higher. In this sense Van Caenegem, for example, concluded on the basis of his research on the practice of the criminal law in Flanders that: "On a nettement l'impression … que dans la période sous revue le droit pénal n'etait appliqué dans toute sa férocité qu'aux étrangers (et notamment aux vagabonds et mendiants)".[51]

Vallerani concluded in a similar manner for the Italian city-states in the late middle ages that judicial torture and the inquisitorial procedure were used far more easily against strangers and vagabonds than against the privileged citizens of the commune. The citizens of a good reputation were, furthermore, given a far greater room to find a resolution for 'crimes' through a monetary composition.[52] The fact that the social reputation was of such significance in the criminal procedural law is not surprising considering the all-pervasive importance of social standing in the late Middle Ages and in the early modern period. It is important to keep in mind that apart from the abstract theory of the evidentiary rules, the reputation of the accused was a factor of great importance in determining the strictness with which the rules were applied in practice. The procedural differentiation on the basis of the reputation of the accused can be seen as late as the end of the eighteenth century. For example, an ordinance created in 1791 which regulated the criminal procedural law for the city of Den Bosch, contained two procedural tracks: one for ordinary citizens and one for strangers and vagabonds. The ordinance explicitly prescribed that judicial torture and other investigative measures could be used far more easily against vagabonds and strangers than against normal citizens.[53]

The *infamia iurius*, on the other hand, referred to the reputation of the accused. When the accused had a bad reputation this could form an important indicium against him. See L.I. Stern, "Public Fame in the Fifteenth Century", pp. 198–214.

51   R.C. Van Caenegem, "La Peine dans les anciens Pays-Bas", pp. 127–128. See also J. Théry, "Fama: l'opinion publique comme preuve judiciaire aperçu *sur la révolucion médiévale de l'inquisitoire (XIIe–XIVe siècle)*". and K. Nehlsen-von Stryk, "Die Krise des 'irrationele' Beweises im Hoch- und SpätMA und ihre gesellschaftlichen Implikationen".

52   M. Vallerani, *Medieval Public Justice*, pp. 250–251.

53   *Reglement en ordonnantie op de crimineele justitie en den styl van procedeeren in Crimineele Zaaken voor den geregte van 's Hertogenbosch*, pp. 65–89.

2.3.2 The Possibilities in Absence of a Full Proof: Judicial Torture, Extraordinary Punishments and the Absolutio ab Instantia

It is easily imaginable that the strict observance of the rules requiring either a confession or the testimony of two irreproachable eyewitnesses would leave many crimes unpunished. It was for this reason that solutions were developed within the system of legal proofs for the situation where strong evidence existed against the accused short of a full proof. The most infamous of these solutions was the possibility of judicial torture. Under certain circumstances, which were regulated in the juridical treatises, the judge could decide that the accused would be tortured in order to obtain his confession. Another solution, when strong evidence short of a full proof existed, was that a less severe or 'extraordinary' punishment could be applied. Finally, a solution was also developed for the situation when there was incriminating evidence which was too weak to apply judicial torture or an extraordinary punishment, but which was felt to be too strong to completely acquit the accused: the *absolutio ab instantia*.

To an extent there was a hybrid approach within the system of legal proofs. On the one hand a strong emphasis was placed on the fact that in criminal affairs and for severe punishments the evidence needed to be clearer than the light of the noonday sun. Aware of the far-reaching effect of punishments there were constant admonitions that the judge needed to be scrupulous in his judgement and abide by the evidentiary rules. On the other hand there was also a clear unwillingness to simply acquit the accused against whom strong incriminatory evidence short of a full proof existed. It was evident that this would make the criminal procedural law too ineffective. For this reason the alternatives of judicial torture, extraordinary punishments and the *absolutio ab instantia* were developed. Judicial torture created the possibility to try and obtain a confession when there was strong incriminating evidence and it was deemed that a capital or severe corporal punishment should be applied. Extraordinary punishments allowed the judge to pronounce a less severe punishment on evidence short of a full proof. This could even be done after the accused was tortured and when he had refused to confess. Even though these options seemed to be in contradiction with the strict evidentiary rules of the system of legal proofs, they were essentially a necessary correction on their rigidity. They provided the system of legal proofs with a flexibility that ensured that the criminal procedural law could function effectively.[54]

---

54   G. Alessi Palazzolo, *Prova legale e pena*, pp. 18–25.

2.3.2.1 Judicial Torture

The most important reason for the use of judicial torture lay in the relative rigidity of the evidentiary rules and the high probative status that was attached to the confession. Nevertheless, already in the earliest treatises which reflected on judicial torture it was recognized that it was a very dangerous and uncertain instrument that should be used only with the greatest caution. In the juridical treatises a lot of attention was paid to the formulation of criteria which dictated when judicial torture could be used and what the effects were if the accused had or had not confessed. First of all, judicial torture could only be used when there was strong evidence against the accused and when there was no other means of arriving at a full proof. The precise evidentiary standard for the use of judicial torture was discussed continuously and differed according to the author. Many authors stated that at least a half proof was required for judicial torture. In the seventeenth and eighteenth centuries in the Netherlands, the formulation was often used that the evidence needed to be 'so strong that nothing appeared to be lacking except for the confession to completely convince the accused'. Although the legal treatises gave many examples under which torture was or was not allowed, they also recognized that in the end this decision had to be left to the discretion of the judge.[55]

A second rule was that judicial torture was allowed solely for crimes which were threatened with a capital or severe corporal punishment. Thirdly, judicial torture could not be used on everyone. Although the categories differed according to the author, a consensus existed that the following groups were exempted: pregnant women, the insane, minors and those who were very old or of a weak physical condition. A fourth rule was that judicial torture needed to be executed in presence of the judge and of a physician. The manner of execution, the duration and the severity of the judicial torture was left to the discretion of the judge. The confession of the accused during judicial torture was not yet valid. The accused needed to repeat the confession afterwards in court. Only in this way, when the confession was repeated outside of the bounds of pain and iron, was it deemed that the confession was given voluntarily (which was necessary for a confession to be valid). The freedom of the accused was, however, largely illusory because judicial torture could be repeated if the accused retracted his confession. Nevertheless, many authors did state that

---

[55] See, for example, S. van Leeuwen, *Costuymen van Rijnland*, pp. 109–110, J. van der Meulen, *Ordonnantie ende instructie op de stijl ende maniere van procederen voor den hove van Utrecht*, p. 342 and P. Bort, *Tractaet crimineel*, p. 513.

judicial torture could be repeated no more than three times if the accused kept retracting his confession.[56]

The rules surrounding judicial torture had to be followed very scrupulously because any transgression on the side of the judge meant that the confession was invalid. A last important question was what needed to be done when the accused did not confess under torture. There were some authors who argued that if the accused did not confess the incriminating evidence against him was purged and that he should be entirely acquitted or at most be given an *absolutio ab instantia*. However, there were also authors who deemed that the strong incriminating evidence was not purged by the fact that the accused had refused to confess, and that the judge could still pronounce an extraordinary punishment. This was, for example, the established practice in the province of Holland in the seventeenth and eighteenth century.[57] It was also institutionalised in France from the seventeenth century onwards in the possibility of using torture *avec réserve des preuves*, which meant that torture was used but that the judge could still pronounce an extraordinary punishment.[58] The use of judicial torture, therefore, did not exclude the possibility of pronouncing an extraordinary punishment or an *absolutio ab instantia*; these measures complemented each other.

2.3.2.2   Extraordinary Punishment and the Absolutio ab Instantia

The normal or ordinary punishment was the name for the punishment which was prescribed for a certain crime in statutes, Roman law or canonical law. For many of the serious crimes in the late Middle Ages the prescribed punishment was the capital punishment or a severe corporal punishment. The 'extraordinary' punishment was the term which designated a punishment that was less severe than the ordinary punishment and which was left to the discretion of the judge.[59] Within the system of legal proofs this distinction became firmly tied to the question whether there was a full proof or less than a full proof. The ordinary punishment, consisting of a capital punishment or severe corporal punishment, could only be applied if there was a full proof. When there was strong evidence short of a full proof, a less severe extraordinary punishment could be applied. Another term for extraordinary punishments that was used in Germany was *Verdachtsstrafe* (literally a punishment for a suspicion). With

---

56   M. Schmoeckel, *Humanität und Staatsraison*, pp. 254–267.
57   S. Faber, *Strafrechtspleging en criminaliteit te Amsterdam, 1680–1811*, pp. 147–149.
58   J-M. Carbasse, *Histoire du droit pénal et de la justice criminelle*, pp. 212–214.
59   On the origins of the distinction between the ordinary and the extraordinary punishments see L. Mayali, "The concept of discretionary punishment in medieval jurisprudence", pp. 299–315.

this term was meant that a lesser punishment could be applied when there was a strong suspicion of guilt, but not a full proof.[60] There were different forms of extraordinary punishments and they varied regionally. Typical extraordinary punishments in the province of Holland in the seventeenth and eighteenth centuries consisted of banishments or the conviction to spend a certain time in a workhouse.[61] In France workhouses were more rare and the accused could, for example, be convicted to work in the galleys.[62]

The evidentiary standard for the application of an extraordinary punishment varied according to the author and was, just as with judicial torture, not very precise. Unlike the question when there was sufficient evidence for judicial torture – which received a lot of attention in the juridical treatises – the question when sufficient evidence existed to pronounce an extraordinary punishment was normally treated only summarily. The evidentiary standard and the form of the extraordinary punishment were left largely to the discretion of the judge. This meant that the judges had a relatively large freedom in giving the accused an extraordinary punishment when the strict requirements for a full proof were not met.

A last option which the judge had beside a full acquittal, was the *absolutio ab instantia*. This meant that the accused was neither convicted nor acquitted and that the procedure could be reinitiated at any moment when new evidence emerged. The judge could pronounce an *absolutio ab instantia* when he deemed the evidence too strong to acquit the accused and too weak for an extraordinary punishment or judicial torture. This possibility gave the judge a significant further flexibility in adjusting his verdict to the strength of the evidence. Schmoeckel states that the measure was useful because the procedural rule of *non bis in idem* (i.e. someone may not be tried twice for the same crime) had become accepted at least since the thirteenth century. Acquitting the accused, therefore, meant that he could not be prosecuted for the same crime again, while an *absolutio ab instantia* kept the possibility open to further prosecute an accused at a later time.[63] Naturally, the downside for the accused was that he was kept in a continuing state of uncertainty because the procedure could be reopened at any time. This downside would later in the eighteenth and nineteenth centuries become the main point of criticism against the *absolutio ab instantia*.

---

60 On this term see, for example, B. Thäle, *Die Verdachtsstrafe in der kriminalwissenschaftlichen Literatur des 18. und 19. Jahrhunderts*.
61 S. Faber, *Strafrechtspleging en criminaliteit te Amsterdam*, pp. 172–178.
62 J-M. Carbasse, *Histoire du droit pénal et de la justice criminelle*, pp. 289–293.
63 M. Schmoeckel, *Humanität und Staatsraison*, pp. 360–409.

2.4 The Thesis of Langbein

So far a rather static picture has been painted of the system of legal proofs as it existed between the late Middle Ages and the nineteenth century. The underlying presumption is that although there occurred important changes in this period, the theory and workings of the system of legal proofs did not change in a fundamental way until the end of the eighteenth century. There are, however, authors who have argued that a system based on the free evaluation of the evidence already developed in practice since especially the sixteenth and seventeenth centuries, and that the abolition of the system of legal proofs during the French revolution merely formed a ratification of this development. The most well-known defence of this idea was presented by Langbein in his *Torture and the law of proof*.

Langbein starts his book by giving a description of the transition from an evidentiary system based on ordeals to the creation of the system of legal proofs. One important thread in this description is that Langbein argues that a very rigid system of legal proofs was developed in the late Middle Ages because there was an anxiety to accept the subjective judgement of the judge for such far-reaching consequences as a capital punishment. Replacing the ordeals with the subjective judgement was not considered acceptable and instead a rigid system of rules was developed which predetermined when there was sufficient evidence for a conviction. Furthermore, according to Langbein, in the late Middle Ages judicial torture was accepted as the sole corrective to the rigidity of the evidentiary rules.[64]

Subsequently, Langbein presents his explanation of how this rigid system was overturned in practice. This explanation consists of two factors. First of all, Langbein explains that the rigid system applied solely to serious crimes, while at the same a free evaluation of the evidence was already accepted for petty crimes (*delicta leviora*) since the late Middle Ages. Judicial torture was not allowed for petty crimes and the judgement of them was left largely to the discretion of the judge. Secondly, Langbein argues that this free evaluation, which at first only applied to petty crimes, was extended to serious crimes from the sixteenth century onwards in the form of extraordinary punishments. He deems that extraordinary punishments were developed only from the sixteenth century onwards and subsequently became more and more commonly used until the end of the eighteenth century. Concerning extraordinary punishments there were virtually no evidentiary rules which bound the judge in his judgement, and he was therefore *de facto* free in the evaluation of the

---

64   J. Langbein, *Torture and the law of proof*, pp. 3–8.

evidence. Langbein contends that the alternative of freely evaluating the evidence and punishing with a less severe penalty than the capital punishment became increasingly more attractive than using judicial torture and eventually made its use obsolete. In this way, the practice of *de facto* freely evaluating the evidence in the use of extraordinary punishments eventually overturned the system of legal proofs and became the common practice between the sixteenth and eighteenth centuries.[65]

With his thesis Langbein reacts against those who had argued that judicial torture was abolished from the late eighteenth century onwards because of the ideological criticisms of authors such as Beccaria and the French *philosophes* who deemed judicial torture a barbarous and inhumane instrument. Langbein even remarked that the explanation of the abolition of judicial torture and the introduction of the free evaluation of the evidence from the ideological reflections of such authors should be considered a 'fairy tale'.[66] This change had, according to Langbein, already developed in practice and was later only ratified by the legislation that abolished judicial torture and the system of legal proofs.

There are two problems with the thesis of Langbein. First of all, Langbein works from the questionable presumption that in the late Middle Ages the system of legal proofs worked as a completely rigid system and that only from the sixteenth century onwards different means such as the extraordinary punishments were created to circumvent this rigidity (which thus made the instrument of judicial torture obsolete). Secondly, it is questionable whether the large judicial discretion in applying extraordinary punishments can be equated with the conscious formulation of a theory based on the free evaluation of the evidence and the explicit rejection of evidentiary rules which occurred between roughly 1750 and 1870.

Concerning the first aspect, it is unlikely that the system of legal proofs ever worked as rigidly in the late Middle Ages as Langbein presumes. Lepsius in particular has argued that it was never expected of the criminal judge to function as an automaton who mechanically applied the evidentiary rules. The judge had a large discretion in the evaluation of the evidence and it was expected that he, for example, substantively evaluated the trustworthiness of the testimony of witnesses and the accused. The mistaken image of a very rigid system of evidentiary rules in this sense strongly derived from a polemical misrepresentation of the system of legal proofs by the reform-minded authors in

---

65 Ibidem, pp. 27–69.
66 Ibidem, pp. 11–12.

the eighteenth and nineteenth centuries who sought to discredit the old criminal law of evidence.[67]

Furthermore, Schmoeckel has shown in an extensive study that instruments such as the extraordinary punishments and the possibility of an *absolutio ab instantia* had already been developed during the late middle ages in the formative period of the system of legal proofs. Particularly explicit is the following conclusion of Schmoeckel: "Es kann ausgeschlossen werden, dass die Entwicklung der Verdachtsstrafen die Aufhebung der Folter beeinflusst haben konnte. Das Gegenteil ist vielmehr richtig. Die Verdachtsstrafe ist nicht nur so alt wie die dogmatische Fassung der Folter im Mittelalter und das Inquisitionsverfahren, sondern wohl auch ein notwendiges Korrelat".[68] In a study on the relationship between the strictness of the evidentiary rules and the possibility of extraordinary punishments, Alessi Palazzolo reached a similar conclusion as Schmoeckel. The use of extraordinary punishments for the situation where less than a full proof existed did not mean that the system of legal proofs was replaced in practice with a system based on the free evaluation of the evidence. On the contrary, she concludes, it is more likely that the use of extraordinary punishments made the system of legal proofs more flexible (comparable to judicial torture) and thereby contributed to its longevity.[69] Rosoni also sees the possibility of applying extraordinary punishments on the basis of less than a full proof as an essential part of the system of legal proofs.[70] The extraordinary

---

67 S. Lepsius, *Von Zweifeln zur Überzeugung*, pp. 36–45 and 171–197.
68 M. Schmoeckel, *Humanität und Staatsraison*, pp. 295–410. These instruments were, furthermore, not the only correctives on the rigidity of the evidentiary rules that were already developed during the late Middle Ages. Certain exceptional categories of crimes were distinguished which justified a less stringent application of the evidentiary rules, for example, very severe or atrocious crimes such as high treason or crimes which were very difficult to prove (such as murders or thefts by night). Particularly in France, the doctrine was developed that for atrocious and difficult to prove crimes a less stringent evidentiary standard could be applied. It became, for example, commonly accepted that with these forms of crimes the judge could hear witnesses that would otherwise be considered reproachable. In the second half of the eighteenth century this logic would be one of the ideas which was severely criticized by the reform-minded authors. They pointed out that it was absurd to loosen the evidentiary standard just because the crime was difficult to prove or because it was a severe crime. On this doctrine see in particular B. Schnapper, "Testes inhabiles. Les témoins reprochable dans l'ancien droit pénal", pp. 594–616.
69 G. Alessi Palazzolo, *Prova legale e pena*, pp. 13–34.
70 I. Rosoni, *Quae singula non prosunt collecta iuvant*, pp. 124–129. Decock aptly remarked on this subject that: "Suarez and the *ius commune* share a remarkable capacity for allowing the exception within the system, for integrating the ordinary and the extraordinary within a logical whole. The symbiosis of the rule and the exception hinge on the *arbitrium judicis*, which holds this system together by reconciling strict law and equity. This is

punishments, therefore, did not make judicial torture obsolete because both instruments were used side by side and complemented each other.

Damaška as well remarks that there are a number of a reasons why Langbein's emphasis on the initial rigidity of the system of legal proofs appears 'prima facie suspect'. One important reason lies in the fact that many of the most prominent late-medieval authors, such as Gandinus, acknowledged in one way or another the possibility of applying less severe punishments on the basis of less than a full proof. The thesis of Langbein presumes that judicial torture became obsolete between the sixteenth and eighteenth centuries because judges could more easily contend themselves with applying a lighter extraordinary punishment. Damaška observes, however, that there are clear indications that even during the eighteenth century there were still many crimes that were considered so atrocious that death was thought to be the only appropriate punishment. Judicial torture was in these situations not obsolete, because the desire to impose a severe corporal or capital punishment (for which a confession was necessary) was still strongly felt.[71] Incidentally, the critique presented in this section does not mean that Langbein was wrong in his emphasis on the importance of a change in penology for the emergence of the free evaluation of the evidence, but it intends to show that the development of the criminal law of evidence was far more complex and cannot be reduced merely to a change in penology. As was stated in the previous chapter, it is, nevertheless, highly likely that the decreased use of the severe corporal and capital punishments in the eighteenth and nineteenth century made it more easy to accept the free evaluation of the evidence in this period.

Langbein argues that the rise of extraordinary punishments in practice led to the fact that by the late eighteenth century judicial torture was considered obsolete. However, even a cursory view of the juridical handbooks of the late eighteenth century shows that judicial judicial torture was far from being

---

illustrated by the distinction between ordinary and extraordinary punishments". See W. Decock, "The Judge's Conscience and the Protection of the Criminal Defendant: Moral Safeguards against Judicial Arbitrariness", pp. 78–79.

71   The comment of Damaška that early modern judges still deemed severe corporal punishments necessary is supported by Spierenburg. Spierenburg shows that public, physical punishments were considered a far more severe form of punishment than a banishment or confinement in a house of correction. Furthermore, the public infliction of punishments was still seen as indispensable well into the nineteenth century. Spierenburg explains that these demonstrations of power were still necessary both as a deterrent to criminals and to show that the authorities had a monopoly on violence. Only in the eighteenth and nineteenth centuries the power of the state power became so well established that it could afford to relinquish these 'spectacles of suffering' and punish criminals indoors. See P. Spierenburg, *The spectacle of suffering*, pp. 66–67 and 200–207.

considered obsolete in this period. In the Netherlands, for example, where the use of extraordinary punishments was widespread, juridical treatises in the late eighteenth century show that a large number of authors were still entirely convinced of the necessity of maintaining judicial torture. Authors such as Van der Keessel and Voorda argued for its retention because they deemed that the criminal procedural law would become ineffective without it.[72] The same can be seen in the juridical treatises in France by, among others, Muyart de Vouglans and Jousse who also defended the continued use of judicial torture.[73]

The fact that judicial torture was not yet deemed obsolete is also visible in other sources. Faber, for example, has shown in his research of the practice of the criminal justice in Amsterdam between 1680 and 1811, that the city government had had a discussion on the question whether judicial torture should be abolished or whether its use should be merely restricted in the late 1770s. A large majority of the alderman was entirely convinced of the continued necessity of the use of judicial torture and torture kept on being used in Amsterdam until it was abolished in 1798. Explicitly refuting the thesis of Langbein, Faber remarks that the abolition in 1798 was not the confirmation of the obsolescence of judicial torture in practice, but in fact formed an important breaking point in the reformation of the criminal law of evidence in the Netherlands.[74]

The second objection against the thesis of Langbein is that it is questionable whether the large judicial discretion in the application of extraordinary punishments can be equated with the introduction of the free evaluation of the evidence. The 'modern' principle of the free evaluation of the evidence – as it developed from the second half of the eighteenth century onwards – contained three important aspects which differentiated it from the large judicial discretion to apply extraordinary punishments under the system of legal proofs. Firstly, it was based on a conscious rejection of the system of legal proofs and the possibility to determine in *a priori* rules when sufficient evidence existed to convict someone. Secondly, it made the internal conviction of the judge or jurors the foundation of the evidentiary decision. Finally, the principle of the free evaluation of the evidence was embedded in a thoroughly altered criminal

---

[72] B. Beinart and P. van Warmelo, *Dionysius Godefredus van der Keessel. Lectures on Books 47 and 48 of the Digest*, vol VI, pp. 1749–1755 and B. Voorda, *De Crimineele Ordonnantien*, pp. 70–79.

[73] M. de Vouglans, *Les loix criminelles de France, dans leur ordre naturel*, pp. 796–798, and D. Jousse, *Traité de la justice criminelle de France, Tome II*, pp. 474–496.

[74] S. Faber, *Strafrechtspleging en criminaliteit te Amsterdam*, pp. 144–147. The fact that the abolition of judicial torture in 1798 in Holland did not form a confirmation of an obsolete practice will be further described in Chapter seven.

procedural law and it was the expression of changed epistemological ideas (which will be further discussed in the following chapter).

The large discretion of the judge in the application of extraordinary punishments can also not be equated with the free evaluation of the evidence because this discretion formed an essential part of the system of legal proofs itself. Until the end of the eighteenth century, the treatment of the system of legal proofs in the juridical handbooks and in the legislation remained largely the same. The focus continued to lie on a description of the criteria for a full proof on the basis of which a capital or a severe corporal punishment could be pronounced and under which circumstances judicial torture could be applied. The possibility to apply an extraordinary capital punishment continued to be treated summarily and as an exception to the situation where a full proof could be acquired. Furthermore, in the juridical literature it was not argued that the pronunciation of an extraordinary punishment was based on the freely formed internal conviction of the judge. Pihlajamäki, who agrees with Langbein in many other respects, similarly argues against his equation of this large judicial discretion with the free evaluation of the evidence:

> I would, however, hesitate to draw from this the conclusion that a "system" of free evaluation existed alongside that of statutory proof. First of all, medieval and early modern jurists did not consciously apply a system of legal proof alongside which another, contrasting system could have been tolerated. The premodern doctrine knew only one law of proof, applicable basically to all categories of crimes, although against some crimes more forceful methods of fact-finding were allowed. The evidentiary system was essentially hierarchical: different standards of proof corresponded to different grades of crime and to the distinct stages of the criminal procedure. However, no consciously formulated theory of free evaluation of evidence existed in continental jurisprudence before the latter half of the eighteenth century.[75]

---

75   H. Pihlajamaki, *Evidence, Crime and the Legal Profession*, pp. 30–31. The same criticism which is presented here against the thesis of Langbein can be directed against authors – such as Schnapper – who argue that the free evaluation of the evidence was practically introduced through a more extended use of indicia in the sixteenth, seventeenth and eighteenth centuries. Although there are indications that in some regions it became more accepted to convict someone to an ordinary or extraordinary punishment on the basis of indicia, this did not mean that thereby the free evaluation was introduced in practice. Firstly, convictions to the ordinary punishment on the basis of indicia continued to be relatively exceptional and the distrust against indicia remained very strong well into the nineteenth century. Secondly, and most importantly, a more extended possibility to

It is, finally, important to emphasize that it is not denied here that significant changes have occurred in practice within the system of legal proofs and penology between the late Middle Ages and the eighteenth century. There are, for example, studies which show that the possibility to convict on the basis of indicia was extended in especially the eighteenth century and that judicial torture was used more restrictively.[76] Furthermore, it is highly likely that the decreased use of severe corporal and capital punishments made the transition to the free evaluation of the evidence more easily acceptable in the eighteenth and nineteenth centuries. The point here is that these changes in practice did not themselves constitute the transition to a system based on the free evaluation of the evidence because they still occurred largely within the confines of the system of legal proofs and the existing procedural law. To a certain extent the changes in practice presaged a development in a new direction and were influenced by the same ideas which led to the eventual introduction of the free evaluation of the evidence.[77] Nevertheless, a crucial and innovative role was played by the reform discussion between 1750 and 1870 in which a consensus

---

convict to the ordinary punishment on the basis of indicia within the confines of the system of legal proofs was not the same as the conscious introduction of the free evaluation of the evidence. As Schmoeckel aptly stated on the extended possibility to convict on the basis of indicia: "diese bedeutete keineswegs die heimliche Einführung der freien richterlichen Beweiswürdigung. Vielmehr liegt darin eine der *typischen Inkonsequenzen*, die den flexiblen Umgang mit der starren gesetzlichen Beweislehre ermöglichte". See B. Schnapper, "Les peines arbitraries du XIIIe au XVIIIe siècle (doctrines savants et usages français", pp. 87–98, and M. Schmoeckel, *Humanität und Staatsraison*, p. 226.

[76] Andrews has, for example, shown that judicial torture and the acquisition of a confession became less important for the *parlement* of Paris the eighteenth century and Durand found that The 'Conseil souverain de Roussillon' (which was the equivalent of a *parlement*) pronounced its last confirmation of judicial torture in 1737. See R.M. Andrews, *Law, Magistracy, and crime in Old Regime Paris, 1735–1789. Vol 1*, pp. 439–455, and B. Durand, "Arbitraire du juge et droit de la torture: l'exemple du Conseil souverain de Roussillon", p. 177.

[77] This can be seen clearly in the conclusion of Ulrich who observed that the *parlement* of Bourgogne increasingly restricted the use of judicial torture in the eighteenth century and that it was used for the last time in 1766. Ulrich states that it is wrong to presume that changes in the criminal procedure took place solely after the French Revolution. They were preceded by a change in practice in the eighteenth century of especially the *parlements*. According to Ulrich, these changes in practice can be at least partially explained by the permeation of the 'enlightened' ideas to the judges of the *parlements* and provincial courts. For the Bourgogne, Ulrich notes that many of the judges were members of a freemason society while a survey of their libraries showed that, for example, the books of Locke, Helvetius, Rousseau, Voltaire and above all Montesquieu, were widespread. As will be described in Chapter seven, there was also a tendency in the Netherlands in the eighteenth century to pose far more restrictive criteria on the use of judicial torture. These changes in practice reflected the increasingly critical attitude towards the system of legal

grew that evidentiary rules should be abolished and that the judge should freely evaluate the evidence. In these discussions and the resulting legislation, the system of legal proofs was consciously replaced with the free evaluation of the evidence.

2.5 Conclusion

In this chapter the contours of the system of legal proofs have been sketched. The system of legal proofs had developed in the juridical discussions in the late Middle Ages and had a surprising longevity. This chapter has attempted to show that the system of legal proofs should not be seen as consisting solely of a group of rigid rules which determined when a full proof existed and when sufficient evidence was present to use judicial torture. As Pihlajamäki stated the system of legal proofs was essentially hierarchical: different standards of proof corresponded to different possible punishments.

This approach led to apparent contradictions within the system of legal proofs which, nevertheless, formed a fundamental part of the system itself. The 'contradictions' essentially derived from two conflicting tendencies. On the one hand there was the tendency to create strict criteria – particularly concerning serious crimes that might lead to a capital or severe corporal punishment – which needed to guarantee that someone was only convicted when the proof was clearer than the light of day. There was, in other words, a strong desire to bind the judge to strict rules to prevent unjustified convictions. On the other hand there was also the conflicting tendency to ensure that the criminal procedural law remained an effective instrument to punish undesirable behaviour effectively. Although the ideal was maintained that for a severe punishment a full proof was necessary, on the basis of the second tendency many exceptions and alleviations to this standard were created. The somewhat awkward instruments of judicial torture, extraordinary punishments and the *absolutio ab instantia* were accepted in this vein and provided a flexibility within the system of legal proofs without which it could not have functioned adequately.[78]

---

proofs and the ideas which underlay them. See D. Ulrich, "La repression en Bourgogne au XVIIIe siècle", pp. 412–437.

78 Furthermore, the possibility to allow extraordinary punishments on the basis of less strong evidence fitted well within the hierarchical logic of the system of legal proofs. It was acknowledged from the start that for civil cases and for petty crimes a lower standard of proof existed because they could only lead to a pecuniary sanction. Conversely, the high evidentiary standard was formulated because of the far-reaching consequences of

In a certain sense the problem of the thesis of Langbein is that he did not sufficiently acknowledge these contradictory tendencies. He presented the image of an ideal type situation in the late Middle Ages where the system of legal proofs supposedly functioned in all its rigidity, which later started to crumble away when instruments were developed which circumvented this rigidity. Another difficulty with the thesis of Langbein is that he equated the existence of a large judicial discretion with the formation of a system based on the free evaluation of the evidence. The thesis of Langbein, nonetheless, touches on one of the most important questions underlying this study, namely to what extent the 'modern' system based on the free evaluation of the evidence differed from the large judicial discretion which already existed under the system of legal proofs.

To answer this question it is first of all important to note that there was indeed in many respects a large room for judicial discretion within the system of legal proofs. Many things were left explicitly to the *arbitrium* (discretion) of the judge.[79] The judge was, for example, largely free in his decision on the question whether there was sufficient evidence to use judicial torture or to pronounce an extraordinary punishment, and he was free in choosing between either options. It was dependent on his *arbitrium* how judicial torture would be applied and if it should be repeated. Even regarding the application of the strict rules for a full proof, in practice much was left to the discretion of the judge. As Lepsius has, for example, demonstrated through the work of Bartolus, it was never expected of the judge to mechanically apply the evidentiary rules. In deciding whether the confession was sufficiently trustworthy and whether the testimony of the witnesses were sufficiently reliable, almost everything depended on the concrete evaluation of the judge.[80] It is, in short, beyond doubt that the judge had a large freedom of evaluation under the

---

the capital and severe corporal punishments. Between these two possibilities it was not difficult to accept the possibility to convict to a less severe, extraordinary, punishment when strong evidence existed short of a full proof.

79   On the important role of the arbitrium of the judge in the *ius commune*, see M. Meccarelli, *Arbitrium. Un aspetto sistematico degli ordinamenti giuridici in età di diritto comune*.

80   S. Lepsius, *Der Richter und die Zeugen*, pp. 126–137. Lepsius has shown that Bartolus had a nuanced stance towards the evaluation of the evidence and that he presented the picture of a judge who had a large freedom in the evaluation of the reliability of witness testimony. Furthermore, in the work of Bartolus the term *fides* in the sense of the internal conviction of the judge played a central role. As Lepsius herself acknowledged, however, Bartolus was relatively exceptional in his ideas and particularly in his view of the importance of the *fides* of the judge he was not followed by later authors. Moreover, it appears that Barolus focused primarily on civil law in his work on the law of evidence and not on the criminal law.

system of legal proofs. He did not function as a kind of automaton who had no room to manoeuvre and who solely applied the evidentiary rules.

The distinction between the system of legal proofs and the principle of the free evaluation of the evidence that emerged between 1750 and 1870 should not be seen as an absolute difference between a very rigid, formalistic system where the judge had little discretion in the evaluation of the evidence and a system where the judge suddenly became completely free. The difference between these two 'systems' was, in many respects, more fluid and gradual. Although the contrast should not be drawn too sharply, there are, nevertheless, certain significant qualitative differences between the large judicial discretion which existed under the system of legal proofs and the free evaluation of the evidence that was introduced in the eighteenth and nineteenth centuries. First of all, the free evaluation of the evidence in the eighteenth and nineteenth centuries was embedded in an altered procedural and penological context. A far more adversarial procedure was introduced between 1750 and 1870 in which the accused acquired the right to legal counsel and the right not to incriminate himself. These changes made it impossible to continue to rely as strongly on the confession of the accused.

Secondly, as will be further discussed in the following chapter, the free evaluation which developed from the second half of the eighteenth century onwards was influenced by changed epistemological ideas.[81] The possibility and usefulness of binding evidentiary rules was explicitly rejected and the internal conviction of the judge or jurors was presented as a central criterion for the question whether sufficient evidence existed to convict someone. Extraordinary punishments and intermediate decision types were abolished and – at least in theory – for all crimes the same evidentiary standard applied. This differed in an essential manner from the system of legal proofs where the focus overwhelmingly lay on the formulation of objective criteria which predetermined when a judge could pronounce a severe punishment. With these rules it

---

81   The changed epistemological presuppositions already meant that the 'modern' free evaluation of the evidence was understood in a very different manner than the discretion that the judge had under the system of legal proofs. This point is aptly summarized by Nobili: "[es gibt] einen weiteren Faktor für die Einführung des neuen Maßstabes der ‚inneren Überzeugung'; er begründet zugleich dessen Selbständigkeit gegenüber allen früheren Systemen freier Beweiswürdigung. Gemeint ist die Übertragung der wissenschaftlichen und philosophischen Erkenntnisse des 18. Jahrhunderts, vor allem der induktiveexperimentellen Methode, in den Bereich richterliche Erkenntnis". This more inductive approach Nobili contrasted with the "systematische und aprioristische Methode der Scholastik". See M. Nobili, *Die freie richterliche Überzeugungsbildung*, p. 73.

was sought to bind the judicial evaluation of the evidence as strictly as possible, even though in many respects a judicial discretion was acknowledged. Among authors who wrote within the tradition of the system of legal proofs it is far easier to find remarks which aimed to bind the judge to the legal evidentiary rules than remarks that referred him to his own conviction. As Schmoeckel observed, it was not the case that there were no references to the conscience or to, for example, the *fides* (belief) of the judge at all, but his conviction was not constitutive for the question whether sufficient evidence existed for a conviction:

> Das Gewissen als rein subjektives Gefühl einer Wahrheit war zwar bekannt, aber nicht geachtet. Das Gewissen stellte nur dann eine Autorität dar, wenn es mit den objektiven Tatsachen übereinstimmte. Auf die Situation des Strafrichters übertragen war seine Überzeugung unmaßgeblich, solange sie nur auf einer subjektiven Überzeugung beruhte. Erheblich wurde sie erst, wenn die gesetzlichen Voraussetzungen vorlagen.[82]

In conclusion, the 'modern' system based on the free evaluation of the evidence has to be considered as something that differed qualitatively from the judicial discretion which existed under the system of legal proofs. Furthermore, the free evaluation of the evidence did not simply grow out of an extension in practice of the judicial discretion – in, for example, applying extraordinary punishments –, but was the fruit of an innovative and complex discussion in the juridical literature and on the legislative level between 1750 and 1870, as will be shown in the subsequent chapters.

---

82   M. Schmoeckel, *Humanität und Staatsraison*, pp. 285–290. Similarly, Rosoni stated on the effect of a full proof: "Le prove piene (dette anche vere, perfette, manifeste, complete), sono quelle cho sono sufficienti di per sé – in quanto offrono una 'perfecta cognitio facti' – a convincere il giudice e constringere la decisione, quale che sia la sua opinione". Carbasse goes even further and remarks that within the system of legal proofs it was attempted to exclude any subjectivity on the part of the judge. He stated on the role of the judge that: "il doit donc se garder de toute impression personnelle et son << intime conviction >>, comme on dira beaucoup plus tard ... n'a aucune valeur". See I. Rosoni, *Quae singula non prosunt collecta iuvant*, p. 74, and J-M. Carbasse, *Histoire du droit pénal et de la justice criminelle*, p. 195.

CHAPTER 3

The Theoretical Framework

3.1 Introduction

In the previous chapter a description has been given of the most important characteristics of the system of legal proofs and how it came into being. This chapter attempts to provide a theoretical framework to help explain the reform of the criminal law of evidence between roughly 1750 and 1870. Although there are many factors which led to or at least influenced the reform of the criminal law of evidence in this period, it is the contention of this study that there were two developments which – at least on the level of the ideas underlying these reforms – had a highly important impact on the reform of the criminal law of evidence. For lack of a better term, in this study these developments are called the 'political-constitutional discourse' and the 'epistemological discourse'. In both discourses a significant transformation occurred which, in their combination, delivered an important part of the ideological foundation for the modern criminal law of evidence. In this chapter a description will first be given of the change in the political-constitutional discourse and then of the changed epistemological discourse. Finally, in the conclusion the relationship between these two discourses and the criminal law of evidence is analysed.

There is, however, an important limitation to this chapter. Naturally, one chapter here can never do justice to the highly complex changes in the epistemological and political-constitutional discourses over the long period from the seventeenth until the nineteenth century. The theoretical framework presented in this chapter is based overwhelmingly on secondary sources concerning the development of the epistemological and political-constitutional discourses in which difficult choices had to be made. Regarding both changes this chapter will unavoidably contain a summary and generalizing overview, leaving out many important nuances, developments and points of discussion. The central goal of this chapter is, nevertheless, to create a theoretical 'lens' through which the evidentiary changes in the eighteenth and nineteenth centuries can be understood. It is, in other words, an attempt to provide a framework to understand the language and ideas which the jurists used in their juridical treatises and in the legislative debates to express themselves in the eighteenth and nineteenth centuries.

3.2 The Political-constitutional Discourse

Even more so than with the epistemological discourse, it is difficult to give a precise delineation of the political-constitutional discourse. The term is meant to designate the general process of the rethinking of the relationship between the state and its citizens which took place between the seventeenth and nineteenth centuries. This process had its roots in a significant change in natural law and social contract theories in the seventeenth and eighteenth centuries.

This section consists of three parts. In the first subsection, a summary description is given of the changes in natural law and social contract theories in the seventeenth and eighteenth centuries. In the second and third subsections the impact of the changed political-constitutional discourse on the criminal law of evidence is discussed. The changed discourse affected the reform of the criminal law of evidence in two important ways. Firstly, the combination of natural law and social contract theories stimulated the emergence of the *nemo tenetur*-principle (i.e. the principle that no one should be obliged to contribute to his own conviction) and contributed to a new emphasis on the presumption of innocence and the defensive rights of the accused. These ideas provided strong arguments for a reform of the secret inquisitorial procedure and against the use of judicial torture. This influence will be discussed in the second subsection. Secondly, from the changed political-constitutional discourse important arguments were derived for the introduction of a jury system. The idea that the sovereignty lay with the people and the desire to limit the arbitrary exercise of power by criminal judges provided important arguments in favour of a jury system. This influence is discussed in the third subsection.

3.2.1 *The Change in Natural Law and Social Contract Theories in the Seventeenth and Eighteenth Centuries*

The purpose of this section is not to give a detailed description of the complex developments in natural law theories in the seventeenth and eighteenth centuries and the many significant differences which existed between different regions and authors. Only some of the most important general ideas in natural law theories will be discussed and how they affected the reform of the criminal procedural law and the criminal law of evidence. Although ideas concerning natural law had a very long history, there is a consensus that a profound change occurred in the way natural law was perceived and in the relative importance of this subject in the seventeenth and eighteenth centuries.[1] Scattola, for example, mentions several significant differences between the notion of natural law in the late Middle Ages and the ideas surrounding natural law in the seventeenth and eighteenth centuries. In the Middle Ages natural law was seen as a set of innate rules engraved upon human beings by God; rules which corresponded to divine reason. It was seen as a collection of principles regarding practical questions and formed a plurality of disparate rules. Unlike the conception of natural law in the seventeenth and eighteenth centuries, it was not conceived as a logically deductive hierarchical system with one general or core principle from which other rules could be derived.[2]

In the late Middle Ages natural law was seen as being part of a universal order instituted by God and forming part of his plan directing all things and acts of the world towards their due end. Herein can be discerned the combination of an Aristotelian teleological view with Christian divine rule, which formed a central tenet of medieval natural law. In this view, in every being's nature is built in a normative ideal end which is part of the eternal or natural law, and in which there is no real conflict possible between the interests of different persons because they operate within one harmonious moral order.[3] In the sixteenth and seventeenth centuries this medieval view on natural law became problematic because it seemed to presuppose a degree of knowledge about God, the world, and human nature which it was only too easy for sceptical criticism to undermine.[4] Not only sceptical thought, but also the Reformation and the religious wars in the sixteenth and seventeenth centuries contributed strongly to undermine the view of the world as a harmonious order. This had an important effect on rethinking the legitimation of political authority

---

1 L. Daston and M. Stolleis, *Natural Law and Laws of Nature in Early Modern* Europe, pp. 2–4. Natural law not only acquired a new and central position in jurisprudence but also in an interdisciplinary discourse ranging from natural philosophy to debates on religion, tolerance, resistance to rulers and sovereignty. As Daston and Stolleis state: "The term [Natural law] has ancient antecedents in both jurisprudence and natural philosophy, but only in the seventeenth century did it suddenly thrust itself onto centre stage in both realms".
2 M. Scattola, "Before and after natural law. Models of Natural Law in Ancient and Modern Times", pp. 1–6.
3 S. Darwall, "The foundations of morality: virtue, law and obligation", pp. 222–223.
4 K. Haakonssen, *Natural Law and Moral Philosophy*, pp. 24–25. On the importance of formulating a response towards scepticism in the writing of Grotius and Pufendorf by founding the natural law on the principle that man naturally seeks to preserve himself, see R. Tuck, "The 'modern' theory of natural law", pp. 107–115 and B. Tierney, *The Idea Of Natural Rights*, pp. 316–324.

because until then the forms of authority and the social divisions within society were explained and legitimized from the ideal of a harmonious order. Precisely because of the interconnectedness of these ideas, the Reformation and the religious wars (where 'legitimate' Christian rulers were deposed) made it possible and to a certain extent necessary to completely redefine the role of natural law.

An important change in natural law theories in the seventeenth and eighteenth centuries was that the theories became increasingly detached from the idea that natural law formed part of a harmonious order instituted and directed by God. This detachment can, for example, be seen in the writing of Grotius, who tried to find a new theoretical footing for some fundamental rules which should be binding even across religious divides. Because the religious unity was lost, Grotius did not search for a central theoretical justification in a shared notion of God's intentions, but in human sociability. From this context also came his famous claim that natural law would be binding even if it was not instituted by God or if God did not exist. God still was the eventual source of all creation and natural law for Grotius, but he made possible a shift in the discussion wherein natural law was seen more in light of 'human nature'. A second innovation which broke with the traditional approach to natural law was the tendency to treat natural law *more geometrico*. Inspired by Cartesianism, the ideal was that natural law could form a logically deductive system starting from one basic principle. The analogy was, furthermore, made that just as God created a physical world that followed certain laws which were discoverable by the physical sciences, there existed a moral world which had certain permanent features obeying general laws based in human nature. These natural laws were not to be discovered through empirical investigation, but were held to be universally and *a priori* true.[5]

To find a foundation and understanding of natural law deriving from 'human nature', writers such as Hobbes, Locke and Pufendorf stated that it was necessary to look at how man behaved in the state of nature. The foundation of natural law was sought in the most important principles which guided man's actions in the situation where every individual as yet lived for himself and did not form part of a society (with governing institutions). Most natural law theorists largely agreed that man's fundamental striving was to preserve himself. Because man noticed that he was worse of on his own, he formed connections with the people around him and made contracts to enter into a civil state and to create a form of authority. The theorizing about the state of the nature and

---

5 K. Haakonssen, *Natural Law and Moral Philosophy*, pp. 38–52.

the transition to a civil state through the creation of a social contract had two important functions in the general rethinking of the relation between the state and its citizens in the seventeenth and eighteenth centuries. Firstly, the idea of the state of nature and the social contract theories were used to discuss under which circumstances the authority of a government was legitimate and, for example, whether citizens had a right to rebel. Secondly, the idea of the state of nature and the social contract theories formed a vantage point from which legislation and practices by the state could be critically evaluated, for example, whether it was rightful for a state to use judicial torture and whether there were certain natural rights which the state should not infringe.

3.2.1.1 Social Contract Theories

A problem with explaining the impact of the change in natural law and social contract theories in the seventeenth and eighteenth centuries, was that there were significant differences between the authors and that they drew very different conclusions from these ideas. In general the natural law and social contract theories were used by different authors to justify both absolute sovereignty and limited state authority, and they were used both to enlarge the sphere of action of the sovereign and to restrict it.[6] A brief overview of some of the most influential authors can serve to illustrate the diverse ideas and conclusions that were derived from natural law and social contract theories.

Hobbes is an important example of someone who used the idea of the state of nature and the formation of a social contract to justify an, at least in theory, (nearly) absolute and limitless authority.[7] In Hobbes's view, in the state of nature man had an equal and unlimited right to everything, even to one another's bodies. In his rather pessimistic perspective people who lived in the state of nature, without a common power over them, were in a state of 'war of all against all'. Hobbes defined this state of war not as a situation where everyone was continuously fighting, but as a state where everyone knew that every other person was willing to fight him. In this state, punctuated by frequent outbursts of violence, there was so little security of life and property that all lived in constant fear and productive work appeared to be useless. Out of a desire to preserve himself and to escape this state of nature, men united themselves into a commonwealth and created a contract in which they made a ruler sovereign

---

6 M. Scattola "Before and after natural law. Models of Natural Law in Ancient and Modern Times", p. 1.
7 Hobbes argued in theory for a transferral of an absolute sovereignty, but also argued for an only relatively limited role of government in practice. See I. Shapiro, *The Evolution of Rights in Liberal Theory*, pp. 29–40.

over them. Hobbes argued that because any intermediate or limited form of sovereignty would have the danger of reigniting conflict and a war of all against all, it was necessary that an absolute and unlimited power was granted to the sovereign in the social contract.[8] Hobbes, in short, deemed that citizens did not retain certain natural rights which the sovereign had to respect or on the basis of which the conduct of the sovereign could be evaluated. Instead absolute sovereignty was transferred to him.

Locke painted a different picture of the state of nature and drew different conclusions from the social contract regarding legitimate state authority. Unlike Hobbes, Locke's contract theory was an anti-absolutist theory – which was generally the tendency of social contract theories – and presented a justification for resistance to 'tyrants'. Central to Locke's theory was the contrast between the state of nature and the civil state. In Locke's state of nature man did not have an unlimited right of freedom as in Hobbes's state, but was bound by natural law to respect other people's life, health, liberty and possessions. In Locke's state of nature there was, therefore, already an extensive set of natural laws to which man was bound and which would ensure peace and security if they were sufficiently respected. The need for a government arose out of the fact that these natural laws were normally not sufficiently respected and could only be respected when there was an authority which could judge and punish breaches of the natural law. Locke argued that through a social contract men had only given a limited authority to the sovereign, essentially in order to defend the natural rights of individuals and the public good. The significant innovation of Locke was that he created the first contract theory that limited political authority on the basis of the idea of inalienable, natural rights. The state authorities were entrusted with defending the rights and welfare of their subjects but when they did not respect the natural rights of the citizens Locke acknowledged a right of resistance.[9]

Pufendorf's theory of the state of nature and the social contract differed in some important respects from that of Hobbes and Locke. Significantly, he disagreed with Hobbes that there was no justice or injustice and no binding moral law in the state of nature.[10] Pufendorf argued that from the state of nature two separate contracts were made. The first contract was made among the people

---

8   G.S. Kavka, "Hobbes War of all against All", pp. 1–5.
9   J. Tully, *An approach to political philosophy: Locke in* context, pp. 9–62 and 281–314, and M. Lessnoff, *Social Contract*, pp. 59–67.
10 Pufendorf also emphasized that because man was a weak and vulnerable creature on his own he depended on mutual assistance and by nature had to be sociable In his idea that man was naturally sociable, Pufendorf strongly agreed with Grotius. See R. Tuck, "The 'modern' theory of natural law", pp. 104–105.

to create a permanent community and the second contract was created between this community and a sovereign to decide by whom and how they would be ruled. In the theory of Pufendorf the subjects appear to be in a relatively stronger moral position vis-à-vis their ruler – who is bound by the contract with the community and by natural law – than in the theory of Hobbes. However, Pufendorf also did not defend the idea of certain natural inalienable natural rights which the sovereign had to respect and he did not argue for a right of resistance when the sovereign violated these rights. As Lesnoff states, while Pufendorf repudiated Hobbes's absolutism and urged rulers to seek the welfare of the people and rule in accordance with natural law, he at the same time inculcated a duty of passive obedience to the sovereign. His thought was very much in line with the so-called 'enlightened absolutism' that developed particularly in the German territories in the eighteenth century.[11]

Different from all the previous social contract theories was the theory of Rousseau, which would be particularly influential during the French Revolution. Rousseau was not concerned with how a social contract actually might have been made, but with an ideal of how the social contract *ought* to have been made for political authority to be legitimate. In contrast to earlier authors, Rousseau had a far more positive view of man in the state of nature and deemed that man was progressively corrupted through the development of a more complex society. He presupposed that man had been free and equal in the state of nature and that no man, by nature, had any legitimate authority over another. In his view that the growth of a more complex society actually led to a moral degeneration of man, Rousseau differed from virtually all the previous social contract theorists. The actual historical creation of contracts of government Rousseau depicted as a cunning manoeuvre in which the mighty and rich institutionalised their power over the poorer and weaker elements of society. The eventual result was a stabilisation of inequality and oppression as it existed, according to Rousseau, in the eighteenth century.[12]

Such a contract could, of course, not be a legitimate one. For a social contract and a government to be legitimate, Rousseau argued that it needed to find "an association which will defend and protect with the whole common force the person and goods of each associate, and in which each, while uniting himself with all, may still obey himself alone, and remain free as before".[13] His solution to this problem was his famous idea of the general will. Each participant

---

11   M. Lessnoff, *Social Contract*, pp. 71–74.
12   Ibidem, pp. 74–79.
13   Ibidem, p. 80.

to the contract had to put his entire person and power under the supreme direction of the general will. Rousseau argued that each would thus become a member of a political society which could act through general assemblies and thereby collectively exercise sovereign political authority. In Rousseau's theory the sovereignty lay and continued to lie with the people. Furthermore, this sovereignty was supreme and unlimited, meaning that the participants to the contract could not retain any of their rights. Through the formation of a social contract man exchanged his natural liberty for civil liberty. Civil liberty for Rousseau essentially meant obeying a sovereign law-making body that consisted of all citizens equally, which made laws that applied to all citizens equally and in this sense embodied the general will of each citizen as a citizen.[14] In short, important in the theory of Rousseau is, first of all, that he very explicitly claimed that the sovereignty lay with the people and that legislation ought to be the expression of the general will of the people. Secondly, he did not deem that man retained certain natural rights upon entering into the social contract, but that instead he gave the sovereign an unlimited and absolute power.

A last important social contract theorist who has to be discussed was Kant. Until Rousseau and Kant it had been largely unclear among most contract theorists to what extent they viewed the formation of the social contract as something that had actually historically occurred or whether it was merely meant as a normative, hypothetical contract. Rousseau presented his idea of the social contract as an *ideal* contract. For Kant as well, the formation of the social contract was not something that had historically taken place, but it was a form of hypothetical reasoning to explain when legitimate authority existed.[15] The idea of the social contract could be used to test the rightfulness of political

---

14 Ibidem, pp. 79–82.
15 In particular the Scottish enlightened authors had shown that political authority could not rest on an actual historical social contract. The first and most important attack on this idea came from Hume in his essay *Of the Original Contract* (1742). He showed that even if there had once been a contract among men 'in the woods and deserts', the original contract had been subverted by a thousand changes of government and princes with the result that virtually all the existing governments have been founded on usurpation or conquest. These governments did not acquire their legitimacy from consent in a contract. The reason that man had an obligation to obey them did not lie in their consent but simply because otherwise a peaceful and orderly society could not exist. Hume hereby showed that the way government may have originated among men was a quite separate question from why men should currently obey their sovereigns. The critique of the social contract by the Scottish enlightened authors discredited the authority of the idea of the social contract and particularly the idea that they had been actual historical events which legitimated current governments. Kant clearly reacted to these ideas when he presented the social contract as a hypothetical idea to test the rightfulness of political institutions. See also M. Lessnoff, *Social Contract*, pp. 85–91.

institutions and laws. These institutions and laws should be such that they *could* have been agreed to by all citizens or that they could have been produced by 'the united will of a whole nation'. Kant did not follow Rousseau in the idea that political authority was only legitimate when it derived from the ideal social contract, but saw it more as a guideline for legislators and rulers. Kant argued that rulers should govern in a way consonant with laws 'which a people of mature rational powers' would prescribe for themselves. The idea of what rational people would consent to was, furthermore, closely connected to Kant's moral theory. He tied what rational men would agree to, to his idea of what morally good beings would agree to. Kant, therefore, used the idea of the social contract not just to describe what an acceptable constitution would be, but what an ideal constitution would be. As Lesnoff remarked, in the end Kant's version of the social contract appears to be, like Rousseau's, not just a hypothetical, but an ideal contract.[16] Importantly, by tying his idea of the social contract to his specific theory of what morally good beings would agree to, Kant divorced the idea of the legitimate social contract from natural law.

3.2.1.2 Conclusion

There were certain general tendencies in the natural law and social contract theories of the seventeenth and eighteenth centuries that were important in rethinking the relation between the state and the citizens and consequently for how the state should relate to a citizen in a criminal trial. A first important tendency lay in the fact that it was stressed that people were naturally free and equal individuals and only later made a social contract to establish an authority. Given the idea that all individuals were originally free and equal in the state of nature, the notion of the social contract was also intimately linked with the emergence of the idea that all men were and should be equal before the law.[17] This stress on the naturally free individual, furthermore, formed a significant departure from the Aristotelian tradition that was common in the late Middle Ages. In this tradition man was seen as a political animal and his natural state was a social state. As Hofmann remarked, the natural law theories of the seventeenth and eighteenth centuries reversed the logical relationship between the (political) community and the individual that had been current up to that time.[18]

A second important and closely connected tendency lay in the fact that the legitimacy of (royal) authority and of the existing social divisions were no

---

16 M. Lessnoff, *Social Contract*, pp. 90–94.
17 M. Forsyth, "Hobbes contractarianism. A comparative analysis", pp. 35–38.
18 H. Hofmann, "Zur Lehre vom Naturzustand in der Rechtsphilosophie", p. 21.

longer taken for granted as an immutable and divinely ordained order. The stress on the originally free and equal people from whom the sovereignty derived through a social contract, created a vantage point from which the exercise of power by the ruler could be critically evaluated. It made it obvious that the ruler needed to rule first and foremost in the general interest of the people, as was recognized in the tradition of enlightened absolutism in the eighteenth century. The natural law and social contract theories had an even more radical potential that was visible, in different ways, in for example the writings of Locke and Rousseau. Locke presupposed that certain natural, inalienable rights existed which limited the power of the sovereign and that there was even a right of resistance if the sovereign did not respect these rights. Rousseau argued that the sovereignty resided in the people and that a citizen could only be legitimately bound by the general will of the collective body of the citizens of which he was an equal member. These ideas contained a radical potential that would strongly influence the reform of the criminal law of evidence between 1750 and 1870.

A third and last important tendency consisted of the fact that a shift took place in the seventeenth and eighteenth centuries from a relatively abstract and teleological understanding of natural law as general precepts to a focus on more concrete individual natural rights. This shift was made possible by the new centrality of the social contract in the legitimation of state authority, which envisioned society as a group of individual contractors who also retained certain fundamental natural rights in the creation of the social contract.[19] Through the social contract these natural rights turned into civil rights which put clear limitations on the power of the state over the individual citizen-contractors. The new centrality of fundamental civil rights as part of a social contract can, for example, be seen very clearly in the *Déclaration des Droit de l'Homme* of 1789. The civil rights were envisioned as certain foundational rules of the social contract which put limitations on the power of the state to intrude in the personal sphere of citizens. The shift to a focus on fundamental civil rights was, of course, very important for the possibility to, for example, understand the *nemo tenetur* principle as a personal right of a citizen not to incriminate himself.

---

19   Westerman has, for example, described well how this change of focus from natural law to natural rights occurred in the work of Grotius, and Shapiro has described this shift in the work of Hobbes. See P. Westerman, *The disintegration of natural law theory*, pp. 157–180, and I. Shapiro, *The Evolution of Rights in Liberal Theory*, pp. 40–69.

3.2.2 The Nemo Tenetur-principle, the Presumption of Innocence and Judicial Torture

Many of the reform-minded authors who wrote treatises on criminal law during the second half of the eighteenth century explicitly started their work with explaining that the powers of the government were based on a social contract and that the people had transferred merely as much power as was necessary to protect society. Reinar and Calkoen, Dutch authors in the second half of the eighteenth century, for example, started their treatises on criminal law with explaining that its foundation lay in a social contract and they defined crimes as breaches of the social contract.[20] Similarly, authors such as Beccaria, Servan, Lacretelle, Brissot de Warville and Marat, argued that the power of government was based on a social contract and conceived of crimes as a breach of the social contract. However, as Lieven Dupont correctly remarked, these authors normally only used a rather rudimentary notion of the social contract. They did not explain whether they followed the social contract idea of, for example, Locke or Rousseau.[21] The frequent usage of the social contract theories, nevertheless, testifies to the importance that this idea had acquired in the second half of the eighteenth century among the authors who proposed to reform the criminal justice system.

There were important differences between the contract theorists such as Hobbes, Locke and Rousseau and they drew very different conclusions from the idea of the social contract, but the reform-minded authors generally used the idea of the social contract in a simpler way. Because most of the reform-minded authors were arguing against the excesses of the secret, inquisitorial procedure, they used the idea of the social contract predominantly in a Lockean way to argue that there were certain limitations to the legitimate exercise of powers by the government. The idea that the legitimacy of the government was essentially based on a social contract in combination with the idea that there were certain inalienable, natural rights, formed a fruitful combination to critically evaluate the powers of the government in the criminal sphere. From this vantage point several important principles were formulated which would underlie the modern criminal procedure. A new emphasis was placed on the idea that nobody should be forced to incriminate himself, that he should have the freedom to defend himself and that the accused should be considered innocent until his

---

20 J.N. Reinar, *Nemesis Rationalis, of redenkundig vertoog over het crimineele recht uit het natuur-recht afgeleid*, pp. III–XIII, and H. Calkoen, *Verhandeling over het voorkomen en straffen der misdaaden*, pp. 1–79.

21 L. Dupont, *Beginselen van behoorlijke strafrechtsbedeling*, pp. 49–50.

guilt had been fully proven. Furthermore, these ideas delivered important arguments against judicial torture and the secret, inquisitorial procedure.

Schmoeckel has shown that phrases which resemble or suggest the *nemo tenetur* principle (that nobody should be forced to incriminate himself) and the presumption of innocence can already be found in legal texts in the late Middle Ages. However, even though these ideas have old antecedents, they never acquired the same importance and meaning as they did in the criminal law of evidence from the eighteenth century onwards. They were phrases – like the maxim that it was better that ten guilty were set free than that one innocent person was convicted – which were generally used to suggest that criminal judges needed to be cautious in convicting someone. However, these ideas did not have as strong an impact in the old criminal procedural law as they would have in the eighteenth and nineteenth centuries. These ideas, for example, did not prevent the use of judicial torture or extraordinary punishments. Schmoeckel concluded that the importance of the *nemo tenetur* principle and the presumption of innocence became far greater within the context of natural law and social contract theories in the seventeenth and eighteenth centuries.[22]

Two ideas in particular gave the presumption of innocence and the *nemo tenetur* principle their new meaning and greater importance in the eighteenth century. For the presumption of innocence this was the fact that crimes were now defined as a breach of the social contract and that the state only acquired the right to punish someone when the breach of the contract had been fully and legally established. The perspective of the social contract gave a more

---

22 M. Schmoeckel, *Humanität und Staatsraison*, pp. 410–439. Helmholz came to a comparable conclusion regarding the privilege against self-incrimination in Anglo-American law. Helmholz has shown first of all that the first English formulations of the idea that an accused should not be forced to incriminate himself were taken from Roman-canon law through the English ecclesiastical courts. The earliest formulations 'sprang from continental sources and not from the immemorial usages of common law'. Secondly, Helmholz concludes like Schmoeckel that the phrases resembling the *nemo tenetur*-principle still had a different and far less absolute meaning in the sixteenth and seventeenth centuries. As on the continent, many far-reaching exceptions were allowed and the idea that someone should not be forced to contribute to his own conviction had a far less absolute character: "The force of the exceptions shows that, however much sixteenth-century arguments resembled some of the modern reasons given for the privilege against self-incrimination, the privilege did not then have an absolute character. Civilians did not regard a defendant's refusal to answer incriminating questions as the exercise of a fundamental personal right, never to be abridged. They regarded it instead as a protection against the exercise of overly intrusive powers by public officials seeking to pry into the private lives of ordinary men and women". See R.H. Helmholz, "Origins of the privilege against self-incrimination: the role of the European *ius commune*", pp. 962–990.

central place to the idea that everyone should be presumed innocent until it had been fully proven that he had committed a crime. The importance of this contractual idea for the presumption of innocence can, for example, be seen very clearly in the writings of Beccaria. From the idea of a social contract he argued that everyone should be presumed innocent and should continue to have his full rights as a citizen until it had been legally established that someone had breached the contract. According to Beccaria, citizens had a *right* to the protection and benefits of society before their guilt was legally proven.[23]

The second idea, which redefined the role of the *nemo tenetur* principle, lay in the central importance that was attached in natural law theories to the natural urge of self-preservation. In most natural law theories it was taken as a first principle that man's most important urge was to preserve himself.[24] This was, however, not only seen as an empirical fact but it was taken as a normative principle that by nature man should, therefore, seek to preserve himself. From this idea, it was increasingly argued in the eighteenth century that it was against natural law for the state to force an accused to contribute to his own conviction. This idea formed the core of what became the *nemo tenetur* principle and was used to argue that the state had no right to use judicial torture or to force the accused to take an oath to tell the truth. Instead, it was argued that by natural law an accused should have the right to freely defend himself. In this sense, Marat, for example remarked that the accused should have every possibility to defend himself and that it was absurd to want force the accused to confess and to use this confession against him. He remarked that the state did not have a right to extract this horrible genre of proof and that "elle en est une contre nature, puisqu'elle blesse le principe de la defense naturelle".[25]

The newfound importance and centrality of the presumption of innocence and of the *nemo tenetur* principle can, of course, also be seen in declarations of rights at the end of the eighteenth century. Thus, for example, the presumption of innocence found expression in Article 9 of the French declaration: "every man being presumed innocent until judged guilty, if it is deemed indispensable to arrest him, all rigor unnecessary to securing his person should be severely repressed".[26] Similarly, the *nemo tenetur* principle found expression in

---

23   J.M. Michiels, *Cesare Beccaria. Over misdaden en straffen*, pp. 41–47 and 79–90.
24   See, for example, R. Tuck, "The 'modern' theory of natural law", pp. 107–115 and W.H. Schrader, "Naturrecht und Selbsterhaltung: Spinoza und Hobbes", pp. 574–583.
25   J-P. Marat, *Plan de la législation en matière criminelle*, pp. 130–131.
26   L. Hunt, *Inventing Human Rights*, p. 220.

most of the declarations of rights of the American states and in the fifth amendment to the American constitution which read "No Person ... shall be compelled in any criminal case to be a witness against himself, nor be deprived of life, liberty or property, without the due process of law".[27] The recognition of the presumption of innocence and the *nemo tenetur* principle as natural or civil rights in the declarations of rights and in the new criminal procedural codifications of the late eighteenth century, are demonstrations of the larger value that was now attached to them.

It is, furthermore, interesting to observe that there are important parallels between the developments in England and in continental European countries. In the eighteenth and nineteenth centuries, in both regions – on the basis of a similar ideological change –, the defensive rights of the accused were significantly strengthened, the privilege against self-incrimination became recognized and the presumption of innocence found a clear expression. Hostettler and Beattie, for example, argue that the presumption of innocence only started to be explicitly formulated in England in the late eighteenth century.[28] Beattie remarks that at least by the 1820s it had become a commonplace idea and it could, for example, be found in Sir Richard Philip's *Golden Rules for Jurymen* (1820) that "[e]very man is presumed to be innocent till he has clearly been proved to be guilty; the onus of the proof of guilt lies therefore on the accuser; and no man is bound, required or expected, to prove his own innocency".[29] Furthermore, in the eighteenth and early nineteenth centuries the accused acquired the right to use defense counsel in felony cases and the privilege against self-incrimination became explicitly recognized in England.[30]

3.2.2.1   Judicial Torture and the Inquisitorial Procedure
The presumption of innocence and the *nemo tenetur* principle together formed a fruitful combination from which the practice of judicial torture and the far-reaching inquisitorial powers of the state were criticized. Both ideas in their own way provided strong arguments against the legitimacy of judicial torture

---

27   R.A. Rutland, *The Birth of the Bill of Rights 1776–1791*, pp. 49–83 and 194–240.
28   J. Hostettler, *The Criminal Jury Old and New*, pp. 83–84.
29   J.M. Beattie, "Scales of Justice: Defense Counsel and the English Criminal Trial in the Eighteenth and Nineteenth Centuries", pp. 248–249.
30   J. Langbein, *The Origins of Adversary Trial*, pp. 253–330. The right to legal counsel in felony cases was already allowed regarding points of law, but in the course of the eighteenth century legal counsel was also allowed to defend the accused on questions of fact. The defensive rights of the accused were further strengthened by the fact that he could now compel witnesses to appear and that the charge against him needed to be made explicit before the trial.

that were repeated by almost all the authors who pleaded for its abolition. Concerning the presumption of innocence, it was stated that judicial torture was in fact a punishment – even though the juridical handbooks generally described it as an investigatory instrument – which was applied before the guilt of the accused was fully and legally established. A good example of this argument can be found with Pufendorf who stated that it was against natural law to do anything more than to preliminarily detain someone who had not yet been convicted: "Il est donc contre la Loi Naturelle de faire souffrir à un Prisonnier, qui n'est encore ni condamné ni ouï, plus de mal que n'en demande la nécessité de le tenir renfermé".[31] Another example is formed by the Dutch author De Witt who stated that judicial torture was in fact a punishment and that it was wrong to punish someone whose guilt had not yet been fully established.[32]

The use of judicial torture appeared to be in blatant contradiction with the presumption of innocence and with the idea that the state had no right to force someone to contribute to his own conviction. The argument that it was against natural law to force a subject to contribute to his own conviction became one of the most important and frequently cited arguments to abolish judicial torture. It was mentioned in virtually all the treatises which touched on this subject. A very typical expression of this argument can, for example, also be found in a declaration of rights of the Dutch province of Gelderland which abolished judicial torture in 1795:

> The custom of applying judicial torture on the accused of a crime is against humanity and the principles of natural equity; it provides only a very weak guarantee for the conviction of the judge because the question whether the accused endures torture depends predominantly on the physical strength of the accused and, therefore, often has the consequence that the innocent suffer a punishment while the guilty avoid their well-deserved punishment; it also runs against the principle of natural law that no one should be forced to become his own prosecutor. It is for these reasons that we for ever abolish torture ... in this province.[33]

---

31   S. Pufendorf, *Le droit de la nature et des gens*, p. 373.
32   C. de Witt, *Bedenkingen over het aanhoudend gebruik van de pijnbank*, pp. 1–28.
33   *Placaat. Vryheid, Gelykheid ... in naame van de provisioneele Vertegenwoordigers van het vrye Volk van Gelderland. September 9 1795*. Similarly, the Dutch author Wittichius held a speech against judicial torture in 1736 and argued that every man was directed by nature to do everything to preserve himself. The central argument of his speech was that the state had no right to force a citizen to confess and that the accused was not obligated to betray himself. Consequently, Wittichius stated that the accused had the right to do

THE THEORETICAL FRAMEWORK 81

The principle that nobody should be forced to contribute to his own conviction was not only used to criticize the use of judicial torture but was also used to criticize the existing inquisitorial procedure as a whole. The inquisitorial procedure was strongly geared towards obtaining a confession of the accused and treated him as an object of investigation with relatively few possibilities to defend himself. In the inquisitorial procedure, furthermore, the accused literally did not have a right to remain silent. From the natural law theories powerful arguments were derived that the inquisitorial procedure was unjust and that an accused should not be forced to incriminate himself. Instead it was argued that he should have the broadest possibilities to defend himself. In this vein many reform-minded authors remarked that the accused should be able to use legal counsel, that he had a right to know the incriminating evidence and that there should be equality of arms between the accused and the public prosecutor. Summarizing, the criticisms derived from the natural law and social contract theories inspired an encompassing reform of the criminal procedural law in which the accused acquired, among other things, the right to use legal counsel and to know the incriminating evidence.[34] Because a confession would be far harder to obtain in this reformed criminal procedural law, the recognition of the *nemo tenetur* principle also contributed to the necessity of expanding the possibility to convict on other kinds of evidence than the confession.

It is, finally, important to observe that the transformation of the *nemo tenetur* principle into a personal right not to incriminate oneself and into a right to remain silent, was a gradual process in the eighteenth and nineteenth centuries. The precise meaning of this 'principle' was strongly dependent on the context in which it developed and it changed over time. At first, during the second half of the eighteenth century it was used predominantly to argue

---

whatever it took to avoid a capital punishment and, therefore, also had the right to lie under torture. Because there was, by natural law, no obligation for the accused to tell the truth, there was also no reason to lend any credence to his statements which made them unreliable as evidence. See J. Wittichius, *Redevoering over de onbillykheid en de onnutheid der pynigingen*, pp. 8–12.

34 A practice in France which was also considered to be in conflict with the *nemo tenetur*-principle was the fact that the accused was obligated to perform an oath to tell the truth under interrogation. This was deemed to conflict with natural law because it forced the accused to either contribute to his own demise or to commit perjury and break his oath. In this sense Brissot de Warville and Boucher d'Argis, for example, remarked that it was a cruel abuse and against natural law to force the accused to take an oath to tell the truth and that the freedom for the accused to defend himself was 'de droit naturel'. See J-P. Brissot de Warville, *Théorie des loix criminelles*, Tome II, p. 192, and M. Boucher d'Argis, *Observations sur les loix criminelles de France*, pp. 12–18.

against judicial torture and the lack of defensive rights of the accused. It can be seen clearly in the French revolutionary period that this idea contributed to a restructuring of the criminal procedure in which the accused acquired the right to use legal counsel and a far larger freedom to defend himself. The position of the accused changed significantly, but the right not to incriminate oneself was not yet seen as a positive right to remain silent.

In the German territories and the Netherlands the development was even more gradual than in France. The idea of the *nemo tenetur* principle was at first, during the second half of the eighteenth century, used predominantly to argue against judicial torture. When judicial torture was abolished in these territories in the late eighteenth and early nineteenth centuries, it was still deemed that the accused had an obligation to answer questions and that the judge should have the possibility to use certain 'corrective measures' to force the accused to answer (though supposedly not anymore to confess). As will be described in Chapter nine, in the Dutch criminal procedural code of 1838 there was, for example, still an Article that stated that the accused had the obligation to answer questions, even though there were no instruments anymore to oblige the accused to speak. The explicit right to remain silent and the caution were only introduced in the Netherlands in the criminal procedural code of 1926. The developments in the German territories were comparable.

In England and the United States, the development of the modern *nemo tenetur*-principle was also relatively gradual. Smith has shown for England that it was a long process during the late eighteenth and nineteenth centuries in which the privilege against self-incrimination acquired its modern shape.[35] Similarly, Moglen and Witt have described the process by which the privilege against self-incrimination developed in the United States, and how it came to form a constitutionalized right to remain silent regarding any question that could incriminate someone.[36] Nevertheless, even though the process towards the recognition of a positive right to remain silent was gradual in most places, the foundations for this development were laid in the eighteenth and early nineteenth centuries and were strongly inspired by the changed political-constitutional ideas. A modern right to remain silent could only develop in the course of the nineteenth and twentieth centuries because the foundation for a

---

35   H.E. Smith, "The Modern Privilege: Its Nineteenth-Century Origins", pp. 145–180.
36   E. Moglen, "The Privilege in British North America: The Colonial Period to the Fifth Amendment", pp. 109–144, and J.F. Witt, "Making the Fifth: The Constitutionalization of American Self-Incrimination doctrine 1791–1903", pp. 825–922.

different procedure had been laid in the late eighteenth century, which was progressively less dependent on the confession of the accused.[37]

Furthermore, it has to be emphasized that the ideas which underlay the *nemo tenetur* principle did not remain unchanged in the long period of the eighteenth and nineteenth centuries. During the second half of the eighteenth century there was, for example, a strong emphasis on the idea that it was against natural law to force someone to contribute to his own conviction. On the basis of this idea it was argued that the inquisitorial procedure should be entirely restructured and that an accused should have the right to freely defend himself. In the nineteenth century the natural law theories became far less prominent and the *nemo tenetur* principle was no longer primarily based on natural law. Instead, the legacy of the natural law and social contract theories was that it had led to a rethinking of the relationship between the state and its citizens which strongly influenced the liberal political tradition of the nineteenth century. In an altered form the political liberals of the nineteenth century continued on the natural law and social contract theories' ideas, and argued that there were certain fundamental civil rights on which the state should not infringe. In this liberal tradition many of the criticisms of the excesses of the inquisitorial procedure of the second half of the eighteenth century – and the idea, for example, that an accused should have a right to legal counsel and not to incriminate himself – were internalized and were used to define the proper limits of how the state could legitimately proceed in criminal cases.

3.2.3 *Political-constitutional Arguments for the Introduction of a Jury System*

The first aspect of the changed political-constitutional discourse placed a new emphasis on the presumption of innocence and the *nemo tenetur* principle. The second aspect of the changed discourse provided important arguments in favour of the introduction of a jury system. A general tendency within the social contract theories had been to argue that the sovereignty lay originally with the people who then transferred it through a contract to the government. Rousseau was the most radical in his claim that the sovereignty continued to

---

37 As Langbein, for example, accurately remarked, the privilege against self-incrimination was dependent on a restructuring of the criminal procedure and particularly on the introduction of defense counsel. If the accused could not make use of legal counsel, the right to remain silent virtually amounted to a right not to defend oneself at all. See J. Langbein, *The Origins of Adversary Trial*, p. 277.

lie with the people. While the idea of Rousseau had not been generally accepted before the French Revolution, it became highly influential during the first years of the revolution when the decision was made to abolish the system of legal proofs and to introduce a jury system. The idea that the sovereignty lay with the people and that it should also find an expression in the judicial branch – where 'the people would be judged by the people' – formed an influential argument in favour of the introduction of a jury system.[38] A good example of the influence of the idea that a jury system was preferable because it formed an expression of the sovereignty of the people, can be found with the French author Servan:

> La société n'a le droit de punir qu'autant qu'elle est offensée: pour savoir si elle est offensée, et jusqu'à quel point elle l'est, il faut qu'elle le déclare elle-même, ou le fasse déclarer par des hommes qui représente suffisamment son opinion. Tel est donc, en un mot, le contrat originaire sur les peines entre chaque homme et tous les autres ; je consens d'être puni par tous, quand nous jugeront que j'ai nui à tous, et que je suis coupable; ce contrat n'est que vraiment consenti, que parce que chacun en le ratifiant, se met de lui-même au rang des juges, et non des accusés; enfin, pour consentir à être jugé par les autres, chacun veut être leur juge à son tour ; donc tous doivent l'être.[39]

A second argument in favour of the jury system derived from the effort in the eighteenth century to find (constitutional) guarantees against a too strong and arbitrary exercise of power by the government. The famous idea developed by, among others, Locke and Montesquieu to create a division of governmental functions to prevent a concentration of powers was also extended to

---

[38] The importance or explicitness of the argument that the jury system formed an expression of popular sovereignty, however, strongly varied over time with the proponents of a jury system. The argument was at first not widely used among the reform-minded authors in the second half of the eighteenth century because it was far from an accepted idea that the sovereignty lay with the people. Similarly, in the first half of the nineteenth century in the restoration period in France, the Kingdom of the Netherlands and Germany, the proponents of a jury system rarely argued that it was an expression of popular sovereignty because popular sovereignty itself was seen by many as dangerous and revolutionary (and it was itself dangerous in this period to plead for popular sovereignty). Nevertheless, the idea of popular sovereignty was particularly important during the French Revolution when the jury system was for the first time introduced and this was itself a defining moment in the history of the criminal law of evidence.

[39] M. Servan, *Réflexions sur quelques points de nos loix*, pp. 136–137.

THE THEORETICAL FRAMEWORK 85

the criminal procedural law.[40] An important criticism of the old inquisitorial procedure by the French revolutionary reformers – and later by many German reformers during the first half of the nineteenth century – was that in the criminal procedure almost all the power was vested in the judge alone.[41] For this reason the French reformers sought to create a division of powers within the criminal procedure. Clear distinctions were made between the roles of the public prosecutor, the judge and the defendant. The role of the public prosecutor was more clearly distinguished and separated from that of the judge, while the accused acquired the role and the freedom to defend himself for which he was granted far greater defensive rights and the use of legal counsel. Most importantly for the criminal law of evidence, however, a division was also created

---

40 Apart from the separation of powers, the desire to prevent arbitrary exercises of power by the government led to another significant innovation which had an important indirect impact on the criminal law of evidence: the codification of the substantive criminal law and the introduction of the legality principle. The fact that the crimes were now explicitly defined by the law and that the judge became bound by these terms through the indictment of the public prosecutor, meant that the criminal judge had to interpret the description of the crime and see if the terms were proven. This formed an important innovation compared to the situation under the *ancien régime* where the crimes were far more loosely defined.

41 The criticism of the too strong position of the judge acquired special significance in the German reform literature of the first half of the nineteenth century. In the old view of the criminal procedural law it was considered quite normal that the judge had to perform a threefold role as prosecutor, judge and to an extent as the defendant of the accused. This idea is, for example, still neutrally expressed by Feuerbach at the turn of the nineteenth century: "Der Richter ist im Untersuchungspocesse als *dreifache Person* zu betrachten, als Stellvertreter des beleidigten Staats, indem er an dessen Statt die Rechte aus Strafgesetzen zu verfolgen verpflichtet ist; als Stellvertreter des Angeschuldigten, indem er zugleich alles, was die Schuldlosigkeit oder geringere Strafbarkeit desselben begründen kann, aufsuchen und darstellen soll, und endlich als Richter, inwiefern er das Gegebene zu beurtheilen und darüber richterlich zu verfügen (oder zu entscheiden) hat". See P.J.A. Feuerbach, *Lehrbuch des gemeinen in Deutschland Geltenden Peinlichen Rechts*, p. 843.
    However, in the reform literature in France in the second half of the eighteenth century and in Germany in the first half of the nineteenth century this threefold role of the judge in the inquisitorial procedure was increasingly criticized, because the judge had a too powerful role and was asked to perform incompatible functions. Typical of the criticism against the idea of the judge as a threefold person was the following remark by Zachariae in 1846: "Dem Inquirenten aber zuzumuten, bald auf die, bald auf die andere Seite zu springen und mit beiden Waffen resp. gegen sich selbst zu fechten, zugleich aber auch als Kampfrichter den Streit zu leiten, ist an sich eine Absurdität". Instead, it was argued that these three functions should be separated in the criminal procedural law. See H.A. Zachariae, *Die Gebrechen und die Reform des deutschen Strafverfahrens*, p. 146. On the idea of creating a separation of functions within the criminal trial in Germany see further Section 3.4. of Chapter 5.

on the level of the judgement itself by separating the question of fact from the question of law. In the new criminal procedural law created by the French revolutionaries, the professional judge was to decide on questions of law (such as the decision regarding the punishment) while the jurors were to decide on the factual question whether the accused was guilty. The explicit goal of this separation was to prevent a too strong concentration of power in the criminal judge alone.

A central driving force behind the desire of the French revolutionaries to create this separation of functions within the criminal procedural law was the fact that there was a strong distrust against the professional magistrates (the *noblesse de robe*). This distrust in the professional judges and the criminal justice system had been fed by several high profile juridical scandals in the period between 1750 and 1789 such as the affaires of *Calas* and the *Chevalier de la Barre*, and by the use of the *lettres de cachet*.[42] These scandals illustrated that the criminal judge was far too powerful in the inquisitorial procedure and that he could arbitrarily exercise his powers. It becomes clear from the discussions of the French reformers that one of the most important reasons behind the search for institutionalized guarantees against the arbitrary exercise of powers lay in the distrust that they held against the government and the professional judges. Because of this distrust in professional judges there was a consensus among the revolutionaries that the judges should not be given the great power of deciding on the question of fact on the basis of their freely formed internal conviction. Instead, the revolutionaries exalted the impartial and disinterested qualities of 'the people' who would render a fair judgement and who could be trusted with the task of freely evaluating the evidence.

3.2.3.1   A Matter of Trust

The question of whether there was trust in the professional judges is one of central themes which reappears throughout the discussions between 1750 and 1870. In the discussion on the question whether a jury system should be introduced or whether the (free) evaluation of the evidence should be left to professional judges, one of the defining factors was consistently whether there was a high level of trust or distrust in the professional judges. The German revolutionaries of 1848, for example, who managed to force the introduction of a jury

---

42 The affaires of *Calas* and the *Chevalier de la Barre* were famous juridical scandals in which Voltaire had demonstrated that they were most likely unjustly convicted. The *lettres de cachet* were orders on the authority of the king to arrest or imprison someone, often without a precise cause or justification. See J-M. Carbasse, *Histoire du droit pénal et de la justice criminelle*, pp. 392–395.

system in most German states, were driven by a similar distrust of the professional judges as the French revolutionaries.[43]

The importance of the factor of trust becomes particularly apparent from the situation in the Kingdom of the Netherlands between 1815 and 1830. In this period a strong distrust existed against the government and the professional judges in the southern provinces. Again, this distrust was exacerbated by juridical scandals in the form of the harsh criminal repression of journalists from the southern provinces who had criticized the government. There was a constant and loud call for the introduction of a jury system in the southern provinces because it was expected that the people would render fair and impartial verdicts while the professional judges were deemed to be entirely under the influence of the 'despotic' minister of justice Van Maanen.[44] Almost all the authors in the northern provinces, however, lauded the objectivity and high moral standards of the judges in the Netherlands. In the north the professional judges were trusted and correspondingly only a very small minority pleaded for the introduction of jury system.

The question of trust in the people judging was, therefore, one of the most important factors in the discussion surrounding the criminal law of evidence between 1750 and 1870. It to a large extent determined whether someone was willing to let professional judges or lay jurors decide on the evidentiary question. The choice for lay jurors, furthermore, had important implications on how the criminal law of evidence was given shape because most authors deemed that lay jurors could not work with a complex system of evidentiary rules.[45] The choice of the French revolutionaries for the introduction of a jury system was one of the decisive catalysts which led to the abolition of the system of legal proofs. Nevertheless, as will be discussed below, it was not the only factor. A fundamental epistemological critique had emerged regarding the possibility to determine the sufficiency of proof in *a priori* rules, which made the system of legal proofs seem increasingly untenable and which made the free evaluation of the evidence appear to be a far more preferable system.

---

43 As will be described in Chapter five, in the German territories this distrust of the professional judiciary was also fed by several high profile juridical scandals in the first half of the nineteenth century.

44 Van Maanen was the minister of Justice in the United Kingdom of Netherlands between 1815 and 1830 and was a highly influential 'conservative' politician in this period. He was despised in the southern provinces because Van Maanen was against many liberal reforms and in particular because of his highly repressive stance concerning the freedom of the press.

45 On the idea that a jury system was incompatible with a system of legal proofs, see P.C. Ranouil, "L'intime Conviction", pp. 90–92.

3.3 The Epistemological Discourse

3.3.1 *The Epistemological Foundations of the System of Legal Proofs*

One of the most well-known descriptions of the epistemological foundations of the system of legal proofs has been given by Lévy in his *La hiérarchie des preuves dans le droit savant du moyen-âge*. Lévy argued that the intellectual roots of the system of legal proofs lie in the combination of Aristotelian philosophy and the scholastic method of categorization. Categories were made for the various possible forms of evidence, and subdivisions appeared which ascribed different values to them, creating a sort of hierarchy of the kinds of evidence. Thus, the rule was formulated that only the confession and the testimony of two irreproachable eyewitnesses could create a full proof, while it was generally deemed that indicia could not create a full proof. The ascription of these values, furthermore, occurred in constant reference to Roman law and the Bible which were used as texts of authority. In this manner, the various possible forms of evidence were fixed in certain categories and rules were formulated which determined *a priori* when sufficient evidence existed for a conviction to a severe corporal or capital punishment.[46] Lévy concluded that within the system of legal proofs virtually no room existed for the internal conviction of the judge:

> Chaque preuve a ainsi reçu sa place et son autorité a été exactement définie. De la sorte le juge n'avait plus d'appréciation personnelle à faire en dehors des questions de détail, où les cas d'espèces sont si différents que la règlementation ne peut le saisir tous. Partout ailleurs son rôle consistait donc uniquement à appliquer la norme obligatoire à chaque procédé de preuve qu'on lui soumettait, sans se demander si sa conscience était suffisamment édifiée.[47]

---

[46] Rosoni described the formation of this system in the following similar manner: "Il sistema die prova legale prende forma a partire dal XIII secolo. I giuristi che lo elaborano, siano essi civilisti o canonisti, utilizzano, come abbiamo visto, le categorie logiche della scolastica. Nasce così una costruzione die pura invenzione intellettuale che rispecchia la concezione filosofica dell'epoca: in un grande albero tassonomico vengono fissate le regole probatorie sparse nelle fonti romane, nei testi legislatvi en nelle dottrina giurida elaborate dai doctores". See I. Rosoni, *Quae singula non prosunt collecta iuvant. La teoria della prova indiziaria nell'età medievale e moderna*, p. 235.

[47] J. PH. Lévy, *La hiérarchie des preuves dans le droit savant du moyen-âge*, pp. 5–9 and 22–31.

In later historical research there has been significant criticism of the fact that Lévy exaggerated the strictness with which the criminal judge was bound to the evidentiary rules and that in fact much was left to the discretion of the judge within the system of legal proofs.[48] Nevertheless, Lévy was right that within the system of legal proofs a strong emphasis was placed on defining and categorizing in objective rules when sufficient evidence existed for a conviction and for the use of judicial torture. Although it is certainly not the case that there was no room at all for judicial discretion in the evaluation of the evidence, it is also clear that in general no central or constitutive role was given to the internal conviction of the judge.[49]

As Lévy correctly observed, the system of legal proofs was firmly rooted in late-medieval Aristotelian philosophy. Within late-medieval Aristotelian philosophy there was a rather absolute division between that which constituted *scientia* or 'knowledge' and that which fell in the realm of *opinio*. For a proposition to be the object of *scientia* it needed to be universally and necessarily true, known on the basis of an affirmative demonstration.[50] *Scientia* was arrived at through a demonstration in the form of a syllogism. Starting from a higher or foundational principle which was regarded as universal, necessary and true, through a syllogism the truth of another proposition could be deduced. The notion of *scientia* was relational because it connotes a structural and necessary link between a given proposition and some foundational principle. Within demonstrative reasoning the truth of a science as a whole reduces to the truth of its (foundational) principles. When the demonstrative syllogism is used correctly, it guarantees the necessity of the conclusion, meaning that it cannot be other than it is. The demonstrated conclusion, therefore, consists of a perfect grasp of a state of affairs which is necessarily and always true.[51] Demonstration is often contrasted with induction. Induction is a form of reasoning where evidence and arguments support a conclusion, but do not by (logical) necessity

---

48   See in particular R. Fraher, "Conviction according to conscience: The medieval jurists' debate concerning judicial discretion and the law of proof", pp. 27–64, and S. Lepsius, *Von Zweifeln zur Überzeugung*, pp. 171–197.
49   M. Schmoeckel, *Humanität und Staatsraison*, pp. 285–290.
50   Pasnau gives the example of John Duns Scotus who defined *Scientia* as "the certain cognition of a necessary truth that is evident through some prior cause that entails its conclusion through a discursive syllogism". See R. Pasnau, "Medieval social epistemology: *Scientia* for mere mortals", pp. 23–25.
51   E.F. Byrne, *Probability and Opinion*, pp. 166–178.

ensure it. While the conclusion of a deduction is certain, the truth of the conclusion of an inductive argument can merely be probable.[52]

Scientia was contrasted with *opinio*. Whereas *scientia* covered knowledge that was necessarily and always true, *opinio* focused on the contingent and was non-necessary. *Opinio* was concerned with contingents as contingent, and thus dealt with propositions that may be either true or false. 'Opiniative knowledge' was based on arguments, the testimony of authority and on what usually happens. Whereas *scientia* provided demonstrative certainty which compelled the mind to assent, *opinio* was often defined as a proposition that was held to be true but which the person holding it feared might be wrong, resulting from an awareness that one's judgment might be fallible. *Opinio* was the best state of knowledge attainable or desirable under the circumstances, but could never attain to true knowledge.[53]

Pasnau explains that *scientia* was the epistemic ideal in the late Middle Ages, but that it was also clear that many fields of knowledge could not meet its demanding standards. There was a tendency in late-medieval thought to relax some of the strict standards of *scientia* dependent on the subject matter and the context of inquiry.[54] The epistemic ideal of *scientia* performed an important function as a role-model of how the truth was conceived that needed to be acquired in criminal cases. Even though it was clear that the criminal law of evidence dealt with contingent matters and, therefore, fell within the realm of *opinio*, it was modelled after the epistemic ideal of *scientia*. The reason that the criminal law of evidence was modelled after this ideal lay in the fact that in criminal cases a very high level of certainty was required (the evidence needed to be clearer than the light of day). It seemed unacceptable that the judge could convict someone to death or a severe corporal punishment on the basis of a mere opinion or an internal conviction. Instead he needed to have a form of knowledge which resembled the demonstrative certainty of *scientia*. Concerning the question whether sufficient evidence existed, the criminal judge had to work predominantly in a demonstrative manner. He had to work from the existing system of rules to deduce whether the evidence fulfilled the

---

52 An often used example of induction is that all ravens are black because every raven that has ever been observed is black. The empirical fact that all ravens that so far have been observed are black, however, does not mean that all ravens are therefore black. This was typically a conclusion that could not fall under *scientia* because the conclusion did not by necessity follow from the premises.
53 E. Byrne, *Probability and Opinion*, pp. 178–187.
54 R. Pasnau, "Medieval social epistemology: *Scientia* for mere mortals", pp. 23–41 and R. Pasnau, "Science and Certainty", pp. 357–368.

criteria of a full proof and whether he could, therefore, convict the accused to a severe corporal or capital punishment. The *a priori* evidentiary rules, in short, formed the principles from which it could be demonstrated in every case whether sufficient evidence existed for a conviction.

Nevertheless, as Pasnau mentioned, it has to be kept in mind that the epistemic ideal of *scientia* was adapted to the specific field of knowledge and context of inquiry. Important factors in the context of inquiry of the criminal law of evidence were that the criminal procedure was directed at ascertaining the veracity of historical events and that the standard of proof should not entirely prevent the effective prosecution of criminals. An inherent tension existed in the system of legal proofs between the high standard of proof and the desire that crimes should not go unpunished. Many exceptions or circumventions – such as judicial torture and extraordinary punishments – of the strict evidentiary rules were thus made to ensure that crimes would not go unpunished while at the same time juridical authors underlined that a very high certainty was necessary for a conviction.

The significance and the reproduction of the general distinction between *scientia* and *opinio* in the criminal law of evidence can be seen in the important distinction that was made between direct or so-called 'inartificial' evidence (i.e. witness testimony or the confession) and indirect or 'artificial' evidence (i.e. indicia). The former constituted *probationes* while the latter were merely *praesumptiones*.[55] It was held that witness testimony and the confession could create a *probatio perfecta* or *probatio plena* that induced the judge to have a *perfecta credencia* or *plena fides* because they directly proved the crime. Indicia, however, were seen as a qualitatively different form of evidence and were relegated to the realm of *praesumptiones*; they could only create a suspicion in the mind of the judge but not a perfect credence. The main reason behind this differentiation was that witness testimony and the confession were supposed to prove the crime based on a direct sensory ascertainment of the fact while indicia required an additional step of reasoning by the judge.[56] This conjecture by the judge was seen as highly unreliable in contrast to direct sensory evidence of the crime.[57] Summarizing, the general distinction

---

55 J. PH. Lévy, *La hiérarchie des preuves dans le droit savant du moyen-âge*, pp. 26–31, and P. Marchetti, *Testis Contra Se*, pp. 36–38.

56 The reliability of the witnesses was, furthermore, seen in light of the social reputation and character of the witnesses.

57 The tendency of jurists to draw a parallel between the full proof with the epistemic ideal of *scientia* while indicia were seen as belonging to the realm of *opinio* and *praesumptiones* has also been noted by Rosoni. See I. Rosoni, *Quae singula non prosunt collecta iuvant. La teoria della prova indiziaria nell'età medievale e moderna*, pp. 64–65.

between *scientia* and *opinio* was, to an important extent, reproduced in the system of legal proofs in the distinction between what constituted a (full) proof and that which constituted mere suspicions or conjectures.[58]

3.3.2 The Epistemological Change

Between the seventeenth and nineteenth centuries something fundamentally changed in the epistemological ideas underlying the criminal law of evidence. Instead of the dichotomy between *scientia* and *opinio* of the late Middle Ages, this period saw the rise of an approach where different forms of knowledge were perceived to fall along a sliding scale of degrees of probability. Regarding the criminal law of evidence it became commonly accepted that a high probability of guilt sufficed for a conviction. The idea that general rules could *a priori* determine that there was sufficient evidence for a conviction in the concrete case came to be seen as implausible. Instead, the judge had to work in a more inductive manner, without pre-established rules, to see whether there was sufficient evidence to make it highly probable that the accused had committed the crime. The central hinge in this new approach came to be formed by the internal conviction of the judge or jurors.

Hacking and Shapiro have described well how the modern idea of probability emerged and how the centuries-old Aristotelian epistemological tradition

---

[58] It is, however, important to stress that even though indicia were thought to create a lesser kind of certainty, they did occupy an important place within the system of legal proofs and it is certainly not true that no value was attached to them at all. Reasoning about indicia and attempts to classify the strength of different indicia formed a significant part of many treatises on the criminal law of evidence. It is, therefore, not unlikely that, as Daston argues, the attempts at classifying the strength of different forms of evidence by jurists, formed a role-model for the emergence in the seventeenth and eighteenth centuries of the idea that forms of knowledge fell along a sliding scale of degrees of probability. Nevertheless, Daston appears to be wrong in the assumption that the confession, witness testimony and indicia were in the late Middle Ages already seen as part of an uninterrupted, sliding scale of degrees of probability. Most jurists argued that no matter how many indicia there were, they could never create the same certainty as the confession or the concurring testimony of two eyewitnesses. Instead, the comment of Daston on the general distinction between *scientia* and *opinio* applies far better to the qualitative distinction that was made in the system of legal proofs between indicia and the confession or the concurring testimony of two eyewitnesses: "Despite such attempts to rank probable assertions by the comparative force of the arguments mustered in their defence, medieval philosophers regarded probability and certainty as *a sort of two-valued logic*". They were, to an extent, seen as incommensurable categories. As will be described below, only in the eighteenth and nineteenth centuries were the confession, witness testimony and indicia increasingly seen as spanning 'a continuous spectrum of probabilities'. See L. Daston, *Classical Probability in the Enlightenment*, pp. 37–47.

that divided 'science', 'knowledge', 'certainty', 'philosophy' on the one hand, from 'opinion', 'probability', 'appearance' and 'rhetoric' on the other hand started to break down. Shapiro argues that the epistemological change started in the seventeenth century and was a reaction of philosophers such as Descartes, Bacon, Locke and Bayle against the discredited scholastic philosophy and the sixteenth century revival of scepticism. Their attempt to overcome the perceived difficulties in finding a secure fundament for 'absolutely certain' knowledge eventually led to a complete remapping of how different forms of knowledge were perceived. Even though the initial concern in the seventeenth century was to formulate a new basis for absolutely certain knowledge – as can be seen with, for example, Descartes and Bacon –, in effect there was eventually created a view of different forms of knowledge falling along a continuum of degrees of probability. The lower reaches were classified as 'fiction, opinion and conjecture', the middle range as 'probable and highly probable' and the apex of probable knowledge was called '*moral certainty*', which was deemed to come close to demonstrable or mathematically certain knowledge.[59]

In the course of the seventeenth century, traditionally used concepts were beginning to be applied in a new way to map the different forms of knowledge. Although there was at first a strong focus on mathematics and syllogistic demonstrability, which was seen as providing 'absolutely certain' knowledge, in effect many of the other forms of knowledge were in its shadow beginning to be evaluated along a sliding scale of probability. It became accepted that the investigation of natural and social phenomena could not yield the absolute certainty and universally true knowledge that was traditionally expected of *scientia*. Conversely, it was asserted that regarding, for example, the physical sciences and human affairs this absolute certainty was also not necessary.[60] Depending on what sort of practical decision was needed – for example, to convict someone accused of a crime – and the quantity and quality of the

---

59 B.J. Shapiro, *Probability and Certainty in Seventeenth-century England*, p. 1–5. In a different work Shapiro also describes that the term moral certainty and the discussions concerning rational decision-making under conditions of uncertainty were not entirely new in the seventeenth century, but also had important roots in the theological tradition of casuistry. See B. Shapiro, *"Beyond reasonable doubt" and "probable cause"*, 13–18. On this development and the importance of moral certainty, see also H. van Leeuwen, *The Problem of Certainty in English thought: 1630–1690*.

60 It is important to note, however, that the idea that no absolute, demonstrative certainty could be achieved did not apply to all fields of knowledge. Similar to mathematics, for example, it was expected that general and certain principals could be achieved by rational deduction in the area of natural law and morality. Here the method of the *mos geometricus* prevailed in the seventeenth and eighteenth centuries, and the ideal continued to be that absolutely certain and universally true knowledge was attainable.

evidence, conclusions could be arrived at which were sufficiently probable to form the basis for human conduct.[61] Shapiro summarizes this development with the conclusion that the quest for certitude was not abandoned, but that it became evident that only mathematics and a few logical, moral and metaphysical principles were capable of demonstration in the strict sense. Instead: "larger and larger portions of intellectual endeavour that once had been expected to attain the status of science by achieving demonstrative truth were now relegated to the domain of one level or another of probability".[62] As a consequence, the notions of probability and opinion, which during the late Middle Ages had had a rather negative connotation and which were defined in contrast to the ideal of *scientia*, acquired a far more positive connotation as a desirable form of knowledge.[63]

Popkin has famously described the important role of the revival of scepticism and the polemics of the Reformation and the Counter-Reformation in this process which subverted the traditional criteria for belief and certainty in the sixteenth and seventeenth centuries. In its place an approach emerged to most forms of knowledge which Popkin has aptly called "constructive scepticism".[64] While most philosophers in the seventeenth and eighteenth centuries conceded the claim that absolute certainty lay beyond human grasp in all but a few areas such as mathematics, they now argued that the conduct of daily life furnished sufficient, if imperfect standards for moral certainty. As Daston furthermore observed, the pragmatic rationality of partial certainty contrasted sharply with the demonstrative certainty demanded by the Scholastics. Instead of following the epistemic ideal of *scientia*, in the seventeenth and eighteenth centuries the decisions of the judge or natural philosopher were no longer viewed as pale copies of absolute certainty, but as ideals that carried their own imprimatur of certainty suited to their subject matter.[65]

The change in the epistemological discourse that is described by Shapiro is supported to a large extent by Hacking's *The emergence of probability*. Hacking's central question was how and why probability emerged as a separate

---

61 Ibidem, pp. 156–157.
62 Ibidem, pp. 4–5.
63 Ibidem, p. 43. Shapiro mentions the example of the Dutch scientist Huygens, who viewed the probable as a positive goal. Regarding natural phenomena, Huygens remarked, certainty was impossible and that "Tis a glory to arrive at probability ... But there are many degrees of probability, some nearer truth than others, in the determining of which lies the chief exercise of our judgement... I do not believe we know anything with complete certainty, but everything probably and to different degrees of probability".
64 See R. Popkin, *The History of Scepticism. From Savonarola to Bayle*.
65 L. Daston, *Classical Probability in the Enlightenment*, pp. xi–xii and 65.

'form of knowledge' in the seventeenth century. Hacking argues that the concept 'probability' had a very different meaning in the late medieval scholastic tradition than it acquired after the middle of the seventeenth century. The crucial characteristics of the medieval concept of 'probability' (in contrast to the later use of this concept) was that something did not primarily become 'probable' because of its support by evidence, but because of approval by respected people or persons of authority. Something was called 'probable' when it was supported by testimony and the writ of authority.[66] This understanding of probability derived from Aristotle's notion of *endoxon* which was translated by the medieval commentators as *probabilia*. Aristotle remarked that "[T]hose opinions are reputable [*endoxa*] which are accepted by everyone or by the majority of the wise – i.e., by all, or by the majority, or by the most notable and reputable of them".[67]

The concept of 'probability' that developed from the seventeenth century onwards was different from the notion that 'probable opinion is that which is attested by authority'. The new notion that 'probability' is a relation between a hypothesis and the evidence for it, or that something is probable if it has 'much evidence of experience in its favour', according to Hacking, only emerged when a new notion of evidence emerged from the seventeenth century onwards. Evidence as testimony and authority already existed in the Middle Ages. However, testimony and authority are conferred by *people*, and what was largely lacking was evidence provided by *things*. The latter concept that was left out is roughly what modern philosophers have come to call 'inductive evidence'. The importance of 'inductive evidence' increased strongly from the middle of the seventeenth century onwards and played an important role in the emergence of a probabilistic approach to knowledge.[68] The fact that inductive evidence, or evidence provided by inference from 'things', was far less important before the seventeenth century is clearly visible within the system of legal proofs. Evidence through testimony by witnesses and the accused were given pride of place within the system of legal proofs and were considered to prove the guilt

---

66   I. Hacking, *The Emergence of Probability*, pp. 22–26.
67   R. Schuessler, "Probability in Medieval and Renaissance Philosophy", *The Stanford Encyclopedia of Philosophy*, Section 3.1.
68   Ibidem, pp. 32–34. Pasnau remarks in a similar vein on late-medieval epistemology that: "The heart of the problem is that epistemology before Buridan had never clearly come to grips with how to incorporate the notion of evidence into a theory of knowledge. Although the *Posterior Analytics* had described knowledge as grounded in a demonstrative syllogism, Aristotle offered no broader theory of evidence into which his syllogistic theory might fit". See R. Pasnau, "Medieval social epistemology: *Scientia* for mere mortals", p. 34.

of the accused directly. Indicia – although they were certainly not completely left out as Hacking argued – were seen as a qualitatively different and far less secure form of evidence.[69]

It is, furthermore, important to note that the concept of probability that emerged in the seventeenth century had a dual character. On the one hand the concept of probability was used more 'objectively' in a statistical manner concerning itself with the frequency of events. Probability in this sense was used in a numerical way to express, for example, the chance that someone will throw the number six with a dice five times in a row. This form of probability attempts to express numerically the chance that certain events occur.[70] On the other hand, the concept of probability was used more 'subjectively', dedicated to *assessing reasonable degrees of belief* in propositions which were not expressed numerically and which were often devoid of a statistical background. How probable a proposition is, based on the existing evidence, determines the degree of belief which it is rational to have. Probability in this sense was used to create a vision of different forms of knowledge falling along a continuum of degrees of probability, in which the lower reaches were classified as 'fiction, opinion and conjecture', the middle range as 'probable and highly probable' and wherein the highest form of probability was called moral certainty. Both meanings of probability have been applied in the criminal law of evidence. The most important one – on which the focus lies in this study – was, nevertheless, what Hacking described as the epistemological version dedicated to assessing reasonable degrees of belief.[71]

Finally, within the epistemic variant of probability two approaches can be distinguished which were used by the jurists. Firstly, it was used to denote that something needed to be highly probable based on the evidence for it. In this

---

69   As will be further discussed below, the new probabilistic conception made it apparent that various forms of evidence could provide different degrees of probability which depended on the circumstances of the case, without being qualitatively different from each other. It was later recognized that even the confession and witness testimony did not prove the crime directly since the judge still had to make a chain of probable conclusions regarding the question whether, for example, the testimony was reliable and whether the testimony actually sufficiently proved the crime. In short, the new probabilistic conception made it clear that to prove the crime and the guilt of the accused, the same form of inferential reasoning was necessary for the confession, witness testimony and indicia.

70   I. Hacking, *The Emergence of Probability*, p. 11–17.

71   Ibidem, pp. 9–12. There were also a number of authors who attempted to apply the statistical concept of probability to the criminal law of evidence in the eighteenth and nineteenth centuries. For example, Jacques Bernoulli and Condorcet. On these attempts see I. Rosoni, *Quae singula non prosunt collecta iuvant. La teoria della prova indiziaria nell'età medievale e moderna*, pp. 265–298.

approach the emphasis was placed less on the subjective conviction of the person judging and more on the grounds for his conviction. Secondly, the epistemic variant was used in such a way that the emphasis lay on the more or less unreasoned feeling of being convinced. Both variants were used by the reform-minded jurists between 1750 and 1870.[72] As will be further discussed in the following subsection, the first variant was used by jurists to argue that the judge needed to have a reasoned conviction based on evidence and on a high probability of guilt. The second variant was used and popularized in particular by the French revolutionaries. They placed a stronger emphasis on having the subjective feeling of a *conviction intime*, and made the internal conviction of the jurors the foundation for a conviction in criminal cases.[73]

Summarizing, an important epistemological change occurred in the seventeenth and eighteenth centuries. The dichotomy of the scholastic-Aristotelian tradition between *scientia* and *opinio* gave way to seeing different forms of knowledge as falling along a continuum of degrees of probability. It became accepted that in the sphere of the natural sciences and social phenomena the relatively absolute epistemic ideal of *scientia* was unattainable and that man had to contend himself with differing degrees of probability. As Shapiro described, this epistemological shift went hand in hand with – and was strongly induced by – the rise and apparent success of a more empirical, experimental and inductive method of research in the natural sciences.[74] The breakdown of the dichotomy between the realms of *scientia* and *opinio* and the emergence of

---

72 Importantly, Daston notes in a similar way that within the epistemic version of probability two variants can be distinguished. One as "the measure and strength of an argument (how evidence weighed in for or against a judicial verdict); and as the intensity of belief (the firmness of a judge's conviction of the guilt or innocence of the accused)". See L. Daston, *Classical Probability in the Enlightenment*, p. 188.

73 The distinction in the use of these two variants among jurists was, nevertheless, a fluid one and one of degrees only. On the one hand, proponents of the 'reasoned' conviction also acknowledged that the conviction in the end depended on the evaluation of the person judging and, therefore, always contained a subjective element. On the other hand, there were only few jurists who would argue for the extreme variant that a conviction should be based entirely on a subjective and unreasoned feeling.

74 In the area of the natural sciences it was increasingly recognized and accepted that the empirical study of natural phenomena could not lead to demonstrative certainty, but that it was only possible to obtain moral certainty or a high degree of probability from the observation of nature. An inductive, experimental method became the norm and was highly important to the scientific revolution of the seventeenth and eighteenth centuries. On this development see B.J. Shapiro, *Probability and Certainty in Seventeenth-century England*, pp. 15–73.

a probabilistic approach to knowledge had important consequences for the criminal law of evidence. The probabilistic terminology started to be taken over by jurists and was increasingly used to argue that it was impossible to determine *a priori* when sufficient evidence existed for a conviction in the concrete case.

3.3.3 *The Adoption of a Probabilistic Terminology by Jurists*

Shapiro not only described the epistemological change but she has also shown that English jurists adopted the new probabilistic terminology from the end of the seventeenth century onwards. The first comprehensive treatises on the (criminal) law of evidence in England appeared in the early eighteenth century and they were clearly influenced by the changed epistemological ideas. They built especially on the terminology of Locke in his *Essay Concerning Human Understanding*, which formed an influential representation of the idea that different forms of knowledge formed a continuum of degrees of probability. The standard of certainty which the jury needed to attain was formulated in the English legal literature on the basis of the probabilistic notion of moral certainty. Before the second half of the eighteenth century there had not been a clear or uniformly used criterion to instruct the jury. In the second half of the eighteenth century variations of the phrase started to be used that jurors needed to be convinced 'beyond a reasonable doubt and to a moral certainty'. The use of this new terminology did not mean, as Shapiro remarks, that juries had not always required convincing proof in criminal cases, but "rather that legal formulations concerning that conviction were increasingly stated in terms which were consistent with reigning epistemological formulations".[75]

The adoption of the new probabilistic terminology in the Anglo-American juridical literature can, for example, be seen in the influential treatise written

---

75 B.J. Shapiro, "'To a Moral Certainty': Theories of Knowledge and Anglo-American Juries 1600–1850", pp. 158–174. In practice the standard of moral certainty and being convinced 'beyond a reasonable doubt' was used for the first time in the second half of the eighteenth century, most likely in the 'Boston Massacre Trials' of 1770. Nonetheless, this formulation only became uniformly applied in the course of the nineteenth century. An influential definition was given in 'Commonwealth vs. Webster': "It is not merely possible doubt; because everything relating to human affairs, and depending on moral evidence, is open to some possible or imaginary doubt. It is that state of the case, which, after the entire comparison and consideration of all the evidence, leaves the minds of jurors in that condition that they cannot say they feel an abiding conviction, to a *moral certainty*, of the truth of the charge … The evidence must establish the truth of the fact to a reasonable and moral certainty; a certainty that convinces and directs the understanding, and satisfies the reason and judgement … This we take to be proof beyond a reasonable doubt".

by Gilbert in 1726. He relied heavily on Locke and began with a passage copied almost verbatim from his treatise:

> There are several degrees from perfect Certainty and Demonstration, quite down to Improbability and Unlikeness ... and there are several Acts of the Mind proportioned to these degrees of Evidence ... from full Assurance and Confidence, quite down to Conjecture, Doubt, Distrust and Disbelief. Now what is to be done in Trials of Right, is to range all Matters in the Scale of Probability.[76]

Similarly, Starkie stated in his *Practical Treatise on the Law of Evidence* that:

> Evidence which satisfies the minds of the jury of the fact in dispute, to the entire exclusion of every reasonable doubt, constitutes full proof of that fact ... Even the most direct evidence can produce nothing more than such a high degree of probability as amounts to moral certainty. From the highest it may decline by an infinite number of gradations, until it produces in the mind nothing more than a mere preponderance of assent in favour of a particular fact.[77]

Similar to Shapiro, Cogrossi has shown that the new probabilistic terminology started to be taken over by jurists in the Italian peninsula who reflected on the criminal law of evidence. On the continent as well, the term moral certainty, which denoted a very high degree of probability, played a central role in the new probabilistic terminology of the jurists.[78] An influential definition of the

---

76   Ibidem, p. 176.
77   Ibidem, pp. 177–185. Shapiro has extensively shown that a probabilistic terminology was adopted by Anglo-American jurists which derived from a broader epistemological change. However, Shapiro appears to mistakenly have thought that this epistemological change was particular to the Anglo-American tradition and had little or no effect on the (criminal) law of evidence on the continent. Shapiro remarked: "Because the philosophical components in the Roman-canon system had been provided by late medieval scholastic philosophers and because the system had become well-entrenched on the Continent during that period, it seems to have been relatively uninfluenced by the epistemological issues that became acute in the early modern period". In fact a probabilistic conception of knowledge was also adopted by continental jurists from the late seventeenth century onwards and was instrumental in the breakdown of the system of legal proofs, as will be further discussed below. See B.J. Shapiro, "'To a Moral Certainty': Theories of Knowledge and Anglo-American Juries 1600–1850", pp. 155–157.
78   C. Cogrossi, "Alle origini del libero convincimento del giudice. La morale certezza in Tommaso Briganti trattatista del primo settecento", pp. 529–532 and C. Cogrossi, *La formazione*

term *démonstration morale* was given by Bayle in his *Dictionnaire historique et critique*:

> la vraie nature de cette espèce de démonstration, … ne consiste pas comme les démonstrations géométriques dans un point indivisible; elle souffre le plus et le moins, et se promène depuis une grande probabilité, jusque à une très-grande probabilité … Il nous arrive tous les jours d'être pleinement convaincus d'une chose; et sans le moindre doute, quoi que nous sachions que le contraire est possible.[79]

Beside describing the epistemological change itself, Cogrossi has shown in a study of the Neapolitan jurist Briganti how the new probabilistic vocabulary was used regarding the criminal law of evidence and how it replaced the traditional terminology of the system of legal proofs. She discusses Briganti's *Pratica Criminale* (1747), which can be seen as a typical juridical handbook that tried to describe the criminal law of evidence as it actually functioned. It was not intended to reform or revolutionize the criminal law (of evidence). While initially following the custom of discussing the works of authority on the criminal law of evidence, Briganti eventually took an innovative step by filling in traditional terms with a new meaning. This becomes particularly apparent in his treatment of the difficult subject of indicia. There had already been a long debate since the emergence of the system of legal proofs whether it was possible to convict someone on the basis of 'undoubtable indicia'. An ordinance created in 1621 for the kingdom of Sicily explicitly allowed the possibility to convict someone to the ordinary punishment on the basis of *indizi indibutati*, but the question was still how this term should be understood. Briganti explained that undoubtable indicia existed when the judge had attained *certezza morale*. Briganti consequently gave an explanation of what this moral certainty was by giving an exact Italian translation of the words (which have been cited above) with which Bayle described moral certainty in his *Dictionnaire historique et critique*.[80] Briganti used this insight to explain that *indizi indubitati* did not

---

della probabilità e del concetto die "certezza" giudiziale nei giuristi-filosofi europei fra il XVII e il XVIII secolo, pp. 7–8.

79 C. Cogrossi, "Alle origini del libero convincimento del giudice. La morale certezza in Tommaso Briganti trattatista del primo settecento", pp. 520–529.

80 Ibidem, pp. 520–521. Briganti stated : "La vera natura … di questa certezza morale non consiste come nelle dimostrazione geometriche in un punto indivisibile, ma soffre il più ed il meno, e si promena da una grande probabilità sino ad una grandissima probabilità: question sono i suoi limiti e per conseguenza include certezza evidente, ma non esclude la possibilità in contrario". This definition of moral certainty gained wide currency and

THE THEORETICAL FRAMEWORK   101

mean that an absolute certainty was necessary, but that only a high probability was required to convict someone.[81]

The research of Cogrossi illustrates the use of a new probabilistic terminology and that this usage clearly derived from a broader epistemological discourse. A similar adoption of a probabilistic vocabulary can be seen among jurists throughout continental Europe. From roughly the second half of the eighteenth century onwards the old terminology of, for example, the *probatio plena* and *semi-plena* started to give way to this new terminology. Many jurists, such as Briganti, at first used the probabilistic terminology to explain the existing system of evidentiary rules and it was not yet used with the intention to reform it. They sought more to 'rationalize' the system of legal proofs in probabilistic terms. The German author Leyser, for example, stated on the kind of certainty which was required to establish the existence of the *corpus delicti*: "Ad corpus delicti *certitudo moralis*, qualis in rebus humanis haberi potest, non mathematica et absoluta, requiritur".[82] Not a mathematical or absolute certainty was required, but only a kind of certainty which one could normally have in human affairs: a high degree of probability which was called moral certainty. Boehmer as well, stated that it was absurd to demand a mathematical certainty in criminal law where only moral certainty was possible. Gmelin similarly stated: "wir würden weder in bürgerlichen noch peinlichen Sachen

---

was repeated by many jurists who tried to explain what certainty was required in criminal cases. Another example of the use of this definition can be found in the German author Weber who used very similar terms in an article published in 1825: "In Vergleichung mit dieser absoluten Gewissheit ist dann freilich jene empirische und insbesondere die historische Gewissheit, der wir uns im Leben doch auch öfters überlassen müssen häufig nur ein unter den gegebenen Umständen nicht weiter zu steigernder *hoher Grad von Wahrscheinlichkeit*. Es wird dadurch die Möglichkeit des Gegenteils nicht ausgeschlossen, aber doch so weit in die Ferne gestellt, dass wir uns nach dem gewöhnlichen erfahrungsmäßigen Lauf der Dinge bei dem Fürwahr halten beruhigen können". Cited by de Bosch Kemper in J. De Bosch Kemper, *Het Wetboek van Strafvordering. Deel III*, pp. 502–507.

81   Ibidem, pp. 517–521 and 542. Similar to the research of Cogrossi, Rosoni also deems that the epistemological changes of the seventeenth century had an important impact on the continental criminal law of evidence and in particular led to a revaluation of the role of indicia : "È indubbio che la fiducia nel metodo scientifico, basato sull'osservazione, l'analisi e l'induzione, abbia riscattato quel genere die prova che fino ad allora era stato tenuto ai margini della certezza", and later "La riflessione epistemologica del XVII secolo, che tenta di legitimare il procedimento del convencimento induttivo, fa maturare, in campo giudiziale, una teoria della certezza morale legata al principio della probabilità, teoria che legittima appieno la struttura logica della prova indiziaria". See I. Rosoni, *Quae singula non prosunt collecta iuvant. La teoria della prova indiziaria nell'età medievale e moderna*, pp. 18–19 and 26.

82   A.M. Ignor, *Geschichte Strafprozess*, pp. 167–168.

jemals ein Urteil fallen können, wenn wir mathematischen Gewissheit forderten, dann auch eine Million von Zeugen bringt keine solche Gewissheit hervor; wir können uns der Notwendigkeit nicht entheben, den Richter nach lauter Wahrscheinlichkeiten handeln zu lassen".[83]

Beside authors such as Briganti, Leyser and Boehmer who tried to explain and reformulate the system of legal proofs in probabilistic terms, there were also many authors who started to use these new epistemological ideas to criticize the plausibility of the system of legal proofs. They argued that moral certainty alone was sufficient for a conviction and that this could not be regulated in general rules. Beccaria in his ground-breaking work *Dei delitte e delle pene* (1764) speaks in probabilistic terms and stated that only moral certainty was required for a conviction. He even remarked that one might ask why he speaks of the criminal law of evidence in terms of 'probability'. Beccaria's answer to this important question is formulated in a very clear 'matter-of-fact' way: "one has to notice when one wants to speak accurately, that *moral certainty* is nothing more than a probability, but a probability that is called certainty because every man of good sense would consider it that way".[84]

Unlike more traditional or 'conservative' authors, Beccaria used the probabilistic ideas to criticize the existing system of evidentiary rules. Brissot de Warville remarked in a similar way that it was in vain that the jurists had searched for 'un thermomètre judiciaire', the foundation for a conviction could not be anything else than moral certitude.[85] Instead of explaining the requirements for a *probatio plena*, the reform-minded authors argued that only a high degree of probability or moral certainty was necessary for a conviction. From this probabilistic conception it was, furthermore, argued that there was no essential difference between the confession, witness testimony and indicia. Globig and Huster, for example, denied in a treatise in 1782 that there was an essential difference between on the one hand the confession and witness testimony, and on the other hand indicia. They argued that indicia could create the same kind of high probability and that convictions to the ordinary punishment on the basis of indicia should also be possible. Globig and Huster concluded that if indicia were unsuited to create the necessary certainty for a conviction, the same would have to apply to the confession and witness testimony:

---

83   C.G. Gmelin, *Grundsätze der Gesetzgebung über Verbrechen und Strafen*, p. 333.
84   J.M. Michiels, *Cesare Beccaria. Over misdaden en straffen*, pp. 62–63.
85   J-P. Brissot de Warville, *Théorie des loix criminelles, Tome II*, pp. 85–88.

> Die gegenseitige Gründe, als ob die indicia nur wahrscheinliche Argumenta wären, folglich aus ihnen niemand überzeugt werden könnte, dass sie leichte trügen könnten, dass sie den Beweis des Gegenteils zuließen etc. Alle diese Gründe sind von keinem Gewicht. Denn da sie eben sowohl wider die stärkste und jede moralische Gewissheit angeführt werden können; so würde daraus folgen, das wir niemalen einer andern, als einer demonstrativen Gewissheit glauben, folglich auch jeden Beweis durch Zeugen für keinen Beweis erkennen müssten.[86]

Importantly, as has been described in the previous section, the epistemic variant of probability could be used both in a more objective and in a more subjective sense. This duality can be seen in the way the concept of moral certainty was used by the jurists. It was used to denote in a more objective sense that it needed to be highly probable that the accused was guilty, and it was used in a more subjective sense to refer to someone being internally convinced of a proposition (meaning that the judge needed to be morally certain). In the last decades of the eighteenth century the idea of moral certainty was often used in the more subjective sense to refer to the internal or 'moral' conviction of the person judging. Particularly by French authors, the subjective conviction of the person judging started to be presented as a sufficient basis for a conviction in contrast to the system of legal proofs. The use of moral certainty to refer to the internal state of being 'morally' convinced can be seen clearly in the discussions of the French revolutionary assembly where the *conviction intime* of the jurors was introduced as the sole criterion for the sufficiency of proof. Thouret, for example, remarked:

> C'est-là essentiellement la *conviction morale* qui ne se commande pas, qui est tout-à-la-fois et au-dessus des préceptes, et plus sûre qu'eux dans l'application. Elle subjugue quand elle est ressentie, elle ne peut être ni dictée ni suppléée quand elle n'existe pas. Elle est le plus sûr *criterium* de la vérité humaine.[87]

---

86 H.E. Globig and J.G. Huster, *Abhandlung von der Criminal=Gesetzgebung*, pp. 351–352. In a similar vein, the Italian jurist Nani argued in 1781 that indicia could climb to such a high degree of probability that they created a moral certainty. The testimony of witnesses and the confession did not provide a different kind of certainty, but could only create a high probability. See T. Nani, *Degl'indizi e dell'uso de' medesimi per conoscere i delitti*, pp. 106–174.

87 I. Rosoni, *Quae singula non prosunt collecta iuvant. La teoria della prova indiziaria nell'età medievale e moderna*, pp. 323–324. Another good example of this change in terminology is present in a Dutch concept criminal ordinance of 1804 that was intended to reform the

The best and perhaps most influential example of the use of moral certainty to refer to the internal conviction in the juridical literature in the late eighteenth century is formed by Filangieri. Filangieri started by stating that moral certainty was absolutely necessary to convict someone and that without moral certainty a conviction would be an injustice. Subsequently, he remarked that there was some confusion surrounding the concept of moral certainty because some authors deemed that the certainty needed to lie in the propositions. Filangieri stated however, that moral certainty was nothing else than the state of mind which consisted of being certain of the truth or falsity of a proposition. Filangieri, in other words, required moral certainty for a conviction and he meant by this that the judge needed to be internally convinced: "Everything that is said, therefore, about certainty in general can be applied in the same way to moral certainty. This, like any other form of certainty, therefore, does not lie in the propositions but in the mind".[88]

3.3.4 The Epistemological Change and the Reform of the Criminal Law of Evidence

The emergence of a probabilistic conception of knowledge furnished two closely related and highly important criticisms of the system of legal proofs. Firstly, it made the distinction between the direct and indirect forms of evidence seem untenable. A central idea within the system of legal proofs was that only the confession and witness testimony could create a full proof. It was thought that they proved the crime 'directly' and provided a different and higher kind of certainty than indicia. From the new probabilistic conception it was argued that the various forms of evidence could merely provide differing degrees of probability which depended on the circumstances of the case, but that they were not qualitatively different from each other.[89] It was recognized

---

criminal law of evidence. The Article dealing with the question 'when a crime is proven', stated: "the existence of a crime and the guilt of the accused are considered proven, when the judge is convinced that the opposite is morally impossible". See O. Moorman van Kappen, *De ontwerpen Lijfstraffelijk wetboek 1801 en 1804. Deel 1*, p. 155.

88   G. Filangieri, *La scienza della legislazione*, Book III, Chapter 13, pp. 96–103. As will be further discussed later, Filangieri did not propose the moral conviction as the sole criterion for a conviction but was in favour of a negative system of legal proofs.

89   Damaška remarks on the distrust against indicia within the system of legal proofs that: "There are many reasons for the preference of direct over circumstantial evidence in the legal theory of proof. What must especially be emphasized, however, is that there was little understanding that all perception is inferential and that the distinction between direct and circumstantial evidence is one of degree only". See M. Damaška, "Book reviews. The Death of Legal Torture", p. 869. On the increased recognition of indicia as an equally certain form of evidence, see also P. Marchetti, *Testis Contra Se*, pp. 169–225.

that even the confession and witness testimony did not prove the crime directly and that the judge still had to draw conclusions regarding the question whether, for example, the testimony was reliable and if the testimony actually sufficiently proved the guilt of the accused.[90]

Secondly, and closely related to the first criticism, from the new probabilistic conception it seemed impossible to determine *a priori* when sufficiently strong evidence existed for a conviction in the concrete case. There was no reason anymore to assume that the confession or the testimony of two eyewitnesses created a full proof or a sufficient certainty while other forms of evidence automatically could not. The question whether there was a sufficiently high probability for a conviction depended on the concrete circumstances of the case and how they related to each other. The impossibility to predetermine the sufficiency of proof in general rules was particularly apparent concerning the matter of indicia because their endless possible variety seemed to defy any strict regulation.

A good example where the combination of these two criticisms led to the rejection of the system of legal proofs can be found in the report of a Prussian committee which advised to retain the jury system and the free evaluation of the evidence in the Prussian provinces on the left bank of the Rhine in 1819.[91] The committee was strongly inspired by the French revolutionary reformers and their report was essentially a summary of the French reforming ideas. The report started with a theoretical explanation of why the system of legal proofs was untenable. The committee first denied that there was a qualitative difference between indicia, eyewitnesses or a confession. They all had the same effect and could only constitute differing degrees of probability but never an absolute certainty. Every historical proof formed merely a 'Kette von Vermuthungen' which in the end was always dependent on and constituted by the

---

90   An example of this conclusion can be seen with Mittermaier who argued in his *Lehre vom Beweise* (1834) that there was no qualitative difference between indicia and other forms of evidence: "Es ist ein Irrthum zu glauben, dass die Beweismittel, durch welche wir den natürlichen Beweis begründen zu können meinen, Augenschein, Geständniss oder Zeugniss, nur auf der sinnlichen Erwiederung beruhen und für uns nun dadurch überzeugend werden, dass wir dem Zeugnisse unsrer Sinne trauen. Es ist überall nur eine Kette von Vermuthungen, worauf wir unsere Ueberzeugung bauen". See C.J.A. Mittermaier, *Lehre vom Beweise*, pp. 402–403.

91   These Prussian provinces had formed part of the Napoleonic Empire until 1813 and the French legislation was, therefore, in force in this region which contained the jury system and the free evaluation of the evidence. After the fall of the Napoleonic Empire the question emerged if the free evaluation and the jury system should be retained, on which this committee presented its advice. On this committee see further Section three of Chapter five.

'subjective' evaluation of the judge (because the probable conclusions did not exist abstractly but had to be drawn by a person judging). The committee denied that it was possible to adequately prescribe the level of certainty necessary for a conviction in *a priori* evidentiary rules. Mathematical demonstrability could never be reached. For this reason only the internal conviction of the judge or jurors – which was based on probable conclusions drawn from the existing evidence – could form the foundation of a conviction. A further important deficit of the system was legal proofs was that it could never do justice to the complexity of the concrete circumstances of a criminal case. The committee, in short, deemed it impossible and useless to predetermine the force of different forms of evidence in abstract rules.[92]

In the example of the Prussian committee it can be seen that the fundamental criticisms of the system of the system of legal proofs went hand in hand with a change in the idea about the role of the judge in the evaluation of the evidence. With the acknowledgement that it was impossible to predetermine in evidentiary rules when there was sufficient evidence for a conviction, the burden fell on the judge or jurors to evaluate whether a sufficiently high probability of guilt existed in the individual case. This is precisely the conclusion that was drawn between 1750 and 1870 when the internal conviction became the central criterion to convict someone. The change is accurately summarized by Padoa-Schioppa:

> c'est la mutation du rôle du juge dans l'évaluation de la preuve. Une attitude nouvelle émerge en effet, destinée à s'affirmer par la suite: le principe de la 'certitude morale', considérée comme le fondement nécessaire et suffisant pour émettre la décision judiciaire. A son tour, la certitude morale résulte du degré de 'probabilité' qu'un fait donné présente aux yeux du juge: *donc, c'est l'attitude du juge par rapport aux preuves qui devient fondamentale dans la notion moderne de certitude morale*.[93]

The foundation of a conviction no longer consisted in the correspondence of the evidence to certain *a priori* criteria that determined the sufficiency of proof, but instead the requirement became a high probability of guilt (moral certainty) that was to be determined by the free evaluation of the evidence by the judge.

---

92   E. Landsberg, *Die Gutachten der Rheinischen Immediat-Justiz-Kommission*, pp. 122–144.
93   A. Padoa-Schioppa, "Sur la conscience du juge dans le ius commune Européen", pp. 122–123.

The rejection of the possibility to predetermine when sufficient evidence existed for a conviction led to the conclusion that the judge or jurors should be free in the evaluation of the evidence so that they could do justice to the concrete circumstances of the case. In effect the internal conviction of the judge or jurors became the foundation for the decision to convict an accused. Stichweh, who described this transition as a "Subjektivierung des Beweisrechts", commented on this development that the internal conviction started to function as the criterion or equivalent of the certainty required in criminal cases. The significance of the new focus on the internal process of 'being convinced' in opposition to applying general binding evidentiary rules is described by Stichweh in the following way:

> Es geht nicht mehr um die Präsentation der gesetzlich festgelegten Beweismittel und die dann ausgesprochene Anerkennung (oder die Verweigerung dieser Anerkennung), dass die Beweismittel den Bedingungen der gesetzlichen Beweistheorie genügen ... Stattdessen beobachten wir eine Verschiebung der für den Beweis relevanten Bestimmungen und Unterscheidungen in den Bereich einer *Semantik mentaler Operationen*; Wir haben es zu tun mit einer *Mentalisierung des Beweises*.[94]

---

94   R. Stichweh, "Zur Subjektivierung der Entscheidungsfindung im Deutschen Strafprozess des 19. Jahrhunderts", pp. 283–292. Interestingly, Stichweh argues that the transition from the system of legal proofs to a system based on the free evaluation of the evidence eventually enabled a more hermeneutical approach to the criminal law of evidence. In the old system of 'legal proofs' the judge had a predominantly analytical approach. What constituted a 'full proof' was predetermined, and a judge predominantly had the task to see whether the evidence in front of him provided a full proof in accordance with the general rules. From the nineteenth century onwards, this analytical approach was in effect replaced by a hermeneutical approach. There was no clear predetermined objective standard anymore of what constituted a sufficient proof and which determined what 'value' the different individual pieces of evidence had; two witnesses could be too little to convince the judge, while several circumstantial forms of evidence could now convince him of the guilt of the accused. As Stichweh states: "Die freie Beweiswürdigung setzt eine Hermeneutik an die Stelle einer Analytik, und wie gerade am Beispiel des Zeugenbeweises sichtbar wird, handelt es sich nicht um eine Texthermeneutik, nicht um eine Technik der Sinnexplication der in schriftliche Form gebrachten Aussagen, vielmehr um eine Hermeneutik der Interaktion, eine Auslegung von in öffentlicher, zudem dialogischer 'Rede' gemachten Aussagen".
As Stichweh rightfully states, the hermeneutics of the criminal judge was not so much a textual hermeneutics, but more one of interaction in the courtroom where the behaviour and expressions of witnesses were being heard. The idea of a 'hermeneutical circle' applies very well to the new situation of the criminal judge wherein the internal conviction (*Überzeugung*) played a central role. Because there was no longer a predetermined value of, for example, a confession or the testimony of a witness, every form of evidence

As has been explained above, the epistemological change made the distinction between, on the one hand, indicia and, on the other hand, the confession and witness testimony appear untenable. The free evaluation of the evidence made it possible for the judge to ground his decision on either form of evidence. It is, however, important to stress that during the eighteenth and nineteenth centuries, oral testimony remained the central and most highly valued form of evidence that was used in the criminal trial. There was still a lingering distrust against indicia in this period. Only during the late nineteenth and the twentieth centuries, with the rise of the forensic sciences, did indicia become a far more highly valued form of evidence. The new methods of investigation that were developed in this period – such as the study of footprints and fingerprints – and the 'scientific aura' of these methods, gave a more important place to the use of circumstantial forms of evidence and the testimony of expert witnesses who analyzed these circumstances.[95] Nevertheless, it was the emergence of the free evaluation of the evidence which had principally cleared the way for the judge

---

became merely an *Indiez* or *Einzelheit* which had to be seen in the context of the whole (the judge's *Gesamteindruck*). Furthermore, the details of a testimony became more important – such as nervous movements by the accused, small inconsistencies or a too 'perfect story' by a witness – because the total trustworthiness of the testimony was seen in light of these individual aspects. The details and individual pieces of evidence, however, only acquired their meaning in the light of the whole, while the whole was an accumulation of the individual parts. This more hermeneutical approach to the criminal law of evidence appears to have emerged largely unconsciously in the nineteenth century in concomitance with the introduction of the free evaluation of the evidence and a stronger emphasis on the orality of the procedure. Incidentally, the *de facto* more hermeneutical approach in the nineteenth century also fitted well with the new importance that was given to proving the criminal intent of the accused. In a criminal case the goal was not merely to give a reconstruction of the fact, but also to understand and interpret the goals and emotional state of the accused.

This change has been commented on in a similar way by Astaing: "Cette liberté nouvelle dans la domaine probatoire amène les juges à procéder à des opérations intellectuelles et psychologique qui ne se réduisent pas à celles qu'impliquait l'ancien système car l'esprit sait ne pas pouvoir espérer une ferme adhésion a une solution infaillible. De manière plus concrète, lors du jugement, la démarche analytique et objective d'appréciation des preuves s'efface: se substitue à elle une approche synthétique et, dans le même temps, subjective et en partie sentimentale des éléments de preuve". See A. Astaing, "Le refus du dogmatisme et du pyrrhonisme: la preuve pénale dans *le traité de la justice criminelle de France* (1771)", p. 81.

95 F. Chauvaud, "Le Sacre de la preuve indiciale. De la preuve orale à la preuve scientifique (XIXe-milieu du XXe siècle)", pp. 221–239. Conversely, while indicia appeared to be more reliable because of the connection with the forensic sciences, new psychological insights during this period made the testimony of witnesses seem to be more unreliable. In some respects indicia started to be seen as a more certain form of evidence than the confession or the testimony of witnesses. Incidentally, the new ideal of the importance and reliability

to ground his decision on any form of evidence. Even with the more central role of indicia the framework of the evidentiary system remained the same. The judge still had to freely evaluate the evidence and his internal conviction remained the central requirement to convict someone.

The fact that the plausibility of the system of legal proofs was denied and that the freely formed internal conviction was increasingly recognized as the foundation for a conviction in criminal cases, did not mean that the discussion was over and that there was suddenly a general agreement in the nineteenth century on how the role of the internal conviction should be understood. Even though a consensus grew in the first decades of the nineteenth century that the internal conviction of the judge or jurors was required to convict someone, there were nevertheless significant differences in the view on how the internal conviction should be understood and what its role should be. A large part of the debate in the nineteenth century revolved around this question. Roughly two visions can be distinguished on how the internal conviction should be understood: the idea of the *conviction intime* and the idea of the *conviction raisonnée*.

3.3.4.1   The Conviction Intime and the Conviction Raisonnée

The roots of the discussion lay in the reform of the criminal law of evidence by the French revolutionaries. They rejected the plausibility of *a priori* evidentiary rules and wanted to introduce the free evaluation of the evidence by lay jurors (mainly because they distrusted professional magistrates). The French revolutionaries presented the necessary *conviction intime* predominantly as a subjective and even intuitive conviction instead of emphasizing that it needed to be a rational conviction based on a more objective high degree of probability. The proponents of a *conviction raisonnée* later reacted against this idea and argued that it had to be a reasoned conviction based on a high degree of probability. To an important extent, the proponents of a *conviction raisonnée* continued to build on the idea, developed in the second half of the eighteenth century, that the moral certainty required for a conviction needed to be a more objective high degree of probability. The subjective interpretation of the internal conviction by the French revolutionaries, formed a rupture within this development.[96] A difficult question is why the French revolutionaries argued so

---

of the scientific analysis of circumstantial forms of evidence in the late nineteenth and early twentieth centuries is, for example, also visible in Arthur Conan Doyle's popular detective stories of Sherlock Holmes.

96   Rosoni even states that the French idea of the *conviction intime* was a rupture within the fertile epistemological development in the juridical science and contained a banalisation of this development in its presentation of the *conviction intime* as the criterion for the free

strongly for the idea of a subjective and intuitive conviction. Two factors appear to be of central importance to explain this interpretation of the internal conviction.

First of all, the choice for lay jurors determined, to a large extent, how the French revolutionaries presented the role of the internal conviction. The revolutionaries put a strong emphasis on the idea that any lay person could, as it were, feel or understand the truth when he sat at the trial and the evidence was presented to him directly and orally. Partially to justify that no legal training was necessary to correctly evaluate the evidence, a strong emphasis was placed on the idea that the internal conviction was not the process of a reasoned evaluation of the evidence, but far more something that could be 'instinctively' felt. The proponents of a jury system often stated that normal common sense and a good, honest character sufficed to judge on the question of fact, and that a layman with his common sense was even better suited to judge on the question of fact than the professional judge who relied on complex legal evidentiary theories which were estranged from reality.[97]

As Ranouil has observed, there was also a clear 'Rousseauistic' tendency among many of the revolutionary reformers which underpinned the exaltation of the honest, simple and uncorrupted way that lay jurors would decide in contrast to the way that professional judges decided on the basis of complex legal rules. A good example of this tendency can be found with the revolutionary Duport who remarked:

> Les jurés, sont une institution primitive qui sent encore les bois dont elle est sortie et qui respire fortement la nature et l'instinct. On n'en parle qu'avec enthousiasme, on ne l'aime qu'avec passion ... Ce qui plaît dans

---

evaluation of the evidence. See I. Rosoni, *Quae singula non prosunt collecta iuvant. La teoria della prova indiziaria nell'età medievale e moderna*, pp. 26–27.

97 Beccaria can be seen as an early and important example of someone who emphasized that moral certainty was more the product of intuitive feelings and common sense than a conscious and rational weighing of the evidence: "For this moral certainty is easier to feel than to accurately indicate with words. This is why I belief it would be good if the law would prescribe that the president of the court should be assisted by *pairs*, which are not appointed by a magistrate but elected by chance. In this situation an uneducated man who judges by his feelings, offers more safeguards than some learned magistrate whose judgment is guided by an evidentiary theory. When the law is clear and accurate ... there is nothing more required to judge on the question of fact than a *normal common sense*". This emphasis of Beccaria on feeling and sentiment in lieu of reason can perhaps be at least partially explained by the fact that he was strongly influenced by Helvétius. See J.I. Israel, *Democratic enlightenment: philosophy, revolution and human rights 1750–1790*, pp. 336–338, and J.M. Michiels, *Cesare Beccaria. Over misdaden & straffen*, pp. 63–65.

> l'établissement des jurés, c'est que tout s'y décide par la droiture et la bonne foi, simplicité bien préférable à cet amas inutile et funeste de subtilités et formes que l'on a jusqu'à ce jour appelé justice.[98]

Secondly, in addition to the fact that the French Revolutionaries wanted to justify that laymen could decide just as well on the question of fact as professional judges and therefore argued that common sense sufficed, the idea of an almost instinctively formed internal conviction fitted well in the high esteem that sentiment and intuition possessed in the French enlightenment. The second half of the eighteenth century in France is aptly coined 'the age of sensibility' by Riskin who has shown that among the philosophes the idea was current that empirical knowledge grew not from sensory experience alone, but from an inseparable combination of sensation and sentiment. There was a virtual 'cult of sensibility' in France which emphasized the importance of sentiment and intuition in lieu of reason.[99]

The emphasis on the importance of sensibility in the acquisition of empirical knowledge in the French enlightenment forms an important part of the explanation of why the *conviction intime* was understood in a largely intuitive and sentimental sense. A typical formulation of this idea that the jurors could almost 'intuitively' feel the truth was presented by Thouret in the revolutionary *Assemblée Constituante*:

> Les jurés sont placés au sein, pour ainsi dire, de la preuve; ils en suivent tous les progrès matériels et moraux; ils voient et entendent l'accusé se défendre, ils voient et entendent les témoins et l'accusé poursuivant, pressant réciproquement, et faisant sortir la vérité par leur débat contradictoire. A mesure que ce débat s'avance et s'anime, ils reçoivent

---

98   P.C. Ranouil, "L'intime Conviction", pp. 90–94.
99   J. Riskin, *Science in the age of sensibility. The sentimental empiricists of the French enlightenment*, pp. 1–17. The importance of sensibility in the French enlightenment is also summarized well by Kennedy: "As the enlightenment explained the workings of nature by imminent processes, so it discarded the mind-body dualism of the Cartesians by underscoring the origins of all mental activity in experience. By 1801 Destutt de Tracy had pushed Lockean sensationalism so far that he could assert that 'to think is to sense and nothing but to sense'. Etienne Bonnot de Condillac and Helvétius had diminished the active role of the intellect, which Locke had retained for reflection, deduction and intuition. Condillac's *Traité des sensations* (1754) argued that thought was 'transformed sensation'". See E. Kennedy, *A cultural history of the French Revolution*, p. 66. On the importance of sensibility see also L. Hunt, *Inventing human rights: A History*.

> une conviction intime, et s'imprègnent de la vérité par tous leur sens, et par toutes les facultés de leur intelligence.[100]

The accent lay, furthermore, on the relatively passive position of the jurors who, more or less, involuntarily saw or sensed the truth as the evidence was presented to them, and not on the internal conviction as the result of a process of rationally evaluating and weighing the evidence. This idea is typically expressed in the following manner by Meyer, a Dutch jurist who pleaded for the introduction of the jury system in 1819:

> la vivacité des débats, la présence à l'instruction orale, peuvent faire naître cette conviction intime, cette certitude morale qui ne laisse aucun doute sur la vérité; l'application de la loi est le résultat d'une combinaison froide et mûrie par la réflexion; le fait se reconnaît par les sens, par un sentiment qui résulte presqu'involontairement de l'examen.[101]

Another telling example of this view on how the internal conviction worked can be found in a speech by De Brouckere, a parliamentarian in the Kingdom of the Netherlands who pleaded for the introduction of a jury system in 1829:

> Mais on décline l'aptitude du jury à l'appréciation du fait, on pose des règles à la conviction. La conviction ne peut être le résultat d'une évaluation factice, elle ne se compose pas d'éléments déterminés; c'est un sentiment, une impression morale qu'on ne peut pas plus tarifer que la conscience.[102]

---

100 I. Rosoni, *Quae singula non prosunt collecta iuvant. La teoria della prova indiziaria nell'età medievale e moderna*, pp. 323–324.

101 See J.D. Meyer, *Esprit, origine et progress des institutions judiciaires des principaux pays de l'Europe. Tom. VI*, pp. 368–369 and 437. The following remark by Meyer, furthermore, shows well how he saw the internal conviction: "Celui qui est chargé d'examiner un fait et ses circonstances doit apprécier les preuves, non d'après des règles fixes et déterminées, mais d'après l'impression qu'elles ont faite sur sa conscience, sa conviction est souvent formée par le maintien, le geste, l'accent de ceux qu'il voit et qu'il entend; le moindre détail peut donner cette persuasion, quelquefois personnelle et dépendante de ce qu'un autre peut n'avoir point aperçu; il est par conséquent très difficile de se rendre raison à soi-même, il est impossible d'instruire un autre, de ce qui entraîné l'opinion. C'est l'ensemble des preuves qui frappe l'esprit; les décomposer c'est en détruire l'effet, les décrire c'est les dénaturer ... La personne qui, d'après sa conscience, juge sur l'existence d'un fait, ne peut pas motiver son jugement".

102 J.J.F. Noordziek, *Geschiedenis der beraadslagingen gevoerd in de tweede kamer der Staten-Generaal over het ontwerp Wetboek van Strafvordering en het vraagstuk der jury 1828–1829, deel I*, pp. 200–201.

The vision of the French revolutionary reformers became known as the idea of the *conviction intime*. Many of the authors, such as Meyer and De Brouckere, who pleaded for the introduction of a jury system in the nineteenth century followed this idea. In accordance with this view they argued that the internal conviction could not and should not be motivated, and that no appeal should be possible. Conversely, many of those who were in favour of retaining professional judges and who deemed that experience and training were necessary to judge in criminal cases, emphasized that the internal conviction should be the result of a reasoned process of weighing the evidence. In contrast to the 'French' idea of a subjective *conviction intime* they argued that a *conviction raisonnée* was required. The authors who supported this view argued emphatically that it was not just the internal conviction which was important, but the grounds supporting the conviction. Although they deemed that is was not possible or useful to create legal evidentiary rules which positively prescribed when sufficient evidence existed for a conviction, they argued that the judge was still bound to follow the general rules of logic and experience on the basis of which his internal conviction could be scrutinized. For this reason they often put a strong emphasis on the fact that the judge should account for his conviction by motivating the verdict and that it should be possible to review the judgement in appeal.

A good example of this view can be found in Von Savigny who denied that the abolition of the system of legal proofs automatically implied that the judge would now have to decide according to some subjective feeling:

> Daraus, dass die Beweisregeln nicht ein für alle Mal gesetzlich festgestellt werden, folgt noch nicht, dass die Richter überhaupt von der Verpflichtung entbunden werden, nach Gründen und Regeln zu urteilen und hiervon Rechenschaft zu geben ... Der Unterschied zwischen Richtern mit und ohne gesetzlichen Beweistheorie besteht lediglich darin, dass in letzteren Falle dem Richter selbst die Auffindung und Anwendung der Beweisregeln, welche die allgemeine Denkgesetze, Erfahrung und Menschenkenntnis an die Hand geben, überlassen wird, während in ersterem Falle gewisse Beweisregeln schon durch das Gesetz selbst ein für alle Mal als unabänderliche Formeln festgestellt und dadurch das Urteil des Richters gefesselt und derselbe gehindert wird, jeden Fall nach seinen Eigentümlichkeiten zu beurteilen.[103]

In a similar vein, the Dutch author Modderman, in 1867, argued for the free evaluation of the evidence by professional judges. The central tenet of his

---

103   F. von Savigny, *Ueber Schwurgerichte und Beweistheorie im Strafprozesse*, p. 484.

argumentation was that legal evidentiary rules were useless and harmful because the high probability required in a criminal case was something purely concrete which could not be predetermined in general rules. No two crimes were alike and it was foolish to try to capture the endless variety of circumstances under some abstract rules which could never do justice to the complexity of the individual case. Modderman aligned himself with authors such as Mittermaier, Jarcke, and Von Savigny, and agreed that everything depended on the grounds for the conviction. Against the idea of the *conviction intime*, he remarked that most German and Dutch authors now acknowledged that abolishing evidentiary rules did not mean that professional judges would no longer have to rationally weigh the evidence and follow the general rules of logic and experience. He argued that it should be presupposed that judges had to follow these general rules, rationally weigh the evidence and give account of their internal conviction through the motivation of the verdict.[104]

Lastly, however, Modderman also rightfully remarked that the distinction between the so-called *conviction intime* and *conviction raisonnée* should not be drawn too sharply. For a long time during the nineteenth century the discussion had been dominated by a flawed dichotomy which derived from two polemical exaggerations. The first exaggeration consisted of the fact that the French revolutionaries and French authors presented the internal conviction too strongly as based on an intuitive, unreasoned, feeling of the truth to justify that lay jurors could just decide on the evidentiary question as well as professional judges. The second exaggeration, which created the dichotomy, was the reaction against this view by, among others, German and Dutch authors who presented the question as if one could only choose between the unreasoned subjective *conviction intime* proposed by the French revolutionaries, or a system based on evidentiary rules in which the judge rationally weighed the evidence. To an extent, therefore, these Dutch and German authors polemically exaggerated the unreasonableness and subjectivity of the French *conviction intime* to contrast this with their supposedly rational conception of how the judge should evaluate the evidence. Modderman remarked that this sharp dichotomy had, nevertheless, been largely superseded in the juridical literature since the 1840s. According to Modderman, most authors now thought that a reasoned conviction was necessary but that there was, nevertheless, always a subjective element involved and that it was never entirely possible to reconstruct why someone was convinced.[105]

---

104   E.A.J. Modderman, *De wetenschappelijke bewijsleer in Strafzaken*, pp. 10–45.
105   Ibidem, pp. 157–177. It is in any case difficult to determine to what extent the French revolutionaries actually had an 'irrational' and subjective understanding of the *conviction intime*. There were some conflicting tendencies in the expressions of the French

Summarizing, the change in the epistemological discourse between the seventeenth and nineteenth centuries undermined the ideological foundations of the system of legal proofs. Between 1750 and 1870 the conclusion was increasingly drawn that it was impossible to determine in *a priori* rules when sufficient evidence existed to convict someone. Instead it was argued that the freely formed internal conviction of the judge or jurors was the best possible criterion of whether there was sufficient proof (i.e. a sufficiently high probability of guilt) in the concrete case. As has been described, a difficult point of discussion which then arose was how this internal conviction should be understood. Generally two views on this question can be discerned: the *conviction intime* and the *conviction raisonnée*. These views to a large extent dominated the discussion in the nineteenth century and how the criminal law of evidence was given shape after the abolition of the system of legal proofs.

3.4 Conclusion

In this chapter a description has been given of the changes in the political-constitutional and the epistemological discourse. A remaining question is how these two discourses interacted in the reform of the criminal law of evidence. To answer this question, it is important to emphasize that the discourses

---

revolutionaries on this subject and the jury instruction, for example, also prescribed the jurors to ask themselves what impression the evidence had made on their 'reason'. Some authors, such as Donovan, disagree with the idea that the French revolutionaries had an irrational or sentimental understanding of the *conviction intime*. Nevertheless, although it is difficult to determine to what extent the revolutionaries actually endorsed an 'irrational' understanding of the internal conviction, it can be stated that they placed a relatively strong emphasis on the intuitive and subjective nature of the conviction. This accent of the French revolutionaries becomes particularly apparent when it is contrasted with the rhetoric of many Dutch and German authors who argued that it is not primarily the conviction that matters but the grounds supporting this conviction, and who deemed that the judge should give account of his conviction in the motivation of the verdict. These German and Dutch authors, however, also acknowledged – particularly from the 1840s onwards – that it was never entirely possible to explain why someone was subjectively convinced. In conclusion, it can be stated that there was at least a significant difference in emphasis between the rhetoric of the French revolutionaries and that of later supporters of the *conviction raisonnée*. It has to be kept in mind, nevertheless, that there was a degree of polemical exaggeration in this contrast and that it is difficult to ascertain to what extent the French revolutionaries really endorsed an 'unreasoned', sentimental conviction. See also J.M. Donovan, *Juries and the Transformation of Criminal Justice in France*, pp. 29–31.

focused on two very different questions. The political-constitutional discourse concentrated on how to legitimate state-authority and how the state should relate to its citizens (in criminal cases). The epistemological discourse focused on what knowledge was and, concerning the criminal law of evidence, what kind of certainty was necessary for a conviction. The new answers given to these questions between the seventeenth and nineteenth centuries worked mutually reinforcing towards the abolition of the system of legal proofs and a comprehensive reform of the criminal procedural law.

The changed epistemological discourse made the system of evidentiary rules seem implausible. Between 1750 and 1870 it was increasingly argued that only a high probability of guilt was required to convict somebody. Furthermore, in this period a consensus grew that it was impossible to predetermine in general rules when this high probability of guilt existed in a concrete case. It was argued that it was logically untenable that, for example, only the confession or the testimony of two irreproachable eyewitnesses could create this high probability. Instead, most authors agreed that the question whether a sufficient probability of guilt existed, should in the end be left to the free evaluation of the judge or jurors.

The epistemological change led to a different understanding of the kind of certainty that was required for a conviction, whereas the political-constitutional change led to a different view of how the criminal procedural law should be regulated and how the state could proceed against an accused. From the changed natural law and social contract theories it started to be seen as unacceptable that an accused could be forced to contribute to his own conviction and that he did not have an adequate right to defend himself. It was argued that an accused should be presumed innocent and that the state could only take away its protection of a citizen when the guilt of that citizen had been fully and legally established. The use of judicial torture, extraordinary punishments and the *absolutio ab instantia* seemed wholly incompatible with these premises. Furthermore, the shift from natural law to a focus on natural rights made it possible to reformulate the *nemo tenetur* principle as a personal right to remain silent and not to incriminate oneself. The increased importance of natural or civil rights was enabled by the new centrality of the social contract in the legitimation of state authority, which envisioned society as a group of individual contractors who also retained certain fundamental individual rights in the creation of the social contract. The changes in the political-constitutional discourse necessitated a reform of the criminal law of evidence precisely because the system of legal proofs was so tightly interwoven with the secret, inquisitorial procedure that focused on extracting a confession from the accused.

Finally, it is important to observe that the changed political-constitutional discourse provided strong arguments in favour of the introduction of a jury system which functioned as a catalyst in the transition from the system of legal proofs to the free evaluation of the evidence. A central motive underlying the political-constitutional discourse was the distrust against professional magistrates. The desire for a separation of powers – in general and within the judicial procedure –, the desire for a public procedure and the desire for a jury system were all driven by the fact that there was a distrust against the possible 'arbitrariness' and abuses of power by the criminal judges. This distrust was exacerbated by juridical scandals which seemed to prove that the criminal judges abused their powers. The distrust in professional judges was a crucial factor which led to the introduction of a jury system which functioned as a catalyst for the abolition of the system of legal proofs. The jury system was, nevertheless, not the only reason for the introduction of the free evaluation of the evidence. Between 1750 and 1870 the epistemological changes had made the system of legal proofs untenable and eventually made the free evaluation of the evidence by either professional judges or lay jurors seem preferable. The political-constitutional and the epistemological discourse therefore worked mutually reinforcing in the reformation of the criminal law of evidence.

CHAPTER 4

The Reform of the Criminal Law of Evidence in France 1750–1870

4.1 Introduction

In 1791 the Constitutional Assembly of France accepted a law which abolished the system of legal proofs and introduced a jury system in which the jurors had to decide on the basis of their freely formed internal conviction. Intermediary decision types such as the extraordinary punishment or the use of judicial torture on the basis of less than a full proof were abolished. The jury could only find the accused guilty or innocent. The introduction of the jury system was, furthermore, part of an encompassing reform of the criminal procedural law. The secret, inquisitorial procedure was abolished and replaced by a public, oral trial where the accused had far stronger defensive rights and where he was allowed to make use of legal counsel. These momentous reforms constituted a significant break with the old criminal procedure and created a new regulation which would subsequently serve as a model for the rest of continental Europe. The central question in this chapter is how and why these reforms occurred.

This chapter starts in Section two with a summary oversight of how the system of legal proofs was regulated in France until the end of the eighteenth century. In the third section the reform literature of the period between roughly 1750 and 1789 is described. In this section it will become apparent that most of the radical reforms which were implemented by the Constitutional Assembly in 1791, were already proposed and discussed in the juridical literature between 1750 and 1789. Strongly inspired by the English procedural law, many French authors in this period proposed to create a public, oral trial in combination with a jury system.

In the fourth section a description is given of the discussion in the Constitutional Assembly between 1789 and 1791 which led to the acceptance of a law that abolished the system of legal proofs and introduced a jury system. The law of 1791 was characterized by the fact that it put a strong emphasis on providing guarantees for the accused against wrongful convictions. The preliminary investigation was made public, a twofold jury system was introduced and the accused was given extensive defensive rights. Firstly, there was an 'accusation jury' which needed to approve that a criminal trial could be started against the accused. Secondly, there was the 'judgement jury' which had to decide on the basis of the criminal trial whether the accused was guilty.

Section five describes the development of the criminal law of evidence from 1791 until the end of the Napoleonic empire in 1815. In the period from particularly 1795 onwards, the attitude towards the criminal procedural law changed and a more repressive atmosphere emerged. While the Constitutional Assembly between 1789 and 1791 was strongly preoccupied with the protection of the accused, from 1795 onwards the focus came to lie more on the creation of an efficient, repressive procedural law. It was especially under the *Directoire* (1795–1799), the *Consulat* (1799–1804) and the *Empire* (1804–1814) that the social disorder and the revolutionary excesses were attributed to the too 'liberal' model of the criminal procedural law of 1791. This attitude can be clearly discerned in the discussion in the *Conseil d'État* between 1804 and 1808 which led to a significant reform of the criminal procedural law in the *Code d'Instruction Criminelle* of 1808. In this code the preliminary investigation was again made secret and the accusation jury was abolished. The *Code d'Instruction Criminelle* was a highly important piece of legislation because it would form the foundation of the French criminal procedural law in the nineteenth and twentieth centuries and would serve as a model for other European countries.

In Section six a summary description is given of the discussions regarding the criminal law of evidence in the period following the defeat of Napoleon until roughly 1848. The focus will lie on the period between 1815 and 1830, because the French discussion in this period would prove to be particularly important for the discussions in the Kingdom of the Netherlands. After 1815 it was decided to maintain the *Code d'Instruction Criminelle* and, even though the jury system was frequently criticized, it was retained as well. The two main points of discussions in the period between 1815 and 1830 were, first of all, who should be eligible to function as a juror and secondly whether the trial by jury should also be extended to political crimes and press offences. The political crimes and press offences had before been attributed to special courts that were staffed by professional judges. This became an important point of contention between the more 'conservative' politicians and the more 'liberal' politicians who wanted to extend the competence of the jury system to include political crimes and press offences. Importantly, although the discussion continued in the nineteenth century on the question whether a system based on professional judges or lay jurors was preferable, the free evaluation of the evidence was never seriously challenged anymore in this period in France.

4.2 The Regulation of the Criminal Law of Evidence in France until 1789

In the course of the late Middle Ages, the system of legal proofs and the inquisitorial procedure were adopted in France. This happened earlier in the southern parts of France, but eventually also in the north the learned roman-canonical law became firmly established. It was taught at the universities and formed the overarching theoretical framework to which the local customary laws were adapted (although important differences continued to exist between the various regional customary laws). From the end of the fifteenth century onwards, the first attempts occurred to regulate and partially unify the criminal procedural law through royal ordinances. The three most important royal ordinances were made in 1498, 1539 and 1670. They were not meant to change the criminal procedural law, but rather to codify the existing procedural practice.[1]

The ordinance of 1498, promulgated by Louis XII, built on the existing customary distinction between the extraordinary and the ordinary procedure. In this ordinance some rules were laid down concerning the secret nature of the procedure and the possibility to use judicial torture, but the ordinance remained silent on many aspects of the criminal procedural law. The ordinance of Francis I of 1539 further elaborated on the ordinance of 1498 and contained a more detailed regulation of the criminal procedure. Articles 139 to 172 dealt with criminal procedural law and made a clearer distinction between the phase of the 'instruction' and the phase of the 'judgment'. In the phase of the instruction or preliminary investigation, a *juge d'instruction* gathered the evidence, heard witnesses and put everything in writing in procès-verbaux. In the judgment phase the accused had to appear before the entire tribunal and questions could be asked to clarify aspects of the earlier testimony of the accused before the *juge d'instruction*. A significant characteristic of the inquisitorial procedure in these ordinances was the great power of the *juge d'instruction* and the written and secret nature of the investigation.[2]

The ordinance of 1539 remained the most important piece of royal legislation until a new ordinance was created in 1670. The ordinance of 1670 contained a far more encompassing and detailed regulation, but did not significantly alter the secret inquisitorial procedure. The ordinance was of particular importance for the further history of the French criminal law of evidence for two reasons. Firstly, it regulated the criminal procedural law until the French

---

1 J-M. Carbasse, *Histoire du droit pénal et de la justice criminelle*, pp. 180–219.
2 A. Laingui en A. Lebigre, *Histoire du droit pénal II. La procédure criminelle*, pp. 81–83.

Revolution and formed a central object of the enlightened criticisms in the second half of the eighteenth century. In fact, the ordinance came to be seen in this period as exemplary for everything that was wrong with the existing criminal procedural law in France. Secondly, the ordinance was used as an important source of inspiration during the creation of the *Code d'Instruction Criminelle* between 1804 and 1808, when the criminal procedural law was again made more repressive.[3]

The ordinance of 1670 divided the criminal procedure in five stages: the initiation of the prosecution, the preparatory instruction, the definitive instruction, the judgment and the phase where there was a possibility for appeal. A prosecution could be initiated through a denunciation, a complaint by the injured party or the *procureur* (public prosecutor), or ex officio by the judge when he was notified about a crime in a different manner. The ordinance contained the obligation for the *procureur* to prosecute all crimes that were threatened with a severe punishment, even if the parties involved had reached a composition. After the prosecution was initiated, it was the responsibility of the *juge d'instruction* to commence the preparatory instruction. In this phase the judge heard the witnesses secretly and separately, of which a procès-verbaux was made. Furthermore, the scene of the crime was investigated and in case of a violent crime a medical report was ordered.[4] In this phase the accused was for the first time interrogated after he had performed an oath to speak the truth. During this preparatory instruction the accused was normally not yet informed of the crime of which he was accused nor was he allowed legal counsel. After the preparatory instruction the *juge d'instruction* had to choose to either follow the ordinary or the extraordinary procedure. For minor crimes which could not lead to afflictive or defaming punishments the ordinary procedure was followed, while for the more serious crimes the extraordinary procedure was prescribed.[5]

When the extraordinary procedure was chosen the definitive instruction commenced. In this phase the accused was confronted with the witnesses and he had the possibility to recuse them if he could, for example, show their partiality. At this moment the accused was for the first time acquainted with the charges against him. After the confrontation and the possibility to recuse witnesses, the definitive instruction was finished and the *juge d'instruction* had to deliver the *sac du procès* (a veritable sack containing the procès-verbaux and other relevant documents) to the tribunal. The *juge d'instruction* also gave a

---

3   Ibidem, p. 87.
4   R.M. Andrews, *Law, Magistracy, and crime in Old Regime Paris, 1735–1789. Vol 1*, pp. 425–428.
5   J-M. Carbasse, *Histoire du droit pénal et de la justice criminelle*, pp. 208–210.

final report to the tribunal which formed a sort of pre-judgment and attests to the important role of the *juge d'instruction*. After this moment the accused had to appear in front of the tribunal where he could make his defence and pose justificatory facts. Because the accused was alone, could not make use of legal counsel and was until a very late stage badly informed, his defensive possibilities were severely restricted.[6]

The tribunal had a variety of sentences it could pronounce which largely corresponded to the scale of decision types that existed elsewhere under the system of legal proofs. In the French legislation these possibilities were, nevertheless, regulated in a more complex and particular manner. The possibility of an *absolutio ab instantia* largely corresponded to the possibilities of pronouncing a *hors du cour* or a *jugement au plus amplement informé*. Both sentences did not completely absolve the accused because they made it possible to reopen the criminal investigation at a later time. In France as well, the judge had the possibility to pronounce an extraordinary punishment or judicial torture when strong evidence short of a full proof existed. Furthermore, the judge also had the possibility to pronounce a punishment even if the accused had not confessed under judicial torture. The option of torturing while retaining the possibility to pronounce a lighter punishment on the basis of the existing evidence was called the *question préparatoir avec réserve de preuves*.[7]

4.2.1   A Change in the Use of Judicial Torture in the Eighteenth Century

Judicial torture existed in two forms in France: the *question préperatoire* and the *question préalable*. The first form was used to extract a confession during the investigation to 'complete' the proof. The second form could accompany death sentences and was used to force the accused to provide information on accomplices. The *question préperatoire* could only be used when there was considerable proof against the accused and for crimes that were threatened with the death penalty.[8] What 'considerable proof' was and what forms of torture could be used, were not defined in the ordinance of 1670. Similarly a precise regulation of the criminal law of evidence cannot be found in the ordinance. The ordinance left the regulation of these questions to the learned law and local customary practice. The ordinance of 1670, nevertheless, did contain one important innovation regarding the use of judicial torture. It put the

---

6   Ibidem, pp. 210–212.
7   On the more complex regulation of the different decision types which essentially corresponded to the various possibilities elsewhere under the system of legal proofs, see M. Schmoeckel, *Humanität and Staatsraison*, pp. 384–406.
8   A. Laingui en A. Lebigre, *Histoire du droit pénal II. La procédure criminelle*, pp. 97–98.

decision to use torture by lower courts under automatic appeal to the higher *parlements*. Henceforward judicial torture could not be used anymore until permission was given by the relevant *parlement*. The automatic appeal to the *parlements* was also installed for any definitive judgment which contained a physical or defamatory punishment.[9]

There have been several studies on the use of judicial torture in the eighteenth century which show that significant changes occurred in practice in this period. Andrews, for example, concluded that for the *Parlement of Paris* the use of judicial torture decreased in this period, and that an extraordinary punishment was used increasingly as an alternative to a capital punishment when a full proof was not present.[10] The diminished use of the *question préperatoire* and the increased use of non-capital punishments when a full proof was absent, is corroborated by several studies of other regions in eighteenth-century France. The *Conseil souverain de Roussillon* (which was the equivalent of a *parlement*) pronounced its last confirmation of a *question préperatoire* in 1737.[11] In Bretagne between 1750 and 1780 the *question préperatoire* was only pronounced eleven times.[12] In the *parlement* for the French part of Flanders, the sentence to use judicial torture passed from twelve percent of the criminal trials between 1721–1730 to only three percent between 1771–1780.[13]

Similarly, the use of the *question préperatoire* diminished in the eighteenth century in the *parlement* of Bourgogne and was used there for the last time in 1766. Ulrich states that it is wrong to presume that changes in the criminal procedural law only occurred after the French Revolution. They were preceded by a change in the juridical practice of especially the *parlements* in the

---

9   J-M. Carbasse, *Histoire du droit pénal et de la justice criminelle*, pp. 212–216. The *parlements* had an important function as higher courts of justice in their respective regions. The most important one was the *parlement* of Paris which had jurisdiction over a very large part of northern France.

10 R.M. Andrews, *Law, Magistracy, and crime in Old Regime Paris, 1735–1789. Vol 1*, pp. 439–455. According to Andrews the *parlement* of Paris functioned as a very important check on the use of torture. Between 1735 and 1749, for example, the subaltern courts ordered 350 interlocutory verdicts to the *question préperatoire* (which represented circa one-third of the prosecutions of capital offences) of which only 41 were admitted by the the *parlement* of Paris. Thus, circa 3.5 percent of those prosecuted for capital offenses were tortured while the subaltern courts requested torture for almost 35 percent of the capital offenses in this period.

11 B. Durand, "Arbitraire du juge et droit de la torture: l'exemple du Conseil souverain de Roussillon", p. 177.

12 L.-B. Mer, "La procedure criminelle au XVIIIe siècle: l'enseignement des archives bretonnes", pp. 9–42.

13 P. Dautricourt, *La criminalité et la répression au parlement de Flandre au XVIIIe siècle*, p. 160.

eighteenth century. The changes in practice can, according to Ulrich, be at least partially explained by the permeation of the 'enlightened' ideas to the judges of the *parlements* and provincial courts. For the Bourgogne, Ulrich notes that many of the judges were members of a freemason society while a survey of their libraries showed that, for example, the books of Locke, Helvetius, Rousseau, Voltaire and above all Montesquieu, were widespread.[14] It can, in short, be reasonably presumed that there had already occurred significant changes in the practice of the criminal procedural law and that judicial torture was used less and less in the eighteenth century in France.

4.3 The Reform Discussion on the Criminal Law of Evidence between 1750 and 1789

In the period between 1750 and 1789 a large number of treatises appeared which criticized virtually every aspect of the existing criminal procedural law and called for radical reforms. The reform of the criminal justice system had become a fashionable topic in this period to which many prize questions were dedicated by enlightened societies. Often it were not the professional or practicing jurists that presented the most important criticisms against the existing criminal justice system, but it were the more general intellectuals or '*philosophes*' such as Voltaire, Beccaria and Rousseau who played a leading role in the reform movement. The reforms which eventually occurred during the French revolution were, to an important extent, the culmination of the reform discussions which had taken place between 1750 and 1789. It was in the reform literature of this period that the idea was developed to abolish the existing inquisitorial procedure and the system of legal proofs, and to replace it with a public, oral trial with a jury system.

There are several factors which help explain why quite suddenly in this period the idea emerged to replace the existing criminal procedural system with a public, oral trial and a jury system. First of all, around the middle of the eighteenth century there was a general current of 'Anglomania' in France which led to an increased interest in the English political and judicial system. The English institutions became a source of inspiration with which the political and judicial institutions of France were now consistently compared. This would prove to be of particular significance for the criminal procedural law. In England the criminal procedure was characterized by the fact that there was a public, oral trial in which a jury decided on the guilt of the accused. This

---

14   D. Ulrich, "La repression en Bourgogne au XVIIIe siècle", pp. 412–437.

contrasted sharply with the secret, inquisitorial procedure in France where the judge decided predominantly on the basis of written documents following a system of evidentiary rules. A rejection of the existing criminal procedural law in France became more easily intelligible because of the existence of an alternative procedural model with which it could be contrasted. In short, the English procedural model became the 'significant other' with which the French procedural system was continuously compared in this period.

The existence of the alternative English procedural system alone, however, does not explain why it came to be seen as the model for reform in the second half of the eighteenth century. The differences had been there since the late Middle Ages, but had never led to any serious discussion in France. The reason why the English procedural system now started to be seen as a preferable system can be found in the underlying political-constitutional and epistemological changes. As has been explained in Chapter three, the secret inquisitorial procedure appeared to be in clear conflict with the changed natural law and social contract theories. From these changed ideas, it was argued that the accused should be considered innocent until his guilt was fully proven and that he should have the right to freely defend himself and not to incriminate himself. The English procedural model appeared to be more in harmony with these ideas. From the epistemological perspective, furthermore, the system of legal proofs came to be seen as logically untenable. Lastly, the jury system, was considered a desirable alternative because it formed an expression of popular sovereignty and because it was deemed that the disinterested 'people' could be better trusted than the aristocratic *noblesse de robe* who had often inherited or bought their offices.

A final important factor which explains the new interest in the reform of the criminal justice system, lay in the occurrence of several juridical scandals. The polemical writings on juridical scandals – of which Voltaire is rightfully seen as the most influential protagonist – and the indignation regarding the use of judicial torture and the *lettres de cachet*, did much to discredit the existing criminal procedural law and created a strong distrust against the criminal judges.[15] According to Schnapper, these juridical scandals caused an emotionally laden atmosphere wherein a larger public became convinced that frequently

---

15   The *lettres de cachet* were orders on the authority of the king to arrest or imprison someone. Since especially the seventeenth century a practice had developed to use the *lettres de cachet* to imprison people without a precise cause or justification. The use of the *lettres de cachet* became one of most hated and criticized instruments in the second half of the eighteenth century which symbolized the arbitrary and overbearing powers of the government. See J-M. Carbasse, *Histoire du droit pénal et de la justice criminelle*, pp. 392–395.

innocent citizens were convicted to death because of a judicial error.[16] There was, in other words, a growing distrust against the large arbitrary powers of the professional magistrates and the abuses which appeared to be possible within the existing criminal procedural framework.

The overwhelming majority of the publications in France between 1750 and 1789 argued for a significant reform of the criminal law of evidence and the criminal procedural law. This reform literature will be treated in the first subsection. There were, however, also more conservative jurists who rejected the reform ideas and who continued to defend the existing criminal procedural law. These conservative reactions are discussed in the second subsection.

4.3.1 *The Reform Literature*

The example of the English procedural model was a crucial factor which helped to critically evaluate the existing procedural system. A first and highly influential treatise in which the English model was compared with the French procedural system, was the *L'esprit des lois* of Montesquieu in 1748. This was the first work in France which contained a thorough and positive description of the English jury system and the public trial, while it also directed the gaze towards how the jury system had functioned in Roman law and supposedly in medieval France before the adoption of the inquisitorial procedure. A significant aspect in Montesquieu's description of the Roman and English jury, was that he argued that the jury in both systems decided solely on the question of fact while the judge decided on the question of law. The idea of Montesquieu that the question of fact and the question of law could be strictly separated would become very influential among the revolutionary reformers, and fitted well into their ideal that thereby a separation of powers could be made within the criminal procedure between the judge and the jurors. The question of fact could be decided by lay jurors while the judge then only had to apply the letter of the law. Montesquieu also saw a great advantage in the fact that the jury was drawn from the people by lot and that it constantly rotated. This prevented a too strong concentration of power in the hands of a group of permanently appointed magistrates.[17]

---

16   B. Schnapper, "La diffussion en France des nouvelles conceptions pénales dans la dernière décennie de l'ancien régime", pp. 410–415. Marion, for example, counts no less than eight judicial scandals in the 1780's preceding the revolution. See M. Marion, *Le Garde des Sceaux Lamoignon et la réforme judiciaire de 1788*, pp. 30–46.

17   A. Padoa-Schioppa, "I Philosophes e la giuria penale", pp. 9–16. In general, as Padoa-Schioppa correctly remarks, Montesquieu only had an approximative knowledge of how the jury in England actually functioned. He does not seem to have been aware of the

From especially the 1760s onwards, a vigorous discussion ensued in France on the iniquities of the inquisitorial procedure and how these could be amended. There is no doubt that the writings of Voltaire on the *Calas affaire* formed a significant turning point and that it focused the attention of enlightened circles in France on the defects and abuses of the existing criminal justice system. Jean Calas was a protestant merchant in the overwhelmingly Catholic Toulouse, who was prosecuted in 1762 for having murdered his son because, supposedly, his son wanted to convert to Catholicism. In reality, his son Marc-Antoine Calas had committed suicide and his father had merely attempted to hide this shameful fact. On very weak evidence the *parlement* of Toulouse prosecuted Calas and applied a harsh form of torture on him. His arms and legs were severely stretched and over thirty pints of water were poured down his throat. During these torments Calas made a confession which he later retracted. Despite this retraction, Calas was convicted to the severe form of the capital punishment of being broken on the wheel. Not long after the death of Calas, Voltaire became interested in the matter. He managed to show that Calas was innocent all along and that he was the victim of religious intolerance and the abuses of the existing criminal justice system. In 1764 the sentence was annulled and later the family of Calas was compensated. Through the passionate writings of Voltaire, the gruesome fate of Calas became known throughout France and would constantly be mentioned as an example in later treatises which pleaded for a reform of the criminal procedural law. Similar to the case of Calas, Voltaire later demonstrated the injustices in the prosecution of, among others, the family of Sirven, the Chevalier de la Barre and general Tally.[18]

Voltaire also presented very important substantive criticisms on the existing criminal law of evidence. He, first of all, severely criticized judicial torture as a barbarous and useless instrument. Secondly, Voltaire ridiculed the system of legal proofs in a polemical way and presented it as an absurd system. He described it as if the judges of Toulouse worked with a complex and arithmetic system of half, quarter and even smaller fractions of proof to calculate when a full proof existed. This was, of course, inaccurate because there were no calculations with one-fourth or one-eighths of a proof within the system of legal proofs. Nevertheless, the work of Voltaire did much to delegitimize the system

---

        important role the presiding judge played nor of the fact that a system of evidentiary rules existed in the English law about which the jurors were instructed by the presiding judge.

[18]   On the important role of Voltaire in these juridical scandals, see E. Hertz, *Voltaire und die französische Strafrechtspflege im 18. Jahrhundert*.

of legal proofs by presenting it as an overly complex and juridical-technical system of rules that was detached from reality.[19]

Voltaire argued that it was impossible and even absurd to try to determine *a priori* when sufficient evidence existed for a conviction in an individual case. While the criticisms of Voltaire were very forceful and undermined the legitimacy of the system of legal proofs, he did not attempt to defend or formulate an alternative. He was better at intellectually demolishing the existing structure than erecting a new one. Voltaire recognized the difficulty of regulating the criminal law of evidence and did not, for example, argue that professional judges should simply be allowed to freely evaluate the evidence.[20] His views on the desirability of a jury system were, furthermore, ambivalent. In his reflections on Beccaria's essay, Voltaire did not even mention the jury system and in his *Histoire d'Elisabeth Canning et des Calas* (1762) he described in a negative tone the credulity of the jurors who convicted someone to death on the basis of unreliable witnesses. On the other hand, in a later letter in 1771 to Beaumont, Voltaire stated that an English jury would never have committed the injustices and atrocities that were committed in France by so many professional magistrates. Despite the ambiguity regarding his opinion on the jury system, in general it can be stated that Voltaire was in favour of the English criminal procedure 'which appeared to be directed towards the protection of the accused, while the French procedure was directed towards their damnation'.[21]

---

19   Voltaire, *Commentaire sur le livre des délits et des peines*. In his commentary on Beccaria's work he remarked: "à Toulouse on admet des quarts et des huitièmes de preuves. On y peut regarder, par exemple, un ouï-dire comme un quart, un autre ouï-dire plus vague comme un huitième; de sorte que huit rumeurs qui ne sont qu'un écho d'un bruit mal fondé, peuvent devenir une preuve complète". This presentation of the system of legal proofs and how professional judges functioned was later often contrasted by other authors with how lay jurors functioned who judged on the basis of their common sense. Furthermore, Voltaire's polemical presentation of how judges worked arithmetically with fractions of proofs later became a standard misconstrued image of the system of legal proofs. Many authors in the nineteenth century in the Netherlands would, for example, use this description of the system of legal proofs in a polemical fashion. See also M. Schmoeckel, *Humanität and Staatsraison*, pp. 211–214.

20   His doubts about a possible solution can be seen well in the following reflection, in which he first criticizes the legal regulation of evidence and then waivers when he considers the possibility of letting magistrates judge after their own conviction: "combien d'horreurs sont sorties du sein des lois mêmes. Alors on serait tenté de souhaiter que toute loi fût abolie, et qu'il n'y en eût d'autres que la conscience et le bon sens des magistrats. Mais qui nous répondra que cette conscience et cette bon sens ne s'égarent pas?". See Voltaire, *Prix de la justice et de l'humanité*, art. XXII, Section II.

21   A. Padoa-Schioppa, "I Philosophes e la giuria penale", pp. 22–23.

The criticisms of the system of legal proofs and particularly of the 'barbaric' institution of judicial torture became more widespread during and after the 1760s. There were also an increasing number of authors who argued for the introduction of a jury system in this period. Rousseau, for example, in his *Du contrat social* in 1762, unequivocally stated that the function of judge could be performed by any citizen who possessed a 'common sense'.[22] In the influential *Encyclopédie*, under the heading of the term *pairs*, De Jaucourt gave a description of the English jury system with a very positive evaluation: "ce droit des sujets anglois ... est sans doute un des plus beaux et des plus estimables qu'une nation puisse avoir". According to De Jaucourt, a jury system even placed the citizens 'outside of the danger of being oppressed'.[23]

Another highly important impulse to the French reform discussion consisted of the work of Beccaria who became very popular among the *philophes*. He was explicitly praised by Voltaire who wrote a laudatory commentary on Beccaria's treatise and he was even invited to come to Paris.[24] Beccaria's work had a large influence and presented very clear, concise criticisms of the secret, inquisitorial procedure, the system of legal proofs and particularly of the instrument of judicial torture. He also presented a significant – although slightly ambiguous – support for the jury system. In the first two editions of his treatise Beccaria had made no mention of the jury system, but in the third edition (published in 1765) Beccaria included a new Chapter XIV 'on indicia'.[25] In this chapter Beccaria first postulated that for every conviction a *moral certainty* of the guilt of the accused was necessary. Subsequently, he remarked that when the laws were clear and precise, the office of the judge consisted of nothing more than to establish the facts and that he preferred that this would be done by a group of the accused's peers. Beccaria can, furthermore, be seen as an early and important example of the idea that the required moral certainty was more the product of intuitive feelings and common sense than a conscious and rational weighing of the evidence:

> For this moral certainty is easier to feel than to accurately indicate with words. This is why I believe it would be good if the law would prescribe

---

22 J-J. Rousseau, *Du contrat social*, IV.3. Rousseau stated on the function of judging: "l'autre convient à celles où suffisent le bon-sens, la justice, l'intégrité, telles que les charges de judicature; parce que dans une état bien constitué ces qualités sont communes à tous les citoyens".

23 A. Padoa-Schioppa, "I Philosophes e la giuria penale", pp. 17–21.

24 On the reception and background of Beccaria's work, see M. Maestro, *Cesare Beccaria and the Origins of Penal Reform*, pp. 3–59.

25 A. Padoa-Schioppa, "I Philosophes e la giuria penale", pp. 20–22.

that the president of the court should be assisted by *pairs*, which are not appointed by a magistrate but elected by chance. In this situation an uneducated man who judges by his feelings, offers more safeguards than some learned magistrate whose judgment is guided by an evidentiary theory. When the law is clear and accurate ... nothing more is required to decide on the question of fact than *normal common sense*.[26]

Apart from this remark, Beccaria offered no argumentation to explain why he preferred judgement by jurors. A last important contribution to the reform literature in the 1760s consisted of a speech held by the advocate-general Servan before the *parlement* of Grenoble, which was also published in 1767. In this speech Servan did not yet give an opinion on the jury system. As will be described below, in the 1780s he became in favour of a jury system. Servan did criticize the lack of equality of arms in the criminal procedure between the prosecution and the accused, and commented that in wise nations the accused was allowed legal counsel. Significantly, in this speech held by a magistrate before a *parlement*, he also remarked that he was against the use of judicial torture.[27] Although Servan did not yet explicitly criticize the system of legal proofs – apart from his remarks against judicial torture –, there is a scepticism visible throughout his work on the possibility to regulate the sufficiency of proof in general rules. Typical is the following observation regarding the criminal judge who has to evaluate the evidence:

> Elle n'a presque plus d'autre guide que l'expérience; ce guide est bien différent pour des lieux, des temps, des hommes différents ... les motifs infinis de probabilité, sont en effet des grains de sable sur lesquels la raison humaine doit imprimer une trace. Cet art n'a point de règles, ou du moins il n'en a que très-peu, et encore sont-elles si générales qu'à peine elles trouvent quelque prise sur les cas qui se présentent surchargés de circonstances particulières.[28]

4.3.1.1 The 1770s and 1780s

After the important first positive evaluations of the jury system in the 1760s, the interest in the English criminal procedural law and the jury system further intensified in the 1770s and 1780s. Significant for a deeper understanding and

---

26   J.M. Michiels, *Cesare Beccaria. Over misdaden & straffen*, pp. 63–65.
27   J.M.A. Servan, *Discours sur l'administration de la justice criminelle*, pp. 79–85.
28   Ibidem, p. 65.

increased popularization of the English criminal procedural law were the publications by DeLolme and the translation of the work of Blackstone into French. Delolme published his *Constitution de l'Angleterre* in 1771, which described the English political institutions and contained a large chapter on the English criminal procedure. Delolme first argued that in any criminal procedure the accused should have a complete freedom to defend himself and that the trial should be public (as was the case in England). He then gave a description of how the accusation jury (the grand jury) and the trial jury (the petty jury) functioned in England, and explained that the accused had the possibility to recuse a large number of jurors and that the jury had to be unanimous in its verdict. Delolme was clearly in favour of a jury system and described it as an admirable institution. Lastly, he also noted that a jury system had the advantage that it prevented the concentration of a too large power in a permanent corps of judges.[29]

Blackstone's magnum opus, *Commentaries on the law of England*, was translated into French in the mid-1770s. It was of special importance because it contained a self-confident description of the jury system as the vestige of English liberty and a strong barrage against the rule of an aristocracy ('the most oppressive of absolute governments'). This latter aspect naturally had a particular resonance in (revolutionary) France where the jury was especially popular because of its political and 'anti-aristocratic' significance. The publications of Delolme and Blackstone became frequently cited sources among most authors who pleaded for the introduction of a jury system in the last decades of the eighteenth century.[30]

In the 1770s and 1780s a large number of treatises and articles appeared which pleaded for the creation of a jury system and a public, oral trial in France. Marat – who would play a prominent role during the revolution – was, for example, in favour of the introduction of a jury system in his *Plan de la législation en matière criminelle* (1778). Regarding the criminal procedure, Marat first of all argued that the accused should have every possibility to defend himself and that it was absurd to force the accused to confess and to use this confession against him. He severely criticized the barbarity of judicial torture, and remarked that the state did not have any right to extract this 'horrible genre of proof' and that "elle en est une contre nature, puisqu'elle blesse le principe de

---

29 J.L. Delolme, *Constitution de l'Angleterre*, pp. 104–135. Delolme, furthermore, remarked that the English system had the great advantage that it did not allow judicial torture: "Enfin, ce qui seul justifierait la partialité avec laquelle les jurisconsultes Anglois donnent à leurs loix la préférence sur le Droit Romain, c'est que ces loix rejettent absolument la torture".

30 A. Padoa-Schioppa, "I Philosophes e la giuria penale", pp. 28–31.

la defense naturelle".[31] Marat, furthermore, pleaded for the complete publicity of the trial and made clear that he was in favour of a jury system. He criticized the venality and heredity of judicial offices and argued that it was inevitable that magistrates appointed for life would form an esprit de corps. Instead, he argued for a jury system which would inspire confidence and trust in the impartiality of the tribunal. He also deemed that common sense was sufficient to judge on the guilt of the accused:

> Pour éviter toute crainte de partialité, et inspirer de la confiance dans l'équité du tribunal, il importe que chacun soit jugé par ses pairs; et qu'on ne dise pas que peu d'hommes sont capables de remplir dignement les fonctions de juge. Qui ne voit qu'elle exigent plus de probité que de lumières ? Et puisqu'elles se bornent à prononcer sur la réalité d'un fait prouvé jusqu'à l'évidence, tout homme qui a le sens commun peut siéger au criminel.[32]

Bergasse – who later became an important protagonist for judicial reform in the revolutionary Constitutional Assembly – also appeared to be in favour of a jury system in his *Discours sur l'humanité des juges* (1778). He placed a particular emphasis on the danger that professional judges would become too harsh through the continuous judgement of potential criminals and that they would acquire a bias to see criminals everywhere. Bergasse saw an important remedy in the publicity of the trial and in the jury system. Although he did not explicitly argue for the introduction of a jury system, he commented favourably on the institution: "En Angleterre, où la loi est si favorables à l'accusé, ce n'est pas le juge qui examine s'il est coupable, mais les jurés ... tant on a redouté les erreurs dans lesquelles l'habitude de juger entraîne le magistrate!".[33]

Brissot de Warville – who became a leading figure of the Girondins during the revolution and who died under la guillotine in 1793 – proposed a complete reform of the criminal procedural law and the introduction of a jury system in his extensive *Théorie des loix criminelles* (1781). In his section on the criminal law of evidence he started with an explicit rejection of the 'scholastic' system of legal proofs which attempted to treat the criminal law of evidence in a generalized and mathematical way that did not suit the subject matter. Like Voltaire, Brissot de Warville presumed that the system of legal proofs worked

---

31   J-P. Marat, *Plan de la législation en matière criminelle*, pp. 130–131.
32   Ibidem, pp. 131–156.
33   M. Bergasse, *Discours sur l'humanité des juges dans l'administration de la justice criminelle*, pp. 40–48.

in a far more mathematical manner than it actually did. He rhetorically asked why one would attempt to divide proof in half's and quarter's as if it were a pound of sugar. His rejection of the possibility to predetermine when sufficient evidence existed for a conviction is clear and forceful, and deserves full citation:

> Une découverte utile pour le genre humain, et qui épargnerait bien des atrocités judiciaires aux tribunaux, ferait l'art de fixer le degré de certitude de chaque preuve, d'en faire une échelle invariable: mais ce thermomètre judiciaire est une chimère aussi impraticable que l'impraticable paix de l'abbé de Saint-Pierre. Le nombre des crimes est si considérable, les circonstances qui les accompagnent peuvent produire tant de milliards de combinaisons différentes, qu'ils est impossible d'estimer le degré de certitude que peut donner la réunion de ces circonstances, même dans des cas donnés. Ne cherchons donc point l'art d'estimer les preuves. C'est la pierre philosophale de la jurisprudence criminelle. Il est impossible de les réduire à un genre déterminé, d'établir des règles fixes et certain pour distinguer une preuve complète d'une incomplète, les indices vraisemblables des incertains. Le flambeau de la raison, le calcul du moraliste, la voix de l'humanité, sont les seuls guides que le juge doit suivre dans ce labyrinthe ténébreuses.[34]

Brissot de Warville continued to explain that for a conviction in a criminal case moral certitude was required. He rejected the attempts that some authors had made to calculate *algébriquement* when moral certainty existed. Although Brissot de Warville was not entirely clear on how he understood (moral) certainty, it appears that he intended it predominantly as a quality of someone's judgement ("qui emporte l'adhésion forte et invincible de notre esprit a la proposition").[35] As has been made clear above, Brissot de Warville strongly

---

34   J-P. Brissot de Warville, *Théorie des loix criminelles, Tome II*, pp. 85–88 and 156. In a later point in his essay Brissot de Warville made clear that he saw the act of judging as a weighing of probabilities. He cited Voltaire in this respect and explained his own view: "<une chose dit-il, est vraie ou fausse, vous êtes certain ou incertain: l'incertitude étant presque toujours le partage de l'homme, vous vous détermineiz très-rarement, si vous attendiez une démonstration. *Essay sur les probabilités en justice,* par M. de Voltaire>. Cependent il faut prendre une partie, il ne faut pas le prendre au hasard. Il est donc nécessaire à notre nature foible, aveuble, toujours sujette à l'erreur, d'étudier les probabilités avec autant de soin que nous apprenons l'arithmétique et la géometrie. Cette étude des probabilités est la science des juges".
35   Ibidem, pp. 91–95.

rejected the possibility to positively regulate when sufficient certainty existed for a conviction. He, nevertheless, did propose to exclude in a negative manner some forms of evidence which he deemed highly unreliable. He sketched as an example a sort of tableau of the different forms of evidence which presented certain minimum evidentiary standards below which a judge could not convict, while above these evidentiary standards the judge would always remain free to absolve the accused if he was not convinced of his guilt. In this sketch he came close to what later would be called a negative system of legal proofs.[36]

Concerning the criminal procedure, Brissot de Warville argued that the accused should have every possibility to defend himself, that he should be able to use legal counsel and that the trial should be oral and public. In his reflections on how the criminal tribunal should be given shape, Brissot de Warville made clear that he was in favor of a jury system. He called the privilege of the English to be judged by one's peers the most firm rampart 'que la liberté puisse élever contre l'autorité arbitraire'. He was strongly concerned with the possibility that the corps of professional judges would become a too mighty and arbitrary power. For this reason he also argued that judges should not be appointed for life (nor should the office be hereditary or for sale), but that they should be elected by the people or appointed by the king for a fixed and not too long term. In his own design, Brissot de Warville proposed that one professional judge, elected for seven years, would preside over the court and decide on the question of law while a panel of jurors would decide on the question of fact.[37]

Another important and innovative author who had become in favor of a jury system was Servan. While in 1767, in his *Discours sur l'administration de la justice*, he had said nothing about the jury system, in 1781 in his *Réflexions sur*

---

[36] Ibidem, pp. 95–167. Most strongly he argued against the forced confession which he deemed completely untrustworthy. Furthermore, it was unjust and a violation of the natural urge of self-preservation to force the accused to 'strangle himself with his own hands'. Brissot de Warville also criticized the exclusion of hearing certain categories of 'reproachable' witnesses under the system of legal proofs. Witnesses who could have information should always be heard and it should be left to the prudence of the judge to decide what value the testimony has. In his discussion of the different forms of evidence Brissot de Warville shows that he was very distrustful of indicia and in particular how they were used within the system of legal proofs. He did not want to allow convictions on indicia alone if they were not at least supported by the testimony of a witness.

[37] Ibidem, pp. 168–263. An important benefit of the jury system was that it prevented the concentration of the judicial power in the hands of a group of professional judges (a concern that was clearly directed against the power of the *noblesse de robe*): "Or, il n'y a point d'esprit de corps là où les pouvoir finissent avec le jugement. L'homme qui m'a jugé hier, peut être jugé par moi demain. Son intérêt personnel le porte donc à être humain, indulgent, éclairé".

quelques point de nos loix he argued unequivocally for the introduction of a jury system. Concerning the criminal law of evidence, Servan started by stating that moral certainty was necessary for a conviction. He refrained from explaining the distinction between, for example, physical and moral certainty, because he deemed it unnecessary now that "Locke a passé Calais, et Condillac a déjà fait le tour de L'Europe avec lui".[38] Servan explained that moral certainty lay in the conviction or in the mind of the person judging ('la certitude moral se mesure toujours dans l'esprit de chaque homme') and that the manner in which someone acquired moral certainty depended on the person. It depends, among other things, on his experience, intelligence and character. Servan concluded that "La certitude morale n'est donc point une mesure fixe et absolue, elles est toujours relative".[39]

Subsequently, Servan posed the question on what kind of moral certainty it was justified to convict someone in a criminal case. This should not depend on the moral certainty of one or two men, he stated, because nobody would have been foolish enough in the 'contrat originaire' to let his life and honor depend on the decision of a single judge. Society alone had the right to punish someone if it was offended by a crime, and society had to declare whether someone was guilty or have its representatives make this decision for her: "Tel est donc le contrat originaire sur les peines entre chaque homme et tous les autres; je consens d'être puni par tous, quand tous jugeront que j'ai nui à tous, et que je suis coupable".[40] In this way Servan presented an original justification for a jury system. Moral certainty was required to convict someone, but it was only justified to convict someone when a large number of his peers (who represented society) had acquired the moral certainty that he was guilty.

Servan also responded to the hypothetical critique that someone might state that the current system of legal proofs was perhaps better than a jury system spatie invoegen because it established in general rules when moral certainty existed. Against this question he stated that it was impossible to determine beforehand when sufficient evidence existed and that the system of evidentiary rules was useless because the judge would still have to evaluate in the individual case whether the witnesses were irreproachable and trustworthy. Furthermore, the rule that for example two irreproachable witnesses were

---

38   J.M.A. Servan, *Réflexions sur quelques point de nos loix*, p. 130.
39   Ibidem, p. 134.
40   Ibidem, pp. 136–139. Servan later continued to explain: "Quel est donc le point où un fait devient *moralement certain* pour toute une nation ? C'est lorsque le plus grand nombre d'hommes désintéressés sur le fait dont il s'agit, s'accordent unanimement à le déclarer *moralement certain*".

sufficient for a conviction could lead to the fact that a too credulous judge would unjustly and too easily convict someone. Servan concluded that the system of evidentiary rules was implausible and useless.[41] Finally, Servan also stated that the trial should be public and he argued strongly against the injustice of the practice in France of the *plus amplement informé* and the use of extraordinary punishments. His rejection of these instruments was closely tied to his idea that society only had the right to punish someone when it had established a moral certainty of his guilt.[42]

A last and important example of someone who argued for a jury system and who rejected the existing system of legal proofs was Dupaty, who was a high magistrate at the *parlement* of Bordeaux. Dupaty had first published a treatise in 1786 entitled *Mémoire justificatif pour trois hommes condamnés à la Roue*. In this memoire he presented a defense for three men who had been convicted to death in a long-drawn-out procedure on very flimsy evidence (and who were later acquitted by a royal pardon). Dupaty used this occasion to severely criticize many defects of the inquisitorial procedure and the arbitrary powers of the criminal judges. It became another famous juridical scandal which again appeared to show, shortly before the revolution, the dangers of the French criminal procedural law.

Subsequently, in 1788, Dupaty published his *Lettres sur la procédure criminelle de la France*, in which he argued more explicitly against the system of legal proofs and in favour of a jury system. Regarding the criminal law of evidence he remarked that it was impossible to prescribe fixed rules on the nature of the different forms of evidence. He stated that Roman law had known the correct principle. Apart from some trivial rules on how witness testimony

---

41   Ibidem, pp. 141–144. A striking remark about the uselessness of evidentiary rules is the following: "indépendamment de l'injustice de ces prétendues règles, l'inutilité en est évidente; c'est en vain que vous prétendez faire une règle de jugement: pour bien appliquer la règle faite par un autre, ne faut-il pas juger autant que per s'en faire une à soi-même ? Vous reculez la difficulté, et vous ne la détruisez pas".

42   Ibidem, pp. 145–214. Servan was one of the authors who most explicitly and vehemently argued that the logic behind extraordinary punishments was entirely unjust. His rejection of extraordinary punishments was, furthermore, closely related to his conception of the moral certainty required for a conviction (as it would also be among the French revolutionaries when they introduced the jury system). Typical of his principal attack is the following remark: "Ce serait ici peut-être le cas de combattre ce principe détestable qui n'a eu que trop d'applications dans nos jugements criminels; c'est qu'on pouvait punir la simple vraisemblance d'un grand crime, par une peine plus légère que celle du crime avéré".

should be evaluated, Roman law "finit par dire, qu'il ne faut pas s'arrêter à une seule espèce de preuve, et que c'est de l'impression que la réunion de toutes aura faite sur l'esprit du juge, que dépend le certain ou le probable".[43] The medieval jurists had foolishly deviated from this correct principle of Roman law. Dupaty continued to argue that the general evidentiary rules on, for example, indicia and witnesses were wrong and that they could not do justice to the complexity of the concrete circumstances. Revealing is the following comment:

> Toutes les règles générales qu'ils prescrivent sont fautives et défectueuses dans la pratique. Quoi de plus insensé, par exemple, que ce qu'ils disent au sujet des indices! Il en faut trois, suivant les uns; deux, suivant d'autres, suffisent pour la condamnation. Cependant toute la force des indices dépend de leur corrélation; et tel indice sera d'une grande considération dans des circonstances données, qui sera d'aucun poids dans des circonstances opposées ou différentes.[44]

After these criticisms of the system of legal proofs, Dupaty remarked that he preferred the English system. At the end of his treatise, Dupaty returned to the subject and stated that he was in favor of the introduction of a jury system. He believed this to be a better and more impartial system despite the criticisms that had been proposed against it. To the rhetorical question who would want to be judged by such a tribunal with a jury system, he answered "ce serait moi".[45] Dupaty, furthermore, argued that the trial should be public and that the accused should have a complete freedom to defend himself and use legal counsel. Lastly, he also presented a rudimentary form of the idea that an 'accusatorial' or contradictory procedure – where the accused was free to defend himself – would function better to elucidate the truth than an inquisitorial procedure:

> Mais, pour s'assurer des vraies circonstances d'un fait, on ne doit établir aucune règle qui puisse les altérer, ou les empêcher de paraître dans leur véritable jour. Ainsi, quand un fait est avancé par une personne, et

---

43 Ch.M. Dupaty, *Lettres sur la procédure criminelle de la France*, pp. 41–46. Dupaty, furthermore, remarked that there were still no good works on the nature of proofs in jurisprudence or philosophy, except for one or two chapters from the work of Locke. This is another significant example, after Servan, of an author who explicitly referred to Locke as an important authority on this subject.
44 Ibidem, pp. 52–55.
45 Ibidem, pp. 172–176.

contredit par un autre, il faut en donnant la première les moyens de prouver son assertion, que vous laissez également à l'autre la liberté de justifier la sienne. C'est en cela que consiste principalement la défense naturelle, parce que comme je vous l'ai fait voir plus haut, un des moyens les plus efficaces de découvrir la vérité, ce sont les témoignages contraires. C'est de leur accord, souvent même de leur opposition qu'on la voit ressortir.[46]

Even though between 1750 and 1789 there were many authors who pleaded for the introduction of a jury system, it can certainly not be said that there was a clear consensus on its desirability among the reform-minded authors. There were also authors who wanted a far-reaching reform of the criminal (procedural) law, but who were not in favour of a jury system. A clear divergence of opinions on this issue is, for example, visible in an epistolary discussion between Condorcet and Turgot. Condorcet was in favour of a jury system, while Turgot made clear that he did not have confidence in the ability of uneducated men to correctly evaluate the evidence: "l'examen des preuves morales est précisément ce qui exige le plus de sagacité et de finesse d'esprit".[47] In contrast to those who pleaded for a jury system and who thought that being judged by the people guaranteed an unbiased and just evaluation, Turgot had a far more pessimistic view of 'the people'. Turgot did think that important changes to the criminal procedural law were necessary, but instead of a jury system he saw the solution in making the trial public, the office of judge elective and by finding a convergence between the system of legal proofs and the internal conviction of the judge: "il faut adopter le principe de l'intime conviction temperée par des preuves légales".[48]

Turgot was not alone in his preference for a 'middle way' in which he rejected the jury system but still desired a significant reform of the criminal procedural law. Boucher d'Argis, Letrosne and Vermeil were, among others, authors who argued for a reform of the criminal procedural law but who did not plead for the introduction of a jury system. Vermeil, for example, published a treatise in 1781 in which he compared the French and the English procedural system and concluded that while the French procedure leaned too heavily towards establishing the guilt of the accused, the English procedure was far too lenient. This resulted in the fact that in England many crimes went unpunished to the detriment of society. He deemed that the defensive rights of the accused in France should be strengthened and that the final hearing of the

---

46   Ibidem, p. 77.
47   A. Padoa-Schioppa, "I Philosophes e la giuria penale", pp. 26–28.
48   P. Braun, "Turgot et la réforme de la procédure pénale", pp. 121–131.

witnesses and the accused should be public. After the initial interrogations, the accused should also have the right to use legal counsel. Vermeil, furthermore, appeared to be in favour of retaining the system of legal proofs and he did not argue for the introduction of a jury system. As he stated, he sought to find a proper equilibrium between the rigours of the French inquisitorial procedure and the too lenient English procedure. Compared to authors such as Brissot de Warville, Dupaty and Servan, Vermeil was quite conservative.[49]

Similarly, Boucher d'Argis (1781) deemed that the 'Anglomania' and the exaltation of the English procedural system had gone too far. He even sarcastically asked whether it was suddenly on the banks of the Thames that the empire of reason had established its domain. Boucher D'argis was rather complacent in his views on the existing inquisitorial procedure and proposed very few significant reforms. He agreed with the abolition of the *question préparatoire* and stated that the *question préalable* should also be abolished. He, furthermore, argued for a significant strengthening of the defensive rights of the accused. However, Boucher d'Argis was against the publicity of the trial and he did not deem the introduction of a jury system desirable.[50] Letrosne (1777) came very close in his ideas to Boucher d'Argis. In a footnote he argued that the criminal procedure in France left too little room for the accused to defend himself – which was 'bien contraire à la liberté naturelle de la défense' –, and that the judge should, therefore, be particularly scrupulous in the examination of the justificatory facts that the accused proposed. Letrosne was also against judicial torture which violated the natural urge of self-preservation. He, however, did not argue for the abolition of the system of legal proofs, the introduction of a jury system, or for the publicity of the trial.[51]

Padoa-Schioppa accurately points out that many of the authors who were against the jury system – such as Vermeil, Boucher d'Argis and Letrosne –, were professional magistrates or lawyers. Although they did argue for some important reforms, these were reforms that could be achieved within the confines of the existing criminal procedural framework. These authors show that there were gradations in the willingness to reform, but also that there was an awareness among at least some professional magistrates that there were serious defects in the existing inquisitorial procedure. Some magistrates, furthermore, were even willing to radically change the existing criminal procedural law such as Servan and Dupaty.[52] As will be discussed in the following subsection, there

---

49   F.M. Vermeil, *Essai sur les réformes à faire dans notre législation criminelle*, pp. 158–262.
50   M. Boucher d'Argis, *Observations sur les loix criminelles de France*, pp. 27–141.
51   M. Letrosne, *Vues sur la justice criminelle*, pp. 40–139.
52   A. Padoa-Schioppa, "I Philosophes e la giuria penale", pp. 48–49.

were also more conservative authors who defended the existing system and who rejected most of the reform ideas.

4.3.1.2 Conclusion

It has been described in this subsection that between 1750 and 1789 a number of treatises appeared that were strongly inspired by the English criminal procedure and which argued for a far-reaching reform of the French criminal procedural law. There was a consensus among the reform-minded authors that, first of all, judicial torture should be abolished and that the defensive rights of the accused should be considerably strengthened. This claim was often supported by the idea that the accused had a natural right to defend himself and not to incriminate himself. Secondly, most of the reform-minded authors argued for the introduction of a jury system and for a public trial. These were highly innovative suggestions that laid the foundations for the revolutionary reforms between 1789 and 1791.

Furthermore, between 1750 and 1789 an explicit polemic emerged against the system of legal proofs. Authors such as Voltaire and Brissot de Warville presented it as an implausible, medieval-scholastic system in which it was tried to calculate a full proof by using half, quarter and even smaller fractions of proof. Apart from these polemical comments, the system of legal proofs also seemed untenable because it was considered impossible by authors such as Servan, Beccaria, Dupaty and Brissot de Warville to predetermine when sufficient evidence existed for a conviction in the individual case. Importantly, while these authors pleaded for the introduction of a jury system and the abolition of the system of legal proofs, they did not present the necessary moral conviction of the lay jurors as a very subjective, intuitive *conviction intime*, apart from Beccaria who did lean more in this direction. This therefore appears to be at least partially an innovative hyperbole of the French revolutionaries in their attempt to polemically argue that lay jurors were, just as well, or even better suited than professional judges to decide on the question of fact.

4.3.2 *Conservative Reactions*

The emphasis in this section has, thus far, been placed on describing the view of the reform-minded authors. The ideas of these proponents of reform would become dominant during the revolutionary period and they were also the most vocal between 1750 and 1789. There were, nevertheless, also authors who defended the existing inquisitorial procedural law, and who only wanted slight incremental reforms within the boundaries of the existing system. These authors were mostly professional jurists, such as Muyart de Vouglans, Serpillon and Jousse, who wrote influential juridical handbooks in which they attempted to explain and defend the existing procedural system. They rarely spoke out directly or in a systematic way against the ideas of the more radical reform-minded authors. According to Schnapper, this phenomenon can be at least partially explained by the fact that most conservative jurists and magistrates were hesitant to enter into a polemical debate which used a very different style of writing than the traditional juridical treatises.[53]

The most famous example of a conservative jurist who did explicitly react against the reform-minded authors, was Muyart de Vouglans. In 1767 he wrote an essay against the treatise of Beccaria entitled *Réfutation des principes hasardés dans le Traité des Délits et Peines*, which was also reprinted in his handbook on the criminal procedural law in 1780. In this essay he strongly attacked Beccaria for having written a dangerous work full of contradictions, and suggested that the censures should take a close look at it.[54] Throughout his essay it is clear that he defended a repressive criminal justice system and that he deemed that the ideas of Beccaria would lead to an ineffective criminal procedure. Instead of Beccaria's self-proclaimed idea that he wrote in defence of humanity, Muyart de Vouglans remarked that he defended "cette malheureuse portion du genre-humain, qui en est le fléau, qui le déshonore, et en est quelquefois même la destructrice"; a comment which shows the harsh attitude of Muyart de Vouglans towards (potential) criminals.[55]

Muyart de Vouglans was particularly incensed by the idea of Beccaria to abolish the capital punishment, judicial torture and certain religious crimes. In his essay he mainly used arguments from within the existing criminal procedural system to show that Beccaria had not understood what he was talking about. This can be seen in his refutation of the idea that judicial torture was unjust and useless. Muyart de Vouglans argued that it was not unjust by explaining the many precautions that existed around the use of judicial torture and that it would, therefore, almost never be applied to someone who was not actually guilty (because the accused already had to be 'plus qu'à demi convaincu du crime'). For the perhaps one or two people who were innocently tortured, the institution assured that thousands of criminals would not escape their just punishments. Moreover, judicial torture was also not useless, according to Muyart de Vouglans, because how else could the accused be 'convinced' when there was strong evidence short of a full proof? As Muyart de Vouglans

---

53   B. Schnapper, "La diffusion en France des nouvelles conceptions pénales dans la dernière décennie de l'ancien régime", pp. 414–415.
54   In fact, Beccaria's treatise was banned almost immediately in France by the *parlement* of Paris because it scorned all laws. See J.I. Israel, *Democratic enlightenment: philosophy, revolution and human rights 1750–1790*, p. 339.
55   M. de Vouglans, *Les loix criminelles de France, dans leur ordre naturel*, p. 811.

concisely remarked: "la découverte qu'elle produirait étant absolument nécessaire pour l'entière conviction du crime, on ne pourrait dire alors que la torture aurait été inutile".[56] Muyart de Vouglans, in short, justified the usefulness of judicial torture by presupposing that a confession was in these situations absolutely necessary to convict the accused. Here the strong divergence between the presuppositions of Beccaria and Muyart de Vouglans can be seen most clearly.[57]

In his juridical handbook, Muyart de Vouglans treated the rules of the system of legal proofs in a very traditional manner. Here he again, briefly, defended judicial torture. A full proof could normally only exist in the confession or the testimony of at least two irreproachable eyewitnesses. He also explained that in exceptional circumstances indicia could be so strong that they constituted undoubtable indicia, on the basis of which the ordinary punishment could be applied.[58]

Although Jousse described the existing system of legal proofs in a comparable manner in his *Traité de la justice criminelle de France* (1771), he was more skeptical about the system of legal proofs and struggled with how it should be understood. Astaing accurately points out that Jousse appeared to be caught between dogmatism and pyrrhonism.[59] On the one hand, he was still clearly attached to the old system. He described in detail the rules of the system of legal proofs and defended a (very limited) use of judicial torture. Furthermore, for Jousse the confession was without doubt the most certain form of evidence one could have. On the other hand, the skepticism and influence of the changed epistemological ideas becomes apparent in his treatment of, for example, indicia. For Jousse it was clear that indicia could cumulate to become sufficiently strong to form a full proof. He remarked that the capacity to distinguish between a full proof and an incomplete proof was a question of an 'estimation morale', which was the hardest part of the art of judging and for which no precise rules could be given. This was particularly the case with indicia and

---

56   Ibidem, p. 824.
57   Ibidem, pp. 811–831. Muyart de Vouglans was also clearly attached to the idea that the king had a divinely ordained sovereignty and rejected the idea of a social contract in strong words: "On ne peut d'abord qu'être révolté de la singularité de ce prétendu *Contrat Social*".
58   Ibidem, pp. 775–810.
59   A. Astaing, "Le refus du dogmatisme et du pyrrhonisme: la preuve pénale dans *le traité de la justice criminelle de France* (1771)", pp. 71–83. Jousse was not attracted to the ideas of the reform-minded authors and made only one small comment on Beccaria throughout his treatise. In his preface he shortly remarks that it is a book which hardly deserves any comment because it is full of paradoxes and errors, and that the more sensible people think the same. See D. Jousse, *Traité de la justice criminelle de France, Tome 1*, p. lxiii.

their evaluation had to be unavoidably left to the estimation of the judge. The aim in this respect should be moral certainty while often only a probability (*vraisemblable*) could be had: "Dans les preuves qu'on acquiert dans les matières criminelles, la plupart des faits ne peuvent être poussés jusqu'à un degré de certitude morale; et il arrive presque toujours que la liaison de ces faits avec le fait principal est seulement vraisemblable".[60]

In conclusion, authors such as Muyart de Vouglans and Jousse did not show a clear distrust in the criminal judges nor did they think that there were significant deficiencies in the existing legislation. While the reform-minded authors criticized the 'arbitrary' powers that the criminal judge had, Muyart de Vouglans and Jousse deemed that these arbitrary powers were useful for the judge to have a certain flexibility in practice. In this way the criminal judge could show clemency to the accused and adjust the punishment to the circumstances of the case. Muyart de Vouglans and Jousse thought that the criticisms of the reform-minded authors were largely incomprehensible, unjustified and dangerous, because they presumed a benevolent judge who scrupulously followed the rules and the formalities of the existing criminal procedure. Furthermore, they did not see great risks in the secret inquisitorial procedure and the large powers of the judge because they deemed these powers necessary for an effective criminal procedural system. The ideas of the reform-minded authors would in their eyes, lead, to a dangerous situation where crimes could no longer be effectively punished.[61]

---

60   D. Jousse, *Traité de la justice criminelle de France, Tome II*, pp. 664–837. A last 'conservative' author that deserves to be mentioned was Séguier, who was the Advocate-General of the *parlement* of Paris. In 1786 he published a treatise entitled *Réquisitoire contre le mémoire justificatif pour trois hommes condamnés à la roue* in which he strongly criticized the *Mémoire justificatif pour trois hommes condamnés à la Roue* from Dupaty. The reaction of Séguier was of special significance because this was one of the most famous juridical scandals of the 1780s. In his treatise Séguier mainly sought to refute the ideas of Dupaty and to argue that reproachable witnesses could and should be heard in case of atrocious or difficult to prove crimes. On Séguier see B. Schnapper, "Testes inhabiles. Les témoins reprochable dans l'ancien droit pénal", pp. 613–615, and P.C. Ranouil, "L'intime Conviction", pp. 87–88.

61   See in a similar sense A. Monti, "Le rôle et les pouvoirs du juge dans l'œuvre de Daniel Jousse", pp. 40–65. Monti remarks that these authors primarily sought the guarantees to protect innocent suspects in elaborating the duties of the judge: "L'historiographie la plus récente a d'ailleurs bien remarqué la tendance des criminalistes – au premier rang desquels Jousse – à concentrer leur attention sur les obligations et les devoirs des juges, dont l'accomplissement était considéré comme la meilleure garantie des droits de la défense".

Incidentally, the strong focus on the person of the judge and how he should behave in the late Middle Ages and early modern times, can perhaps be at least partially explained from the fact that there was a significant general concern with how a good Christian judge

4.3.2.1 The Legislative Attempts to Reform

Similar to the stance of authors such as Muyart de Vouglans and Jousse, there was for a long time only a very limited willingness to reform the criminal procedural system on the side of the royal authority. The government was not entirely unreceptive to the criticisms of the criminal procedural law, but did not attempt any encompassing reform of the criminal procedural law or the criminal law of evidence before the revolution. One important reform was achieved in 1780, however, when the government decided to abolish the use of the *question préperatoire* in a royal declaration. The reasons presented for this abolition lay not in the inhumanity or barbarity of judicial torture, but in the inefficiency of the institution. It was mentioned that judicial torture only rarely resulted in truthful confessions and it was remarked that, moreover, a confession was not absolutely necessary in practice for the judge to pronounce a severe punishment.[62]

Due to the mounting public criticisms of the criminal justice system, the government finally saw itself forced, in 1788, to announce a more thorough revision of the criminal ordinance of 1670. In his declaration Louis XVI called upon all those interested to submit observations and input which could enlighten the government. The declaration also announced some important provisional reforms which showed that Louis XVI was now willing to improve the criminal justice system. To make it possible for those convicted to death to effectively use the possibility to appeal for a royal pardon, a delay of three months was established between the conviction and the execution. The declaration stated that judges would be required to motivate their verdict and forbade judges to convict an accused with the simple phrase "pour les cas résultant du procès" (which was the common practice). Furthermore, the declaration abolished the use of the *question préalable*, replacing it with a normal interrogation without the use of physical force. Because the *parlements* subsequently refused to 'register' the ordinance, the provisional ordinance never came into

---

should behave in cases which could lead to severe corporal or capital punishments. As Whitman has stressed, there existed a clear moral anxiety surrounding the decision of such cases and a fear of the responsibility attached to convictions to capital punishments. There had, in other words, always been a particular focus in explaining how the judge should conduct criminal trials which was focused at the same time on the salvation of the judge and on the protection of the potentially innocent accused. The often repeated phrase that the judge should incline towards leniency when there was doubt (*in dubio pro reo*), was typically a thought that was not only intended for the benefit of the accused, but also for the conscience of the judge. See J.Q. Whitman, *The origins of reasonable doubt*, pp. 93–123.

62 R.M. Andrews, *Law, Magistracy, and crime in Old Regime Paris, 1735–1789*. Vol 1, pp. 460–462.

effect. The refusal by the *parlements* to support the judicial and fiscal reforms led to the famous convocation of the *États Généraux* in July 1788 and the request to submit grievances through the traditional form of the *cahiers de doléances*.[63]

4.4   The Discussions in the Constitutional Assembly (1789–1791)

To a large extent the *cahiers de doléances* concerning the criminal procedural law represented a sort of vulgate of the ideas that had been expressed by the reform-minded authors. Generally repeated the requests that the trial should be made public, that the accused could make use of legal counsel and that his defensive rights would be strengthened. Furthermore, it was often stated that judicial 'arbitrariness' should be limited and that punishments should be made less severe. Finally, the desire was frequently expressed that a jury system should be introduced. A first response to these requests by the Constitutional Assembly can be found in the *Déclaration des droits de l'homme et du citoyen* of 26 august 1789, which contained several articles that directly touched upon the criminal procedural law. Of general importance were the provisions that were directed at the exclusion of judicial arbitrariness, such as the creation of a separation of powers, the introduction of the legality principle and the provision which contained the presumption of innocence.[64]

The Constitutional Assembly was well aware of the general desire for a thorough reform of the criminal procedural law and commenced with this task almost immediately. The earliest report which was concerned with a reformation of the judicial organisation came from the *Comité de constitution*. The report defined the jury system as the only measure capable of satisfying 'the voice of reason and of humanity', but did not yet contain concrete plans for the introduction of a jury system. On 10 September 1789 a different committee was created specifically for the reform of the criminal procedural law containing seven members among whom Lally-Tollendal, Thouret, Target, Tronchet and Beaumetz. The report they produced was soon integrally accepted by the Constitutional Assembly as a law and contained several important provisional reforms to the criminal ordinance of 1670. The procedure became public and contradictory, the use of legal counsel was admitted freely and the judge was to be supervised by two lay *adjoints* chosen from the "citoyens des bonnes moeurs

---

63   A. Laingui en A. Lebigre, *Histoire du droit pénal II. La procédure criminelle*, pp. 104–105 and 129–130.
64   J-M. Carbasse, *Histoire du droit pénal et de la justice criminelle*, pp. 406–412.

et de probité reconnue". The law was meant as a provisional measure awaiting a more complete remodelling of the criminal procedural law and, for example, did not yet touch on the subject of the system of legal proofs or the introduction of a jury system.[65] It did, however, clearly show the intention of the Constitutional Assembly to rapidly reform the criminal procedural law.

The real discussion on the introduction of a jury system occurred between 1790 and 1791 in two phases. The first phase consisted of a discussion in the Constitutional Assembly from 24 March until 30 April in 1790 and focused on the question whether a jury system should be introduced at all. This phase, which is treated in the first subsection, closed with the vote on 30 April 1790 to adopt a jury system in criminal trials but not in civil trials. The second phase – which is treated in the second subsection – lasted from November 1790 until February 1791 and contained a more detailed discussion on the form and functioning of the jury system. In the second phase a more explicit discussion took place on whether the system of legal proofs should be abolished and how the jury system should function. In addition to the discussion on the jury system, a discussion was held in which it was decided to abolish the intermediary decision types. This discussion is dealt with in the third subsection. Finally, in the fourth subsection the new procedural system as it was regulated in the law on the *Police de sûreté, la justice criminelle et l'établissement des jurés* is described.

4.4.1   The First Phase of the Discussion on the Jury System

The discussion in the Constitutional Assembly on the introduction of a jury system was preceded by the publication of several designs for the regulation of a jury system in 1789 and 1790. The first design came from the *Comité de constitution* in December 1789, two months after their presentation of the provisional reforms to the criminal ordinance. It stated that the jury system should be one of the cornerstones of the French constitution and contained ten articles on how the jury system should be organized. The jury system was, in this proposition, only foreseen for criminal trials and would consist of twelve jurors where at least a majority of 5/6 would be necessary for a conviction. Sieyès, who was part of the *Comité de constitution*, did not agree entirely with the proposal of the committee and for this reason published his own design to reform the criminal procedural law in March 1790. Sieyès proposed a jury system for criminal as well as civil cases and in his design the jurors could decide on matters of fact and on matters of law. Besides Sieyès, two other members of the

---

65   A. Laingui en A. Lebigre, *Histoire du droit pénal II. La procédure criminelle*, pp. 133–134.

Constitutional Assembly, Chabroud and Duport, published designs on the jury system before the debates started.[66]

On 24 March the discussion on the most important characteristics of a law that would create a new judicial organisation started in the Constitutional Assembly. The law, which was finished five months later, introduced the criminal jury, the electivity of judges, a new organisation of appeals and cassation, and regulated the powers of the public prosecutors and the judges of the peace. The debate on the jury system became of primary concern after Duport had presented his alternative design to the design by the *Comité de constitution*. The central premise of Duport's design was that every verdict was the result of a syllogism – where the ascertainment of the fact delivered the minor premise and the rule of the law formed the major premise – and that a formal separation of the question of fact from the question of law was necessary and possible. The first question should be answered by lay jurors and the second by elected, ambulatory judges. The verdict of the jury on the question of fact would be final and appeal would only be possible in cassation against a wrong application of the law. The finality of the verdict of the jury also meant that an acquittal or conviction of the accused was in principle definitive. There would be no room anymore for the old extraordinary punishments or the decision of *plus amplement informé*. This coherent ensemble proposed by Duport would in his opinion exclude the judicial arbitrariness of the old system.[67]

After the proposition of Barrère on 31 March, it was decided that the discussion would henceforth be conducted on several principal questions which would underlie the new judicial organisation. The first question was: "etablira-t-on des jurés?". When the discussion started a few days later, it seemed that the introduction of a jury system in the criminal trials was already a foregone conclusion. A clear and strong majority appeared to be in favour of a jury system in criminal trials. Padoa-Schioppa explains this by reference to the fact that all the designs so far included the criminal jury (which made it seem natural that the criminal jury would be created) and because there was an influential, active and vocal core within the Constitutional Assembly that wanted the introduction of

---

66   A. Padoa-Schioppa, "La giuria all'Assemblea Costituente francese", pp. 68–75. The influential Sieyès had also already clearly stated his preference for a jury system in his essay 'Qu'est ce que le tiers état', where he stated on the jury system that: "Cette méthode de rendre la justice est la seule qui mette à l'abri des abus des pouvoir judiciaire". In addition to the influential designs of the three member of the constitutional assembly, a number of 'private' brochures and designs were published in these months on the jury system. One design was published by Jeremy Bentham (which, however, did not seem to have played a significant role during the discussions itself).

67   Ibidem, pp. 83–86.

a jury system. The question of the desirability of a criminal jury was for this reason not intensively debated, and the discussion soon focused on the question how the jury should function and whether a civil jury should be introduced as well.[68]

Tronchet, for example, took the introduction of the criminal jury as a given and only concentrated on arguing against a civil jury. He stated that while a jury system might be useful in criminal trials, it was unnecessary for civil cases because the risk of the abuse of power was far less great here. Furthermore, he argued that the separation of the questions of fact and of law was far more difficult in civil cases because of the complexity of civil law. On the other side, influential members such as Barnave and Lameth defended the jury system for civil law as well. Typically, they put the question in broader 'political' terms – they saw the jury as an instrument to limit the power of the magistrates – and denied the validity of the more 'juridical-technical' arguments which raised doubt about whether the question of fact and the question of law could be separated. Barnave, for example, remarked in this vein "les jurés sont nécessaires à la liberté", while Robespierre stated that "sans cette institution je ne puis croire que je suis libre". Robespierre, who was a practising jurist himself, also remarked that discarding the civil jury meant "aider à la renaissance de cet esprit aristocratique qui se montre chaque jour avec l'assurance qu'il avait perdue depuis plusieurs mois".[69] In spite of the efforts of in particular Duport, Barnave and Lameth to establish a civil as well as a criminal jury, some twenty days later the view of Tronchet received a majority in the Constitutional Assembly. On 30 April 1790 the introduction of a criminal jury was approved by a grand majority and was received with applause, while the creation of a civil jury was rejected on the same day.[70]

4.4.2 The Second Phase of the Discussion on the Jury System

Four months after the vote which approved the introduction of a jury system in criminal cases, the newly established *Comité de constitution et du jurisprudence criminelle* introduced its design for a law on the *Police de sûreté, la justice*

---

[68] Ibidem, pp. 87–90. Although Padoa-Schioppa states that there seems to have been a clear majority for the criminal jury, there were certainly also opponents against the criminal jury. The criticisms not only came from the more conservative right, such as Cazalès, Desessarts and Lanjuinais, but also from an influential reformer such as Tronchet who made it known that he was not in favour of the jury. Especially critical was Brillat-Savarin who stated that the jury was: "dangéreux dans leur essence, inutiles dans leurs effets, inconvénients à nos moeurs actuelles".

[69] Ibidem, pp. 91–102.

[70] Ibidem, pp. 98–102.

criminelle et l'établissement des jurés in the Constitutional Assembly. The law contained fourteen titles which, among other things, gave an innovative regulation of how the criminal jury would function. The law was discussed in twenty-four sessions between December 1790 and February 1791 and was eventually almost integrally approved. Nevertheless, an important discussion took place on the question whether the procedure before the jury should be entirely oral or if (parts of) the preliminary investigation could be presented to the jury in written form. In the Constitutional Assembly the question of the orality of the procedure became closely linked to the question whether the system of legal proofs should be completely abolished and whether jurors should decide freely according to their internal conviction.[71]

The report of the committee clearly stated that witness testimony should be presented directly and orally in front of the jury while the use of 'secret and written' testimonies was to be abolished. According to the committee, the jurors had to be able to evaluate with all their senses the veracity of the testimony. Furthermore, the report stated that a written procedure would help revive the system of legal proofs. The committee, however, wanted to replace the system of legal proofs with the freely formed internal conviction of the jurors. Lastly, the committee also argued that the transcription of the testimony of witnesses was useless because appeal against the verdict of the jury was impossible and written testimonies would only make the debate 'artificial'.[72]

From December 1790 until January 1791 the Constitutional Assembly discussed, with an unusual intensity, in fifteen sessions the question of allowing written testimony and whether the system of legal proofs should be discarded as a whole.[73] Prugnon started the discussion with the critical remark that the absence of written testimony made the control and comparison of different testimonies practically impossible. Chabroud, on the other hand, insisted that witness testimony was more reliable when it was not first passed through 'la filière de la rédaction' but was perceived directly by the jurors. The idea that there was a close connection between allowing written forms of evidence and the retention of the system of legal proofs was subsequently put into words by Robespierre, who was himself against the complete abolition of the system of legal proofs:

> La loi ne peut pas abandonner à la seule conscience du juge le droit de décider arbitrairement ... la loi pose des règles pour l'examen et pour

---

71   Ibidem, pp. 102–105.
72   Ibidem, pp. 102–105.
73   M. Nobili, *Die freie richterliche Überzeugungsbildung*, p. 124–126.

l'admission de ces preuves ... Le moyen de constater [l'obersvance de ces règles] c'est l'écriture. Il faut ... réunir et la confiance qui est due aux preuves légales et celle que mérite la conviction intime du juge.[74]

Robespierre, in short, proposed a combination of evidentiary rules with the internal conviction of the jurors. He thought that the defensive rights of the accused were best guaranteed when the jurors had an internal conviction that the accused was guilty and when the requirements of some minimum evidentiary standards were met. To create this combination, Robespierre argued that allowing written testimony was necessary because only then compliance with the evidentiary rules could be scrutinized. This stance of Robespierre led to a peculiar 'alliance' on this point between the more conservative parliamentarians who were against the jury system, and a left flank in the Constitutional Assembly who wanted to strengthen the defensive position of the accused by allowing written testimony.[75]

It was against this view that on 4 January 1791 Duport held a compelling speech regarding the injustices and flaws of the system of legal proofs in general. Duport stated that it was not only absurd to determine in advance how to prove a fact which had not yet occurred, but it was also barbaric to constrain a judge to convict when two witnesses à charge were present. Under the system of legal proofs, according to Duport, it was not investigated whether a fact was true but only if a fact was proven. After discrediting the system of legal proofs Duport stated that with the jury system everything would be different. The jurors would work without prejudice and, unlike professional judges, the people trusted them. He argued, furthermore, that they were capable to decide on the question of fact using their common sense.[76] Later in his speech, Duport stated that the debate before the jury had to be entirely oral because otherwise the debate would become 'artificial' and the jurors would only focus on the written testimonies as did the old judges of the *parlements*.[77]

Duport's speech certainly did not silence those in favour of evidentiary rules and the use of written testimony. Goupil reacted by posing the question if there was anything more arbitrary than the mere internal conviction of the jurors. He then remarked that the system of legal proofs provided guarantees for the accused and that in the old procedural law judges in fact were not forced to convict against their conscience. The most influential speech against

---

74   A. Padoa-Schioppa, "La giuria all'Assemblea Costituente francese", pp. 106–107.
75   Ibidem, pp. 106–107.
76   M. Nobili, *Die freie richterliche Überzeugungsbildung*, pp. 128–129.
77   A. Padoa-Schioppa, "La giuria all'Assemblea Costituente francese", pp. 108–109.

the design of the committee, however, came from Tronchet, who argued that writing down the testimonies was indispensable to diligently compare them and to avoid false testimonies. He further stated that the supposed incompatibility between written forms of evidence and the principle of the internal conviction was incorrect. Tronchet, therefore, proposed a combination of oral and written evidence: "L'instruction de la procédure criminelle se fera publiquement en présence des juges et des jurés, elle sera écrite et ensuite remise aux jurés pour y avoir tel égard que de raison".[78]

Five days later, on 12 January 1791, when the discussion was reopened, Thouret held an important speech in line with Duport to regain the support of the Constitutional Assembly for the design of the committee by refuting the objections of Tronchet. He stated that with a written procedure the jury system could not survive more than a year because the procedures would become far too long. Thouret also remarked that the defendants of the system of legal proofs incorrectly gave the impression that the judge in the old procedure could evaluate the evidence according to his conscience. The judge was, according to Thouret, obligated to convict someone under the system of legal proofs when there was a confession or when there were two concordant eyewitnesses ("cette doctrine n'est donc pas une simple reverie").[79] Thouret then contrasted the system of legal proofs with the system based on the *intime conviction* (in a largely similar way as Duport had done in his speech on 4 January) and gave a homage to the superiority of the *conviction morale*. Part of this speech merits a longer citation because it is revealing of how the proponents of a completely oral procedure juxtaposed the new jury system with the old system of legal proofs:

> On a appelé preuve légale ce que la loi ou une doctrine ayant acquis le même crédit que la loi déclare être probant. Ainsi la preuve légale est factice et artificielle; elle peut, dans bien des cas, n'avoir rien de commun avec la vérité intrinsèque du fait. La preuve morale, au contraire, est celle

---

78 Ibidem, pp. 108–109.
79 A. Padoa-Schioppa, "La giuria all'Assemblea Costituente francese", p. 121–122. Padoa-Schioppa remarks that during the debates the system of legal proofs was generally associated with the procedure of the old regime and partially misrepresented. The important changes in practice which had diminished the rigidity of the system of legal proofs in the eighteenth century were more or less polemically ignored by those who wanted a completely new procedure on the basis of a jury system. Rosoni similarly notes the absence of knowledge in the Constitutional Assembly on the changes that had already occurred in the praxis of the criminal procedure. See I. Rosoni, *Quae singula non prosunt collecta iuvant. La teoria della prova indiziaria nell'età medievale e moderna*, p. 315.

qui, indépendante de toute règle ou de toute préoccupation étrangère à la vérité intrinsèque des faits se puise sur chaque fait particulier dans toutes les circonstances qui produisent, par l'assentiment libre, une conviction uniforme sur le très grand nombre des hommes impartiaux ... Les jurés sont placés au sein, pour ainsi dire, de la preuve; ils en suivent tous les progrès matériels et moraux; ils voient et entendent l'accusé se défendre, ils voient et entendent les témoins et l'accusé poursuivant, pressant réciproquement, et faisant sortir la vérité par leur débat contradictoire. A mesure que ce débat s'avance et s'anime, ils reçoivent une conviction intime, et s'imprègnent de la vérité par tous leur sens, et par toutes les facultés de leur intelligence. Cette conviction-là, dont les éléments sont simples et vrais, qui est principalement de sentiment, qui est celle de tous les hommes non-légistes, non savants, non exercés, mais qui ont, avec un cœur droit, un jugement sain, est la conviction humaine dans sa pureté, dans sa sincérité naturelle. C'est là essentiellement la conviction morale qui ne se commande pas, qui est tout-à-la-fois et au-dessus des préceptes, et plus sûre qu'eux dans l'application. Elle subjugue quand elle est ressentie, elle ne peut être ni dictée ni suppléé quand elle n'existe pas. Elle est le plus sûr criterium de la vérité humaine.[80]

Thouret further concluded that even though evidentiary rules were a necessary guarantee to circumscribe the judicial discretion of professional magistrates under the old procedural law, the guarantees of judgement by the people and the electivity of the judges made it possible to abandon them in favour of the freely established internal conviction.[81]

An important characteristic of the second phase of the debate was that parliamentarians such as Thouret and Duport emphasized the complete incompatibility of a jury system and an oral procedure with evidentiary rules and written testimony. In their view the *intime conviction* of the jury had to be based entirely on an immediate oral procedure and could not be motivated. There was a clear desire to abolish every remnant of the old system of legal proofs. Any form of written evidence was suspected of re-establishing evidentiary rules through which the verdict of the jury could be scrutinized. This relatively extreme position on the jury system, although it eventually prevailed in the Constitutional Assembly, was fiercely criticized during the debates. Parliamentarians such as Tronchet, Robespiere, Rey and Maury contended that

---

80   I. Rosoni, *Quae singula non prosunt collecta iuvant. La teoria della prova indiziaria nell'età medievale e moderna*, pp. 323–324.
81   Ibidem, p. 110–113.

written evidence formed a safeguard for the accused and that it was not incompatible with a jury system. Maury even remarked that without written evidence Calas could never have been rehabilitated.[82]

After the speech of Thouret, the discussion was closed again for several days, until the final discussion took place between 17 and 19 January in 1791. During this debate by and large the same arguments were expressed. The assembly decided to close the debate and force a decision by vote. Apart from some minor adjustments to the original proposal, Thouret and Duport got their way. The Constitutional Assembly decided that the procedure before the jury would be entirely oral and public, and that the system of legal proofs would be completely abolished.[83]

4.4.3   *The Discussion on Intermediary Decision Types*

During the discussions on how the jury system should function, on 3 February 1791 a brief but significant discussion was held as well on the question whether any intermediary decision types – such as the extraordinary punishments and the *absolutio ab instantia* – should be retained. The discussion was started by Maury. He noticed that in the proposed regulation the jury could only pronounce the verdicts guilty or not guilty and that the intermediary decision types were not mentioned. Maury did not attempt to justify or argue for the use of extraordinary punishments. The use of extraordinary punishments would, in any case, clearly not have fitted in the ensemble of the proposed criminal legislation because the idea was to prescribe fixed punishments for the different crimes which the judge would have to pronounce when the guilt of the accused was proven. Maury did, however, think it was unwise to abolish the *hors du cour* and the *jugement au plus amplement informé* (which were forms of the *absolutio ab instantia*).

Maury, remarked that everyone knew that there were many instances in England where people boldly bragged about crimes they had committed after they were acquitted by a jury because they knew that they could not be prosecuted again. This was a situation that should be avoided in France. Maury also argued that there were many cases in which the evidence was as yet insufficient to convict someone but where it would be dangerous to fully acquit that person. In these situations Maury deemed that an intermediary decision type

---

82   P.C. Ranouil, "L'intime Conviction", pp. 89–98. The extreme position on the jury system of, among others, Duport and Thouret was not only criticized during the debates in the Constitutional Assembly, but would also become an important point of contention in the discussions on the jury system in the Netherlands and in the German territories.
83   A. Padoa-Schioppa, "La giuria all'Assemblea Costituente francese", p. 113–120.

was necessary whereby the accused would be released but where the trial could still be reopened. Whether this decision should also entail the deprivation of certain civil rights, Maury wanted to leave to the wisdom of the assembly.[84]

It was Robespierre who reacted against the suggestion of Maury and unequivocally rejected it. His important speech on this subject merits full citation:

> Il [Maury] demande que vous introduisez dans votre jurisprudence criminelle une troisième formule qui ne soit ni absolution, ni la condamnation, mais qui laisse l'accusé dans un état de soupçon. Cet état-là, Messieurs, est déjà une peine infamante ; car dès qu'un homme est accusé et qu'il n'est pas déclaré innocent, il est dès lors flétri dans l'opinion publique ; il est pour jamais dépouillé de la considération publique. Il n'y a jamais que deux alternatives ; ou bien la société a prouvé contre un citoyen accusé qu'il était coupable et qu'il devait être privé de ses droit de citoyen, ou elle ne l'a pas prouvé. Si elle l'a prouvé, il est coupable; sinon, il jouit de tous ses droits et il est déclaré innocent. Remarquez qu'une pareille motion tend à altérer entièrement l'esprit du juré. En effet, quand des jurés ont à prononcer si dans leur conscience ils croient un accusé coupable ou non, alors ils déploient tous les ressorts moraux possibles; ils examinent avec une attention religieuse les motifs de la décision qu'ils vont rendre sur le sort de l'accusé; mais si vous leur laissez une autre alternative, ils sont moins scrupuleux. Sous prétexte qu'ils ne sont pas obligés de condamner, ils se laissent aller nonchalamment à prendre un parti moyen; et sur des présomptions et indices faibles et incertains, ils se portent à flétrir un accusé qu'ils auraient absous.[85]

Robespierre here presented three important arguments against an intermediate decision type in the form of an *absolutio ab instantia*. Firstly, he stated that this third road, after all, was a form of punishment that shamed the citizen. As long as someone was accused but not entirely acquitted that person would be deprived of his public esteem. Secondly, he argued that jurors would be less conscientious in their examination because they could just pronounce an *absolutio ab instantia* whenever they were not entirely certain. Third, and perhaps most importantly, he deemed that this intermediary decision type was incompatible with the spirit of the jury system. This last argument must be

---

84   *Archives Parlementaires de 1787 à 1860, Tome XXII*, pp. 726–727.
85   Ibidem, p. 727.

seen in light of the proposition to abolish the system of legal proofs and introduce a system based on the freely formed *conviction intime*. The *absolutio ab instantia* was a useful instrument under the demanding rules of the system of legal proofs but had no place in a system based on the free evaluation of the evidence. Furthermore, society did not have the right to keep the accused in suspense if it had not been able to prove his guilt.[86]

The speech of Robespierre was received with applause and shortly afterwards the motion of Maury was rejected. This short discussion shows that an explicit decision was made to abolish the intermediary decision types which were seen as belonging to the system of legal proofs. In effect a far more absolute distinction was thereby created between the verdicts guilty and not-guilty. As Robespierre remarked "there are always only two alternatives", and it was an injustice for society to let the sword of Damocles continue to hang over someone's head whose guilt had not been fully proven.

4.4.4 *The New Procedural Regulation*

The law on the *Police de sûreté, la justice criminelle et l'établissement des jurés* was approved between 16 and 29 September 1791, and was complemented by the decree *En forme d'instruction pour la procédure criminelle*. These laws together contained a precise regulation of the new criminal procedural law and of the jury system. They formed part of a broader reform programme of the judicial organisation and of the substantive criminal law in the *Code Pénal* of 25 September – 6 October in 1791. The judicial organisation had been changed in such a manner that France was divided into eighty-three districts, which each contained a criminal tribunal (the courts of assizes). In the *Code Pénal* a tripartite distinction was made between *contraventions*, *délits* and *crimes*. *Crimes* were the most serious category that were dealt with by the courts of assizes. The lesser *délits* were tried by correctional judges who were professional magistrates and who also decided after their freely formed internal conviction. The jury would only be used in the courts of assizes in case of a *crime* which was threatened with a punishment of more than two years imprisonment. The preliminary investigation was entrusted to a judge of the peace who would make an *acte d'accusation* that was subsequently handed over to a judge of the tribunal charged with the function of *directeur du jury*. The preliminary investigation entailed the gathering of evidence and the hearing of the accused and witnesses by the judge of the peace.[87]

---

86   See also W.F. van Hattum, *Non bis in idem*, pp. 221–224.
87   J-M. Carbasse, *Histoire du droit pénal et de la justice criminelle*, p. 414–415. The relative competence of the different courts were determined on the basis of one criterion: the

Two different juries were established in the new regulation: the 'accusation jury' and the 'judgement jury'. The accusation jury consisted of eight members who were selected by the *directeur du jury* by chance. They had to decide, on the basis of a simple majority, whether the evidence presented in the *acte d'accusation* was sufficiently strong to proceed to a trial before the criminal tribunal. Their purpose was, therefore, solely to judge whether the evidence was strong enough to merit a criminal trial. The accusation jury formed an extra safety valve which would protect the citizens against an unjustified criminal procedure. When the accusation jury deemed the evidence sufficiently strong, the case was brought before the court.[88]

The court was composed of an elected 'president' of the court, three elected judges and the 'judgement jury', which had twelve jurors. The procedure before this tribunal was oral, public and contradictory, while the accused had complete liberty in his defence. The public prosecutor could only start to prepare his case after the decision of the accusation jury and then stood opposed to the accused during the trial. The public prosecutor, therefore, had no role in the preliminary investigation. The 'president' directed the debates during the trial after which the jury had to decide on three questions with a yes or no answer: whether they were convinced that the accused had committed the alleged crime, whether he had had the necessary 'criminal intent' and if justificatory facts were absent. Ten positive votes on these questions were required for a conviction. Subsequently the judges had to apply the law which consisted predominantly of convicting the accused to the rigidly prescribed punishments in the *Code Pénal*.[89] As had been decided in the Constitutional Assembly, the system of legal proofs was abolished and the jurors had to base their decision solely on their internal conviction.

There were several important differences between the English and the French jury system. With the prescription that the jurors had to decide on several separate questions regarding the facts, the Constituent Assembly consciously deviated from the English model where jurors had to decide in one general verdict whether they deemed the accused guilty. The revolutionaries followed Montesquieu in the idea that the jurors should decide on one fact at a time which supposedly would simplify the task for them to judge solely on the question of fact. The French jury system also differed from the English

---

severity of the punishment. Simple *contraventions* with a maximal punishment of 500 francs or 8 days imprisonment lay in the competence of the *Police municipal*. The intermediary *délits* with a maximum punishment of two years lay in the competence of the *police correctionelle*. *Crimes* were judged by the criminal tribunal of the district.
88   J-M. Carbasse, *Histoire du droit pénal et de la justice criminelle*, p. 414–415.
89   A. Laingui en A. Lebigre, *Histoire du droit pénal II. La procédure criminelle*, pp. 137–139.

model in the fact that unanimity among the jurors was not required but that a majority of ten votes out of twelve was sufficient (in later legislation the necessary majority was decreased even further). Finally, a last important difference was that while the French jurors were completely free in the evaluation of the evidence, in England the jurors were bound by a system of exclusionary rules of evidence.[90]

4.4.4.1 The Jury Instruction

The decree *En forme d'instruction pour la procédure criminelle*, composed by Beaumetz in 1791, famously gave the following instruction to the jurors, which was retained in the later *Code d'Instruction Criminelle* and remained largely unchanged under the criminal procedural code of 1958:

---

90 J.M. Donovan, *Juries and the Transformation of Criminal Justice in France*, pp. 28–32. The exclusionary rules of evidence which are so characteristic of the modern Anglo-Saxon adversarial trial – such as the hearsay rule and the rule that no evidence regarding former crimes of the accused may be introduced – were only developed during the eighteenth and nineteenth centuries. These evidentiary rules developed in concomitance with the growth of the lawyer-dominated adversarial trial. Before the eighteenth century the accused could normally not make use of legal counsel and his defensive position was weak. The accused was expected to speak for himself and his testimony was considered a vital source of information on which the jurors could base their decision. In the course of the eighteenth and nineteenth centuries, the lawyers of the accuser and the accused began to dominate the criminal trial while the formerly very influential criminal judge became more passive. The acceptance of legal counsel in criminal trials fundamentally changed the nature of the criminal procedure.

Langbein has given an explanation of how and why the exclusionary rules of evidence were formulated in the eighteenth and nineteenth centuries. He argues that the judges started to formulate these rules in response to the increasingly lawyer-dominated nature of the trial. Before the eighteenth century these rules were unnecessary because the judge had a leading role in the interrogation of the witnesses and the accused, and on the development of the proceedings. He could guide the jurors far more in their evaluation of the evidence. Essentially the exclusionary rules were formulated because the judges lost this dominant position and out of fear that the jurors could be swayed too easily by the cross-examinations and the sophisticated argumentation of the lawyers. For this cautionary reason the criminal judges formulated the exclusionary rules to prevent unjustified convictions by unexperienced jurors. The jurors remained free to evaluate the evidence that was presented to them, but the exclusionary rules prevented certain dubious forms of evidence – such as hearsay evidence and evidence concerning past offences – to be heard at all. Although the rules were formulated by the bench, this most likely happened under the stimulation of the lawyers who argued that certain forms of evidence should not be used against their clients. On this development and the emergence of the adversarial trial, see J. Langbein, *The Origins of Adversary Trial*, pp. 178–251, and J.M. Beattie, "Scales of Justice: Defense Counsel and the English Criminal Trial in the Eighteenth and Nineteenth Centuries", pp. 232–233.

> Le loi ne demande pas compte aux jurés des moyens par lesquels ils se sont convaincus; elle ne leur prescrit point de règles desquelles ils doivent faire particulièrement dépendre la plénitude et la suffisance d'une preuve; elle leur prescrit de s'interroger eux-mêmes dans le silence et le recueillement, et de chercher, dans la sincérité de leur conscience, quelle impression ont fait sur leur raison, les preuves rapportées contre l'accusé et les moyens de la défense. La loi ne leur dit point: vous tiendrez pour vrai tout fait attesté par tel ou tel nombre de témoins, ou: vous ne regardez pas comme suffisamment établie toute preuve qui ne sera pas formée de tant de témoins, ou de tant d'indices. Elle ne leur fait que cette seule question: Avez-vous une intime conviction?.[91]

In this formulation, the system of legal proofs was rejected and it was stated that the jurors had to decide solely on the basis of their *conviction intime*. It is visible from the discussion in the Constitutional Assembly that this conviction was understood in a largely subjective manner. The proponents of a jury system exalted the common sense of lay jurors over the judgement according to a system of legal rules by professional magistrates. This was, for example, apparent in the following remark of Thouret: "Cette conviction-là, dont les éléments sont simples et vrais, *qui est principalement de sentiment*, qui est celle de tous les hommes non-légistes, non savants, non exercés, mais qui ont, avec un cœur droit, un jugement sain, est la conviction humaine dans sa pureté, dans sa sincérité naturelle".[92]

As explained in the previous chapter, this subjective understanding of the *conviction intime* reflected the belief of the revolutionaries that the sentiment and common sense of an upright and impartial juror was less subject to error than the 'artificial' judgement of a professional judge. There was a clear 'Rousseauistic' tendency in this exaltation of the judgment of the honest and unlearned citizen, who was not yet corrupted by the prejudice and sophistry of civilized existence.[93] Moreover, the idea of an almost instinctively formed internal conviction fitted very well in the high esteem that sentiment and intuition possessed in the French enlightenment. The emphasis on the importance of sensibility in the acquisition of empirical knowledge helps to

---

[91] A. Padoa-Schioppa, "I Philosophes e la giuria penale", p. 135.
[92] I. Rosoni, *Quae singula non prosunt collecta iuvant. La teoria della prova indiziaria nell'età medievale e moderna*, p. 323–324.
[93] P.C. Ranouil, "L'intime Conviction", pp. 90–94. See also in this sense E. Berenson, *The Trial of Madame Caillaux*, pp. 39–40.

explain the subjective and sentimental understanding of the *conviction intime*.[94] Nevertheless, it is clear that apart from the importance of sensibility and the 'Rousseauistic' tendency, the exaltation of the judgement of the common man in comparison to that of the learned judge was also largely used in a polemical fashion by the French revolutionaries to discredit the system of legal proofs and to make sure that the jury system would be adopted. To justify that no legal training was necessary to correctly evaluate the evidence, a strong emphasis was placed on the fact that the internal conviction was not the product of a reasoned evaluation of the evidence, but far more something that could be 'instinctively' felt after viewing the direct oral presentation of the evidence.

In conclusion, the ensemble of the laws of 1791 created a momentous and encompassing reform of the old criminal procedural law and criminal law of evidence, which formed a decisive rupture in the history of the criminal law of evidence. It essentially consisted of three major changes. First of all, the system of evidentiary rules was abolished and the jurors now decided solely on the basis of their freely formed internal conviction. This meant that no principal distinction was made anymore between the value of different kinds of evidence such as the confession, witness testimony and indicia. Several indicia or even one indicium could be sufficient for a conviction, as long as it convinced ten or more jurors. Secondly, the scale of decision types which was closely connected with this system of evidentiary rules, was abolished. It was no longer allowed to convict the accused to an extraordinary punishment or an *absolutio ab instantia* on the basis of less than a full proof. Finally, the new criminal law of evidence was embedded in a completely different procedural structure. The jury now had to form their internal conviction on the basis of a public, oral trial where the evidence was presented directly to them and where the accused had a complete freedom to defend himself. The trial had become far more accusatorial and the underlying idea was that the truth would best come out through the contradictory debate.

4.5 The Development of the Criminal Law of Evidence between 1791 and 1814

It is a well-known phenomenon that not long after the creation of the new criminal procedural framework in 1791, strong repressive tendencies developed

---

94   J. Riskin, *Science in the age of sensibility. The sentimental empiricists of the French enlightenment*, pp. 1–17.

under the guise of the need to defend the 'revolution and the republic'. For those who were considered counter-revolutionaries or 'enemies of the people' the presumption of innocence was turned into a presumption of guilt. These mistrusted groups were not judged in the regular criminal tribunals but in special courts where the normal criminal procedural law was suspended (the most famous was the *Tribunal criminelle extraordinaire*).[95] It is not the purpose of this section to treat these turbulent years with its many extraordinary trials, which can to a large extent be attributed to the relatively extreme circumstances of the time. Of greater interest here are the continuities and discontinuities in the 'regular' criminal procedural law between 1791 and 1814.

Between 1791 and 1795 the criminal procedural law did not change significantly. From roughly the 'Thermidorian reaction' in 1795 until 1814, a more repressive approach to the criminal procedural law developed. Where the period between 1789 and 1791 saw the creation of an overwhelmingly accusatorial procedure with strong defensive rights and guarantees for the accused, from 1795 onwards the perspective of effectively punishing and preventing crimes came more to the foreground and the criminal procedure again turned more inquisitorial. The effects of this more repressive climate on the criminal law of evidence between 1791 and 1814 is the subject of this section.

4.5.1   *The Period of the Directoire and Consulat (1795–1804)*

Under the *Directoire*, from 1795 until 1799, the pretention was at least that a return was made to a constitutional government, a separation of powers and the 'rule of law'. Nevertheless, many extraordinary tribunals remained in force and would continue to do so until 1814. The most important extraordinary jurisdiction was formed by the military tribunals. With a simplified criminal procedure the military tribunals were assigned the task to combat the roaming bands of vagabonds and militant royalists who were menacing the countryside.[96] In the new *Code des délits et des peines* (also known as the code 'Merlin' after its creator) of 1795, the revolutionary laws of 1791 were harmonized in one code but they were not significantly changed. The code regulated the procedural and substantive criminal law and largely retained the many guarantees and defensive rights of the accused that existed under the laws of 1791. Although the *Directoire* proposed some modifications to the jury system and the criminal procedural law between 1795 and 1799, these were rejected by the

---

95   J-M. Carbasse, *Histoire du droit pénal et de la justice criminelle*, pp. 419–424.
96   J-L. Halpérin, "Continuité et rupture dans l'évolution de la procédure pénale en France de 1795 à 1810", pp. 114–119. This problem had become especially acute since the unemployment had risen sharply during the revolution and the conscription laws forced many young men to flee into the arms of marauding bands.

Council of five-hundred and the chamber of the *Anciens*. Both remained loyal to the principles of 1791 and still held the jury system in high esteem. According to Halperin it is, therefore, not accurate to speak of a 'rupture' during the period of the *Directoire*, because significant reforms to strengthen the role of the public prosecutor or to reform the jury system were not yet made in this period.[97]

It was especially from 1799 onwards, under the *Consulat* and the *Empire*, that the social disorder and the revolutionary excesses were increasingly attributed to the too 'liberal' criminal procedural law which supposedly made the criminal justice system ineffective. Under the *Consulat* the executive power was strengthened in diverse ways in the area of criminal justice and the liberal principles of 1791 started to be criticized in a rather polemical fashion. According to Berger, in the discussions during the period of the *Consulat* the system of 1791 was described as being too theoretical and composed of abstract idealistic formulations, while its creators were typified as 'philosophes' and 'moralists'. A typical attack on the principles of 1791 came from François de Nantes, a representative of the *Consulat* government, which shows the changed attitude towards the criminal procedural law:

> Que l'on descende, pour un moment, des sommités nébuleuses de ces théories (où l'on est tellement élevé qu'on n'aperçoit plus rien de ce qui se passe sur la terre) dans les prisons où sont entassés ces êtres féroces ... N'est-ce donc pas assez la rude expérience que nous avons faite pendant dix ans sur l'abus de ces abstractions, qui supposent tous les hommes bons, sensibles, désintéressés, sans vouloir commencer un nouveau cours de ce genre? Et n'est-il pas temps de revenir aux maximes pratiques d'un sage gouvernement, qui veut s'assurer la paix de tous les citoyens par la punition de tous les assassins?.[98]

Summarizing, the main criticism during the period of the *Consulat* and subsequently under the *Empire* was that in 1791 there had been too much attention for the rights of the accused to the detriment of the security of society and the state. Similarly, the jury system itself was not criticized because it was thought to lead to judicial errors, but because the jurors were deemed too indulgent in their verdicts. Berger calls the criticisms of the laws of 1791 partially unjustified because they took insufficiently into account the pragmatism and the desire to maintain the public order that was also present in the discussions of the

---

97   Ibidem, pp. 120–121.
98   E. Berger, *La justice pénale sous la Révolution. Les enjeux d'un modèle judiciaire libéral*, pp. 13–14.

Constitutional Assembly between 1789 and 1791. Nonetheless, Berger observes that there was a distinctly more repressive climate from the period of the *Consulat* onwards, which was continued under Napoleon and later between 1814 and 1830 under the restauration monarchy.[99]

Not only did the discourse on the inefficacies of the criminal procedural law become more critical during the period of the *Consulat*, but this period also saw the creation of several important repressive innovations. In 1801 a law was promulgated which significantly modified the criminal procedural law. The law strengthened the role of a new 'public prosecutor' in the form of the *substituts*, who were now to be appointed by the central government. The *substituts* were made the chiefs of the *police judiciaire* and responsible for the investigation of crimes, while the judges of the peace were made only auxiliary to the *substituts*. The *substituts* were later renamed *procureurs*. The investigation under the direction of the *substituts* was, furthermore, made secret and written again. The accusation jury heard almost no witnesses anymore and now had to decide on the basis of written documents gathered during the preliminary investigation by the *substituts*.[100] With these legislative changes an important step was taken to reintroduce a secret preliminary investigation and to marginalize the role of the accusation jury.

4.5.2   The Creation of the Code d'Instruction Criminelle of 1808

From the beginning of the period of the *Consulat*, Napoleon had decided to replace the code Merlin of 1795 – which he considered to be too lenient – with a more repressive and effective criminal procedural law. The project was designated to a committee of five – composed of Vieillard, Target, Oudart, Treilhard and Blondel – who designed new codes for the substantive and the procedural criminal law in the first three months of 1801. Even though some modifications were proposed, the design left the jury system largely unchanged. Before the discussion started in the *Conseil d'État* on 22 Mai 1804, the cassation court, the courts of appeal and the criminal tribunals were given the chance to present their opinion on the design of a new criminal procedural law. The view of the cassation court was negative regarding the jury system and in careful terms proposed a re-evaluation of whether the jury system should be retained. The cassation court, however, did not propose an outright abolition of the institution. Its principle criticism regarding the jury system – 'si belle en théorie' – was that it was inefficacious in practice and that it let

---

99   Ibidem, pp. 16–20. On this development, see also J.M. Donovan, *Juries and the Transformation of Criminal Justice in France*, pp. 34–40.
100 A. Laingui en A. Lebigre, *Histoire du droit pénal II. La procédure criminelle*, pp. 140–141.

many crimes go unpunished.[101] Furthermore, the president of the cassation court, Muraire, posed the question whether 'common sense' was really sufficient to decide on the question of fact and whether the jury system was compatible with the French national character.[102]

Among the courts of appeal, twelve courts spoke out against the jury system, five wanted to retain it and five did not give their opinion on this question. The courts of appeal that were against the jury system were even harsher in their criticisms than the cassation court, and contained several points of criticism that would resurface during the debates in the *Conseil d'État*: the jury members were too inexperienced, hesitant and led by their passions. Furthermore, they were not effective in suppressing crimes, it was impossible to establish traditions or a fixed jurisprudence and the written procedure (supposedly incompatible with a jury system) was deemed superior. Lastly, the 'Anglomania' of the Constitutional Assembly was criticized in the reports – after many years of war with England – and it was stated that the jury system was incongruent with the customs and habits of the French. Instead, some courts of appeal remarked that a closer realignment with the old national tradition should be sought. A combination of the criminal ordinance of 1670 with the reforms of 1789 was suggested wherein the defensive rights of the accused were guaranteed and where the trial would remain public. The courts of appeal that were in favour of the jury system predominantly repeated the arguments that had led to its introduction between 1789 and 1791. They also stated that if the jury system had not yet functioned properly this was mostly to blame on the turbulent circumstances of the times.[103]

A striking contrast can be seen between the opinions of the courts who were against the jury system and the reform-minded authors and revolutionaries in the period between 1750 and 1791 who were in favour of a jury system. The reformers had expressed great admiration for the English system and were adamant on transplanting it to France. The critical courts, on the other hand, were far less 'universalistic' in their approach and stressed the incompatibility

---

101 A. Esmein, *Histoire de la procédure criminelle en France*, pp. 481–486.
102 P. Feldhausen, *Zur Geschichte des Strafprozessrechtes in Frankreich*, pp. 140–147. The committee of five had already stated – in a memorandum that accompanied the design for a new criminal procedural – that it did not think that the jury system was unsuited for the national character of the French. The committee even proposed that the jury system would function better if the English example would be followed more closely.
103 A. Esmein, *Histoire de la procédure criminelle en France*, pp. 485–504. The seventy-five lower criminal tribunals were more equally divided on the jury question. Twenty-six were against the jury system, twenty-six were in favour of maintaining it and twenty-three did not give an opinion.

of this 'English' institution with the French national character. After ten years of experience with the jury system they also presented the criticism that the jurors had proven themselves to be too lenient and that they made the criminal procedural law ineffective. Furthermore, now that there was more distance to the criminal procedure of the *Ancien régime* and a stronger desire for an effective repressive apparatus, the criminal ordinance of 1670 was looked upon more favourably by a large part of the courts.

The discussion in the *Conseil d'État* on the design of a new criminal procedural code can be divided into two periods. The first lasted from Mai 22 1804 until December 20 1804, and – after a long break – the second period lasted from January 23 1808 to march 5 1808. From the very beginning a central point of discussion was whether the jury system should be maintained. Importantly, during the discussions of the *Conseil d'État* it soon became clear that almost everyone was in favour of the continued abolition of the system of legal proofs. The free evaluation of the evidence was at first introduced in concomitance with the jury system and only deemed acceptable by the revolutionaries because it would be exercised by lay jurors (of whom it was supposed that they could be trusted because they were impartial and disinterested). More than ten years later, however, the judgement on the basis of the freely formed *intime conviction* was an established practice and the focus now turned on the question whether this could be best done by professional judges or by lay jurors.[104]

Siméon, Dupuy, Portalis and Bigot-Préameneu in the *Conseil d'État* pleaded unequivocally for a system based on the free evaluation of the evidence by professional judges. Their position was mainly to return to the criminal procedural law of the criminal ordinance of 1670, modified and softened with some of the reforms made between 1789 and 1791. Siméon held an important speech in the beginning of the sessions in which he proposed to abolish the jury system and where he enumerated all the known arguments against this institution which had also been expressed by the courts of appeal. He, furthermore, stated that the true protection of individual liberty lay in the publicity of the procedure and the better defensive possibilities of the accused, not in the jury system. Under these conditions, he argued, an accused would be better protected when he was judged by professional magistrates than by the people.[105]

Berlier, Treilhard, Defermon, Cretet, Bérenger, Frochot and Regnaud de Saint-Jean d'Angély, on the other hand, were in favour of retaining a jury system. They saw the jury system as one of the most significant acquisitions of the revolution and stated that it was popular among the people. Their most

---

104 M. Nobili, *Die freie richterliche Überzeugungsbildung*, pp. 143–144.
105 A. Esmein, *Histoire de la procédure criminelle en France*, pp. 506–510.

important argument was, nevertheless, that only a jury system was compatible with an evidentiary system based on the freely formed *conviction intime* – which virtually everyone in the council wanted to retain –, because the power of professional magistrates would become far too great if they could also decide on the question of fact while having to give no other motivation than that they were internally convinced.[106] Those in favour of a jury system gained an initial victory when the decision was made that in principle both the accusation and the judgment jury would be retained. As long as Bigot-Préameneau (who was opposed to the jury system) was president of the legislative committee, however, the retention of the jury system was made the object of renewed discussion throughout the sessions of 1804. Only when in 1808 the debates reopened with Treilhard as the president of the legislative committee, did those in favour of a jury system gain the decisive victory.[107]

During the discussions in the *Conseil d'État* the eyes were naturally fixed on Napoleon. It was clear that the jury system could not survive if Napoleon would decidedly speak against it. Napoleon showed a vivid interest in the discussions on the jury system and, for example, asked for a further response to the statement of Siméon that professional judges were more apt to judge according to their internal conviction than lay persons. In the first phase in 1804, Napoleon did not take a clear side and ambiguously stated that "Sa Majesté admet le jury s'il est possible de parvenir à le bien composer".[108] At the end of the sessions of 1804 the majority of the *Conseil d'État* appeared to be in favour of the jury system and Napoleon remarked that it might be unwise to abolish this institution when public opinion seemed to be in favour of it. At this point, however, rather suddenly the discussions on the concept criminal procedural code were suspended and only reopened three years later in 1808. Esmein explains this peculiar turn of events by the fact that Napoleon was actually against the jury system but wanted to wait for a more appropriate time to abolish it.[109] Feldhausen, however, states that Esmein is wrong in his presupposition that Napoleon was against the retention of the jury system all along. Napoleon seemed to be wavering and not entirely sure on this matter. Furthermore, Feldhausen states that the explanation of Esmein is improbable, because in 1808 Napoleon did eventually decide in favour of the retention of the jury. He claims that it is

---

106   Ibidem, pp. 506–510. Treilhard, furthermore, made the for Napoleon important remark that the nation might be surprised that such a liberal institute would be abolished by an emperor who was known for his liberal sentiments.
107   P. Feldhausen, *Zur Geschichte des Strafprozessrechtes in Frankreich*, pp. 153–155.
108   A. Esmein, *Histoire de la procédure criminelle en France*, pp. 510–521.
109   Ibidem, pp. 510–521.

more probable that Napoleon had to focus on foreign affairs which led to a long pause in the legislative activities of the *Conseil d'État*.[110]

The exact (evolution of the) opinion of Napoleon remains unclear. He seems not to have been decidedly in favour of a jury system but had a largely opportunistic and careful approach to this subject. When he noticed that the institution was relatively popular in France and that it might seem as though he was trying to curb back this liberal acquisition of the revolutionary period, he prudently decided to retain it. The fact that he was not a strong proponent of the jury system becomes clear from his legislative activity in the newly created Italian Kingdom. In 1807 he approved the creation of a criminal procedural code for this kingdom which contained the free evaluation of the evidence by professional judges. This code was promulgated on 8 September 1807. According to Nobili, Napoleon did not desire to introduce a jury system in his Italian kingdom, but instead abolished the system of legal proofs and created a system in which professional judges decided solely on the basis of their internal conviction. Napoleon did not give a clear motivation for this decision, but merely remarked in a speech that the current political situation in Italy did not lend itself for the introduction of a jury system.[111] In any case, the criminal procedural code for the Kingdom of Italy was the first time that the system of legal proofs was explicitly abolished and replaced by the free evaluation of the evidence by professional judges.

On 23 January 1808 the discussion was reopened in the *Conseil d'État* and the debate on the jury system was started anew. Doubts were again cast on the retention of the jury system in the first sessions and it was again decided in principle that the jury system would not be abolished. Finally, Napoleon clearly spoke out in favour of retaining the judgment jury and to abolish the accusation jury. Although Napoleon did not elaborate on his reasons in favour of the judgment jury, he did at this point mention the argument that professional judges would become harsher and would start to see criminals everywhere because of their continuous judgements in criminal cases. Jurors would not have this negative effect because of their constant rotation. Napoleon subsequently stated that the accusation jury was not suited for its task and was an unnecessary institution. A central criticism was that the accusation jury often transgressed the limits of its role and tended to already judge on the guilt of the accused. Furthermore, while the accusation jury was introduced out of suspicion against judicial arbitrariness, it was stated that this was no longer a real danger under the present magistrates. Instead, the decision on the accusation of an

---

110   P. Feldhausen, *Zur Geschichte des Strafprozessrechtes in Frankreich*, pp. 166–168.
111   M. Nobili, *Die freie richterliche Überzeugungsbildung*, pp. 164–167.

accused would now be made by the *procureur général* which subsequently had to be approved by three judges. In this way at the beginning of March 1808, a definitive solution was found out of the impasse regarding the jury question which was then laid down in the *Code d'Instruction Criminelle*. The instruction for the judgment jury to decide according to their freely formed internal conviction was copied almost verbatim from the earlier decree of Beaumetz. It was also decided that the procedure before the tribunal would remain oral, public and with equality of arms between the public prosecutor and the defendant.[112]

Even though the judgment jury was retained in the *Code d'Instruction Criminelle*, it has to be emphasized that it now functioned in an altered procedural context. The most important reforms in the code concerned the preliminary investigation, which was again modelled after the preparatory instruction of the criminal ordinance of 1670. In general, the weight of the preliminary investigation had increased strongly in the *Code d'Instruction Criminelle* and was placed under the control of a public prosecutor who was no longer elected but appointed by the executive branch. The preliminary investigation was again made secret and written, the witnesses could be heard separately by the *juge d'instruction* without the presence of the accused and the accused himself could be interrogated without a notification of what he was accused of. All this meant that during the eventual public trial in front of the judgment jury, the actual balance of power had shifted dramatically in favour of the public prosecutor when compared with the procedural system of 1791. The improvements of the defensive position of the accused that had been achieved in 1791 remained in force, but their effect was largely limited to the phase of the main public trial. The preliminary investigation was made more inquisitorial in character, while the main trial remained accusatorial. As Esmein observed on the difference between these two phases of the trial: "on passe de l'obscurité au plein jour".[113]

Summarizing, the *Code d'Instruction Criminelle* can be typified as trying to find a balance between the principles of 1791 and the desire for more repressive rigour which could be found in the old criminal procedural ordinance of 1670. Crucial for the criminal law of evidence was, nevertheless, that the *Code d'Instruction Criminelle* retained the two most important revolutionary changes in this area: the abolition of the system of legal proofs and the introduction of a jury system. The regulation in the *Code d'Instruction Criminelle* of the criminal law of evidence would, furthermore, prove to be very influential because it

---

112   A. Esmein, *Histoire de la procédure criminelle en France*, pp. 521–527.
113   Ibidem, pp. 530–539.

was predominantly through this code that other areas outside of France would become acquainted with the jury system and the public, oral trial.

4.6 The Criminal Law of Evidence between 1815 and 1848

In 1814, Article 65 of the charter of Louis XVIII confirmed the continued existence of the jury system. The charter was intended as a constitution that was granted by Louis XVIII to the people and was of a relatively conservative nature. The *Code d'Instruction Criminelle* remained in force and the regulation of the jury system was left largely unchanged. Regarding the criminal law of evidence, the period between 1815 and 1848, to a large extent, inherited the discussion points and preoccupations that had crystallized in the period between 1795 and 1814. Although there were again voices that called for the abolition of the jury system and for its replacement by professional magistrates, there appears to have been no real desire to return to the old system of legal proofs. The free evaluation of the evidence was firmly established and the latter option seemed to be a closed chapter in France.

After 1815 the discussion concerning the jury system focused on three questions. The first question was whether jurors should be allowed to decide whether there were mitigating circumstances on the basis of which the judge would have to pronounce a less severe punishment. The other two questions were closely dependent on a general political division between 'conservatives' and 'liberals'. The second question was whether the jury system should also be extended to political and press offences. Under the Napoleonic criminal code, political and press offences fell under the category of *délits* which were tried by the correctional courts. They were, therefore, treated in lower courts which were staffed by professional judges and which did not have a jury system. The third question was what the criteria should be for someone to be eligible to function as a juror.[114]

4.6.1 *The Possibility to Ameliorate Punishments*
A central principle of the jury system as it was erected between 1791 and 1814, was that the jurors could only decide on the question of fact. They were not allowed to take the possible penal consequences of their verdicts into consideration and could only decide whether the facts were proven or not. In the first decades of the nineteenth century it became clear, however, that the jurors did take the penal consequences into consideration and often acquitted when

---

114. B. Schnapper, "Le jury français aux XIX et XXème siècles", pp. 182–184.

they deemed the punishment to be too severe. This happened rather frequently for two reasons. Firstly, the substantive criminal codes, in particular Napoleon's *Code Pénal* of 1810, contained relatively severe punishments. The second reason was that there were very few possibilities to adjust the punishment to the circumstances of the case. As Donovan observed, acquittals by the jurors formed a sort of revolt against the 'classical' system of penology that was inscribed in the revolutionary and Napoleonic criminal codes. In classical penology, based on the work of authors such as Beccaria and Bentham, it was assumed that criminals were reasonable persons who normally possessed a sufficiently free will to be held morally responsible for their crimes. Accordingly, the substantive criminal codes punished the crime rather than the criminal, and prescribed punishments for crimes that would be equally applicable to all individuals who committed it, regardless of the character of the individual and the circumstances under which someone had committed a crime.[115]

The revolutionary and Napoleonic criminal codes were thus characterized by the fact that the punishments were rigidly fixed by the law and that there was very little leeway for the judge to alter the punishment based on the circumstances of the case. The fixation of the punishment supposedly had two benefits. Firstly, potential criminals could know what punishment would await them so that they could calculate whether the costs of the crime would outweigh the benefits. Secondly, and most importantly, the rigid prescription of the penalty would prevent the possibility of judicial arbitrariness. Unlike in the old system where the judge had a relatively large freedom to adjust the punishment, the revolutionary reformers wanted to prevent judicial arbitrariness and create a situation where the judge would only have to apply the letter of the law in an almost mechanical way.

Almost from the start cracks appeared in this rigid framework. It was noticed that jurors tended to acquit when they deemed that the punishment was too severe. Napoleon was the first who sought to remedy this situation. The *Code Pénal* of 1810 partially broke with the rigid revolutionary codes. With the explicit aim of stimulating juries to convict more, the *Code Pénal* of 1810 instituted minimum and maximum punishments that could be moderated by the judges. A second important step was taken in 1824 with the creation of a law that made it possible for judges to soften the punishment for a limited number of offenses when they deemed that there were extenuating circumstances. Both of these measures did not have the desired effect and jurors continued to

---

115   J.M. Donovan, *Juries and the Transformation of Criminal Justice in France*, pp. 45–48.

frequently acquit, apparently because the jurors could not be certain that the judge would actually soften the sentence as they deemed appropriate. A very important reform was finally achieved in the law of 1832 which revised the *Code Pénal*. This law transferred the power to decide on extenuating circumstances from the judges to the jurors and made it applicable to all crimes. In this way, jurors, for the first time, gained a significant legal power to determine the punishment of those they convicted. The Ministry of Justice pointed out in 1832 that the reform had become necessary because of the tendency of jurors to acquit when they deemed the punishment too severe.[116]

The law of 1832 broke with the rigid and stern system of punishments of the revolutionary and Napoleonic codes. The juries now had the possibility to take into account the personal characteristics of the accused, his motives and, for example, his chances of rehabilitation.[117] The jury's verdict was no longer a simple decision on the guilt or innocence of the accused, but focused more on the individual circumstances and the intent of the accused. While the reform was aimed at ensuring higher conviction rates, it was also inspired by and conformed to a change in ideas about penology. Since the restoration a new movement in penology had emerged which is often called the 'neoclassical' school. This school built on the ideas of the classical school of, among others, Beccaria and Bentham, but argued that more attention should be paid to the individual circumstances of the criminal. Above all Pellegrino Rossi became the most important protagonist of the neoclassical doctrine. As Vielfaure remarked, the ideas of the neoclassical school and the law of 1832 formed an important step in the individualisation of the punishment, and in paying more attention to the intentions and the state of mind of the accused.[118]

---

116   Ibidem, pp. 47–62.
117   Ibidem, pp. 59–65. According to Donovan, the reform also significantly enhanced the use of psychiatric reports in criminals trials to assess the mental state of the accused. Apart from the possibility to better individualize the punishment through extenuating circumstances, the law of 1832 also decreased the severity of many of the punishments in the *Code Pénal*. The number of capital offenses was, for example, reduced from thirty-six to twenty-two.
118   P. Vielfaure, *L'évolution du droit pénal sous la monarchie du juillet. Entre exigences politiques et interrogations de société*, pp. 26–29 and 340–344. This 'subjectivisation' of the substantive criminal law in the first decades of the nineteenth century has also been noted by Pihlajamäki. While in France it had the effect that it was decided to allow jurors to judge on extenuating circumstances, in the German territories (as in the Netherlands) the increased importance of the subjective side of the crime was used as an argument in favour of the introduction of the free evaluation of the evidence. The increased need to prove the precise level of the criminal intent of the accused and to modify the punishment

4.6.2 The Judgement on Political- and Press Offences

Donovan observed that there was most likely no other era in which the awareness of the political role of the jury was stronger than during the Bourbon restoration (1815–1830) and the July Monarchy (1830–1848). This awareness was heightened by the sharp political controversies of this period. The fierce liberal support for the jury system as the 'palladium of liberty' reached its peak during this period. Not only in France, but in most parts of continental Europe which followed the example of France.[119] The political group which can broadly be designated as 'conservatives', was largely opposed to the jury system. They deemed that lay jurors did not have the necessary skills to judge on the question of fact and that, professional magistrates were far more efficacious in repressing crimes. Furthermore, they argued that the jury system was a foreign institution and they saw it as a fruit of the despised revolution. The liberals, on the other hand, considered the jury system an important acquisition of the revolutionary period which they wanted to protect. The jury system, in short, became the object of a broader political discussion and of the different interpretations of the legacy of the revolution.[120]

A central concern of the liberals during the restoration period lay in the attempt to extend the competency of the jury system to the *délits politiques et de presse*. The political *crimes* which were threatened with a minimum of five years imprisonment were normally already judged by the courts of assizes with a jury system. The lesser *délits* were judged by the lower correctional courts. These *délits* constituted mainly what could be called crimes of opinion in speech and press. The liberals argued that these offenses should be tried by a jury because they deemed that jurors would be far more impartial and more

---

accordingly made it clear that the system of legal proofs was too inflexible to deal with the subjective side of the crime. It was argued that a more free evaluation of the evidence and particularly a free use of indicia was necessary for the judge to be able to deduce the criminal intent of the accused from the proven circumstances. Conversely, only a more free evaluation of the evidence made it possible for the judges in the Netherlands and Germany to more adequately adjust the punishment to the precise level of the criminal intent of the accused. As Pihlajamäki remarked, there was, therefore, also an important connection between the 'subjectivisation' of the substantive criminal law and the development of the modern criminal law of evidence. See H. Pihlajamäki, *Evidence, Crime and the Legal Profession*, pp. 5–6 and 128–131.

119 J.M. Donovan, *Juries and the Transformation of Criminal Justice in France*, p. 49.
120 B. Schnapper, "Le jury français aux XIX et XXème siècles", pp. 180–185. Important in these discussions was that the jury system came to be seen a safeguard to protect civil liberty but that jurors were also often too lenient, while repressive efficiency was seen as an attribute of professional magistrates.

independent from the government than the appointed correctional judges.[121] The liberals, in short, did not trust the professional judges to safeguard the liberty to express political opinions and (correctly) feared that the government could use the correctional tribunals to harass journalists and political opponents. The significance that was attached to the extension of the competency of the jury trial to political- and press offenses during the restoration period should also be seen in light of the central importance that freedom of speech and public opinion had in the liberal ideology. Public opinion was seen as a sort of fourth power that was crucial to keep the government in check and to prevent the arbitrary use of its power. To make sure that public opinion could exercise this function, adequate safeguards of the freedom of speech were necessary.[122]

The liberals attained a first success in 1819, after they had increased their representation in the Chamber of Deputies during the election of 1818. Under the ministry headed by Élie Decazes, a law was passed in May 1819 which granted a jury trial to persons accused of *délits de presse*. However, after the assassination of the Duke of Berry in 1820 the government clamped down harder on the opposition again and in 1822 the law which extended the jury trial to the *délits de presse* was abolished. The liberals, naturally, opposed this measure. After they came to power during the July Revolution in 1830 they managed to extend the jury trial to both political- and press offenses. The liberals had thereby finally achieved their much desired reform.[123]

4.6.3 Who should be Allowed to be Jurors?

A significant part of the discussion between 1815 and 1848 focused on the question who should be allowed to perform the function of juror. The composition of the jury panels had been an important concern from the moment the jury system was introduced and played a crucial role in the trust which was given to the jury system. In the early revolutionary period the jury was introduced

---

121   J.M. Donovan, *Juries and the Transformation of Criminal Justice in France*, pp. 53–55.
122   The example and the ideas of the French liberals in the restoration period also formed an important role model for liberals in the Netherlands and in the German territories. It became an article of faith among most of these liberals that a jury trial should be instituted for at least political- and press offenses. Benjamin Constant was one of the most important liberal protagonists in France in the restoration period who fought tirelessly for the extension of the competency of the jury trial to political- and press offenses (both in his publications and in parliament). On the important role that public opinion and the jury system played in his ideas, see for example B. Fontana, *Benjamin Constant and the post-revolutionary mind*, pp. 81–97.
123   J.M. Donovan, *Juries and the Transformation of Criminal Justice in France*, pp. 54–56.

because in a general abstract manner the 'people' were trusted more than the professional magistrates. As soon as it was clear that a jury system would be adopted, the question became who this 'people' should be and thereby who should be allowed to function as jurors. During the early revolution, the discussion on this question was dominated by, on the one hand, the more radical or egalitarian democrats who wanted a very large section of the population to judge, and on the other hand the more conservative side who wanted a far more restricted accessibility. Apart from a short period under the leadership of Robespierre, the criteria for the possibility to function as a juror were restrictive and only a small portion of society was eligible for jury duty. The restrictive criteria were understandable because for many people the jury system would not have been acceptable if the uneducated and poor could perform the function of juror. The importance of the restrictive criteria could, for example, also be seen during the discussions in the *Conseil d'État* between 1804 and 1808. Napoleon remarked that he would allow the retention of a jury system "s'il est possible de parvenir à le bien composer". By this he meant that he would only find the jury system acceptable when a restricted group would be allowed to perform this function.[124]

During the period between 1815 and 1848 the discussion on the question who should be eligible to perform the function of juror was dominated by the more general political discussion between conservatives and liberals. The criteria for the selection of jurors were mostly formulated in terms of income and occupation, and closely followed the discussions on who should have the right to vote. It is not the goal here to give an extensive overview of the fluctuations in the criteria, but it is sufficient to observe that between the period of the 1815 and 1848 the jurors were selected predominantly from the relatively rich proprietors and those who had a degree of a university. The income criteria aside, the fact that the jurors were not remunerated for their function already made it difficult for a large portion of society to perform this function.[125]

The group which was eligible to fulfil the function of juror was extended at the beginning of the reign of Louis-Philippe from around 100.000 to 250.000 people, but remained a relatively small portion of society.[126] For a short period, during the Second Republic, which was formed in February 1848, universal manhood suffrage was introduced whereby every adult male could also perform the function of juror. Following the election of a more conservative National Assembly in April, however, this measure was repealed. During the

---

124   B. Schnapper, "Le jury français aux XIX et XXème siècles", pp. 165–182.
125   Ibidem, pp. 189–193.
126   R. Martinage, *Punir le crime. La repression judiciaire depuis le code pénal*, pp. 140–141.

authoritarian reign of Napoleon III (1852–1870) the modest attempts to democratize the jury panels under the Second Republic were rescinded, and a return was made to the situation under the July Monarchy. Only during the Third Republic a precocious democratization of the jury panel again occurred.[127]

Finally, a last comment has to be made on a development that eventually strongly undermined the importance of the jury system: 'correctionalization'. As Donovan has shown, particularly under the reign of Napoleon III the government took significant steps to 'correctionalize' many of the *crimes*. The punishments for a large number of crimes were lowered which meant that they would henceforward have to be tried by the correctional courts and no longer by the courts of assizes. The process of correctionalization was partially inspired by the distrust and dissatisfaction of the government of Napoleon III with the jury system, and partially by the desire to prosecute offenses more efficiently and less costly. In effect, the legislative correctionalization of many of the *crimes* diminished the importance of the jury trial and had the effect that only the most serious crimes would still be tried by jurors.[128]

4.7 Conclusion

A description has been given of the reform in revolutionary France whereby the system of legal proofs was replaced by the free evaluation of evidence by lay jurors. This was part of a complete reform of the criminal procedural law in 1791, in which the secret, written inquisitorial procedure was replaced by a public, oral trial where the defendant was given far more freedom to defend himself. Moreover, the old scale of decision types that formed a fundamental part of the system of legal proofs was abolished and it was now only possible for the jurors to find the accused guilty or to acquit him. The reforms of 1791 were characterized by their relatively liberal character and focus on creating guarantees to strengthen the position of the accused. Nevertheless, during the Napoleonic era some of the revolutionary reforms were rescinded. The possibility to elect the judges and the institution of the accusation jury were abolished. Furthermore, the preliminary investigation was again made secret and the defensive rights of the accused in this phase were weakened. A division was made, therefore, between the more inquisitorial preliminary investigation and the more accusatorial public, oral trial.

---

127 J.M. Donovan, *Juries and the Transformation of Criminal Justice in France*, pp. 87–140.
128 Ibidem, pp. 87–110.

It has been shown in this chapter that the revolutionary reforms were inspired by a change in the underlying epistemological and political-constitutional ideas. Already in the reform literature between 1750 and 1789 it could be seen that for many authors the system of legal proofs had become logically untenable. Authors such as Voltaire, Beccaria, Brissot de Warville, Servan and Dupaty argued that it was impossible to determine beforehand in general rules when sufficient evidence existed for a conviction in the individual case. These authors polemically ridiculed the medieval-scholastic and artificial nature of the system of legal proofs with which supposedly the judges worked in an almost mathematical way to calculate a full proof. These criticisms were taken even further during the discussions in the Constitutional Assembly, where the artificial and incomprehensible system of legal proofs was constantly contrasted with the way honest, upright citizens would judge using their common sense. In short, the changed epistemological ideas undermined the plausibility of the system of legal proofs, and instead it was argued that the foundation of a conviction could only be the *conviction intime* of the person judging.

The polemic against the system of legal proofs and the inquisitorial procedure was also strongly inspired by a distrust in the professional magistrates and a change in the political-constitutional ideas. The changed political-constitutional ideas and the contrast with the English criminal procedure made it clear that there were severe defects in the existing inquisitorial procedure. Many authors – even the relatively conservative authors such as Vermeil and Letrosne – remarked that the existing inquisitorial procedure contradicted the 'natural right' of the accused to defend himself. They argued that the accused should have a complete liberty to defend himself and that he should have the right to use legal counsel. Furthermore, almost all the reform-minded authors agreed that judicial torture was a gruesome, useless practice which violated the natural urge of self-preservation. The criticisms which were expressed on the basis of these changed political-constitutional ideas made an encompassing reform of the inquisitorial procedure seem highly desirable. The reforms of the criminal procedure, however, would have made the system of legal proofs (with its focus on acquiring a confession) largely ineffective and, therefore, also necessitated a reform of the criminal law of evidence.

Finally, the distrust in the professional magistrates had a pervasive influence on the direction of the reform-discussion. The distrust in professional judges, first of all, inspired many authors to argue that the trial should be completely public. The publicity of the trial was seen as one of the most effective remedies against the possible arbitrary abuses of power by the judges. Secondly, the distrust in the professional judges led to the idea that a separation of powers could and should be made within the criminal trial. Inspired by the ground-breaking work of Montesquieu, the idea was popularized that a clear distinction could be made between the question of law and the question of fact. The revolutionaries deemed that a too strong concentration of power and judicial arbitrariness could be largely excluded when lay jurors decided on the question of fact and the judge would only have to apply the law (i.e. pronounce the punishment that was rigidly prescribed in the *Code Pénal*). The distrust in professional magistrates remained in the first half of the nineteenth century, and it became an article of faith among the liberals that the retention of a jury system was absolutely vital as the 'palladium of civil liberty'.

In France the discussion on the reform of the criminal law of evidence was radical and occurred in a relatively short period of time. The revolutionary abolition of the system of legal proofs and the introduction of the free evaluation of the evidence were here intimately tied to the introduction of the jury system. Because of the desire to introduce a jury system and the presupposition that lay jurors could not work with a complex system of evidentiary rules, the subjective and almost 'instinctive' *conviction intime* of lay jurors was exalted over the technical and artificial way judges decided on evidentiary questions. As will be described in the following chapters, the discussion on the criminal law of evidence developed in a far more gradual way in the German territories and in the Netherlands. Nevertheless, the French revolutionary reforms and their idea of the *conviction intime* had a profound influence on the discussion in the German territories and the Netherlands.

CHAPTER 5

The Development of the German Criminal Law of Evidence 1750–1870

5.1 Introduction

Compared to France, the discussion on the reform of the criminal law of evidence developed far more gradually in the German territories.[1] The change from the system of legal proofs to the free evaluation of the evidence between 1750 and 1870 can be roughly divided into three successive stages. They will be described in the following three sections of this chapter. The first phase lasted from roughly 1750 until 1812, the second phase lasted from 1812 until 1848 – also called the *Vormärz* period referring to the revolutions starting in March 1848 – and the third phase from 1848 until the 1870s. As in France, the reform of the criminal law of evidence in the German territories was part of a broader reform of the criminal procedural law. In the German historiography this transition is commonly designated as the change from the old 'inquisitorial procedure' to the modern 'reformed criminal procedure' (*reformierte Strafprozess*) or *Anklageprozess*. Characteristic of the *reformierte Strafprozess* was the free evaluation of the evidence with a public, oral trial and a public prosecutor. The reformed procedure was in place in all the German states in the 1870s, but it had taken a long time and much discussion to get there. The central question in this chapter is how this change occurred.

During the first phase, the Germans were still relatively uncritical of the existing procedural system and the willingness for reform remained modest. Even though sporadically some German authors – such as Möser and Von Justi – argued for more far-reaching reforms, the mainstream of authors only sought limited reforms within the boundaries of the existing procedural framework. The central point of debate in the first phase concerned the question

---

1   The terms 'Germany' and 'the German territories' are used interchangeably in this chapter and throughout this book. Nevertheless, it is important to keep in mind that throughout the period between 1750 and 1870 there was not one unified German state but many German speaking states and that the term 'Germany' is, therefore, not meant to refer to a unified German state for this period. Furthermore, it has to be remarked that the focus in this chapter lies on the German territories and states that would, after 1871, form part of the unified German state. Far less attention will be paid to German speaking Austria and the development of the criminal law of evidence in the German parts of the Austro-Hungarian Empire.

© KONINKLIJKE BRILL NV, LEIDEN, 2020 | DOI:10.1163/9789004415027_006

whether judicial torture should be abolished and what should come in its place. It was clear to the German authors that if judicial torture would be abolished, some solution would have to be found for the difficult cases where strong evidence existed against the accused but not yet a full proof. Broadly two solutions were suggested for this problem. The more 'conservative' side wanted to extend the practice of extraordinary punishments and *Ungehorsamstrafe*.[2] The more 'progressive' authors proposed to allow convictions to the ordinary punishments on the basis of indicia in certain situations. Even though a consensus grew in the first phase that judicial torture should be abolished, most German authors remained strictly tied to the system of legal proofs and were still highly suspicious of the use of indicia.

During the second phase the nature of the debate changed entirely. The scope of the discussion broadened to include more and more radical options to reform the criminal law of evidence. Since the 1810s the real intellectual confrontation with the ideas of the French revolutionaries started. An important stimulus was the fact that the German territories on the left-bank of the Rhine retained the French legislation after Napoleon was expelled. The presence of the French procedural system created a 'significant other' in the German discussions. It presented a mirror to hold up to the existing criminal procedural system, which led to a deeper and more conscious evaluation of the existing criminal law of evidence. One important change, therefore, was the simple fact

---

[2] *Ungehorsamsstrafe*, which is here meant as encompassing the *Lügenstrafe* as well, were disciplinary punishments which could be used when the accused obstinately refused to cooperate with the investigation, when he refused to answer questions under interrogation or when it was clear that he was lying. The punishments could consist of worsening the circumstances of the imprisonment and, according to some, it could also consist of several strikes with a whip. In the literature they were often expressly distinguished from judicial torture and extraordinary punishments, because they were not in the first place meant to extract a confession but only to punish the accused who had not cooperated. Fundamentally, it was argued that the accused had an obligation to tell the truth and that lying was a punishable form of disobedience to the court. According to some authors, however, the *Ungehorsamsstrafe* were more clearly seen as a less severe substitute for judicial torture through which pressure could be put on the accused to confess. In any case, the often rather vague terms in which they were regulated and the fact that they could be used against an accused who was lying or not cooperating with his own prosecution, meant that in practice they could be used in a very similar way as judicial torture. Furthermore, the view that it was meant as a punishment for lying and not to extort a future confession was not a very tenable distinction in practice. After all, with *Lügenstrafe*, the punishment occurred with the clear intention of making the accused tell the (incriminating) truth. See N. Knapp, *Die Ungehorssamstrafe in der Strafprozesspraxis des frühen 19. Jahrhunderts*, pp. 28–53.

that the French example showed the possibility of a completely different way of organizing the criminal law of evidence, which was supported by influential political-constitutional ideals. The central question in the second period became whether the jury system should be adopted, or if not at least a far-reaching reform of the existing evidentiary system should be introduced. Importantly, just as in France, the option of reforming the criminal law of evidence was not treated in isolation, but was always discussed in the context of a broader reform of the criminal procedural law.

The discussion during the second phase was dominated by two sides. On the one side there emerged a group of 'liberals' who demanded a complete reform of the criminal procedural law and the introduction of a jury system on the basis of predominantly political-constitutional ideas.[3] This group contained many journalists, politicians and some jurists as well. They largely followed the reform ideals of the French revolutionaries. On the other side, a clear majority within the more 'scientific-juridical' discussion was opposed to the jury system and had become in favour of professional judges in combination with a negative system of legal proofs. This period generally saw an increasingly critical attitude towards the system of legal proofs, the use of extraordinary punishments and the secret, inquisitorial procedure as a whole. Eventually a consensus grew that extraordinary punishments should be abolished and that convictions on the basis of indicia should be possible. Furthermore, during the second phase the internal conviction of the judge was given a far more central role in the criminal law of evidence through the acceptance of a negative system of legal proofs. This meant that the judge should only convict if he was internally convinced of the guilt of the accused and if the minimum evidentiary standards were met.

Finally, a further important development occurred during the end of the second phase in the 1840s. Several authors started to question the existing

---

3 As Pihlajamäki states, the term 'liberalism' is not easy to circumscribe, especially in the first half of the nineteenth century. He quotes Sheehan who suggests that it should be seen as "a family of ideas and behaviour patterns which overlapped more or less, enabling the modern observer to recognize a liberal much the same way as the contemporary liberals recognize each other". In this chapter, this rather broad understanding of the term liberal is used following the use of this term as it mostly recurs in the German historiography. It was not a clearly circumscribed group, but they were connected in their, for this time, progressive constitutional-political ideals. Relevant for the criminal law of evidence was that they strove for a better protection of civil rights – through, among other things, a constitution and a separation of powers – and for representative governmental institutions (which positively inclined them towards a jury system). See Pihlajamäki, *Evidence, Crime, and the legal profession*, p. 124.

dichotomy in the debate wherein it was presumed that only jurors should be able to judge on the basis of their freely formed internal conviction and that professional judges had to be bound by a (negative) system of evidentiary rules. These authors, who were against a jury system but argued that the system of legal proofs was untenable, now proposed to let professional judges decide on the basis of their freely formed internal conviction. Although this was still only the opinion of a minority in the juridical debate in the 1840s, it became far more broadly supported between 1848 and 1870.

The second phase ended in march 1848 with the outbreak of a revolutionary atmosphere in the German territories. The winds suddenly turned in favour of the 'liberals' who desired the adoption of a jury system and a public oral trial mainly out of political-constitutional motives. During this revolutionary period, and in the years shortly afterwards, the authorities of most German states adopted a jury system in concomitance with the introduction of a public, oral trial and a public prosecutor. The jury system was, for example, introduced in the new procedural codes in the early 1850s in Bavaria, Baden, Wurttemberg and Prussia. In the revolutionary period of 1848 and 1849 the reforms occurred in a sudden and high tempo in the German territories and they were motivated predominantly by political-constitutional motives. Even though the internal development within the scientific juridical debate was not the *direct* decisive factor for the reforms in 1848 and 1849, it did help pave the way for these reforms in an important way. Before 1848 the increasingly critical academic discussion had strongly delegitimized the existing inquisitorial procedure and the system of legal proofs. The juridical discussion had thus contributed to the growing feeling that a large scale reform of the criminal procedural law was necessary.

The fact that the internal development in the juridical debate was increasingly directed towards the abolition of the system of legal proofs, becomes especially apparent from the continuation of the discussion in the third phase lasting from 1848 until 1870. There was still no consensus on the desirability of a jury system in the juridical literature in this period, but the discussion had evolved in such a way that the question was now predominantly whether lay jurors or professional judges should judge on the basis of their freely formed internal conviction. To these two options the new idea of *Schwurgerichte* was added in the third phase, which meant that a professional judge would decide in combination with one or more lay judges. In conclusion, during the third phase the supporters of a legal theory of proof had definitively become a minority opinion, and the free evaluation of the evidence by either professional judges, lay jurors or *Schwurgerichte* was now regarded as one of the principles of the *reformierte Strafprozess*.

5.2   1750–1812: The Abolition of Judicial Torture and the Start of the Reform Debate

The starting point of the discussion in the German territories regarding the criminal law of evidence in the second half of the eighteenth century was somewhat different from that in France. Whereas in France the criminal ordinance of 1670 appeared to allow at least a limited possibility to convict someone on the basis of 'undoubtable indicia' to the ordinary or full punishment, in the German territories a more strict version of the system of legal proofs existed which explicitly prohibited this possibility. The stricter German variant can be traced back to the *Constitutio Criminalis Carolina* (CCC) of 1532. The CCC was the main ordinance which regulated the substantive and procedural criminal law in the German territories. Even though the German states could give prevalence to their own particular criminal regulation above the CCC, it had a significant authority in the German territories until well in the nineteenth century. Crucial was Article 22 of the CCC which explicitly forbade the pronunciation of a *peinliche Strafe* on the basis of indicia alone. According to the ordinance a full proof could only be based on the testimony of at least two eyewitnesses or a confession.[4]

The prohibition to convict to the ordinary punishment on the basis of indicia was repeated in the German handbooks of the seventeenth and eighteenth centuries. The most influential handbook on criminal procedural law in the seventeenth century was Carpzov's *Practica nova Imperialis Saxonica rerum criminalum*. Carpzov stated that indicia could not suffice for an ordinary punishment. He also taught that a more lenient extraordinary punishment could be pronounced on the basis of indicia if they created a very strong suspicion. This was a subject on which the CCC had remained silent.[5] Most authors who wrote handbooks on the criminal procedural law in the eighteenth century did not deviate from the evidentiary standards proposed by the CCC and Carpzov. Influential writers such as Boehmer and Meister the elder, for example, both taught that a full proof could only consist of a confession or the testimony of two eyewitnesses.[6] The same evidentiary standards could also still be found in the criminal legislation for Bavaria in 1751 and Austria in 1768.[7]

---

4   A.M. Ignor, *Geschichte Strafprozess*, pp. 41–44 and 62–64.
5   K. Michels, *Der Indizienbeweis in Übergang vom Inquisitionsprozess zum reformierten Strafverfahren*, pp. 23–30.
6   B. Thäle, *Die Verdachtsstrafe in der kriminalwissenschaftlichen Literatur des 18. und 19. Jahrhunderts*, pp. 29–34.
7   K. Michels, *Der Indizienbeweis in Übergang vom Inquisitionsprozess zum reformierten Strafverfahren*, pp. 37–43.

Even though eighteenth century authors still repeated the same evidentiary standards as the CCC and Carpzov, they did start to use a new probabilistic terminology to describe what kind of certainty was required in criminal cases. Ignor has observed this changed terminology in, for example, the works of Boehmer and Leyser. Ignor describes this new terminology as the placement of dogmatic explosives under the system of legal proofs that would eventually lead to the destruction of the traditional evidentiary system. Leyser, for example, stated on the kind of certainty which was required to establish the existence of the *corpus delicti*: "Ad corpus delicti *certitudo moralis*, qualis in rebus humanis haberi potest, non mathematica et absoluta, requiritur".[8] Not a mathematical or absolute certainty was required, but only a kind of certainty which one could normally have in human affairs: a high degree of probability which was called moral certainty. Boehmer as well, stated that it was absurd to demand a mathematical certainty in criminal law where only a moral certainty was possible.[9] Ignor, furthermore, refers to Gmelin (1785) who remarked: "wir würden weder in bürgerlichen noch peinlichen Sachen jemals ein Urteil fallen können, wenn wir mathematischen Gewissheit forderten, dann auch eine Million von Zeugen bringt keine solche Gewissheit hervor; wir können uns der Notwendigkeit nicht entheben, den Richter nach lauter Wahrscheinlichkeiten handeln zu lassen".[10]

Ignor sees the use of this new probabilistic terminology as the beginning of a change which eventually led to the abolition of the rigid system of legal proofs to the acceptance of a system based on the free evaluation of evidence. The change started in the second half of the eighteenth century with the abolition of judicial torture and the increasing recognition of indicia, and ended with the acceptance of the free evaluation of the evidence in the German territories after 1848.[11] The emergence of a probabilistic conception was an

---

8   A.M. Ignor, *Geschichte Strafprozess*, pp. 167–168.
9   Ibidem, p. 166–168. Incidentally, Ignor mentions that in this period a "Lehre von der 'moralische Gewissheit'" seems to have been spreading and he notes that Beccaria propagated it as well. Ignor, however, does not give an explanation for the origins of this new terminology and does not seem to have been aware that it was a general phenomenon throughout continental Europe. He, for example, only tries to explain why it is unlikely that Beccaria acquired this terminology from Boehmer, and that he might not have been the first to propagate a "Lehre von der 'moralische Gewissheit'".
10 C.G. Gmelin, *Grundsätze der Gesetzgebung über Verbrechen und Strafen*, p. 333.
11 Ignor describes the underlying epistemological change in the criminal law of evidence as follows: "Von den Indizien hatte man immer behauptet, dass sie nur 'Wahrscheinlichkeiten' begründen könnten, niemals die 'Wahrheit'. Wie konnte man davon abrücken? Faktisch war es so, dass die verwendeten Begriffe umdefiniert wurden. Man fand, 'Wahrheit' sei im Grunde 'Wahrscheinlichkeit'. Die Wahrheit einer Tat – das, was wirklich

important factor in the eventual move from the system of legal proofs to a system based on the free evaluation of the evidence. As Ignor himself remarked, however, this was not a change which happened overnight and the 'epistemological change' was certainly not the only factor that helped shape the eventual reform of the criminal law of evidence. Similar to France, the reform was shaped to a significant extent by political-constitutional motives and was, moreover, firmly embedded in a broader change of the criminal procedural law.

5.2.1   *The Start of a Reform Discussion*
The reform debate on the criminal procedural law in Germany started to take off in the second half of the eighteenth century. Although it was still moderate in tone compared to France, there was an evidently growing dissatisfaction with aspects of the inquisitorial procedure. Judicial torture came under particular criticism. In the period from roughly the 1740s until the 1810s, a consensus grew that the practice of judicial torture was as inefficient as it was unjust, and that it should be abolished. During this phase judicial torture was in fact abolished in almost every German state. This happened (at least partially) in Prussia in 1740, in Baden in 1767, Mecklenburg in 1769, Austria in 1776, Bavaria and Württemberg in 1806 and Hannover in 1822. The decrees which abolished judicial torture, however, most often contained no provisions on what should take its place and altered nothing to the existing procedural framework or the system of legal proofs. It remained largely for the judicial practice and theory to fill in this void.[12]

Despite the growing consensus that judicial torture should be abolished, a difference of opinion remained in the juridical literature on the question what should take its place. In this period roughly two views can be distinguished in the juridical literature. One side consisted of the more conservative authors who did not want to change the existing system of legal proofs except for the – sometimes grudgingly accepted – abolition of judicial torture. The other, more progressive, side wanted to abolish judicial torture and extend the possibility for the judge to convict on the basis of indicia, but normally still within the bounds of a legal theory of proof which prescribed when the indicia were

---

vorgefallen ist – können man überhaupt nicht herausfinden, weder durch ein Geständnis oder zwei Tatzeugen, noch durch eine Millionen Zeugen. Einzig erreichbar sei eine *subjektive Gewissheit*, die im Grunde auf mehr oder weniger 'Wahrscheinlichkeit' beruhe, auch im Falle eines Geständnisses oder zweier Tatzeugen". See A.M. Ignor, *Geschichte Strafprozess*, pp. 167–167.

12   K. Michels, *Der Indizienbeweis in Übergang vom Inquisitionsprozess zum reformierten Strafverfahren*, pp. 37–43.

sufficient for a conviction. The more conservative authors remained unwilling to accept the possibility to convict on the basis of indicia and would rather just extend the use of extraordinary punishments and the so-called *Lügenstrafe* and *Ungehorsamstrafe* (punishments for 'lying' and for 'disobedience'), when there was strong evidence short of a full proof.

Important representatives of the more progressive side were Globig and Huster. They worked together on the *Abhandlung von der Criminalgesetzgebung* which in 1782 won the prestigious prize question of the *Berner Ökonomischen Gesellschaft*. This prize question, which asked 'what is the best way to organize the criminal law', was a significant event. It was supported by Voltaire – who for this purpose wrote his small treatise *Prix de la justice et de l'humanité* (1777) –, and had a large number of participants, among whom Marat, Servin and Brissot de Warville. The treatise of Globig and Huster contained many new enlightened ideas. It started with a theoretical part which derived the right to punish from a social contract and argued for an encompassing codification of the criminal law. Compared to French contemporaries, Globig and Huster were more conservative regarding the criminal procedural law. They by and large wanted to retain the existing inquisitorial procedure.[13]

Concerning the criminal law of evidence Globig and Huster reasoned from what they called 'the principle of probability'. They contended that in criminal cases no demonstrative or mathematical certainty could be reached, and that the certainty required for a full proof could only consist of a high degree of probability. Against the common opinion in the literature they argued that this could also be brought about by indicia. They stated that even when a judge uses the testimony of an eyewitness, he in fact grounds his decision on the multiple indicia which can be found in the testimony: "Der Richter gründet sein Urtheil auf die Indicia; es ist ihm einerley, ob er sie durch die Aussage zweyer Zeugen, oder auf eine andere Art erhalte".[14] Globig and Huster denied that there was an essential difference between the confession, witness testimony and indicia. Furthermore, against the common opinion they argued that these forms of evidence could all create the same kind of high probability and that if indicia were unsuited to create the necessary certainty, the same applied to witness testimony:

---

13   S. Schmidt, *Die Abhandlung von der Criminal=Gesetzgebung von Hans Ernst von Globig und Johann Georg Huster*, pp. 22–63 and 152–165.

14   H.E. Globig and J.G. Huster, *Abhandlung von der Criminal=Gesetzgebung*, pp. 301–314. Globig and Huster defined indicia as an „Umstand, von welchem sich ein Schluss nach den Regeln der Wahrscheinlichkeit auf das begangenen Verbrechen, oder den Täter machen lässt".

> Die gegenseitige Gründe, als ob die indicia nur wahrscheinliche Argumenta wären, folglich aus ihnen niemand überzeugt werden könnte, dass sie leichte trügen könnten, dass sie den Beweis des Gegenteils zuließen etc. Alle diese Gründe sind von keinem Gewicht. Denn da sie eben sowohl wider die stärkste und jede moralische Gewissheit angeführt werden können; so würde daraus folgen, das wir niemalen einer andern, als einer demonstrativen Gewissheit glauben, folglich auch jeden Beweis durch Zeugen für keinen Beweis erkennen müssten.[15]

Even though Globig and Huster wanted to allow the ordinary punishment on the basis of indicia, they certainly did not want to introduce a system based on the free evaluation of the evidence. Instead, they established a theory of indicia which was meant to supplement the already existing rules of the CCC that two eyewitnesses or a confession delivered sufficient certainty for a conviction. These rules they deemed to be the most certain rules on what constituted a sufficiently high probability: "diese Vorschriften ... [sind] aus einem so reifen Nachdenken geflossen, dass man nach scharfer Ueberlegung noch keine sicherere Regeln hatte finden können".[16] Globig and Huster defended their theory of evidence by arguing that the high degree of probability necessary for a conviction was not grounded in the subjective conviction of the judge, but in objective qualities of the indicia which followed general rules. Notwithstanding that they continued to support a system of evidentiary rules, their willingness to allow convictions to the ordinary punishment on the basis of indicia was in itself an innovative stance. Furthermore, Globig and Huster generally rejected extraordinary punishments and measures to press the accused to confess.[17]

Unlike Globig and Huster, the German authors on the conservative side argued that there was in fact a qualitative difference between on the one hand indicia and on the other hand the confession and witness testimony, and stated that indicia were a too uncertain form of evidence to substantiate a severe corporal or capital punishment. They saw the solution for the lacuna of judicial torture predominantly in extraordinary punishments and other measures

---

15   Ibidem, pp. 351–352.
16   Ibidem, p. 264.
17   K. Michels, *Der Indizienbeweis in Übergang vom Inquisitionsprozess zum reformierten Strafverfahren*, pp. 54–62. The rejection of extraordinary punishments by Globig and Huster was limited, however, because they still did not want the accused to be set free if there was a strong suspicion against him. In the situations of strong evidence short of a full proof they proposed to allow certain 'security measures' which were in effect hard to distinguish from extraordinary punishments.

to persuade the accused to make a confession. They reasoned from the existing evidentiary framework and often used the argument that Article 22 of the CCC forbade the use of the ordinary or *peinliche Strafe* on the basis of indicia. Regarding extraordinary punishments, such as fines or prison sentences, however, it was deemed that they had not been forbidden by this article. Typical representatives of this conservative side were Quistorp and Meister the Younger. They both pleaded for the abolition of judicial torture, but did not want to enlarge the possibility to convict to the ordinary punishment on the basis of indicia. Instead, they saw the use of extraordinary punishments or 'security measures' as an adequate surrogate for the situation where previously judicial torture had been possible. Meister the younger, for example, stated that extraordinary punishments are a necessary and useful instrument to replace the use of judicial torture.[18]

On the conservative side, a continued adherence was visible to the idea that there was a qualitative difference between indicia on the one hand, and the confession and witness testimony on the other hand. The reasoning behind this distinction can be seen well in the work of Kleinschrod. He defined an indicium as a proven circumstantial fact (*Umstand*) from which the probable conclusion can be drawn that a crime has been committed and who the culprit was. This was already a relatively sharp definition, because many authors such as Quistorp and Boehmer more generally defined indicia as an insufficient proof (*unvollständigen Beweis*). Kleinschrod stated that the confession and eyewitnesses could form a full proof because they were able to create a direct and 'objective' proof. They were based on *sinnliche Evidenz*. Indicia, on the other hand, were necessarily an indirect and 'subjective' proof, because they were dependent on the conclusions that the particular judge still had to draw from the proven circumstantial fact. The certainty which could be acquired from indicia was, therefore, only a subjective certainty which differed from

---

18 B. Thäle, *Die Verdachtsstrafe in der kriminalwissenschaftlichen Literatur des 18. und 19. Jahrhunderts*, pp. 34–41. Meister the younger did acknowledge, like Globig and Huster, that there was no essential difference between indicia and other forms of evidence and that they could only create differing degrees of probability. Indicia could equally create moral certainty: „Dass durch starke, insbesondere gehäufte und zusammenhängende Anzeigen, ein hoher Grad der Wahrscheinlichkeit, folglich moralische Gewissheit und Beweis, nach Vernunftgrunden gewirtet werde, leidet keinen Zweifel". However, for Meister the younger indicia alone could not suffice for the ordinary punishment because Article 22 of the CCC explicitly forbade this. As an alternative extraordinary punishments could be used for the situations where a 'hoher Grad von moralische Gewissheit' existed, as a more suitable alternative to judicial torture. See G.J.F. Meister, *Practische Bermerkungen aus dem Criminal= und Civilrechte; vol. 1*, pp. 1–6.

person to person and which could never be generally or objectively true.[19] Because every person could draw different conclusions from indicia and drawing the right conclusions was often difficult, Kleinschrod considered indicia to be incapable of constituting a full proof. As Kleinschrod prescribed in his *Entwurf eines peinlichen Gesetzbuches* for Bavaria in 1802, indicia could never create a full proof but only a lower degree of probability. For this reason, his design for a criminal code did not allow convictions to the ordinary punishment on the basis of indicia.[20]

At the turn of the nineteenth century, the topics under discussion remained largely the same. The central question still was whether the judge should be allowed to convict on the basis of indicia or whether an extension of the use of extraordinary punishments sufficed after the abolition of judicial torture. There was, nevertheless, a growing uneasiness discernible among German authors concerning the use of extraordinary punishments and the discrepancies of the existing system. Revealing of this uneasiness was a prize question organized by Klein and Kleinschrod in 1798 which asked: "Inwiefern lässt sich eine außerordentliche Strafe, welche nicht als bloßes Sicherungsmittel, sondern als eigentliche Strafe erkannt wird, rechtfertigen?". In their motivation for this prize question they tentatively remarked that the extraordinary punishments are only excusable as an emergency measure (*Notbehelf*). Was it in the long-term not unjustifiable because it was too lenient for the truly guilty and too harsh for the innocent?[21]

In 1800 Eisenhart won the prize question with a contribution which, according to Michels, represented the leading opinion of most jurists on indicia and extraordinary punishments in the early nineteenth century. In the introduction Eisenhart stated that to answer the question, first a clear definition needed to be given of what constitutes a full proof. He distinguished the simple natural proof where the crime was proven directly by witnesses or the confession from the artificial proof where the crime was proven indirectly through

---

19 Ibidem, pp. 65–67. The idea of a qualitative difference between indicia and witness testimony and the confession was a fundamental presupposition of the system of legal proofs which was given up only very slowly during the second phase. It still found many supporters even in the 1840's. Welcker, for example, warned in 1840 against allowing judges to decide on the basis of indicia: "d.h. nach ihrem subjektiven Meinen zu verurteilen". Woringen similarly stated in 1845 that the free use of indicia would let subjectivity reign and would make objective justice impossible. See E. Schwinge, *Der Kampf um die Schwurgerichte bis zur Frankfurter Nationalversammlung*, pp. 82–83.
20 G.A. Kleinschrod, *Entwurf eines peinlichen Gesetzbuches*, pp. 308–326.
21 B. Thäle, *Die Verdachtsstrafe in der kriminalwissenschaftlichen Literatur des 18. und 19. Jahrhunderts*, pp. 105–106.

reasoning and conclusions. Just as Kleinschrod, Eisenhart used a sharp definition of indicia as circumstantial facts from which conclusions could be drawn about the crime and its culprit. He divided indicia in remote and near indicia, which depended on the strength and 'closeness' of the connection between the indicium and the crime. Significantly, Eisenhart argued that indicia could be so strong and mutually supporting that they created 'certainty' – which he termed 'absolutely near indicia' – and were therefore sufficient for the ordinary punishment. He deemed that this exception was also acknowledged in Article 22 of the CCC because this article only excluded indicia when they created a high probability, not indicia which were so strong that they created certainty. Still reasoning from within the framework of the system of legal proofs, Eisenhart came to a limited acceptation of the possibility to convict the accused to the ordinary punishment on the basis of indicia.[22]

Comparable to Globig, Huster, and Kleinschrod, Eisenhart stated that extraordinary punishments should not be allowed when strong evidence short of a full proof was present, because a punishment should only be pronounced when someone's guilt was fully proven. Just like them, however, Eisenhart could not accept the situation that someone would be completely acquitted against whom strong evidence existed. While many authors simply opted for the use of extraordinary punishments and the *absolutio ab instantia*, the growing uneasiness with this solution is visible in the work of Eisenhart, Kleinschrod, Klein, and Globig and Huster. They principally did not want to allow *punishments* on the basis of a suspicion alone, but they also did not want the accused to be fully acquitted when a strong suspicion pressed on him. This was considered too dangerous to society. With considerable mental gymnastics they tried to find the solution in 'security measures' which, nevertheless, substantively almost always amounted to the same thing as extraordinary punishments. The security measures could, just like extraordinary punishments, consist of confinement in a prison or workhouse and the possibility to apply them depended on the existence of a strong suspicion against the accused.[23]

Vezin, in the treatise that he submitted for the prize question of Kleinschrod and Klein, also tried to argue against extraordinary punishments and for 'security measures'. He first remarked that either an accused had been proven guilty or not, and that no (extraordinary) punishment should be allowed when someone's guilt was not proven. Subsequently, however, he remarked that instead

---

22   K. Michels, *Der Indizienbeweis in Übergang vom Inquisitionsprozess zum reformierten Strafverfahren*, pp. 81–86.
23   B. Thäle, *Die Verdachtsstrafe in der kriminalwissenschaftlichen Literatur des 18. und 19. Jahrhunderts*, pp. 48–56 and 121–128.

security measures could be applied in "den Fällen, da man sonst zu der ausserordentlichen Strafe seine Zuflucht nahm, mithin gegen zwar unüberführte, aber doch durch ihre Schuld verdächtige und gefährliche Personen ... der Inquisit [müsse] so belastigt sein, dass vormals die Tortur gegen ihn erkannt worden wäre".[24] The demand of Vezin that a level of suspicion needed to be present which formerly would have sufficed for judicial torture, clearly shows the connection between the idea of the 'security measure' and the void left by judicial torture. The wrestling with this problem was symptomatic for the difficult dilemma which remained as long as a more free evaluation of evidence was not allowed and the strict evidentiary criteria were upheld. As Kleinschrod and Klein remarked, however, the solution of extending the use of extraordinary punishments remained unsatisfactory because it was too lenient for the truly guilty and too harsh for the innocent.

Finally, the prevailing attachment to the old system of legal proofs in the first decade of the nineteenth century can be seen clearly in the work of two young jurists who would later play a central role in the debates which led to a more free evaluation of the evidence: Feuerbach and Mittermaier. In his *Lehrbuch des gemeinen in Deutschland peinlichen Rechts* (1801), Feuerbach taught that *volle juristische Gewissheit* could only be brought about by non-artificial forms of evidence (witnesses, the confession and documents). According to Feuerbach, convictions on the basis of indicia were not allowed, as was dictated in Article 22 of the CCC.[25] In his *Theorie des Beweises im Peinlichen Processe* (1809) and in the two volumes of his *Handbuch des Peinlichen Processes* (1810–1812), Mittermaier as well came to the conclusion that indicia could not constitute a full proof. First, like Feuerbach he argued that Article 22 of the CCC was still in force and that it forbade convictions on the basis of indicia. Secondly, for a full juridical proof 'certainty' was necessary and indicia could never create certainty because they were dependent for their effect on subjective reasoning and conclusions drawn by the judge. It did not matter how many indicia were present because they could only create a high degree of probability, and all probabilities added up could still never amount to certainty. Summarizing, Mittermaier still held firm to the idea that only witnesses and the

---

24   Ibidem, pp. 128–137 and 175. Thäle here cited Henke who in a treatise on the history of the criminal law (1809) criticized the simple replacement of security measures for extraordinary punishments: "Kann den der bloße Name in der Sache etwas andern? Sind die von der Polizei zu verfügenden Maßregeln weniger Strafen, weil sie Bloß den Namen Sicherungsmittel führen? – Beruhen nicht diese Sicherungsmittel auf demselben Prinzip, wie die so verabscheute Tortur?".

25   K. Michels, *Der Indizienbeweis in Übergang vom Inquisitionsprozess zum reformierten Strafverfahren*, pp. 89–90.

confession were capable of creating certainty and that they were qualitatively different from indicia.[26]

5.2.2 The Legislative Changes

Characteristic of the relatively conservative character of the German debate and the difficulty of finding a replacement for judicial torture were the developments in Prussia. The first and most famous abolition of judicial torture in the German territories occurred in Prussia under the direct command of Frederick the Great. Shortly after his ascension to the thrown in 1740, he forbade the use of torture in an ordonnance leaving just a few exceptions. In further ordonnances in 1754 and 1756 he entirely abolished judicial torture. This significant leap of Frederick the Great, taken against the advice of his cabinet and the common opinion of Prussian jurists, also directly showed the problem which arose with the removal of one of the pillars of the system of legal proofs. It was the central problem in the period between 1750 and the 1810s: if torture was to be abolished what would then be done in the situation where strong evidence short of a full proof existed against the accused? Frederick the Great gave a radical and pragmatic answer to this question. He stated that 'when such strong indicia existed against the accused that he should be held for completely convinced and nothing seemed to be missing but the confession', the ordinary punishment should be applied '*as if* a confession was present'. This shows that Frederick the Great was still so strongly tied to the old evidentiary system that he felt the need to make use of the fiction that a confession was present under these circumstances. When the indicia created a strong suspicion but they did not yet completely 'convince the accused', a lighter extraordinary punishment should be applied.[27] In short, Frederick the Great was aware of the lacuna that the abolition of torture would create and therefore at the same time enabled the possibility to convict to the full, even capital, punishment on the basis of indicia.

The measures of Frederick the Great represented an extraordinary step which suddenly created a far more free evaluation of the evidence. He did not ground this freedom of evaluation on any theoretical footing or, for example, explicitly gave a central place to the internal conviction of the judge. He just created a large factual freedom for the criminal judge by making it possible to

---

26 Ibidem, pp. 98–103. The inconsistency in Mittermaier's view becomes apparent when he remarks in his handbook that indicia can create such a high degree of probability that this de facto equals certainty. Here he acknowledges that certainty is only gradually different from a high probability which could be brought about by indicia, but he did not further elaborate on when indicia could be so strong that they de facto created certainty.

27 M. Schmoeckel, *Humanität und Staatsraison*, pp. 19–49.

convict to the ordinary punishment on the basis of indicia. Michels states that the Prussian jurists were still too accustomed to the system of legal proof as it was developed in the CCC and by Carpzov and Boehmer, to really accept this solution. Precisely because there was no new theoretical foundation for the free evaluation of the judge and because the distrust of the Prussian jurists against indicia had not subsided, Frederick the Great eventually saw himself forced to take a step back and to abolish the possibility to convict to the ordinary punishment on the basis of indicia. He did so in an ordonnance in 1776 which read: "In Criminalfällen, wenn kein vollkommener Beweis wider den Angeschuldigten vorhanden ist, muss niemals aus bloßen Anzeigen, wenn sie auch noch so dringend erscheinen, auf die ordentliche Strafe, sondern auf temporäres Gefängnis nach Befinden der Umstände erkannt werden".[28]

The continued attachment to the system of legal proofs and the limited willingness to reform the criminal law of evidence is also still visible in the criminal legislation of the early nineteenth century. Within the timespan of ten years, the three most important states in the German realm acquired new criminal legislations: Austria in 1803, Prussia in 1805 and Bavaria in 1813. These legislations all held tight to the secret, inquisitorial procedure and the system of legal proofs and would remain in force until the 1840s.

The Austrian legislation was one of the first that allowed convictions to the ordinary punishment on the basis of a complexly regulated system of indicia. While the legislation made it possible to prove who committed the crime by indicia, it was not entirely clear whether the *corpus delicti* could also be proven by indicia alone. To prove who the culprit was through indicia, the legislation gave the very strict standard that 'after the normal and natural course of events it was impossible to believe that anyone other than the accused was the culprit'. This demand was explicated in further rules which regulated what kind of indicia were at least necessary for a conviction. Concerning crimes other than murder and assault (which contained a special regulation), the legislation required that the way of living of the accused made him appear as someone who could be expected to have committed the crime, and that at least two other indicia were present from the list of indicia enumerated in the legislation. Only under these restrictive circumstances could an ordinary punishment be pronounced on the basis of indicia. The remaining distrust of indicia is also visible in the rule that the punishment on the basis of indicia could not exceed twenty

---

28   K. Michels, *Der Indizienbeweis in Übergang vom Inquisitionsprozess zum reformierten Strafverfahren*, pp. 109–110.

years of imprisonment and that a capital punishment was not allowed on the basis of indicia.[29]

The ordinance of 1805 was the first extensive criminal codification for Prussia and remained very conservative in the regulation of the criminal law of evidence. The ordinary punishment could solely be pronounced on the basis of a confession or two eyewitnesses. Against an accused who remained silent under questioning or who was evidently lying, *Ungehorsamsstrafe* could be applied to persuade the accused to speak the truth. Indicia could not suffice for an ordinary punishment. It was left to the careful scrutiny and evaluation of the judge whether he deemed the indicia sufficiently strong for an extraordinary punishment.[30] Importantly, the relevant articles of the Prussian code dictated that the severity of the extraordinary punishment depended on the seriousness of the crime, the level of suspicion and the reputation of the accused:

> Bei Bestimmung einer außerordentlichen Strafe muss der Richter nicht allein auf die Größe des Verbrechens und der darauf bestimmten ordentlichen Strafe, sondern zugleich auf das Gewicht der gegen den Angeschuldigten vorhandenen Beweise, je nachdem sie der vollständigen Ueberführung sich mehr oder weniger nähern, ganz besonders aber auf den Charakter und die bisherige Lebensart des Angeschuldigten sorgfältig Rücksicht nehmen.[31]

More progressive was the criminal codification of Bavaria in 1813, of which Feuerbach was the main author. Like the other ordinances, it was still strongly directed towards obtaining a confession and allowed *Ungehorssamsstrafe*.

---

29 Ibidem, pp. 116–120.
30 Ibidem, pp. 120–123.
31 E. Landsberg, *Die Gutachten der Rheinischen Immediat-Justiz Kommission*, pp. 144–145. The requirement in the Prussian and Austrian legislation that the accused needed to have a bad reputation or that 'the way of living of the accused made him appear as someone who could be trusted to have committed the crime', was a circumstance which was still given a lot of weight in the regulation of indicia. This is not surprising considering the role that the social standing or *Leumund* had always played within the system of legal proofs. The Austrian and Prussian legislation reveal the continuing importance of the reputation of the accused in the criminal law of evidence. This importance can, for example, also be seen in the concept criminal ordinance made by Kleinschrod for Bavaria in 1802. Article 1990 made the strength of indicia generally dependent on the character of the accused: "Anzeigungen können nur dann einen bedeutenden Grad von Wahrscheinlichkeit bewirken, wenn derjenige, die sie betreffen, ein solcher Mensch ist, auf den Verdacht dieses Verbrechen mit Grunde fallen kann". See G.A. Kleinschrod, *Entwurf eines peinlichen Gesetzbuches*, p. 314.

Similar to the ordinance of Austria, the Bavarian legislation made it possible to convict to the ordinary punishment on the basis of indicia, excluding the death penalty.[32] It did not leave the judge free in the evaluation of the strength of indicia, but instead contained a detailed regulation of indicia. Multiple indicia needed to combine in such a way that 'after the normal course of events it could not be otherwise than that the crime was committed and that the accused was the culprit'. The Bavarian codification took an important step towards the recognition of indicia as a sufficient form of evidence to support an ordinary punishment. The remaining distrust of this form of evidence and of the greater freedom of evaluation for the judge which it might create are, nevertheless, evident in the detailed regulation of indicia and in the fact that the capital punishment was still not permitted on the basis of indicia. Because of the generally innovative character of the Bavarian legislation, which more closely aligned with the general opinion in the juridical literature, it became an important role model for many German states in the first decades of the nineteenth century.[33]

5.2.3   *Conclusion and Different Perspectives*

In this section it has been described that even with a growing consensus to abolish judicial torture, the mainstream of the German authors remained firmly attached to the system of legal proofs. The conservative authors wanted to change as little as possible and preferred to fill the void left by the abolition of judicial torture with an increased use of extraordinary punishment and measures such as *Lügenstrafe* and *Ungehorssamsstrafe*. The more progressive authors opted for the possibility to convict to the ordinary punishment on the basis of indicia. Nonetheless, even the progressive side was still very suspicious of indicia and generally held it for a less certain form of evidence than witness testimony or the confession. They only wanted to allow convictions on the basis of indicia in relatively exceptional cases and within a legal framework which prescribed for the judge when sufficient indicia were present.

In the beginning of this section, Ignor has been cited who stated that in the eighteenth century many authors had adopted a probabilistic conception of the truth, and that this placed dogmatic explosives under the system of legal proofs in the long term. During the first phase, however, the new probabilistic conception did not yet lead to any demands for fundamental reforms.

---

32   C. Blusch, *Das Bayerische Strafverfahrensrecht von 1813*, pp. 101–129.
33   K. Michels, *Der Indizienbeweis in Übergang vom Inquisitionsprozess zum reformierten Strafverfahren*, pp. 124–127.

The reason was that most German authors in this period believed that the high probability necessary for a conviction could and should be regulated in general objective rules. Even though many German authors now stated that in criminal cases – as in general in human affairs – no 'mathematical certainty' could be reached but only 'moral certainty', they either did not tie this moral certainty to the internal conviction of the judge or they stated that the subjective or moral conviction of the judge alone was not sufficient and that 'juridical certainty' was necessary. The former had a more objective understanding of moral certainty and filled in the concept of moral certainty with the existing evidentiary criteria, while the latter distinguished between moral certainty and juridical certainty.

The prevailing idea that the necessary high probability or 'moral certainty' could be captured in general objective rules can be seen clearly in the work of Globig and Huster. They took the 'principle of probability' as their starting point and stated that moral certainty was necessary for a conviction. However, in their view, this moral certainty was not dependent on the subjective conviction of the judge but followed general objective rules. Even for the complex matter of indicia they proposed that general rules could and should pre-establish when a sufficiently high probability was reached for a conviction.

There were also authors who distinguished between juridical certainty and moral certainty. Juridical certainty was the certainty which existed when the pre-established legal evidentiary criteria were met. Moral certainty was only the high degree of probability which normally convinced people and on the basis of which they made their decisions. This distinction was used to emphasize that moral certainty alone was insufficient for an ordinary punishment and that the more 'objective' juridical certainty, defined by the rules of the system of legal proofs, was necessary. A lighter, extraordinary punishment could be pronounced when only moral certainty existed. In this manner Kleinschrod had, for example, argued that the ordinary punishment should be pronounced on the basis of a full juridical proof, while an extraordinary punishment or a *bürgerliche Strafe* for small crimes could already be given when there was a mere moral certainty.[34]

The mainstream of authors, in short, started to use a new probabilistic terminology in the eighteenth century but filled in this concept with the objective general rules of the system of legal proofs. Nevertheless, there were also a few authors in the late eighteenth century who more fundamentally questioned

---

34   B. Thäle, *Die Verdachtsstrafe in der kriminalwissenschaftlichen Literatur des 18. und 19. Jahrhunderts*, pp. 51–54.

the system of legal proofs. The innovative character of their work can best be seen in their conception of the certainty which needed to be attained in criminal cases and in their ideas for procedural reform. There were only a few German authors who argued that the moral certainty necessary in the individual case could not be regulated in general rules and who made the existence of moral certainty dependent on the internal conviction of the judge. One of them was Von Justi. In a treatise in 1760 he stated that the certainty which was necessary to prove the *corpus delicti* was nothing other than "die volkommene Überzeugung des Richters, dass eine Missethat wahrhaftig geschehen sei".[35] From this idea Von Justi argued that the judge should make free use of indicia, and that the criterion for the certainty necessary in a criminal case should lie in the complete personal conviction of the judge.[36]

In 1792 Soden made a similar point in his *Geist der peinlichen Gesetzgebung Teutschlands*. He stated that all the categorizations in half proof, full proof and more than a half proof were useless distinctions. The proof of a crime was nothing else than the "Überzeugung, dass eine strafbare Handlung von einem bestimmten Individuum begangen sey".[37] Only the reason of the judge could guide him to see if in the individual case that level of certainty was acquired – "die Stufe der Überzeugung erricht sey" – that excluded the possibility that the accused was innocent.[38] The opinions of Von Justi and Soden were, however, minority opinions which found little resonance in the German territories in this period.

The ideas of Von Justi and Soden do show great parallels to the work of Beccaria, Filangieri and that of the French 'philosophes', and were a harbinger of things to come.[39] In the work of Von Justi and Soden a crucial step can be seen wherein the main criterion for the existence of moral certainty was to be found in the (subjective) conviction of the judge. For these authors moral certainty existed when the judge was 'morally convinced'. During the first phase the mainstream of German authors still filled the concept of moral certainty with the existing system of 'objective' evidentiary rules. As will be described in the

---

35 A.M. Ignor, *Geschichte Strafprozess*, p. 168.
36 K. Michels, *Der Indizienbeweis in Übergang vom Inquisitionsprozess zum reformierten Strafverfahren*, pp. 49–50.
37 A.M. Ignor, *Geschichte Strafprozess*, p. 187.
38 Ibidem, p. 187.
39 Unlike Beccaria and many of the French authors, however, Filangieri argued that there should also be minimum evidentiary standards for a conviction and that the internal conviction of the judge alone was not sufficient to convict someone. Filangieri argued for what later would be called a negative system of legal proofs. See G. Filangieri, *La scienza della legislazione*, Book III, Chapter 13, pp. 96–103.

following section, however, during the second phase the internal conviction was given an increasingly more central place within the criminal law of evidence. Like Filangieri, most German authors wanted to retain certain minimum evidentiary standards as a guarantee against judicial arbitrariness and now opted for a negative system of legal proofs. In effect, through the negative system of legal proofs the internal conviction of the judge became one of the two central pillars of the criminal law of evidence.[40]

5.3 The German Discussion between 1812 and 1848

During the second phase the foundations were laid for the *reformierte Strafprozess*. Eventually, in the late 1840s a large part of the professional jurists argued for the introduction of a public, oral trial with a public prosecutor and the free evaluation of the evidence by either professional judges or lay jurors. The reforms of 1848 were not just a sudden reception of the French reform ideals in a revolutionary period in Germany. It was the fruit of a long process of contemplating and discussing the French reform ideals and the existing system of legal proofs. The rather complex development of the German discussion during the second phase will be treated in this section in four subsections. The first subsection describes the development of the debate between 1812 and 1820. In this period the first important reflections occurred on the French revolutionary reforms and the first works appeared discussing the jury system and the free evaluation of the evidence.

The second subsection describes the period from roughly 1820 until 1840. In this period two groups dominated the discussion: those in favour of the jury system and those in favour of a negative system of legal proofs with professional judges. The third subsection focuses on the developments in the juridical literature in the 1840s. In this period for the first time proponents of the free evaluation of the evidence by professional judges emerged. In the first three subsections the discussion on the criminal law of evidence is treated in relative isolation from the political background and the overarching criminal procedural context. Finally, in the fourth subsection the connection between

---

40   During the first phase there was virtually no author that argued for the introduction of a jury system in Germany. There was, however, one exception in the form of Justus Möser (1720–1794) in his *Patriotischen Phantasien* (1774–1786). His work, nonetheless found little resonance in the German territories in this period. See N. Lieber, *Schöffengericht und Trial by Jury*, pp. 139–140.

the criminal law of evidence and the political and procedural context will be described, and how the reforms were eventually given shape during the revolutionary period of 1848 and 1849.

5.3.1 *The First Reflections on the Jury System 1812–1820*

The second decade of the nineteenth century saw the appearance of two important works on the jury system, which, to a large extent, shaped the discussion in the German territories in the following thirty years. One work was Feuerbach's *Betrachtungen über das Geschworenengericht* (1812), which was the first extensive treatise on the jury system in the German territories. The second work was the report of a committee called *Der Rheinischen Immediat-Justiz-Kommission* (1819), which was given the task to investigate whether the French criminal procedural law should remain in force in the Prussian territories on the left-bank of the Rhine. Although Feuerbach was not principally opposed to a jury system, his highly critical treatment of especially the French version of the jury system provided many arguments against the jury system in general. The opponents of the jury system would, in the following decades, take over many of his ideas in their argumentation against a jury system.[41]

5.3.1.1 Feuerbach

Feuerbach argued that in considering the merits of a jury system two viewpoints needed to be strictly separated: the political perspective and the 'technical' perspective of the criminal law. This was a distinction which would be followed by many later authors. From a political perspective, Feuerbach argued that the jury system was an important guarantee for civil liberty in democratic and 'constitutional' states, but not in states where the sovereignty rested exclusively in the monarch. According to Feuerbach, the essence of a democratic state demanded that representatives of the people decided in criminal cases and not professional judges. In the constitutional or 'mixed' state – which Feuerbach saw as a state based on Montesquieu's principle of a separation of powers where the sovereignty was shared between the monarch and one or more representative organs – the jury was necessary to guarantee an objective judiciary. Feuerbach explained that in the German states, where in his conception mostly absolute monarchies existed, the jury system did not fit in the political system. All the sovereignty rested with the monarch and the jury system could not provide any real protection against his will. Feuerbach argued that in

---

41 E. Schwinge, *Der Kampf um die Schwurgerichte bis zur Frankfurter Nationalversammlung*, pp. 6–10.

the monarchical state, independent professional judges who were appointed for life were a more appropriate solution because they could better safeguard civil liberty than jurors.[42]

Feuerbach subsequently gave a very critical evaluation of the juridical-technical aspect of the jury system which focused on the way it was given shape in France. His two main criticisms were directed against the typically French idea that a strict separation could be made between the question of fact and the question of law, and against the French conception of the *conviction intime*. The presupposition that the questions of fact and of law could easily be distinguished was instrumental in the idea of the French reformers that a strict separation of powers could be realised within the criminal procedure. Supposedly, the jurors would decide on the question of fact using their common sense and then the professional judge would simply subsume the proven facts under a certain criminal law and apply the correct punishment. Feuerbach did not agree with this view and argued that a clear separation between the question of fact and the question of law was impossible to make. The question of 'guilty or not-guilty' was principally a mixed question. The jury was always asked whether they deemed a fact proven which fell under a certain legal prescription. This meant that the jury decided on the veracity of the facts and at the same time they had to interpret the meaning of juridical terms. Feuerbach was the first to sharply and convincingly argue that the distinction between the question of fact and the question of law was, therefore, largely illusory. This provided an important argument against the jury system, because it was highly questionable whether untrained lay jurors had the necessary knowledge to deal with these technical juridical questions.[43]

Feuerbach was, furthermore, very critical of the French conception of the *conviction intime*. As has been described in the previous chapter, several French revolutionaries described the formation of the internal conviction as the result of an 'unreasoned process of feeling the truth', and not as a reasoned process of weighing and analysing the evidence. Feuerbach criticized the idea that laymen had an 'instinct' to feel the truth, which automatically and unconsciously worked as the evidence was presented to them during an oral and public trial. He was highly sceptical of this kind of truth finding and argued that it did not give any guarantees for its veracity: "auch die lebendigste innigste Überzeu-

---

42 P.J.A. Feuerbach, *Betrachtungen über das Geschworenengericht*, pp. 47–80.
43 Ibidem, pp. 167–178. See also E. Schwinge, *Der Kampf um die Schwurgerichte bis zur Frankfurter Nationalversammlung*, pp. 8–14.

gung, werde diese von noch so vielen Personen geteilt, ist darum keine Bürgschaft für ihre Wahrheit und Richtigkeit".[44] Instead of the French idea of a passive instinct for the truth, Feuerbach explained the distinction between the way in which the 'juridical-technical' evaluation by professional judges worked from how the lay evaluation of the evidence worked in the following way:

> Bei jenem ist sich der Verstand seiner Gründe bewusst, nicht bei diesem. Hier urtheilt und schließt das Gemüht wie dort, bedient sich derselben Mittel, derselbe Materialien, um daraus seine Ueberzeugung zu bauen; aber er beobachtet nicht sein eigenes Thun, sieht nicht den Weg, den es nimmt, findet sich beim Resultate, ohne bestimmt zu wissen, wie? Fühlt sich durch Ueberzeugung gebunden, ohne zu wissen, warum? Das wissenschaftlichen gelehrte erkennen hingegen, geht von deutlicher Erkenntnis des Allgemeinen aus und findet aus dem Allgemeinen das Besondere ... Die Erkenntnis des gemeinen Verstandes kommt übrigens mit dem Antriebe eines Instinctes allerdings darin überein, dass so wie sich dieser seines Wirkens nicht bewusst ist, so auch nicht jene des ihrigen.[45]

Through his argumentation – and his distinction between 'juridical-technical' and 'lay evaluation' – Feuerbach helped to spread the idea that there was a fundamental difference between the decision of jurors who were unconscious of how their own conviction came about, and professional judges who decided according to a conscious analysis and process of reasoning. He gave the impression that a choice had to be made between either jurors who judged by their freely formed conviction or professional judges who were bound by rules of evidence. Jurors supposedly could not work with rules of evidence and it was too dangerous to let professional judges decide without evidentiary rules. This dichotomized view, to which Feuerbach contributed, would dominate the discussion for the coming decades and was shared by the proponents as well as the opponents of a jury system.[46]

Importantly, Feuerbach did acknowledge the argument of the French reformers that evidentiary rules could never prescribe when that degree of probability existed which would create a moral certainty for the judge of the guilt of the accused in the individual case.[47] He, therefore, stated that it was wrong for

---

44   P.J.A. Feuerbach, *Betrachtungen über das Geschworenengericht*, p. 135.
45   Ibidem, pp. 122–123.
46   E. Schwinge, *Der Kampf um die Schwurgerichte bis zur Frankfurter Nationalversammlung*, pp. 17–18.
47   Feuerbach agreed with the French reformers that the necessary truth in criminal cases could only consist of a high degree of probability and that this could not be regulated in

the lawmaker who tried to create general rules which precisely determined when the necessary level of certainty existed under which the judge had to convict. However, the lawmaker could create general rules which prescribed a *minimum* standard of evidence which was necessary so that the judge did not solely follow his internal conviction:

> Die Beweistheorie eines Gesetzgebers, der von diese Gedanken ausgeht, wird daher mehr negative, als positive seyn; wird nicht sowohl bestimmen wo die Ueberzeugung zu suchen, als vielmehr wo sie nicht zu suchen ist; wird nicht an nakte allgemeine Regeln die Ueberzeugung binden und jene unbedingt von Gesetzeswegen gebieten, sondern innerhalb der sehr weiten Grenzen, welche das Gebiet der Wahrheit umschließen, dem eigenen Urtheil des Richters seinen gemessenen Spielraum lassen.[48]

The judge should only have to convict when he was internally convinced of the guilt and when the minimum evidentiary requirements were met. The minimum evidentiary standards would create at least some guarantee that the judge did not follow a too easily acquired internal conviction. The idea of Feuerbach that minimum evidentiary standards should be created clearly derived from the insight that the level of probability which was necessary in the individual case could not be determined in general rules and in the end needed to be left to the internal conviction of the judge. Feuerbach was the first to call this constellation – which was very similar to the ideas of Filangieri – a 'negative system of legal proofs'. He acknowledged that beside fulfilling the minimum evidentiary requirements, the internal conviction of the judge was necessary for a conviction. In the following decades this idea of a negative

---

general rules: "Jede Historische Gewissheit, so wie die moralische, nach welcher wir über menschliche Handlungen entscheiden, *ist wie sie sehr richtig bemerken*, zuletzt aus bloßen Elementen der Wahrscheinlichkeit zusammengesetzt ... Zwar giebt es eine Wissenschaft des Wahrscheinlichen ... [aber] es giebt keine Wissenschaft, welche die Elemente der Gewissheit auch nur einfach, geschweige in ihren Mischungen und unendlichen Zusammensetzungen darstellen, und im Allgemeinen bestimmen könnte, wo die Gewissheit, wo die Wahrscheinlichkeit zu finden [ist]". Characteristic of Feuerbach's rhetoric was his conclusion that "Im Voraus die Beweise und die Kraft bestimmen, welche sie für den Verstand des Richters haben sollen, ist nicht vernünftiger als der Plan, den Ozean der Natur in einen Eimer zu fassen. Solche Gesetze sagen immer zu wenig und zu viel, sind entweder zu eng oder zu weit". See P.J.A. Feuerbach, *Betrachtungen über das Geschworenengericht*, pp. 123–126.

48 P.J.A. Feuerbach, *Betrachtungen über das Geschworenengericht*, pp. 123–133.

system of legal proofs became widely supported by the opponents of a jury system in the German territories.[49]

5.3.1.2 Der Rheinischen Immediat-Justiz-Kommission

After Feuerbach, the second significant work concerning the criminal law of evidence was the report from the *Rheinischen Immediat-Justiz-Kommission*. The report was written because the Prussian minister of Justice, Von Kircheisen, wanted to replace the French legislation with Prussian law in the newly acquired territories on the left-bank of the Rhine. Due to the opposition from the Rhine provinces it was decided that a committee would research whether the Prussian legislation should be introduced there. After two years the committee presented its report and recommended to let the French legislation remain in force at least until the Prussian legislation would be reformed. The committee, which also contained Prussian members, had in the meantime become very positive about the jury system after their inspection of the French legislation. Their argumentation in the report focused on the juridical-technical aspects and in many instances sought to refute the criticisms of Feuerbach against the jury system. Aware of the fact that the Prussian government saw the French procedural system as the result of revolutionary ideas, the committee downplayed the political importance of the jury system. They, nevertheless, also attempted to refute the political-constitutional idea of Feuerbach that the jury system could not function under a monarchy. A further significant non-technical argument that they presented for a jury system was that, unlike professional judges, the jury system had the trust of the people in the Rhine provinces.[50]

The two most important 'juridical-technical' arguments in the report were directed against the usefulness of the system of legal proofs in general, and against the doubts cast by Feuerbach on the question whether jurors were capable of evaluating the question of fact. Regarding the latter, the committee agreed with Feuerbach that, to a certain extent, questions of fact could not be separated entirely from questions of law. However, when the laws were formulated clearly and in the vernacular, jurors should be (more than) capable to apply them on the basis of their normal common sense. Feuerbach had had too little confidence in the capabilities of jurors. Subsequently, the committee stated that lay jurors were often even more suited than professional judges to

---

49   W. Küper, *Die Richteridee der Strafprozessordnung und ihre geschichtlichen Grundlagen*, pp. 139–142.
50   E. Schwinge, *Der Kampf um die Schwurgerichte bis zur Frankfurter Nationalversammlung*, pp. 19–27.

decide on questions of fact because they were better able to understand the vicissitudes of everyday life than the learned judge. The jurors did not have the unavoidable prejudices of a criminal judge who, through constant practice, would acquire a habit to find more evidence for the guilt than for the innocence of the accused. Furthermore, the committee remarked that it was unjust if citizens would be convicted on the basis of laws and for crimes which they themselves could not understand. According to the committee, the best proof that the accused should be able to understand the criminal law would lie in the fact that twelve of his peers are able to convict him on the basis of these laws.[51]

The significance of epistemological ideas for the reform of the criminal law of evidence becomes can be seen well in the report of the Prussian committee. The report started with a philosophical-theoretical explanation of why the system of legal proofs was untenable and why the free evaluation of the evidence was preferable. The committee denied that there was a qualitative difference between indicia, eyewitnesses or a confession. They all had the same effect and could only constitute differing degrees of probability, never a complete certainty. Every historical proof formed merely a 'Kette von Vermuthungen' (a chain of probable inferences), which is in the end always dependent on and constituted by the concrete evaluation of the judge. From all forms of evidence probable conclusions still needed to be drawn so that the distinction between indirect and direct forms of evidence was based on thin air. The committee denied that it was possible to determine the level of certainty necessary for a conviction in *a priori* evidentiary rules. They stated that the decision whether certain facts were proven in a criminal case solely rests on a 'historische Überzeugung', which was based on probable elements. Mathematical demonstrability could never be reached. For this reason they stated that only the internal conviction of the judge or jurors – which was based on probable conclusions drawn from the existing evidence – could form the foundation for a conviction. A further important deficit of the system was legal proofs was that it could never do justice to the concrete circumstances of a criminal case. According to the committee, because there are an endless variety of different facts which can create differing degrees of probability, it was impossible to predetermine the force of different forms of evidence in abstract rules. The 'historische Überzeugung' could always only be the result of an individual evaluation of the particular facts.[52]

According to the committee, a system of evidentiary rules was merely obstructive in the process of truth finding and did not effectively bind the judge

---

[51] Ibidem, pp. 24–30.
[52] E. Landsberg, *Die Gutachten der Rheinischen Immediat-Justiz Kommission*, pp. 122–144.

because even evidentiary rules eventually always relied on the evaluation of the judge and his internal conviction. The question, for example, whether a confession or the testimony of a witness was reliable and if it sufficiently proved the crime always depended on the internal conviction of the judge. The guarantee against arbitrariness which the system of legal proofs supposedly provided was, therefore, illusory. The system of legal proofs was built on the mistaken presupposition that evidentiary rules could in general prescribe when sufficient certainty existed for a conviction as if they were mathematical formulas. The committee also criticized Feuerbach's idea of a negative evidentiary system. They stated that it was a half measure and that it was contradictory to on the one hand give such a central role to the internal conviction of the judge, but on the other hand still distrust the judge so strongly that he needed to be bound by minimum evidentiary standards. The committee did agree with Feuerbach that only jurors and not professional judges could be trusted enough to judge after their freely formed internal conviction.[53]

Importantly, like Feuerbach, the committee contributed to the idea that there was a fundamental difference between the way lay jurors and professional judges decided on the evidentiary question. In the view of the committee, the judge who was bound by the system of legal proofs worked in an analytical manner. He had to consciously individualize the different forms of evidence and then categorize them according to the objective rules. The lay juror, deciding after his internal conviction, did not work in this way and did not atomize the different forms of evidence in front of him. In a more unconscious manner, the interplay of all the forms of evidence presented in a public, oral trial, would constitute in the mind of the juror a *Totaleindruck* or *Totalanschauung*. The orality or 'immediacy' of the presentation of the evidence was deemed a necessary prerequisite for a jury system, because the jurors needed to get a direct and complete impression of the accused, the witnesses and the other forms of evidence. Supposedly, the *Totaleindruck*, and thereby the internal conviction, of a juror was formed by an 'unmittelbare Sinnesanschauung' of all the different forms of evidence during the trial, while a judge rationally reflected on the individual forms of evidence presented to him in writing. The committee emphasized that for judging on the basis of this *Totaleindruck* no special juridical knowledge was necessary, only a normal common sense.[54]

The idea that lay jurors decided on the basis of an internal conviction formed by an unreasoned *Totaleindruck*, became a commonly held view in the

---

53   Ibidem, pp. 130–144.
54   P. Landau, "Schwurgerichte und Schöffengerichte in Deutschland im 19. Jahrhundert bis 1870", pp. 281–282.

juridical discussion in the following three decades among proponents as well as opponents of the jury system.[55] Even though this German idea of a *Totaleindruck* emphasized less than the French idea of the *conviction intime* the element of a 'feeling' or instinct for the truth, it also saw the formation of the internal conviction as a largely unreasoned process of which the jurors could give no rational account. This German view of how the jury system functioned was clearly inspired by and showed strong similarities to the French idea of the *conviction intime*. As Glaser stated – although there were nuances –, in the German as well as in the French conception there was a tendency to understand the internal conviction as "einer orakelhaften moralischen Überzeugung".[56] Schwinge cites the view of Zentner in a treatise, published in 1834, which very well exemplifies this idea of the *Totaleindruck*. Zentner stated on jurors that:

> der gemeine gesunde Menschenverstand findet die Wahrheit nicht, wie der wissenschaftlich gebildete verstand, durch Zergliederung und Vereinzelung der Begriffe; sie offenbart sich ihm durch den unmittelbaren Eindruck der äußeren Gegenstände, der Verhandlungen auf sein Gefühl, dessen Reinheit und Richtigkeit ihm in der Evidenz stärkere Gewissheit gewährt, als dem wissenschaftlich Gebildeten die Prüfung jedes einzelnen Momentes an den abstrakten Regeln der Schule und der Theorie. Der einfache, natürliche Verstand, verbunden mit dem unverbildeten Gefühl, fasst das Ganze richtiger in der Totalanschauung auf, als in einzelnen, zersplitterten, ihm besonders vorgehaltenen Punkten, weil er die Handlungen leichter und besser versteht, als die abgezogenen Begriffe.[57]

Lastly, an important conclusion of the committee was that extraordinary punishments and alternatives such as 'security measures' should be entirely abolished. Either the jury was convinced that the accused was guilty and he should be punished with the ordinary punishment or the jury was not convinced and the accused should be acquitted. There should be no middle way.[58] The internal conviction hereby became the sole and definitive criterion for the question whether someone was guilty or not. In the view of the committee, there should be no more gradations in between which could justify an *absolutio ab instantia* or an extraordinary punishment.

---

55   E. Schwinge, *Der Kampf um die Schwurgerichte bis zur Frankfurter Nationalversammlung*, pp. 85–87.
56   J. Glaser, *Beiträge zur Lehre vom Beweis im Strafprozess*, pp. 17–20.
57   E. Schwinge, *Der Kampf um die Schwurgerichte bis zur Frankfurter Nationalversammlung*, pp. 85–87.
58   E. Landsberg, *Die Gutachten der Rheinischen Immediat-Justiz Kommission*, pp. 144–169.

5.3.2 *The Discussion on the Criminal Law of Evidence between 1820 and 1840*

The work of Feuerbach and the report of the committee shaped the contours of the discussion in the following decades in a significant manner. They helped create the dominant view that there was a qualitative difference in the way that lay jurors and professional judges evaluated the evidence. Jurors supposedly decided on the basis of their *Totaleindruck* in a manner which could not be rationally construed, while judges as trained jurists reasoned in an analytical way whereby they individualized the different forms of evidence and fit them into general evidentiary categories. This idea of a qualitative difference inspired the strongly dichotomized view in the following decades that it was a choice of either-or. The discussion between 1820 and 1840 became dominated by the proponents of a jury system on one side and the proponents of a negative system of legal proofs in combination with professional judges on the other side. Supposedly the free evaluation of the evidence could only coexist with a jury system and evidentiary rules only with professional judges. In his *Betrachtungen über die Öffentlichkeit und Mundlichkeit der Gerechtigkeitspflege* (1821–1825), Feuerbach further contributed to this idea and warned for the danger that if the evidentiary rules would be abolished, the judge would necessarily start to act as a juror who gave his judgment on the basis of his *Totaleindruck* without motivation or the possibility of appeal. This, he stated, was a very dangerous situation for civil liberty.[59]

5.3.2.1 The Supporters of a Jury System

After the works of Feuerbach and the report of the Prussian committee, in a short time until 1825 a large number of treatises and articles were published on the question whether a jury system should be introduced. Then the interest subsided for some time until in the late 1830s the question returned to the centre of attention again. In the period between 1820 and 1840, two main groups can be distinguished who most ardently pleaded for the introduction of a jury system. Firstly there was the group that can be described as the 'constitutional-liberals' who wanted a jury system on the basis of predominantly political-constitutional motives. Secondly, there was the group of Hegel and his followers who pleaded for a jury system on the basis of his philosophical ideas.

---

59   P.J.A. Feuerbach, *Öffentlichtkeit und Mundlichkeit*, p. 76. He also remarked that this situation existed in the Netherlands and in the French lower criminal courts: "da ist, soweit solche Einrichtung reicht, nichts anderes zu finden als die Justiz der Willkür".

The authors belonging to the first group argued for a jury system following the political ideals of the French reformers. This group of 'liberals' wanted the jury system on the basis of essentially two reasons. Firstly, it would create a division of power within the criminal procedure and would thereby diminish the possibility of judicial arbitrariness. This was especially desirable because, unlike professional judges, jurors could be trusted to be impartial and unbiased. Secondly, a jury system would create an element of democratic or popular representation in the judicial system. The people would judge themselves. Besides these political-constitutional motives, the liberals used the substantive criticisms against the system of legal proofs that can be found in the report of the Prussian-Rhenish committee and in the French reform literature. This group wanted a complete reform of the criminal procedural law consisting of the introduction of a jury system and a public, oral trial with a public prosecutor. They were highly critical of the secret, inquisitorial procedure and distrusted the professional judges. According to Schwinge, this group of authors was largely repetitive in their argumentation and added almost nothing new.[60] Nevertheless, throughout the second phase they formed a very important and vocal group who defended a radical reform of the criminal procedural law and offered criticisms which tore at the foundations of the system of legal proofs.

The second group demanded a jury system on the basis of Hegel's ideas. Hegel himself had argued in his *Grundlinien der Philosophie des Rechts* (1821) that a jury system was preferable, because only a jury could ensure "das Recht des Selbstbewusstseins der Partei" in a criminal trial. He was against any utilitarian conception of punishing because it made a means out of a person instead of respecting him as a rational and free human being. For this reason he did not want the accused to stand as a mere object of investigation before a professional, inquisitorial judge. An accused needed to have trust in the persons who judged him and this trust could only be based on the fact that the jurors were free men and equals of the accused. Only 'Standesgleichen' that judged the accused could guarantee "das Recht des Selbstbewusstseins der Partei". The fact that the accused trusted the jurors to decide on his fate legitimized this system, while against professional judges the accused would stand in a relationship of serfdom. Two important followers of Hegel who pleaded for the jury system were Gans and Köstlin. In general Landau states that the

---

60   E. Schwinge, *Der Kampf um die Schwurgerichte bis zur Frankfurter Nationalversammlung*, pp. 66–74.

Hegelian argumentation for a jury system found relatively little resonance.[61] Nevertheless, it provided an important legitimation to the proponents of a jury system that such an influential philosophical current seemed to support their demands.[62]

5.3.2.2   The Proponents of a Negative System of Legal Proofs 1820–1840
The vocal proponents of a jury system changed the discussion on the criminal law of evidence by providing an alternative for the system of legal proofs. This was an important new feature of the German discussion during the second phase. Many of the proponents of a jury system were politicians or journalists who desired the jury system predominantly on political-constitutional grounds (although there were also practicing jurists among them). Nevertheless, within the more 'scientific-juridical discussion' a clear majority of the authors remained against a jury system.[63] The mainstream of the German juridical authors wanted to retain some form of the system of legal proofs and continued to discuss the topics that were under discussion in the first phase between 1750 and 1812, namely, whether judges should be allowed to convict to the ordinary punishment on the basis of indicia and whether the intermediate decision types should be abolished. Even though there was some continuity in the scientific-juridical discussion between the first and the second phase, there also emerged influential new ideas which changed the understanding of the system of legal proofs.

During the period between the 1810s and 1840, three important changes occurred in the 'scientific-juridical discussion' in comparison to the discussion in the first phase. Firstly, many authors now turned decisively against the use of extraordinary punishments and the so-called 'security measures' which often amounted to the same thing (although many authors were still in favour of retaining some form of an *absolutio ab instantia*). Secondly, it was increasingly accepted that convictions to the ordinary punishment should be possible on

---

61   P. Landau, "Schwurgerichte und Schöffengerichte in Deutschland im 19. Jahrhundert bis 1870", pp. 251–254.
62   In a similar manner, the large number of treatises between 1820 and 1848 which attempted to show that historically the jury system had Germanic roots and was not a 'foreign' institution, provided additional legitimation to the proponents of a jury system. These ideas would never form the main reason for the introduction of a jury system, but they did provide a significant additional support to the political-constitutional ideals. For the German discussion on the historical origins of the jury system, see E. Schwinge, *Der Kampf um die Schwurgerichte bis zur Frankfurter Nationalversammlung*, pp. 38–43 and 92–9
63   Ibidem, pp. 66–74.

the basis of indicia. Thirdly, a majority of the authors became in favour of what was now described as a 'negative system of legal proofs'. It was argued by most authors that a positive system of evidentiary rules was untenable – among other reasons because the endless possible variety of indicia could not be adequately regulated – and that in the end the question whether sufficient evidence existed in the concrete case should be left to the internal conviction of the judge. The conviction of the judge thereby became a central and constitutive requirement to convict someone while at the same it was argued that the evidentiary rules should be understood only as minimum evidentiary requirements. This constituted a highly important reinterpretation of the system of legal proofs.

The presupposition that there was a fundamental difference in the way jurors and professional judges operated, remained the dominant view in the 1820s and 1830s among proponents of a negative system of legal proofs as well as proponents of a jury system. However, this period also saw the emergence of a different understanding of the system of legal proofs and the jury system which challenged this dichotomy. In several influential treatises, a view started to be espoused which showed that there was in fact no essential difference in the way a judge or juror decided on the evidentiary question. Through this new understanding the gap which was perceived between a jury system and professional judges would eventually become smaller and smaller. A significant break-through in the idea that the judge and jurors actually decided on the evidentiary question in a very similar manner can be found in the works of Jarcke and Mittermaier. Their work was also highly influential in their argumentation for a negative system of legal proofs and in undermining the idea that there was a qualitative difference between on the one hand indicia and on the other hand witness testimony and the confession.

The perceived difference between the way jurors and professional judges operated started to break down because on the one hand it was argued that jurors in fact did not decide intuitively on the basis of a *Totaleindruck*, but like judges through a rational process of evaluating the evidence. On the other hand, a fundamental criticism against the system of legal proofs began to show that in the end the decision of the professional judge also always depended on his internal conviction and not simply on an analytical application of objective evidentiary rules. While the criticisms against the system of legal proofs increased, it was at the same time becoming more accepted that the way the judge evaluated the evidence was not so different from that of a juror. Although this was at first a minority opinion it would, from the 1840s onwards, become the dominant view.

The break-through in the idea that judges and jurors actually decided in a similar manner was formed by the works of Jarcke and Mittermaier. The first important work was Jarcke's article *Bemerkungen über die Lehre vom unvollständigen Beweise* (1825). It attempted to show that, contrary to the common opinion, there was no essential difference in the way jurors and professional judges decided on the evidentiary question. Jarcke started his treatise with the question 'what is truth'. He answered this question by following Kant and stated: "Die Wahrheit liegt in der Übereinstimmung der Überzeugung des urtheilenden Subjects mit dem erkannten Objecte".[64] As Küper explains, this statement was directed at what Jarcke saw as the two wrongful conceptions of what constituted truth in criminal cases. Firstly, it was directed against the presupposition underlying the system of legal proofs that the truth lay 'in der Sache selbst'; meaning that it was something which could be known *objectively* and *independently* of the judge himself and that it could be regulated in general rules. As stated in the definition of Jarcke, there could be no truth without the conviction of the person judging. Secondly, it was also directed against the idea of the supporters of the *conviction intime* that the truth was to be found solely in the internal conviction of the judging person. Because the internal conviction was only a 'subjektiven Fürwahrhaltens', it did not in itself give a guarantee for its veracity.[65]

Then, Jarcke came to the central question: what guarantee does someone have that his internal conviction corresponds with "mit dem erkannten Objecte"? His answer was:

> Die einzige Garantie dafür kann nur in den *Gründen* liegen; sie kann namentlich nicht in der Überzeugung selbst liegen, sonst hätte der Mensch bei sich und bei Andern nur zu untersuchen, ob er oder ob der Andere überzeugt sey ... Das Prüfen und Abwägen dieser Gründe ist aber ein Geschäft der Reflexion und folglich des Verstandes.[66]

Subsequently, Jarcke denied that there existed in this matter an essential difference between jurors and professional judges:

---

64 C.E. Jarcke, "Bemerkungen über die Lehre vom unvollständigen Beweise", p. 98.
65 W. Küper, *Die Richteridee der Strafprozessordnung und ihre geschichtlichen Grundlagen*, pp. 222–223.
66 C.E. Jarcke, "Bemerkungen über die Lehre vom unvollständigen Beweise", pp. 100–103.

> Wollen die Geschworenen sich eine Überzeugung bilden, und eine Garantie für die Richtigkeit ihrer Überzeugungen haben, so stehen sie hierin ... *dem deutschen Richter ganz gleich*. Sie müssen sich der Gründe ihrer Erkenntnis bewusst werden, diese einzeln prüfen und prüfen, ob dieselben in ihrer Gesamtheit zu einem Urtheil hinreichen Dies Alles ist ein Geschäft der Reflexion, demnach können die Geschwornen also die Gewissheit, dass ihr Urtheil richtig sey, nur durch Reflexion gewinnen.[67]

To summarize, for Jarcke the only guarantee that a conviction was true, lay in the grounds for the conviction. The formation of a conviction was necessarily the consequence of a reasoned process of reflexion on the all the forms of evidence in themselves and in relation to each other. In this respect the judge and lay jurors functioned exactly the same. He argued that the system of legal proofs should be seen as forming only a group of general logical rules which guided the judge in his rational process of evaluating the evidence. For Jarcke, the question whether a sufficient certainty existed to convict someone was in the end always dependent on the internal conviction – which needed to rest on sufficient grounds – of the judge or jurors concerning the particular case.[68]

A further influential contribution to the insight that jurors and judges decided in a similar way came from Mittermaier, who by this time had become one of the most preeminent authorities on the criminal procedural law. It is striking in Mittermaier's *Lehre vom Beweise* (1834), that his language focuses not on objective qualities of the different forms of evidence and when they could form a full proof necessary for a conviction. Instead, his language concentrates far more on explaining how the evidence worked in the internal or mental process by which a judge became convinced. In the work of Mittermaier the development is particularly apparent of what Stichweh has called a *Mentalisierung des Beweisrechts*.[69] Mittermaier, for example, described how the different forms of evidence worked as "ein Kampf von Gründen für und wider eine Ansicht [in dem Gemüthe des Urtheilenden], und aus diesem

---

67 Ibidem, pp. 103–104.
68 W. Küper, *Die Richteridee der Strafprozessordnung und ihre geschichtlichen Grundlagen*, pp. 222–230.
69 R. Stichweh, "Zur Subjektivierung der Entscheidungsfindung im Deutschen Strafprozess des 19. Jahrhunderts", p. 285. Stichweh stated on this development: „Es geht nicht mehr um die Präsentation der gesetzlich festgelegten Beweismittel und die dann ausgesprochene Anerkennung (oder die Verweigerung dieser Anerkennung), dass die Beweismittel den Bedingungen der gesetzlichen Beweistheorie genügen ... Stattdessen beobachten wir eine Verschiebung der für den Beweis relevanten Bestimmungen und Unterscheidungen in den Bereich einer *Semantik mentaler Operationen*".

Kampfe entwickelt sich erst die Ueberzeugung".[70] He constantly emphasized that the strength of any form of evidence was not something which could be determined *a priori*, but was always dependent on a chain of probable inferences ('Kette von Vermuthungen') drawn by the judge in the particular case. Mittermaier, in short, treated the different forms of evidence very much in relation to the formation of an internal conviction.

Mittermaier stated that truth consisted of the correspondence of our conviction of something 'mit dem wirklichen Wesen desselben'. Like Jarcke, he argued against the idea that the truth required in criminal cases lay exclusively in the subjective conviction or that it was possible to determine in general objective rules when a sufficient certainty of a historical fact existed. The internal conviction was not something purely subjective, but rested on grounds and was therefore the result of a reasoned process: "Einen Zustand aber, in welchem unser Fürwahrhalten auf völlig befriedigenden Gründen beruht, deren wir uns bewusst sind, nennen wir Überzeugung".[71] In this respect professional judges and jurors functioned in a similar way and had to form their internal conviction on the basis of a reasoned process of weighing the evidence. He stated that it was a mistake to belief that jurors necessarily had to decide after an unreasoned subjective conviction. Even if this view underlay the French reforms, it did not belong to the essence of a jury system that jurors had to decide on the basis of a purely subjective conviction. To substantiate this claim, he also referred to the fact that the English jurors did follow a 'law of evidence', which consisted of evidentiary rules which had developed over a long time.[72]

Beside his insight that jurors and judges decided on the evidentiary question in essentially the same manner, Mittermaier also argued that there was no qualitative difference between indicia and the so-called 'direct' forms of evidence such as the confession and witness testimony. In close resemblance to the argumentation of the *Rheinischen Immediat-Justiz-Kommission*, Mittermaier stressed throughout his treatise that every form of evidence could only provide links in a chain of probable conclusions. All forms of evidence created qualitatively the same kind of certainty and indicia were, therefore, just as capable of creating a sufficiently high degree of probability as other forms of evidence. He refuted the distinction between indicia as indirect evidence, and witness testimony and the confession as direct evidence. In fact, witness

---

70 J.A. Mittermaier, *Lehre vom Beweise*, p. 60.
71 Ibidem, p. 70.
72 Ibidem, pp. 109–114. See also W. Küper, *Die Richteridee der Strafprozessordnung und ihre geschichtlichen Grundlagen*, pp. 222–224.

testimony and the confession themselves only provided indicia, because from this testimony the judge still needed to make probable conclusions concerning the question whether the testimony was trustworthy and if the testimony actually sufficiently proved the criminal fact:

> Es ist ein Irrthum zu glauben, dass die Beweismittel, durch welche wir den natürlichen Beweis begründen zu können meinen, Augenschein, Geständniss oder Zeugniss, nur auf der sinnlichen Erwiederung beruhen und für uns nun dadurch überzeugend werden, dass wir dem Zeugnisse unsrer Sinne trauen. *Es ist überall nur eine Kette von Vermuthungen, worauf wir unsere Ueberzeugung bauen.*[73]

Because it was still necessary with any form of evidence that the judge drew probable conclusions from them, the question whether sufficient evidence existed to convict someone was in the end always dependent on the conviction of the judge. The fact that with witness testimony and the confession everything in the end also depended on the reasoning and the perception of the judge, furthermore, implied that the protection that the system of legal proofs offered against judicial arbitrariness, was largely illusory.[74] For Mittermaier the

---

[73] C.J.A. Mittermaier, *Lehre vom Beweise*, pp. 402–403 and 435–437. Mittermaier, furthermore, stated against those who deemed it impossible to create a full proof from indicia: "Alle diese Gründe verlieren aber ihr Gewicht, wenn man den Irrtum der Voraussetzungen, von welchen die Gegner ausgehen, näher betrachten. Sie setzen nämlich einen schroffen Gegensatz von Gewissheit und Wahrscheinlichkeit in der Art voraus, dass Gewissheit nur durch Gründe entstehen könne, welche sich auf sinnliche Evidenz stutzen. Wir erinnern aber an unsere oben gelieferte Entwicklung, nach welcher die Gewissheit jener Zustand von Überzeugung ist, in welchem Jemand aus einem Zusammenhang von Gründen, die die Gründe für die Annahme des Gegenteils ausschließen, eine gewisse Tatsache für wahr hält. Wir erinnern zugleich an die Ausführung über die Quellen der Gewissheit, wo wir gezeigt zu haben glauben, dass wir nicht unseren Sinnen, sondern nur dem Resultate der Verständigen auf gewisse Schlüsse gebauten Prüfung des Ergebnisses der Sinnen trauen, so dass jener schroffe Gegensatz, nach welchen wir in einigen Fällen nur auf sinnliche Evidenz und in anderen Fällen nur dem Zusammentreffen von Schlüssen trauen, irrig ist".

[74] Importantly, Mittermaier also acknowledged that the question if and when a judge would be internally convinced, was unavoidably dependent on the personality of the person judging: "Allein mit Unrecht würde man das wahre Verhältnis verkennen … dass überall, wo eine Person über die Wahrheit zu urteilen hat, es zugleich die Individualität dieser Person ist, welche die Überzeugung begründet. Diese Person ist es, welche die Einzelheiten, auf welchen der Beweis beruht, zu betrachten, mit einander zu verbinden, daraus die Schlüsse abzuleiten und nach der Vergleichung aller für und wider streitende Gründe bei sich den Schluss über das Resultat der ganzen Geistesoperation zu fassen hat. Bei allen unseren Handlungen aber ist es immer unsere Persönlichkeit, unsere ganze

necessary foundation for every conviction had to be the internal conviction of the judge. In 1834, Mittermaier was, nevertheless, not prepared to give up evidentiary rules all together and wanted to retain a negative system of legal proofs as a, albeit imperfect, guarantee against judicial arbitrariness. He conceived of these evidentiary rules more as guidelines which should provide minimum standards and never force the judge to decide against his internal conviction. Lastly, Mittermaier also made a more absolute distinction between guilty and not-guilty. He argued that all intermediate decision-types such as extraordinary punishment, security measures and the *absolutio ab instantia* should be abolished. The judge was either convinced or he was not.[75]

5.3.2.3 Conclusion

Küper remarks that the increasing recognition of the possibility to convict on the basis of indicia and the support for a negative system of legal proofs as envisioned by, for example, Mittermaier and Jarcke so strongly resembled a system based on the free evaluation of the evidence that it was reduced to a mere gradual difference.[76] The treatises of Jarcke and Mittermaier in this respect represented relatively 'progressive' views in the 1820s and 1830s, but were part of a broader change wherein the idea of a negative system of legal proofs gained more and more ground. According to Schwinge as well, a negative theory of proof in one way or another had become generally accepted in the juridical literature by the start of the 1840s.[77]

Unlike, for example, Globig and Huster who believed that the existence of moral certainty could be regulated in general evidentiary rules, most authors now presumed like Filangieri that the criterion for the existence of moral certainty was to be found primarily in the 'moral' or internal conviction of the judge. The internal conviction became the central hinge on which everything depended in the criminal law of evidence. With this new central role, the strength of forms of evidence was seen as essentially dependent on their 'Überzeugungskraft für den Richter', and not on predetermined general qualities of the forms of evidence themselves. In other words, all forms of evidence

---

Individualität, welche dabei tätig ist, und daher auch auf das Ergebnis unserer geistigen Operationen einwirkt". See C.J.A. Mittermaier, *Lehre vom Beweise*, p. 67.

75 Ibidem, pp. 467–504.
76 W. Küper, *Die Richteridee der Strafprozessordnung und ihre geschichtlichen Grundlagen*, p. 231.
77 E. Schwinge, *Der Kampf um die Schwurgerichte bis zur Frankfurter Nationalversammlung*, pp. 74–76.

provided merely chains in a 'Kette von Vermuthungen', which in the end was always dependent on the concrete evaluation of the judge.

The change was clear in the work of Jarcke and Mittermaier who argued that the internal conviction of the judge was the decisive foundation for every conviction, while the evidentiary rules were perceived by them more as guidelines which should only negatively bind the judge. It also became the dominant view in the juridical literature in the period between 1820 and 1840. As Küper observed, however, in general the acceptance of a negative theory of proof in this period did not so much occur as a conscious formulation of a new theory or a legislative change, but was the consequence of a reinterpretation of the role of the internal conviction of the judge and of the system of legal proofs in practice and in the juridical literature:

> vielmehr bedingt durch die Art und Weise, wie Gesetzgebung und Wissenschaft bei der Formulierung und Auslegung der gesetzlichen Beweiskriterien nunmehr die Überzeugung des Richters mitberücksichtigen, nahm die herrschenden Beweislehre immer deutlicher die Gestalt der sogenannten negativen Beweistheorie an, die zwar schon seit Feuerbach bekannt war, aber bisher nur sehr geringe praktische Bedeutung gehabt hatte.[78]

Similarly, in 1845, Mittermaier stated on the negative theory of proof that "sie liegt jetzt, *als durch die Praxis und die Wissenschaft ausgebildet*, dem gemeinen Recht zu Grunde".[79]

Although the internal conviction of the judge had now acquired a far more central role, it has to be kept in mind that most authors still desired to retain at least a negative system of legal proofs and were fearful of creating a truly free evaluation of evidence by professional judges. Küper may be right that the negative system of legal proofs strongly resembled a system based on the free

---

[78] W. Küper, *Die Richteridee der Strafprozessordnung und ihre geschichtlichen Grundlagen*, pp. 229–230. The negative theory of proof was not introduced through new legislation, but this appears to have had much to do with the general failure to reform the criminal procedural law. The concept-ordinances which were made tended to explicitly take a negative theory of proof as their fundament. This was the case in, for example, the concept-ordinances of Prussia in 1828, Bavaria in 1831 and Baden in 1835 and 1845, and Wurttemberg in 1843, which never acquired force of law. See H. Krieter, *Historische Entwicklung des „Prinzips der freien Beweiswürdigung" im Strafprozess*, pp. 20–42. As will be discussed in the following chapters, in the Netherlands in 1838 a legislative change did occur in which a negative theory of proof was adopted.

[79] C.J.A. Mittermaier, *Handbuch des Strafverfahrens*, p. 535.

evaluation of the evidence, but there were as yet no authors in the 1820s and 1830s in the German territories who were willing to allow a professional judge to decide on the basis of his freely formed internal conviction. The negative system of evidentiary rules was taken seriously and was deemed absolutely necessary to prevent judicial arbitrariness.

The fear of a too free evaluation of the evidence by the judge can be seen especially well in the continuing discussion between 1820 and 1840 on the question whether judges should be allowed to convict to the ordinary punishment on the basis of indicia. It was clear that convictions to the ordinary punishment would have to become possible on the basis of indicia if the extraordinary punishments were abolished. Furthermore, it was commonly recognized in the juridical debate that the use of indicia was indispensable for an effectively functioning criminal procedural law. The legislative committee of Baden, for example, argued that convictions on the basis of indicia were unavoidable "wenn die Gesellschaft gegen den verstockten Verbrecher nicht Schutzlos sein soll".[80] In 1846 Savigny similarly remarked on indicia that "Ohne seine Zulassung müsste man fast auf die Handhabung der Kriminal-Justiz verzichten".[81] In short, the question of the indicia was perceived as a difficult predicament where a choice had to be made between either a relatively ineffective criminal law or the danger of a (too) large judicial discretion.

Michels states that even though a majority within the juridical debate started to accept the possibility to convict to the ordinary punishment on the basis of indicia in the 1820s and 1830s, there were still many authors that remained highly distrustful of this form of evidence. Authors like Schede, Kircheisen, Siegen and Abegg still maintained that there was a qualitative difference between indicia and 'direct' forms of evidence, and did not want to allow convictions to the ordinary punishment on the basis of indicia. They stated that unlike witness testimony and the confession, indicia could not create certainty. Abegg, for example, stated in his *Lehrbuch des Gemeinen Criminal-Processes* (1833) that from indicia "nur eine für das Subject möglicherweise vorhandene, in der Sache selbst aber nicht existierende Wahrscheinlichkeit [hervorgehe]".[82] Furthermore, these authors also still argued that it was not allowed by Article 22 of the CCC to convict to the ordinary punishment on the basis of indicia.[83]

---

80 A.M. Ignor, *Geschichte Strafprozess*, pp. 252–254. See F. von Savigny, *Die Prinzipien in Beziehung auf eine neue Strafprozessordnung*, p. 488.
81 F. von Savigny, *Die Prinzipien in Beziehung auf eine neue Strafprozessordnung*, p. 488.
82 B. Thäle, *Die Verdachtsstrafe in der kriminalwissenschaftlichen Literatur des 18. und 19. Jahrhunderts*, pp. 224–225.
83 K. Michels, *Der Indizienbeweis in Übergang vom Inquisitionsprozess zum reformierten Strafverfahren*, pp. 134–162.

The fearfulness of allowing professional judges to convict on the basis of indicia also existed among proponents of a jury system. It was an important and often repeated argument from their side that it was too dangerous to let professional judges decide on the basis of indicia and that only jurors could be trusted enough to do this. Schwinge, for example, cites Welcker (1840) – an influential liberal politician and proponent of a jury system – who stated in strong words that if professional judges were allowed to decide on the basis of indicia "d.h. nach ihrem subjektiven Meinen zu verurteilen, so gebe man ihnen damit die Ermächtigung zu Justizmorden".[84]

In short, the insight of, among others, Mittermaier and the *Rheinischen Immediat-Justiz-Kommission* that there was no essential difference between indicia and other forms of evidence was certainly not yet completely accepted.[85] There was also as yet nobody who wanted to allow professional judges to decide on the basis of their freely formed internal conviction. This started to change, however, from the 1840s onwards. For the first time in the German territories there appeared authors who took the bold step to propose to let professional judges decide on the basis of their freely formed internal conviction.

5.3.3   *The Development of the Juridical Discussion in the 1840s*

The works of Mittermaier and Jarcke had refuted the common presupposition that a professional judge, who was left free to evaluate the evidence, would necessarily have to decide as a juror on the basis of an 'unreasoned' subjective conviction. They had argued that both jurors and judges in fact formed their conviction on the basis of a reasoned process of weighing the evidence. Furthermore, the works of Mittermaier and the Prussian-Rhenish committee had shown that there was no essential difference between indicia and other forms of evidence. Instead, from all forms of evidence probable conclusions still needed to be drawn which in the end depended on the evaluation of the judge or juror. In this respect, the supposed guarantees of the system of legal proofs appeared to offer only a very limited protection. These insights opened the door to consider to allow professional judges to decide on the basis of their freely formed internal conviction. Although Mittermaier himself did not yet

---

84   E. Schwinge, *Der Kampf um die Schwurgerichte bis zur Frankfurter Nationalversammlung*, pp. 82–83.
85   The Prussian committee and Mittermaier argued in a similar fashion that there was no qualitative difference between indicia and other forms of evidence, but until the 1840s Mittermaier did not agree with the committee on the desirability of a jury system. As has been described earlier, in the 1830s Mittermaier was still in favour of a negative system of legal proofs.

draw this conclusion and wanted to retain negative evidentiary rules, this conclusion was drawn in the 1840s and became accepted rather quickly in the period after 1848.

One of the first to plead for the introduction of the free evaluation of the evidence by professional judges in the German territories was Möhl in his articles *Über das Urtheilen rechtsgelehrter Richter ohne gesetzliche Beweistheorie* (1842) and *Über die Wertlosigkeit einer gesetzliche Beweistheorie* (1844). In these works he was strongly inspired by Bentham and Mittermaier, who are quoted many times. Möhl argued that in a public, oral trial, the system of legal proofs was not only unnecessary, but it was even counterproductive and should be abolished. He remarked that in criminal cases mathematical certainty could never be reached, only *geschichtliche Gewissheit*. Like Mittermaier, Möhl stated that this historical certainty was constituted by the internal conviction of the judge which rested on grounds and always remained 'mehr oder weniger subjektiv'. The only purpose of a negative theory of proof could be to legally prescribe certain general *Vernunftwahrheiten* and rules of experience which bound the judge in his evaluation. This, however, offered little guarantees against judicial arbitrariness and was in fact counterproductive because it was impossible to determine in general rules "wann und wie weit man einem Beweismittel Glauben schenken oder an dessen Glaubwürdigkeit zweifeln solle ... Nur die Individualität des einzelnen Falles kann über die Momente der Beweiskraft der Beweismittel entscheiden".[86]

Möhl argued that it was impossible to state beforehand that a certain group of witnesses was generally untrustworthy, just as it was impossible to determine in general when witness testimony or the confession provided sufficient certainty for a conviction. This impossibility was even more apparent in the vain attempts to regulate the complex matter of indicia. Evidentiary rules could never do justice to the complexity of the individual case and always said either too much or too little. Inherently, even under the negative system of legal proofs, evidentiary rules on occasion forced judges to decide against their internal conviction. Möhl did not deny that judges had to follow rules of logic and of experience in their evaluation, but he argued that they should not be prescribed in binding legal rules. Instead, the judge should only have to follow a non-binding theory of proof developed by legal scholars, of which it was left to his discretion how he applied it in the individual case. Möhl stated that it was necessary to put more trust in the person of the judges: "Das Richteramt ist

---

86   A. Möhl, „Über das Urtheilen rechtsgelehrter Richter ohne gesetzliche Beweistheorie", pp. 282–291.

nothwendig ein Fideicommissum, dem Wissen und Gewissen des Richters (religioni judicantis) ist das Meiste überlassen".[87]

Importantly, Möhl argued that the guarantees against judicial arbitrariness should not be sought in evidentiary rules, but in the introduction of a public, oral trial, the obligation to motivate the verdict and in the possibility of appeal. These measures were, according to Möhl, far more capable of ensuring impartial and objective verdicts than any system of evidentiary rules. Möhl was one of the first to seek a guarantee against judicial arbitrariness in the motivation of the verdict. The reason he could find a guarantee in stating the grounds for a verdict was the fact that he – like Jarcke and Mittermaier – did not think that judges would automatically decide on the basis of an unreasoned *Totaleindruck* if the evidentiary rules were abolished. Because the internal conviction was based on a reasoned process, the judge should be able to explain the grounds for his decision for which he could then be held accountable.[88]

Möhl was soon followed by a number of authors who pleaded for the free evaluation of the evidence by professional judges on similar grounds. Like Möhl, they deemed the system of legal proofs to be untenable and thought that better guarantees could be found in the introduction of a public, oral trial, and the obligation of the judge to motivate his verdict. Küper mentions the treatises of Hayen (1843), Foelix (1843), Höpfner (1844) and Wächter (1845), who argued for the free evaluation of the evidence by professional judges.[89] An important plea for the introduction of the free evaluation of the evidence by professional judges can, furthermore, be found in a memorandum written by Von Savigny in 1846. The memorandum contained a reflexion on a Prussian ordonnance of 1846 which for the first time explicitly introduced the free evaluation of the evidence by professional judges and a public, oral trial with a public prosecutor in the German territories. The ordinance, however, did not apply to the Prussian territories in general but was only intended for the *Kammergericht* and the *Kriminalgericht* of Berlin.[90] This ordinance formed a ground

---

87   Ibidem, pp. 289–294.
88   Ibidem, pp. 296–304. As Schwinge stated, it is highly remarkable that almost no author until the 1840s considered the motivation of the judge in his verdict as a (sufficient) guarantee against arbitrariness if the system of legal proofs would be abolished. The reason was that the prejudice was too strong that the free evaluation of the evidence would automatically make of the judge a juror who decided on the basis of a *Totaleindruck* of which no rational account could be given. See E. Schwinge, *Der Kampf um die Schwurgerichte bis zur Frankfurter Nationalversammlung*, pp. 72–85.
89   W. Küper, *Die Richteridee der Strafprozessordnung und ihre geschichtlichen Grundlagen*, p. 235.
90   A.M. Ignor, *Geschichte Strafprozess*, pp. 263–275. The direct cause for creation of the ordinance was the fact that a conspiracy for an uprising in the Polish territories led to a very

breaking piece of legislation and can, according to Ignor, be considered as the *normative Geburtsstunde* of the free evaluation of the evidence in Germany. The ordinance prescribed that the evidentiary rules would be abolished and that from now on the judge had to decide if the accused was guilty "nach seiner freien, aus dem Inbegriff der vor ihm erfolgten Verhandlungen geschöpften Ueberzeugung".[91] The words of this prescription have remained virtually unchanged in the present German criminal procedural legislation.

Although Von Savigny was the Prussian minister who was responsible for the revision of the legal codes at the time, he had almost no influence on the creation of this ordinance. His memorandum was also not published in 1846 and was probably only read by a few higher officials in the Prussian ministry.[92] Nevertheless, it forms a revealing source for how the perception had changed of the system of legal proofs from one of the most influential German jurists in the nineteenth century. In 1858 the part of his memorandum was published which focused on the criminal law of evidence. Here Von Savigny first presented a thorough argumentation against the jury system. Subsequently he gave an oversight of the current state of the debate on the criminal law of evidence and explained why he was in favour of letting professional judges decide after their freely formed internal conviction. Like Jarcke and Mittermaier, Von Savigny denied that the abolition of the system of legal proofs would automatically mean that the judge would have to decide according to some subjective feeling:

> Daraus, dass die Beweisregeln nicht ein für allemal gesetzlich festgestellt werden, folgt noch nicht, dass die Richter überhaupt von der Verpflichtung entbunden werden, nach Gründen und Regeln zu urtheilen und hiervon Rechenschaft zu geben ... Der unterschied zwischen Richtern mit und ohne gesetzlichen Beweistheorie besteht lediglich darin, dass in letzteren Falle dem Richter selbst die Auffindung und Anwendung der Beweisregeln, welche die allgemeine Denkgesetze, Erfahrung und Menschenkenntniss an die Hand geben, überlassen wird, während in ersterem Falle gewisse Beweisregeln schon durch das Gesetz selbst ein für

---

large number of criminal trials which had to take place for the *Kammergericht* of Berlin. Significantly, one central reason to create a public, oral trial with a public prosecutor and a free evaluation of the evidence, was to ensure effective and fast trials. The Prussian ministry wanted to avoid the vicissitudes of the long and slow, written inquisitorial procedure.

91 Ibidem, pp. 263–280, p. 252.
92 Ibidem, pp. 263–275. Ignor has described that in fact the *Justizverwaltungsminister* Uhden and the official Friedberg (later minister of justice of the German empire), were the ones mainly responsible for the ordinance of 1846.

allemal als unabänderliche Formeln festgestellt und dadurch das Urteil des Richters gefesselt und derselbe gehindert wird, jeden Fall nach seinen Eigenthümlichkeiten zu beurtheilen.[93]

With or without legally prescribed evidentiary rules, the judge essentially formed his conviction in the same way, following general rules of logic and experience. According to Von Savigny, the only difference was that a system of legal proofs inflexibly chained the decision of the judge to certain *a priori* prescriptions of what constituted a full proof, which prevented him from doing justice to the concrete circumstances of the individual case. Subsequently, in a crucial passage which touches the heart of the problem, Von Savigny explains why it was impossible to codify when sufficient evidence existed for a conviction in the individual case:

> Die Regeln, wonach der reflektirenden Verstand sein Urtheil bildet und die sich andrängende Meinung prüft, beruhen auf Sätzen der Erfahrung und auf Kenntnis der sittlichen und sinnlichen Natur des Menschen. Allerdings kann die Wissenschaft hierin Erfahrungen verbreiten, Prinzipien entwickeln und dem Richter und der Gesetzgebung vorarbeiten; allein sie kann dem Gesetzgeber keine allgemein gültigen und erschöpfenden Regeln an die Hand geben, *weil es sich großenteils um Elemente der Wahrscheinlichkeit handelt,* deren Regeln sich nach allen Richtungen hin auf die mannigfaltigste Weise durchkreuzen. Der Gesetzgeber kann keine spezielle Beweisregeln hinstellen ohne das Bewusstsein, dass in vielen Fällen durch deren Befolgung die Wahrheit verfehlt werden wird, in welchen sie nicht verfehlt sein würde, wenn die Regel nicht bestanden hätte ... Das was wir Gewissheit einer Tatsache nennen beruht auf so vielen einzelnen, in ihrer Zusammenwirkung nur dem einzelnen Fall angehörenden Elementen, dass sich dafür gar keine wissenschaftlichen allgemeinen Gesetze geben lassen.[94]

Here Von Savigny principally argued that the legislator could not predetermine in general rules when a sufficiently high probability of guilt existed for a conviction. These rules would only inhibit the process of truth finding in the individual case. He also denied that the system of legal proofs was capable of

---

[93] F. von Savigny, *Ueber Schwurgerichte und Beweistheorie im Strafprozesse*, p. 484.
[94] Ibidem, pp. 485–486. See also W. Küper, *Die Richteridee der Strafprozessordnung und ihre geschichtlichen Grundlagen*, pp. 235–237.

offering any effective guarantees against judicial arbitrariness, because in the end their application still overwhelmingly depended on the concrete evaluation of the judge. Like Möhl, Von Savigny stated that the real guarantee against judicial arbitrariness had to be sought in trustworthy, professionally capable judges, and in the orality and publicity of the trial, the obligation for the judge to motivate his verdict and the possibility of appeal. Von Savigny argued that when these guarantees existed, there was no reason to fear judicial arbitrariness of professional judges who decided on the basis of their freely formed internal conviction. Interestingly, he also mentioned practical examples which had shown that under these circumstances no judicial arbitrariness had to be feared. Von Savigny referred to the situation in the Netherlands between 1813 and 1838 where professional judges had decided on the basis of their freely formed internal conviction, and which had apparently functioned outstandingly.[95]

As Pihlajamäki has accurately stressed, there was also another argument for the free evaluation of the evidence which became more important in the 1830s and 1840s. This argument had its foundation in the development towards a subjectification of the criminal *Tatbestände* in the nineteenth century, which is visible in the works of, among others, Feuerbach and Mittermaier. The need to prove the precise level of the criminal intent of the accused and to modify the punishment accordingly became a far more important objective in this period. It was, however, clear for most authors that the system of legal proofs was woefully inadequate and too inflexible to deal with the subjective *Tatbestände* of the crime. It was argued that a more free evaluation of the evidence and particularly a free use of indicia was necessary for the judge to be able to infer the criminal intent of the accused from the proven circumstances of the case.[96] In this sense, Mittermaier for example remarked that the use of circumstantial evidence was indispensable to prove the '*inneren Merkmalen*' of the crime.[97]

The idea was also very prominent in the work of Welcker, Von Gneist and Köstlin. Köstlin argued that a negative theory of proof could only cover the objective *Tatbestände* of the crime. Evidence needed to be evaluated freely, however, in order to determine the '*subjective Seele der Handlung*'. If there was no confession, the judge needed to be able to draw conclusions from the other

---

95 E. Schwinge, *Der Kampf um die Schwurgerichte bis zur Frankfurter Nationalversammlung*, pp. 91–92. This evaluation of the situation in the Netherlands stands in sharp contrast to the remark of Feurebach twenty years earlier, who stated on the Netherlands that "da ist, soweit solche Einrichtung reicht, nichts anderes zu finden als die Justiz der Willkür". See P.J.A. Feuerbach, *Öffentlichtkeit und Mundlichkeit*, p. 76.

96 H. Pihlajamäki, *Evidence, Crime, and the legal profession*, pp. 128–129.

97 C.J.A. Mittermaier, *Handbuch des Strafverfahrens*, p. 404.

sources of evidence to determine what went on inside the head of the accused.[98] Welcker remarked that there were many things relevant to the imputation of guilt that could not be perceived directly. It is particularly in the work of Von Gneist that the impossibility of combining a system of legal proofs with the possibility to adequately prove the criminal intent, is most apparent. The system of legal proofs could only sufficiently deal with the objective *Tatbestände* of the crime but not with the subjective elements. Witnesses, for example, could not prove conclusively that the accused had a malicious intent. Instead, Von Gneist remarked that "der Beweis des inneren Thatbestandes nur aus den Umständen zu entnehmen sei".[99]

In conclusion, the argument that the free evaluation of the evidence was necessary to be able to prove the criminal intent of the accused, shows that there was also an important interconnectedness between the development of the substantive criminal law and the development of the criminal law of evidence. As Pihlajamäki has observed the division of *Tatbestände* into objective and subjective components is an essential element of the modernization of the substantive criminal law. The underlying idea of the 'classical criminal law' was that individuals were free agents who were morally responsible, and that they had to be punished according to the exact amount of responsibility – based on the level of criminal intent – that could be imputed to them. To be able to do this it was necessary to get 'inside the head of the accused', and for this the free evaluation of the evidence was deemed indispensable.[100]

The view of authors such as Möhl, Foelix and Von Savigny who argued that jurors and judges decided on the evidentiary question in essentially the same manner and that the free evaluation of the evidence was compatible with professional judges was, in the 1840s, still decidedly a minority opinion. A majority of the authors held the view that unlike professional judges, jurors decided on the basis of a *Totaleindruck*, and that it was far too dangerous to let judges decide after their freely formed internal conviction. In the 1840s the two main sides of the debate still consisted of those who wanted to retain professional judges and a negative system of proofs, and those who desired the introduction of a jury system combined with a complete reform of the criminal procedural law. An important change in especially the 1840s, nonetheless, was that the call for a jury system became louder and that the system of legal proofs was under increasing attack.

The change was partially due to the growing momentum of the liberal-constitutional movement after 1830, and partially due to the stronger criticisms

---

98   S.R. Köstlin, *Das Geschworenengericht, für Nichtjuristen*, p. 127.
99   R. von Gneist, *Die Bildung der Geschworenengerichten in Deutschland*, p. 64.
100 H. Pihlajamäki, *Evidence, Crime, and the legal profession*, pp. 128–131.

of the system of legal proofs within the scientific-juridical debate. The increased importance of the internal conviction of the judge and the recognition of the possibility to convict to the ordinary punishment on the basis of indicia in the juridical literature at the same time heightened the fear for judicial arbitrariness by professional judges. This fear was further exacerbated by the fact that little control was possible on the professional judges who still functioned within a secret, inquisitorial procedure. Even though there was an increasing recognition that indicia could create the same probability as witness testimony and the confession, the distrust of indicia had not diminished. The distrust remained because it became clear to most authors that it was virtually impossible to effectively regulate indicia in general rules. The attempts, in especially the legislation of the southern German states, to regulate indicia had proven to be largely unsatisfactory. The fact that indicia were very difficult to regulate and the growing understanding that in the end the application of evidentiary rules still depended on the internal conviction of the judge, helped create the feeling that the system of legal proofs was not capable of providing sufficient guarantees against judicial arbitrariness.

In the 1830s and 1840s the 'indicia-question' was considered one of the central problems by proponents of a negative system of legal proofs as well as by proponents of a jury system. The fact that indicia proved so difficult to regulate and the fear of a too free evaluation of the evidence created a strong argument for the proponents of a jury system for reform. As in France in the second half of the eighteenth century, the distrust in professional judges was heightened by several juridical scandals which attracted nationwide attention in this period. One notorious trial, which started in 1830, was conducted against Wendt who was convicted on the basis of indicia of having poisoned his wife. During the seven years in which Wendt was imprisoned, he was first convicted to death, then in appeal he was absolved from the instance and in a further appeal he was entirely acquitted. Because a year after the final trial someone else confessed to the murder it became clear that Wendt was innocent all along. Wendt had, however, been convicted to death in the first instance on the basis of indicia. Naturally, the story of Wendt gave important ammunition to the proponents of a jury system and was commented on in many pamphlets and treatises. Welcker, for example, commented that this trial shows "was man von dem jetzt zur Mode gewordenen Indizienbeweis ... vor gelehrtem Juristengericht zu erwarten hat".[101]

Another important trial was conducted against the famous politician Jordan in 1843. He was, after a four year during investigation, convicted to five

---

[101] E. Schwinge, *Der Kampf um die Schwurgerichte bis zur Frankfurter Nationalversammlung*, pp. 81–82.

years of imprisonment on the basis of a highly dubious constellation of indicia. Both trials attracted a lot of commentary and clearly showed to the larger public the dangers of allowing professional judges to convict on the basis of indicia. The proponents of a jury system used these trials as a propaganda tool and presented the jury system as the only remedy for the unavoidable dangers of judging on the basis of indicia. Schwinge cites among others Michelsen, who was representative for the jurists that saw the jury as the sole solution for the problem of judging on the basis of indicia. Michelsen stated in 1847 on the jury that it was "das Organ, um den Indizienbeweis zu liefern ... das ist es eigentlich, was durch die Jury gelöst worden ist und wird".[102] However, the main reason that authors such as Michelsen argued that only a jury system could solve the problem of indicia was fundamentally a question of trust. Most authors recognized the necessity of the possibility to convict on the basis of indicia in order to maintain an effective criminal procedural law but simply did not trust professional magistrates enough to grant them this power. Especially not within the context of a secret, written inquisitorial procedure. Professional magistrates were deemed to be too dependent on the government while only the people could really be impartial and unbiased.

To summarize, by the late 1840s the (negative) system of legal proofs came under increasing criticism. Michels states that during the 1840s the arguments of Mittermaier against the system of legal proofs became widely shared in the German literature.[103] This led to a growing recognition that the system of legal proofs was built on an untenable theoretical foundation and that it was inable to provide strong guarantees against judicial arbitrariness. As will be further discussed below, it was nevertheless the revolutionary atmosphere and predominantly political-constitutional motives which finally led to largescale legislative reforms in 1848 and 1849.

5.3.4 *Political-constitutional Motives, the Procedural Framework and the Reforms of 1848*

So far the development of the discussion on the criminal law of evidence has been treated in relative isolation from the political-constitutional background and the criminal procedural law as a whole. In the juridical treatises the criminal law of evidence was, however, almost never treated in isolation but always in connection with the criminal procedural law. The importance of this connection becomes especially clear when it is considered that the demand for

---

102   Ibidem, p. 149.
103   K. Michels, *Der Indizienbeweis in Übergang vom Inquisitionsprozess zum reformierten Strafverfahren*, p. 180.

the introduction of the free evaluation of the evidence was invariably accompanied by the demand for the introduction of a public, oral trial with a public prosecutor. This applied to those who desired the free evaluation of the evidence by professional judges as well as to those who preferred a jury system. Möhl and Von Savigny, for example, only wanted to allow the free evaluation of the evidence by judges if at the same time a public, oral trial was introduced, possibilities for appeal were created and the judge was obligated to motivate his verdict. Suggestions to reform the criminal law of evidence were always part of a reform package which broadly beheld the principles of what would come to be known as the *reformierte Strafprozess*.

As in France in the second half of the eighteenth century, in Germany the desire to reform the criminal procedural law came forth out of predominantly political-constitutional motives. The 'liberals' sought better guarantees to protect civil liberty and were in agreement that the existing secret, inquisitorial procedure did not offer these guarantees. The opinion that the existing procedural law contained structural flaws and needed to be reformed became widespread during the period between 1812 and 1848. The criticisms focused on three points. First of all, it was increasingly recognized that the system of legal proofs was unable to strictly bind the judge and that it was particularly problematic to regulate the use of indicia. Secondly, the secret nature of the procedure made control by the public impossible. Thirdly, the concentration of functions in the professional judge was considered to constitute a very dangerous situation. The inquisitorial judge gathered the evidence in the preliminary investigation and then either decided on the evidentiary question himself, or handed over the evidence in written form to a tribunal – of which the inquisitorial judge was often a member – that decided on the evidentiary question. The possibility for the accused to defend himself or to make use of legal counsel were very limited. In the 'old' view in Germany this situation was not seen as particularly problematic. This changed however during the first half of the nineteenth century.[104]

In the old view the powerful position of the judge was not deemed problematic because the judge was generally trusted and it was thought that the accused was sufficiently protected by the three roles that the judge was expected to perform (combined with the system of legal proofs). It was considered natural that the judge performed the role of public prosecutor, of judge, and finally the role of defendant all at once. Typical of the positive evaluation of this threefold position of the judge in the inquisitorial procedure is the following

---

104 W. Küper, *Die Richteridee der Strafprozessordnung und ihre geschichtlichen Grundlagen*, pp. 179–183.

remark by Feuerbach, in his handbook on criminal law, at the beginning of the nineteenth century:

> Der Richter ist im Untersuchungspocesse als *dreifache Person* zu betrachten, als Stellvertreter des beleidigten Staats, indem er an dessen Statt die Rechte aus Strafgesetzen zu verfolgen verpflichtet ist; als Stellvertreter des Angeschuldigten, indem er zugleich alles, was die Schuldlosigkeit oder geringere Strafbarkeit desselben begründen kann, aufsuchen und darstellen soll, und endlich als Richter, inwiefern er das Gegebene zu beurtheilen und darüber richterlich zu verfügen (oder zu entscheiden) hat.[105]

Particularly during the 1830s and 1840s, this concentration of three roles in the inquisitorial judge started to be seen as a dangerous situation, while at the same time it became clear that the system of legal proofs was incapable of providing the guarantees which were once expected from it. Typical of the criticism against the idea of the judge as *dreifache Person* was the following remark of Zachariae in 1846: "Dem Inquirenten aber zuzumuten, bald auf die, bald auf die andere Seite zu springen und mit beiden Waffen resp. gegen sich selbst zu fechten, zugleich aber auch als Kampfrichter den Streit zu leiten, ist an sich eine Absurdität".[106] The recognition of these flaws in the inquisitorial procedure, which made it incapable of providing sufficient guarantees against judicial arbitrariness, created the feeling that an encompassing reform of the criminal procedural law was necessary.

Furthermore, the sense that the existing inquisitorial procedure was dangerous for civil liberty, was significantly heightened by the political trials which attracted nationwide attention. It has been mentioned in the previous subsection that there were several trials which showed the supposed unreliability of indicia. Similarly, there were many political trials and criminal prosecutions which infringed the freedom of the press and showed to a larger public the dangers of the secret, inquisitorial procedure. One of the most famous of these trials was the case of Weidig who was prosecuted for treason in 1834. He was imprisoned for three years in a dark, damp dungeon while harsh *Ungehorsamsstrafen* were used to force him to confess, which he resisted. In 1837 Weidig, still imprisoned, took his own life and wrote with his blood on the dungeon walls: "Da mir der Feind jede Vertheidigung versagt, so wähle ich einen

---

105   P.J.A. Feuerbach, *Lehrbuch*, p. 843.
106   H.A. Zachariae, *Die Gebrechen und die Reform des deutschen Strafverfahrens*, p. 146.

schimpflichen Tod von freien Stücken".[107] The case of Weidig and other political trials naturally became the rallying point for liberals to show the dangers of the inquisitorial procedure and were pernicious for the trust in professional magistrates. They helped shape the public perception of the inquisitorial procedure and created an atmosphere where an often emotional and principal stance was taken against the inquisitorial procedure as a whole. These trials, in short, strongly induced a sense of urgency for a largescale reform.[108]

The solution for the perceived deficiencies of the inquisitorial procedure was sought in the creation of a jury system and a public, oral trial with a public prosecutor. Concomitant important reforms were the strengthening of the defensive rights of the accused and the abolition of intermediary decision types such as *Ungehorsamsstrafen*, extraordinary punishments and, to a lesser extent, the *absolutio ab instantia*. In the following subsection, first the discussion on the principles for an encompassing reform of the criminal procedural law and the desire to abolish extraordinary punishments will be described. In the second subsection, the reforms in and shortly after 1848 will be discussed which led to the introduction of a jury system.

5.3.4.1   The Reform of the Criminal Procedural Framework

Parallel to the reflections on the free evaluation of the evidence between 1812 and 1848, there had been a continuous discussion in the German juridical literature on the principles of orality and publicity, and the introduction of a public prosecutor. At first, these principles were closely associated with a jury system and were seen as necessarily connected to each other. It was, for example, argued that the principle of orality was required for jurors because they needed to hear and see the witnesses and the accused directly to form a *Totaleindruck*. On the other hand, it was argued that a professional judge could work better with written evidence because he reasoned in an analytical way and had to reflect on the evidence. There was at first a dichotomized view wherein it was argued that the principles of orality and publicity only worked with a jury system. However, in the course of particularly the 1830s and 1840s this dichotomized view began to break down. Just as it was increasingly deemed possible that professional judges could work with a system based on the free evaluation of the evidence, so it was also argued that the principles of orality and publicity could be combined with a system based on professional judges.

---

107   A.M. Ignor, *Geschichte Strafprozess*, p. 225.
108   E. Schwinge, *Der Kampf um die Schwurgerichte bis zur Frankfurter Nationalversammlung*, pp. 45–50.

Unlike the demand for a jury system, which was seen as a more difficult and political question on which the opinions remained strongly divided, by the late 1840s there had grown general support within the juridical literature for the public, oral trial with a public prosecutor. Proponents of a jury system as well as proponents of a system based on professional judges now both argued for these reform principles. Even though the dichotomized view did not disappear entirely, the value of the reform principles was increasingly recognized. In this subsection it is not possible to describe in detail the development of the complex discussion on the reform principles between 1812 and 1848. Instead, a brief oversight will be given of the most important ideas supporting these principles and how they were meant to reshape the criminal procedural law.

The proponents of the public, oral trial with a the public prosecutor and the motivation of the verdict used an array of arguments which were closely intertwined and which were all directed against certain perceived flaws of the secret, inquisitorial procedure. First of all, however, it has to be kept in mind that these principles were normally intended only for the main trial. A division was made between the preliminary investigation and the main trial. The preliminary investigation would still remain secret and would be conducted by an investigative judge with the help of the police. On the basis of the results of this investigation, the public prosecutor would formulate his accusation and present it during the public, oral trial. Ignor states that this division was given an important theoretical foundation by presenting it as an attempt to find a correct balance or harmony between on the one hand the goal of effectively prosecuting crimes, and on the other hand the goal of safeguarding the civil liberty of the citizens.[109]

---

109 A.M. Ignor, *Geschichte Strafprozess*, pp. 231–237. Although the concern for guaranteeing civil liberty against a too powerful state and judicial arbitrariness was often the focal point of discussion, it must not be forgotten that creating an *effective* criminal procedural system was equally important. In the rethinking of the relationship between the state and its citizens from a constitutional-liberal point of view, it was always a matter of finding a balance between these two goals. This concern can also be seen well in, for example, the work of Beccaria, who was not only preoccupied with protecting citizens against judicial arbitrariness, but perhaps even more so with laying the foundations for an efficient criminal procedural law. His criticism of judicial torture was not only that it was unjust to torture someone before his guilt was fully established, but even more that it was unnecessary and inefficient to search for a confession when the guilt of the accused was sufficiently established. The reform principles were often also understood as creating a more efficient procedure. Typically, the first encompassing procedural reform in 1846 in Prussia was predominantly motivated by the desire to efficiently prosecute the large number of treason cases.

In Germany the attempt to find this balance or middle road was often treated in terms of general principles. The idea was that the 'inquisitorial principle' would dominate in the preliminary investigation and the 'accusatorial principle' in the main trial. Möhl typically formulated this search for the right balance as follows:

> Die Herstellung des richtigen Verhältnisses in dem Strafverfahren zwischen dem inquisitorischen und dem accusatorischen Prinzip ist das Streben der neueren Zeit ... Nur die Verbindung beider Prinzipien miteinander in zweckmäßiger Wechselwirkung aufeinander, so dass in dem Vorverfahren die inquisitorische Form, in dem Hauptverfahren aber die accusatorische Form hervortritt, verbürgt die sichere gerechte Bestrafung der wahren Schuld und den notwendigen Schutz der Unschuld.[110]

Of the reform principles, the argumentation for the principle of publicity was perhaps the most straightforward. It was directed against the secret nature of the inquisitorial procedure. The two main arguments presented for this principle were that it would enable the public to scrutinize the judge and would thereby increase the trust of the people in the criminal justice system.[111] Another argument was the idea that the public trial would contribute to the general prevention of crimes. The possibility for the people to see the distressed situation of criminals on trial would supposedly have a deterring effect. The principle of publicity was perceived to be in close connection to the principle of orality, because the scrutiny of the judge by the public would be very difficult if the evidence was not presented orally during the trial.[112]

There were several arguments which were proposed in favour of the principle of the orality or 'immediacy' (*Unmittelbarkeit*) of the trial, as it was also often called. Most importantly, the oral testimony of witnesses and the accused during the trial would enable the judge to acquire better and more complete information than through written documents. In contrast to the dead letter of

---

110 A. Möhl, *Über das Urtheilen rechtsgelehrter Richter ohne gesetzliche Beweistheorie*, pp. 277–280. By some authors, such as Mittermaier and Zachariae, the search for this balance was even presented as the result of a dialectical historical process. They stated that there were two *Grundsysteme* in the criminal procedural law: the accusatorial and the inquisitorial system. In this view the early Germanic law was dominated by the accusatory principle and later under the absolutistic state the inquisitorial principle came to dominate completely. It was now time to find the correct synthesis between these two principles. See A.M. Ignor, *Geschichte Strafprozess*, pp. 234–236.
111 E.J. Wettstein, *Der Öffentlichkeitsgrundsatz im Strafprozess*, pp. 17–34.
112 A.M. Ignor, *Geschichte Strafprozess*, pp. 242–244.

documents where testimony was transmitted through the filter of the investigating judge, the oral statements made it possible for the judge to see the expression and demeanour of the accused and witnesses directly.[113] In other words, the oral presentation of the evidence was deemed to create a more genuine impression on the judge or jurors than the mediated representations in writing by the investigative judge. Especially the proponents of a jury system argued that a jury could only function in an oral procedure. It was stated that for them to form a correct *Totaleindruck* they needed to see and hear the witnesses and the accused directly. Another argument for the principle of orality was that it would increase the speed of the procedure and that it would improve the defensive options of the accused. The latter aspect was of particular importance. With the orality of the trial the judge or jurors could see and hear the accused defend himself and the accused could ask questions to the witnesses directly in front of the court.[114]

Lastly, the accusatorial principle (*Anklageprinzip*), which implied the introduction of a public prosecutor, acquired a central significance within the German reform movement. The accusatory principle contained three aspects. First, it meant that the accusation, presented by the public prosecutor, had to specify precisely which crime would be the subject of the trial. The judge or jurors could subsequently only decide on the basis of the charge of the public prosecutor and the evidence that was presented during the public trial. This was a highly important innovation for the defensive position of the accused and enhanced the significance of the principles of orality and publicity. In the existing secret, inquisitorial procedure the judge was not forced to make the charge concrete and had relatively much leeway to change the crime for which the accused was prosecuted. The judge was not even obligated to inform the accused of what crime or for what constellation of facts he was being prosecuted. The *Anklageprinzip* entailed that the charge needed to be specified before the public, oral trial which created far better defensive possibilities for the accused.[115]

The second aspect of the *Anklageprinzip* consisted of a strengthening of the defensive rights of the accused. Besides the improvement of his position by

---

113 As Feuerbach, for example, stated "Wie vieles müsste an Mitteln der Ueberzuegung verloren gehen, wenn die geschwornen diese nicht aus dem vollen Strome der Verhandlungen selbst, sondern nur aus dem abgeleiteten versandeten Kanale eines Gerichtsprotokols schöpfen dürften!". See P.J.A. Feuerbach, *Betrachtungen über das Geschworenengericht*, p. 30.
114 A.M. Ignor, *Geschichte Strafprozess*, pp. 237–241.
115 J.F. Henschel, *Die Strafverteidigung im Inquisitionsprozess des 18. und im Anklageprozess des 19. Jahrhunderts*, pp. 88–102.

the fixation of the charge and the principle of immediacy, it was argued in the juridical literature that a right to legal counsel and a right to be informed of the incriminating evidence (*Akteneinsicht*) should be introduced. Furthermore, the defendant should be allowed to pose questions to the witnesses during the public trial and be given more room to present witnesses or other forms of evidence in favour of his innocence. These defensive rights were meant to be general and guaranteed by the law, and not, as it was under the secret, inquisitorial procedure, dependent on approval by the inquisitorial judge.[116] The goal was to make the accused less an object of investigation and more a party to the procedure in opposition to the public prosecutor, and in front of a more neutral judge. This can also be seen in the growing demand in especially the 1830s and 1840s for the abolition of *Ungehorsamsstrafe* and the increased recognition of the right of the accused not to incriminate himself.[117] The expected effect of the stronger defensive position of the accused was, furthermore, that it would better enable the judge to find the truth, because he would be presented with a more complete picture of the evidence for and against the accused.

The third aspect of the accusatory principle was that the charge should be presented during the main trial by a public prosecutor. The purpose of the stronger defensive rights of the accused and the introduction of the public prosecutor was to counteract the dangerous situation which existed under the secret, inquisitorial procedure where the judge had to perform three roles. The argumentation for the introduction of a public prosecutor was at first dominated by the political-constitutional idea that a separation of powers within the judicial branch was necessary to prevent judicial arbitrariness. Later it was also stated that the performance of three roles put the judge in a psychologically untenable situation. From this perspective it was argued that the fact that the judge had to perform the role of public prosecutor, defendant and judge at the same time, inhibited him psychologically from being impartial. Both perspectives worked mutually reinforcing and led to the conclusion that a separation of functions would prevent judicial arbitrariness and would be conducive to the process of truth finding. The central idea of the accusatory principle was that the truth could be better established when two opposing parties presented the arguments for and against the guilt of the accused, while the judge remained impartial and stood more neutrally above the parties.[118]

There were other reasons which were proposed for the introduction of a public prosecutor as well. It was argued that a public prosecutor would make

---

116   Ibidem, pp. 103–154.
117   D. Mauss, *Die „Lügenstrafe" nach Abschaffung der Folter ab 1740*, pp. 48–64.
118   A.M. Ignor, *Geschichte Strafprozess*, pp. 244–248.

the criminal procedure more efficient and that it was a necessary consequence of the creation of a public, oral trial. The judge needed to be and appear impartial, and it would give a wrong impression to the accused and the people if in a public trial the judge also had to perform the role of public prosecutor. It has to be kept in mind that it was in this period not yet seen as the job of the public prosecutor to lead the preliminary investigation. This remained the responsibility of a separate investigative judge. The fear was that otherwise the public prosecutor would become a too powerful instrument of repression. He should only formulate and present the charge during the main trial. The public prosecutor was, furthermore, not proposed in the Anglo-American manner as a party to the process. Comparable to the French view, he was supposed to be more impartial and obligated to strive for the 'objective truth' and, for example, was also required to present the evidence which pleaded in favour the innocence of the accused.[119]

5.3.4.1.1   *Intermediary Decision Types and the Nemo Tenetur-principle*
By the late 1840s the *Anklageprinzip* and the principles of orality and publicity had acquired widespread support in the juridical literature. These principles were understood as strongly intertwined with each other and with the introduction of the free evaluation of the evidence. Closely related to the reform principles, there was also a general demand for the abolition of the use of extraordinary punishments, *Lügenstrafe* and *Ungehorsamstrafe*. Although there were also criticisms of the *absolutio ab instantia*, this instrument still had a relatively widespread support.[120] The desire to abolish extraordinary punishments and other disciplinary measures to force an accused to answer questions, was an essential part of the broader reform package of the criminal procedural law. It entailed the creation of a more absolute distinction between guilty and not-guilty, and was closely linked to the rise of the free evaluation of the evidence. As has been described in the previous section, the growing recognition of the possibility to convict to the ordinary punishment on the basis of indicia made the use of extraordinary punishments superfluous. Thäle concludes that by the 1830s and 1840s the demand for the abolition of extraordinary punishments had become generally accepted in the juridical literature.[121] The

---

[119] W. Wohlers, *Entstehung und Funktion der Staatsanwaltschaft*, pp. 90–129 and 202–207.
[120] For the discussion on the extraordinary punishments and particularly on the continued support for the *absolutio ab instantia*, see O. Elben, *Die Entbindung von der Instanz vom dogmengeschichtlichen und allgemein rechtlichen Standpunkt aus erörtert. Ein Beitrag zur Geschichte und Gesetzgebung des deutschen Strafverfahrens*.
[121] B. Thäle, *Die Verdachtsstrafe in der kriminalwissenschaftlichen Literatur des 18. und 19. Jahrhunderts*, pp. 223–235.

reformers in the late 1840s proposed that someone should only receive the legally prescribed punishment if the judge or jurors were fully convinced of the guilt of the accused. If not, he should be acquitted and no extraordinary punishments or 'security measures' should be allowed. Furthermore, until his guilt was fully proven the accused should be considered innocent.

As in France, the free evaluation of the evidence, the idea of an absolute distinction between guilty and not-guilty, and the presumption of innocence worked fruitfully together as arguments against extraordinary punishments. They also enabled the abolition of *Ungehorssamstrafe* in the form of punishing the accused for lying or remaining silent.[122] The presumption of innocence and the idea that the accused had a right not to incriminate himself were used as important arguments against *Ungehorssamstrafe*. Knapp, for example, cites Welcker who stated: "Der eigentliche positive Rechtsgrund gegen eine bürgerliche Strafbarkeit der Antwortverweigerung ... liegt [darin], dass einestheils jeder Bürger bis zum vollen Beweis seiner Schuld als ganz schuldlos zu behandeln ist, und das andernteils rechtlich nicht der Angeklagte gegen sich selbst Zeugnis und Beweis zu liefern verbunden ist".[123]

Lastly the discussions in the German territories show that the recognition of the *nemo tenetur* principle as a positive right to remain silent was a relatively gradual process. At first, in the late eighteenth and early nineteenth centures, the idea that nobody should be forced to incriminate oneself was used as an important argument for the abolition of judicial torture. At this time the use of physical torments to force an accused to confess came to be seen as illegitimate but *Ungehorsamstrafe* and extraordinary punishments were still deemed acceptable. It was thought that the accused had at least a moral obligation to answer questions. In the course of the nineteenth century, and particularly with the growing support for the *Anklageprozess* in the 1830s and 1840s, this changed. The idea became increasingly accepted that the accused should be more a party to the procedure, that he had a right to remain silent and that he

---

[122] The necessity of punishments for lying became particularly superfluous with the recognition of the possibility to convict on the basis of indicia. This effect can be seen very well in the concept criminal ordinance of Baden in 1845 which abolished disciplinary punishments for lying and stated: "Verweigert der Angeschuldigte entweder alle Antwort oder die Antwort auf bestimmte Fragen, so kann dieses die Wirkung einer für seine Schuld sprechende Anzeige haben". See D. Mauss, *Die „Lügenstrafe" nach Abschaffung der Folter ab 1740*, pp. 29-31.

[123] N. Knapp, *Die Ungehorssamstrafe in der Strafprozesspraxis des frühen 19. Jahrhunderts*, p. 48.

also had a right to be considered innocent until his guilt had been fully proven. A first important recognition of this idea can be seen in the reform legislation of 1848 and 1848 where the *Ungehorsamstrafe* and extraordinary punishments were abolished almost everywhere. In the criminal procedural ordinance of 1877 for the unified German state an article also explicitly acknowledged that the accused was not obligated to answer questions. The requirement to give the caution to accused that he had a right to remain silent before being interrogated was, however, not yet introduced by this time.[124]

5.3.4.2 The Revolution of 1848 and the Legislative Reforms of the Criminal Procedural Law

The introduction of a jury system and a public, oral trial with a public prosecutor had already been proposed and discussed multiple times before 1848 in the parliaments of particularly the southern German states of Baden, Wurttemberg and Bavaria. With intervals the subject was raised in the parliaments – in the German states that had one – by the 'liberal' representatives and caused intense discussions. Until 1848, however, these proposals led to virtually no attempt by the governments of the German states to adopt the reform principles. Exceptions were the Prussian ordinance of 1846 and the creation of a reform-ordinance in Baden in 1845, which combined a negative system of legal proofs with a public, oral trial and the introduction of a public prosecutor. Although the ordinance in Baden was approved by both chambers of parliament, it was never promulgated because it was tied to a broader reform of the court system in Baden that failed.[125] Apart from the attempt in Baden and the ordinance in Prussia in 1846 (which has been discussed previously), it was only during and after 1848 that comprehensive legislative reforms in the German states started to follow each other in rapid succession. It took the politically revolutionary atmosphere of 1848 to create the necessary momentum for these reforms.

Beside the revolutionary atmosphere, there was also an important event before 1848 which appeared to give added 'juridical-scientific' legitimation to the introduction of a jury system. This was the *Lübecker Germanistenversammlung* in 1847, a conference for the advancement of German language, history and law. The conference attracted nationwide attention and many of the most renowned German scholars attended it. During the *Germanistenversammlung* a year earlier, in Frankfurt in 1846, it had been decided that a committee would

---

124 See also K. Rogall, *Der Beschuldigte als Beweismittel gegen sich selbst*, pp. 91–103.
125 H. Krieter, *Historische Entwicklung des „Prinzips der freien Beweiswürdigung" im Strafprozess*, pp. 28–38.

write a report on the jury question, which subsequently became one of the central subjects of debate during the conference in 1847. The report of the committee contained a resounding recommendation for the introduction of a jury system. Very significant was the fact that Mittermaier, who was a member of the committee, declared that he had changed his opinion and that he was now in favour of a jury system. He explained that his change of opinion was based on his observations in the German territories and other countries. Everywhere experience had shown him that the system of legal proofs was untenable and that unlike professional judges, jurors did have the trust of the people. He now also argued that only a jury system was compatible with a public, oral trial. Furthermore, Mittermaier went out of his way to show through statistical evidence that a jury system did not entail a less effective repression and that jurors did not acquit more often than professional judges. This was an important point, because many of the opponents of a jury system had raised the fear that jurors would be too lenient.[126] Summarizing, the *Lübecker Germanistenversammlung* was an important event, because at a decisive moment before the revolution of 1848, it gave the impression to the larger public that now even within the scientific-juridical debate the objections against the jury system were being abandoned.

Similar to the reforms in France, the wave of reforms in the German territories started in a revolutionary atmosphere. In this atmosphere the governments of the German states were no longer capable of controlling the 'liberal-revolutionary' elements in society and saw themselves forced to make concessions to reform. For decades it had been an article of faith of the liberal movement that a jury system with a public, oral trial should be introduced and that the secret, inquisitorial procedure should be abolished. As Schwinge stated, the introduction of a jury system was "eine der großen Forderungen der 48er Revolution, die in allen Sturmpetitionen als eine Selbstverständlichkeit wiederkehrt".[127] Characteristic of how broadly the demand for a jury system was shared among the liberal revolutionaries, was the fact that the national assembly in the Pauls church in Frankfurt accepted the introduction of a jury system and the *Anklageprozess* (meaning a public, oral trial with a public prosecutor) without any discussion. The *Grundrechte des deutschen Volkes* which the assembly created, included the provision that: "Das Gerichtsverfahren soll öffentlich und mündlich sein. In Strafsachen gilt der Anklageprozess. Schwurg-

---

126 E. Schwinge, *Der Kampf um die Schwurgerichte bis zur Frankfurter Nationalversammlung*, pp. 146–148.
127 Ibidem, p. 153.

erichte sollen jedenfalls in schwereren Strafsachen und bei allen politischen Vergehen urteilen".[128]

The provisions of the national assembly never acquired force of law because its authority was not recognized by the German states. Instead, it was on the level of the individual states that the actual reforms occurred. Under the revolutionary pressure most German governments in 1848 and 1849 saw themselves forced to enact provisional ordinances which promised the introduction of a public, oral trial with a public prosecutor and a jury system. In the following years, most governments kept their promise and enacted ordinances which comprehensively reformed the criminal procedural law. Hannover, Kürhessen, Brunswick and the Thuringian states already created new criminal ordinances between 1848 and 1850 which introduced a public, oral trial with a public prosecutor and jury system. Provisional ordinances introduced the public, oral trial and the jury system in Bavaria and Hessen-Darmstadt in 1848, and in Prussia, Wurttemberg, Baden and Nassau in 1849. The provisional ordinances were replaced in the following years by new procedural codes which retained the public, oral trial with a public prosecutor and jury system in these states.[129]

Even though the French version of the jury trial had often been criticized in the juridical literature in the preceding decades, the new procedural systems in the German states were modelled strongly after the French legislation. The reason to take over the French model lay in the fact that the German discussion about the jury system had largely been a discussion of principle about the question whether a jury system should be introduced or not. Very little attention had been paid to the question how the jury system should actually be given shape once it was accepted. When suddenly, during the revolutionary storms of 1848, the possibility emerged to introduce a jury system, there was no well-developed alternative idea in the juridical literature of how the jury system should be regulated. Because the reformers wanted to make use of the momentum and quickly reform the criminal procedural law, the French model was followed which was best known. Furthermore, there was already a lot of experience with the French legislation and it was deemed easier to apply in Germany than the English version of the jury system. The idea prevailed that the English version was difficult to transplant because it had grown organically

---

128 H. Krieter, *Historische Entwicklung des „Prinzips der freien Beweiswürdigung" im Strafprozess*, p. 11. The national assembly in the Pauls church in Frankfurt was a revolutionary assembly which gathered to create a constitution for a unified German state, which they hoped would be created in the near future. Its authority was not recognized by the governments of the individual German states and once the revolution was brought under control militarily, the parliament dissolved.

129 Ibidem, pp. 18–69.

in England and was too strongly embedded in their particular judicial institutions and culture.[130]

The jury system made a quick and triumphant procession throughout the German territories, but there also remained a significant part of the German states which did not adopt the jury trial. Austria and Saxony only introduced a jury system under revolutionary pressure for a short period. Soon new criminal procedural codes were made in Austria (1853) and Saxony (1855) without a jury system. They were, nevertheless, modernized criminal codes that contained a public, oral trial with a public prosecutor. While the Austrian legislation returned to a negative system of legal proofs, the Saxon code explicitly acknowledged a system based on the free evaluation of the evidence by professional judges. Article 10 of the code in Saxony read: "Soweit die Richter über tatsächliche Verhältnisse zu urteilen haben, sind sie nur an ihre durch die vorliegenden Beweise gewonnene Überzeugung gebunden". Mecklenburg, Holstein, Lippe and the Hanseatic cities resisted the pressure to reform and, for the time being, retained the secret inquisitorial procedure.[131]

Summarizing, by the early 1850s a public, oral trial with a public prosecutor and a jury system had replaced the old inquisitorial procedure in most German states. However, there also remained a significant minority of states which did not adopt a jury system. The discussion on the merits of the jury system and the system based on professional judges, therefore, continued unabated in the 1850s, 1860s and 1870s.

5.3.4.2.1 *Conclusion*
There is a consensus in the historiography that political-constitutional motives were the most decisive *direct* cause of the introduction of the jury system in the revolutionary period of 1848 and 1849. Schwinge, for example, states that the decisive arguments for the jury system were political ones: "Endgültig wurde der Kampf nicht innerhalb der Grenzen der Wissenschaft, sondern auf politischen Gebiete entschieden ... als Verwirklichung einer programmatischen Forderung des deutschen Liberalismus hielt es seinen Einzug in Deutschland".[132] Lieber as well, argues that although philosophical and juridical arguments played an important role and were closely intertwined with the

---

130 P. Landau, "Schwurgerichte und Schöffengerichte in Deutschland im 19. Jahrhundert bis 1870", pp. 268–290.
131 Ibidem, pp. 18–69.
132 E. Schwinge, *Der Kampf um die Schwurgerichte bis zur Frankfurter Nationalversammlung*, pp. 153–155.

political motives, the political reasons in the end predominated among the proponents of a jury system.[133]

As has been stated before, the jury system was demanded by the liberals in Germany for essentially three reasons. Firstly, it would create a division of power within the criminal trial and would thereby diminish the possibility of judicial arbitrariness. Secondly, a jury system would create an element of democratic representation in the judicial system. The third and perhaps most important reason was the question of trust in the persons judging. Comparable to the distrust in France against the *noblesse du robe*, the jury system was predominantly demanded by the liberals in Germany because of a lack of trust in the professional magistrates. The distrust had been significantly strengthened as a consequence of the many sensational political trials which attracted nationwide attention. Time and again it was stated that only jurors had the trust of the people, that they were unbiased and impartial and that they would form a palladium of civil liberty. In short, the distrust against the professional magistrates was the underlying crucial factor which inspired the political-constitutional demand for the introduction of a jury system with a public, oral trial and a public prosecutor.

Although the political-constitutional motives were in the end the decisive direct cause which led to the reforms of 1848, they were closely intertwined with and supported by the changed epistemological ideas. The works of, among others, Mittermaier, Möhl, Savigny and the Prussian-Rhenish committee had shown that there was no essential difference between indicia and other forms of evidence, and that even with a negative system of legal proofs in the end almost everything still depended on the conviction of the judge. This meant that the evidentiary rules could only provide a limited protection against judicial arbitrariness. The changed understanding of the system of legal proofs and the recognition of its structural flaws in the juridical literature supported the feeling that a comprehensive reform of the criminal law of evidence was necessary. In the revolutionary atmosphere of 1848 and 1849 this reform acquired the shape of the introduction of a jury system. However, there was still no final consensus after 1848 on the desirability of a jury system, but there was a growing consensus that the (negative) system of legal proofs should be abolished. After 1848 the main point of discussion now became whether the free evaluation of the evidence should be exercised by professional judges or by lay jurors.

---

133   N. Lieber, *Schöffengericht und Trial by Jury*, pp. 158–159. See also, for example, K. Michels, *Der Indizienbeweis in Übergang vom Inquisitionsprozess zum reformierten Strafverfahren*, p. 180.

5.4 The Discussion on the Criminal Law of Evidence between 1848 and the 1870s

In the phase after the revolutionary reforms of 1848, two important changes occurred in the discussion on the criminal law of evidence. Firstly, as experience was gained with a public, oral procedure and the free evaluation of the evidence, the support for a return to a (negative) system of legal proofs and the secret inquisitorial procedure disappeared at a remarkable pace. The idea that the system of legal proofs was untenable acquired widespread support and in a short time the free evaluation of the evidence was considered an essential part of the *reformierte Strafprozess*. The second change consisted of the fact that the jury system, which had been idealized for several decades by the liberals, came under critical scrutiny during this period. With the increased criticisms of the jury system, it was discussed if perhaps professionals judges or the intermediary solution of *Schöffengerichten* – a combination of professional judges with lay jurors – were more suited to decide on the evidentiary question.

Concerning the first change, after 1848 the argumentation of Jarcke, Möhl and Von Savigny gained increasing support that on the one hand the system of legal proofs was logically untenable, and on the other hand that the abolition of evidentiary rules did not mean that professional judges would necessarily have to decide on the basis of some unreasoned *Totaleindruck*. Instead, the view became widely accepted that even without legal evidentiary rules, jurors and judges would still have to decide on the basis of a reasoned process of weighing the evidence. This meant that the perceived dichotomy between jurors deciding on the basis of their subjective conviction and judges following a system of evidentiary rules, dissolved rapidly. Glaser was struck by this development after 1848 and commented in 1883: "Was einst so gegensätzlich schien, stand nun nebeneinander ... Jury und rechtsgelehrte Richter, beide gleichmäßig von Beweisregeln entbunden".[134]

The increasing acceptance of the view of Jarcke, Möhl and Von Savigny that without evidentiary rules the judge would still have to decide on the basis of a reasoned process of weighing the evidence, opened the way to look for guarantees against judicial arbitrariness in the motivation of the verdict and the possibility of appeal. Furthermore, their idea gained support that even without legal evidentiary rules the judge would still be bound by general rules of logic and experience. Authors appeared after 1848 which pleaded for the creation of a theory of evidence in juridical scholarship instead of a binding system legal

---

134 J. Glaser, *Beiträge zur Lehre vom Beweis im Strafprozess*, pp. 23–24.

system of proofs. Nobili remarks on this development that the common opinion in the German territories started to follow the path of Jarcke and Von Savigny, and began to promote the view that: "nach Abschaffung der gesetzlichen Beweisregeln die Rationalität der Überzeugungsbildung von der Übernahme unverbindlicher wissenschaftlicher Anweisungen abhänge, unter denen Denkgesetze, Erfahrung und Menschenkenntnisse besonders hervorzuheben seien".[135]

It was argued that the 'scientific' theory was to consist of flexible 'guidelines' which would not rigidly prescribe when sufficient evidence existed for a conviction. Representatives of this view were, among others, Planck with his *Systematische Darstellung des deutschen Strafverfahrens auf Grundlage der neueren Strafprozessordnungen seit 1848* (1857), Ortloff's *Beweisregeln und Entscheidungsgründe im Strafprozesse* (1860) and Arnold's *Prüfung der Beweise ohne gesetzliche Beweistheorie* (1858). Ortloff, for example, stated that the function of this scientific theory was to form „einer Anleitung zum Gebrauch eines Maßstabes der richterlichen Erkenntnis und Entscheidung, welcher jedoch elastisch sein und der Beurteilung nach der Individualität der Fälle weichen muss".[136]

Concerning the second change, Landau states that it is clear that the jury system had lost much of its popularity after 1848. He mentions two factors which appear to have been of particular importance in this reconsideration of the jury system. First of all, it became apparent that the separation of the question of fact and the question of law led to difficulties in practice. In the juridical literature it was argued that the German criminal law was too complex and that the jurors were not skilled enough to subsume the proven facts under the juridical terms of the criminal law. The second factor consisted of the fact that the strong distrust of professional judges seemed to diminish rapidly during the period after 1848. One of the most important reasons for the popularity of the jury system lay in the strong conviction that professional judges could not be trusted, but now this argument increasingly lost its appeal. Landau mentions two possible explanations for this development. The public, oral trial and the motivation of the verdict may have increased the trust in professional judges, and during this period the professional judges were recruited more and more from the middle and upper-middle classes. Landau states that the judges

---

135 M. Nobili, *Die freie richterliche Überzeugungsbildung*, pp. 160–161.
136 H. Ortloff, „Beweisregeln und Entscheidungsgründe im Strafprozesse", p. 596.

were increasingly seen as a part of the *bürgerlichen Gesellschaft* against whom no special protection was necessary.[137]

The practical problems with the jury system and the growing trust in the professional judges led to the discussion whether professional judges or perhaps *Schöffengerichten* were not more suited to decide on the evidentiary question. Especially the new option of *Schöffengerichten* quickly gained in popularity. The idea of *Schöffengerichten* had been virtually absent from the debate before 1848. Due to the supposed fundamental difference in the way judges and jurors decided on the evidentiary question it was never seriously considered that they could work together on this point. When this dichotomy disappeared, the *Schöffengerichten* for the first time came to be seen as a good intermediary solution which combined the advantages of lay jurors and professional judges. In particular the problem of the separation of the question of fact and the question of law could be solved through the introduction of *Schöffengerichten*, because the professional judges could explain the meaning of the legal terminology to the lay judges. This technical-juridical argument, for example, appeared in the influential work *Geschworenengericht und Schöffengerichten* (1864) of Schwarze.[138]

The *Schöffengericht* was introduced for the first time in Hannover in 1850 for less severe forms of crimes. The example of Hannover was soon followed in Oldenburg (1857), in Kurhessen and Bremen (1863), in Baden (1864) and in Saxony and Wurttemberg (1869). Although the *Schöffengericht* was at first introduced only for less severe crimes, its positive reception opened the way to consider the option of generally replacing the jury system with *Schöffengerichten*. Importantly, the replacement of the jury system with *Schöffengerichten* was proposed in the concept criminal procedural code for the unified German empire in 1873. This concept ordinance led to an intense debate wherein, among others, Zachariae argued for the introduction of *Schöffengerichten*. It was due to Bavaria and Wurttemberg – who made clear that they would not accept a new criminal procedural code without a jury system – that the concept ordi-

---

137 P. Landau, "Schwurgerichte und Schöffengerichte in Deutschland im 19. Jahrhundert bis 1870", pp. 303–304. This shows important parallels to the idea of Pihlajamäki that the free evaluation of the evidence by professional judges became more acceptable in the course of the nineteenth century because the jurists were drawn more from the middle and upper-middle classes and because they increasingly became 'professional' jurists (in contrast to, for example, the hereditary *noblesse de robe* in eighteenth century France). See H. Pihlajamäki, *Evidence, Crime and the Legal Profession*, pp. 5–6 and 123–125.
138 Ibidem, pp. 295–296. A further important argument that was used in favour of the *Schöffengerichten*, was the fact that it was seen as a form of judicial organisation which had deep roots in German legal history.

nance was eventually changed. In the end, the criminal procedural code for the German empire of 1877 contained the jury system for severe crimes and *Schöffengerichten* for less severe crimes. Nevertheless, Landau states that after 1870 the jury system was constantly put into question. Eventually, this would lead to the complete replacement of the jury system with *Schöffengerichten* for severe crimes in the reform of the criminal procedural law of 1926. In all this time, however, the free evaluation of the evidence was not seriously questioned anymore and had become an integral part of the modern German criminal procedural law.[139]

5.5   Conclusion

It has been described in this chapter that through a long and gradual process the system of legal proofs was replaced by a system based on the free evaluation of the evidence in the German territories between 1750 and 1870. Furthermore, the secret inquisitorial procedure was replaced by the public, oral trial with a public prosecutor and extraordinary punishments were abolished. Three phases can be distinguished in this process. In the first phase, which lasted from 1750 until 1812, the discussion focused predominantly on the question whether judicial torture should be abolished and what should come in its place. During the second phase, lasting from 1812 until 1848, the French reform ideals became known and the central point of debate became whether a jury system should be adopted with the free evaluation of the evidence or whether professional judges in combination with a negative system of legal proofs was preferable. Finally, in the third phase, which lasted from 1848 until the 1870s (although it could also be extended to, for example, 1926) the discussion focused on the question whether it was better to let lay jurors, professional judges or a combination of the two in the form of *Schöffengerichten*, decide after their freely formed internal conviction. The choice was first made for a jury system in the criminal procedural code of 1877, but subsequently in the code of 1926 *Schöffengerichten* were preferred. During the third phase, furthermore, the free evaluation of the evidence became firmly established as an important principle of the German criminal procedural law.

It has become clear throughout this chapter that the reforms of the criminal law of evidence and of the criminal procedural law were inspired, to a very large extent, by the changed epistemological and political-constitutional ideas.

---

[139]   Ibidem, pp. 293–303.

Concerning the first aspect, Ignor has been cited who accurately remarked that the adoption of a probabilistic conception of the certainty required in criminal cases 'laid dogmatic explosives that would eventually lead to the destruction of the system of legal proofs'.[140] In the German discussion it can be seen very well how the new epistemological ideas were adopted and how they were used to question the plausibility of the system of legal proofs. On the basis of the changed epistemological ideas it was argued – by, for example, Mittermaier and the Prussian-Rhenish committee – that there was no essential difference between indicia and other forms of evidence, which undermined one of the central presuppositions of the system of legal proofs (especially how it was applied in the German territories where convictions were forbidden on the basis of indicia). Furthermore, it was argued on the basis of the new probabilistic ideas that it was impossible to determine in general rules for the individual case when there was a sufficiently high probability of guilt to convict someone. This conclusion was increasingly drawn in the course of the nineteenth century and it was used to argue that instead it was better to let lay jurors or professional judges decide on the basis of their freely formed internal conviction.

Concerning the second aspect, it is clear that the changed political-constitutional ideas played a crucial role in the reformation of the inquisitorial procedure and in the argumentation for the adoption of a jury system. From the political-constitutional discourse the idea was derived that the accused should not be forced to contribute to his own conviction, but that he should have the broadest possibility to defend himself and make use of legal counsel. Furthermore, the new concern with the dangers of judicial arbitrariness induced many authors to argue that the trial should be made public and that a clear separation should be made between the functions of public prosecutor, defendant and judge. Finally, the political-constitutional ideas and the distrust of the professional magistrates provided the most important motives for the introduction of a jury system. In this respect the German liberals were ideologically indebted to the French revolutionaries. As will be discussed in the following five chapters, the development of the discussion regarding the criminal law of evidence in the Netherlands between 1750 and 1870 followed a very similar path as the German discussion. This was partially the case because the German discussion was highly influential as a role-model in the Netherlands in this period. There were, nevertheless, also significant differences between the developments in the Netherlands and Germany.

140　A.M. Ignor, *Geschichte Strafprozess*, pp. 167-167.

PART 2

*The Development of the Criminal Law of
Evidence in the Netherlands 1750–1870*

∴

CHAPTER 6

The Criminal Law of Evidence in the Dutch Republic between 1600 and 1795

6.1 Introduction

In this chapter a description is given of how the criminal law of evidence was regulated in the seventeenth and eighteenth centuries in the Dutch Republic and how it functioned in practice. The aim is not to give an exhaustive account of the criminal law of evidence in this period, for that would require one or more separate studies. The purpose of this chapter is to provide a general overview and understanding of the criminal law of evidence as it existed in the Dutch Republic until the end of the eighteenth century when it increasingly became the object of discussion and reform. The importance of this chapter lies in the fact that the nature and extent of the reforms which occurred from the end of the eighteenth century onwards can only be understood and appreciated in contrast to what existed before.

The criminal law of evidence is described in two sections. Section two consists of an analysis of a selection of juridical handbooks and describes how the criminal law of evidence was treated in these theoretical works. Section three focuses on how the criminal law of evidence functioned in practice and to what extent this differed from how it was treated in the juridical literature. The third section is based primarily on existing (archival) studies of how the criminal procedural law functioned in practice in the Dutch Republic. Both sections concentrate on how the criminal law of evidence functioned in the 'normal' criminal procedure which was used for severe crimes (threatened with a corporal or capital punishment). This means that the treatment of less severe crimes and some less common procedural possibilities will not be discussed. No attention will be paid, for example, to the procedural law for military courts and other special tribunals, or to the special rules which applied when an accused was contumacious.

It is, furthermore, important to bear in mind that it is only possible to a certain extent to describe 'the' criminal law of evidence in the Dutch Republic in the seventeenth and eighteenth centuries. An important characteristic of the Dutch Republic was the retention of a large local autonomy and the development of limited (legislative) powers on the level of the province and the Republic as a whole. Every local rural or city court possessed its own customarily determined 'style' and there existed significant differences between the provinces as well.[1] In other words, regional diversity was an essential characteristic of the criminal law of evidence (and the law in general) in the Dutch Republic.[2] Nevertheless, because the Roman-canonical system of legal proofs had been received since the late Middle Ages, there was also an overarching framework concerning the criminal law of evidence that was shared throughout the Republic.

The criminal law of evidence in the Dutch Republic of the seventeenth and eighteenth centuries can, therefore, best be understood as consisting of a common core of presuppositions, rules and maxims which were repeated in the various handbooks and statutes, on which consensus existed, and a peripheral grey area of questions where consensus did not exist and which were often answered differently by the various authors and customary styles of the courts. A further characteristic of the criminal law of evidence in the Dutch Republic in the seventeenth and eighteenth centuries, is the fact that there was continuity in how it was treated in the juridical handbooks and statutes. At least outwardly, in their formulations and structure, a significant transformation is difficult to discern. Even during the late eighteenth century, authors from the sixteenth century such as Wielant and De Damhouder remained important sources of authority.

6.1.1 *The Sources*

This chapter does not aim to be exhaustive and, for this reason, not all the juridical treatises and statutes which were created in the seventeenth and eighteenth centuries have been used. Instead, a selection is made of several important juridical handbooks which span the entire period and multiple provinces. Apart from the handbooks written in the seventeenth and eighteenth

---

1 These courts often had the highest form of criminal jurisdiction, while there was only a very limited possibility for appeals in the Republic, although this differed among the provinces. Egmond, for example, counts two-hundred courts with high criminal jurisdiction in the province of Holland and ninety in the Dutch part of Brabant during the seventeenth and eighteenth centuries alone. See F. Egmond, "Fragmentatie, rechtsverscheidenheid en rechtsongelijkheid in de Noordelijke Nederlanden tijdens de zeventiende en achttiende eeuw", pp. 9–15.

2 The focus of this chapter, furthermore, lies on the description of the criminal law of evidence in the province of Holland. This bias is, to an important extent, caused by the available sources. Most of the juridical handbooks were written by authors from this province and most of the secondary sources describe the criminal procedural practice of cities in the province of Holland.

centuries, some works are used from the sixteenth century which continued to be important sources of authority in the seventeenth and eighteenth centuries. This was particularly the case with the works of Wielant (1440–1520) (*Corte instructie in materie criminele*) and of De Damhouder (1507–1581) (*Praxis rerum criminalum*). Although they wrote on the procedural practice in fifteenth and sixteenth century Flanders, they remained very influential in the Dutch Republic throughout the seventeenth and eighteenth centuries.[3]

The period from around the 1630s until the end of the seventeenth century was the time in which the most influential works were written on the criminal law, while during the first half of the eighteenth century only very few new works were published on this subject. The authors used most intensively for this period are Matthaeus from Utrecht, Bort and Van Leeuwen from Holland, and Huber from Friesland. Besides these Dutch authors, frequent use will also be made of the work *Practica nova rerum criminalium* from the German author Carpzov which was published in 1635. This work had a large influence in the Republic and was referred to by almost all Dutch authors in the seventeenth and eighteenth centuries. Carpzov's work was even translated into Dutch in 1752.

A second important period of reflection on the criminal law of evidence occurred in the last four decades of the eighteenth century, which can be seen as a period of transition. In this chapter some references will be made to the work of Voorda, Van der Keessel and Lievens Kersteman, in as far as they described or explained the criminal law of evidence as it functioned. In this period, however, criticisms of the criminal law started to increase and these authors also gave their opinion on how the criminal law could be reformed. They will, in this chapter, only be used to show how the criminal law of evidence was regulated in the late eighteenth century. Their criticisms and ideas for reform will be treated in the following chapter, although the descriptive and normative parts of their work cannot always be separated entirely.

A last and rather difficult source which is used in this chapter are the criminal ordinances of 1570. These ordinances are included because they were often discussed and referred to in the juridical handbooks, and remained an influential source of legislation throughout the seventeenth and eighteenth centuries. Even as late as 1792, for example, Voorda still dedicated an entire work to show how the criminal ordinances should be interpreted and used in the Republic. The ordinances can be treated well besides the juridical handbooks, because,

---

[3] It has to be noted, however, that the work of De Damhouder was for the most part an unoriginal Latin translation of the work of Wielant. Nonetheless, he made some important expansions and additions, particularly regarding the subject of the criminal law of evidence.

as Faber stated, they themselves possessed something like the authority of an 'important juridical handbook'.[4] The criminal ordinances consisted of three separate ordinances which were meant to form one coherent whole. They were promulgated in 1570 under the authority of king Philip II for the then seventeen provinces of the Netherlands. The ordinances focused predominantly on the criminal procedural law, while a regulation of the substantive criminal law was not included. The precise juridical status of this first significant attempt at criminal procedural unification in the Netherlands remained a point of debate in the Dutch Republic in the seventeenth and eighteenth centuries, as well as in the contemporary historiography. The confusion was caused by the fact that it was unclear whether they were promulgated correctly and if they were completely or only partially suspended by the Dutch revolt. Two sides can be discerned in the historiographical debate on the status of the ordinances. On the one hand, Van de Vrugt holds the opinion that the ordinances did have 'legal validity' in the Dutch Republic in the seventeenth and eighteenth centuries, but she does not base this statement on archival research which shows what this legal validity consisted of and to what extent the ordinances were followed in practice.[5]

Studies that are based on archival research of the actual practice of the criminal law, on the other hand, conclude that the criminal ordinances were not treated as strictly binding but only had a difficult to grasp authority which varied according to the province and the different courts. Archival studies in different regions show that customary practices and provincial or city statutes often continued to be followed even when they were in conflict with the ordinances of 1570. Faber has, for example, found that in Amsterdam a certain authority of the ordinances was recognized, but that many customary practices contrary to the ordinances continued to be followed.[6] Huussen notes for the province of Friesland that the criminal ordinances merely had a strong authority. The primary source which the high court of Friesland used, however, was the compilation of provincial statutes, ordinances and customary laws of 1602

---

4 S. Faber, *Strafrechtspleging en criminaliteit te Amsterdam*, p. 224.
5 M. van de Vrugt, *De criminele ordonnantiën van 1570*, pp. 159–169. The obfuscation was caused by Article five of the 'Pacification of Gent' in 1576 wherein the criminal ordinances were suspended. This article is, however, vaguely formulated so that it could have meant that the ordinances were suspended completely or only in so far as they pertained to the prosecution of heresy. It was, furthermore, unclear for some provinces whether the ordinances had been promulgated correctly and, therefore, if they had ever even acquired force of law.
6 S. Faber, *Strafrechtspleging en criminaliteit te Amsterdam, 1680–1811. De nieuwe menslievendheid*, pp. 222–225.

and later of 1723.[7] Overdijk remarks that in the *Kwartier van Nijmegen* – consisting of several districts in the province of Gelderland – the criminal ordinances were mentioned only very sparsely, while the German Carolina was referred to more frequently.[8] In conclusion, it can be said that the criminal ordinances did not have a strictly binding status in the Dutch provinces but that they did have the authority of, at least, an influential juridical handbook. It is, therefore, useful to look at how they regulated the criminal law of evidence.

6.2 The Regulation of the Criminal Law of Evidence in the Juridical Literature

Similar to the rest of continental Europe, the criminal law of evidence in the Dutch Republic not only described what was sufficient evidence for a conviction, but formed a complex system of rules which presented different evidentiary thresholds for the various procedural steps. The evidentiary rules regulated what kind of procedural path could be followed, when judicial torture could be used and what kind of punishment was possible on what evidentiary basis. There was a scale of decision types which corresponded to different evidentiary standards. Generally, a severe corporal or capital punishment could only be applied when there was a full proof, while judicial torture, a less severe extraordinary punishment or an *absolutio ab instantia* could be pronounced on the basis of less strong evidence. The evidentiary thresholds were, furthermore, never treated on the basis of the existing evidence alone, but were always judged in the light of two other important factors: the social reputation of the accused and the severity of the crime. In this section, three central procedural and evidentiary questions are treated in three subsections. First the difference between the ordinary and the extraordinary procedure is described and it is explicated how the choice of the procedural path was connected with the evidence. In the second subsection, the evidentiary requirements for the use of judicial torture are discussed. Lastly, in the third subsection the rules regulating the sufficiency of proof for the various possible forms of punishments are analysed.

---

7 A.H. Huussen, *Veroordeeld in Friesland. Criminaliteitsbestrijding in de eeuw der verlichting*, pp. 81–83. Voorda, furthermore, remarked that he had never seen that the criminal ordinances were used by the high court of Friesland while he practiced there. See B. Voorda, *De Crimineele Ordonnantien*, p. 17.
8 D.A.J. Overdijk, *De gewoonte is de beste uitleg van de wet*, pp. 61–73.

6.2.1 The Distinction between the Ordinary and the Extraordinary Procedure

One question which is fraught with difficulty, is what the distinction was between the ordinary and the extraordinary procedure in the Dutch Republic in the seventeenth and eighteenth centuries. A clarification of this distinction is particularly difficult because there existed significant differences between the various provinces and local courts on this point, and in many cases it is relatively unclear what the distinction precisely entailed. Monballyu has done much to clarify this distinction for sixteenth century Flanders, and how this distinction was intended in the criminal ordinances of 1570. This explanation forms a useful starting point because it appears to clarify, at least to an important extent, how the distinction was understood in the Dutch Republic.

As Wielant and De Damhouder explain, one first of all has to distinguish between civilly and criminally instituted criminal trials. Secondly, within the criminally instituted criminal trials a distinction can be made between the ordinary and the extraordinary procedure. The civil criminal trials were used for lighter offences that could only give rise to small punishments such as a fine, an *amende honorable* (i.e. a performance of public penitence or an open apology, sometimes combined with some form of a reparation to the victim) or a short banishment. Examples of these lighter offences were not paying certain customs or verbal insults. The civil criminal trial followed the procedural and evidentiary rules of a normal civil trial. In this procedure both parties had to openly present their evidence, the accused could make use of legal counsel and he was almost never arrested. The criminal ordinances of 1570 do not apply to the lighter offences and do not regulate the civilly instituted criminal trials. This procedural type will not be further discussed in this chapter.[9]

The criminally instituted criminal trials were used for offences which were threatened with a long-term banishment, a severe corporal punishment or a capital punishment. There were significant differences between the civilly and criminally instituted criminal trials. In the civil criminal trials, the prosecutor and accused were equal parties and the judge was relatively passive. In the criminally instituted criminal trials, on the other hand, the accused was an object of investigation and the judge had to actively investigate the truth. To achieve this goal the judge could use various procedural measures (often on the instigation of the public prosecutor) such as the hearing of witnesses, confronting witnesses with the accused and judicial torture. As Wielant, De

---

9 J. Monballyu, "Het onderscheid tussen de civiele en de criminele en de ordinaire en de extraordinaire strafrechtspleging in het Vlaamse recht van de 16ᵉ eeuw", pp. 124–125.

Damhouder and the criminal ordinances explain, *the criminally instituted criminal trials* could be conducted ordinarily or extraordinarily.

The ordinary procedural form meant that the procedure was longer and resembled the normal civil procedure (hence 'ordinary'). In the ordinary procedural form the accused could make use of legal counsel and he was given more ample opportunities to defend himself. The extraordinary form was not essentially different from the ordinary procedure but consisted of a more summary procedure wherein many of the defensive possibilities of the accused were restricted. The term 'extraordinary' is somewhat misleading because this was in fact the procedural form that was used most frequently for severe crimes. The purpose and structure of both procedural types were in many respects the same, but in the extraordinary procedure parts of the ordinary procedure were skipped because the case was deemed sufficiently clear. According to the criminal ordinances of 1570 the case was, for example, sufficiently clear when there was a confession or the testimony of two reliable eyewitnesses. In this situation the more summary extraordinary procedure should be followed.[10]

According to Monballyu, the distinction between the ordinary and the extraordinary criminal procedure did not lie in how the preliminary investigation was conducted. As a rule, every criminally instituted criminal trial began with a preliminary investigation (*informatie précédente*). In this phase the witnesses, including persons who had made a complaint or denunciation, were questioned secretly and under oath. Furthermore, the judge could visit the place of the crime, search the house of the accused and order a surgeon to inspect the corpse of the victim.[11] The distinction also did not lie in the possibility

---

10 Ibidem, pp. 124–127.
11 Ibidem, pp. 126–127. A preparatory investigation could not be started without a good reason. If during the preparatory investigation sufficient incriminating evidence had arisen, the accused could be apprehended after permission was given by the criminal judge. Article 4 of the *Ordonnantie op de manier van procederen in criminele saecken* prescribed that "a half proof, vehement or probable suspicion ... after the quality of the crime and or the person" was required to apprehend the suspect. This standard was not further clarified and referred to Roman-canonical law for its more specific criteria. When the standard was not met the suspect could not be apprehended but had to be summoned to appear before the court. However, no special permission of the judge was needed to apprehend the suspect when he was caught *in flagranti delicto* ('red-handed'). Shortly after his apprehension or summoning the suspect was interrogated. This could be repeated as often as the judge deemed necessary. The suspect was interrogated on 'articles' (question points) to which he was required to answer with yes or no. The suspect did not have a right to remain silent but was obligated to answer. Although the suspect was required to answer with a simple yes or no, he could at the end or during the interrogation state facts to his defence (for example, proposing an alibi or declaring that he was acting in self-defence). Witnesses were questioned on articles in the same way. The hearing on articles

to use judicial torture or in the 'inquisitorial' role of the judge. In both the ordinary and the extraordinary criminal procedure, the judge could decide to use judicial torture and he performed an active investigative function (unlike in civil trials where the judge was more passive). The possible decisions were also the same: the judge could acquit the accused, pronounce an *absolutio ab instantia* or convict the accused to an ordinary or extraordinary punishment. Thus, the difference lay purely in the fact that the extraordinary procedure was more summary and that the accused had less defensive rights than in the ordinary procedure.[12]

Importantly, the distinction between the ordinary and the extraordinary procedure as it was made in Flanders, and also in the Dutch Republic in the seventeenth and eighteenth centuries, was not the same as the distinction between the ordinary and extraordinary procedure which was generally made in the late Middle Ages when the inquisitorial procedure first emerged (as described in Chapter two). At this time the ordinary procedure was a procedure which was conducted on the basis of the complaint of a private party, while the extraordinary procedure was a procedure conducted *ex officio* on the basis of the initiative of the judge or 'public prosecutor'. In Flanders and in the Dutch Republic, however, the ordinary and extraordinary criminal procedure were almost always conducted *ex officio* without the complaint of a private party (by the sixteenth century this had become a firmly established practice). Within this inquisitorial *ex officio* procedure a distinction was now made between the ordinary form (where the accused had better defensive possibilities and which more resembled the civil procedure) and the summary extraordinary form.[13]

The extraordinary or shorter procedure was used when the evidence turned out to be sufficiently clear for the judge after the preparatory investigation to make a (definitive) decision. For example, when there was a full proof or when the evidence was so weak that the accused had to be acquitted. The extraordinary procedure was the procedure that was normally used in criminal cases. As

---

occurred in largely the same manner throughout the seventeenth and eighteenth century in the Dutch Republic. Article 14 of the ordinance, furthermore, prescribed that the accused could not use legal counsel or provide written documents to his defence unless the judge gave permission. See M. van de Vrugt, *De criminele ordonnantiën van 1570*, p. 115–116.

12   J. Monballyu, "Het onderscheid tussen de civiele en de criminele en de ordinaire en de extraordinaire strafrechtspleging in het Vlaamse recht van de 16e eeuw", pp. 130–131.

13   A similar distinction appears to have been made in the seventeenth century in Castile. See A.L. Sabadell da Silva, *Tormenta juris permissione*, pp. 67–73.

Article 32 of the *Criminal ordinance on the style* stated, a criminal procedure should be conducted extraordinarily unless the evidence was of a great 'obscurity and darkness', in which case an ordinary procedure should be followed. In other words, the ordinance of 1570 prescribed that the ordinary procedure should solely be used for certain exceptional cases where the evidence or the qualification of the crime was particularly unclear. In this situation the judge could allow a further discussion on the evidence, also from the side of the accused, before he made his decision. Naturally, the ordinary procedure was a more time-consuming and costly effort which the criminal ordinances sought to limit to exceptional cases (partially) out of fiscal motives.[14]

Lastly, Monballyu also reflects on a point which was of a particular importance for the criminal law of evidence in the northern provinces. In general, the criminal ordinances of 1570 were not intended to change the criminal procedural law in the seventeen provinces, but to codify the existing practice and make it more uniform. Nevertheless, there were also some 'abuses' or customary practices that ran against the common opinion in the learned law, which the ordinances sought to abolish. One such abuse was the customary practice, which was followed by many courts, that someone could only be given a severe corporal or capital punishment when he had confessed the crime. This was contrary to the common opinion in the learned law, according to which an accused should be convicted to the ordinary punishment when there were two or more reliable eyewitnesses (and according to some authors even when there were undoubtable indicia). De Damhouder also explicitly complained of this 'abuse', and remarked that there were many courts in Flanders which did not convict the accused to the ordinary punishment when a full proof in the form of two reliable eyewitnesses was present, but instead still proceeded to torture him to obtain a confession.[15]

This was one of the 'customs against justice and good manners' which the criminal ordinances of 1570 intended to abolish. The criminal ordinances made

---

14   J. Monballyu, "Het onderscheid tussen de civiele en de criminele en de ordinaire en de extraordinaire strafrechtspleging in het Vlaamse recht van de 16ᵉ eeuw", pp. 127–131.

15   Ibidem, pp. 129–130. This practice of using torture even when a full proof was present in order to obtain a confession was not unique to the Dutch Republic. Lévy, for example, mentions a remark by Baldus who complained in a similar manner as De Damhouder that suspects were still being tortured to obtain a confession even where there was a full proof. Schmoeckel, furthermore, mentions several other examples where the practice persisted that torture was used even though a full proof was present. He states that this was still done, among other reasons, because the confession was deemed to give a higher form of certainty and for the practical reason that the confession made appeal impossible. See J. PH. Lévy, *La hiérarchie des preuves dans le droit savant du Moyen-Age*, pp. 57–58 and Schmoeckel, *Humanität und Staatsraison*, pp. 441–443.

clear that the accused should be convicted to the full, even capital punishment in the extraordinary procedure when there was a full proof according to the learned law (i.e. when two reliable eyewitnesses were present), and that he should not be tortured in this situation to obtain a confession. It is not clear whether the ordinances also intended to allow convictions to the ordinary punishment on the basis of 'undoubtable indicia', which was an important point of discussion within Roman-canonical law. The criminal ordinances simply referred to the learned law but did not contain an explicit decision on this point which the German *Carolina*, for example, did contain.[16]

Monballyu's analysis offers a useful explanation of how the distinction between the ordinary and extraordinary procedure was understood and intended by Wielant, De Damhouder and the criminal ordinances of 1570. The neat distinction between the ordinary and extraordinary procedure as described by Monballyu, cannot be found in the same way in the Dutch Republic in the seventeenth and eighteenth centuries. Significant differences existed on this point between the various provinces. For the important province of Holland, the distinction between the ordinary and the extraordinary procedure was relatively clear and in many respects resembled the distinction as described by Monballyu. Nevertheless, the distinction in the province of Holland deviated in one very important way from how it was understood and intended by Wielant, De Damhouder and the criminal ordinances of 1570, which was closely connected to the criminal law of evidence.

In the province of Holland, the customary rule had developed that it was normally a necessity that the accused had to confess before a capital or severe corporal punishment could be inflicted. The extraordinary procedure, which was the regular procedure, was understood in Holland as 'proceeding on the confession' of the accused alone. The 'abuse' which De Damhouder mentioned and which the criminal ordinances attempted to abolish, had, therefore, persisted in Holland. Most authors stated that in an extraordinary procedure a conviction to the ordinary punishment could only be given on the basis of a confession. Convicting on the basis of two reliable eyewitnesses or undoubtable indicia to the ordinary punishment was not allowed within the extraordinary procedure, but an extraordinary punishment or the use of judicial torture was possible on the basis of these forms of evidence.[17] In other respects, the

---

16 Wielant was clearer on this subject and stated that an accused "cannot be criminally convicted on the basis of indicia, because in criminal law the evidence has to be clearer than the sky". See J. Monballyu, *Filips Wielant verzameld werk 1*, p. 126.
17 As will be described below, a conviction to a severe corporal or capital punishment was possible on the basis of two reliable eyewitnesses in the ordinary procedure in Holland.

distinction between the ordinary and extraordinary procedure in Holland was the same as that described by Monballyu. In the ordinary procedure the accused was allowed legal counsel and had a better opportunity to defend himself, while the extraordinary procedure was more summary and here the accused did not have these rights.

This conception of the ordinary and extraordinary procedure in Holland can be seen clearly in the works of Van Leeuwen, Bort and Voorda. In his *Roomsch-Hollandsch-Regt* (1656), Van Leeuwen gave a succinct description of the criminal procedural law. The criminal procedure could start in two ways after the preparatory investigation, either by apprehension or by summoning. Van Leeuwen states that when the crime is threatened with a corporal or capital punishment, when it is clear that the crime has been committed (meaning that the *corpus delicti* can be proven) and when there is sufficiently strong evidence against the accused, the procedure had to be conducted extraordinarily. Extraordinarily, Van Leeuwen remarked, means 'summarily and on his confession'.[18] For Bort as well, proceeding extraordinarily meant 'proceeding on the confession' of the accused.[19] In 1792, Voorda strongly criticized this, according to him, fundamentally wrong interpretation of the criminal ordinances by Bort and Van Leeuwen. He deemed that the criminal ordinances had clearly prescribed that in the extraordinary procedure, convictions should also be possible on the basis of a full proof in absence of a confession. However, as he himself observed and regretted, the practice in Holland was that proceeding extraordinarily still meant proceeding exclusively on the confession of the accused.[20]

The understanding of the extraordinary procedure as meaning to proceed on the confession of the accused may also have prevailed in the province of Utrecht. An indication hereof can be found in a commentary by Van der Meulen on the statute regulating the criminal procedure for the high court of Utrecht (1707). Article 8 of this statute mentioned that the extraordinary procedure could be transformed in an ordinary procedure if the court found the case to be so disposed. Van der Meulen explains in his commentary on this

---

18 S. van Leeuwen, *Roomsch-Hollandsch-Recht*, pp. 504–511.
19 P. Bort, *Tractaet crimineel*, pp. 409–503.
20 B. Voorda, *De Crimineele Ordonnantien*, pp. 2–30. The fact that in Holland convictions to the ordinary punishment were possible on the basis of a full proof in absence of a confession in the ordinary procedure, while convictions to a severe capital or corporal punishment in the extraordinary procedure were only possible on the basis of a confession (even though extraordinary punishments could be pronounced in this procedure on the basis of lesser evidence), shows how closely interwoven the criminal procedural path, the possible punishments and the criminal law of evidence were.

article that the extraordinary procedure meant 'proceeding on the confession of the accused'. He furthermore stated that the case could be transformed in an ordinary procedure on account of the 'importance, obscurity and darkness' of the material (the exact wordings of Article 32 of the *Criminal ordinance on the style* of 1570).[21]

For many other regions in the Dutch Republic, however, the distinction between the ordinary and the extraordinary procedure remains relatively unclear and was not defined in the handbooks or regulated in the statutes. Overdijk, for example, mentions that she could not find a definition or clear criterion for this distinction in the legislation or in the practice of the *Kwartier van Nijmegen*.[22] In comparison to Holland, the standard procedural path in other regions appears to have been more of a mixed type where convictions were possible on the basis of a full proof in absence of a confession and where the accused at the same time had better defensive rights. In Friesland, for example, most crimes were dealt with in a procedural form which resembled the ordinary procedure. This meant that convictions to the ordinary punishment were possible on the basis of a full proof in absence of a confession and that the accused had relatively large defensive possibilities. According to Huussen, an extraordinary form was only used in Friesland when the accused had confessed or when the evidence was clear enough for the judge to promptly pronounce a verdict.[23]

In conclusion, there is still much unclear regarding the way in which the ordinary and extraordinary procedure were distinguished in the different provinces of the Republic in the seventeenth and eighteenth centuries. Further (comparative) research needs to be done between and within the provinces on the differences in the criminal procedural styles and, for instance, on how the procedural paths related to the criminal law of evidence and the possible punishments. Despite the variations in procedural styles between the provinces, there are nevertheless two important commonalities. Firstly, the extraordinary procedure – when it was distinguished as such – was everywhere a more summary procedure with less defensive possibilities for the accused and its use depended on the state and clarity of the evidence (with a sufficient

---

[21] J. van der Meulen, *Ordonnantie ende instructie op de stijl ende maniere van procederen voor den hove van Utrecht*, pp. 319–336.

[22] D.A.J. Overdijk, *De gewoonte is de beste uitleg van de wet*, pp. 127–128.

[23] A.H. Huussen, *Veroordeeld in Friesland*, pp. 41–43. Huber in his juridical handbook on Friesland stated: "when the crime is confessed in a manner that a verdict can be given, the accused will be promptly convicted; not having confessed, the procedure will be conducted ordinarily on evidence and the accused will be given time to present his counter-evidence". See U. Huber, *Heedendaegse Rechtsgeleertheyt*, p. 945.

confession a more summary procedure was the norm). Secondly, the evidentiary standards for the different forms of punishments and procedural steps appears to have been largely the same between the provinces and everywhere a strong emphasis was placed on acquiring a confession (although in some provinces, such as Friesland, it did appear to be more acceptable to convict to the ordinary punishment on the basis of a full proof in absence of a confession than in Holland).

6.2.2 *Evidentiary Standards for the Use of Judicial Torture*
As elsewhere in continental Europe, judicial torture formed an important part of the criminal law of evidence in the Dutch Republic. Almost every juridical handbook under consideration contained at least one separate section on the use of torture. In such a section the following subjects were usually treated: for which crimes judicial torture could be used, what level of incriminating evidence was necessary, who were exempted from judicial torture and lastly how judicial torture should be applied and how often it could be repeated. Judicial torture was often dealt with quite extensively in the juridical handbooks. One reason for the large amount of attention which was paid to judicial torture lay in the fact that it was considered a dangerous and far-reaching instrument which needed to be regulated as precisely as possible. From the juridical literature it becomes clear, furthermore, that judicial torture was perceived as an important instrument and a necessary evil precisely for those hard cases where strong evidence short of a full proof existed and where it was desired that a severe corporal or capital punishment could be applied. Huber, for example, stated in this vein: "the common wealth and the tranquillity of the people could not be well safeguarded if all crimes which could not be proven fully, would remain unpunished; for the majority of the crimes are committed in such a way that they cannot be proven through written documents or witnesses".[24] Judicial torture formed an essential part of the criminal procedural law. This was especially the case in those provinces, such as Holland, where a confession was generally deemed a necessity for the infliction of a capital or severe corporal punishment.

Judicial torture was treated in a critical manner and with much circumspection in the juridical handbooks. There were certain cautionary tropes which were repeated in almost all treatises to warn the judge against a too light-hearted use of judicial torture. One such trope, which could be found in most handbooks, was the remark from Ulpian that judicial torture is a dangerous and uncertain instrument because it could very well lead innocent people

---

24   U. Huber, *Heedendaegse Rechtsgeleertheyt*, p. 948.

of a weak constitution to confess to crimes that they had not committed out of fear of pain, while guilty persons of a strong constitution could endure torture without confessing and thereby seem innocent. These cautionary remarks – for example, that the judge was liable to penalties for the unlawful use of judicial torture – showed the consensus that this far-reaching measure should be used with great care.

Precisely because of the dangers inherent in the use of judicial torture, there was a detailed description of the (evidentiary) requirements to prevent its light-hearted use. The treatment of these requirements often started with the acknowledgement that not every situation could be described beforehand and that, therefore, the decision in the end needs to be left to the *arbitrium* or discretion of the judge (in Dutch: *willekeur*). This *arbitrium*, however, was a technical term and did not mean that the judge was left entirely free in his decision. Instead, after this acknowledgment the legal requirements were described which needed to be fulfilled before torture could be used. There were three essential requirements for the use of judicial torture: the crime needed to be punishable by death or a severe corporal punishment, it had to be clear that a crime had been committed (the *corpus delicti* needed to be proven) and, finally, there had to be sufficiently strong evidence against the accused that he had committed the crime.

Regarding the first requirement, it needed to be possible that at least a severe corporal punishment could be inflicted for the crime in question. As some authors explained, it would be unjust when the use of judicial torture was more severe than the possible punishment.[25] Unlike the authors in the seventeenth century, Kersteman and Voorda – writing at the end of the eighteenth century – stated more restrictively that judicial torture was only possible when the crime was threatened with a capital punishment. This more restrictive requirement can also be found in provincial and city ordinances that were created in the second half of the eighteenth century. In these statutes it was prescribed that judicial torture was allowed only if a death penalty would necessarily follow upon a conviction.[26]

---

25   M.L. Hewett, *On crimes. A commentary on books XLVII and XLVIII of the digest by Antonius Matthaeus volume IV*, p. 548–549 and U. Huber, *Hedendaegse Rechtsgeleertheyt*, p. 949. Matthaeus, for example, observed: "natural reason dictates that prior to the conviction the accused should not be treated with greater severity than he would be treated after conviction".

26   Kersteman, *Hollands Rechtsgeleerd Woordenboek*, sub Pijnbank, and Voorda, De *Criminele Ordonnantiën*, p. 77. See, for example, *Reglement en ordonnantie op de crimineele justitie en den styl van procedeeren in Crimineele Zaaken voor den geregte van 's Hertogenbosch* (1792), pp. 65–89.

The second requirement was that normally the *corpus delicti* – meaning the existence of the crime itself – needed to be proven beforehand. As Van Heemskerk explained, the 'natural order' demands that it is first proven that a crime has been committed before it can be proven who has committed it. He then explained that this rule does have some exceptions. Such exceptions were necessary because the *corpus delicti* was sometimes very difficult to prove, for example, when the presumed stolen object or the corps of the victim could not be found. In such situations it sufficed if there was strong evidence that a crime had been committed or when the accused had the reputation of a well-known malefactor.[27] Similarly, Van der Keessel stated: "for if it is probable from suitable evidence that an offence was committed, the *corpus delicti* can be established, even though, to take an example, the body of the killed person is not produced".[28] It was, furthermore, common practice that against vagabonds and beggars judicial torture could be used more easily even when the *corpus delicti* was not proven.[29]

It was the third requirement – that sufficiently strong evidence against the accused needed to be present – which offered the most difficult and most elaborately discussed problem surrounding the use of judicial torture. There was a standard formulation of the necessary level of incriminating evidence which could be found, with slight modifications, in almost every juridical handbook. Article 42 of the *Criminal ordinance on the style* of 1570 formulated this standard neatly and was used in the same words by Bort, Van der Meulen and Van Leeuwen: "the case needs to be so clear and the proof so apparent, that nothing appears to be missing but the confession of the accused to undoubtedly convince him".[30] The ordinance in its original wording then continues "but

---

27 J. van Heemskerk, *Batavische Arcadia*, pp. 487–488.
28 B. Beinart and P. van Warmelo, *Dionysius Godefredus van der Keessel. Lectures on Books 47 and 48 of the Digest*, pp. 1855–1859.
29 P. van Heijnsbergen, *De pijnbank in de Nederlanden*, p. 48. Besides these two first important requirements, there were also some additional rules which needed to be followed. Torture could only be used after an interlocutory verdict from the judge. It could not be used if the accused had already confessed, and not before the accused had been previously interrogated in a normal way without the use of torture. Wielant and the criminal ordinances also state that torture should not be used when the crime has already been fully proven by two irreproachable witnesses. As has been remarked before, however, this demand was not followed in the province of Holland. Matthaeus also stated that it was unlawful to use torture when the crime was already fully proven by either circumstantial evidence, witnesses or documents. See M.L. Hewett, *On crimes. A commentary on books XLVII and XLVIII of the digest by Antonius Matthaeus volume IV*, p. 553.
30 S. van Leeuwen, *Costuymen van Rijnland*, pp. 109–110, J. van der Meulen, *Ordonnantie ende instructie op de stijl ende maniere van procederen voor den hove van Utrecht*, p. 342 and P. Bort, *Tractaet crimineel*, p. 513. Hubert stated similarly: "that the accused is not con-

where there is not a full half proof, or when the evidence is certain and undoubtable, we forbid the application of torture". The complexly formulated article, therefore, only allowed judicial torture when there was a full half proof (i.e. very strong evidence) and at the same time forbade judicial torture when there was already a full proof (i.e. when the evidence was 'certain and undoubtable').

Infamously, the influential jurist Van Leeuwen mistakenly changed the words of the ordinance in his handbook into 'torture is not allowed when there is not a full or a half proof, or when the proof is uncertain and doubtable'. The effect of this change was that in the view of Van Leeuwen judicial torture was allowed when there was already a full proof – for example, two eyewitnesses – as was the practice in Holland, while this was explicitly forbidden in the criminal ordinances of 1570 and in the Roman-canonical doctrine in general. Van Leeuwen does note in passing by at a different point in his handbook that the learned law does not seem to allow the practice of torturing when there was a full proof and that the custom in Holland does not accord with the learned law. The mistake by Van Leeuwen, nevertheless, confirmed the practice in the province of Holland to torture in extraordinary procedures when there was already a full proof purely to acquire a confession. Regarding the minimum evidentiary standard (i.e. 'a full half proof') before torture could be used, Van Leeuwen referred to the learned law in general.[31]

The standard of a (full) half proof or that the evidence needed to be 'so apparent that nothing seemed to be missing but the confession', was normally not further specified in the Dutch handbooks. What is characteristic for most Dutch handbooks, is that they are relatively summary on when this evidentiary threshold was met. They do not contain long lists where a plethora of situations and forms of evidence are discussed and qualified as being either sufficient or insufficient for the use of judicial torture, which can be found in the treatises of many Italian, French and German authors. Instead, most Dutch handbooks simply refer the reader to the treatises of, for example, Clarus, Farinacius, Marsiliis, Gomez and Carpzov. The exemplary status of these foreign authors is clearly acknowledged and relied on by most Dutch authors. A more difficult question is how strictly binding the Dutch jurists interpreted the prescriptions for the use of torture which can be found in these treatises.

The famous foreign writers on criminal law differed among themselves on when precisely judicial torture was allowed. Hotly disputed questions were, for

---

vinced entirely, but he is pressed by such strong presumptions that the judge has no doubt that he is guilty". See U. Huber, *Heedendaegse Rechtsgeleertheyt*, p. 949.

31 S. van Leeuwen, *Roomsch-Hollandsch-Recht*, pp. 511–512.

example, whether one witness of a good reputation, who had seen the crime, was enough for the use of judicial torture and under what circumstances an extra-judicial confession was sufficient. Furthermore, in these treatises it is noted that the evidentiary requirements differ according to several factors such as the reputation of the accused, the severity of the crime and whether the crime would be difficult to prove otherwise. For instance, judicial torture was allowed more easily when the crime was particularly heinous and committed at night or in absence of witnesses. Generally, the treatises intended to formulate minimum evidentiary standards for when torture could be used but they did not dictate that torture had to be used when this standard was met. Whether the evidence was sufficient in the concrete case was in the end left to the discretion of the judge. The Dutch authors appeared to interpret the criteria and examples in the works of foreign authors merely as guidelines which more or less bound the judge in what was minimally required. This approach in the Dutch Republic is perhaps most clearly formulated by Van der Keessel at the end of the eighteenth century:

> The matter, therefore, comes to this that it ought not to be laid down in a general rule, at least not in our courts where the legislator implicitly refers us to the Roman Law, which evidence can be described as proximate in the sense that it is regarded as adequate for ordering torture, but the whole matter must be left to the discretion of a prudent judge who alone, by consulting his conscience and the duties of his office, ought to know and to decide for himself in every case which comes before him, whether there is sufficient probability for him to consider that recourse must or must not be had, to that step which is necessary, indeed, but, nevertheless, harsh and uncertain. Consequently, we ought not to be misled by the authority of the German jurists who, being compelled to observe the Caroline Constitution, cannot in this regard use as great a freedom of opinion as falls to the jurists in the Netherlands by reason of the fact that our law has laid down no definite and special kinds of evidence as fit for decreeing torture.[32]

Van der Keessel here points out an important difference between the Dutch jurists and the German jurists who took the Carolina as their starting point. The Carolina described in much more detail in which situations torture could be used, whereas the criminal ordinances of 1570 only contain the abovementioned rather unspecific standard. Even though Van der Keessel first points out

---

32   B. Beinart and P. van Warmelo, *Dionysius Godefredus van der Keessel. Lectures on Books 47 and 48 of the Digest*, pp. 1890–1891.

that the question whether torture should be used is ultimately left to the discretion of the judge, he does continue – as one of the few Dutch authors – to then extensively treat thirty-four forms of evidence and under which circumstances these can be sufficient for torture. He describes these forms of evidence as they are discussed by the 'doctors of the criminal law', dividing them in proximate and remote forms of evidence. This shows that Van der Keessel still found it useful to describe the learned discussions as exemplary guidelines, but he did not treat them as strictly binding.[33]

Besides Van der Keessel, it was Matthaeus who most extensively discussed the requirements for the use of judicial torture. Matthaeus critically evaluated some points of contention in the learned law, such as the question whether one undoubtable form of proof could be sufficient to torture someone. He explained that the standard in Roman law was that the evidence needed to be such as to make the crime seem probable, so that almost nothing else appeared to be lacking except the confession of the accused. He then remarked that it is highly unlikely that a single form of (circumstantial) evidence could render the commission of the crime so probable that nothing but the confession of the accused would seem to be lacking. Matthaeus, furthermore, remarked that the Roman-canonical authors often mistakenly spoke of 'one sufficient indicium' for the use of torture, when they actually described several forms of circumstantial evidence. For example, the often-mentioned 'indicium' of a man with a blood-stained sword who had been seen fleeing from a house where a crime had been committed, in fact consisted of multiple indicia.[34]

Matthaeus had little sympathy for the discussions in the learned law concerning judicial torture and made clear that it all depended on the cogency of the circumstantial evidence. After having described several forms of circumstantial evidence such as the reputation of the accused and the motive, he remarked "let it suffice to have cited these as examples only. For the rest, how almost uncountable are the instances of circumstantial evidence and arguments and this can better be gathered from everyday experience than from theory".[35]

Apart from the juridical handbooks, the fact that the discussions and examples in the learned law were taken seriously as a guiding principle in practice can also be seen in the published *consilia* or advices in the Dutch Republic.

33   Ibidem, pp. 1891–1953.
34   M.L. Hewett, *On crimes. A commentary on books XLVII and XLVIII of the digest by Antonius Matthaeus volume IV*, pp. 551–554.
35   Ibidem, pp. 549–551.

In some parts of the Dutch Republic it was a regular practice for the (often lay) criminal judges to ask for an advice of a professional jurist when a difficult juridical question arose. For some courts there was even a duty to ask for the advice of a trained jurist for certain decisions, which can be compared to the German *Aktenversendungspflicht* (the obligation to send the juridical question to one or two professional jurists for advice). Some of these advices or *consilia* have been published in bundles. They are especially interesting because here a jurist applies the theory to a concrete case. In one such bundle, collected by Barels and published in 1778, an advice dating from 1712 is given on the question whether judicial torture could be used. In this advice, the jurist scrupulously demonstrated that all the requisites were fulfilled for the use of torture. The crime was severe enough, the *corpus delicti* was proven and the advice demonstrated how the different pieces of circumstantial evidence coalesced to create a strong enough suspicion. As concerns this last aspect, authors such as Mascardus, Menochius and Althusius are cited to show that the evidence was so strong that nothing appeared to be lacking but the confession.[36]

In a similar manner, Schomaker published an advice dating from 1738 where his conclusion was that sufficient circumstantial evidence was not present. This advice reads almost as a small treatise on the use of torture. Schomaker argued that although the question of the sufficiency of proof is left to the *arbitrium* of the judge because no certain rules can be given, this did not mean that the judge could decide on the basis of his own feelings and thoughts (*pro suo sensu et cerebro*). Instead, he had to follow the law as it was explained in the learned treatises.[37] Naturally, the ideal-typical advice of trained jurists – especially the published ones – are not meant here to be representative of how normally a criminal judge would make his decision on whether or not to use torture. This is in fact very hard to ascertain for the Dutch Republic because the decision to use torture was normally not motivated. Furthermore, there most likely existed excesses in practice and differences in style between the different courts.[38] Nevertheless, what the published *consilia* do show is how the decision should ideally be made when judicial torture was to be used.

---

36   J.M. Barels, *Crimineele advysen*, pp. 71–104.
37   J. Schomaker, *Consilia et responsa juris. Vierde deel*, pp. 723–739. Van Hasselt gives a more summary advice in a different case, also coming to the conclusion that torture should not be used. In this case because Van Hasselt expected that the punishment after a confession would not have been severe enough to justify the use of torture. See J.J. van Hasselt, *Onderricht over het houden van krygsraad*, pp. 323–336.
38   De Damhouder, for example, notes that in Flanders judges in practice applied torture abusively on the basis of infamy alone when a specific *corpus delicti* has not even

Finally, there are three further subjects which are treated in most juridical handbooks regarding judicial torture: under which circumstances judicial torture could be repeated, who were exempted from judicial torture and what needed to be done when someone had not confessed under torture. The last subject will be treated in the following subsection. Regarding the first subject, the rule was generally that someone who had undergone judicial torture without confessing should not be tortured again unless new indicia had emerged. In the situation where an accused had confessed under torture but afterwards revoked or denied his confession he could be tortured again. The reason was that the confession strengthened the existing evidence. Most authors stated that there should be a maximum of three repetitions of judicial torture.[39]

Concerning the second subject, there were multiple categories of persons who were exempted from judicial torture. Most Dutch authors acknowledged that pregnant women, old persons who were no longer of a strong constitution and sound mind, and children should not be tortured.[40] The precise definitions and extent of these categories differed among the authors. De Damhouder, for example, remarked that 'juridical doctors' and high dignitaries were exempted from torture as well.[41]

6.2.3   *The Sufficiency of Proof for a Conviction*

In the seventeenth and eighteenth centuries in the Dutch Republic, as elsewhere in continental Europe where the system of legal proofs applied, a scale of decision types existed which corresponded to the strength of the evidence. In general, the principle was acknowledged that only guilty persons should be punished, but the handbooks and the juridical practice testify to the fact that different possible punishments could be used depending on the strength of the evidence. In comparison, the modern criminal law of evidence contains a more 'absolute' distinction between guilty and not-guilty. When the crime is not sufficiently proven the accused is normally entirely acquitted. During the seventeenth and eighteenth centuries in the Dutch Republic the logic was different. When a strong suspicion pressed on the accused but the crime could

---

been established. pp. 64–65 and P. van Heijnsbergen, *De pijnbank in de Nederlanden*, pp. 48–49.

39   See, for example, U. Huber, *Heedendaegse Rechtsgeleertheyt*, p. 952 and M.L. Hewett, *On crimes. A commentary on books XLVII and XLVIII of the digest by Antonius Matthaeus volume IV*, pp. 556–557.

40   See, for example, U. Huber, *Heedendaegse Rechtsgeleertheyt*, p. 951.

41   J. de Damhouder, *Practycke in criminele saken*, pp. 64–65 and P. van Heijnsbergen, *De pijnbank in de Nederlanden*, p. 59.

not be proven 'fully', the judge had the possibilities of judicial torture, an extraordinary punishment or an *absolutio ab instantia*.

6.2.3.1 The Regulation of a Full Proof

There was a consensus in the Dutch juridical literature that a severe corporal or capital punishment should only be pronounced on the basis of a full proof. A feature which the Dutch juridical handbooks had in common with the learned law in general, is that very little attention was paid to the circumstances under which an extraordinary punishment or an *absolutio ab instantia* could be pronounced. These options, which were very important in practice, were left largely to the *arbitrium* of the judge. The juridical handbooks focused predominantly on explaining the criteria which prescribed when a full proof existed and when judicial torture could be used. Regarding the criteria for a full proof, the Dutch authors generally followed the opinion of authors such as Farinacius, Clarus, Gomez and Carpzov and frequently referred to them.

Concerning the sixteenth century, the approach to the existence of a full proof can be seen in the criminal ordinances and in the works of Wielant and De Damhouder. The ordinances of 1570 make clear that an accused could be convicted on the basis of his confession or on the basis of multiple, irreproachable eyewitnesses. They did not explicitly pronounce themselves on the question whether a full proof could also be formed by undoubtable indicia. Wielant, however, unequivocally stated that "no one can be convicted on indicia, however strong they are, because in criminal cases the proof needs to be clearer than the light of day".[42] De Damhouder, on the other hand, did not reject the possibility of 'undoubtable indicia' entirely. He merely stated that according to some authors this was allowed and that it was in dispute.[43]

Even though in general the authority of authors such as Farinacius and Carpzov was followed, there existed important differences between the provinces in the Republic in the seventeenth and eighteenth centuries. In the province of Friesland, for example, it appears that it was possible to convict someone to the ordinary punishment on the basis of two reliable eyewitnesses and on the basis of 'undoubtable indicia'. Huber, who wrote on the criminal procedural law in Friesland, stated that: "for convicted must be held not only those accused persons who are convinced by witnesses or instruments [documents],

---

42 J. Monballyu, *Filips Wielant verzameld werk 1*, pp. 128–129 and M. van de Vrugt, *De criminele ordonnantiën van 1570*, pp. 126–127.

43 J. de Damhouder, *Practycke in criminele saken*, pp. 64–65 and P. van Heijnsbergen, *De pijnbank in de Nederlanden*, pp. 52–53.

but also those who are convinced by undoubtable indicia".[44] He further explains that there is no reason why arguments or indicia should have less probative force than witnesses or written documents, as long as the circumstantial evidence is so strong that it leaves no room for the judge to doubt. When the evidence was very strong but still left doubt in the mind of the judge, the instrument of judicial torture could be used. Nevertheless, Huber remarks that judicial torture should not be used when the crime is already fully proven by either witnesses or undoubtable indicia because the use of judicial torture is only allowed if the truth cannot be known in any other way.[45] Thus, it appears that in Friesland it was recognized that a full proof could be formed by eyewitnesses as well as by undoubtable indicia. That this was possible in Friesland may be partially explained by the fact that the procedure that was

---

44   U. Huber, *Heedendaegse Rechtsgeleertheyt*, pp. 949. This use of the word 'convinced' by Huber is interesting and typical for the juridical handbooks of this period. Authors used the word convinced predominantly to describe that when certain evidence existed the accused or the judge was convinced (or *overtuigd*) by the evidence. It was normally not used to refer to an internal conviction of the judge. Lepsius observed a similar tendency in the work of Bartolus: "Auffällig sind allerdings mehrere passive Formulierungen, mit denen Bartolus die Überzeugungsbildung des Rechters charakterisiert. Stets ist in passivischer Syntax die Rede davon, dass der Richter zur Überzeugung gebracht werde (*ad fidem adducitur*) ... Der Richter übernimmt also keine Ermittlungstätigkeit, sondern wird überzeugt". See S. Lepsius, *Von Zweifeln zur Überzeugung*, pp. 18–19.

Lepsius draws the conclusion from these formulations that Bartolus was most likely focused on civil procedures in which the judge was relatively passive. This seems an unlikely explanation because the word convinced was used in a similar passive way in the Dutch treatises in the seventeenth and eighteenth centuries which were focused solely on the criminal procedure. It is probable that the passive use of the word convinced was typical for the 'objectifying' tendency within the system of legal proofs. As the use of this word in the Dutch treatises make clear, when the objective evidentiary standards were met then the accused or the judge 'was convinced'. It was not yet used to refer to the internal conviction of the judge because this was not constitutive for the question whether there was sufficient evidence to convict someone. Incidentally, the 'objective' or 'passive' etymological roots of this use of 'convincing' may lie in the traditional meaning of the Dutch and German equivalent words of *overtuigen* and *überzeugen*. These words referred to the old Germanic procedure where you could literally bring more witnesses or oath-helpers to the trial and thereby 'overwitness' the opponent (*über* means 'over' and *zeug* means 'witness', hence 'overwitness'). That is why it was the accused that was 'convinced' and not primarily the judge. Only later did the meaning of this word shift and was it increasingly used to refer to the (internal) conviction of the judge. This shift in meaning is a reflection of what Stichweh aptly called the 'Mentalisierung des Beweises' in the eighteenth and nineteenth centuries. See R. Stichweh, "Zur Subjektivierung der Entscheidungsfindung im Deutschen Strafprozess des 19. Jahrhunderts", pp. 283–292.

45   Ibidem, pp. 949–950.

normally followed in Friesland strongly resembled the ordinary procedure where the accused had relatively strong defensive rights.

The situation was different for authors commenting on the practice in the province of Holland. As has been stated before, in Holland the customary rule had remained in force that someone could not be convicted to a capital or severe corporal punishment in the *extraordinary* procedure if he had not confessed to the crime. Within the extraordinary procedure, two eyewitnesses nor undoubtable indicia sufficed for a severe corporal or capital punishment. Instead, an extraordinary punishment or the use of judicial torture could be pronounced. As will be further discussed below, it does seem, however, that in the exceptional cases where an ordinary procedure was used, convictions were possible on the basis two eyewitnesses or undoubtable indicia in absence of a confession in Holland.

The practice in Holland that within the extraordinary procedure a full proof could only be formed by a confession deviated from the doctrine in the learned law. The Dutch authors, such as Van Leeuwen and Bort were well aware that the practice in Holland deviated from what the 'general school of thought' prescribed and they recognized this fact in their handbooks. Van Leeuwen, for example, remarks that to torture someone when the evidence was clear and undoubtable was prohibited in the learned law and in the criminal ordinances of 1570, but that the customary rule nevertheless had not changed in Holland. He, thus, rather ambiguously acknowledged that the practice in Holland was not in accordance with the learned law, but he did not explicitly condemn this practice. Instead, he went on to give an explanation for the 'popularity' of this customary rule. The reason for its popularly, Van Leeuwen remarked, was that when there was a confession, the accused could not appeal (*confessus non appellat*).[46] The impossibility to appeal was of special significance for the cities that were zealous of retaining their (juridical) autonomy and did not want any interference from higher authorities.

In his handbook, Bort as well observed that, according to many authors, nobody can be given a capital or corporal punishment unless he has confessed to

---

[46] S. van Leeuwen, *Costuymen van Rijnland*, pp. 107–108, S. van Leeuwen, *Roomsch-Hollandsch-Recht*, pp. 511–512 and P. van Heijnsbergen, *De pijnbank in de Nederlanden*, pp. 52–53. The first article of the custom of Rijnland on which van Leeuwen gave his commentary read: "No one shall be convicted to die unless the delinquent has confessed to his crime, notwithstanding that the crime is notorious and knowable through witnesses or other indicia". Van Leeuwen, however, stated that this statement should not be taken as absolutely true and that there were exceptions.

the crime. But this, he contended, 'is not always and universally true'. Bort was more explicitly critical of the practice in Holland than Van Leeuwen. He remarked that a capital punishment could also be pronounced when 'the accused is convinced by notorious and irrefutable evidence, even when he obstinately refuses to confess'. He did not, however, further elucidate when this 'notorious and irrefutable evidence' existed but simply referred at this point to a large number of authors such as Carpzov and Gomez. Another critical observation from Bort was that he stated that the accused should not be tortured when a full proof was present solely to obtain a confession.[47]

The practice to only impose a capital punishment in the extraordinary procedure when there was a confession remained in force throughout the eighteenth century in Holland. This can be seen from the works of, among others, Lievens Kersteman and Van der Keessel in the second half of the eighteenth century. Lievens Kersteman observed that there is a customary rule which is commonly followed that no one should be given the capital punishment unless he has confessed the crime.[48] Van der Keessel as well remarked that the practice in Holland exists that the capital punishment can only be applied when there is a confession. He himself, however, disagreed with those who deemed 'that capital punishment ought to be imposed only on those who have confessed'. He continued to explain:

> I consider, therefore, that the rule stated in C.9.47.16, which requires either a confession by the accused or his conviction and full proof of the crime, is consistent with legislative wisdom. And to me it seems harsh that when the crime has been fully proven that the accused is still tortured so that he may confess to the crime.[49]

The practice in Holland in the seventeenth and eighteenth centuries, therefore, was that the full ordinary punishment could only be applied in the extraordinary procedure when there was a confession. It appears, however, that in the ordinary procedure the full punishment could be applied on the basis of witnesses and indicia in absence of a confession. This occurred in at least two famous cases in the eighteenth century in Holland. Both Jaco (1718) – who had been tortured two times – and Van Goch (1777) were received in an ordinary procedure after an extraordinary procedure in which they had not confessed.

---

47   P. Bort, *Tractaet crimineel*, pp. 570–572.
48   Lievens Kersteman, *Der jonge Practisyns*, pp. 105–106.
49   B. Beinart and P. van Warmelo, *Dionysius Godefredus van der Keessel. Lectures on Books 47 and 48 of the Digest*, p. 1767.

These ordinary procedures were highly exceptional in the juridical practice of Holland. Thuijs, for example, only counts five cases between 1690 and 1730 which were continued ordinarily after an extraordinary procedure.[50] Jaco and Van Goch were eventually convicted to death on the basis of witnesses and indicia, after which they appealed first to the high court of Holland, then to the supreme court and lastly for revision to the provincial government of Holland (appeal was possible in criminal cases in Holland, after an ordinary procedure, when the accused had not confessed). Particularly the case of Van Goch gives an interesting insight in the ideas underlying the distinction between the ordinary and extraordinary procedure and its connection with the criminal law of evidence.

Unusually, the pleas from the public prosecutor and the lawyer representing Van Goch were published in a magazine in 1778 (in the *Nieuwe Nederlandsche Jaerboeken*). A large part of the argumentation of the lawyer representing Van Goch was aimed at demonstrating that in an ordinary procedure a capital punishment could only be pronounced on the basis of a confession or a full proof which consisted of the testimony of multiple eyewitnesses, but never through 'arguments or indicia'. He remarked that it had not been allowed in any law or custom. He also referred to Gothodfredus, Böhmer and Bruneau, and stated that it is clear from divine law – 'no truth shall exist but on the mouth of two or three witnesses' – and from Roman law that "the judge can acquire no certainty of the truth through conjectures or so called indicia alone".[51]

The public prosecutor, on the other hand, argued that the combination of the different forms of evidence amounted to "such a high degree of probability, yes of certainty, that the honourable judges ... cannot doubt for a moment of

---

50 F. Thuijs, *Op zoek naar de ware Jaco*, pp. 246–248 and 276–278. Faber, who counted with ten year intervals between 1680 and 1811, comes to an average frequency of less than one time per year that an accused was admitted to an ordinary procedure. S. Faber, *Strafrechtspleging en criminaliteit te Amsterdam, 1680–1811. De nieuwe menslievendheid*, p. 33.

51 *Nieuwe Nederlandsche Jaerboeken (mei 1778)*, pp. 382–404. Of particular interest is a passage from Bruneau which the lawyer of the accused cited to substantiate that indicia could not create a full proof sufficient in criminal cases: "Il y a deux sortes de science aussi biens, qu'il y a deux sortes de convictions: il y a la science qui produit une *certitude morale*; il y a science qui produit une *certitude physique*. La science qui produit une certitude morale est celle, qui dépend du raisonnement, et telle est la science, qui n'est fondée sur des indices et présomptions. La science, qui produit une certitude physique est celle, qui dépend immédiatement des sens, telle qu'est celle des témoins, qui ont vu commettre le crime ... Or la science et la conviction morale sont bien capables de fonder un jugement en matière civile, mais elles ne suffisent jamais en matière criminelle". The work of Bruneau to which lawyer referred here was *Observations et maximes sure les matières criminelle* (1715).

its truth".[52] The public prosecutor extensively demonstrated that Roman law did allow capital punishments on the basis of undoubtable indicia, and that this was also accepted in the contemporary Dutch law.[53] Subsequently, he gave a revealing argumentation of why convictions to the capital punishment on the basis of indicia were permitted in ordinary procedures while they were not in extraordinary procedures:

> In regard of this question careful distinction is necessary between the ordinary and extraordinary procedure; yes in extraordinary procedures, where only on the confession definitive sentences can be given, indicia cannot come into further consideration than in respect of the use of torture: the reason is clear, in an extraordinary procedure the accused cannot make use of legal counsel and he cannot appeal; it would therefore be a *pessimi exempli* to definitively convict someone in an extraordinary procedure on the basis of indicia. But when the accused finds himself in an ordinary procedure, it is entirely different: because then all legitimate forms of evidence may be used *contra reum* and among them also indicia ... the purpose of the ordinary procedure whereto the accused is allowed in absence of a full confession, is on the one side to allow him to present his defence with the help of legal counsel, and on the other side to give the *accusatores publici* opportunity to prove through *testes et argumenta* what was lacking in the confession.[54]

In short, the public prosecutor argued that in the ordinary procedure capital punishments could be pronounced on the basis of witnesses and undoubtable indicia because here the accused had ample opportunity to defend himself and make use of legal counsel. The public prosecutor won the trial, and the verdicts of the lower courts were confirmed without motivation. It can, therefore, be concluded that convictions to a capital punishment on the basis of multiple eyewitnesses and undoubtable indicia were possible in Holland in the ordinary procedure. Nevertheless, the reasoning of the public prosecutor also shows that the ordinary course of events was that first everything needed to be done in the extraordinary procedure to acquire a confession. Furthermore, the fact that the lawyer of the accused spent such a large part of his plea

---

52   Ibidem, p. 532. The plea and defence of the lawyer and the public prosecutor have been published integrally in the magazine *Nieuwe Nederlandsche Jaerboeken*.
53   Ibidem, pp. 478–500. Importantly, the public prosecutor also remarked in passing by that the criminal ordinances of 1570 were used in Holland only as a guideline, and that practices contrary to the ordinance were not invalid. See pp. 545–546.
54   Ibidem, pp. 498–499 and 534.

to show that convictions on indicia were not permitted, testifies to the fact that this was not yet a clearly settled question even in 1777.

Finally, it is important to note that not every confession was sufficient for a conviction. There were several criteria for a valid confession on which most handbooks agreed. The confession had to be made in court in front of the judge. The confession also needed to be credible on the basis of supporting (circumstantial) evidence, and the confessed crime needed to be sufficiently qualified. An extrajudicial or an as yet insufficient confession could be a reason to use judicial torture if the accused refused to confess before the judge.[55] Furthermore, the confession needed to have been made 'freely'. The confession made under the influence of judicial torture was not yet sufficient for a conviction. After someone had confessed under torture, he needed to repeat or 'ratify' his confession within a short period, often twenty-four hours, before the judge and 'outside of pain and bonds of iron'. The 'freedom' in this confession was, of course, largely illusory because the accused who retracted his confession after the use of judicial torture, could be tortured again. Most authors agreed that the accused who kept retracting his confession after the use of torture, could be tortured to a maximum of three times.[56]

6.2.3.2 Extraordinary Punishments and the Absolutio ab Instantia

The important question under which circumstances sufficiently strong evidence existed to pronounce an extraordinary punishment or an *absolutio ab instantia* was given relatively little attention in the juridical literature. In the situation where strong evidence short of a full proof existed it was left largely to the *arbitrium* of the judge to decide whether he deemed that judicial torture, an extraordinary punishment or an *absolutio ab instantia* should be pronounced. The juridical handbooks predominantly treated these discretionary powers of the judge when they discussed what needed to be done when judicial torture had been applied but the accused persisted in stating that he was innocent. Already in 1570 Article 41 of the *Criminal ordinance on the style* presented the four options of what the judge could do in this situation, which were largely repeated in the juridical handbooks of the seventeenth and eighteenth centuries. This article stated that judicial torture could not be reapplied without new indicia. Instead the judge had to make a decision to either fully acquit the accused, to absolve him from the instance (*absolutio ab instantia*),

---

55 P. Bort, *Tractaet crimineel*, pp. 499–500.
56 J. van der Meulen, *Ordonnantie ende instructie op de stijl ende maniere van procederen voor den hove van Utrecht*, pp. 345–346 and M.L. Hewett, *On crimes. A commentary on books XLVII and XLVIII of the digest by Antonius Matthaeus volume IV*, pp. 556–557.

to pronounce an extraordinary punishment or to 'decide otherwise after the exigency of the case'.

Authors such as Bort, Van Leeuwen and Hubert attest to the relative lack of clarity which of these sentences should be applied under what circumstances. Van Leeuwen, in his commentary on this article, observed that there exists a difference of opinion between those who state that he who has endured torture without confessing should be completely absolved, and those who state that at least a lesser punishment could be pronounced or an *absolutio ab instantia*. Van Leeuwen continued to explain that a distinction had to be made between the situation where an accused was tortured on the basis of only a half proof and the situation where there was already nearly a full proof but the accused was tortured solely to acquire a confession so that a capital punishment could be applied. In the first scenario, normally a complete acquittal or an *absolutio ab instantia* should be applied. In the second situation, however, Van Leeuwen stated that the accused should be punished with a lesser, extraordinary penalty.[57] In a different work Van Leeuwen remarked that someone who had withstood judicial torture should be acquitted or punished with an extraordinary punishment 'after the exigency of the case and the strength of the evidence'.[58]

Bort was of the opinion that the accused should be acquitted if the indicia had been sufficiently purged by the endurance of torture and that otherwise the accused should be punished extraordinarily after the exigency of the case and *pro arbitrio judicis* (to the discretion of the judge).[59] Huber too, described the differences of opinion on this point. He noted that some authors found that the accused should be acquitted entirely or at least be absolved from the instance when he had endured torture. Other authors were of the opinion that when the accused was 'infamous' and the judge still believed he was guilty even though he had withstood torture, he should be punished extraordinarily.[60] A more restrictive approach can be seen in Article 10 of the statutes for the high court of Utrecht which stated that someone who had endured torture

---

57 S. van Leeuwen, *Manier van procedeeren in civile en crimineele saaken*, pp. 326–327.
58 S. van Leeuwen, *Roomsch-Hollandsch-Recht*, pp. 519–520. Here van Leeuwen also reiterates that: "it is uncertain if and how the accused should be punished when he has endured torture, and on this matter there is no uniformity of opinion".
59 P. Bort, *Tractaet crimineel*, p. 503.
60 U. Huber, *Heedendaegse Rechtsgeleertheyt*, p. 953.

should be acquitted entirely or absolved from the instance 'after the exigency of the case'.[61]

The juridical handbooks reveal that the judges had a lot of leeway in deciding what decision to make when there was strong evidence short of a full proof. Even when judicial torture had been applied, most authors were of the opinion that the judge could still decide to pronounce an extraordinary punishment. This was a largely unregulated area which can be seen from the fact that most authors acknowledged that it had to be left to the *arbitrium* of the judge and, for example, in the often repeated phrase that the judge had to decide 'after the exigency of the case'. Although it was left to the discretion of the judge, three factors clearly played a central role in the decision of the judge: the strength of the evidence, the gravity of the crime and the reputation of the accused. Here it has to be kept in mind that the social reputation of the accused was a highly significant factor throughout the criminal procedure. Vagabonds and beggars could be tortured and given an extraordinary punishment far more easily than citizens who had a good reputation.

6.2.3.3   Antonius Matthaeus

Matthaeus was without a doubt the most original and critical writer on the criminal law in the Dutch Republic of the seventeenth century, and his work *De criminibus* (published in 1644) became internationally renowned. Matthaeus merits a separate treatment because, particularly regarding the criminal law of evidence, his views differed in many ways from that of the other Dutch authors. Matthaeus was well aware of his innovative approach and consciously distanced himself from many of the commonly held opinions of the 'learned doctors'. As Matthaeus himself stated, instead of following them he went back more directly to the sources of the Roman law and presented a different interpretation thereof. His consciously critical stance towards the 'learned doctors' can, for example, be seen in the following remark: "the reader will not be able to employ himself better than by abandoning these name droppers (for I may so call those who spend all their time citing learned authorities and none quoting laws and jurisprudence) and by looking rather at the laws and the reasons for the laws".[62]

---

61   J. van der Meulen, *Ordonnantie ende instructie op de stijl ende maniere van procederen voor den hove van Utrecht*, pp. 343–344.
62   M.L. Hewett, *On crimes. A commentary on books XLVII and XLVIII of the digest by Antonius Matthaeus volume IV*, p. 550.

Matthaeus opens his chapter 'on arguments and circumstantial evidence' with the observation that the 'general school of thought' holds that an accused cannot be convicted on the basis of arguments and circumstantial evidence. Within this group there are also those who find that someone cannot be convicted to the statutory (i.e. the ordinary) penalty on the basis of circumstantial evidence, but that he can be given an extraordinary punishment. Matthaeus continues: "abandoning both views, we will cleave to the very few, who think that one convicted by circumstantial evidence and arguments can be punished with the statutory penalty just as if he was convicted by witnesses".[63]

Matthaeus agreed that the evidence needed to be 'clearer than the light of day' for a conviction in criminal cases, but he disagreed with the idea that this clarity could not be created by arguments and circumstantial evidence. He rejected this notion because he found that Roman law did allow for this possibility and because reason appeared to dictate it as well. Matthaeus explained that an argument was nothing other than a reason which gives credence to a doubtful fact. Several circumstantial forms of evidence can combine to form sufficient evidence to convict someone just as well as two eyewitnesses or a confession. Matthaeus poignantly argued that, in contrast to what most doctors held, this was the normal practice under Roman law:

> They raise their second objection "the range of evidence is so great that it cannot be brought to certainty unless it is left to the discretion of the judge. This, however, will be odious for the judge, and harmful to the accused". I am astonished that there are persons who object in this way, since Papinian has openly replied in two texts to what they regard as absurd. Indeed, in D.48.16.1.4 and D.50.1.15 he says that a question of fact is left to the discretion of the judge, but the penalties are reserved for the authority of the law. I am also astonished that they have not taken notice of what Callistratus has remarked in general concerning testimonies and proofs in D.22.5.3. Namely that the judge knows best how much trust must be put in witnesses. And that no definite limit can be set as to which arguments suffice for proving a specific point, and that therefore an enquiry must not be bound to one kind of proof, *but the judge must decide in his own mind what he either believes, or what he regards as not sufficiently proven.*[64]

---

63 Ibidem p. 530.
64 Ibidem, pp. 531–533.

This innovative approach of Matthaeus also had significant further consequences for how he evaluated several of the core principles of the 'general school of thought'. He did not treat the confession as a sacrosanct form of evidence but regarded the confession as something which could be very convincing when it was 'probable' enough. His approach also helps explain his scepticism towards the instrument of judicial torture. He stated that he did not understand how the use of torture was an appropriate measure to extract the truth from someone and on this point disagreed with Roman law which did allow for judicial torture. Matthaeus even came to the tentative conclusion that judicial torture should be abolished when he remarked: "for when, in the scale of reason, we balance the arguments which are produced on both sides, both for and against torture, those by which torture is attacked seem stronger than those by which it is defended".[65]

Finally, Matthaeus also advocated a far more absolute distinction between guilty and not-guilty than that which existed within the system of legal proofs. This can, for example, be seen in his rejection of the idea that circumstantial evidence alone does not suffice for the statutory penalty but could be enough for an extraordinary punishment: "A crime is either proven by arguments or it is not proven. If it is proven there is no reason why the statutory penalty must not be imposed. If it is not proven, there is no place left for punishment".[66] It can also be seen in his treatment of the question whether someone who had endured torture without confessing should be absolved from the instance (*absolutio ab instantia*) or acquitted entirely. Matthaeus did not agree with those who argued that "Just as an accused must not be convicted if the accuser does not prove the crime, so he must not be absolved from the crime if he himself does not prove his innocence, for it would be inequitable that a man of suspect innocence, if he were prosecuted again, should defend himself with the exception of *res judicita* [D.9.2.51]".[67] Instead, Matthaeus argued that when the crime had not been sufficiently proven, the accused needed to be acquitted entirely: "For if an accused person has been tortured three times or if the accuser cannot prove the charge, it is far more equitable that the accused be acquitted [completely] than that he suffer perpetual suspense about his life and safety".[68]

In conclusion, it can be said that the work of Matthaeus was relatively exceptional. His views differed from that of most Dutch authors who more

---

65   Ibidem, pp. 553–562. Matthaeus also emphatically condemns the custom whereby torture is used when the crime is already proven otherwise (either by witnesses or circumstantial evidence).
66   Ibidem, p. 534.
67   Ibidem, pp. 557–558.
68   Ibidem, p. 558.

closely followed the 'general school of thought'. Even though most Dutch authors did not follow the deviating opinions of Matthaeus regarding the criminal law of evidence, his work did have great authority in the Republic and was often referred to throughout the seventeenth and eighteenth centuries.[69] His work is, furthermore, difficult to place in comparison to, for example, the French reformers who introduced the free evaluation of the evidence in the second half of the eighteenth century. Unlike the French revolutionaries, Matthaeus did not entirely reject the usefulness of evidentiary rules and did not plead for a completely free evaluation of the evidence. Matthaeus argued that the existing system of evidentiary rules was based on an incorrect understanding of Roman law and seemed to be contrary to 'what reason dictated'. He presented his view, in which the judge would have a far larger room to evaluate the evidence, as a more correct understanding of Roman law and still relied heavily on its authority. Summarizing, it can be said that the approach of Matthaeus, in which he rejected large parts of the existing system of legal proofs, was highly innovative but at the same time went too far for many of his contemporaries.[70]

6.3   The Practice of the Criminal Law of Evidence in the Dutch Republic

Because of the legal fragmentation it is difficult to make general statements about the practice of the criminal law of evidence in the Dutch Republic. The possibility to ascertain the uniformity or diversity between different regions is further hampered by the fact that so far relatively little research has been done on how the criminal procedural law actually functioned in different parts of the Republic. One significant exception to this relative dearth of information is a study on the practice of criminal justice in Amsterdam between 1680 and 1811 by Faber. This study will be discussed in this section to describe how the

---

[69]   One important example of an author who did follow Matthaeus was Huber who wrote on the criminal law in Friesland. Regarding the criminal law of evidence he frequently and approvingly cited Matthaeus. See U. Huber, *Heedendaegse Rechtsgeleertheyt*, pp. 949–953.

[70]   The work of Matthaeus in this sense shows significant parallels to the work of Bartolus as described by Lepsius. Matthaeus, like Bartolus, frequently used the term *fides* in the sense of the conviction of the judge. Like Bartolus, however, his innovative approach was not followed by the mainstream of the authors (a fact of which Matthaeus was well aware). These authors, nevertheless, show that there were significant divergences concerning the criminal law of evidence within the tradition of the *ius commune*, and that there were some authors who pleaded for a far more free evaluation of the evidence. See also S. Lepsius, *Von Zweifeln zur Überzeugung*, pp. 171–197.

criminal procedure functioned in the eighteenth century, but it cannot be taken as (entirely) representative for the criminal justice in the entire Republic. Nevertheless, it offers a significant example of the characteristics of the practice of the criminal procedural law in the province of Holland.[71]

In Amsterdam there was a college of nine *schepenen* which formed the criminal court. The function of the *schout* can be equated to some extent with that of a public prosecutor, although the modern 'duality' between public prosecutor and judge was not yet fully in place. The final judgment was left solely to the *schepenen*. The *schout* led the investigation, he demanded a certain punishment and was responsible for the execution of the sentence. Besides these two main actors, there were also numerous clerks, police agents, night watches and the *substitute-schouten* which need not be discussed in detail here. Finally, there was one hangman in the pay of the province of Holland who performed the public executions, and one *binnen-scherprechter* who executed the non-public corporal punishments and applied judicial torture.[72]

In Amsterdam a procedural distinction was made between cases that were treated *below* in the dungeons of the town hall, and cases that were treated *above* in the courtroom. The difference between these two options corresponded largely to the general distinction between the extraordinary and the ordinary procedure, although procedures *above* could also be conducted extraordinarily. The procedure *below* was used for offences threatened with a corporal or capital punishment. For these crimes the suspect was in most cases apprehended and confined in the dungeon of the town hall. He was normally not allowed legal counsel. The *schout* questioned the suspect in the interrogation room of the dungeon in the presence of two *schepenen*. If the suspect denied the allegations and if there was strong evidence against him, the *schepenen* could decide in an interlocutory verdict that judicial torture would be applied. After these proceedings the *schepenen* pronounced their final verdict. The procedure above was normally only used for civil cases, minor offences and for more severe crimes when the accused was contumacious. The minor offences and crimes of violence which were dealt with above appeared on the *schoutsrol* and were prosecuted extraordinarily. In these instances, in contrast with the

---

71 There have also been written two interesting studies on the criminal procedural practice in the cities of Haarlem and Amsterdam in the late Middle Ages by Boomgaard and Müller, which shed light on how the inquisitorial procedure developed and was used in this period. See J.E.A. Boomgaard, *Misdaad en Straf in Amsterdam*, and M. Müller, *Misdaad en straf in een Hollandse stad: Haarlem, 1245–1615*.

72 S. Faber, *Strafrechtspleging en criminaliteit te Amsterdam, 1680–1811. De nieuwe menslievendheid*, pp. 27–28.

procedure below, the accused was not put into custody and could not be tortured.[73]

Judicial torture has been used in Amsterdam since the late Middle Ages and continued to be used until 1798 when the *Staatsregeling* (constitution) of the Batavian Republic forbade judicial torture. A distinction was made between 'big torture', which most often consisted of a tightening of metal screws or hoisting the accused on a pole and thereby (painfully) extending his limbs, and 'small torture' which entailed whipping. Another possibility was for the *schepenen* to allow only the frightening of the accused with torture (*territio*) by bringing him into the torture chamber. In a selection of circa 20 years spanning the eighteenth century, Faber finds that on a total of 2619 criminal cases, 139 times (5.3%) the *schout* requested the use of torture which was allowed in 80 cases (3.6%). The data of Faber further shows that the use of big torture diminished slightly in the second half of the eighteenth century and that the use of small torture remained largely the same until 1798. Faber, however, does not explain the diminished use of big torture by an increased reluctance to use torture in the second half of the eighteenth century. According to Faber, the reason lay in the fact that there occurred less crimes for which big torture would normally have been applied.[74] Judicial torture in Amsterdam seems, therefore, not to have withered away in practice due to changing sensitivities of the judges. As will be discussed in the following chapter, it also becomes clear from the juridical literature of the late eighteenth century that judicial torture was not considered obsolete and still had many supporters among jurists in the Dutch Republic.

There were two important incentives for the use of judicial torture in the province of Holland. Firstly, there was a strong incentive to use torture because a confession prohibited the possibility of appeal to the high court of Holland and thus protected the autonomy of the cities. Secondly, even when a full proof was present, a confession was normally still a necessity for any public form of a corporal or capital punishment (*schavotstraffen*).[75] The handbooks

---

73 Ibidem, pp. 29–33 and 260–267.
74 Ibidem, pp. 111–136. Faber also remarks that these numbers only show the use of judicial torture which was transcribed in the 'confession books'. It does not show the effects of the threat of torture in the preliminary investigation by the *schout* and his officers or (physical) harassments that might have taken place. These practices naturally remain a dark number. Incidentally, the emphasis on acquiring a confession in the extraordinary procedure can also be seen in the fact that the name of the register in which the judicial documents and evidence of criminal cases was kept, was called the 'confession books'.
75 Amsterdam appears to be a relative exception in the sense that in most parts of the Republic a confession was only necessary for a capital punishment, but not for public

that describe that no corporal or capital punishment was allowed in Holland in the extraordinary procedure in absence of a confession is therefore corroborated by the research of Faber. He has found only very scarce exceptions to this rule in which a minor corporal punishment was applied without a confession, but not once in the eighteenth century was a death sentence pronounced without a confession after an *extraordinary* procedure. He concludes that this rule was strictly applied until 1798.[76]

The practice of the criminal procedural law of Amsterdam shows, furthermore, in accordance with the juridical literature, that there existed several different possible sentences which depended on the strength of the incriminating evidence. When there was almost no evidence the accused could be acquitted entirely. When some evidence was present but the judges deemed it insufficient to continue the procedure, the accused could be released *onder handtasting* (which was the Dutch term for an *absolutio ab instantia*). In this case the accused had to promise to appear again before the court when requested, under the threat that if he did not come he would be considered guilty (*sub poena confessi et convicti*). In the situation where a confession was not present but when there was strong evidence against the accused, the *schepenen* could pronounce an extraordinary punishment in the form of a banishment or a confinement in one of the workhouses (the *rasp- or spinhuis*). Such a sentence could also be given after the accused had refused to confess under the pressure of torture. In fact, this happened more often than not. Of 63 cases where a confession could not be acquired through torture, 54 ended in a non-corporal punishment while only 9 of the accused were entirely acquitted. It is not well possible to determine what constituted sufficient evidence for the conviction to an extraordinary non-corporal punishment. The *schepenen* did not motivate their verdicts or give a clear explanation of the kinds of evidence that led to their verdict.[77]

The research of Faber shows that judicial torture was not used automatically when strong evidence against an accused, short of a confession, was present. To use judicial torture permission was necessary from the *schepenen*. The *schepenen* often did not allow the use of torture but simply decided to apply an extraordinary, non-corporal punishment instead. Faber states that judicial torture was only used when the *schepenen* deemed that a non-corporal

---

corporal punishments as well. See P. van Heijnsbergen, *De pijnbank in de Nederlanden*, pp. 65–66.

[76] S. Faber, *Strafrechtspleging en criminaliteit te Amsterdam, 1680–1811. De nieuwe menslievendheid*, pp. 169–174.

[77] Ibidem, pp. 29–31 and 169–174.

punishment was too light a penalty. Here the two-sided nature of torture becomes apparent according to Faber, and he agrees with Langbein that judicial torture was used 'both as a means of investigation and as a species of punishment'.[78] The *schepenen* knew that in many cases the tortured accused would not confess but in this way he had at least undergone some of the desired physical punishment. In other words, judicial torture was primarily used because the *schepenen* wanted to pronounce a severe corporal or capital punishment and deemed an extraordinary punishment too light. Otherwise, when sufficiently strong evidence was present, a sentence of confinement in a workhouse or a banishment would be pronounced when the accused refused to confess.[79]

The results of the research of Faber are similar in many respects to the results of a research on the city of The Hague between 1700 and 1811 by Van Weel, and a research on the city and region of Heusden (both in the province of Holland) by Van de Mortel. Van Weel and Van de Mortel also observe the centrality of the confession in the extraordinary procedure. In most cases judicial torture was not used but the accused confessed voluntarily or after a 'lighter form of persuasion'. Van Weel mentions, in this respect, the possibilities of confronting the accused with other witnesses, threatening with judicial torture, confinement in a dark cold dungeon and forms of lighter physical abuse which did not qualify as judicial torture. The extraordinary procedure was used in the Hague for the most serious offences and the punishments could consist of public whipping, banishment, confinement in a correction house, branding or a capital punishment. For less serious forms of crime the so-called *resolutie-procedure* was used in The Hague, in which the punishment could consist of banishment, confinement in a correction house or a non-public whipping. It seems to have been possible to convert an extraordinary procedure in a *resolutie-procedure* when the accused did not confess, and subsequently to convict the accused to an extraordinary punishment in the form of a banishment or confinement. Van Weel mentions at least one example hereof, but he does not further reflect on the conditions under which this was possible.[80] An interesting aspect of the

---

78   Langbein, *Torture and the law of proof*, p. 67.
79   S. Faber, *Strafrechtspleging en criminaliteit te Amsterdam, 1680–1811. De nieuwe menslievendheid*, pp. 147–149 and 172–178.
80   A.J. van Weel, "De strafvonnissen van de Haagse Vierschaar in de periode 1700–1811", p. 144–173. The same applies to a similar research by Van Haastert for the city Breda in the North of Brabant between 1626 and 1795. The juridical organisation, the procedural steps and the modes of punishments for the different forms of crimes show large similarities to Amsterdam and the Hague. Van Haastert, however, does not give an analysis of the

research of Van de Mortel is that he observes that even in the seventeenth and eighteenth centuries there are still many examples of manslaughter and severe physical abuses which were settled through a monetary composition.[81]

A research by Overdijk on the practice of the criminal procedural law in the *Kwartier van Nijmegen* shows some differences with the procedural practice in Holland.[82] According to Overdijk, the distinction between the ordinary and the extraordinary procedure was particularly unclear in this region. In both procedural types the preliminary investigation was secret and judicial torture was possible. After the preliminary investigation was closed, the accused was informed of the accusation against him and of the incriminating evidence. In contrast to Holland, here in both procedural types the accused was allowed legal counsel to present his defence. The accused who could not finance his own legal assistance was even required to be given a counsellor *pro deo*.[83] An important difference seems to have existed in the criminal law of evidence as well. Overdijk states that in the *Kwartier van Nijmegen* a conviction to a corporal or capital punishment was normally possible on the basis of a full proof consisting of the testimony of two or more reliable eyewitnesses, in absence of a confession. A precise standard for the use of judicial torture could not be distilled from the archives. Overdijk did find an article in the provincial statutes which prescribed that torture could only be used when there were indicia and arguments that constituted more than a half proof. Those who did not confess after the use of torture could not be given a corporal or capital punishment, but they could be banished or confined in a workhouse. On a

---

frequency of judicial torture or the application of extraordinary punishments. The possibility to convict to an extraordinary punishment after withstanding judicial torture did seem to be possible here, because Van Haastert describes a case in 1734 where 'Keeske le Monde' was sentenced to an imprisonment after not having confessed under the pressure of judicial torture. The research by Van Haastert does very little to elucidate the workings of the criminal law of evidence and under which circumstances what forms of punishment could be applied. See J. van Haastert, "Beschouwingen bij de criminele vonnissen van de schepenbank van de stad Breda uit de jaren 1626 tot 1795", pp. 69–99.

81 H. van de Mortel, *Criminaliteit, rechtspleging en straf in het Hollandse drostambt Heusden*, pp. 92–93.

82 D.A.J. Overdijk, *De gewoonte is de beste uitleg van de wet*, pp. 15–26. The province of Gelderland consisted of three regions called *Kwartieren*. In the *Kwartier van Nijmegen* some of the jurisdictions were subjected to obligatory approval by the high court of Gelderland for the use of judicial torture and for final verdicts in criminal cases. In the other two *Kwartieren* the high court of Gelderland had acquired an even stronger position as judge of appeal.

83 Ibidem, pp. 123–134.

total of 500 cases Overdijk has found 34 instances where judicial torture was used (6.8%).[84]

Within the Republic, the province of Friesland deviated the most from the other provinces in its juridical organisation and its criminal procedural practice. In contrast to the other provinces, here a stronger centralisation had occurred during the sixteenth century. Since this period Friesland had one high court with an exclusive competence over crimes threatened with a corporal punishment for the whole province. No appeal was possible because no court stood above the provincial high court. Locally, *grietmannen* were responsible for punishing lesser crimes and for sending those accused of serious crimes, with the results of their preliminary investigations, to the high court. In the eighteenth century the high court had twelve counsel men who were required to have a legal education. The *procureur-generaal* at the high court performed the role of public prosecutor. The high court of Friesland had a far more important role in criminal cases than its counterparts in other provinces and decided in more than 7500 cases between 1701 and 1811. In contrast, the high court of the combined territories of Holland, West-Friesland and Zeeland judged only 800 cases in the same period.[85]

According to the research of Huussen, severe crimes were dealt with in an ordinary procedure far more frequently in Friesland than in other provinces. The ordinary procedure as practiced by the high court of Friesland had several crucial advantages for the accused in contrast to the summary extraordinary procedure. The accused was not the object of a secret investigation but party to a public trial and the accused could make use of legal counsel. Similar to other provinces, however, the use of extraordinary punishments also appeared to be a standard practice in Friesland when there was strong evidence short of a full proof.[86] As has been stated before, in Friesland capital punishments appeared to have been possible on the basis of a full proof consisting of witnesses or

---

84   Ibidem, pp. 174–187.
85   A.H. Huussen, "Jurisprudentie en bureaucratie: het Hof van Friesland en zijn criminele rechtspraak in de achttiende eeuw", pp. 244–256. Here it has to be kept in mind, furthermore, that the high court of Holland, West-Friesland and Zeeland covered a far larger population – in 1795 a population of approximately 783.000 inhabitants in opposition to 157.000 in Friesland – and never acquired the same monopoly on severe crimes.
86   A.H. Huussen, *Veroordeeld in Friesland. Criminaliteitsbestrijding in de eeuw der verlichting*, pp. 41–45 and 141–149. Huussen, for example, mentions several sodomy cases where the accused did not confess and was subsequently sentenced to a banishment or a confinement in prison. Furthermore, in the second half of the eighteenth century, the high court made it a regular practice to convict children below the age of twelve to lighter punishments by *resolutie*.

undoubtable indicia. Van Heynsbergen, furthermore, states that the high court of Friesland made more reluctant use of judicial torture than the courts in Holland and that judicial torture was prohibited when a full proof was present. Van Heynsbergen does not, however, give any data to substantiate that torture was used more reluctantly by the high court of Friesland.[87] The fact that capital punishments were possible on the basis of eyewitnesses and indicia in Friesland may be, at least partially, explained by the fact that the ordinary procedure was used far more frequently here and by the fact that no appeals were possible to a higher court in any case (so that the advantage of *confessus non appellat* did not apply here).

6.4 Conclusion

In conclusion, the criminal law of evidence in the Dutch Republic functioned in a largely similar way as in other countries in continental Europe. As elsewhere, the system of legal proofs in the Republic consisted of a common core of presuppositions, rules and maxims which were repeated in the various handbooks and statutes about which a relative consensus existed, and a peripheral grey area of questions which were treated differently by the various authors and provinces. One very important deviation existed in the province of Holland, where a conviction to a capital or severe corporal punishment was only possible in the extraordinary procedure on the basis of a confession. This differed from the consensus in the learned law and also from the practice in other countries and other provinces of the Dutch Republic, such as Friesland.

Nevertheless, the most important characteristics of the system of legal proofs were adhered to in the Dutch Republic. First of all, the extraordinary procedure was strongly directed towards obtaining a confession (which applied particularly in Holland). In the extraordinary procedure which was normally followed, the accused had very limited defensive rights and was predominantly an object of investigation. The 'secret' nature of the procedure was visible in the fact that the procedure was often not public and that the accused was informed relatively late about the incriminating evidence and why he was under investigation The written nature of the procedure which was, for example, characteristic of the criminal procedure in France, appears to have been less prevalent in most parts of the Dutch Republic where the *schepenen* or other local judges normally heard the witnesses and the accused themselves.

---

87   Ibidem, p. 147.

The second important characteristic of the system of legal proofs which applied in the Republic, was the fact that there was a scale of decision types which corresponded to the level of the incriminating evidence. A severe corporal or capital punishment could normally be applied only when there was a full proof, while judicial torture, an extraordinary punishment or an *absolutio ab instantia* were possible when there was strong evidence short of a full proof. In the Republic, as well, the judge appears to have had a large discretion in deciding what to do when there was strong evidence short of a full proof.

Importantly, the juridical handbooks also make clear that the system of legal proofs was not a homogenous set of rules which the judge merely had to apply mechanically to a specific case, and which supposedly excluded all judicial discretion. As was described in Chapter two, there were important conflicting tendencies within the system of legal proofs and there were significant differences of opinion among the authors. While many authors, such as Van Leeuwen, advocated a relatively strict interpretation of the system of legal proofs which was strongly focused on the acquisition of the confession, there were also authors such as Matthaeus and Huber who argued for a far less rigid variant in which convictions on the basis of witnesses and indicia were possible. These differences of opinion are reflected in the differences in practice between, for example, the province of Holland and Friesland. It has also become apparent that the evidentiary rules were applied far less strictly in Holland in the ordinary procedure because in this situation the accused had more room to defend himself, which testifies to the important connection between the criminal procedural law and the criminal law of evidence. Although there were, therefore, important conflicting tendencies within the system of legal proofs, the relative consensus was that normally the confession or the testimony of two eyewitnesses were required for a conviction. The use of the ordinary procedure was highly exceptional and it becomes clear from the juridical literature that there was still a lot of circumspection surrounding indicia. For example, even in 1777, in the Van Goch case, a large part of the defence of the lawyer of Van Goch was devoted to arguing that convictions were not allowed on the basis of indicia alone and – as will be described in Chapter seven – in later discussions convictions on the basis of indicia remained a difficult subject.

Despite the conflicting tendencies, it can be concluded that the focus in the juridical literature overwhelmingly lay on the formulation of objective criteria which predetermined when a judge could pronounce a severe corporal or capital punishment. It is far easier to find remarks in these works which intended to bind the judge to the legal evidentiary rules than remarks which referred him to his internal conviction. As has been described in Chapter two, it was not the case that there were no references to the conscience or to, for example, the *fides* (belief) of the judge at all, but his conviction was normally not constitutive for the question whether sufficient evidence existed for a conviction.[88] The conflicting tendencies, the many exceptions to the general rule and the large judicial discretion were an essential part of the system of legal proofs and the early modern criminal procedure.[89] Furthermore, the system of legal proofs and the criminal procedural law seem to have remained largely unchanged – at least on the juridical-dogmatic level – in the seventeenth and eighteenth centuries. As will be described in the following chapters, it was only in the course of the late eighteenth and nineteenth centuries that a fundamental change in the criminal procedural law and the criminal law of evidence occurred.

Finally, a last conclusion that can be drawn, is that the juridical practice appears to correspond largely with how the criminal law of evidence was described in the juridical handbooks. At least, the archival studies of Faber, Van Weel, Overdijk and Huussen confirm to a significant extent what is written in the juridical literature. According to Faber, the rule described in the handbooks concerning Holland that no one could be given a severe corporal or capital punishment in the extraordinary procedure without a confession, was consistently applied in Amsterdam. Similarly, the different practice in Friesland that Huber described is corroborated by the research of Huussen. There was, nevertheless, one difference in emphasis between the juridical handbooks and the juridical practice. The handbooks paid relatively little attention to the possibility of extraordinary punishments while this was a highly important instrument in the juridical practice. Conversely, much attention was paid to judicial torture while this instrument was used far less frequently in practice.

---

88   M. Schmoeckel, *Humanität und Staatsraison*, pp. 285–290.
89   As Decock aptly remarked on this subject: "the *ius commune* [has] a remarkable capacity for allowing the exception within the system, for integrating the ordinary and the extraordinary within a logical whole. The symbiosis of the rule and the exception hinge on the *arbitrium judicis*, which holds this system together". See W. Decock, "The Judge's Conscience and the Protection of the Criminal Defendant: Moral Safeguards against Judicial Arbitrariness", pp. 78–79.

CHAPTER 7

The Criminal Law of Evidence under Discussion: 1750–1795

7.1 Introduction

In the previous chapter a description has been given of the juridical literature in the seventeenth and eighteenth centuries. Although some points of criticism could be found in these works, they were predominantly descriptive and explanatory in character. An exception was the relatively unique work of Matthaeus. In this chapter the focus lies on treatises which were aimed at a reform of the criminal law of evidence.

In the 'reform literature' concerning the criminal law of evidence in the Dutch Republic two phases can be distinguished. The first phase, which is treated in Section two, contains the works written in the Dutch Republic from the beginning of the seventeenth century until the 1750s. The treatises in this period were almost exclusively aimed at the abolition of judicial torture. The second phase, described in the third section, lasted from the late 1750s until 1795 when the Batavian Republic came into being. In this phase the works of, among others, Beccaria and Montesquieu were seeping into the Dutch discussion and a more comprehensive reform of the criminal justice system in the Netherlands started to be discussed. Finally, the fourth section describes several attempts at reform of provincial and city ordinances in the second half of the eighteenth century. This last section serves to illustrate to what extent there was a willingness to reform the criminal procedural law among the provincial and city authorities before 1795.

The reform literature in the first phase was relatively limited in scope and did not present a comprehensive critique of the existing evidentiary or procedural system. These works argued for the abolition of judicial torture, but they did not give an answer to the question how the difficult cases – where strong evidence existed short of a full proof – should then be dealt with. The main point of criticism consisted of the unreliability and injustice of the forced confession, and the fact that it should not be used by a 'good Christian judge'. Apart from the fact that the use of judicial torture was unjust, the idea also prevailed that if a crime could not be fully proven in a normal way and the culprit could, therefore, not be punished in the temporal realm, this should be left to the later judgment of God from whom nothing could be hidden. An understanding of the literature against judicial torture written before the 1750s is useful because it makes it possible to compare to what extent the discussion during the second half of the eighteenth century changed.

The reform literature in the second period differed in several important respects from the older literature against judicial torture. The works of Beccaria, Sonnenfels, Montesquieu and Voltaire were received in the Republic and stimulated a change in the discussion on the criminal law of evidence. The abolition of judicial torture became the object of a more general debate and there was an increased willingness to allow convictions 'on evidence' in absence of a confession. Another new point in the second phase was that authors started to propose that the defensive rights of the accused should be improved and that the possibility of appeal should be extended. The Dutch discussion, nevertheless, remained moderate in comparison to the discussion in France. The idea, for example, to abolish the system of legal proofs entirely and to replace it with a jury system was not seriously discussed in the Netherlands in this period. The Dutch authors appeared to be relatively complacent regarding the existing procedural system and only proposed limited and incremental reforms. As will be shown in the fourth section, this complacency was reflected in the attempts at reform of provincial and city ordinances which took place during the second half of the eighteenth century. The new ordinances contained only limited reforms of the criminal law of evidence and in none of the ordinances was judicial torture completely abolished before 1795.

Lastly, an important feature of the Dutch reform discussion in the second half of the eighteenth century consists of the fact that there was a clear tendency in the juridical literature to 'transplant' features of the ordinary procedure to the extraordinary procedure, such as the extension of defensive rights of the accused and the possibility to convict to the ordinary punishment on the basis of a full proof in absence of a confession. The strong emphasis on the need for a confession in the extraordinary procedure and the use of judicial torture were no longer taken for granted. While the French reformers used the English criminal procedure as their model to reform the criminal procedure, the Dutch jurists used the more 'adversarial' ordinary procedure as their reform model in which the accused was allowed legal counsel, the possibility of appeal and where he was given far more room to defend himself. Although there were differences, both models were attractive because they appeared to be far more in accordance with the demands of the changing political-constitutional ideals.

7.2   Criticisms on the use of Judicial Torture 1600–1750

In his *Humanität und Staatsraison*, Schmoeckel has shown that a critical stance towards judicial torture has a long tradition in continental Europe. In Roman times, for example, it was already a common practice in the rhetorical schools to discuss the arguments for and against the use of judicial torture. In different ways, authors such as Cicero, Ulpian and (later) Augustin commented on the insecurities and dangers inherent in the use of judicial torture. Famously, Ulpian stated that torture led the innocent of a weak constitution to confess crimes they did not commit, while the guilty of a strong composition remained resilient in their denial. Overall, however, they did not argue for a complete abolition of judicial torture. These sorts of warnings became commonplaces in the discussions on judicial torture to explain that it should be used with caution and only when there was no other way to prove the guilt of the accused. According to Schmoeckel, until the sixteenth century no works explicitly aimed at the abolition of judicial torture appeared in continental Europe. Authors who wrote on judicial torture showed themselves more or less critical – some as Erasmus at least seemingly tending towards its prohibition –, but they did not present a comprehensive critique aimed at the abolition of judicial torture.[1]

Explicit argumentations for the abolition of torture only appeared from the sixteenth century onwards. Schmoeckel mentions the humanist Vives as the first to do so in his commentary on *De civitate Dei*. At the critical passage of Augustine on the use of torture, Vives reflected on the usual criticisms regarding the insecurities attached to this instrument. Innovatively, he concluded from the criticisms of Augustine on the harshness and unreliability of judicial torture that it is in fact of no use and that a forced confession has no evidentiary value. He goes on to state that abolishing torture would cause no damage to the state or society and refers to countries which functioned well without using torture. Furthermore, Vives characterized torture as a pagan instrument which contradicted Christian values. It was against Christian *charitas* to apply such gruesome pains, often worse than death, on fellow human beings. Montaigne as well, was highly critical of the instrument of judicial torture in the sixteenth century. Schmoeckel states that this innovative attitude is no coincidence, but

---

1   M. Schmoeckel, *Humanität und Staatsraison*, pp. 93–112.

must be seen in the light of the more critical humanistic approach and the emphasis which, for example, Vives put on the concept of *humanitas*.[2]

A further significant impulse to a more critical attitude was given by the excessive use of judicial torture in the witch trials in the sixteenth and early seventeenth centuries. The most famous response to these excesses was the *Cautio Criminalis* (1630/31) by Von Spee, in which he criticized the witch trials and the frequent use of judicial torture which made many suspects confess to crimes they could not possibly have committed. Van Heijnsbergen remarks that much attention was given to the work of Von Spee in the Dutch Republic and that it was translated into Dutch in 1657. Another example of a well-known work against the prosecution of witchcraft and which was critical of the use of torture was *De praestigiis daemonum et incantationibus ac veneficiis* (1563) by Wier, a doctor from the Dutch city of Arnhem.[3]

While Vives was the first to openly call for the abolition of judicial torture, it was Graevius who was the first to write a complete monograph aimed solely at the abolition of judicial torture. Graevius, born in Cleve, was a priest who adhered to the Calvinist strand of Arminius and refused to follow the instructions of the Synod of Dordrecht (1619). For this reason he came into conflict with the Dutch authorities and fled to the German border town of Emmerich, where he was arrested and tortured. During his imprisonment in Emmerich he wrote his monograph against torture in Latin, called *Tribunal Reformatum* (1624). Although Graevius was a priest, his work shows a great knowledge of the juridical rules concerning judicial torture and he cited extensively from an array of jurists including Baldus, Clarus, Farinacius and De Damhouder. Graevius also made use of Vives and Montaigne, and further elaborated on their ideas. He stated that judicial torture was a pagan practice, irreconcilable with Christian values and that no mention of it was made in holy scripture. He acknowledged that the proponents of judicial torture argued that it was a necessary evil to effectively punish difficult to prove crimes. Graevius, however, argued for a more restricted duty of the temporal authorities to punish crimes. He stated that some hidden crimes which could not be proven should not be uncovered

---

2 Ibidem, pp. 112–131. Schmoeckel also remarks that Montaigne's treatment of judicial torture reflects his sceptical approach. To a certain extent it can be said that his sceptical questioning of existing prejudices formed a precursor to the more comprehensive questioning of the system of legal proofs in the second half of the eighteenth century. Furthermore, in France Montaigne's approach was very influential and was followed closely by his student Pierre Charron in his *Traité de la Sagesse* (1601).

3 P. van Heijnsbergen, *De pijnbank in de Nederlanden*, p. 107.

at any expense, while it had to be kept in mind that true justice would eventually prevail before the judgment of God.[4]

Complementing these 'theological' arguments, Graevius also used more 'juridical' arguments. He remarked that the consequences of judicial torture are irreparable when the accused turns out to be innocent, and that the maxim *in dubio pro reo* (in case of doubt the judge has to decide in favour of the accused) should apply here. He also stated that the evidentiary rule *actore non probante, reus absolvitur* (if the accuser does not prove his claim, the accused has to be absolved) should be followed when a crime could not be sufficiently proven. This formed a new interpretation of this rule, which was normally interpreted restrictively as applying only to the situation where the accuser had not proven anything. Furthermore, Schmoeckel states that Graevius appears to have been the first author who postulated the idea in this context that according to natural law no one should be forced to testify against himself. The idea that it was unjust to force someone to contribute to his own demise was repeated many times after Graevius. From the end of the seventeenth century onwards it became of even greater importance among the proponents of natural law theories who consistently emphasized that it was a natural urge to safeguard one's own life.[5] Finally, besides the significant array of theological and juridical arguments which Graevius presented in his work, he also described many gruesome examples of innocent people who had confessed under torture and compared this instrument to the old medieval ordeals.[6]

In the seventeenth century, several works appeared in the Dutch Republic that followed in the footsteps of the work of Graevius.[7] Van Heemskerk, who studied law in Leiden and became a judge in the supreme court of Holland and Zeeland, published his *Batavische Arcadia* in 1637. Although this work was meant as a novel, it also contained a large section in which he gave an extensive exposé against the abuses of judicial torture. As was shown in the previous chapter, Matthaeus argued against judicial torture in his *De criminibus* (1644). Jonctijs, who had studied medicine and later became a *schepen* in Rotterdam, published *De pynbank wedersproken en bematigt* in 1651. This was a monograph

---

4   Ibidem, pp. 137–141.
5   Ibidem, pp. 418–421.
6   Ibidem, pp. 139–142.
7   Graevius's work gained further recognition outside of the Dutch Republic through Pierre Bayle. He discussed 'Grévius' under a separate lemma in his *Dictionnaire* and described him as the writer of the first monograph against judicial torture. Although Bayle did not explicitly pronounce himself against judicial torture, Schmoeckel remarks that his true position was clear and that he was seen as one of the most famous opponents of judicial torture. See M. Schmoeckel, *Humanität und Staatsraison*, pp. 142–143.

based largely on the work of Graevius which also argued for the abolition of judicial torture. Lastly, in 1655 Van Aller, a lawyer in the province of Holland, published a general handbook on civil and criminal law which contained a separate appendix, in which he pleaded against judicial torture, entitled *Een nauwkeurige verhandeling van de pynbank*. Significantly, all these authors wrote in the vernacular (except Matthaeus), and all were trained jurists or had experience as a judge. Their works also had in common that they only wrote against the practice of judicial torture and did not further criticize the existing evidentiary or criminal procedural system.

Joncktijs, Van Heemskerk and Van Aller relied heavily on the work of Graevius and stressed the fact that judicial torture was a pagan practice irreconcilable with Christian values. A character in Van Heemskerk's novel, for instance, stated that it is an abuse to be all too prone to extort confessions of presumed crimes, and that he is surprised that present-day Christians still follow this cruel pagan practice which is unknown to divine law and was only used by the Romans on slaves 'for as long as true Roman freedom lasted'.[8] The argument that the Romans used torture exclusively on slaves and only later started to extend this practice to free persons under tyrannical emperors is repeated in most treatises against judicial torture. Van Aller, for example, similarly remarked that judicial torture became a normal practice only under the tyrannical emperors Diocletian and Maximian when they were prosecuting Christians. This argument was meant to delegitimize the fact that Roman law allowed the use of judicial torture by showing that it was merely an aberration which was instituted under tyrannical emperors.[9]

All three authors followed Graevius in rejecting the supposed necessity of judicial torture to prevent difficult to prove crimes from remaining unpunished. The most important three arguments of the 'abolitionist' treatises were directed against this claim. Firstly, they stressed that a forced confession was a highly unreliable form of evidence which gave no added certainty to the judge. The treatises argued that there was no reason to believe that people would be

---

8 J. van Heemskerk, *Batavische Arcadia*, pp. 446–462. He also called judicial torture a "remnant of slavish oppression of the innocent". It is, however, not entirely clear whether Van Heemskerk pleaded for a complete abolition or only for a very restricted usage of judicial torture. The reason that Van Heemskerk, nevertheless, merits attention lies in the fact that he showed himself highly critical of judicial torture and because he approvingly cited almost all the known authors against judicial torture. Furthermore, because of his condemnatory statements on judicial torture, he was perceived by later authors to be a critic of judicial torture and he was often cited by others who argued for the abolition of judicial torture.

9 K. van Aller, *Een nauwkeurige verhandeling van de pynbank*, pp. 367–374.

more steadfast in their denial because of their innocence, while it was in fact more likely that guilty persons would sooner endure torture because of their malevolence. Joncktijs in this vein poignantly asked "is it normally not impossible for the judge to distinguish, who endures torture by a clear conscience and tranquil innocence, and who endures it by an insurmountable strength of the body even though he is guilty?".[10] It was also argued that judicial torture was a highly dangerous instrument because innocent people could perish. The treatises substantiated this claim by giving many examples of tragic stories where people were forced to confess and later turned out to be innocent.

The second central argument against judicial torture consisted of the idea that not every crime needed to be punished at any cost, and that crimes which could not be proven without judicial torture should be left to divine judgment. The authors argued that the limits of earthly justice needed to be recognized. Joncktijs, for instance, stated that it was not necessary that every crime would be punished to safeguard public order, but that it was better that some crimes which could not be proven remained unpunished. He added that it was, furthermore, "known to everybody that many crimes are saved for the divine court, and that not all the wrong-doers get the punishment for their sins in this lifetime".[11] The best formulation of the argument that some crimes should be left to divine punishment can, however, be found in the work of the French author Nicolas Augustin (1682):

> S'il n'y a ni Dieu ni providence dans le train du monde, ils seront sans doute impunis; mais s'il y en a, comme nostre foy et la lumiere naturelle nous l'enseignent, ils seront punis à son temps ... [si] ces crimes ne peuvent venir à l'evidence par des témoignages dignes de foy, il en faut laisser le chatiment à Dieu. Il saura les moyens de nous les rendre evidens, s'il veut que nous en fassions le chatiment; si non, c'est un signe evident qu'il en s'en reserve le jugement.[12]

10　D. Joncktijs, *De pynbank wedersproken en bematigt*, p. 152.
11　Ibidem, pp. 1–3 and 42–43.
12　A. Nicolas, *Si la torture est un moyen sur a verifier les crimes secrets*, pp. 64–65. This treatise against judicial torture was published in Amsterdam in 1682 by Nicolas, a judge in the parlement of Franche-Comté. The work was often cited by later Dutch authors who wrote against judicial torture and was translated into Dutch in 1702 by Johannes Kitto. It can to a certain extent be typified as a transitional work wherein the reasoning from natural law started to play a larger role. Nicolas also placed a particularly strong emphasis on the fact that judicial torture was irreconcilable with Christian values and that divine law only allowed crimes to be proven by witnesses or a voluntary confession. If these were not present, God had clearly retained punishment for himself.

The third important argument was that no one should be punished before his guilt was fully established, and that judicial torture was in fact a form of punishment even though the jurists generally described it as an instrument of investigation. Van Aller, for example, stated that judicial torture was a punishment, even when it was only intended to obtain a confession, and that it was against divine and natural law because no one is obliged to betray or endanger himself.[13] The question whether judicial torture was a form of punishment or an investigative tool remained a point of contention between the opponents and proponents of judicial torture until the end of the eighteenth century, and it was touched upon in most treatises. Apart from the three central arguments there were several other arguments against judicial torture which were repeated by most authors. They observed, for example, that the English and reputedly many other peoples did not use torture, and that there was no reason to assume that crimes were more frequent there. Lastly, it was also often remarked that none of the regulations in theory could prevent the inherent abuses of this instrument in practice by overzealous judges who would often go too far to acquire the confession they needed.[14]

7.2.1   *A New Emphasis on Natural Law*

After Graevius the argument became more commonplace that no one should be forced to testify against himself. This argument grew in importance especially among the proponents of natural law theories since the last decades of the seventeenth century. They argued that it was a natural urge to safeguard one's own life and that it was, therefore, against natural law to force someone to contribute to his own demise. There are many examples of the increased influence of the argument that no one should be forced to testify against

---

13   Ibidem, pp. 340–349. See also D. Joncktijs, *De pynbank wedersproken en bematigt*, p. 38. Matthaeus stated similarly in his arguments against torture: "it is utterly abhorrent to natural equity for anyone to be tortured before it is established that he is guilty. *For all physical pain is punishment, even if it is inflicted before sentence.* However, there ought to be no punishment where there is no offence since punishment is retribution for an offence". See M.L. Hewett, *On crimes. A commentary on books XLVII and XLVIII of the digest by Antonius Matthaeus volume IV*, p. 560.

14   D. Joncktijs, *De pynbank wedersproken en bematigt*, pp. 104–124 and J. van Heemskerk, *Batavische Arcadia*, pp. 449–531. Besides these arguments, Joncktijs mentioned many more. For example, he stated that it was a suitable mechanism for tyrants to prosecute their enemies under false pretences, and he argued that judicial torture often led a desperate accused to commit the terrible sin of suicide to prevent himself from being tortured.

himself. Famously, for example, the president of the *parlement* of Paris, Lamoignon, argued during the deliberations on the criminal ordinance of 1670 against the obligation for the accused to swear an oath to tell the truth because this oath conflicted with the natural urge of self-preservation. The oath forced the accused either to commit perjury and betray his religion or to confess and contribute to his own demise. The modern principle of *nemo tenetur* (no one should be held to contribute to his own conviction) developed from these ideas and an early form thereof can already be discerned in the motivation of Lamoignon against the oath: "Nul n'est tenu de se condamner soi-mêmes par sa bouche". In a similar fashion Pufendorf stated: "Mais on n'est nullement obligé de s'accuser ou de s'exposer soi-même à la peine".[15]

Although in the first half of the eighteenth century almost no treatises against judicial torture were published in the Dutch Republic, the increased importance of the argument that no one should be forced to testify against himself can be seen in a speech by Wittichius. Wittichius became a professor of philosophy at the university of Leiden in 1718 and held his speech against judicial torture in 1736, during the ceremony when his term as Rector ended. Wittichius started by explaining that every man was directed by nature to do everything to preserve himself. The central argument of his speech was that the state had no right to force a citizen to confess and that the accused was not obligated to betray himself. Consequently, Wittichius stated that the accused had the right to do whatever it took to avoid a capital punishment and, therefore, also had the right to lie under torture. Because there was by natural law no obligation for the accused to tell the truth, there was also no reason to lend any credence to his statements under torture which made them unreliable as evidence.[16]

After stating that the forced confession was a highly unreliable form of evidence and that judicial torture was gruesome and unjust, Wittichius remarked that it was also unnecessary. He pointed out that the English and the early Romans did not use torture and that there was no reason to believe that public order was any less well preserved among these peoples. Wittichius stated that just as among the Romans and English, the judge should only decide on the basis of witnesses and other forms of evidence. He subsequently acknowledged that without judicial torture some godless criminals would perhaps go

---

15   M. Schmoeckel, *Humanität und Staatsraison*, pp. 418–425.
16   J. Wittichius, *Redevoering over de onbillykheid en de onnutheid der pynigingen*, pp. 8–12. The address of Wittichius was translated from Latin into Dutch by Hendrik van Damme and published in 1736.

unpunished, but he argued that this was not a sufficient reasons to maintain the institution. Instead, Wittichius remarked that "the vigilance of the government and its severity in punishing are the only means by which crimes can be suppressed".[17]

Summarizing, there are several commonalities in the Dutch works against judicial torture in the seventeenth and early eighteenth centuries. First, it is striking that the authors continuously repeat and refer to the existing works against torture, just as the juridical handbooks refer to the established authorities. The Dutch works consistently mentioned Vives, Montaigne, Graevius and later Van Heemskerk and Joncktijs. Secondly, and more importantly, the works from this period did not present the criticism on judicial torture in a wider context of evidentiary or procedural reform. They acknowledged and supported the necessity of a full proof clearer than the light of day for a conviction. The works argued against judicial torture because of its inherent uncertainty and gruesomeness and stated that torture was unnecessary – predominantly on theological grounds – because not every crime had to be punished. In other words, these authors proposed to acknowledge the limits of earthly justice and to constrain the sphere of criminal investigations. Finally, from the late seventeenth century onwards the argumentation started to focus more on the notion derived from natural law that people should not be forced to contribute to their own demise. This can be seen in the speech of Wittichius, who reasoned from natural law that the state had no right to force a citizen to confess. A shift of focus can be seen here, wherein the limits of earthly justice were derived from a different perspective than the theological grounds which had predominated among the earlier writers such as Graevius and Joncktijs.

7.3   The Reform-literature between 1750 and 1795

This section gives an analysis of the published works which discussed the criminal law of evidence in the Republic between approximately 1750 and 1795. Unlike the older works which had merely criticized judicial torture, the overall approach towards criminal justice had changed in a significant way. As has been observed in Chapter three, many works published after the 1750s took as their starting point that the criminal law was the result of a social contract which was aimed at effectively increasing the happiness and safety of the citizens. The authority of Roman law and authors such as Farinacius and Carpzov had become far less self-evident, while proposals could now be heard that the

---

17   Ibidem, pp. 12–27.

criminal law should be accessible in the vernacular. Furthermore, a distinct laicization took place in the discussion on criminal justice in this period and the question became more prominent how to increase the effectiveness of the criminal procedural law.[18] This meant, for example, that the older 'theological' argument of the abolitionists that judicial torture should not be used because those guilty of hidden crimes would receive their due punishment from God, was heard less frequently. It became of greater importance for those against judicial torture to formulate a practical alternative which ensured that those guilty of difficult to prove crimes would not remain unpunished when judicial torture would be abolished. As will be shown in this section, the greater willingness to abolish judicial torture was one of the reasons for many authors to propose to enhance the possibility to convict an accused to the ordinary punishment on the basis of other forms of evidence than the confession.

When the discussion in the Republic between 1750 and 1795 is compared to the one taking place in France in the same period, it becomes evident that the Dutch authors were far less radical in their ideas of reform and that they reasoned more strongly from the existing procedural system than the French authors. They appeared to be relatively satisfied with the existing criminal procedural law and predominantly searched to improve it in an incremental manner. It is, therefore, no coincidence that virtually no author in the Dutch debate proposed to abolish the system of legal proofs as a whole or to adopt a jury system. The strong sense of dissatisfaction with the judicial system and the accusations of arbitrariness of the *noblesse de robe* which occurred in France, were largely absent in the Republic between 1750 and 1795. The tone of the discussions was moderate and the reception of ideas for reform from other countries was relatively limited. Nevertheless, the works of several authors and reformers, such as Beccaria, Montesquieu, Sonnenfels, Frederick the Great and Catherine II, were discussed frequently and had a significant influence on the Dutch debate.[19] The treatises of radical French reformers such as Marat,

---

18 This 'laicization' should off course be understood in a relatively limited sense. In reasoning from natural laws or a social contract it was often explicitly acknowledged that these existed by the will of God or in the framework of his creation. The point is that there emerged more room for a (functionalistic) argumentation which did not reason from religious precepts. This can also be seen in the increased willingness to decriminalize offences such as sorcery, heresy, suicide and blasphemy, in as far as these acts did not actually damage society. See also J.W. Bosch, "Quelques remarques sur la sécularisation du droit pénal au XVIIIe siècle en Belgique et aux Pays-Bas", p. 557–569.

19 The reforms of Frederick the Great were known in the Republic through his work *Dissertation sur les raisons d'etablir et d'abroger les loix*, which was cited by several authors. The famous *Nakaz* of Catherine II (strongly inspired by Beccaria and Montesquieu), was

Servan, Brissot de Warville and Dupaty, however, were hardly discussed in the Dutch works of this period. At least, no mention of them was made and the Dutch authors appeared to be largely unaware of the ideas of the French authors to completely reform the criminal procedural law.

In short, the Dutch discussion between 1750 and 1795 shows that there was a reception of 'enlightened' reform-ideas and a change of approach as compared to the period before the 1750s, but also that the overall tone of the discussion remained moderate and the willingness to reform limited. A distinction in the reform debate can be made between on the one hand the more 'progressive' authors who strongly pleaded for the abolition of judicial torture, for stronger defensive rights and for an increased possibility to convict an accused without a confession, and on other hand, the more 'conservative' authors who defended judicial torture and the existing criminal law of evidence. The ideas of the proponents of a significant reform of the criminal law of evidence will be discussed in the first sub section and the more conservative authors are dealt with in the second subsection.

7.3.1 *The 'progressive' Supporters of Reform*

In the discussions regarding the criminal law of evidence, the question of abolishing judicial torture remained one of the central points of debate between 1750 and 1795. The approach to this question and the criminal law in general had, however, changed in an important way. Many of the works now started by explaining that the government and the criminal laws were founded on a social contract which was concluded by men who were at first free in a state of nature. It was no longer taken for granted that the government had certain far-reaching powers over their citizens – such as the right to torture – when it was not clear that these powers were an effective way to protect the 'common good'. The approach from 'natural law' and from 'reason' created room to rethink and criticize the existing criminal procedural law, as well as its foundation in a complex patchwork of Roman, customary and statutory laws. This changed approach can, for example, be seen in the work *Nemesis Rationalis, of redenkundig vertoog over het crimineele recht uit het natuur-recht afgeleid* by Reinar (1778). In his prologue Reinar started by explaining that the foundation of the criminal law lay in a social contract – often citing Pufendorf – and then made the following observation:

---

translated even twice into Dutch. Once in 1769, and again in 1794 as *Berigschrift van Catharina de tweede ter vervaardiging van een ontwerp voor een nieuw Russiesch wetboek*.

> According to this theory I have written my Nemesis; not with prejudice or according to the authority of Roman law or the dictates of human institutions, but according to reason and understanding. Although I judge all the criminal laws which contribute to public tranquillity with great equity ... I cannot understand how men have killed so many people on the authority of a Carpzovius, Farinacius and Julius Clarus, yes even on the basis of the *Constitutio Criminalis Carolina* ... The cruelty of punishments has always been rejected by reasonably thinking legislators on the basis of human kindness (*Menschlieventheid*), which is a resultant of enlightened reason.[20]

Although Reinar did not explicitly argue for the abolition of judicial torture, it becomes evident from his reflections on this subject that he was strongly against this instrument. He approvingly cited Sonnenfels and the fact that judicial torture had been abolished in Prussia and Russia, and later remarked that through this unreliable institution no certain truth could be acquired. Instead of judicial torture, Reinar proposed to allow convictions on other forms of evidence in absence of a confession. He at least wanted to allow crimes to be proven through witnesses but he was more circumspect and unclear regarding indicia. First, he stated that one has to be very careful with indicia and pointed out its uncertainties. Subsequently, however, he rhetorically posed the question 'why then am I speaking of indicia?', and answered "the reason is that they can be of use to a judge in a criminal case, by letting him through ascending *gradations of probability* reach a certain truth".[21] A little earlier he also observed that "there are such indicia and presumptions that, when they are at least proven by two reliable witnesses, they sufficiently and undoubtedly prove the fact".[22] Lastly, Reinar argued more clearly for reform on a different point. He remarked that it was against natural law that the accused could not defend himself

---

20 J.N. Reinar, *Nemesis Rationalis, of redenkundig vertoog over het crimineele recht uit het natuur-recht afgeleid*, pp. III–XIII. After the prologue, the first part of Reinar's treatise is focused on substantive criminal law. Here he strongly stressed that for a conviction it was not only necessary that the accused had committed the fact, but also that the fact could be morally imputed to the accused. In agreement with Pufendorf, he stated that a person needs to have been able, through the use of his reason, to have wanted the evil deed. Reinar deemed it necessary that the judge had a certain discretion to proportion the punishment to the gradation to which the crime was morally imputable and the circumstances of the case. In this respect the judge should not be bound rigidly to the words of the law, but judge by its spirit adapted to the individual case. Reinar differed on this point from many of the French reformers who abhorred these sorts of arbitrary powers.
21 Ibidem, pp. 75–77 and 108–116.
22 Ibidem, p. 73.

properly in extraordinary procedures. Even when an accused had confessed, Reinar deemed it necessary that he should have the possibility to defend himself by making use of legal counsel and having the right to appeal.[23]

Similar ideas can be found in many of the works which proposed a reform of the criminal law of evidence between 1750 and 1795. The changed attitude can in particular be seen in works directed against judicial torture which tried to formulate an alternative evidentiary solution for the difficult to prove cases. A short treatise against judicial torture by De Witt shows these characteristics most evidently. De Witt started by repeating many of the arguments against judicial torture that were presented in the older literature, often citing Graevius. After explaining the unreliability of forced confessions and stating that it was against natural law to punish someone whose guilt had not yet been fully established, De Witt unequivocally concluded for its abolition in the following manner:

> Does reason itself not teach that, when the abuses of a law or custom are greater than its utility, even if they were just, that such a law or custom needs to be promptly destroyed? This applies even more for such a thing as the rack, which above the abuses that are inherent to it, is also an uncertain, unjust, dangerous and cruel instrument.[24]

Importantly, however, De Witt did not stop after his plea for the abolition of judicial torture. He continued to answer the question what needed to happen when a judge knew the accused to be guilty of a capital crime which he refused to confess. De Witt refuted the dichotomy of either torturing such an accused or necessarily letting him go. He asked rhetorically: "Is there not a safer measure, through which the guilty are more likely to be punished and the innocent set free; a measure, although not mathematically certain, nonetheless endlessly more certain, more just, less dangerous and more humane?".[25] De Witt proposed that those accused of a severe crime who refused to confess, but against whom existed multiple witnesses or a chain of indicia, should be

---

23   Ibidem, pp. 119–123.
24   C. de Witt, *Bedenkingen over het aanhoudend gebruik van de pijnbank*, pp. 1–28. It is apparent that for De Witt 'arbitrary' had become a very negative term. He also had no faith in the possibility of *a priori* regulating the use of judicial torture and criticized those who took their refuge in the "cruel Spanish, Italian and German doctors, or similar contemporary Draco's".
25   Ibidem, p. 34.

prosecuted in an ordinary procedure. Then the accused had the possibility to make use of his natural right to defend himself, he had a right of appeal, and innocence had a better chance to show itself. Furthermore, when after thorough investigation in this procedure two irreproachable eyewitnesses testified against the accused, the normal punishment should be applied. De Witt was more hesitant when it came to indicia. For the situation where such clear, probable and mutually reinforcing indicia were present that nothing seemed to be lacking but the confession of the accused, he stated that the ordinary punishment should not be applied. Instead, he deemed that it accords with equity and the nature of these cases that in such a situation an extraordinary punishment could be pronounced in the form of a confinement or a banishment.[26]

De Witt referred in his work to, among others, Beccaria, Montesquieu and Sonnenfels. His stance corresponded most closely to that of the Austrian Sonnenfels whose treatise was translated into Dutch just two years earlier: *Verhandeling over het afschaffen der Pynbank* (1776). The Dutch author who translated this work strongly agreed with Sonnenfels and in the prologue called it an essay which 'honours humanity and sound reason'. After a lucid and lengthy argumentation against the uncertainty and cruelty of judicial torture, Sonnenfels presented his alternative. This alternative was essentially that judges should be allowed to convict an accused on the basis of the testimony of witnesses or indicia when they were so probable that they convinced the judge of the guilt of the accused and left no room for him to doubt. This was also largely the solution adopted by de Witt, although De Witt showed more hesitancy regarding indicia.[27]

In the Dutch reform literature, one of the most 'radical' pleas for reform came from the young lawyer Amalry in his book *Beschouwinge der crimineele zaaken* (1777). Amalry was an adamant follower of Beccaria and in many respects uncritically reproduced his ideas. The work reads, like the treatise of Beccaria, as a synthesis of new ideas to completely reform the criminal justice system. Amalry started by remarking that no one of common sense could deny that all creatures are endowed with a natural urge to increase their happiness. In the social contract, which was created to achieve this happiness, the participants only relinquished as much of their freedom as was necessary for this purpose. According to Amalry, all civil institutions and laws could be judged on

---

26 Ibidem, pp. 28–43. De Witt also substantiated the claim that the abolition of judicial torture would not lead to an increase in crime by referring to other countries where torture had already been abolished. Most notably Prussia where he admiringly cited Frederick the Great's *Dissertation sur les raisons d'etablir et d'abroger les loix*.
27 J. Sonnenfels, *Verhandeling over het afschaffen der Pynbank*, pp. 1–x and 85–91.

the basis of this principle. From this point of view he deemed it incomprehensible that the criminal laws were written in Latin. Criminal laws should be written in the vernacular so that every citizen could understand them and adjust his behaviour accordingly.[28]

Regarding punishments as well, Amalry followed Beccaria and stressed that the certainty of punishments was far more efficacious than their severity, and that they should be proportionate to the crimes and no more severe than was necessary to prevent them. He also condemned in very strong words the possibility of arbitrary or extraordinary punishments when the crime was not fully proven. According to Amalry, extraordinary punishments were against natural law and common sense because an accused has to be considered innocent as long as his guilt was not fully proven. At this last point he also stated that it makes of the judge the lawmaker, while the judge should only be 'la bouche qui prononce les paroles de la loi'.[29]

In Chapter 9 of his treatise, Amalry criticized the extraordinary procedure and pleaded for the general usage of the ordinary procedure where the accused has room to defend himself and make use of legal counsel. He had no trust in the idea that in an extraordinary procedure the judge would *ex officio* find the truth and remarked that it was the natural way to bring as much light as possible on both sides so that nothing remains hidden or unchallenged. Amalry, furthermore, found it incomprehensible that in extraordinary cases the accused could not appeal to a higher court when he was convicted, and he pleaded for the publicity of criminal trials.[30]

It will, finally, come as no surprise that Amalry was also a fierce opponent of judicial torture. He remarked that torture was an inhumane instrument and deemed the forced confession completely unreliable. It is apparent from his argumentation that instead Amalry wanted to allow convictions on the basis of witnesses and perhaps on the basis of indicia (he does not pronounce himself explicitly on this subject). His stance concerning the criminal law of evidence is, however, somewhat unclear. He first observed that in every criminal case it had to be proven that the fact constituted a crime, and secondly that it was committed by the accused not only *physice* but also *moraliter* (i.e. the fact has to be imputable). He then stated that the theory of evidence is one of the most complex and hard to understand parts of the law, and he appeared to lament the fact that it was not regulated precisely enough in the law. Amalry stated that it was unfortunate that the terms of 'half proof' and 'vehement suspicion'

---

28   S. Amalry, *Beschouwinge der crimineele zaaken*, pp. 1–45.
29   Ibidem, pp. 1–45. The last remark was a quotation of Montesquieu.
30   Ibidem, pp. 30–47.

still had to be filled in *lege probabilitas* by the arbitrary judgment of the judge. He subsequently remarked that to correctly understand and apply this complex theory a sharp mind and long study were required, and that mere common sense did not suffice. After these remarks it then comes as a surprise to see that Amalry stated in a footnote that to him the most pleasing composition of the court would be the form wherein *pairs* judge on the facts and jurists on the question of law.[31]

7.3.2 Conservative Reactions and Supporters of 'moderate' Reforms

So far, several authors have been discussed who argued for the abolition of judicial torture and for important changes in the criminal procedural law. These authors can be characterized as belonging to the 'progressive' side of the debate. It can, however, not be said that there was a consensus between 1750 and 1795 in the Republic on the need to abolish judicial torture and to comprehensively reform the criminal law of evidence. There were many conservative authors who preferred to retain judicial torture and who only desired minor reforms to the existing criminal procedural law. The lack of consensus on this subject can be seen in two disputes concerning judicial torture and in the important publications by Calkoen, Van der Keessel and Voorda.

7.3.2.1 Two Discussions on Judicial Torture

One of the disputes on judicial torture arose as a consequence of a work published in 1777 by Schorer, who was a judge in Zeeland. His treatise led to a very critical reaction by the young lawyer Vitringa in the same year. Although the work of Schorer focused largely on civil law, he also devoted some attention to criminal law. He sharply criticized the fact that the 'chaotic and incoherent mass of Roman law' still played such a prominent role in the Dutch Republic. Two particular points of criticism were that its complexity led to many and long procedures, and that it was in understandable for most citizens because it

---

31   Ibidem, pp. 13–29 and 93–103. This remark by Amalry formed one of the few allusions to a jury system which were made in the Dutch discussion before 1795, although it is not entirely certain that he actually referred to a jury system with this remark. It appears to have been taken directly from Beccaria who in a similar way stated that he deemed judgement by pairs on the facts the most agreeable form of adjudication. In any case, Amalry did not further explain this claim and it seems to be in direct contradiction to his earlier statements. Bossers also finds it doubtful whether Amalry actually meant a jury system when he spoke of pairs in this instance. See G. Bossers, *Welk eene natie, die de jurij gehad heeft, en ze weder heeft afgeschaft*, pp. 22–29.

was written in Latin. To remedy these defects, he proposed to make a national or provincial codification in the vernacular. Schorer's criticisms concerning the criminal law concentrated on two points: judicial torture and the fact that the punishments were often disproportionate to the crimes. His section against judicial torture mainly formed a repetition of the traditional arguments but he was exceptionally vehement in his condemnatory rhetoric. Schorer, for example, started by stating: "I tremble to touch this terrible cesspool of injustice. For at its entrance I encounter a nature-raping monstrosity arising out of the sulphurous pits, which is created in Hell by an honourless tyrant to the demise of the innocent; I mean a cursed torture or the rack".[32]

The treatise of Vitringa formed a conservative and rather outraged reaction where he attempted to refute the ideas of Schorer point by point. In contrast to Schorer, Vitringa was very positive about the existing judicial system in the Dutch Republic and argued that Roman law was full of reason without which there would truly be chaos. He did not principally object to the idea of a national or provincial codification, but deemed it – because of local and provincial privileges – entirely impossible that such a codification could be created in the Republic. Vitringa opened his section on criminal justice with the acknowledgement that because in recent times men have learned to reason more humanely, this part of the law was most in need of reform. He disagreed, however, with the idea of Schorer that judicial torture should be abolished. He stated that he had often been surprised that the 'abolitionists' evaluated this instrument only from the negative side, stressing its abuses, without acknowledging its usefulness. The fact that sometimes innocent people were convicted through judicial torture was an objection which could be made to the use of all forms of evidence. Even if sometimes an innocent person had been convicted, thousands of guilty criminals had received their just punishment because of the use of judicial torture. Vitringa did not continue to reflect more deeply on the evidentiary necessity of a forced confession, but it is clear that he thought that the benefits of the instrument far outweighed its downsides.[33]

The treatise of Vitringa soon led to a bitter reaction in a new work by Schorer, and thereafter again to a retaliation by Vitringa. These two new works do

---

32 W. Schorer, *Vertoog over de ongerymdheid van het samenstel onzer hedendaagsche regtsgeleerdheid en praktyk*, pp. 79–135. Furthermore, in response to the often-stated requirement that for the use of judicial torture the evidence needed to be so clear that nothing seemed to be lacking but the confession, Schorer curtly remarked that then obviously the confession was unnecessary and superfluous.

33 L.J. Vitringa, *De eer der Hollandsche natie*, pp. 112–142.

not merit further treatment because they predominantly formed a superficial repetition of the same arguments.[34] It is, however, interesting to note that in a short time the dispute between Vitringa and Schorer led to three anonymous reactions. The first treatise did not state anything regarding the criminal law but supported the good intentions of Schorer. The second treatise also had nothing to say on the criminal law but contained a strong plea for a national codification in the vernacular. The author showed himself surprised that such an enlightened age with so many learned societies had not yet attempted to create a clear and understandable codification.[35] The third author was far more critical of Schorer and disagreed with his criticisms on Roman law and the criminal law. He believed that in general the criminal justice system in the Republic was equitable and functioned very well. The author, furthermore, regarded it as a just requirement that the confession was necessary in extraordinary procedures, because it was the most certain form of evidence and protected innocent citizens against wrongful convictions. The author for this reason pronounced himself in favour of the retention of judicial torture, while he deemed that the alternative of convictions to (capital) punishments in absence of a confession would be far more dangerous.[36]

The second discussion concerning judicial torture was waged within a juridical dictionary, written by several authors under the editorship of Lievens Kerstemans. The first part of the dictionary, published in 1768, contained a plea against judicial torture under the lemma *Pijnbank* (i.e. the rack). In a second part of the dictionary, published in 1772, a refutation hereof was written under the lemma *Confessie*. The plea against judicial torture consisted largely of a repetition of the traditional arguments described in the previous section. The author did not propose any further evidentiary reforms to make it possible to convict on the basis of evidence in absence of a confession in concomitance with the abolition of judicial torture. Unlike Amalry and De Witt, this author relied solely on older works against judicial torture, such as Graevius, Joncktijs, Matthaeus, Nicolas and Wittichius, while no mention was made of more 'modern' authors such as Beccaria, Sonnenfels or Montesquieu.[37]

---

34   W. Schorer, *De jonge practisyn ontmaskerd*, and LJ. Vitringa, *De valschelijk ontmaskerde jonge practizyn*.
35   [L.P. van der Spiegel], *Gedagten over het samenstel onzer hedendaagsche burgerlyke regtsgeleerdheid*, p. 5.
36   *Algemene Bibliotheek* (1777), pp. 187–201 and 328–343.
37   F. Lievens Kersteman, *Hollandsch Regtsgeleerd Woorden-boek*, pp. 387–397.

The author of the refutation argued that judicial torture was absolutely necessary for the maintenance of public order in a country with so many strangers and vagabonds. He did not agree with the idea that judicial torture formed a punishment before the guilt had been established but stated that judicial torture was of the same nature as preliminary detention and that it was not meant as a punishment. Furthermore, he remarked that it has to be kept in mind that most of the accused were not tortured by chance, but by their own fault because a strong suspicion had arisen against them which was often due to their criminal way of living. Judicial torture should not be judged on the basis of its abuses and the very rare cases where innocent citizens had perished, but on the basis of the overall benefits for public order which its careful and scrupulous usage has had. Interestingly, the author also remarked that in Holland the greatest privilege of the cities, meaning the possibility to proceed extraordinarily on the confession without the possibility of appeal, was tied up in such a manner with judicial torture that once abolished this privilege would become meaningless.[38]

The argumentation of this author reveals that for him – as it was for many others – the abolition of judicial torture was difficult to conceive because it formed an integral part of the existing criminal procedural edifice which was intimately tied to the autonomy and privileges of the cities. The presupposition here remained that a confession – even a forced one – was the surest form of evidence and should continue to be a central requirement for any conviction to a severe corporal or capital punishment. The confession was perceived as a requirement which actually safeguarded the citizens against light-hearted convictions and protected the innocent.

7.3.2.2   Calkoen

The lack of consensus on the need to reform the criminal law of evidence has been demonstrated in the disputes above, but it can also be seen in one of the most sophisticated and comprehensive publications on criminal justice in the period between 1750 and 1795 in the Dutch Republic. This was a work written by the lawyer Calkoen from Amsterdam, entitled *Verhandeling over het voorkomen en straffen der misdaaden* ('treatise on the prevention and punishment of crimes'). The work was the winning treatise in a price question in 1778

---

[38] F. Lievens Kersteman, *Aanhangzel tot het Hollandsch rechtsgeleerd woorden-boek*, pp. 154–178. The author even approved of the practice to torture suspects whose crime had been fully proven to attain a confession. He also found it just that when the tortured suspect did not confess in this situation, that he could still be punished extraordinarily because strong evidence was present.

of the society *Floreant Liberales Artes*, which read "What are the best ways to punish crimes in a 'cultivated' society, with a special regard towards this Republic?". Calkoen had a distinctly modern approach and proposed many reform ideas which covered almost all aspects of criminal justice. He was, however, a pragmatic realist who also placed a strong emphasis on the protective or repressive function of the criminal law. On some subjects, such as the criminal law of evidence, he was even outright 'conservative'.

His stance can best be typified as he has done himself. He accused Beccaria and similar authors of being too idealistic and approaching the subject only from the side of the accused. The criminal laws were there, however, for the protection of decent citizens and their interests must never be neglected. He posited himself as someone who was speaking from knowledge in practice and who approached the subject with sober realism. More than once he remarked that he intended to find a middle road which was, for example, visible in his statement in the prologue that: "Without letting me get swept away by too great a respect for what is old, or letting me get enticed by the apparent beauty of novelties – which are often as impossible as they are impracticable –, I have tried to walk a wholesome middle road".[39] Overall, it has to be kept in mind that Calkoen was convinced that the criminal justice system in the Dutch Republic was already working well and that he deemed it remarkable how safe the Republic was in comparison with other countries. He, therefore, did not intend to propose any radical changes to the existing system, but only to make recommendations to further perfect it.[40]

In the first part of his treatise, Calkoen stated that the main purpose of all civil societies was to establish a greater security, safety and prosperity for its citizens. He remarked, furthermore, that crimes were punished not because they constituted a *moral* evil, but because they constituted a *civil* evil. Society has a responsibility to punish and prevent them. Because punishments were a necessary evil and should be a last resort, he devoted the first section of his treatise to non-juridical measures which could prevent crimes. According to Calkoen, these measures needed to combat the causes of crimes, meaning for instance laziness, greed, poverty and lack of education and control of one's passions. He proposed an extensive array of reforms which could help prevent

---

39 H. Calkoen, *Verhandeling over het voorkomen en straffen der misdaaden*, pp. VI and 142–144.
40 Ibidem, pp. 36–39. Nonetheless, Calkoen did admit already in the prologue that he had been strongly inspired by the work of Beccaria, and that many good ideas are to be found in it. His treatise can certainly not be described as a conservative refutation of Beccaria, for he openly integrates many of Beccaria's reforming ideas in his work. The best characterisation remains that he tried to find a middle road.

crimes. Firstly, public training and education had to be facilitated for orphans and children of the poor to learn to read and practice a particular craft. Work needed to be provided for the poor and handicapped to prevent begging and laziness, following the credo 'everyone who can work, must work'. He stated that public orphanages should be created where one could anonymously bring children to prevent the murder of infants. Furthermore, public schools should be erected and moral and religious lectures should be given to educate the people in their responsibilities as men and as citizens.[41] The reforming measures which Calkoen proposed to prevent crimes show the enlightened optimism he had of the ability to form man and modify society through education and work. Typical in this respect is his remark that: "many people die on the scaffold who could have been useful citizens to society under different circumstances".[42]

Calkoen started the second part of his treatise with the observation that preventive measures could never eliminate all crimes. An appropriate severity in punishing must, therefore, continue where the humane preventive measures fail. The second part of his work consisted of the recommendation to create a national codification of the criminal law, and an explanation of how this codification should be given shape. Calkoen stated that the codification had to be created by the lawful sovereign, representing, as it were, the will of society in its laws. It needed to be adapted to the characteristics and spirit of the inhabitants, and written in the vernacular in clear, precise and understandable formulations. Referring to Beccaria, he remarked that the laws had to be published and made known to the people so that they could adjust their behaviour to them. The codification needed to encompass all the different crimes in all their different modifications, followed by their punishments, so that when a certain fact had been committed it would always be possible to determine which crime it constituted and what punishment should be applied. Precision was necessary so that the law alone convicted the accused and as little arbitrary judicial discretion as possible remained. The only task of the judge should be to determine whether the crime was proven and to apply the law. Calkoen did not agree with Beccaria that the judge should not be allowed any room at all to interpret the laws. He deemed it unavoidable that a certain limited judicial discretion would have to remain.[43]

After discussing the criteria concerning the form of the codification, Calkoen continued with formulating substantive criteria concerning the crimes and

---

41   Ibidem, pp. 1–79.
42   Ibidem, p. 15.
43   Ibidem, pp. 80–88 and 100–104.

punishments. Matters of religion should not be regulated by the criminal law as long as they did not harm the rights or safety of others. These were subjects that belonged to the inner conscience of each citizen over which only God had power. The codification should exclusively include crimes which constituted a civil evil, meaning that they harmed the safety and prosperity of society. For this reason, Calkoen stated that the belying of god and suicide should not be penalized as long as these acts did not harm others. In agreement with Beccaria, he remarked that punishments needed to be as minimally severe as was necessary to prevent crimes and that they should be proportionate to the crimes. In contrast to Beccaria, however, Calkoen deemed the capital punishment entirely justified. Lastly, Calkoen was against the use of banishments because these only led to an ineffective exchange of criminals between different regions.[44]

In the third part of his treatise Calkoen discussed the criminal procedural law. He directly made clear that he preferred the extraordinary over the ordinary procedural form, 'despite the criticisms which have recently been uttered against it'. This opening remark shows that he was well aware that there was a discussion taking place about the criminal procedural law and that many authors were dissatisfied with the existing extraordinary procedure. Calkoen did not argue for an increased possibility for the accused to defend himself or for a general right to legal counsel in the extraordinary procedure. Instead, he stressed that it was the role of the judge to seek the truth, that he should hold the accused innocent for as long as possible and that he needed to seriously investigate whatever the accused proposed in his defence. In the eyes of Calkoen, the judge had to function, as it were, as the lawyer of the accused which would provide adequate safeguards for the accused. This view, in contrast to the French reformers, attests to the large confidence Calkoen had in the Dutch magistrates.[45]

Calkoen, furthermore, presented a comparison with England to illustrate the superiority of the Dutch extraordinary procedure. In the first place, he remarked that while the ordinary procedure may be sufficient for public safety on an island, it was unsuitable for a country such as the Dutch Republic where many foreign vagabonds and criminals could be found. Secondly, in England an accused could be convicted when several circumstantial forms of evidence were present which appeared sufficient to the jury, notwithstanding the most ardent denial of the accused. According to Calkoen, however, innocence was better protected in the extraordinary procedure in Holland. At this point, Calkoen's relentless faith in the confession as the surest form of evidence

---

44 Ibidem, pp. 117–184.
45 Ibidem, pp. 191–202.

becomes apparent. This faith makes clear why he perceived the necessity of the confession as a safeguard for citizens against unjust convictions, and why he did not desire any significant changes in the criminal law of evidence.[46] He remarked:

> Through the extraordinary procedure one acquires the suspects' own confession, the most certain evidence of guilt one can have. This takes away all doubt and makes all eventualities apparent to the judge, even those that are in favour of the accused. The confession puts his mind at ease, so that he knows that he cannot make a mistake in his judgement. The evidence is now, so to speak, a mathematical demonstration, while all other forms of evidence – of what nature they may be – can accumulate only to a highest degree of probability but never to an actual certainty ... The law which demands one's own confession is, whatever others may think on this matter, a cornerstone of civil surety and safety, through which innocence – threatened by probability – can be protected.[47]

Later in his treatise, Calkoen mentioned two options in the hypothetical situation where strong evidence against the accused existed but where he refused to confess: "[When] it is so *morally certain*, for as far as proofs of this nature can be, that Titus is truly guilty ... Only two paths are open, either the prosecutor is allowed to use torture, or he must be admitted to an ordinary procedure (wherein convictions can be pronounced on the evidence, even without a confession) and where the accused can defend himself *ex carcere*".[48] Calkoen defended the careful usage of judicial torture in this situation. The extraordinary procedure was for him the norm and he wanted to allow convictions 'on evidence' in ordinary procedures only for relatively exceptional cases. He acknowledged that some intelligent authors have pronounced themselves against judicial torture – he mentioned Graevius, Joncktijs, Heemskerk and Beccaria – but deemed that they had approached torture too one-sidedly from the perspective of the accused which they presumed to be innocent. Calkoen argued that judicial torture was overall justified for the benefit of society and then continued to treat the criteria for judicial torture in a very restrictive manner. He stated that when these criteria were prudently applied, he could not imagine a situation where an innocent person would be tortured.[49]

---

46   Ibidem, pp. 191–219.
47   Ibidem, pp. 219–220.
48   Ibidem, pp. 244–245.
49   Ibidem, pp. 245–262 and 275–277.

Calkoen also asked himself the rhetorical question: why – when there is sufficient evidence of guilt – proceed to use torture, why press for a confession? His answer was that, first of all, this requirement protected civil safety. Secondly, without (the threat of) judicial torture the extraordinary procedure would become largely ineffective.[50] Thirdly, judicial torture was the least dangerous measure. With the last argument he meant that in comparison to the ordinary procedure where someone could be convicted to a capital punishment on the basis of strong evidence in absence of a confession, judicial torture was a far less dangerous method in this situation because here the accused could at least save his life by enduring torture without confessing. Calkoen, furthermore, emphasized that the forced confession alone was never sufficient. It needed to be very probable and confirmed by other forms of evidence.[51]

In conclusion, Calkoen shows a mixture of a relatively modern or 'enlightened' approach and innovative ideas – for example, to create a codification of the criminal law in the vernacular and decriminalize suicide –, with a relatively conservative stance regarding the criminal law of evidence. Furthermore, his treatment of the criminal law of evidence makes clear that a probabilistic conception of evidence did not necessarily lead one to criticize the system of legal proofs and relativize the importance of the confession. Where many reformers came to the conclusion that in human affairs no absolute certainty could be attained and that, therefore, only a very high probability (moral certainty) was necessary for a conviction, Calkoen used a similar terminology to claim that the confession created a certainty which virtually amounted to a 'mathematical demonstration' and contrasted this with other forms of evidence that could only lead to different degrees of probability. Evidence amounting to a 'moral certainty' was for Calkoen a standard sufficient to use judicial torture but not to convict someone to a capital punishment. He saw the necessity of the confession as a criterion which safeguarded citizens against unjust convictions. For this reason, he wanted to retain the extraordinary

---

50   Calkoen and other authors who wished to maintain judicial torture clearly saw judicial torture as an integral part of the existing criminal procedural structure. As, for example, Mittermaier and later Fiorelli observed, there was a fear to remove this stone from the procedural edifice because it might weaken or destroy the structure as a whole. See P. Fiorelli, *La tortura giudiziaria nel diritto commune*, vol. *II*, p. 224 and A. Mittermaier, *Lehre vom Beweise*, p. 42.

51   Ibidem, pp. 268–274 and 278–301.

procedure as the standard procedural form. He did leave room for convictions 'on evidence' without a confession in ordinary procedures, but this was to be highly exceptional (as was also the practice in Holland at this time).[52]

The example of Calkoen also shows that he did not consider the English jury trial as a suitable alternative for the extraordinary procedure.[53] Calkoen, like other Dutch authors of this period, did not seem to be aware of the debate in France where the introduction of a jury system was being discussed. At least, Calkoen does not explicitly reflect on this idea or compare the extraordinary procedure to the reform ideas which circulated in France.[54]

7.3.2.3   Van der Keessel

In the lectures which Van der Keessel gave in the last decades of the eighteenth century as a professor in Leiden, he expressed a similar view on the criminal law of evidence as Calkoen. His position becomes particularly clear from his treatment of judicial torture. In his lectures Van der Keessel treated the subject of judicial torture in a traditional way and gave an overview of its regulation in the learned law. Besides his explanation of the existing rules concerning judicial torture, he also presented a comprehensive oversight in his lectures of the arguments for and against judicial torture of older and modern authors. As proponents of judicial torture he mentioned Voet, Leyser, Boehmer and Muyart de Vouglans. As opponents he mentioned, among others, Grevius, Joncktijs, Matthaeus, Beccaria and Sonnenfels, and remarked:

---

[52] Incidentally, Calkoen shows that he was very well aware of the difficult dilemma to either allow judicial torture and require the confession or abandon this practice and convict on, in his perception, less certain forms of evidence: "when one cannot enforce the investigation and interrogation by the use of torture, then one either has to complacently let many crimes go unpunished or be less demanding on the evidentiary requirements. One has to proceed on lesser grounds of probability". See pp. 208–281.

[53] Ibidem, pp. 197–201.

[54] An exception to this relative disinterest in the jury system among Dutch authors is formed by Meerman, who devoted a short passage to the jury system in his book on England and Ireland (1787). He remarked that he did not agree with the 'multitude of foreign writers' in their admiration for the English jury system. Instead, he deemed it preferable when judges had acquired legal training and remarked that he would much rather stand trial for the high court of Holland than for an English jury. See J. Meerman, *Eenige berichten omtrent Groot-Brittannien en Ierland*, pp. 252–257.

so many eminent men, forming a phalanx, as it were, and with which it is still attacked daily, especially in our present century, in which the pursuit of humanitarianism, as they call it, and of compassion, as well as philanthropy, is so widely flaunted and fostered, and it has invaded the minds not only of the public (or of private citizens) who generally are the judges, but also the minds of certain legislators.[55]

Van der Keessel was not convinced by the arguments of the opponents of judicial torture. He stated that with the abolition of judicial torture it would become necessary to let many of the more serious crimes go unpunished while there was no suitable alternative. Referring to the province of Holland, he remarked that this argument was especially important because capital punishments could not be imposed here without a confession.[56] Van der Keessel deemed a carefully circumscribed use of torture entirely justified:

> if we look at the matter correctly, there will only be injustice in torture, if it is applied to a person of whom it has not clearly been established whether he is guilty or innocent ... There is, therefore, nothing to make a judge apprehensive of the injustice of torture, if he observes the injunction of Leyser in the aforesaid spec., medit. 6, p. 66, and he does not order torture unless he is fully convinced in his own mind that the accused has committed an offence, and he considers that only legal certainty is lacking.[57]

Significantly, the reasoning of Van der Keessel shows that he made a distinction between 'moral certainty' which reflected the internal conviction of a judge, and 'legal certainty' which represented evidence that met the legal

---

55   B. Beinart and P. van Warmelo, *Dionysius Godefredus van der Keessel. Lectures on Books 47 and 48 of the Digest*, pp. 1744–1749. See also P. van Warmelo, "Van der Keessel en Beccaria", pp. 573–583. Van der Keessel was a professor in Groningen from 1762 until 1769, and in Leiden from 1769 until 1815. The lectures discussed here encompass the period until roughly 1795–1798, after which a new procedural law was promulgated for Holland and judicial torture was abolished. The discussion of these procedural changes are treated by Van der Keessel in separate parts of the lectures and will be further discussed in the following chapter. See T.J. Veen and P.C. Kop, *Zestig juristen*, pp. 185–189.

56   Ibidem, pp. 1749–1753. He remarked, in this respect, that: "certainly in those regions where such a rule has been received, a measure other than torture can hardly exist. And, indeed, some consider the rule that capital punishments can only be exacted on those who have confessed as so valuable that they hold that torture ought for that reason alone either to be retained, or even to be introduced".

57   Ibidem, p. 1755.

evidentiary standard required for a severe, ordinary punishment. Van der Keessel like Calkoen, therefore, adopted a probabilistic terminology but did not use this to criticize the system of legal proofs. While moral certainty or a high probability was sufficient for judicial torture or an extraordinary punishment, a full legal proof was necessary for the ordinary punishment. As it was described in Chapter three, Van der Keessel and Calkoen are representative of the group of authors who in this transitional period adopted a probabilistic terminology and who merely attempted to reinterpret the evidentiary rules in light of these terms. They contrasted moral certainty with 'legal certainty' to make clear that something more than a normal high probability of guilt was necessary for a conviction to the ordinary punishment and did not use the probabilistic terminology to criticize the system of legal proofs. They argued that for 'legal certainty' the demands of the evidentiary rules needed to be fulfilled:

> For under the Civil Law there is the prerequisite of *legal certainty* before punishment can be decreed. It is, therefore, not repugnant to natural equity to order torture for someone who *morally* ought to be regarded as a criminal; nor is it unjust to satisfy the wish of the sovereign authority who for other serious reasons does not wish punishment to be publicly imposed except where there is *legal certainty* in addition to *moral certainty*.[58]

Van der Keessel, in short, distinguished moral certainty from legal certainty, and just as Calkoen deemed that while moral certainty was sufficient to use judicial torture, legal certainty was necessary to apply the ordinary punishment. Unlike Calkoen, however, Van der Keessel placed less emphasis on the necessity of a confession and appeared far more willing to allow crimes to be proven through witness testimony and indicia. He stated that interrogations by judicial torture must never be employed if the truth could be lawfully discovered and proven in another way. He explicitly disagreed with those who argued that capital punishments ought to be imposed only on those who have confessed:

> I willingly acknowledge that in proof which appears to be clearer than the light of day there can be some falsity and thus some uncertainty can exist, nevertheless, since *in human affairs* it can hardly be otherwise, a judge will be able to be satisfied by a very great *probability* even in this

---

58   Ibidem, p. 1755.

very serious matter... And to me it seems harsh that when the crime has been fully proved the accused is still tortured.[59]

Summarizing, Van der Keessel argued that it should be possible to pronounce capital punishments in absence of a confession on the basis of a full proof, which according to him can consist of testimony which is above all exception and of 'undoubted evidence'. He approved that a restricted use of judicial torture should, as a necessary evil, remain possible in order to punish 'covert crimes'. Van der Keessel, furthermore, stated that the abolition of judicial torture would mean that the extraordinary procedure would also have to be abolished, or, at any rate, would become useless. He warned against this danger, stating that if the extraordinary procedure would be abolished, the state would not only be burdened with very great expenses but also that lawsuits would be protracted and its great force as a deterrent would vanish. Lastly, it is interesting to note that Van der Keessel explicitly rejected the possibility of a judgement on the basis of the internal conviction as an alternative for judicial torture:

> As regards the other alternative, namely that the law permits capital punishment to be imposed if the judge is persuaded of the commission of the offence, even where juridical proof of the crime is not present, who cannot see and recognize that this method is far more iniquitous and contains more danger than torture itself?[60]

Van der Keessel, like Calkoen adopted a probabilistic terminology of the certainty required in criminal cases, but did not draw the conclusion from this that the system of legal proofs should be abolished. As it was stated in Chapter three, there were still many authors in the eighteenth century who predominantly sought to reinterpret the system of legal proofs in probabilistic terms but who did not yet fundamentally criticize the system of legal proofs on the basis of the changed epistemological ideas. As in the German territories, this shift occurred more prominently in the nineteenth century in the Netherlands.

---

59 Ibidem, p. 1767 and 1871. Later in his lectures Van der Keessel disagreed with the German doctrine as expounded by Boehmer that indicia could not constitute a full proof: "But we follow the Civil Law more closely, and according to that, as we have stated above, even in capital cases a conviction can be pronounced on the basis of *indicia* which are plain and clearer than the noonday light. From the celebrated decision in the criminal case of Van Goch one can consider that the judges of Holland do not seem to be opposed to that view".

60 Ibidem, p. 1773.

7.3.2.4 Voorda

A last author of this period that merits special attention is Voorda. He was a professor in Franeker from 1755 until 1765 and thereafter in Leiden until 1788. He was fired in 1788 because he did not want to sign a declaration of allegiance to William V, but was reinstated again in 1795 and continued in this function until he died in 1799. In 1792 Voorda published a large treatise on 'the understanding of the criminal procedural ordinances of 1570'. His goal was to show to the judicial magistrates in Holland that a significant reinterpretation of the criminal ordinances could be used to strongly improve the criminal procedural law, without any legislative change being necessary. Voorda stated that the improvements he suggested in his treatise could and should be implemented by the courts on their own authority so that an improved and uniform criminal procedural law would function throughout the province of Holland. Until a new and better criminal ordinance would be made on the provincial level, these improvements could alleviate many of the abuses in the extraordinary procedure and give this recently much criticized procedure a better reputation.[61]

The strategy of reform of Voorda was a peculiar one. Instead of formulating general criteria for a new criminal codification, he wanted to reform the existing system from within the courts via a reinterpretation of the criminal ordinances of 1570 (which were only partially followed in Holland). In general, Voorda was relatively conservative in the reforms which he suggested. He predominantly wanted to return to the extraordinary procedure as he thought that it was actually regulated in the ordinances of 1570, which he deemed an excellent and just piece of legislation. The ordinances merely needed to be cleansed of the, according to Voorda, wrong interpretations that authors such as Van Leeuwen and Bort had given of it in the seventeenth century and which were unfortunately followed in practice. His main criticism was directed at the fact that the extraordinary procedure had degenerated into a secret procedure where the accused was not allowed any legal counsel or opportunity of defence, and where everything was geared towards extracting a confession of the accused at any expense. His condemnatory remarks of this situation were far from mild. He, for example, asked "would I speak too strongly if I called this procedure a hideous monstrosity instead of a well-regulated form of adjudication?".[62]

---

61 B. Voorda, *De Crimineele Ordonnantien*, pp. 2–5.
62 Ibidem, pp. 6–30 and 100–101. Voorda also dedicated a large part of his introduction to argue that the criminal ordinance was in fact a source of law which had never lost its validity in the province of Holland. As has been discussed in the previous chapter, this was in fact a rather contentious claim.

Voorda was highly critical of the practice in Holland and the works of Van Leeuwen and Bort who 'misinterpreted' the ordinance by stating that in extraordinary procedures convictions could only follow on the basis of a confession. In line with this misinterpretation they had described the extraordinary procedure as consisting only of different steps to acquire a confession, while the accused was kept in the dark and had virtually no defensive possibilities. According to Voorda, this interpretation ran against the rules of Roman law, sound reason and the meaning of the criminal ordinances of 1570. Bort and Van Leeuwen had, in particular, misunderstood Articles 2 to 17 as describing the entire extraordinary procedure (these only described the preliminary investigation according to Voorda), and considered the subsequent articles as pertaining only to the ordinary procedure. When the ordinance was interpreted correctly, however, it followed that the extraordinary procedure should be directed at convictions on the basis of confessions as well as 'on evidence' (witnesses and indicia), and that the accused should be left a far larger room to defend himself during the procedure. In short, according to Voorda, characteristics had been attributed to the ordinary procedure which actually were intended to apply to the extraordinary procedure as well. The effects of this misinterpretation were further exacerbated by the fact that the ordinary procedure was used only in exceptional cases. This meant that in practice a far too strong emphasis was placed on acquiring a confession, while the defensive rights of the accused and the possibility to convict on evidence were neglected in the extraordinary procedure.[63]

The mistaken idea that in extraordinary procedures convictions to a severe corporal or capital punishment could only be based on the confession was accompanied by a wrongful use of judicial torture. In his treatise Voorda has shown that Article 42 of the ordinance originally stated that judicial torture could be used only when there was a 'full half proof' but not when there was already a full proof (i.e. when 'the evidence was certain and undoubtable'). As has been described in the previous chapter, Van Leeuwen had changed these words to mean that judicial torture was allowed when there was a half proof or a full proof. Voorda criticized this misinterpretation but was not against judicial torture in general. He was a proponent of a limited and carefully circumscribed use of judicial torture. His principle idea for reform was that judicial torture should never be used when a full proof could be acquired otherwise. He emphatically argued throughout his treatise that in an extraordinary procedure, when there was a full proof consisting of evidence by witnesses or indicia which were 'irrefutable and clear as the noonday sun', the judge had to

---

63   Ibidem, pp. 34–70.

convict to the ordinary punishment. Voorda made clear that the confession was certainly not an absolute necessity for a capital punishment, and that judicial torture should merely be used as a last resort when very strong evidence existed which did not constitute a full proof.[64]

Summarizing, Voorda deemed that the extraordinary procedure should consist of a full procedure conducted 'on evidence', wherein the accused was allowed to defend himself properly and was given more information on what evidence existed against him. He argued for a greater possibility to use legal counsel and stated that appeal should always be open for the accused unless he had confessed voluntarily. Furthermore, according to Voorda, when a confession could not be acquired, convicting on the basis of witnesses or indicia should become the norm and judicial torture should be an instrument used only as a very last resort. Voorda, therefore, proposed several very significant reforms to the extraordinary procedure as it was practiced in Holland. He also remarked that through these modifications the procedure in Holland would become very similar to the procedure as it was practiced by the high court of Friesland, which Voorda found to be the most humane of the Republic.[65]

7.4 Reforms of (criminal) Ordinances in the Second Half of the Eighteenth Century

There have been multiple reforms and attempts at reform of provincial and city-ordinances in the second half of the eighteenth century before 1795. These reforms, just as the juridical literature, reflect a concern with judicial torture and a desire to improve the criminal procedural law. Nevertheless, all off these reforms remained firmly within the confines of the existing procedural system and no ground-breaking changes were made before 1795. Some of them, such as the province of Groningen (1749–1771) and the city of Den Bosch (1791), saw the creation of a far more detailed criminal procedural ordinance which strictly circumscribed the use of judicial torture. Other new ordinances, such

---

64 Ibidem, pp. 70–79. Voorda remarked on judicial torture that, after careful consideration, he was of the opinion that the benefits for public safety outweighed the criticisms formulated against it. He briefly mentioned Beccaria only once in his entire treatise of more than six hundred pages as an opponent of torture.

65 Ibidem, pp. 15–18 and 83–101. Voorda also pleaded for a more restrictive use of extraordinary punishments when an accused had endured judicial torture without confessing. This should only be allowed, if in spite of the denial a lesser crime was already fully proven. See B. Voorda, *De Crimineele Ordonnantien*, pp. 364–368.

as that of Zwolle (1794) and the concept-ordinances for the province of Holland (1732–1736 and 1773–1774), were more limited in their innovations but also revealed a desire to improve the regulation of the criminal procedural law. In this section several reforms will be analysed to show too what extent there was a willingness to reform the criminal procedural law in the Republic before 1795.[66]

The province of Groningen implemented significant innovations in the (criminal) procedural law after the promulgation of the *Reglement reformatoir* in 1749. The *Stadhouder* Willem IV acquired more extensive competencies during this turbulent period in the Dutch Republic and heeded the appeals for a reform of the judicial system in Groningen. On his instigation, the jurisdiction of the high court of the province was greatly expanded and appeals were made possible to the provincial high court in criminal cases (except for cases in which the accused had confessed). Between 1749 and 1756, furthermore, new criminal procedural ordinances were made for the provincial high court of Groningen and for the courts in the countryside. The reforms were of particular importance for the countryside where criminal justice had remained in the hands of local laymen who possessed a certain amount of land. Here judicial power was often exercised by the local judge alone which led to many complaints about abuses. In the new ordinances appeals were made possible to the high court which was staffed by trained jurists and the local lay judges were forced to acquire the advice of two or three professional jurists when they wanted to use judicial torture or convict an accused to a severe punishment. The reforms, therefore, also meant an increased professionalization and hierarchization of the criminal justice system in the province of Groningen.[67]

The new ordinances reveal a relatively large concern for the public prosecutor and the judges to pay attention to evidence in favour of the accused, and they clearly intended to restrict the use of judicial torture. Articles 27 to 33 of the criminal ordinance for the *Ommelanden* (part of the countryside in the province of Groningen) of 1756, for example, prescribed that judicial torture should only be used for atrocious crimes for which the death penalty would undoubtedly follow. Furthermore, the evidence needed to be very probable, establishing more than a half proof so that nothing appeared to be lacking but the confession of the accused. These articles also made clear that a capital

---

66   This section does not aim to exhaustively discuss all reforms of provincial and city-ordinances during the eighteenth century but will indicate the general characteristics of the reforms during this period. There appear to have been no reforms in the Republic which went further in their innovations than the reforms discussed here. In no place, for example, was judicial torture outright abolished in the Dutch Republic before 1795.
67   K. Hildebrand, *Het reglement reformatoir in de stad en lande in de praktijk*, pp. 123–125.

punishment was possible when a full proof was present in absence of a confession and that extraordinary punishments could be applied when a strong suspicion existed against the accused.[68]

The intention to restrict the use of judicial torture and to extend the possibility to convict without a confession can be found most emphatically in the revised ordinance for the provincial high court of Groningen of 1771. This ordinance contained an Article on judicial torture which was almost identical to that of the ordinance for the *Ommelanden* of 1756. However, the revised article was even more restrictive and contained an added passage that stated:

> And torture, being a subsidiary form of evidence, shall not be used when the truth of the crime has been established through such incontestable forms of evidence that they constitute a full proof according to law; in which case the court shall have the right to convict the accused to death without needing the confession of the accused.[69]

Just as older ordinances in the Republic, the ordinances of Groningen did not themselves define when a 'full proof' existed, but for this question referred implicitly to the learned law. Nevertheless, the ordinances unequivocally recognized the possibility to convict to a capital punishment in absence of a confession and forbade the use of judicial torture when there was already a full proof.

The new criminal ordinance of 1791 of the city of Den Bosch was substantively very similar to the ordinances of Groningen. After regulating the preparatory investigation and the hearing of witnesses in general, Chapter 5 of the ordinance gave two separate procedural paths for on the one hand citizens and on the other hand strangers and vagabonds. The first were allowed a relatively large room to summon witnesses and present their defence, while strangers and vagabonds were to be prosecuted in a more summary procedure without these defensive possibilities. The distinct procedural treatment of these two groups continued in Chapter 6 'on torture'. Article 3 of this chapter prescribed that the *schepenen* shall always take into consideration the reputation of the accused and differentiate between residents of good name and fame, and vagabonds or known 'evil-doers' who have committed crimes before.[70] This different treatment of strangers and vagabonds was, of course, not specific to the court of Den Bosch and was applied everywhere in the Dutch Republic, but it

---

68 *Reglementen, ordonnantien, instructien, en proces-ordres*, pp. 133–134.
69 Ibidem, pp. 55–56 and 165–166.
70 *Reglement en ordonnantie op de crimineele justitie en den styl van procedeeren in Crimineele Zaaken voor den geregte van 's Hertogenbosch*, pp. 65–89.

is significant to see that still in 1791 distinct procedural paths were codified in this criminal ordinance.

Judicial torture was regulated very restrictively in the ordinance of Den Bosch concerning normal citizens. Judicial torture was allowed only when the *corpus delicti* was proven, when the death penalty would necessarily follow upon conviction and when the evidence constituted almost a full proof. It was forbidden on the basis of the testimony of one accomplice or one witness alone, unless there were supporting indicia. According to Article 5 torture could, furthermore, not be applied when the crime was already fully proven because judicial torture was deemed a subsidiary measure. The ordinance explicitly allowed capital punishments on the basis of a full proof in absence of a confession. Lastly, when the accused had endured judicial torture without confessing, the ordinance permitted the judge to pronounce an extraordinary punishment or an *absolutio ab instantia* after 'the exigency of the case'.[71]

In the province of Groningen and the city of Den Bosch a clear tendency is discernible to restrict the use of judicial torture and to enhance the possibility to convict to the ordinary punishment on the basis of a full proof in absence of a confession. This tendency can also be seen in the concept ordinances for the province of Holland, which were eventually never promulgated. In 1732 the province of Holland created a committee to reform the criminal procedural law which worked intermittently until 1736. The committee did not finish its work, but did leave a concept-ordinance which was used by a new committee with the same assignment between 1773 and 1774. The committee of 1773–1774, for unclear reasons, also did not finish its work and only left a concept-ordinance which strongly resembled the concept-ordinance of the first committee. The concept-ordinance of 1736 consisted of two parts. The first part contained 23 Articles and mainly regulated subpoena's. The second part contained 112

---

71   Ibidem, pp. 63–105. In 1794 a new ordinance on civil and criminal law for the city of Zwolle was promulgated, of which the fourth part regulated the criminal law. This ordinance gives a far less detailed regulation of the criminal procedural law than the ordinances of Groningen and Den Bosch but also appears to further restrict the use of judicial torture. The ordinance of Zwolle leaned towards the use of the ordinary procedure wherein the accused was allowed legal assistance. The ordinance prescribed that after the preparatory investigation an extraordinary procedure would only follow when three quarters of the judges deemed the case fit for this procedure. Article 16, furthermore, stated that judicial torture could be used solely in cases for which the death penalty would surely follow and when at least two thirds of the judges deemed its use necessary. Lastly, Article 20 prescribed that when the crime was not fully proven, a lesser extraordinary punishment could be applied. See *Stadsrecht van Zwolle, en reglement voor het edel schoutengerichte*, pp. 405–422.

Articles and regulated the preliminary investigation, incarceration, interrogations and the use of judicial torture. The committee was also supposed to present rules on the defensive rights of the accused, but discontinued its work at this point. Although the concept-ordinances never acquired force of law, they do show the intention in the province of Holland to improve the criminal procedural law and to create a far more detailed and uniform procedure for the whole province. They are also of importance because they were used later as an example in the national codification attempts on the criminal procedural law in 1799 and 1809.[72]

The concept-ordinances of 1736 and 1774 were almost identical on the point of judicial torture. The ordinances prescribed that judicial torture may only be used after deliberation by the full court. Article 92 stated that the *corpus delicti* had to be proven, the crime needed to be threatened by a capital or severe corporal punishment, and the proof needed to be so strong that it 'almost constituted a full proof'. Furthermore, Article 93 contained the important rule that it was forbidden to use judicial torture when the crime was fully proven, because judicial torture was only meant as an aide to discover the truth in absence of a full proof. This article, in other words, condemned the practice in Holland to use judicial torture to acquire a confession even when a full proof was present and made clear that capital punishments should be possible when a full proof already existed. Article 94, furthermore, dictated that torture was not allowed on the basis of one (irreproachable) eyewitness, but that supporting indicia were necessary.[73]

Although the concept-ordinance of 1736 did not explicitly state that an accused could be convicted to a capital punishment in an *extraordinary* procedure on the basis of a full proof without a confession, the discussions of the first committee do shed light on this question. Some members deemed that it should be possible in an extraordinary procedure to convict someone to a capital punishment on the basis of a full proof without a confession, while others stated that this should only be possible in an ordinary procedure. Subsequently the committee found it necessary to define the meaning of 'full proof'. They came to the conclusion that a full proof could not consist of indicia alone but

---

72 J.W. Bosch, "Aantekeningen over de inhoud der Hollandse Hervormingsplannen van de criminele ordonnantiën van 1570 in de 18de eeuw", pp. 197–212. Bosch remarks that the committee-members of 1732 owed their juridical education to the works of Matthaeus, Bort, Van Leeuwen and Huber, while they only once cited a legal source not from Holland (the ordinance of *het Rijk van Nijmegen* of 1686).

73 J.W. Bosch, "Aantekeningen over de inhoud der Hollandse Hervormingsplannen van de criminele ordonnantiën van 1570 in de 18de eeuw III", pp. 267–283.

could be formed by two irreproachable eyewitnesses who testified consonantly. After further debate the committee decided that in the extraordinary procedure a conviction to the ordinary punishment should be possible on the basis of two irreproachable eyewitnesses but not on the basis of indicia. These ideas were eventually not written down in articles of the concept-ordinance because the committee discontinued its work during these discussions. These deliberations, nevertheless, reveal the prevailing distrust of indicia in Holland.[74]

Both attempts at reform of the committees of 1732–1736 and 1773–1774 remained just that, attempts. However, the general willingness to restrict the use of judicial torture and to enlarge the possibility to convict on the basis of strong evidence in absence of a confession can be found in other instances in the province of Holland as well. Faber has, for example, discovered a discussion within the council of the *schepenen* of Amsterdam in 1772 which was instigated by a memorandum of the *schepen* Graafland. Graafland proposed to make it possible to convict an accused who refused to confess in the extraordinary procedure on the basis of 'entirely convincing evidence'. Graafland gave the following motivation: "the purpose of torture [is] ... to discover the truth; does it then not run against equity and charity (*menschlievendheid*) to cause pain to an accused to acquire a confession which is superfluous for the conviction that he is guilty?".[75] Graafland was thus not against judicial torture per se, but against its unnecessary application. Only one other *schepen* consented with him. The other seven *schepenen* did not agree and deemed that it was "safer and more prudent to remain with the old customs and the existing practice".[76]

Summarizing, this section has shown that there have been some reforms on the level of the provinces and of the cities in the Dutch Republic in the second half of the eighteenth century. The reforms were aimed at restricting the use of judicial torture and enhancing the possibility to convict to an ordinary punishment on the basis of a full proof in absence of a confession. The ordinances of Groningen, Den Bosch, and to a certain extent the concept-ordinances for

---

74 J.W. Bosch, "Aantekeningen over de inhoud der Hollandse Hervormingsplannen van de criminele ordonnantiën van 1570 in de 18de eeuw IV", pp. 179–198. The committee also deliberated on the question if and to what extent the accused in an extraordinary procedure had the right to present his defence. The majority of the committee seemed to be unwilling to allow the accused to defend himself after he had confessed out of fear off delays and the possible retraction of his confession. Some committee members were furthermore especially unwilling to allow a defence to accused persons who were convicted to judicial torture. These discussions show that the committee members were still very hesitant about enlarging the possibility for debate and defence in an extraordinary procedure.
75 S. Faber, *Strafrechtspleging en criminaliteit te Amsterdam, 1680–1811*, pp. 141–142.
76 Ibidem, pp. 142–143.

Holland, clearly reveal this intention. Nevertheless, there does not appear to have been a sense of urgency among the magistrates to comprehensively reform the existing criminal procedural system, as is, for example, shown by the discussion of the *schepenen* of Amsterdam and the failed reform attempts at the provincial level in Holland. Looking at the reforms as a whole, they contained relatively limited amendments to the existing procedural system with no discernible intention to radically change it. The centrality of the confession and the evidentiary rules was not challenged and, for example, the possibility to convict an accused to an extraordinary punishment remained in force in all the ordinances. The approach of the reforming magistrates, in this respect, showed strong parallels to the opinions expressed in the reform literature by the more conservative authors.

7.5 Conclusion

In this chapter it has been described that there was a new and qualitatively different interest in the reform of the criminal procedural law and the criminal law of evidence between 1750 and 1795 in the Dutch Republic. However, in comparison to the reform discussion in France in this period, the Dutch reform discussion remained relatively moderate. Unlike in France, there were no authors who looked at the English procedural model and discussed the idea of introducing a public, oral trial in combination with a jury system. There also appears not to have been a strong distrust in the professional judges in the Dutch Republic. Here most authors were relatively satisfied with the existing criminal justice system. The discussion in the Dutch Republic, in this respect, much more resembled the discussion in the German territories during the second half of the eighteenth century.

Even though the Dutch discussion did not contain the radical ideas that were being discussed in France, there were significant innovations in the period between 1750 and 1795 in comparison to the period before 1750. Under influence of natural law theories and the idea that the criminal law derived from a social contract, the existing criminal justice system was criticized and many significant ideas for a reform of the criminal procedure were discussed. Often referring to natural law and to the idea that the criminal law was based on a social contract, many authors argued for the abolition of judicial torture, an improvement of the defensive possibilities of the accused in the extraordinary procedure and the possibility of appeal. Some authors also showed the desire for a general codification of the criminal law in the vernacular to which the judge would be strictly bound to limit judicial arbitrariness. An important change in this period was, furthermore, that the authority of authors such as Farinacius, Carpzov and Wielant was no longer self-evident. Instead, the sources of inspiration became, for example, Beccaria, Sonnenfels and Montesquieu, who pleaded for a significant reform of the criminal procedural system.

Regarding the criminal law of evidence, there was an increased desire to extend the possibility to convict on the basis of evidence (witnesses and indicia) in absence of a confession. The proposals in the juridical literature to enlarge this possibility stood in a close relationship to the role of judicial torture and were often presented as a remedy for the situation when judicial torture would be abolished. The main arguments against judicial torture in this period were derived from the idea that it was against natural law and that the state did not have a right to force someone to confess. Furthermore, it was frequently remarked that a confession obtained under the influence of judicial torture was highly unreliable and that it was also unnecessary when there was already a full proof. Even authors who wanted to retain judicial torture, such as Voorda and Van der Keessel, made abundantly clear that first every possibility should be explored to convict on evidence and that judicial torture should only be used as a very last resort. The reform literature and the changed ordinances, in short, show a slight but significant shift in the understanding of the criminal law of evidence.

Nevertheless, especially compared to the discussion in France, the suggestions for reform in the Dutch Republic regarding the criminal law of evidence remained largely within the confines of the system of legal proofs. This can be seen, for example, in the continued adherence of many authors to the necessity of judicial torture in situations where strong evidence short of a full proof existed. There were as yet no authors who pleaded for the free evaluation of the evidence or for the necessity of the internal conviction of the judge as a constitutive requirement for a conviction. Furthermore, the existence of a scale of decision types in which, for example, an extraordinary punishment could be applied on the basis of less than a full proof, was also not fundamentally criticized in the period between 1750 and 1795. Importantly, although a probabilistic conception of the certainty required in criminal cases was adopted by many jurists in the second half of the eighteenth century, this new conception was not yet used to fundamentally criticize the existing evidentiary rules. Instead the system of legal proofs was reinterpreted in light of the probabilistic terminology and a distinction was made by some authors between 'moral certainty' and 'legal certainty'. Similar to the approach of some German authors, it was deemed that while a high probability of guilt was sufficient for an extraordinary punishment or the application of judicial torture, only evidence that was in accordance with the requirements of the evidentiary rules could create legal certainty (on the basis of which the ordinary punishments could be pronounced). As will be described in the following chapter, this situation changed between 1795 and 1813 when the probabilistic terminology was used increasingly and more explicitly to criticize the logical tenability of the system of legal proofs.

Finally, the important conclusion can be drawn that there was a clear tendency in the juridical literature in the second half of the eighteenth century to 'transplant' features of the ordinary procedure to the extraordinary procedure, such as the extension of defensive rights of the accused and the possibility to convict to the ordinary punishment on the basis of a full proof in absence of a confession. The strong emphasis on the need for a confession in the extraordinary procedure and the use of judicial torture were no longer taken for granted. Comparable to France, the changed political-constitutional ideas made the existing inquisitorial procedure seem illegitimate and it was deemed that reforms were necessary to find a balance within the criminal procedure in which the defensive rights of the accused would be better protected. While the French jurists took the English adversarial criminal procedure as their model, the Dutch jurists took the more 'civil' ordinary procedure as their model in which the accused was allowed legal counsel, the possibility of appeal and where he was given far more room to defend himself.

As will be shown in the following chapter, the discussion on the criminal law of evidence evolved further in this direction in the period between 1795 and 1813. Particularly after the general abolition of judicial torture in 1798, the possibility to convict on the basis of witness testimony and indicia was extended and the internal conviction of the judge acquired a more central place within the criminal law of evidence. Furthermore, in the concept criminal procedural ordinances of 1799 and 1809 an attempt was made to actually transplant several features of the ordinary procedure to the extraordinary procedure as was suggested in the juridical literature between 1750 and 1795.

CHAPTER 8

The Criminal Law of Evidence in the Franco-Batavian Period 1795–1813

8.1 Introduction

In the unusually cold month of January 1795 the rivers in the Netherlands froze, allowing the French army to cross the rivers and swiftly conquer the Dutch Republic. In many cities revolutionary committees took over power and opened their gates to the French army. The main objective of the revolutionary groups was to destroy the existing governing system of the *Stadhouder* and the aristocratic regent class. The idea was widely shared among the Dutch revolutionaries that a new, written constitution should be created for the Batavian Republic, which was based on the sovereignty of the people and which recognized the equality of all citizens before the law. This constitution was, furthermore, meant to form the embodiment of a new social contract. In 1795, revolutionary committees took over power at the level of the cities and the provinces and directly started to make reforms on the municipal and provincial level. In the meantime, the intention existed among the revolutionaries to elect a national Constituent Assembly which would create a constitution for the Batavian Republic as a whole. After a protracted discussion of the provincial representatives in The Hague – which foreshadowed many of the difficulties that would resurface in the discussions of the Constituent Assembly – an agreement was reached to hold elections for the Constituent Assembly. Elections were held in February 1796, and on 1 March 1796 the first elected Constituent Assembly in Dutch history started its work.[1]

It is, however, not the purpose of this chapter to describe the general historical developments in this interesting period in detail, but only in as far as it is relevant to understand the changes in the criminal law of evidence. This chapter will consist of three parts. The first part describes the different stages of the legislative discussion regarding the reform of the criminal law of evidence at the national level between 1795 and 1810. The second part discusses the juridical literature which reflected on the criminal law of evidence in this period.

---

1   J. Rosendaal, *De Nederlandse Revolutie*, pp. 97–102 and J. Oddens, *Pioniers in Schaduwbeeld*, pp. 82–100.

The third and last part describes the impact of the incorporation of the Netherlands into the French empire between 1810 and 1813 on the criminal law of evidence.

The legislative discussion regarding the reform of the criminal law of evidence between 1795 and 1810 occurred in several stages which were closely connected with the general political-constitutional developments in the Dutch Republic. The first stage consisted of the debates in the Constituent Assembly between 1796 and 1798. In this period, which eventually led to the promulgation of a national constitution in 1798, there were two important points of discussion in the Constituent Assembly that had a direct relevance for the criminal law of evidence. The first point of discussion was whether a jury system should be introduced for criminal cases and the second question was whether judicial torture should be abolished. As will be described in section two, the Constituent Assembly decided to abolish judicial torture but not to create a jury system. Apart from the abolition of judicial torture, the constitution of 1798 also contained the important provision that a committee was to be appointed which would create a national codification of the civil and criminal law.

While between 1796 and 1798 the central question was whether judicial torture should be abolished, the question subsequently became what should come in its place. This was a question which had to be answered by the codification committee and which led to a discussion which provides significant insights into the understanding of the criminal law of evidence in this period. Between 1798 and 1804 the codification committee worked on the codification and in November 1804 it send its designs to the national government and to the Supreme Court which had to evaluate the designs. Crucially, in the concept codification the decision was made that henceforward the internal conviction of the judge was always necessary to convict someone, while the evidentiary rules were turned into minimum evidentiary standards. Furthermore, the judge was explicitly allowed to convict to the ordinary punishment on the basis of indicia as well as witness testimony. However, the concept codification never acquired force of law.

When the commentary was finally provided by the Supreme Court in 1806, it gave its advice to the by this time newly installed king Louis Napoleon. The commentary was very negative and Louis Napoleon decided to create a new committee which had to reform the concept codification of the criminal law of 1804. The discussions in the new committee and in the Council of State led to the creation of the *Crimineel Wetboek voor het Koninkrijk Holland* (criminal code for the kingdom of Holland) in 1809. In essence it contained a more summary version of the regulation of the criminal law of evidence of the concept code of 1804 but it did not significantly alter its basic principles. This first criminal codification for the Netherlands, which contained a negative system of legal proofs, only functioned for a short period of two years because Napoleon decided to incorporate the Netherlands into the French empire.

The third section describes the discussions in the juridical literature between 1795 and 1810. Somewhat surprisingly, the discussion on the reform of the criminal law of evidence in the national legislature was not accompanied by an intense debate in the juridical literature in this period. There were, nevertheless, several important treatises which reflected on the question of how the criminal law of evidence should be given shape now that judicial torture was abolished. Finally, in the fourth section the period is discussed in which the Netherlands was incorporated into the French Empire. This period, which lasted from July 1810 until the French were driven out in November 1813, saw the introduction of the French criminal legislation in the Netherlands. This meant that a public, oral trial with a jury system was introduced for the first time in the Netherlands.

8.2   The Reform of the Criminal Law of Evidence in National Legislation 1795–1810

Directly after the instalment of the Constituent Assembly on 1 March 1796, a special committee of 21 members was created which was given the task to create a concept constitution. The committee presented its concept in November 1796. It was then discussed and amended in the Constituent Assembly until a new concept constitution was finished and presented to the people for a national referendum in August 1797. In the Constituent Assembly there were several important ideals which were widely shared but also a few important points of discussion which formed the principle dividing lines in the assembly. Ideas that were widely shared were, for example, that there should be a representative democracy, that the sovereignty lay with the people, that a division of powers between a legislative, administrative and judicial branch had to be created, that there needed to be a separation between the state and the church and that there should be equality of all citizens before the law.[2]

The perhaps most important point of discussion was the question whether the Batavian Republic should take the form of a federation wherein the sovereignty was presumed to lie with the peoples of the different provinces, or if a

---
2   M. Rutjes, *Door gelijkheid gegrepen*, pp. 205–220. See also J. Oddens, *Pioniers in schaduwbeeld*, pp. 195–236.

unitary state should be created based on the sovereignty of one Batavian people. Concomitant to the second option was that an amalgamation of the debts of the different provinces would take place which was disadvantageous for some provinces.[3] Those who were in favour of a unitary state were often also in favour of the more radical revolutionary and democratic ideas. This group identified themselves as the 'Republicans' in opposition to the group of 'Federalists' who were often more conservative and in favour of a larger provincial autonomy. The dividing lines in the Constituent Assembly are, nevertheless, not easy to draw. There was not a general opposition between revolutionary Republicans and conservative Federalists, because there were also many moderate or 'conservative' representatives who were in favour of a unitary state. Generally, however, the Republicans can be clearly identified as a vocal and influential group in the assembly which pleaded for more radical revolutionary principles and the creation of a unitary state. The frontman of the Republican group in the Constituent Assembly was Vreede.[4]

In the referendum of August 1797 a relatively large part of the adult male population was allowed to vote with the possibility to either accept or reject the concept constitution. The constitution was turned down by a great majority in this referendum after which a second Constituent Assembly was elected which started its work in September 1797. The most important reason why the constitution was turned down appears to have been that the constitution was too much a compromise which did not really satisfy the Republicans or the Federalists. While the Federalists largely supported the concept constitution as being a better option than having no constitution at all, the Republicans actively campaigned for its rejection in the referendum. In the second Constituent Assembly the Republicans had acquired a minor electoral victory and now formed a slightly larger group. They were, nevertheless, still in a minority and the stalemates of the first Constituent Assembly remained largely the same in the second assembly. These stalemates induced the Republicans to seek the help of the French government to commit a coup d'état and to purge the assembly of conservatives and Federalists on 12 January 1798. The French, who up to that point had interfered little in the Dutch constitutional process, decided to support the Republicans in order to create a unitarian and more effectively governed ally which could better support them in their war with England. In

---

3 In the period before 1795, even during the patriotic revolution of 1780 until 1787, the idea that there should be a unitary Dutch state was almost unheard of. The call for a unitary state was something largely new and strongly inspired by the French revolutionary ideal of the unity and indivisibility of the people.

4 J. Oddens, *Pioniers in schaduwbeeld*, pp. 101–146 and 195–236.

an agreement to support the coup, the French negotiated an important set of terms which the Republicans needed to follow in the creation of the new constitution.[5]

Within a few months the Republicans managed to produce a new concept constitution which was approved in a referendum in April 1798. It has to be noted, however, that the electorate was purified during this referendum from many voters who the Republicans feared would vote against the concept constitution. The Dutch, nonetheless, had acquired their first written constitution for the Republic as a whole. The Republicans who created this constitution could not enjoy the fruits of their work for long. With the support of France, where a more conservative government had just come into place, a group of moderate Republicans managed to commit another coup d'état on 22 June 1798 in which the radical Republicans were ousted. Even though the radical Republicans were now out of play, the constitution remained in force until 1801 when a revision occurred. A significant tendency in the coups that occurred from 1798 onwards, was that the French influence on the internal affairs of the Batavian Republic continuously increased, and that the administrative branch was strengthened to the detriment of the power of the legislative branch.

8.2.1 The Discussions on the Jury Trial and Judicial Torture 1795–1798
8.2.1.1 The Question of the Jury System

It has been described in the previous chapter that there had not been any significant debate in the reform literature in the Dutch Republic on the introduction of a jury system before 1795.[6] Now that the example of the French revolutionary reforms existed and the Dutch had their own Constituent Assembly, for the first time a discussion occurred on the desirability of a jury system. This discussion took place on 30 June and 1 July 1796 in the special committee of the Constituent Assembly which was designated to create a constitution. Of this discussion only a summary transcription has been made containing the most important arguments that were presented by the opponents and the proponents of a jury system. In this transcription it is striking that the arguments for a jury system were largely of a political-constitutional nature while the

---

5 Ibidem, pp. 271–322.
6 The idea to introduce a jury system had also been proposed in one 'sketch for a new constitution' which was made by patriots who were in exile in France after the failed patriotic revolution between 1780 and 1787. This sketch was made in November 1792 by Abbema, Van der Capellen and Van der Marsch in the expectation that the Netherlands would soon be 'liberated' by the French. In the summary sketch there is no further information on why they wanted a jury system or in what way, but it is likely that they envisioned a French model. See M.W. van Boven, *De rechterlijke instellingen ter discussie*, pp. 59–62.

arguments against its introduction were predominantly of a more technical-juridical nature.

Those in favour of a jury system stated, first of all, that a jury system appeared to be more in accordance with a democratic form of government than professional judges. The most important argument of the proponents, however, was that when the jurors were chosen from the people and when the accused had the right to recuse a certain number of jurors this would increase the *trust* in the criminal justice system. Furthermore, a jury system entailed that the evidence would have to be presented in a public trial which would also increase the trust of the people and of the accused in the criminal procedure. Another argument for the jury system was that more impartiality was to be expected from jurors than from professional judges who were appointed for life and among whom often a certain *esprit de corps* would form. Lastly, it was remarked that a jury system would help prevent the harmful influencing of judicial trials by 'political organs'.[7]

The opponents of a jury system, on the other hand, doubted whether a jury system would be effective enough in combatting crimes. It was remarked that the English jury system appeared to have been instituted more to protect the accused and the liberty of the people, while the procedural system in the Dutch Republic seemed to be directed more at discovering crimes. There were, furthermore, three main arguments proposed against the jury system. Firstly, it was argued that jurors lacked the necessary technical capabilities such as the skill to hear and confront witnesses, to judge on the existence of the *corpus delicti* and to decide whether witnesses were reproachable. This problem was feared to be especially acute in the rural districts where it would be even more difficult to find sufficiently capable jurors. Significantly, the opponents of the jury system also mentioned that the technical capabilities were important because the jurors would "strictly speaking, have to judge on questions of fact as well as on questions of law".[8]

The second argument was that according to 'the strict rules of the law', the internal conviction of the jurors about the guilt of the accused did not provide a sufficient basis for the judge to pronounce a punishment. The third and perhaps most important argument against the jury system consisted of the fact that the opponents found that the professional judges functioned very well in the Netherlands and had the trust of the people. The jury system was deemed unnecessary and its benefits highly uncertain. The opponents of the jury system acknowledged that there were some aspects of the criminal procedural

---

[7] L. de Gou, *Het plan van constitutie van 1796*, p. 145.
[8] Ibidem, pp. 145–146.

law which needed to be reformed, but they did not think the jury system was an alteration for the better. As improvements they recommended that 'certain institutes of the English, American and French procedural law which were advantageous to liberty in general and the accused in particular' would be introduced, and that a good codification of the criminal law should be made.[9]

After the deliberations where the arguments for and against the jury system were presented, no final decision was made on the jury question in the committee. Instead, a special subcommittee was instituted which had to make the chapter of the constitution which dealt with the judicial branch. The subcommittee was also instructed to advise on the desirability of the jury system and on what ways the criminal procedural law could be improved. Unfortunately, the report which the subcommittee presented on 22 September 1796 is lost, and the transcription of the discussion in the general committee gives little information on the subsequent discussion concerning the jury question. Only the provisional conclusion of this discussion is clear from the transcription of 2 November 1796 where it was stated that if a jury system should be introduced at all, it should only be created for cases of high treason and crimes against the freedom of the press. When the committee finally presented its design for a constitution to the Constituent Assembly on 10 November 1796, however, no mention was made anymore of the creation of a jury system. The Articles on the judicial branch in the concept constitution were formulated in such a manner as to keep the option open of introducing a jury system, but during the meetings of the Constituent Assembly there was no further discussion on this subject.[10]

The concept constitution was rejected in the referendum, and after the coup d'état of 12 January the Republicans started to work on a new concept constitution. As was stated before, to acquire the support of the French government the Republicans were forced to agree to certain terms of the French concerning the new constitution. The French representative in the Netherlands, Delacroix, had received a document from the *Directoire* entitled *Projet de constitution pour la République Batave* which was written by Danou. Danou himself was the principal author of the French constitution of 1795 and a member of parliament. He made clear that he did not deem it wise to force the jury system upon the Batavian Republic because it was an institution which was entirely unknown in the Netherlands and it appeared that there was no desire for it: "Il parait que les Bataves ne connaissent point cette institution ou qu'ils ont contre elle des preventions que n'a pas du dissiper. Il en faut convenir l'expérience

---

9   Ibidem, pp. 146–147.
10 G. Bosser, "*Welk eene natie die de jurij gehad heeft, en ze weder afschaft!*", pp. 26–27.

que nous en avons faite depuis six ans. Nous avons cru devoir garder la silence sur les jurés".[11] The Dutch Republicans who created a new constitution also did not propose to introduce a jury system of their own accord. Thus, no further discussion took place on the desirability of a jury system and it was not introduced in the constitution which was approved in April 1798. Furthermore, no discussion appears to have taken place on the jury system during the subsequent revisions of the constitution in 1801, 1805 and 1806.

Apart from the relatively short debate on the desirability of a jury system on the national level, there was also one instance where the introduction of a jury system was considered on the provincial level. In the province of Groningen a committee was given the task to create a plan for a new constitution for Groningen, which the committee presented on 9 June 1796. Regarding the criminal procedure, the committee stated that, 'following the English, French and North-Americans', they deemed the procedural order safest in which the judgment on the facts was separated from the decision on what punishment should be given. They proposed that a body of jurors should decide on the facts and that the judge should, on the indictment by the public prosecutor, apply the punishment determined by the law. Furthermore, the procedure needed to be public and the accused should be allowed to use legal counsel. Although the committee mentioned that they wanted to follow the example of England, North-America and France in establishing a jury system, they strongly followed the French model in their proposal. The discussion on this plan for a constitution for Groningen was postponed because priority was given to first create an ordinance regulating the provincial elections for a new government. Eventually the proposal to introduce a jury system was shelved and never effectuated. One important reason for this was the fact that it was uncertain whether the new national constitution would leave any room for these provincial plans.[12]

There are several conclusions which can be drawn from the Dutch discussion on the jury system between 1795 and 1798. Firstly, it is a significant fact in and of itself that in Groningen and in the national constitutional committee – under influence of the example of the French revolutionary reforms – it was

---

11   L. de Gou, *Ontwerp van constitutie 1797*, pp. 438–439.
12   M.W. van Boven, *De rechterlijke instellingen ter discussie*, pp. 62–69 and 293–298. See also H.A. Kamphuis, *Stad en Lande tijdens de Bataafse Republiek*, pp. 32–44. The plan of Groningen to create new codifications and reform the judicial organisation on the provincial level was not unique. After the liberation in 1795 it was still uncertain whether a Unitarian or a Federalist state would be created. In this uncertainty most provincial revolutionary committees started to work on reforming the governmental and judicial system in their own province. In Friesland, for example, it was also considered to create codifications for the province alone.

for the first time seriously considered in the Dutch Republic to introduce a jury system (which would necessitate a significant reform of the criminal law of evidence). From the discussion in the constitutional committee it becomes apparent that there were proponents of a jury system on predominantly political-constitutional grounds: it seemed to conform better to a democratic form of government and it would increase the trust of the people in the criminal justice system. Another argument was that it would mean that the procedure would have to become public which would further increase the trust in the impartiality of the procedure.[13]

The second conclusion pertains to the question why the jury question was only briefly considered during the beginning of the revolution and afterwards was not mentioned anymore in the period between 1798 and 1810. Not only was the attention for this subject limited on the level of the national legislature, but there were also no publications on this subject in the juridical literature and there appears to have been virtually no popular demand for the introduction of a jury system in the Dutch Republic (in contrast to, for example, the support shown in the French juridical literature and the *cahiers des doléance* for the jury system). This is remarkable because the political-constitutional ideals of the sovereignty of the people and the desire for a separation of powers which underlay the introduction of the jury system in France were widely shared among the Dutch reformers. Nevertheless, the answer to the question why the demand for a jury system was largely absent in the Netherlands in this period appears to be relatively clear. It can be seen in the counterarguments of those in the constitutional committee who did not want the introduction of a jury system. The fundamental difference between the French and the Dutch situation was that there was not a strong distrust against the professional judges in the Netherlands.[14] In the discussion in the national legislature and in the juridical literature many remarks can be found which praised the judicial system and the impartiality of the judges in the Dutch Republic. Here it again becomes apparent how important the matter of trust in the criminal justice system was for the willingness to support such a far-reaching reform as the introduction of a jury system.

---

13   The principle of publicity or the demand to make the criminal trial public was only treated as a consequence of the introduction of a jury system. During the further debates and reforms between 1795 and 1811 there was not an independent demand for the publicity or orality of the trial. This was not a subject of discussion in this period. See also L. van Lent, *Externe openbaarheid in het strafproces*, pp. 30–34.

14   Bossers and Van Boven come to the same conclusion. See M.W. van Boven, *De rechterlijke instellingen ter discussie*, pp. 83–84 and G. Bosser, "*Welk eene natie die de jurij gehad heeft, en ze weder afschaft!*", pp. 24–29.

8.2.1.2   The Abolition of Judicial Torture and its Consequences

Although there were many authors who had argued strongly against judicial torture before 1795, there had been no clear majority in the literature in favour of the abolition of judicial torture and there were no attempts to abolish judicial torture from any of the city or provincial governments. Its use was circumscribed more restrictively in several local ordinances before 1795, but this also implied a conscious decision that judicial torture should be retained. The situation changed in the period after 1795. There still remained many who doubted whether it was prudent to abolish judicial torture and who warned that if it was abolished a new regulation of the criminal law of evidence would become necessary. However, the opponents who emphasized that judicial torture was against natural law, that it was unreliable and that it was unnecessary, now acquired a majority and the momentum after 1795 to force the abolition of judicial torture. Unmistakably, the revolutionary and optimistic atmosphere of the Batavian revolution, wherein it was thought possible to get rid of the abuses of the criminal procedural law, and the rhetoric wherein judicial torture was constantly designated as an unenlightened, barbaric and inhumane institution were important factors in the abolition of judicial torture. Nevertheless, the reformers who wanted to abolish judicial torture were well aware that this could not be done without significant changes to the criminal law of evidence.

Before judicial torture was abolished for the entire Republic in the constitution which was promulgated on 1 May 1798, it had already been abolished in two provinces. The first was Gelderland on 9 September 1795 and the second was Brabant on 11 October 1796.[15] The proclamation which announced the abolition of judicial torture in Gelderland used an array of arguments which can be found among most of the abolitionists. It stated that:

> The custom of applying judicial torture on the accused of a crime is against humanity and the principles of natural equity; it provides only a very weak guarantee for the conviction of the judge because the question whether the accused endures torture depends predominantly on the physical strength of the accused and, therefore, often has the consequence that the innocent suffer a punishment while the guilty avoid their well-deserved punishment; it also runs against the principle of natural

---

15   J.W. Bosch, "Aantekeningen over de inhoud der Hollandse Hervormingsplannen van de criminele ordonnantiën van 1570 in de 18de eeuw, deel III", p. 284.

law that no one should be forced to become his own prosecutor. It is for these reasons that we forever abolish torture ... in this province.[16]

In this proclamation it can be seen very clearly that it was a combination of epistemological and political-constitutional considerations which led to the abolition of judicial torture. On the one hand it is remarked that the forced confession is a highly unreliable form of evidence, and on the other hand it is stated that it is, furthermore, against natural law to force someone to contribute to his own conviction.

The first mention of a proposal to abolish judicial torture for the entire Batavian Republic can be found in the discussion of the constitutional committee on 7 October 1796. Unfortunately there is no transcription of the discussion about the initial proposal and acceptance of the relevant Article which read "The use of judicial torture shall no longer take place".[17] A few days later, on 12 October, the question of judicial torture again surfaced when the instruction for the new supreme court was discussed. Article 20 of this instruction stated that, until a new procedural law would be created, the supreme court would follow the existing procedural law of the high court of Holland with the exception that judicial torture could no longer be used. The transcription of the discussion about this article shows that some members pointed out that this might lead to severe difficulties because in Holland the confession was required in extraordinary procedures. It was recommended that the subcommittee on the judicial branch would take another look at this article.[18] Besides this short remark, there is no further information on the discussion surrounding the abolition of judicial torture in the constitutional committee. Only the result is clear. The concept constitution which the committee presented to the Constituent Assembly in November 1796 contained Article 651 which read that judicial torture should be abolished in the entire Republic.

The next point in time that the abolition of judicial torture was discussed, was on 24 February 1797 when the Constituent Assembly held a plenary debate on Article 651 of the concept constitution. The parliamentarian Schimmelpenninck reacted negatively and remarked that he could understand that the constitutional committee proposed this article out of a 'philosophical spirit', but that it was impossible to effectuate this article as long as a new criminal procedural law was not created and the confession was still necessary. Subsequently,

---

16 *Placaat. Vryheid, Gelykheid ... in naame van de provisioneele Vertegenwoordigers van het vrye Volk van Gelderland.* September 9 1795.
17 L. de Gou, *Het plan van constitutie van 1796*, p. 302.
18 Ibidem, pp. 313–314.

Bacot reacted and agreed with Schimmelpenninck on the point that the abolition of judicial torture would inevitably have to encompass the relinquishing of the absolute requirement of the confession. Bacot, however, strongly criticized Schimmelpenninck for making it seem as if the demand for the abolition of judicial torture was the fruit of an all too careless philosophical spirit which did not understand the practical problems to which it would lead. Bacot argued that while Schimmelpenninck made it appear as if judicial torture was a necessary evil for the effective prosecution of crimes, there were examples of other countries which showed that this was not the case. He stated that judicial torture had already been abolished in several provinces and that this had not led to the endangerment of public safety. He, furthermore, spoke in strongly condemnatory words of the cruel and humanity-dishonouring institution of judicial torture.[19]

After Bacot, Ten Berge remarked that if there was anything which flows from the 'rights of man', it was that judicial torture should be abolished immediately. He stated that it was a useless institution because in as far as the complete conviction of the judge was necessary for a punishment, the judge would acquire this out of the existing evidence or he would not. If the judge acquired this conviction and a full proof was present, the confession was irrelevant. If there was not a full proof, then judicial torture was also useless because it was only dependent on the temperament of the accused whether he could withstand the torments. Ten Berge stated that a modification of the criminal procedural law should not be an obstacle to the abolition of judicial torture. A resounding condemnation of judicial torture also came from Nuhout van der Veen. He exclaimed that he had never expected that 'we citizens, representatives of a free people would still differ of opinion on the abolition of such a horrific and cruel monster as judicial torture; this malignant remnant of slavery which to the shame of the Netherlands was still being used to extort confessions'. Judicial torture was presented by Nuhout van der Veen as a barbaric instrument which did not differ from the backward ordeals of fire and water, and which ran counter to natural law.[20]

Subsequently, Vitringa remarked that he thought that there was a consensus among the representatives that judicial torture was against natural law because it forced someone to contribute to his own demise. He then stated that he understood that there were practical problems tied to the abolition of judicial torture – especially in Holland where the confession was demanded in the

---

19 *Dagverhaal der handelingen van de nationaale vergadering representeerenden het volk van Nederland,* 1797, p. 10.
20 Ibidem, pp. 10–11.

extraordinary procedure – but that these problems were only of a transitory nature until a new procedural law would be created. In an enlightened age such as the present one, these obstacles should no longer prevent the abolition of judicial torture. Furthermore, he stated that he was of the opinion that a new criminal procedural law would have to change the demand for a confession before a severe punishment could be pronounced. Vitringa also remarked that in the provinces of Friesland, Groningen and Gelderland the confession was no longer an absolute requirement for the ordinary punishment and that the criminal justice system seemed to be functioning fine there. Reyns, on the other hand, stated that he thought it unwise to abolish judicial torture before a new procedural law was created. Lastly some representatives spoke in favour of keeping the Article in the constitution so that the makers of the new criminal codification were at least clearly bound by the decision to abolish judicial torture. After this discussion the Article was put to the vote and approved by the Constituent Assembly.[21]

However, the concept constitution, which contained the Article that abolished judicial torture, was rejected in the referendum of August 1797. When the second Constituent Assembly revised the concept constitution the Article abolishing judicial torture was, nevertheless, retained without further discussion as Article 36 of the new constitution.[22] After the coup d'état of 22 January 1798 the Article also remained unchanged. At the end of April 1798, the constitution was finally approved by a referendum. The new constitution acquired force of law on 1 May and thereby, for the first time, judicial torture was officially abolished for the Dutch Republic as a whole. Importantly, Article 28 of this constitution also prescribed that a committee would be formed which would create a codification of the substantive and procedural criminal law.

8.2.1.2.1   *The Alternative for Judicial Torture*
As several representatives had already foreseen, as long as a new criminal procedural law was not yet created the abolition of judicial torture would be especially problematic for the province of Holland. For most other provinces the abolition of judicial torture was easier to cope with because they already allowed the possibility of convicting to a severe corporal and sometimes even capital punishment on the basis of a full proof in absence of a confession. However, for the important province of Holland, which represented around forty percent of the population of the Dutch Republic, it meant the removal of an instrument which was considered crucial in the extraordinary procedure. It

---

21   Ibidem, pp. 11–12.
22   L. de Gou, *Ontwerp van constitutie 1797*, p. 282.

did not take long before a letter was sent by the city of Amsterdam to the central government with the question what they had to do in this transitory period with the prisoners who refused to confess, now that judicial torture was abolished. This was an important practical point, because as Faber has shown, even after the revolution of 1795 judicial torture continued to be used in the province of Holland until 1798. In Amsterdam, for example, judicial torture was still applied several times between 1795 and 1798.[23]

On 24 July 1798, the government (*Intermediar Uitvoerend Bewind*) presented an advice to the new legislator – which now consisted of two chambers – concerning the question of Amsterdam. The government presented four possible solutions to the practical problem caused by the abolition of judicial torture: 1. The legislator could decree that all those who did not confess would have to be admitted to an ordinary procedure. 2. The legislator could authorize the courts to do justice 'on conviction' in the extraordinary procedure. The terminology of doing justice 'on conviction' is somewhat misleading. With this it was not meant that the judge could decide on the basis of his freely formed subjective conviction like the French jurors. It had the same meaning as doing justice 'on evidence' and it was intended as a contrast to doing justice 'on the confession'. Doing justice 'on conviction', in other words, meant that the judge could decide on the basis of a full proof (through indicia or witness testimony) in absence of a confession. 3. If the legislator deemed the second option too dangerous for civil liberty, it could create an intermediary law which would prescribe a different procedure. 4. The legislator could decide that the Article abolishing judicial torture would come into force only at the moment when a new criminal procedural codification was promulgated. The government then commented that the first option appeared impracticable because the costs and duration of the ordinary procedure would be too great. The second option seemed more practical, but they remarked that it might have the consequence that civil liberty was more in danger than it was when judicial torture was allowed. The third option was deemed unconstitutional because a special committee was already supposed to create a new codification. The government recommended either to allow the judges to decide 'on conviction' or to follow the fourth option, but left the choice to the legislator.[24]

The legislator appointed a special committee to present a report on this question which was read by Steyn Parvé on 17 August 1798. The committee

---

23 S. Faber, *Strafrechtspleging en criminaliteit te Amsterdam, 1680–1811. De nieuwe menslievendheid*, pp. 120–125.
24 *Dagverhaal der handelingen van de nationaale vergadering representeerenden het volk van Nederland,* 1798, pp. 587–588.

recommended that judicial torture should be abolished only from the moment that a new criminal procedural law was created in accordance with Article 28 of the constitution. In the report it was stated that judicial torture was used seldomly and solely in cases which were threatened with a severe punishment. Furthermore, it was remarked that judicial torture was used merely when the judge was already morally convinced of the guilt of the accused in order to a acquire the confession which was legally required for a conviction to a severe punishment.[25]

On 21 August 1798 an intense discussion ensued in the first chamber of the legislator on the question posed by the city of Amsterdam. Several representatives used the occasion to again speak out in strong terms against the barbarity and uselessness of judicial torture and argued that it should not be allowed to function even in the transitory phase. In this vein Van Galen, for example, spoke out against judicial torture which should be forbidden in a free republic, and described it as a backward institution which was created in times of superstition when witches were prosecuted. He stated that it was better and more natural that the judge who holds sufficiently strong evidence for judicial torture to either convict the accused to the punishment decreed by the law or to an extraordinary punishment. Van Galen did not agree with those who saw a great danger in doing justice on conviction. It was already an accepted practice in ordinary procedures. The real problem, he stated, was that the ordinary procedure was too costly and always took far too long. Subsequently, Verbeek held a similar plea, condemning the cruelty of judicial torture and argued that the accused should be admitted to an ordinary procedure instead.[26]

Vitringa remarked that the question was not whether judicial torture should be reintroduced, but only if this practice should be allowed to continue until a new criminal procedural code was created. He then stated that as long as the rule existed that a confession was necessary for a conviction, the extraordinary procedure would be ineffective without judicial torture. He observed that there was also no pressing need to directly abolish judicial torture, because the criminal justice system in Holland had thus far functioned in such an equitable manner that it in fact formed a role model for other nations. Van Hall, who had functioned as a public prosecutor in Amsterdam, did not want to put into question whether judicial torture should be abolished, but argued that it should be allowed in this transitory phase. He contended that it might be possible to create a better alternative than judicial torture, but that this was more

---

25 *Dagverhaal der handelingen van de nationaale vergadering representeerenden het volk van Nederland,* 1798, pp. 199–203 and 235.
26 Ibidem, pp. 230–235.

difficult than some representatives seemed to think and certainly not possible within a short time span. Van Hall continued to argue that in practice in Holland the use of judicial torture had been a lot more equitable and less cruel than was contended by many of the representatives. Besides, he remarked, a single example of a person unjustly tortured in Holland could not be mentioned, while many examples could be given of innocent persons who were convicted to death in England where the demand of the confession of the accused did not exist.[27]

Similar to Van Hall, Van Foreest stated that judicial torture was not such a horrific instrument if one imagined that judicial torture was only used in the situation where, if one did justice 'on conviction', the accused would be convicted to death. Furthermore, he remarked that even in those provinces where judicial torture had been abolished all kinds of harsh measures were still being used to press the accused to confess. For these reasons he did not see any objections to the continued use of judicial torture in the transitory phase. At the end of the debate, the first chamber decided that by way of a compromise judicial torture would still be allowed in Holland until a special committee had created a new criminal procedural ordinance.[28] On 23 August 1798, however, the second chamber of parliament rejected this proposition. It argued that Article 36 of the constitution had directly abolished judicial torture and that it should not be permitted anywhere anymore. On 27 August the first chamber accepted this rejection and gave the assignment to the high court of Holland and Zeeland to create a provisional solution of how to proceed in Holland now that judicial torture was abolished.[29]

On 5 and 6 October in 1798, the first and second chamber approved a provisional ordinance created by the high court of Holland and Zeeland. This provisional ordinance proved to be an important piece of legislation because it remained in force in the province of Holland until in 1811 the *Code d'Instruction Criminelle* acquired force of law. The ordinance contained 18 Articles. Article 1 consisted of two parts. The first part expressly reiterated that judicial torture was abolished and that the judge was under no circumstance allowed to hurt or pressure the accused to confess. The second part of this article, however, stated that the judge was permitted to use 'such means as he thought necessary' to force the accused to answer to questions when the accused obstinately refused to speak. This shows similarities to the German *Ungehorsamstrafe*. The accused could no longer be pressured to confess, but he could be forced to

---

27   Ibidem, pp. 235–239.
28   Ibidem, pp. 241–243.
29   Ibidem, pp. 286–287 and 319–322.

answer by such measures as the judge saw fit. It is obvious that this far from clear formulation created a certain room for the judge which could be abused to pressure the accused. Furthermore, the discussion surrounding this article shows that even though judicial torture was abolished, it was still deemed that the accused had an obligation to answer questions and that the judge should have some corrective means to force him to answer.[30] As it has been stated in Chapter three, the development of the *nemo tenetur* principle was a gradual process in the Netherlands. The abolition of judicial torture was a first important step, but it did not mean in this period that a 'right to remain silent' was positively acknowledged.

The following Articles regulated the different possibilities a judge had now that judicial torture was abolished. First of all, if there was a sufficiently reliable confession the judge had to convict. If the accused did not confess and the evidence made it unlikely that the accused was guilty he had to be absolved. If there was a stronger level of suspicion the judge could pronounce a form of an *absolutio ab instantia*. If, and this was the innovative part, there was no confession but the evidence produced by the public prosecutor was so strong that it seemed to fully prove the crime, the judge could allow the public prosecutor to ask for a conviction in an extraordinary procedure on this basis. The judge was now permitted in an extraordinary procedure to convict on the basis of a full proof in absence of a confession. However, the high court had taken into account the dangers of this situation and made provisions which significantly strengthened the defensive position of the accused under these circumstances. From the moment that the judge permitted the public prosecutor to ask for a conviction in absence of a confession, the accused was allowed legal counsel. If he could not afford legal counsel it had to be given to him on behalf of the court. The accused and the legal counsel then had a right to see the incriminating evidence, to hear witnesses and to produce their defence. The provisional ordinance makes clear that this all had to take place within short terms which were to be determined by the judge, while no appeal was allowed.[31]

---

30 Faber has shown that this second part of the Article was inserted only later by the high court under pressure of a letter from Amsterdam which explained that they had difficulties with an accused who refused to answer questions. See S. Faber, *Strafrechtspleging en criminaliteit te Amsterdam, 1680–1811. De nieuwe menslievendheid*, pp. 124–128.

31 *Dagverhaal der handelingen van de nationaale vergadering representeerenden het volk van Nederland*, 1798, pp. 761–765. It is apparent that the ordinance attempted to incorporate the benefits of the ordinary procedure while creating a faster and more efficient procedure. The ordinance did continue to allow the judge to refer a case to the ordinary procedure under the circumstances under which this had normally been possible, but this needed to remain an exception.

Summarizing, the provisional ordinance changed the nature of the extraordinary procedure in Holland in two crucial ways. The judge was now allowed to convict to the ordinary punishment in absence of a confession, and the accused was given legal counsel and far better possibilities to defend himself when the public prosecutor proposed to convict him 'on conviction' (i.e. witness testimony and indicia). These were significant innovations which were directly related to the abolition of judicial torture.[32] The research of Faber shows that the provisional ordinance was duly followed in the city of Amsterdam. Furthermore, he has discovered only two cases between 1798 and 1811 where the second part of Article 1 was applied to an accused who refused to speak. In both situations the whip was used on an accused who had refused to answer questions by the judge.[33]

8.2.1.2.2 Conclusion

In conclusion, it can be observed that in the period after 1795 a clear momentum existed to abolish judicial torture. In the constitutional committee and the Constituent Assembly there were majorities for its abolition, and it appeared to be an unpopular opinion to speak out for the retention of judicial torture. This opinion was only voiced by some parliamentarians in careful wordings that stressed the practical problems which might arise out of its abolition, while the opponents of judicial torture used far stronger and emphatic rhetoric. The arguments used against judicial torture corresponded largely to those which had been expressed in the juridical literature between 1750 and 1795. The most important arguments were, first of all, that it was an inhumane and cruel instrument. Many representatives stressed its barbaric and unenlightened character, and stated that it was incompatible with civil freedom. Supposedly, throughout history it was typically used by repressive tyrants and within the context of superstitious practices such as the persecution of witches. Furthermore, the idea was voiced by some that judicial torture was just as absurd as the medieval ordeals. Although the criticism that judicial torture was a cruel, inhumane practice was certainly not new in the second half of the eighteenth century, it was voiced more frequently and it is likely that this argument

---

[32] The influence of the provisional ordinance was eventually not limited to Holland. It also applied to the province of Zeeland and was copied almost verbatim in the instruction for the high court of Brabant on 15 November 1803. See J.W. Bosch, "Aantekeningen over de inhoud der Hollandse Hervormingsplannen van de criminele ordonnantiën van 1570 in de 18de eeuw, deel III", pp. 286–288.

[33] S. Faber, *Strafrechtspleging en criminaliteit te Amsterdam, 1680–1811. De nieuwe menslievendheid*, pp. 128–132.

started to weigh heavier in this period due to changing sensibilities concerning the use of violence, as Spierenburg has argued.[34]

A second important argument, which was also voiced in the ordinance of Gelderland, was that judicial torture was contrary to natural law. It was stated that no one should be forced to act against nature and contribute to his own demise. Finally, the last argument which was frequently used against judicial torture reveals the underlying epistemological change. It was argued that judicial torture was unnecessary and unreliable. It was considered unnecessary because many of the reformers deemed that other forms of evidence could create the same kind of certainty required for a conviction as the confession. Public safety was guaranteed just as well or even better when the judge was allowed to convict someone 'on conviction'. It can be concluded that three factors decisively influenced the abolition of judicial torture. It was abolished due to a combination of political-constitutional and epistemological considerations, and due to a change in sensibilities.

Nevertheless, the further discussions in 1798 in parliament regarding the provisional ordinance for the province of Holland show that there was still some hesitation whether it was prudent to abolish judicial torture outright. Those in favour of its retention now voiced their concerns regarding the abolition of judicial torture more prominently. Although all agreed that judicial torture should remain abolished, the discussion in parliament shows that there were many representatives who did not seem to think that judicial torture was such a horrific and useless instrument. It is clear in the speeches of, among others, Van Hall and Van Foreest that they still thought judicial torture was a necessary evil and that it was a good rule that the confession was required for a conviction in Holland. The alternative of allowing the judge to decide 'on conviction' appeared to them to be far more dangerous. This stance is typical for those who held firm to the traditional idea that the confession was the only truly certain form of evidence. An opinion which could also be seen in, for example, the work of Calkoen which has been discussed in the previous chapter.

Another conclusion which can be drawn, is that the representatives were well aware of the fact that the abolition of judicial torture meant that the existing extraordinary procedure would become untenable. There was still a certain hesitation in this period of what should come in its place. This hesitation can be seen in the advice which was given by the government to the legislator, where four options were mentioned but where the government did not dare to

---

34 P. Spierenburg, *The spectacle of suffering*, pp. 183–190.

give a strong recommendation of which option it deemed best. While there were some representatives who simply wanted to allow the judge to decide 'on conviction' in the extraordinary procedure, this was considered a very dangerous and unsatisfactory option by many representatives. Here the important connection between the criminal law of evidence and the procedural law becomes especially apparent. The option of allowing the judge to convict someone 'on conviction' was deemed acceptable only in the ordinary procedure where the accused had far better possibilities to defend himself. Turning the extraordinary procedures into ordinary procedures, which took far longer and would be very costly, was thought to make the criminal justice system entirely ineffective. For those representatives who wanted to allow the judge to decide 'on conviction', it was, therefore, first of all necessary to create a new procedural law which would be more efficient and which would introduce better defensive rights to the accused. A significant breakthrough out of this impasse was reached with the provisional ordinance for Holland of 1798 which introduced for the first time the combination of allowing the judge to decide 'on conviction' with better defensive rights for the accused. The hope was that a better and more permanent solution could be found in the new substantive and procedural criminal codes that still had to be created.

8.2.2 *The Discussions in the Codification Committee 1798–1804*

Throughout the period of 1795 until 1798 there was a broadly shared desire for the creation of a codification of the criminal law.[35] In the constitution of 1798 the legality principle found expression that no one should be punished for crimes which were not prescribed by law. Article 28 of the constitution of 1798 stated that a special committee had to be formed which would create a codification of the civil law and criminal law. Subsequently, in September 1798 a general codification committee of twelve renowned jurists was appointed by the government to design this codification. Already in May 1799, a subcommittee of this committee produced a concept ordinance for the criminal procedural law. This procedural ordinance is the subject of the first subsection. Later, in the period between 1798 and 1804, the general committee finished a concept codification of the laws of evidence and of the substantive criminal law. These are dealt with in the second subsection. Finally, it is important to keep in mind that during the reform discussions between 1798 and 1804, the codification committee was bound by the two fundamental decisions – which had been

---

35 O. Moorman van Kappen, "Uitwendige schets der wordingsgeschiedenis van het ontwerp-Lijfstraffelijk Wetboek 1804", pp. 116–119.

made earlier by the Constitutional Assembly between 1795 and 1798 – that there would be no jury trial and that judicial torture would remain abolished.[36]

8.2.2.1 The Concept Criminal Procedural Ordinance of 1799

The general codification committee, appointed in September 1798, consisted of Bondt, Walraven, Farjon, Kreeft, Reitz, Craeyvanger, Gockinga, Reuvens, In de Betouw, Cras, de Beveren and Donker Curtius. Apart from the general codification committee, another committee was charged with the creation of a law on the judicial organization in 1798. Because the latter committee stated that it could not function properly until more clarity on the new procedural law existed, it was decided that a subcommittee of the general codification committee would first have to create a concept ordinance on the civil and criminal procedural law within six months. The subcommittee was created on 16 November 1798 and succeeded within a surprisingly short time. On 3 May 1799 it presented a concept ordinance for the civil and criminal procedural law. The subcommittee consisted of five members, Bondt, Farjon, Walraven, Reuvens and Kreet, of whom Reuvens and Kreet were responsible for the criminal procedural law. Unfortunately, no transcription of the discussions concerning the criminal procedural code have survived so all that remains is the concept criminal procedural code itself.[37]

Essentially, the criminal procedural code of 1799 brought only limited innovations and formed a codification of the procedural practice which existed for the provincial high court in Holland. De Bosch Kemper has observed that the procedural code of 1799 was modelled after the concept procedural ordinance for the province of Holland created between 1773 and 1776 (which has been treated in the previous chapter). This concept ordinance was itself largely a codification of the existing procedural practice of the high court of Holland.[38] The concept ordinance of 1799 gave a more detailed regulation of the different procedural steps than the concept ordinance created in the 1770s, and it no longer contained the possibility of judicial torture. Nevertheless, the distinction between the ordinary and the extraordinary procedure was retained and the inquisitorial procedure remained secret. Furthermore, the powerful role of the inquisitorial judge also stayed largely the same. The ordinance, in short,

---

36   The decision that there would be no jury trial was not made explicit in the constitution of 1798, but the codification committees seems to have presumed that they should not introduce this institution without an explicit mandate. At least there appear to have been no discussions on the topic of the introduction of a jury system in the criminal codification committee between 1798 and 1804.
37   M.W. van Boven, *De rechterlijke instellingen ter discussie*, pp. 113–120.
38   J. de Bosch Kemper, *Wetboek van Strafvordering I*, pp. CXXXIII–CXXXIX.

was not intended to fundamentally alter the existing procedural practice in the Republic.

The most important reforms that the procedural ordinance of 1799 contained, corresponded to the changes which can be found in the provisional ordinance for Holland of 1798. Article 89 repeated that judicial torture was abolished. Article 110 stated that in absence of a confession, the judge could convict the accused when the evidence "was complete and of such a nature, that the crime was fully proven after the requirements of the law".[39] As in the provisional ordinance for Holland of 1798, the accused had the right to legal counsel in this situation. The legal counsel was allowed to hear witnesses and to present the defence of the accused, all within short time frames to be determined by the judge. It was also still possible for the judge, if he thought the crime was not yet entirely proven or the situation too unclear, to turn the case into an ordinary procedure. A further parallel to the provisional ordinance was that Article 62 allowed the judge – again in very vague terms – to use such disciplinary measures as he deemed necessary against an accused who refused to answer questions. This was formulated as a measure to 'persuade the accused to fulfil his obligation', meaning that the accused did not have a right to remain silent but was obligated to answer.[40]

Summarizing, the concept procedural ordinance of 1799 made it possible to convict in an extraordinary procedure on the basis of a full proof in absence of a confession, but for this situation the defensive rights of the accused were strongly enhanced. This reflects the fear of the 'danger for civil liberty' which existed when the judge was allowed to decide 'on conviction'. It also becomes clear from this ordinance that a special and important position was still attached to the confession of the accused. When a sufficient confession existed, the accused was not allowed legal counsel or the extended defensive rights, and he was also not allowed to appeal to a higher court. The latter was possible solely when the accused was convicted 'on conviction' in an extraordinary procedure, although the high court could reject this appeal summarily. The continued importance of the confession is, furthermore, visible in the possibility to force the accused to answer and in a peculiar novelty which can be found in Article 126. This article prescribed that when the accused was convicted to death in absence of a confession, sometime before the execution the accused needed to be brought before the judges and for a last time it would be tried to

---

39   *Algemeene Manier van Procedeeren in civiele en crimineele zaaken*, p. 284.
40   Ibidem, pp. 263–288.

persuade him to confess his crime while it was explained to him that the death penalty was now in any case unavoidable.[41]

Interestingly, a concept criminal procedural ordinance was also made by Van Houten, a lawyer from Amsterdam. He sent this concept to the National Assembly as a suggestion of how the criminal procedural law could be regulated. The design by Van Houten showed many similarities to the provisional ordinance of 1798 and the concept criminal procedural ordinance of 1799. Important differences were that on the one hand Van Houten did not seem to want to allow legal counsel to the accused, and that on the other hand he did propose that the accused should have the right not to answer questions (the silence of the accused would have to be seen as a denial of the charges). The concept of Van Houten also proposed to allow the judge to convict 'on conviction' now that judicial torture was abolished.[42]

The concept civil and criminal procedural ordinances were approved by the first chamber of the legislator on 22 July and by the second chamber on 22 August in 1799. Van Boven states that there was much appreciation for the short and clear redaction of the articles. Nevertheless, the concept procedural ordinances of 1799 were never promulgated because their coming into force was tied to the ordinance which would reorganize the judicial organisation of the Republic. While the creation of the latter ordinance was still in progress, the concept procedural ordinances were shelved. As it turned out, the reorganization of the judicial system proved such an arduous task that the criminal procedural ordinance eventually never came into force.[43]

8.2.2.2 The Criminal Codification Committee of 1798–1804

The concept criminal procedural ordinance of 1799 contained a relatively summary regulation of the criminal law of evidence which sanctioned the change that a judge could convict in the extraordinary procedure in absence of a confession. It did not give a more detailed regulation of the question when sufficient proof existed or, for example, when witnesses were admissible. It only created the procedural contours. The more detailed regulation of the criminal law of evidence was to take place in a special part still to be created by the criminal codification committee. Of the twelve general committee members appointed in 1798, the following five were selected to codify the criminal law:

---

41   Ibidem, pp. 283–310.
42   On this concept ordinance of Van Houten, see G. Bossers, "Een ontwerp *manier van procederen in criminele zaken* uit 1798", pp. 97–119.
43   M.W. van Boven, *De rechterlijke instellingen ter discussie*, pp. 117–120. As was mentioned before, this was also the reason why the provisional ordinance created by the high court of Holland and Zeeland remained in force for the entire period between 1798 and 1811.

Reuvens, In de Betouw, Cras, De Beveren and Donker Curtius. By the time the criminal committee started its work in 1799, however, the members of the committee had changed to become: in de Betouw, de Beveren, Donker Curtius, Elout and Kreet. The dominant member of this committee was Elout, who often wrote the first drafts for the more difficult theoretical parts.[44]

The attempt to reform the criminal law of evidence by the codification committee can be divided into two phases. The first phase between 1798 and 1801 consisted of the creation of the concept substantive criminal ordinance. This concept ordinance contained four parts. A first, general part, of which the third chapter regulated the criminal law of evidence, and three other parts which regulated the substantive criminal law. The chapter on the criminal law of evidence was written by Elout. After the concept criminal ordinance was finished it was sent to the civil committee for commentary in 1801. Because the civil committee did not stop its own work to review the criminal ordinance, it took two years before they finally gave their commentary in 1803. The most important comments were provided by Cras. The second phase consisted of the discussion on this commentary and the transposition of the criminal law of evidence into a general concept codification of the laws of evidence for the civil as well as criminal law between 1803 and 1804. The main authors of the new separate ordinance on the laws of evidence were Cras and Elout. At the end of 1804 the separate concept ordinances for the laws of evidence and for the substantive criminal law were finished and sent for further commentary to the Supreme Court.[45]

Substantively, the regulation of the criminal law of evidence in the concept ordinances of 1801 and 1804 showed no great differences. The rules regarding the different sources of evidence and on the evaluation of the evidence by the judge were largely the same. In both designs the criminal law (of evidence) is regulated in a very extensive and 'didactic' manner. Instead of succinct and clear formulations, the Articles are long and saturated with definitions and the treatment of many possible modifications and exceptions. The committee tried to explain what intention they had with the Articles and often even used examples within the Articles themselves to illustrate what they meant. The supreme court, unsurprisingly, later severely criticized the concept ordinances for their lengthiness and the fact that they read more like a juridical handbook which gave instruction norms to the judge, than as clear positive prescriptions.

---

44   O. Moorman van Kappen, "Uitwendige schets der wordingsgeschiedenis van het ontwerp-Lijfstraffelijk Wetboek 1804", pp. 122–131.

45   Ibidem, pp. 123–131.

This was especially problematic for the substantive criminal law, which was meant to be written in a way that it could be understood by the people.[46]

The ordinances of 1801 and 1804 show in style many similarities to the treatises on natural law which deductively reasoned from certain general principles.[47] The similarity is understandable in light of the sources that the codification committee used. Somewhat surprisingly, almost no mention is made in the discussions of French authors – except Montesquieu –, and virtually no use seems to have been made of the French or any of the other recent codifications. The authors which are cited most frequently are Dutch and German authors from predominantly the second half of the eighteenth century, in particular Pestel, Leyser, Böhmer, Kleinschrod, Meister and Gmelin. The work, however, which seems to have had the greatest influence, was the *Science of Legislation* by Filangieri. He was cited approvingly many times and was of a particular importance for the discussions on the criminal law of evidence. Also, some older Dutch criminal handbooks from the seventeenth century were used, particularly Matthaeus, Voet and Huber. As Moorman van Kappen accurately characterized, the codification committee appears to have been standing with one leg in the existing criminal law of the Dutch Republic, and with the other leg in the 'new ideas of the enlightenment' as they were given shape by particularly the German and Italian jurists of the late eighteenth century.[48] It was on the basis of this combination that the committee tried to create a codification of the criminal law of evidence. As will be described in the following chapter, the French revolutionary ideas about the criminal procedural law and the jury system only became of a greater influence after the 1810s.

Both designs of the criminal law of evidence of 1801 and 1804 started with a general definition of when a crime was proven and with mentioning the different sources of evidence which could be used. In the subsequent chapters these forms of evidence were regulated in more detail. Article 2 of the ordinance of 1801 gave the following definition of when a crime was proven: "the existence

---

46 O. Moorman van Kappen, *Ontwerp-Lijfstraffelijk Wetboek 1804*, pp. 401–422.

47 The high regard for writers on natural law and the idea that through their analytical approach the law could be improved, can be seen well in a short memorandum by Cras. Cras remarked that it was 'philosophy' which had destroyed the demons of superstition, and it was the same philosophy which through the wise teachings of among others Grotius, Pufendorf and Montesquieu had purified legal scholarship from many prejudices. The subject of the laws of evidence was difficult, Cras remarked, but the confused concepts have sprouted out of the lack of a proper analytical approach. See J. Th. Smidt and A.H. Huussen, *Bronnen van de Nederlandse codificatie sinds 1798 I*, pp. 491–492.

48 O. Moorman van Kappen, "Bijdrage tot de codificatiegeschiedenis van ons strafrecht rond het begin van de negentiende eeuw: het ontwerp-lijfstraffelijk wetboek van 1804", pp. 317–322.

of a crime and the guilt of the accused are considered proven, when the judge has acquired the conviction that the contrary is morally impossible". Article 6 adds to this definition: "A judge cannot obtain the required certainty, and may therefore not convict someone, unless he has a full proof". The commentary on Article 2 by Cras is very instructive of how this norm was to be understood. Cras questioned the use of the word 'conviction' and proposed that instead the word 'certainty' should be used. The reason was that, as Cras understood it, conviction was normally used in a more subjective sense and certainty had a more objective meaning.[49] In the ordinance of 1804, Cras now used the term juridical certainty and gave the following definition of when a crime was proven in Article 5: "Juridical certainty lies in the judge's conviction of the truth of the alleged facts, grounded on the general and specific rules which have been prescribed to him for the formation of his judgment".[50]

In a similar way Farjon, a member of the civil committee, commented on Article 2 of the ordinance of 1801 that "the moral conviction of the judge alone does not seem sufficient in itself. There also needs to be a juridical certainty: that is the moral conviction of the judge needs to be acquired by such means, which according to the rules of the law, provide a full proof".[51] What the Articles 2 and 6 of the ordinance of 1801 show – and what was made even more clear by the comments of Farjon and Cras – was that the subjective conviction of the judge alone was deemed insufficient. Although not sufficient, Article 4 of the ordinance of 1804 did state that the conviction of the judge was seen as a necessary prerequisite to convict someone. The moral conviction of the judge needed to be acquired in accordance with the legal evidentiary rules to form a 'juridical conviction' or 'juridical certainty'. The moral conviction alone was deemed insufficient because this was considered to be too uncertain.

Importantly, both the designs of 1801 and 1804 make clear that it was by no means the idea of the committee that it could be positively and exhaustively prescribed beforehand when the evidence was sufficiently strong to form a 'juridical certainty'. Article 24 of the ordinance of 1804 – and similarly Article 62 of the ordinance of 1801 – explicitly stated in general that "because it is impossible to determine in advance what constitutes a sufficient proof in every individual case, the judge has to evaluate internally, informed by the rules of law, what appears to him as true or probable".[52] Apart from this explicit remark, it can also be seen throughout the concept ordinances in the treatment of the

---

49   O. Moorman van Kappen, *Ontwerp-Lijfstraffelijk Wetboek 1801*, pp. 155–157.
50   J. Th. Smidt and A.H. Huussen, *Bronnen van de Nederlandse codificatie sinds 1798 I*, p. 405.
51   O. Moorman van Kappen, *Ontwerp-Lijfstraffelijk Wetboek 1801*, pp. 156–157.
52   J. Th. Smidt and A.H. Huussen, *Bronnen van de Nederlandse codificatie sinds 1798 I*, p. 410.

different forms of evidence that the intention was not to positively prescribe when a full proof existed. The view of the committee, in this respect, shows strong similarities to the ideas of Filangieri, and in effect was identical to what later would be called a 'negative theory of proof'. The codification committee sought, like Filangieri, alignment with the traditional evidentiary rules, but everywhere made room for what was seen as the 'unavoidable' judicial freedom of evaluation in the individual case.

The ordinances recognized the following sources of evidence: the confession, witness testimony, written documents and indicia. The ordinance of 1804 also mentioned oaths as a fifth form. Both ordinances prescribed that a confession could constitute a full proof when it had been made voluntarily in court, when it was sufficiently specific and clear, and corroborated by some other form of evidence. The testimony of two irreproachable eyewitnesses *could* also make a full proof, while a full proof could not exist in the testimony of one witness. Furthermore, there were many rules in the concept ordinances which determined when witnesses were reproachable. Among others, the following persons could not be regarded as irreproachable witnesses: persons under the age of twenty, fellow culprits, enemies of the accused, friends and relatives of the accused and those with a mental illness. Although the testimonies of these persons could not have the force of a witness testimony, this did not mean that they could not be heard at all. Similar to an insufficient confession, the witness testimony of reproachable persons could still have the force of an indicium. The ordinances also stated that the probative force of witnesses did not simply lie in their number, but also in the extent to which they confirmed each other and in the trustworthiness of the witnesses.[53]

The regulation of the confession and witness testimony corresponded largely to the traditional rules from the system of legal proofs about which a broad consensus existed in the juridical literature. The more difficult part lay in the question how indicia should be regulated. There was an important difference on this subject between the ordinances of 1801 and 1804. The first ordinance was far more restrictive regarding the use of indicia, while the second design wanted to allow more room for convictions on the basis of indicia. Particularly the regulation of indicia in the ordinance of 1804 shows the fundamental openness and 'negative' character of the criminal law of evidence intended in this ordinance.

The ordinance of 1801 was relatively summary on indicia and contained only five Articles. In Article 56 the ordinance defined indicia as 'circumstances from

---

[53] O. Moorman van Kappen, *Ontwerp-Lijfstraffelijk Wetboek 1801*, pp. 159–176 and J. Th. Smidt and A.H. Huussen, *Bronnen van de Nederlandse codificatie sinds 1798 I*, pp. 408–446.

which the crime and the guilt of the culprit could be inferred'. Article 58 stated that "when the indicia stand in a direct and necessary connection to the presumed crime or culpability of the accused, they provide a full proof. When, for example, a married woman, whose husband has been absent for two years, has a child, the crime of adultery is fully proven".[54] The following Article stated that when there was not a necessary connection between the indicia and the crime, they could never provide a full proof; regardless of how many indicia there were and how suspicious they may seem. Then the Article gave the confusing example of two people who slept in an inn in a room together. The following morning one person was found dead while the other one had left early and was later found with a knife covered in blood. The Article of the concept ordinance of 1801 concluded that "Never can a moral certainty be born hereof that the latter person was the culprit".[55]

Donker Curtius criticized this example because it might be difficult to understand for most judges. Cras went even further and questioned whether under these circumstances – and when, for example, the accused was found with stolen goods of the victim – the indicia were not strong enough to create the necessary certainty. He also commented that it was clarifying to read Filangieri on this subject, because he gave very useful prescriptions on how indicia can cumulate to become a sufficient proof. Article 61, finally, stated that when the indicia are so strong that the probability of the innocence of the accused disappears, and they were combined with the confession of the accused or other forms of evidence, they *could* create a full proof. Donker Curtius commented on this article that he wanted the word 'could' changed in 'should', because in his opinion indicia were a strong form of evidence and could often have more probative force than witness testimony. Elout replied that he agreed that indicia could be very strong, but that it was not well possible to determine *a priori* when indicia 'should' create a full proof, but only when they 'could' create a full proof. These articles need to be seen in combination with the Articles of the following chapter containing 'general remarks on the law of evidence'. The opening Article 62 stated that it is impossible to determine beforehand what provides a sufficient proof in every individual case, and Article 64 stated that "the judge has to inspect every form of evidence and then evaluate in his mind what he considers to be proven".[56]

The chapter on indicia of the concept of Cras in 1804 contained several significant modifications and additions to the design of Elout of 1801. In a far

---

54   O. Moorman van Kappen, *Ontwerp-Lijfstraffelijk Wetboek 1801*, pp. 176–177.
55   Ibidem, p. 177.
56   Ibidem, pp. 177–180.

larger chapter of eighty-five Articles on indicia, Cras defined indicia in Article 3 as all 'objects, events or circumstances which provide a suspicion through their necessary or more or less probable connection to the subject under investigation'. Article 5 then stated "Even though not everything can be predetermined regarding indicia because of the endless possible variety of circumstances and much therefore needs to be left to the discretion of the judge, the rules in this chapter aim to guide his judgement".[57] Unlike Elout, Cras gave a large enumeration of different types of indicia which could also typically be found in many of the traditional juridical handbooks. He categorized indicia in proximate and remote indicia, of which the first had a very close connection to the crime and the latter a more remote connection. He further subdivided them in general indicia and indicia specific for certain crimes. A general proximate indicium was, for example, finding someone on the scene of the crime with the weapon with which the crime has been committed. General remote indicia were, among other things, the bad reputation of the accused and the refusal of the accused to answer questions during the judicial interrogation.[58]

The lengthiness of the chapter on indicia by Cras was largely due to the enumeration of the indicia he provided. As Cras explained in Article 79, however, the enumeration of the indicia was not limitative or meant to bindingly prescribe the force of the different indicia. On the contrary, their strength had to be determined by the judge for each individual case. The chapter on the 'strength of indicia' opened with Article 74 which stated "The force of indicia is generally that they can work to strengthen other forms of evidence, and also that they can, through their number and through their internal corroboration, climb to reach the strength of a [full] judicial proof".[59] Article 77 and 80 further confirmed that when indicia stood in a direct causal connection to the alleged crime, they could provide a full proof. Article 78, however, expressly warned that in convicting someone on the basis of indicia, the judge had to use the utmost care and circumspection and he had to be aware that 'his conscience was severely charged' with this decision (a warning that was absent regarding other forms of evidence). Lastly, the chapter contained three Articles on indicia relating to the innocence of the accused. They stated that the judge needed to research whether there were indicia which pointed at the innocence of the

---

57 J. Th. Smidt and A.H. Huussen, *Bronnen van de Nederlandse codificatie sinds 1798 I*, pp. 493–495.
58 Ibidem, pp. 493–509.
59 Ibidem, pp. 510–512.

accused, and that the reverse situations of incriminating indicia could often provide clues of his innocence.[60]

On the most important premises of how the criminal law of evidence should be regulated there did not seem to have been a fundamental difference of opinion between the members of the criminal committee or later that of the civil committee. At least, in the very limited sources of the internal communications which remain, there is no evidence of strong differences of opinion. On the contrary, the comments by the civil members on the concept ordinance of 1801 were predominantly directed at relatively minor points and the concept ordinance of Cras of 1804 did not substantially deviate from the design of Elout of 1801, apart form the subject of indicia. An important difference was, nevertheless, that Cras was often more elaborate and seems to have worked from a more clearly articulated theoretical idea of how the criminal law of evidence should be given shape, while Elout had a more practical approach.[61] The concept ordinance of Cras was accepted by the general codification committee within a short time span in 1804, which suggests that a consensus on this design was quickly reached. Importantly, there does not appear to have been any serious further discussion on the question whether indicia could form a full proof and this possibility was accepted.

Unfortunately, of the work of Elout only his finished design of 1801 and some minor comments have been preserved. There are no memoranda or earlier designs which shed light on his thought process in creating the concept ordinance. For Cras the situation is different. His commentaries on the design of Elout and a memorandum he wrote to Elout in 1802 or 1803 wherein he presented his 'views on the law of evidence' have been preserved. The memorandum forms an interesting exposé of his theoretical ideas regarding the (criminal) law of evidence. He started his memorandum with explaining that the goal of every judicial investigation was certainty and he distinguished between mathematical and moral certainty. Because of the difference in subject matter, Cras remarked, the reflections of Leibniz, Bernoulli and Voltaire on mathematical certainty were of little use to the judge. However, Cras did find the idea of Leibniz very useful where he used a graph to visualize the different degrees

---

60   Ibidem, pp. 512–513.
61   The difference between the more theoretical approach of Cras and the practical approach of Elout can be partially explained by their background. Cras had been a teacher in law since 1771 at the Athenaeum Illustre of Amsterdam and had in this period developed a strong interest in natural law. Elout, on the other hand, was far younger than Cras and had always been a practicing jurist – first as a lawyer and later as a judge – since he finished his study. On Cras see C.J.H. Jansen, "H.C. Cras (1739–1820), hoogleraar en natuurrechtsgeleerde in hart en nieren", pp. 287–309.

ranging from certainty to the lowest angle of mere suspicion. In his memorandum to Elout, Cras even made a drawing of a graph in which he showed how the different degrees of certainty ranged from suspicion, to presumption to a high probability.[62]

Concerning moral certainty, Cras remarked that there could be either absolute certainty or merely a high level of probability. Absolute certainty, he stated, existed when there was a necessary causal connection. For example, a woman who is pregnant must have had intercourse, and a baby who has breathed after its birth must have been alive. In most situations, however, no absolute certainty was obtainable but only a high probability. Cras stated that when many reasons for a certain fact exist, their probability could increase as steps on a ladder to a higher level of probability. This was, however, not entirely comparable to the field of mathematics where everything could be expressed in numbers. In moral cases this was different and much depended not on the number of reasons but on their intensity and their internal corroboration. A single indicium could be as pertinent as six others. He then stated that in the courts one must often be satisfied with probabilities, although in the most important affairs a very high probability had to exist. This, Cras remarked, is what was called juridical certainty, 'which the law cannot define in any exactness but which it can guide by particular rules'.[63]

The theoretical reflections of Cras on what kind of certainty was required in criminal cases had a direct relevance for his view on how the criminal law of evidence should be regulated. This becomes especially apparent from his reflections on indicia. Cras did not – as for example some contemporary German authors – think that there was a qualitative difference between indicia and other forms of evidence. Precisely because he saw the necessary certainty for a conviction as a high form of probability which formed part of a sliding scale, Cras stated on multiple occasions that indicia could cumulate to reach the required high probability or 'juridical certainty' and expressed this view in Article 74 of his concept ordinance.[64] Furthermore, because Cras thought that the probative force of indicia depended on an endless variety of circumstances and because he thought that the probative force was not quantifiable, he deemed that they could not be circumscribed in numbers as would be possible in the field of mathematics. These are the reasons why Cras did not propose any strict criteria on how many indicia would be necessary for a conviction, and why he explicitly left this to the discretion of the judge.

---

62 J. Th. Smidt and A.H. Huussen, *Bronnen van de Nederlandse codificatie sinds 1798 I*, p. 539.
63 Ibidem, pp. 540–541.
64 Ibidem, pp. 510–513.

The discussion on the concept ordinances of 1801 and 1804 show that the epistemological changes which have been described in Chapter three, played an important role in how the criminal law of evidence was reformed. This can be seen in particular in the comments and the approach of Cras. He remarked that a high probability of guilt was necessary to convict someone and that it was impossible for the legislator to prescribe *a priori* when this high probability existed. To a large extent this had to be left to the discretion of the judge. Furthermore, from his probabilistic conception of the certainty required in criminal cases, he argued that there was no fundamental difference between indicia and other forms of evidence. He observed that indicia, like witness testimony and the confession, could merely provide differing degrees of probability dependent on the circumstances of the case and that, therefore, it should be possible to convict someone on the basis of indicia. Cras was the most outspoken member of the codification committee and went furthest in his idea that there was no qualitative difference between indicia and other forms of evidence. The other members of the committee, such as Elout, appear to have had stronger reservations regarding this subject. A last important aspect of the concept ordinances was that they explicitly gave a more central role to the (moral) conviction of the judge which was now required to convict someone. Nevertheless, the conviction of the judge alone was not sufficient and there was a consensus that it needed to be in accordance with the evidentiary rules to form a 'juridical conviction'.

8.2.2.2.1 *Extraordinary Punishments and the Absolutio ab Instantia*
In the codification of the substantive and procedural law between 1798 and 1804 there did not appear to have been a specific discussion on the use of extraordinary punishments (as was the case in the German territories in this period). From the new constellation of the proposed substantive and procedural criminal law, it becomes clear that the use of extraordinary punishments would be forbidden. The intention was to codify the different crimes and their punishments, and when the crime was proven the judge had to apply the prescribed punishment. Similar to the French *Code Pénal*, the use of extraordinary punishments simply did not fit in the system of a clear codification of the crimes and their punishments. On the proscription of extraordinary punishments there appears to have existed a relative consensus.

This was not the case for the *absolutio ab instantia*. There was a discussion on the use of the *absolutio ab instantia* in the codification committee of 1798–1804 and there was an intention to abolish or limit its use when a trial had taken place. The Articles which prohibited the use of the *absolutio ab instantia* were, however, vague and appeared to leave room for some form of an *absolutio ab instantia*. In the design for the criminal code of 1809 the Articles which appeared to abolish the *absolutio ab instantia* were removed and the possibility was, therefore, reintroduced in this code. Van Hattum concludes that the work of the committee of 1798–1804 shows that there was a concern to limit the use of the *absolutio ab instantia* but that the Dutch jurists were not yet ready to completely abolish this intermediate decision type. It was, therefore, retained in the Dutch legislation.[65]

8.2.2.2.2   Conclusion

Finally, some important conclusions can be drawn from the first attempt at a codification of the criminal law of evidence between 1798 and 1804. First of all, it is striking that even though the German authors of the second half of the eighteenth century were known and frequently used, their 'dogmatic' conservatism on the subject of the criminal law of evidence was not followed by the codification committee. In the German territories there was still a heated debate in this period whether indicia could create a sufficient certainty for a conviction, and many authors continued to make the traditional distinction between direct evidence (the confession and witness testimony) and indirect evidence (indicia). This distinction was drawn less sharply in the Dutch discussion and it appeared to be more accepted that indicia could create a sufficient certainty for a conviction to the ordinary punishment. In his memorandum, Cras observed only one time and briefly that some authors made use of the distinction between direct and indirect evidence and then stated "but they seem to me, not to have fully understood or accurately analysed the subject".[66]

The German dogmatic approach and its strong emphasis on the idea that there was a qualitative difference between indicia and other forms of evidence was not shared in the Dutch committee. There was, nevertheless, still a clear distrust against letting the judge too free in his evaluation and relying solely on his 'moral' conviction. For this reason, and because of the supposed inherent uncertainty of indicia, there remained a clear uneasiness surrounding the use of indicia. This can be seen in the explicit warnings to the judge that he had to use the utmost circumspection when convicting someone on the basis of indicia. This distrust did not go as far as the attempts in, for example, the Austrian and Bavarian legislation of the early nineteenth century to prescribe how many and what kinds of indicia had to be present before they could form a full

---

65   For a detailed description of the attempts to limit or abolish the use of the *absolutio ab instantia*, see W.F. van Hattum, *Non bis in idem*, pp. 289–361.
66   Ibidem, p. 544.

proof. Unlike the German legislations, furthermore, the Dutch concept ordinances did allow the death penalty on the basis of indicia.

Instead of the German dogmatic categorizations of the different forms of evidence, there was a far more sober 'common sense' approach in the codification committee.[67] It was recognized that a degree of judicial discretion in the evaluation of the evidence was unavoidable and that it was futile to try to regulate the strength of the endless variety of indicia. Under these circumstances it is not surprising that Filangieri was cited so often and approvingly within the codification committee. Regarding the criminal law of evidence, he provided a theoretical foundation which perfectly suited what the committee wanted; namely, to find a proper middle road. Filangieri taught that it was unavoidable that in the end the question whether a sufficient proof existed had to depend on the concrete evaluation of the judge in the specific case. However, like the codification committee he also thought that it was too dangerous to simply allow the judge to decide on the basis of his internal conviction. For this reason, he wanted at least some minimum evidentiary standards which bound the judge and this is also precisely what the Dutch codification committee desired. As will be discussed in the following section, the approach of the codification committee and the absence of the overly dogmatic categorizations was also characteristic for the discussion in the juridical literature in the period between 1795 and 1810.

8.2.3 *The Substantive Criminal Ordinance of 1809*

In October 1804 the codification committee presented three concept ordinances to the government of the Batavian Republic. One ordinance on the substantive criminal law, one on the laws of evidence for the civil and criminal law and one introductory ordinance on laws in general. These concept ordinances were then sent to the Supreme Court for commentary. The Supreme Court finally submitted their commentary on the concept ordinances on 24 October 1806. Because of the changes in government which had in the meantime taken place in the Netherlands, the advice was now given to the recently 'appointed' king Louis Napoleon. The criticisms of the Supreme Court were severe. The Supreme Court argued that the ordinances were far too lengthy and that they

---

67   It has to be reminded here that the German juridical tradition had acquired a strong predilection against convicting on the basis of indicia because of it prohibition in the CCC. Jurists such as Carpzov and Böhmer not only justified the distinction between indicia and other forms of evidence on the basis of the supposed qualitative difference, but also on the simple fact that the CCC seemed to clearly forbid convictions to severe punishments on indicia. In the Netherlands such a general prohibition of convicting on indicia did not exist.

looked more like a philosophical juridical handbook than like an actual codification of positive laws. The criticisms were not unjustified. The substantive criminal ordinance alone, for example, contained over nine-hundred articles.[68]

Despite the generally severe criticisms on the criminal ordinance and especially on the style it was written in, the Supreme Court was less critical of the ordinance on the laws of evidence. The Supreme Court acknowledged that the didactic or explaining style on this subject could, to a certain extent, not be missed.[69] In the commentary of the Supreme Court on the individual Articles of the ordinance on the laws of evidence it can be seen that the Supreme Court agreed with the substance of most Articles and that its criticisms focused predominantly on the formulation of some of the articles. One point of criticism was that the judge should have more freedom in determining to what extent he wanted to make use of a reproachable witness. For the rest the Supreme Court agreed with the regulation of when a sufficient proof existed for a conviction and with the fact that indicia could amount to a full proof.[70]

Soon after Louis Napoleon received the commentary of the Supreme Court, he decided to revive the codification project and to start a revision of the concept criminal ordinance. The decision was made to focus on the substantive criminal law. Between 14 February and 24 September in 1807, around fifty sessions of the Council of State – which was often presided over by Louis Napoleon – were dedicated to the revision of the concept criminal ordinance. In these sessions the commentary of the Supreme Court was used and it was attempted to strongly reduce the ordinance in size by eliminating unnecessary Articles and making the redaction of the remaining Articles shorter and clearer. By September the Council of State realized that they were performing a hopeless task and that the elimination of unnecessary Articles had resulted in an incongruent whole. While in September the Council of State realized that a different approach was necessary, Louis Napoleon was being pressured by his brother to adopt the French legislation. Louis Napoleon, however, had acquired a peculiar affection for the Netherlands and wished to keep his

---

68 O. Moorman van Kappen, *Ontwerp-Lijfstraffelijk Wetboek 1804*, pp. 401–422.
69 Ibidem, p. 422.
70 J. Th. Smidt and A.H. Huussen, *Bronnen van de Nederlandse codificatie sinds 1798 I*, pp. 405–515. The Supreme Court also criticized the fact that the word 'indicium' was used in two different meanings. Cras used indicium to refer to a source of evidence as opposed to witnesses, documents and the confession, but he also used indicium as meaning 'an incomplete proof' in juxtaposition to a 'full proof'. The supreme court found that this led to a certain confusion and that indicium should only be used to refer to the kind of evidence as distinct from witnesses, documents and the confession.

kingdom as independent as possible. For this reason, Louis Napoleon appointed three codification committees on 18 November 1807 (instead of simply adopting the French legislation). One committee would have to create a new law on the judicial organisation and the procedural law, one would have to codify the substantive criminal law and one would have to write an adaptation of the French *Code Civil* for the Netherlands.[71] The committee designated with the creation of a law on the judicial organisation and the procedural law finished its work in 1809. Importantly, concerning the criminal procedural law this concept ordinance made no significant changes to the concept procedural ordinance of 1799 and maintained the distinction between the ordinary and the extraordinary procedure.[72]

The three members of the criminal committee were Reuvens, Van Musschenbroek and again Elout. After working continuously from the end of November in 1807 onwards, the committee delivered a finished concept criminal ordinance on 29 March 1808. A memorandum shows that the committee made their concept ordinance on the basis of a combination of three sources: the work of the earlier codification committee, the commentaries of the Supreme Court and the discussions in the Council of State in 1807. The committee used these sources to create a far shorter concept substantive criminal ordinance of which the theoretical and didactic style of the design of 1804 was largely removed. The ordinance now contained only 394 Articles of which 16 Articles regulated the criminal law of evidence.[73]

In September and October 1808, the Council of State discussed the concept criminal ordinance and evaluated it Article by Article. These discussions of the Council of State were published on the order of Louis Napoleon under the name *Précis des discussions, et des deliberations du Conseil d'Etat sur le Code Criminel* in 1810.[74] In the concept criminal ordinance, which predominantly

---

71 O. Moorman van Kappen, "Het Crimineel Wetboek voor het koningrijk Holland van 1809 in het licht van zijn wordingsgeschiedenis", pp. 204–209.

72 The concept ordinance was published in 1809 under the title *Wetboek van regterlijke instellingen en regtspleging in het koningrijk Holland*. The concept ordinance was approved and ratified by king Louis Napoleon on 14 July 1809. Eventually, because of the incorporation into the French empire in 1810 and the practical difficulties with changing the judicial organisation the concept ordinance was never effectuated. See M.W. van Boven, *De rechterlijke instellingen ter discussie*, pp. 216–217.

73 O. Moorman van Kappen, "Het Crimineel Wetboek voor het Koningrijk Holland van 1809 in het licht van zijn wordingsgeschiedenis", pp. 209–214.

74 On the *Précis* see also M.E. Kluit, *Cornelis Felix van Maanen*, p. 441.

regulated the substantive criminal law, the chapter on the criminal law of evidence had a peculiar position. The Dutch codifiers did not appear to have had a very clear view on the question whether the criminal law of evidence should be placed in the procedural law, in the substantive law or in a separate ordinance. In the concept ordinance of 1801 it was placed in the general part of the substantive criminal ordinance, but in 1804 it was placed within a general ordinance on the laws of evidence.[75]

The lack of clarity of where the criminal law of evidence belonged is also visible in the discussions of the codification committee of 1807. In a memorandum accompanying the concept criminal ordinance, the committee stated that they had doubted to what extent they should make use of the ordinance on the laws of evidence of 1804 and that it was difficult to decide whether the criminal law of evidence should be regulated in the substantive or in the procedural ordinance. The committee responsible for the substantive criminal code explained that it eventually chose to insert in their chapter on the criminal law of evidence only those prescriptions which were of a general and undisputed nature and 'which at least had to be regulated somewhere by the lawmaker'. Furthermore, they had tried to shape the Articles in such a way that they would be adaptable to any criminal procedural ordinance that might be created. The committee stated that it did not deem it wise to go any further in their regulation because then they might collide with the work which was reserved for the committee on the judicial organisation and the procedural order.[76] These considerations of the criminal codification committee left a clear mark on the regulation of the criminal law of evidence in their ordinance. It was regulated in only fourteen Articles and in relatively general terms.

---

75   Cras called the law of evidence a *tertium juris objectum* and thought that the laws of evidence needed to be treated as an independent subject which could be separated from procedural and substantive law. He remarked in a memorandum that in his concept ordinance of 1804 nothing of the procedural law was regulated and that the laws were formulated in such a way that they were universally applicable in any court. See J. Th. Smidt and A.H. Huussen, *Bronnen van de Nederlandse codificatie sinds 1798 I*, pp. 491–492.

76   W.C. van Binsbergen, *Algemeen Karakter van het Crimineel Wetboek voor het Koninkrijk Holland*, pp. 30–31. Peculiarly, no coordination had taken place between the codification committees about the question where the criminal law of evidence should be regulated, and during the debates in the Council of State the question was left completely undiscussed. Because the concept ordinance on the judicial organisation and procedural law of 1809 largely followed the concept procedural ordinance of 1799, the criminal law of evidence was also not regulated in any more detail in the procedural law.

Article 359 of the substantive criminal code opened the chapter on evidence and stated that nobody could be convicted unless the existence of the crime and the guilt of the accused were proven. Article 360 then stated that "Both these aspects need to be proven completely and indubitably in accordance with the law and to the satisfaction of the judge; nobody may be convicted on mere suspicions or incomplete evidence".[77] Article 361 mentioned the four legal sources of evidence – witness testimony, written documents, indicia and the confession – and remarked that they could serve separately or in combination with one another to form judicial certainty. After these three general Articles, the different kinds of evidence were treated. Article 362 prescribed that witness testimony *could* create a full proof, when there were two or more irreproachable eyewitnesses who declared under oath and with sufficient motivation. They had to declare what they had actually seen and hearsay evidence was, therefore, inadmissible. Article 363 merely stated that everyone who was not qualified to testify under civil law was also reproachable under criminal law, and the same applied to persons under the age of twenty (in civil law the age limit was 14). The following Articles regulated that witness testimony could be weakened by contrary evidence and that the judge always had to scrupulously examine the reliability of the witnesses. Furthermore, Article 364 stated that public functionaries in general deserved credence in relation to the subjects which belonged to their occupation.[78]

On written documents it was prescribed that they could serve as evidence when the crime consisted of the falsification or abuse of a written document, or when it could be deduced from the written document in itself or in combination with other circumstances that a crime had been committed. On the confession it was stated that a sufficiently specific confession in court, which was corroborated by other evidence, could create a full proof. A simple confession of guilt, which was not supported by any other circumstances, could never be sufficient to convict someone. The complex matter of indicia was regulated in a mere three Articles. Article 370 defined indicia as all the actions, things, events and circumstances from which one could infer that a crime had been committed and/or who the culprit was. Article 371 stated that indicia had to be proven themselves, after the nature of the case, by either the inspection of the judge, by a report of an expert, by written documents, witness testimony or

---

77 *Précis des discussions, et des deliberations du Conseil d'Etat sur le Code Criminel*, pp. 309–310.
78 Ibidem, pp. 311–317.

the confession of the accused. This enumeration appears to have been meant exhaustively and to exclude the possibility of proving indicia by indicia, which formed an important limitation on the use of indicia.[79] Finally, Article 372 stated that "It is left to the discretion of the judges to determine what strength the indicia have in each particular case. Their conscience is severely charged with using the utmost care and circumspection in this evaluation".[80] The negative system of legal proofs in the criminal code was, therefore, intended to create some important minimum evidentiary standards.

In the meetings of the Council of State in September and October of 1808 there was virtually no discussion on the regulation of the criminal law of evidence. Almost all the Articles, even on the sensitive subject of indicia, merely have the short remark "est adopté sans discussion". There was also no debate on the doubts raised in the memorandum of the committee on where the criminal law of evidence could best be regulated and how the relation should be between the substantive and the procedural law. In short, there seems to have been a relative consensus on the most important rules of the criminal law of evidence, while only minor points relating to witness testimony raised some discussion.[81] After the meetings were finished and Van Maanen had made the

---

[79] As will be described in the following chapter, this significant limitation that indicia could not be proven by indicia was also part of the negative system of legal proofs in the criminal procedural ordinance of 1838.

[80] Ibidem, pp. 318–322. It is important and revealing that regarding indicia it was specifically remarked that the judge's conscience (*geweten*) was severely charged with this decision. It shows a lingering distrust towards indicia, but the words also suggest a continued concern with the moral salvation – or at least the 'clear conscience' – of the judge, specifically when he had to decide on the basis of indicia. A similar preoccupation is visible in the concept criminal procedural ordinances of 1799 and 1809 which prescribed that an effort had to be made to acquire a confession, even when there was already sufficient evidence, 'for the reassurance of the mind of the judge'. In this feign it was regulated that it had to be attempted to extract a confession from a convicted accused before his execution, not because it was juridically necessary but to sooth the conscience of the judge. These considerations show that there was still an important concern with the moral salvation and good conscience of the judge who had to decide in criminal cases, and that the confession was the best means to reassure him.

[81] *Précis des discussions, et des deliberations du Conseil d'Etat sur le Code Criminel*, pp. 309–322. The subject which did lead to a discussion was related to the question of the irreproachability of witnesses and the evaluation of witness testimony. Louis Napoleon raised the question whether the parents of an accused should be excluded from giving testimony. Van Maanen responded that it was better not to completely exclude them but leave it to the discretion of the judge to determine how reliable their testimony was. Furthermore, Van Maanen proposed to reduce the age limit of 20 to 18, but after some discussion accepted to leave the Article as it was. Finally, there was a long discussion on the question to what extent public functionaries should have a special role as witnesses.

necessary changes in accordance with the discussions of the Council of State, the ordinance was presented to the legislative chamber which confirmed the ordinance without any substantial criticisms at the end of December in 1808. The chapter on the criminal ordinance for the Kingdom of the Netherlands came into force on 1 February 1809 with a chapter on the criminal law of evidence that was virtually the same as that presented in the design by the committee.[82] This was the first criminal codification for the Netherlands as a whole and the first time that there was one uniform regulation of the criminal law of evidence. It remained in force until in March 1811 the French criminal legislation was promulgated. How the criminal code was actually applied by the courts in the Netherlands in this short period of two years and to what extent it changed the practice of the criminal law of evidence is, nevertheless, uncertain and still open to investigation.

8.3   The Juridical Literature between 1795 and 1810

The events in the period between 1795 and 1810 do not seem to have provoked a significant rise in the number of publications concerning the criminal law (of evidence). Even important events such as the abolition of judicial torture in 1798 or the publication of the concept criminal ordinance in 1804 attracted relatively little commentary. There were, for example, almost no treatises which made proposals for the new criminal codification or which pleaded for the introduction of a jury system. In general, the interest in the criminal law seems to have been rather limited in this period in the juridical literature and there is no strong sense of urgency discernible that the criminal procedural law needed to be comprehensively reformed (as was the case in revolutionary France).

The literature that did appear in this period can be divided into two phases. The works published between 1795 and 1798 – before the abolition of judicial torture – were still hesitant of making any fundamental changes to the existing criminal law of evidence. They show the remaining concern of what should come in the place of judicial torture and the fear that the criminal procedural law might be severely crippled by abolishing judicial torture. The treatises that were published after the promulgation of the constitution in 1798, however, appear to have quickly come to terms with the new situation where judicial

---

82   O. Moorman van Kappen, "Het Crimineel Wetboek voor het koningrijk Holland van 1809 in het licht van zijn wordingsgeschiedenis", pp. 214–216 and W.C. van Binsbergen, *Algemeen Karakter van het Crimineel Wetboek voor het Koninkrijk Holland*, pp. 19–20.

torture was abolished and where the judge was allowed to decide 'on conviction'. The main topic in the literature after 1798 was to understand and explain what this doing justice 'on conviction' precisely meant, and on interpreting how the relation should be understood between the judge's conviction and the system of evidentiary rules. Importantly, most treatises which were published in this period were written by authors reflecting on the criminal procedural law in the province of Holland.

8.3.1 The Literature between 1795 and 1798

Three works which reflected on the criminal law of evidence were published before the abolition of judicial torture. The first of the three works was a juridical handbook by Van der Linden which was published in 1798. In this book he summarily described the criminal procedural practice in the province of Holland in one chapter. The chapter treated the different steps of the extraordinary procedure as it was still being practiced until 1798 and which was strongly focused on acquiring a confession. Nevertheless, Van der Linden made two interesting remarks. Firstly, he stated that there had been a lot of discussion recently on the question whether judicial torture should be abolished. He deemed that the severe form of judicial torture could be abolished without any practical difficulties, but strongly doubted whether it would be prudent to also abolish another measure which was often used in the criminal courts: the whipping of the accused to force him to confess. Van der Linden was in favour of the retention of a lighter form of physical coercion in the situation where strong evidence was present but the accused refused to confess. The second point of interest, is a remark where Van der Linden stated that in his opinion it should also be possible to convict on the basis of a full proof in absence of a confession in the extraordinary procedure.[83]

The second work was a treatise by Van Hall and Van Hamelsveld, published in 1798, which focused on the question under which circumstances a crime was imputable. The book opens with a quotation of Filangieri stating that an act without the necessary criminal intent is not a crime and that the criminal intent without the act is not punishable. The treatise was written as a reflection on the case of Harmen Alfkens which had occurred in Amsterdam in 1795. Harmen Alfkens had gruesomely murdered two of his young daughters and then turned himself in to the authorities and confessed the crime he had just committed. Alfkens, who had never committed any crimes before, appears to have committed this crime in a state of severe mental confusion or 'melancholy', as

---

83 J. van der Linden, *Verhandeling over de judicieele practijcq of form van procedeeren voor de Hoven van Justitie in Holland gebruikelijk, deel II*, pp. 220–239.

it was called. Van Hall and Van Hamelsveld used this case to show that there were gradations in the forms of criminal intent – depending on the question whether the accused was 'morally free' to determine his will – to which the severity of the punishment should be adjusted. In this case they argued that because of the mental state of Alfkens, the death penalty was too harsh a punishment. Instead, they thought that a lifelong imprisonment was better suited which was intended more as a 'security measure' than as a punishment.[84]

In Chapter two Van Hall and Van Hamelsveld reflected on what had to be proven in a criminal case. In this chapter they stated that when there was a voluntary confession and there were indicia that corroborated this confession, the 'judge may consider himself morally convinced'. Subsequently, they asked the question what needs to happen in the extraordinary procedure when there was a full proof but not a confession. Their answer was that it was commonly accepted in Holland that in this situation one may not be convicted in the extraordinary procedure, but the judge can order the use of judicial torture. In a footnote they stated, however, that they agreed with Voorda that this consensus was erroneous and that the judge should be allowed to convict in this situation. Subsequently, they explained that when the accused had refused to confess under torture or had later revoked his confession, the judge had to pronounce either an acquittal, an *absolutio ab instantia* or an extraordinary punishment.[85] In short, Van Hall and Van Hamelsveld simply described the procedural practice as it still existed in Holland until 1798 with solely the criticism that convictions should also be possible in extraordinary procedures on the basis of a full proof in absence of a confession.

---

84 M.C. van Hall and W.Y. van Hamelsveld, *Harmen Alfkens of eene wijsgeerige en rechskundige bijdrage tot de geschiedenis van het lijfstraffelijk recht*, pp. 1–95.
85 Ibidem, pp. 15–32. Van Hall and Van Hamelsveld also presented a short observation on judicial torture. They stated that they would not mingle themselves in the debate on the question whether judicial torture should be allowed among a 'free and enlightened people'. They only wanted to remark that how desirable it may seem to any reasonable person that judicial torture should be abolished, they at least hoped that judicial torture would not be abolished before a codification had been made of a new criminal procedural law. Because abolishing judicial torture without a concomitant change in the procedural law would gravely endanger the state and lead to many crimes going unpunished. Lastly, Van Hall and Van Hamelsveld placed great emphasis on the fact that not only the *corpus delicti* and the guilt of the accused needed to be proven, but also that the crime had to be morally imputable. In other words, the criminal intent needed to be proven. According to Van Hall and Van Hamelsveld the judge had to deduce the level of criminal intent from the moral character and the situation of the accused and adjust the punishment according to the severity of his intent. The preeminent question on which the judge had to orientate himself was whether 'the culprit was morally free when he committed the act'.

A third work of interest, published early in 1798, was a short treatise by Kleyn, a judge from Gelderland, on 'the duties of a criminal judge'. Kleyn argued that a diligent judge does not need to act hostile against the accused but that it is better to try and gain his trust so that he will speak more openly. Concerning the criminal law of evidence, the work of Kleyn is of interest because it shows that he perceived the criminal procedure as focused essentially on obtaining a confession from the accused. Kleyn considered the confession by far the most certain form of evidence and stated that even when there is the most complete proof which convinced the judge, he should still do everything in his power to persuade the accused to confess.[86]

8.3.2 The Literature between 1798 and 1810

The first work dedicated to the criminal law of evidence written after the abolition of judicial torture was a treatise published in 1800 by Aansorgh, a judge from the province of Utrecht. The main part of this work consisted of an 'essay on the juridical conviction concerning crimes'. Aansorgh began his essay with expressing his satisfaction that since the 'revolution' many important reforms had been made, such as the extension of the freedom of the press and the abolition of the guilds. He also praised the abolition of judicial torture which many wise men, he mentioned Beccaria and Sonnenfels, had criticized so strongly. He remarked that the abolition of judicial torture was an improvement because it ran against natural law to demand of the accused that he confesses his guilt. Furthermore, Aansorgh remarked that a new concept ordinance on the criminal procedural law had been made in 1799 which would create a uniform procedural law for the Republic and entail many improvements. One important improvement of the ordinance was that it would allow the judge to decide 'on conviction' even when there was not a confession. Something which was not yet allowed 'in the province of Holland and several other places in the Republic'.[87]

---

[86] B. Kleyn, *Vrymoedige gedachten over den plicht een's rechters in crimineele zaaken*, pp. 1–21. Another work which was published before the abolition of judicial torture, was a treatise of Van der Marck, a professor of natural law in Groningen, containing suggestions for the upcoming codifications. It focused predominantly on civil law, but also contained a small part on criminal law. Regarding the criminal law of evidence, the treatise only contained a short passage which pleaded for the abolition of judicial torture. This passage merely convicted judicial torture as a cruel and unjust practice which should not exist among the civilized Batavians in this enlightened age. Besides proposing its abolition Van der Marck presented no further reflections on what should come in its place. See F.A. van der Marck, *Schets over de rechten van den mensch*, pp. 263–275.

[87] S. Aansorgh, *Eenige bijdrage tot de wijsgeerige rechtskunde. Bestaande in eene proeve over de rechterlijke overtuiging betrekkelijk misdaden*, pp. 1–3.

After his observation that it was an improvement that judicial torture had been abolished and that the judge was allowed to decide 'on conviction', Aansorgh presented the main objective of his work. He acknowledged that it can be hard to distinguish the guilty from the innocent. The inherent danger of judging 'on conviction', however, was less striking when one considered that a full proof was still required and that the judge still had to follow certain evidentiary rules in his judgement to obtain 'juridical certainty'.

He first described how this juridical certainty could be acquired through witness testimony and then dealt with the subject of indicia. When the indicia were sufficiently proven Aansorgh, thought that they could provide the same kind of certainty as direct witness testimony and could even justify the capital punishment. Finally, it is important to note that Aansorgh used a rather 'objective' approach when he discussed the criteria according to which a judge could acquire juridical certainty and that he did not deem the subjective conviction of the judge alone sufficient to convict someone.[88]

A similar rejection of the idea that judging 'on conviction' meant deciding on the basis of a subjective conviction can be found in three works published in 1801 by Calkoen, Deiman and Van Houten. These three works were written in relation to a criminal case where two Jewish men were convicted for falsifying bonds in Amsterdam, and they provide some important reflections on how the provisional ordinance for Holland of 1798 should be understood. This provisional ordinance prescribed that accused persons who were prosecuted in an extraordinary procedure and who did not confess, had to be allowed legal counsel to defend themselves. Calkoen, the writer of the award-winning treatise in 1778, became their lawyer. Because Calkoen deemed that there were certain irregularities in the procedure, he decided to publish his defence memorandum. This publication of Calkoen attracted two published reactions in 1801 which tried to refute the work of Calkoen in detail. One reaction came from the lawyer Deiman, and another from Van Houten who was a judge in the court of Amsterdam.

At a certain point in his memorandum, while arguing that the guilt of an accused could not be deduced from his flight, Calkoen touched on the question what was meant with doing justice 'on conviction'. He acknowledged that now that judicial torture had been abolished, a judge could do justice on conviction in the extraordinary procedure. Calkoen then emphatically argued that this, however, did not mean that the judge could do justice on his 'particular' or mere 'cerebral' conviction and stated that one scares at the thought that the life, honour and goods of citizens could depend on such a conviction. Instead,

---

88   Ibidem, pp. 36–47.

he remarked that a 'juridical conviction' was required, i.e. a conviction which was acquired in accordance with the evidentiary rules. At this point Calkoen did not further elaborate on the question what the evidentiary requirements were for a juridical conviction. He did refer approvingly to the work of Voorda which had shown that it was in accordance with the criminal ordinances of 1570 to convict someone in the extraordinary procedure, even in absence of a confession, when there was a full proof of the guilt of the accused. Lastly, at the end of his memorandum Calkoen made another remark of importance for the criminal law of evidence. He concluded that the guilt of the two accused persons had not been fully proven, and that it could only be said that some suspicions existed against them. However, citing Farinacius, Calkoen argued that it was not allowed by law to convict someone to a corporal punishment on the basis of mere presumptions or indicia.[89]

In his refutation of the argumentation of Calkoen, Deiman also reflected on the question what doing justice 'on conviction' meant. Deiman stated that he agreed with Calkoen that a juridical conviction was required and not solely the internal conviction of the judge. He deemed, however, that Calkoen had drawn incorrect conclusions from this distinction. Deiman stated that, depending on the subject matter, the conviction could be called mathematical or moral, and that when normally one speaks of a conviction, a moral conviction is meant. According to Deiman, a juridical conviction was merely a species of the general 'moral conviction' and that what applied to a moral conviction also applied to a juridical conviction (but not necessarily the other way around). He stated that a juridical conviction was, therefore, always 'an internal conviction based on moral grounds of probability'. The only difference was that with a juridical conviction these grounds needed to be proven in accordance with the evidentiary rules and that the juridical formalities had to be followed. Witness testimony could, for example, only be used when the witness was heard under oath and when the accused has had the chance to react to the testimony. Deiman found that Calkoen drew two incorrect conclusions. Firstly, Calkoen did not seem to fully understand that a juridical conviction was essentially the same as what was normally called a moral conviction and that they come about in a similar manner. Secondly, Calkoen suggested that a full proof necessary for a juridical conviction could not be created by indicia alone. This

---

[89] H. Calkoen, *Twee gevangenen tegen de aanklacht van Mr. Reinier Willem Tadama ... verdeedigd*, pp. 135–138 and 161–164. Nevertheless, it has to be reminded that Calkoen proposed this idea in the context of a memorandum of defence on behalf of his clients, and it does not necessarily reflect his own ideas on the subject of indicia.

second misconception Deiman discussed later in a special section of his treatise.[90]

Deiman opened this section with the remark that common sense and Roman law taught that a crime could be proven not only by irreproachable witnesses, but also through undoubtable indicia. Indicia, he stated, were nothing other than the more or less probable conclusions drawn from proven circumstances in relation to the crime. Furthermore, when the terms undoubtable indicia or the necessity of 'proof clearer than the light of day' were used, this emphatic expression only meant, first of all, that the circumstances from which one reasoned needed to be proven themselves. Secondly, that these circumstances had to stand in an apparent connection with the alleged fact and, thirdly, that a single indicium or ground of suspicion was not enough. Multiple corresponding indicia needed to exist which all pointed in the same direction 'and appeared to flow together into one point'. Finally, Deiman stated that it was entirely impossible for the legislator to predetermine for all the individual cases when and under what circumstances indicia could suffice for a conviction. The evaluation of the strength of indicia and whether they were sufficient had to be left to the *religio judicantis* (the discretion of the judge). If the indicia, which had been proven in accordance with the law, combined to create such a high probability that they amounted to a moral certainty, the judge could and should convict to the ordinary punishment.[91]

In his treatise, Deiman also presented some important observations on how the provisional ordinance of 1798 had changed the relation between the ordinary and the extraordinary procedure in Holland. He remarked that the abolition of judicial torture had created the need for significant changes in the extraordinary procedure. Allowing judges to convict 'on conviction' in absence of a confession in the extraordinary procedure had, according to Deiman, become a necessity to make sure the procedure would not become entirely ineffective. This also meant that the accused was now given a far better opportunity to defend himself in the extraordinary procedure. Deiman deemed that with the changes created by the provisional ordinance the difference between the extraordinary and the ordinary procedure had become very small and that, for this reason, the option of admitting the accused to an ordinary procedure should be used even more rarely. A difference which did remain in

---

90 A.J. Deiman, *De zaak der beleedigde gerechtigheid voldongen voor de vierschaar van het kundig en onzijdig publiek*, pp. 30–33.
91 Ibidem, pp. 206–213. Deiman cited several passages from Roman sources, among them the often cited rescript of Hadrianus, to substantiate his claim that indicia could suffice for a conviction, and also referred to Mattheus and Böhmer.

the provisional ordinance was that only in the ordinary procedure appeal was possible.[92]

Van Houten, in his treatise, reacted curtly that he did not need a lesson from Calkoen to know that a mere 'moral or cerebral conviction' of the judge was insufficient and that a juridical conviction was necessary. Like Deiman, Van Houten stated that indicia could create the same juridical certainty as a confession or witness testimony.[93] At a later point in his treatise Van Houten also presented a strong criticism of the proposition of Calkoen that no corporal punishment was permitted on the basis of indicia:

> The idea that it is notorious by law that on this basis no corporal punishment can be pronounced goes against all common sense and all legal principles. Shall the preaching of this incongruent idea not finally end? Shall the expired credit of a Farinacius and other old-fashioned criminalists, since the time that people have started to think for themselves, still be proposed against sound reason and law? One does not need the authority of legal writers to combat such an incongruent idea which has been rebutted completely by, among others, Matthaeus. It is enough to consider what the law wants punished. Is it not a crime, a proven crime? And can crimes not be proven just as well through indirect evidence, indicia, as through the confession or testimonies? Is this not decidedly certain?[94]

Van Houten continued to state that only one conclusion was possible, either the crime was fully proven and the punishment had to be pronounced, or the crime was not sufficiently proven and the accused should be released through an *absolutio ab instantia*. When the crime was proven it did not matter whether it was by indicia or by other kinds of evidence. He concluded with the remark that "partial punishment for partial evidence is a preposterous idea".[95] Summarizing, Van Houten presented a sharp criticism of the idea that indicia were qualitatively different from 'direct evidence' and entirely rejected the authority of Farinacius and other 'out-dated criminalists' on this subject.

---

92 Ibidem, pp. 21–24 and 321–333.
93 B.A. van Houten, *Rechtsgeleerd advis van Mr. B.A. van Houten*, pp. 148–151. Earlier in his treatise, Van Houten came to a similar conclusion as Deiman that since the introduction of the provisional ordinance the difference between the ordinary and the extraordinary procedure had all but disappeared. See B.A. van Houten, *Rechtsgeleerd advis van Mr. B.A. van Houten*, p. 23–27.
94 Ibidem, pp. 271–272.
95 Ibidem, p. 272.

Furthermore, his concluding remark seems to imply that he rejected the use of extraordinary punishments and that he only considered the *absolutio ab instantia* permissible in cases of uncertainty.

A rejection of the 'older criminalists' can also be found in a juridical handbook by Van der Linden, published in 1806. In his introduction he explained which works were still worth reading:

> On the subject of criminal law almost none of the older writers deserve our recommendation. They often contain a stockpile of remarks which confuse more than that they elucidate. Especially since the subject of the punishing of crimes has started to be treated from a more philosophical and humane perspective, it has acquired a completely different shape.[96]

The authors that Van der Linden recommended as still worthy of reading were, among others, Matthaeus, Böhmer, Meister, Putman, Beccaria and Grolman. Montesquieu and Filangieri were mentioned as authors on the subject of 'natural and constitutional law'.[97] This is a quite representative enumeration of the authors which were referred to in the Dutch juridical literature of this period. It shows the strong orientation towards the German literature of the second half of the eighteenth century and the continued authority of Matthaeus.

Just as in his previous handbook, published in 1798, Van der Linden treated the criminal procedural law summarily in one chapter in his handbook of 1806. While Van der Linden had remarked in 1798 that he deemed some form of physical coercion to extract a confession indispensable in extraordinary procedures, he now only neutrally stated that judicial torture was abolished. Subsequently he treated the changes in the procedural law in Holland which had been made by the provisional ordinance of 1798, and observed that doing justice 'on conviction' in the extraordinary procedure had taken the place of judicial torture. Regarding indicia, Van der Linden, remarked that there had been much controversy on this subject among legal scholars. He deemed, however, that these discussions could be resolved easily if one understood indicia as such acts or circumstances, which had been proven sufficiently themselves, and from which by a necessary connection the guilt of the accused could be inferred. When indicia were thus understood, there was no reason why they could not form a full proof.[98]

---

96 J. van der Linden, *Regtsgeleerd, practicaal, en koopmans handboek,* p. LXIII.
97 Ibidem, pp. LXIII–LXIV.
98 Ibidem, pp. 266–272 and 387–418.

A further source of reflection on the changes in the criminal law of evidence can be found in the lectures by Van der Keessel. As a professor in Leiden he gave lectures on the criminal law of evidence between 1770 and 1815. In the previous chapter it has been stated that in his lectures before 1798 he was a proponent of a limited use of judicial torture. In the notes he kept of his lectures there are several appendices which show that after 1798 he also explained in his classes what reforms had been made regarding the criminal law of evidence. In his remarks concerning the provisional ordinance for Holland of 1798, Van der Keessel showed himself to be sceptical of the abolition of judicial torture and allowing convictions in the extraordinary procedure 'on conviction'. He argued that through the vague formulations in this ordinance, which permitted the use of corrective measures to force the accused to answer questions, the legislator had in fact opened a backdoor for the continued use of physical coercion.[99] Subsequently, in an appendix of a later date, a commentary by Van der Keessel can be found on the chapter concerning the criminal law of evidence in the criminal ordinance of 1809. Of particular interest is his observation on Article 361 which enumerated the admissible kinds of evidence:

> Here are listed as legitimate proof witnesses, written documents, real evidence [indicia], and a confession, of which it is stated that both separately and together they can provide full proof, that is, legal certainty. In this rule, or rather in its third part at the end of the article, there is a clear settlement of the well-known controversy which, I am accustomed to discuss fully in the title *on proof* (D.22.3), namely whether in criminal cases a full proof which would suffice for imposing the ordinary penalty, including the capital penalty, can be constituted solely by the concurrence of several pieces of proper and cogent evidence [indicia plura idonea et verisimilia]. I think that this must be answered in the affirmative ... since in the various cases so much and such weighty evidence can come together as to constitute *so great a degree of probability* that it is not only equal to, but is even superior to, the legal certainty which the law presumes from the concurring testimony of two witnesses who are above exception.[100]

---

99 B. Beinart and P. van Warmelo, *Dionysius Godefredus van der Keessel. Lectures on Books 47 and 48 of the Digest*, pp. 1779–1789.
100 Ibidem, p. 2055. The Latin terms used by van der Keessel have been put between brackets, because the English translation of indicia into 'real evidence' by Beinart and Warmelo appears rather confusing.

Summarizing, Van der Keessel showed himself a proponent of the criminal ordinance of 1809 which allowed convictions on the basis of indicia. He deemed that indicia could create a similarly high degree of probability as could be found in, for example, the testimony of two eyewitnesses. Van der Keessel also remarked that the article 'settled the controversy' regarding the use of indicia, which shows that the possibility to convict on the basis of indicia had still been a matter of discussion.

Lastly, Van der Keessel commented favourably on Article 372 which stated that the evaluation of the strength of the indicia in the individual case was left to the discretion of the judge. In his observation he testified to the fact that there was a large trust in the criminal judges and that he deemed it impossible to determine *a priori* when sufficient evidence existed for a conviction:

> Our present Code left out all divisions of evidence and an enumeration of them, and very wisely refrained from any judgement on their value, firstly, indeed, since it had confidence that those who would decide criminal cases would plainly not be ignorant of this subject as diligently handed down by celebrated teachers of criminal law, and this is also the reason why it has set out the matter as above. But, secondly, because in questions of fact it is not possible to prescribe rules for the mind of the judge by which he can pass judgement on the degree of probability. Deservedly, therefore, the whole judgment of this has been left to the conscience of judges.[101]

A last work which deserves to be mentioned, is a published version of the criminal code of 1809 with an introduction and commentary by Kemper. It was intended to consist of two volumes but Kemper eventually did not write the second part (which would have provided commentary on the chapter concerning the criminal law of evidence). The significance of the work of Kemper lies in the fact that it is the first Dutch work which provides a (brief) history of the attempts at codifying the criminal law in the Republic and in several other continental European countries. Kemper attempted to show that the codification of the criminal law was not just the product of recent revolutions and the enthusiasm of some misguided philosophers, but that in fact the creation of codifications had deeper roots and had taken place in the last half century under all different kinds of governmental systems (from revolutionary France to Prussia, Austria and Lombardy). Kemper described the criminal

---

101   Ibidem, p. 2065.

codifications as the result of the more developed and enlightened level that the criminal juridical science had recently attained.[102]

The treatise of Kemper shows that among legal scholars there was an awareness that the criminal legal 'science' had underwent a great transformation in the past fifty years. He, for example, remarked that the new spirit was visible in the Netherlands in the work of natural law teachers such as Cras and Pestel and in the award-winning treatise of Calkoen. Furthermore, he stated that in the last decades of the eighteenth century: "One now heard before the courts almost as often the quotation of philosophical German and French writers, as one would hear before only the names of a De Damhouder, Matthaeus and Carpzovius ... Nevertheless, the philosophical principles of our time often stood in the most preposterous contrast with the existing laws".[103]

8.4 The Incorporation of the Netherlands into the French Empire 1810–1813

On 9 July 1810 the Netherlands was incorporated into the French Empire through a simple decree. The French legal codes acquired force of law on 1 March 1811 and at the same time the French administrative and judicial system was implemented.[104] This formed a monumental rupture in the history of the Dutch criminal justice system in two ways: it completely reformed the structure both of the judicial organisation and of the criminal procedural law. First of all, the introduction of the French judicial system provided a centralisation, a rationalisation and a professionalization of the Dutch judicial organisation. Before 1811, in the province of Holland alone there had been over two hundred criminal jurisdictions. In the Republic, in most cities the city-council (*schepenbank*) formed the criminal court while in rural districts the criminal jurisdiction was often in the hands of a local notable. Except for the more professional provincial high courts and the courts of the bigger cities, most judges were lay judges who often needed the help of legal counsel. The public prosecutor, if there was one, formed part of the city government and was closely

---

102   J.M. Kemper, *Crimineel Wetboek voor het Koningrijk Holland met eene Inleiding en Aanmerkingen*, pp. 1–184.
103   Ibidem, pp. 80–81. Beside the lectures of Van der Keessel and the treatise of Kemper there appear to have been no further substantive reflections on the criminal codification of 1809. There is, nevertheless, also a small book by Van Swinderen in which he gave an explanation of the most important principles of the criminal codification for children. See Th. Van Swinderen, *Schoolboek der Strafwetten van Ons Vaderland* (1810).
104   A.G. Bosch, "Het Openbaar Ministerie in de periode van 1811–1838", pp. 1–4.

attached to the city-council. Furthermore, except for some limited possibilities of appeal to the provincial high court, there was no overarching organisation of the criminal courts or of the public prosecutors. Many local courts had an exclusive criminal jurisdiction with no possibility of appeal (although this varied strongly within the different provinces).[105]

This situation changed entirely after 1811. A centralized hierarchical system was created for the courts as well as for the public prosecutors. The introduction of the French judicial organisation meant a radical reduction of the number of criminal courts and created a clear uniformity and hierarchy within the courts. In the province of Holland, for example, the over two hundred courts with criminal jurisdiction were reduced to around ten courts with a lower or higher criminal jurisdiction.[106] Importantly, the courts became specialized institutions and the judges could no longer simultaneously have administrative and judicial functions (as often happened in the old *schepenbanken*). The competence of the criminal courts was tied to the tripartite division of crimes in the French *Code Pénal*. Severe *crimes* would now be treated only before the departmental courts of assizes, the less serious *délits* before the courts of the arrondissements, and the mere *contraventions* before the justices of the peace. The judges of the courts of assizes and of the arrondissements had to be professional jurists.[107] The former Dutch Republic was divided in seven departments and every department acquired one court of assizes, which meant that these courts had the exclusive jurisdiction concerning severe crimes over a relatively large area. Above the courts of assizes stood the imperial court in The Hague and the imperial court of cassation in Paris.[108] The centralized hierarchical structure of the courts was mimicked by the structure of the public

---

105   M.W. van Boven, "Een blijvend domein van juristen. De rechtspraak vóór en na de Bataafse omwenteling van 1795", pp. 135–142.

106   S. Faber, "Straffen in Nederland sedert 1811", pp. 169–170. This entailed, for lack of a better term, the introduction of an 'economy of scales' into the criminal courts. Instead of a very high number of small courts which often treated only a few criminal offences a year (staffed by mostly lay judges), there were now professional courts which covered a far larger area. As will be discussed in the following chapter, this 'professionalization' and specialisation was mirrored in the education of the criminal law at the universities and the emergence of special scientific magazines dedicated to criminal law.

107   M.W. van Boven, *De rechterlijke instellingen ter discussie*, pp. 247–266. There was continuity in personnel because a large part of the judges appointed in 1811 had had previous experience as judges in the Republic. On the order of Napoleon most public prosecutors, however, came from the Belgian provinces. Van Boven states that this order probably came forth out of Napoleon's distrust of the willingness of the Dutch to follow the French regulations on contraband and taxes.

108   G. Bossers, *"Welk eene Natie, die de jurij gekend heeft, en ze weder heeft afschaft!"*, pp. 32–34.

prosecution service which stood under control of the Ministry of Justice. The public prosecution was now, for the first time, given shape as one hierarchical centralized institution which covered the whole of the Netherlands and which was functionally differentiated from the criminal judges.[109]

The second aspect of change concerned the criminal procedural law. The introduction of the *Code d'Instruction Criminelle* meant that there was now a separation between the secret preliminary investigation and the public, oral main trial. The old distinction between the ordinary and the extraordinary procedure disappeared. Furthermore, a jury system was instituted for the courts of assizes. These courts would work with a clear functional separation. The preliminary investigation was conducted under the authority of a judge of investigation (*juge d'instruction*). After approval was granted to present an accusation, the documents containing the incriminating evidence were send to the public prosecutor.[110] During the main trial the public prosecutor delivered his criminal indictment and presented the incriminating evidence. The accused had the right to use legal counsel and to present his defence during the public main trial. The trial was conducted orally; every written form of evidence had to be read aloud and every witness had to repeat his testimony in court. At the end of the trial, the jury decided on the question of fact and the criminal judges decided on the question of law. The legal evidentiary rules were abolished and the jurors had to decide after their freely formed *conviction intime*. They could only pronounce that the accused was guilty or not-guilty, after which the criminal judges would have to apply the punishment prescribed in the *Code Pénal*. Extraordinary punishments were no longer allowed.[111]

---

109   A.G. Bosch, "Het Openbaar Ministerie in de periode van 1811–1838", pp. 1–6. There had, of course, been several important attempts during the period of 1795 until 1810 to create a new centralized system of courts but these attempts had thus far not brought any significant changes. It took the incorporation into the French Empire to forcefully break with the old judicial organisation. On the many Dutch attempts to reform the judicial organisation see M.W. van Boven, *De rechterlijke instellingen ter discussie*.

110   The permission to present an accusation had to be given by the imperial court in the Hague which now performed the role of the former *jury d'accusation*. For each severe crime, the judge of investigation had to send the evidence to the imperial court. If the imperial court deemed that an accusation should be made it would then give this assignment to the relevant public prosecutor. This centralized system remained in force after 1813 until a new criminal procedural code was made in 1838. See S. Ruller, "Franse strafwetgeving in Nederland", pp. 59–68.

111   G. Bossers, "*Welk eene Natie, die de jurij gekend heeft, en ze weder heeft afschaft!*", pp. 34–43.

The jury system was officially abolished by a decree of the newly installed Dutch king William I on 11 December 1813, after the French were driven out. The jury system, therefore, only functioned a short two years in the northern part of the Netherlands. In a detailed investigation of the jury system in this period, Bossers states that it is not possible to determine whether the jury system functioned well in the sense that they convicted the guilty and acquitted the innocent. Nevertheless, what can be said is that there were no great organisational problems and that the courts of assizes and the jury system appear to have functioned relatively smoothly in this period. There were, for example, almost no cases where the quorum of jurors was not attained and there were no outspoken complaints of innocent people being convicted.[112] As will be discussed in the next chapter, the *Code d'Instruction Criminelle* remained in force in the Netherlands largely unchanged until 1838 (with the exception of the abolition of the jury system). Most of the far-reaching changes in the Dutch criminal justice system described in this section would, therefore, long outlive the period of French occupation.

8.5 Conclusion

The period of 1795 until 1813 was of momentous importance for the development of the Dutch criminal law of evidence. With the creation of the Batavian Republic there was a strong momentum to abolish judicial torture and to reform the criminal of evidence, and there was for the first time an institution which had the power to legislate for the Republic as a whole. Although many authors had doubted before 1795 whether judicial torture could and should be abolished, it is striking how quickly almost all the jurists came to terms with the abolition of torture after 1798. The focus now shifted to the question how the difficult cases should be regulated where strong evidence existed but the accused refused to confess. In the legislative debates and the juridical literature between 1798 and 1810, the solution to this problem was found in allowing the judge to convict on the basis of a full proof in the form of witness testimony or indicia in the extraordinary procedure, while at the same time the accused was given far stronger defensive rights and the right to use legal counsel. This possibility to convict in absence of a confession was, somewhat misleadingly, called doing justice 'on conviction'. By this it was not meant that the judge could decide on the basis of his subjective or moral conviction, but on a juridical conviction which was acquired in accordance with the evidentiary rules.

---

112 Ibidem, pp. 46–78.

In the discussions in the legislature and in the juridical literature between 1795 and 1810 it can be seen that the change in the epistemological ideas, in the form of the emergence of a probabilistic approach to the criminal law of evidence, acquired a more pronounced character. This is particularly visible in, for example, the (philosophical) reflections of Cras, Deiman and Van der Keessel when they attempted to justify that convictions should be possible on the basis of indicia. Cras, for example, explained in his memorandum that convictions on the basis of indicia should be possible because indicia did not qualitatively differ from other forms of evidence. He stated that in human affairs normally only a high probability was attainable and that this sufficed for a conviction. Indicia could, just as well as other forms of evidence, through their cumulation ascend to this high degree of probability. With these sorts of reflections, the reform whereby convictions became possible in the extraordinary procedure on the basis of other forms of evidence than merely the confession, was justified. Significant is, furthermore, that the view of Cras was eventually accepted by the codification committee and implemented in the regulation of indicia in the concept code of 1804 and the promulgated criminal ordinance of 1809. A similar view was expounded by Van der Keessel when he stated that indicia could suffice to pronounce even a capital punishment because they could create 'so great a degree of probability that it was not only equal to but even superior to the legal certainty which the law presumed to flow from the concurring testimony of two witnesses'.[113]

The importance of the changed epistemological ideas is also visible in the new and more central role which was given to the internal conviction of the judge in the criminal law of evidence. In the codification committees it was acknowledged that it was impossible to regulate and positively prescribe when sufficient evidence existed to convict someone in the individual case. Instead, it was now stated that in the end this depended on the conviction of the judge. Importantly, in the concept code of 1804 and in the criminal ordinance of 1809, the conviction of the judge was for the first time explicitly made into a constitutive requirement to convict someone.

Nevertheless, even though the conviction of the judge acquired a more important place, this did not mean that a system of evidentiary rules was rejected between 1795 and 1810. In contrast to the radical ideas of the French revolutionaries who completely abolished the system of legal proofs, it was still self-evident for everyone in the Dutch discussion that a system of (negative) evidentiary rules should be retained. The discussion in the Netherlands between 1795 and 1810 focused far more on reconciling the 'moral' conviction of the

---

113   B. Beinart and P. van Warmelo, *Dionysius Godefredus van der Keessel. Lectures on Books 47 and 48 of the Digest*, p. 2055.

judge with a system of evidentiary rules, in a similar way as Filangieri had done. Like Filangieri, the Dutch reformers still adhered to the authority of the old system of legal proofs – which was to a large extent retained in the evidentiary rules of the Dutch criminal ordinances between 1795 and 1810 –, while at the same time they gave a far more prominent role to the conviction of the judge which changed the role of the evidentiary rules. The evidentiary rules were now interpreted more as guiding and shaping the 'juridical conviction' and containing minimum requirements.

Besides the epistemological discourse, there was also a significant influence from the changed political-constitutional discourse. The political-constitutional discourse had a particularly prominent impact on the abolition of judicial torture and the reform of the criminal procedural law. This can be seen in the importance of the idea that the state did not have the right to force the accused to confess and thereby to contribute to his own conviction. The argument that judicial torture was against natural law was often repeated in the Dutch legislative discussions between 1795 and 1798. Furthermore, arguments were derived from the political-constitutional discourse which justified that the accused should have a right to defend himself and use legal counsel. Although it had become unacceptable to force the accused to confess, it was not yet recognized that he also had a positive right to remain silent. Instead it was deemed that the accused had an obligation to answer questions and, to a certain extent, to cooperate with the investigation.

Apart from the importance of the political-constitutional discourse in the abolition of judicial torture and in the extension of the defensive rights of the accused, it was also highly important in determining the direction that the Dutch reforms did not take between 1795 and 1813. In contrast to revolutionary France, it can be seen that almost all the Dutch reformers had a high level of trust in the professional magistrates and that they were relatively satisfied with the criminal justice system in the Republic. The fact that they had trust in the judges and the criminal justice system entailed that they did not feel the need to make radical alterations to the criminal procedural law. This becomes very clear from the discussions regarding the jury system in the committee that created the concept constitution of 1797. A majority did not want to introduce the jury system predominantly because they thought that the professional judges were trusted and already functioned well. Throughout the period of 1795 until 1813, virtually no radical proposals for reform were made in the juridical literature as well, because most authors did not deem this necessary.

As will be described in the following chapter, the situation again changed significantly between 1813 and 1830. Firstly, in this period a large group emerged in the Belgian provinces that strongly distrusted the professional judges and demanded the introduction of a jury system. In this period, the political-constitutional motives would play an even more prominent role in the discussions surrounding the criminal law of evidence than between 1795 and 1813. Secondly, the discussion changed significantly after 1813 due to the momentous reforms that the introduction of the French legislation brought about in the Netherlands between 1810 and 1813. While the reforming ideas of the French revolutionaries had played only a small role in the Dutch discussions between 1795 and 1810, this changed after 1813. The question to what extent the French legislation should be modified or retained now became the central topic of debate.

CHAPTER 9

The Criminal Law of Evidence in the United Kingdom of the Netherlands 1813–1830

9.1   Introduction

On 11 December 1813, soon after William I's ascension to the throne in the Northern Netherlands, a decree was issued which declared that the French criminal legislation would remain in force until the creation of new national substantive and procedural codes. The decree also made several important changes to the substantive and procedural criminal law. The jury system was abolished and the publicity of the trial was restricted to the final discussions, meaning that the hearing of witnesses and the presentation of other forms of evidence now occurred behind closed doors.[1] Henceforward five judges would sit in the courts of assizes and a simple majority of three judges was sufficient for a conviction. Until new rules concerning the criminal law of evidence would be made, the judges had to decide in accordance with article 342 of the *Code d'Instruction Criminelle,* originally prescribed for jurors. This entailed that until a new criminal procedural code was promulgated the evidentiary rules remained abolished and judges had to decide according to their freely formed *conviction intime*. After the Belgian provinces had been incorporated into the United Kingdom of the Netherlands on 1 August 1814, these changes in the criminal procedural law were also extended to these provinces.[2]

The precise reason why the jury system was abolished remains uncertain. There was no reason given for the decision in the decree of 1813. It only mentioned that it aimed to take away certain 'inconveniences' of the French legislation. The reasons for the abolition can also not be found in the scant documentation left by the three creators of the decree, Van Maanen, Philipse and Van Gennep, who had all been highly placed jurists at the imperial court. Nevertheless, there are most likely several reasons which culminated in the desire to directly abolish the jury system. In 1813 there were strong anti-French

---

1 S. van Ruller and S. Faber, *Afdoening van strafzaken in Nederland sinds 1813,* pp. 42–45. Another important change was that the exact and mandatory prescription of the punishments for crimes in the *Code Pénal* was replaced by a system which gave a far larger discretion to the judge to give a lesser punishment on the basis of ameliorating circumstances.
2 G. Bossers, *"Welk eene Natie, die de jurij gekend heeft, en ze weder heeft afschaft!",* pp. 86–95.

sentiments. The guillotine was directly abolished and French custom houses were burned to the ground. It is likely that the jury system was also considered a typical institution of the French oppressors and was, at least partially, abolished for this reason. Furthermore, the high trust in the professional judges in the northern provinces was probably a central reason for the fact that a jury system was deemed undesirable. As Bossers observed, the desire to remove this form of lay participation may have been particularly prevalent among the highly placed jurists – Van Maanen, Philipse and Van Gennep – who created the decree and who may have felt that the jury system was a sign of distrust against the professional magistrates.[3]

The abolition of the jury system at first attracted virtually no attention or discussion in the United Kingdom of the Netherlands; not even in the Belgian provinces which had known a jury system for almost twenty years since their incorporation into France in 1795. In the debates on the Dutch constitution of 1814 and 1815 there was also no discussion on the question of the jury system. In the first years of the new kingdom there were no appeals for the reintroduction of a jury system. Delbecke states that the general relief surrounding the removal of the autocratic Napoleonic regime probably prevailed at this time in the northern and southern provinces, and the new constitution seemed to offer sufficient guarantees for an independent judiciary.[4]

In the course of the period between 1815 and 1830 the situation changed and the question of how the criminal law of evidence should be given shape and whether a jury system should be introduced became an important point of discussion. A large number of publications started to appear which addressed the question whether a negative system of legal proofs should be created with professional judges or if a jury system should be introduced. While most of the jurists in the northern provinces were in favour of professional judges bound by a negative system of evidentiary rules, the reintroduction of a jury system became one of the central demands of the reform movement in the southern provinces. Especially between 1825 and 1830 a clear division in the discussion emerged between the southern and the northern provinces. Besides the discussion in the juridical literature, the question came to the fore in the

---

3   Ibidem, pp. 90–95. This explanation is even more probable when it is considered that many of the reforms of the decree of 1813 were directed against institutions which were created out of a distrust against the judiciary. After all, the jury system, the publicity of the trial and the exact prescription of the punishments, leaving no room for judicial discretion or arbitrariness, were all introduced by the French revolutionaries out of distrust against professional judges.
4   B. Delbecke, "<<Le fruit du terroir?>>. The Debate on Trial by Jury in the United Kingdom of the Netherlands (1814–1831)", pp. 89–97.

parliamentarian debates on new substantive and procedural criminal codes between 1827 and 1830. This culminated in an important discussion in parliament which lasted for three days, where in the end a majority voted against the introduction of a jury system. Eventually, after some modifications due to the separation of Belgium from the Netherlands, a new criminal procedural code was promulgated in the Netherlands in 1838 which contained a negative system of legal proofs. In the newly created Kingdom of Belgium, however, a jury system was introduced almost directly after its separation from the Netherlands in 1830.

In this chapter the development of the discussion on the criminal law of evidence in the (juridical) literature and in the legislature between 1813 and 1830 will be described. In the second section a description is given of the discussions in the juridical literature in the northern and the southern provinces in this period. In the third section the parliamentarian debates on new substantive and procedural criminal codes which took place between 1827 and 1830 are analysed. Finally, in the fourth section a short description is given of the consequences of the separation between the southern and the northern provinces for the criminal law of evidence.

9.2   The Development of the Discussion in the Juridical Literature between 1813 and 1830

The discussion on the criminal law of evidence which developed in the United Kingdom of the Netherlands between 1813 and 1830 contained some important innovations which distinguish it from the discussion between 1795 and 1813 in the northern Netherlands. In the earlier period, after the abolition of judicial torture, there was a consensus that, in essence, a negative system of legal proofs should be created (although it was not yet called this way). There was a consensus that on the one hand rules should prescribe minimum evidentiary criteria of when legal certainty existed, and on the other hand that the internal conviction of the judge was always necessary to convict someone. The idea to introduce a jury system, was almost entirely absent from the discussion in the northern provinces in the period between 1795 and 1813, apart from a short discussion in the Constitutional Assembly between 1795 and 1798. The 'technical-juridical' ideas were dominant and the debate – in the literature as well as in the codification committees – was conducted predominantly by professional jurists. In the period between 1813 and 1830 the spectrum of ideas under discussion significantly broadened. With the idea of a jury system there was now a serious alternative present in contrast to a (negative) system of legal proofs. The alternative was, furthermore, supported by influential political-constitutional ideals and a theoretically substantiated criticism of the usefulness of evidentiary rules. Lastly, in this period a third option started to be proposed as well in the Netherlands: a system based on professional judges unbound by evidentiary rules.

Before 1813, the ideas of the French reformers about the jury system had not yet significantly penetrated the Dutch discussion. Now that these ideas started to find a broad group of supporters, the proponents of a negative system of evidentiary rules were forced to re-evaluate and defend their own position, which until that time had been largely undisputed. They had to react to the political-constitutional ideas which were proposed in favour of the jury system and they had to react to the criticism that it was futile to try to bind the judge by evidentiary rules because in the end everything still depended on the internal conviction of the judge. Furthermore, the presupposition that the question of fact could just as well be answered by lay persons on the basis of common sense, and the 'French' ideas surrounding the *conviction intime* led to the situation that the proponents of a negative system of legal proofs now had to compare their ideas with the 'French' ideas.

In the period between 1813 and 1830 the demand for a jury system in accordance with the French model came increasingly from the southern provinces, while a large majority in the northern provinces was in favour of a system based on professional judges in combination with either a negative system of proofs, or completely unbound by evidentiary rules. To a large extent two different, although interacting, discourses developed. In the northern provinces the discussion was dominated by professional jurists and took place mostly within juridical treatises. A large majority of the participants were not in favour of a jury system and argued against it on the basis of predominantly technical-juridical grounds. The northern jurists were, furthermore, orientated more strongly towards the discussion in Germany and influenced by authors such as Feuerbach and Mittermaier. Nevertheless, there was also a significant reception of the French ideas and French authors among these professional jurists in the northern provinces.

In the southern provinces the discourse was different. In the 1820s the discussion became increasingly dominated by 'liberal' journalists and a generation of young lawyers. In general, they were more strongly orientated towards discussions that were taking place in France and to French liberal writers such as Constant, Guizot and Rémusat. Unlike the more technical-juridical debate in the northern provinces, in the south the political-constitutional arguments dominated the discussion. In particular in the last years of the 1820s, among 'liberals' as well as among Catholics, there was a far stronger distrust of the government of William I than in the north. The distrust of the judicial system was exacerbated by prosecutions of prominent liberals and Catholics for press offences, who were given severe punishments for criticizing the government. Similar to the French and German liberals in the restoration period, the demand for a jury system – especially regarding press and political offences – became part of a broader package of demands for constitutional reforms among the liberals from the southern provinces.

From the discussion in the southern provinces it again becomes apparent how decisive the question of trust in the judicial system was for the demand of a jury system. The main argument proposed in favour of jurors was that they were more independent and impartial than professional judges. In the north, on the other hand, there was a relatively high level of trust in the judicial system and there were only few proponents of a jury system. In the following two subsections the development of the discussion in the northern and southern provinces between 1813 and 1830 will be described and subsequently compared.

9.2.1   *The Discussion in the Northern Provinces between 1813 and 1830.*

The discussion on the criminal law of evidence and the desirability of a jury system in the northern and southern provinces between 1813 and 1830 can be divided into two periods. The first period lasted from 1813 until roughly 1826 and the second period from 1826 until 1830. During the first period, virtually no publications appeared on the criminal law of evidence or the jury system in either parts of the Netherlands until 1819–1820. The interest in this subject was aroused in both parts of the Netherlands around the same time by two different events. In the southern provinces the interest in the jury system was sparked by an intense discussion in France concerning the question whether a jury system should be used to decide on press offences.[5] In the northern provinces, on the other hand, the interest in the jury system was inspired by the discussions on this topic in the Prussian Rhine provinces and by the publication of the report of the *Immediat Justiz Kommission*.[6] Because of these events the interest in the jury system increased in the Netherlands and several publications on this subject started to appear. Nevertheless, the question of the jury system did not yet become the object of a highly politicized debate in the first period and the number of publications on this subject still remained relatively small. This changed in the second period, lasting from 1826 until

---

5   Ibidem, pp. 97–100.
6   See Section 3.1. of Chapter five on this report.

1830, when the discussion became more politicized and the number of publications regarding the criminal law of evidence increased sharply.

9.2.1.1   The Discussion in the Northern Provinces between 1813 and 1826

In 1819, Tydeman, a professor of law at Leiden University, asked Meyer to provide him with more information on the discussion taking place in the Prussian Rhine Provinces on the jury system. Meyer, a jurist from Amsterdam, was living in Cleves which formed part of the Prussian provinces at that time. Meyer answered the question of Tydeman by giving an extensive summary in Dutch of the reports of the Prussian committee and spoke appreciatively of the conclusions of the report which recommended the retention of the French jury system. Because the letters between Tydeman and Meyer were published in 1819, as *Briefwisseling van eenige regtsgeleerden*, a broader public was enabled to take notice of this summary of the reports of the *Immediat Justiz Kommission*.[7]

In a later letter, which was also published, Tydeman responded to the summary of Meyer. He did not clearly pronounce himself for or against a jury system, but he did remark that in his opinion the jury system and the publicity of the trial had been abolished in the Netherlands without due consideration simply because they were seen as products of French oppression. He stated that people in the northern provinces did not even seem to realize that the jury system and the publicity of the trial were in fact 'liberal' institutions stemming from the early revolution and that they were disliked by Napoleon. Tydeman also remarked that the prejudices against the jury system and the publicity of the trial had to do with the 'aristocratic spirit of our judges', which predisposed them against being held accountable for their actions to the public. Nevertheless, Tydeman noted that recently the prejudices against these institutions had started to slowly give way to a more open and impartial evaluation. Lastly, it is significant that already in 1819 Tydeman observed a difference in attitude between the southern provinces who were more appreciative of a jury system and the northern provinces which were against the institution.[8]

---

7   H.W. Tydeman and J.D. Meyer, *Briefwisseling van eenige regtsgeleerden*, pp. 471–53. Interestingly, when he discussed the idea of the Prussian committee that evidentiary rules were superfluous and that it would be better to leave everything to the internal conviction of the judge, Meyer remarked in a footnote that this idea so far never seems to have occurred to the Dutch law makers, not even to the committee of 'wise jurists' of 1798–1804. Meyer also summarized the arguments of the Prussian committee against extraordinary punishment. In a footnote he briefly remarked that extraordinary punishments used to exist in the Netherlands, but did no longer appear in the new criminal code of 1809.
8   Ibidem, pp. 567–582.

The new interest in the jury system prompted the University of Leiden to devote its annual prize question to this subject. In 1819 the question was posed whether the introduction of a jury system was desirable. Five students submitted an answer to the question, of which Cock won the first prize. All five manuscripts argued against the jury system. They treated the matter in a relatively superficial way and predominantly repeated the most important arguments which Feuerbach had presented against the institution, namely, that jurors lacked the necessary legal experience to answer the question of fact and that they were too impressionable. After the prize question there was also a student who argued in favour of a jury system in his dissertation in 1821.[9] Although the prize question did not lead to a more in-depth discussion on the jury system and the merits of a system based on evidentiary rules, it does attest to the growing interest in this subject and the reception of the ideas of Feuerbach.

The most influential work written in favour of a jury system in the northern provinces in the nineteenth century came from Meyer. This exceptionally erudite jurist from Amsterdam published a six volume work, *Esprit, origine et progress des institutions judiciaires des principaux pays de l'Europe*, between 1818 and 1823 which described the history of the judicial system in France, Germany, England and the Netherlands going back to the time of the Germanic tribes and the Roman empire. In the fifth part he gave a detailed and positive description of the way the jury system was introduced during the French revolution and what the underlying ideas were behind its introduction. In his description of the criminal procedural law of the Dutch Republic, Meyer also gave a very critical evaluation of the old inquisitorial procedure. He deemed the Dutch inquisitorial procedure even harsher than the criminal procedural law in pre-revolutionary France. He remarked that this very harsh system was only ameliorated by the high moral standards of the Dutch judges.[10]

In the sixth part of his work, Meyer ended his descriptive work and defended an array of reforms to the Dutch (criminal) justice system. Meyer pleaded for, among other things, the introduction of a jury system, the necessity of a completely public and oral trial and for a further improvement of the defensive rights of the accused. In particular in his argumentation for the publicity of the trial, Meyer showed that he had high expectations of the controlling function of the people which he deemed a 'censeur éclairé, juste et impartial'

---

9   B. Delbecke, "<<Le fruit du terroir?>>. The Debate on Trial by Jury in the United Kingdom of the Netherlands (1814–1831)", pp. 96–97 and G. Bossers, *"Welk eene Natie, die de jurij gekend heeft, en ze weder heeft afschaft!"*, pp. 102–103.

10   J.D. Meijer, *Esprit, origine et progress des institutions judiciaires des principaux pays de l'Europe. Tom. IV*, pp. 292–293 and 408–411.

and later called 'un moniteur incorruptible'. The publicity of the trial would force judges to act impartially and in accordance with the law. He deemed the orality of the procedure necessary to make the scrutinizing function of the public effective and to enable the judges to directly see the movements and conduct of the witnesses and the accused, which provided important information for the evaluation of their trustworthiness. He, furthermore, pleaded for the greatest freedom of defence of the accused and, quite remarkably, for a complete publicity of the preliminary investigation.[11]

Meyer subsequently devoted several chapters to his recommendation of a jury system, treating the institution first from a juridical and then from a political-constitutional point of view. It cannot be said that Meyer was very original in his argumentation for the jury system or that he proposed important new arguments in favour of this institution. Nevertheless, he provided by far the most elaborate argumentation for the jury system published in the Netherlands between 1813 and 1830. Meyer was strongly influenced by the ideas of the French reformers of the second half of the eighteenth century and largely followed the argumentation of the Prussian *Immediat Justiz Kommission* (which itself was inspired by the French reform ideas). Like the Prussian committee, Meyer started by arguing that it was impossible to predetermine in evidentiary rules when sufficient evidence existed for a conviction. Legislators had in vain tried to describe positive or negative rules to determine when sufficient evidence existed in the concrete case, because in the end everything still unavoidably depended on the evaluation and the conviction of the judge. Meyer, furthermore, followed the view of the French reformers and the Prussian committee that it was not possible to give a rational reconstruction of why someone was convinced and that it was, therefore, impossible to give a motivation for this conviction (either by judges or by jurors).[12] Meyer also emphasized the necessity of the orality of the procedure so that the forms of evidence could work 'directly' on the conscience of the judges or jurors:

> Celui qui est chargé d'examiner un fait et ses circonstances doit apprécier les preuves, non d'après des règles fixes et déterminées, mais d'après

---

11 J.D. Meijer, *Esprit, origine et progress des institutions judiciaires des principaux pays de l'Europe. Tom. VI*, pp. 119–151 and 293–338. Meyer also argued that the public prosecutor needed to have an entirely separate function in the procedure to ensure the impartial role of the judges. In his treatment of the public prosecutors, Meyer stated that they should be seen as part of the administrative branch of government and not the judicial branch. In his view public prosecutors were subordinated to the government and the government should have the possibility to give binding instructions to the public prosecutors.

12 Ibidem, pp. 361–368.

l'impression qu'elles ont faite sur sa conscience, sa conviction est souvent formée par le maintien, le geste, l'accent de ceux qu'il voit et qu'il entend; le moindre détail peut donner cette persuasion, quelquefois personnelle et dépendante de ce qu'un autre peut n'avoir point aperçu; il est par conséquent très difficile de se rendre raison à soi-même, *il est impossible d'instruire un autre, de ce qui entrainé l'opinion. C'est l'ensemble des preuves qui frappe l'esprit; les décomposer c'est en détruire l'effet, les décrire c'est les dénaturer* ... La personne qui, d'après sa conscience, juge sur l'existence d'un fait, ne peut pas motiver son jugement.[13]

In short, just as the French reformers and the Prussian committee, Meyer placed a strong emphasis on the importance of the direct impression which the oral presentation of the evidence made and argued that it was impossible to rationally reconstruct how an internal conviction was precisely formed. It is not so much the case that this was an entirely 'irrational' concept of truth finding, even though critics of the French idea of the *conviction intime* did describe it as such. After all, the famous French instruction for the jurors asked them to consider what effect the presented evidence had made on their 'raison'. As argued in Chapter three, it is, however, true that this view put a strong accent on the 'unconscious' formation of the internal conviction and the unavoidably subjective, individual nature of this conviction. The accent lay, furthermore, on the relatively passive position of the jurors who, more or less, saw and sensed the truth as the evidence was presented to them directly, and not on the internal conviction as the result of a process of a rational evaluation of the evidence. This idea is very typically expressed in the following manner by Meyer:

la vivacité des débats, la présence à l'instruction orale, peuvent faire naître cette conviction intime, cette certitude morale qui ne laisse aucun doute sur la vérité; l'application de la loi est le résultat d'une combinaison froide et mûrie par la réflexion; *le fait se reconnaît par les sens, par un sentiment qui résulte presqu'involontairement de l'examen.*[14]

As in Germany, this conception of the nature of the internal conviction would became one of the principal points of criticism of the opponents of a jury system

---

13 Ibidem, pp. 368–369. At a later point Meyer criticized the idea of trying to decompose the different forms of evidence and analyse their degree of certainty by attributing values of full, half, or one-thirds, or a quarter to the different forms of proof. Like the French reformers he contrasted the workings of the internal conviction sharply against what he conceived of as the old system of legal proofs. See pp. 379–380.

14 Ibidem, p. 437.

in the northern provinces. The opponents placed a far greater emphasis on the possibility of 'rationally' analysing and comparing the different forms of evidence and to follow certain general rules of logic and experience. Consequently, the opponents of a jury system argued that it was possible and useful to follow minimum evidentiary standards and to give at least some motivation of the internal conviction.

In close concomitance with the idea that it was impossible to follow general evidentiary rules, Meyer stressed time and again that no specific training or juridical knowledge was necessary to judge on the question of fact. Only common sense was required:

> il n'est point nécessaire de se former par des études préliminaires, il n'est pas de connaissances qu'on doive acquérir, et le bon sens, la droiture, l'impartialité suffisent; dans plus d'un cas ces qualités naturelles, *une espèce d'instinct*, sont des guides plus sûrs que les idées les plus savantes ou abstraites.[15]

Meyer also argued that the question of fact and the question of law could be separated and that allowing ordinary people to judge on the question of fact provided more guarantees for the accused. Especially if the criminal laws were clear and precise, there would be no problem for the jurors to understand what was asked of them. In his treatment from a juridical point of view, Meyer also stressed that although individual jurors could sometimes be too easily persuaded, a great number of jurors formed a sufficient safeguard for correct decisions.[16]

The defence of the idea that lay jurors offered more guarantees than professional judges belonged to the 'political-constitutional' part of Meyer's argumentation. He proposed several arguments for this idea. First of all, a jury system prevented a concentration of power in the judge who normally decided on both the question of fact and the question of law. Secondly, and this was the most important reason, Meyer expected a greater impartiality and independence from lay jurors. Because of the continually new selection of jurors it was impossible that an *esprit de corps* could form among them and they would have nothing to gain or to lose by judging in a certain manner, in contrast to professional judges who might be swayed to judge in a certain way to please the government. Thirdly, the judgement by jurors would, like the publicity of the trial, increase the trust of the people in the judicial system. Fourthly, Meyer

---

15   Ibidem, p. 376.
16   Ibidem, pp. 371–387.

mentioned the often-repeated arguments that jurors were more apt to judge on the question of fact because they stood closer to the everyday life of normal people than the more estranged judges, and that judges had often become too harsh in their judgement because through their work they had acquired a habit of seeing criminals everywhere. A final important political argument which Meyer mentioned in favour of the jury system was that it would increase the public spirit and the interest of the citizens in public affairs. The acquaintance of the people with the laws would help them better identify with these laws and increase their patriotic spirit. Meyer also saw the jury system as a useful form of representation of the people in the judicial branch, and as a necessary complement in a constitutional monarchy where the sovereign shared his power with the people.[17]

The summary of the report from the Prussian committee and the six volume historical work by Meyer were an influential starting point of the debate on the jury system in the northern provinces and it already framed an important part of the discussion regarding the criminal law of evidence. Although Meyer represented a minority opinion in the northern provinces, he was highly respected for his erudition and intellect by proponents as well as opponents of the jury system. Because of his thorough argumentation, the work of Meyer became a central point of reference in the discussion on the criminal law of evidence. The opponents of the jury system sought to refute his arguments while the proponents often quoted him and repeated his arguments. The significance of the work of Meyer can also be seen in the parliamentarian debate on the jury system in 1829. He was frequently referred to in this debate by delegates from the southern as well as the northern provinces.

Besides the five answers to the prize question in Leiden which all argued against the jury system, the two earliest explicit publications against the jury system came from Van Heusden, a judge in Breda, in 1822 and from Van der Meer Mohr, a lawyer in Goes, in 1823. Van Heusden stated that two systems could be distinguished within the criminal law of evidence: one based on evidentiary rules and one based on the freely formed internal conviction. He then remarked that in his opinion, the best system consisted of a combination of these two systems. Van Heusden was against the jury system because he deemed it impossible for lay jurors to follow evidentiary rules and he found

---

17   Ibidem, pp. 388–415. After treating the jury from a political perspective, Meyer devoted a separate chapter to the composition of the jury. Here it can be seen that Meyer was in favour of a very broad census for selecting jurors, while he criticized the French system for having too restrictive criteria. See J.D. Meijer, *Esprit, origine et progress des institutions judiciaires des principaux pays de l'Europe*. Tom. VI, pp. 414–436.

their judgement based solely on their internal conviction too dangerous. He also disapproved of the existing situation in the Netherlands where the judge was left entirely free in the evaluation of the evidence. Because Van Heusden deemed it impossible to completely determine in evidentiary rules when sufficient evidence existed for a conviction, he argued that the best solution was a system based on a combination of evidentiary rules and the requirement of the internal conviction.[18]

A more elaborate argumentation against the jury system was provided by Van der Meer Mohr. First of all, he offered a new argument against the jury system, viz that a jury system was unconstitutional in the Netherlands. He remarked that the creators of the constitution had nowhere discussed or expressed the idea of introducing a jury system and that the Articles on the judicial branch in the constitution only spoke of 'judges appointed for life'. This argument of the unconstitutionality of the jury system would become one of the central arguments against the jury system in the parliamentarian debate in 1829. Subsequently, Van der Meer Mohr continued to explain why he, in general did not find a jury system desirable by discussing the arguments of the Prussian committee (which he knew through the summary provided by Meyer). His first important argument was that he did not believe that lay persons were capable of answering the complex question of guilty or not-guilty which unavoidably contained juridical elements. Especially the difficult question whether the crime was imputable required a long training and juridical practice. He also remarked that he himself had experienced the incompetence of lay persons in this respect between 1811 and 1813. Van der Meer Mohr stated that whenever there was a person with legal knowledge in the selected jury everybody normally waited for him to give his opinion and then overwhelmingly followed this opinion.[19]

The second argument Van der Meer Mohr presented against a jury system was that he had a high trust in the 'capable, impartial and morally' outstanding judges of the Netherlands. While *esprit de corps* may have been a problem among the old *parlements* of France, such manifestations had never occurred in the Netherlands. Furthermore, he did not believe that lay persons had a better understanding of the affairs of everyday life and that judges were estranged from society, nor that experience as a criminal judge had hardened them to see criminals everywhere. In his own long experience as a lawyer he had not found

---

18   C.J. van Heusden, *Merkwaardige voorbeelden uit de hedendaagsche lijfstraffelijke regtspleging*, pp. 1–16.
19   J.C. van der Meer Mohr, *Bedenkingen over het grondwettige, nuttige en noodzakelijke der jury in Nederland*, pp. 8–28.

these claims to be true. For these reasons he rejected the conclusions of the Prussian committee and was against the introduction of a jury system. Even though he was against a jury system, van der Meer Mohr did remark that he was strongly in favour of the publicity of the main trial. He believed that a public trial was just as compatible with a system based on professional judges as with a system based on lay jurors, and that all the benefits attributed to the publicity of the trial were applicable to a trial with professional judges in the same manner.[20]

9.2.1.2   The Discussion in the Northern Provinces between 1826 and 1830
The interest in and the number of publications on the criminal law of evidence sharply increased in the northern provinces between 1826 and 1830. The reason for the growing interest was twofold. Firstly, the designs for new substantive and procedural criminal codes became known and were discussed in parliament in this period. As will be further discussed in the following section, a chapter regulating the criminal law of evidence in the form of a negative system of legal proofs – which was very similar to that of the criminal ordinance of 1809 – was included in the design for the code of substantive criminal law of 1827 (which was later transposed to the procedural code in 1828). In this negative system of legal proofs the internal conviction of the judge was always required and the negative rules were again formulated very broadly. The second reason for the increased interest in the criminal law of evidence, was the fact that there was a growing appeal from the southern provinces in this period for the introduction of a jury system, especially for press offences. This clamour was intensified by several prosecutions of journalists for press offences which attracted nationwide attention. In short, the combination of these events triggered the jurists in the northern provinces to take up a position either for or against a jury system.

In the reaction of the jurists from the northern provinces three views can be distinguished which will be treated with below. One group of authors argued for a system based on professional judges without evidentiary rules which they deemed useless. Another group was in favour of professional judges in combination with a negative system of legal proofs as was proposed in the concept criminal codes. Although they differed in opinion concerning the necessity of evidentiary rules, these two groups together created a large majority in the northern provinces in favour of professional judges and against a jury system. Finally, a small but vocal minority constituted the third group in the northern provinces which desired the introduction of a jury system.

---

20   Ibidem, pp. 30–59.

9.2.1.2.1 *Proponents of Professional Judges Unbound by Evidentiary Rules*

Van Hamelsveld, Van Rappard and Den Tex all argued against the introduction of a jury system, and they were the first to declare that they preferred a system based on professional judges unbound by evidentiary rules. In 1826 a long article appeared by Van Hamelsveld, a judge at the Supreme Court in the Hague, which discussed the question whether the introduction of a jury system was desirable in the new criminal legislation for the Netherlands. He started by remarking that he was not against the jury system out of some narrow-minded prejudice against anything French, or out of an aristocratic spirit which desired to make an arcane secret out of the workings of the judicial system. In fact, he remarked, he was strongly in favour of the publicity of the main trial.[21] He continued to state that the most important reason which could justify the introduction of lay jurors would be that they were more impartial than professional judges. This, however, he deemed not to be the case in the Netherlands. He remarked that he had full confidence that in the Netherlands the judges were just and impartial. Furthermore, the constitution guaranteed the independence of the judicial branch.[22]

Unlike most opponents of a jury system, Van Hamelsveld agreed with the Prussian report that nothing more was required than common sense to decide on the question of fact. Nevertheless, Van Hamelsveld fundamentally disagreed with the idea of the report that lay people were better suited to answer the question of fact than professional judges. He deemed it a very strange conclusion that supposedly judges lost their capability to decide on the basis of their common sense simply because they had acquired a legal training. He denied the validity of the argument that professional judges were estranged from everyday life and more harsh in their judgement because they acquired the habit of seeing criminals everywhere. At least, in his own long experience as a judge he found no proof of this. He concluded that there was no need for a jury system because all the reasons which were proposed in favour of its introduction applied just as well to professional judges. Furthermore, he argued that jurors might offer even fewer guarantees for a correct judgement because they were more easily impressed by the eloquent and deceitful orations of lawyers.[23]

---

21 W.Y. van Hamelsveld, "Zoude de wederinvoering der jurij, bij de nieuwe wetgeving van lijfstraffelijke regtspleging voor ons te noodzakelijk en te wenschen zijn?", pp. 75–78.
22 Ibidem, pp. 81–95. Van Hamelsveld spoke specifically on the desirability of a jury system in the Netherlands. He acknowledged that this institution might be useful in other countries, especially in places where the judges were less impartial.
23 Ibidem, pp. 87–120.

A final important aspect of the article of Van Hamelsveld, was that he appeared to agree entirely with the idea of the Prussian committee that it was impossible to create evidentiary rules which prescribed when sufficient evidence existed for a conviction. He remarked that he preferred the existing situation where judges decide after their freely formed internal conviction, and that it had not given rise to any complaints in the Netherlands. Van Hamelsveld argued that because of the progress which legal science had made since 'the times of superstition and prejudices', no judge would be foolish enough to follow the distinctions between full, half and quarters of proof of the old legal theory. On the contrary: "as highly inappropriate and useless in criminal cases he will shove them aside and determine the strength of the evidence solely on the basis of the conviction which the evidence provides him, and decide accordingly".[24] Van Hamelsveld, in short, was in favour of a complete abolition of evidentiary rules. Although he did not provide any further arguments for this point of view, it seems that he came to this conclusion following the idea of the Prussian committee and the French reformers that it was impossible to regulate the strength of the evidence in pre-established rules.

Van Hamelsveld's remark that he did not wish to return to the old evidentiary system where distinctions were made between full, half and quarters of proof, is very interesting. He was one of the first to give this misrepresentation of the 'old' system of legal proofs in the Netherlands, but this characterization would later be often repeated.[25] This misrepresentation derived from the polemical rhetoric of authors in the second half of the eighteenth century such as Brissot de Warville and Voltaire, who criticized the system of legal proofs in this vein. The remark of Van Hamelsveld is interesting because it shows that he already historicized what he perceived as the 'old system of evidentiary rules'. He deemed that such progress had taken place in legal science that there had been a rupture with this old evidentiary system (which had apparently taken place in the preceding decades). He, and other jurists in this period, clearly perceived 'their' criminal law of evidence as something largely new and fundamentally different from the old system of evidentiary rules.

---

24   Ibidem, pp. 121–123.
25   In the parliamentary discussion this characterization was, for example, given by van de Kasteele in 1829, and later Lipman and Modderman made a similar comment. See J.J.F. Noordziek, *Geschiedenis der beraadslagingen gevoerd in de tweede kamer der Staten-Generaal over het ontwerp Wetboek van Strafvordering en het vraagstuk der jury 1828–1829, deel I*, p. 104, S.P. Lipman, *Wetboek van Strafvordering, vergeleken met het Romeinsche en Fransche regt*, pp. 210–216 and E.A.J. Modderman, *De wetenschappelijke bewijsleer in Strafzaken*, pp. 10–49.

The comment of Van Hamelsveld is, furthermore, typical of the process whereby the 'old' system of evidentiary rules was increasingly historicized and presented as something of the past. From around the 1810s onwards, a large number of publications started to appear on the history of the criminal law of evidence – particularly in the German territories – whereby a more or less 'developmental' outlook on the history of the criminal law of evidence emerged. Roughly three phases were distinguished in these works. In the early Middle Ages the system of ordeals dominated, then in the late Middle Ages the 'scholastic' system of legal proofs developed and finally the contemporary approach to the criminal law of evidence developed during the enlightenment when 'the times of superstition and prejudices' were left behind. As will become apparent in the following chapter, particularly in the period between 1830 and 1870, almost every publication on the criminal law of evidence devoted a large part to the historical development of the criminal law of evidence. In these publications the image was constantly repeated that the 'old' system of legal proofs positively prescribed when sufficient evidence existed and that it was based on a scholastic division of the different forms of evidence in full, half and quarters of proofs. In short, it was already in the early nineteenth century that the system of legal proofs became historicized and that it was envisioned – on the basis of the polemical misrepresentations of the enlightenment – as something far more formalistic and rigid than it had actually been.[26]

Van Rappard, a public prosecutor, was even more unequivocal in his rejection of evidentiary rules than Van Hamelsveld. In his commentary on the concept substantive criminal code of 1827, he argued that the supposed 'negative' evidentiary rules were formulated so broadly that they left everything to the conviction of the judge. This he deemed a good thing. He stated that the French jury system had been mistakenly accused of allowing convictions on a mere 'subjective' or 'intuitive' feeling. In fact, he remarked, the French system demanded that jurors asked themselves what impression the evidence had made on their 'reason'. They were not permitted to convict on the basis of mere suspicions or an 'irrational' feeling. Van Rappard argued that the differences between the French system and the proposed negative system of legal proofs were negligible, because in the latter everything was in the end also still left to the internal conviction of the judge. Superficially, the regulation seemed to deviate from the French system, but actually the evidentiary rules in the chapter

---

26   It is this view which has predominated in the legal historical literature for a long time and which was still very clearly visible in the work of, for example, Lévy. Only in the last decades has this view been increasingly nuanced. See J. PH. Lévy, *La hiérarchie des preuves dans le droit savant du Moyen-Age*.

should be interpreted as forming only guidelines which still left everything to the conviction of the judge.[27]

In several passages Van Rappard put forth as an unquestionable axiom that it was impossible to create rules which predetermined when sufficient evidence existed for a conviction in the concrete case and that the evidentiary rules in the concept criminal code were superfluous. This was not the domain of the legislator but should be left to legal science. In line with the French idea of the *conviction intime*, he remarked that in criminal cases a 'historical certainty' was required and that this certainty consisted of that state of mind in which someone fully believes a certain fact: "the certainty does not lie in the thing itself, but in the internal feeling".[28] The required certainty, therefore, had to be found in the feeling or internal conviction of the person judging. Unlike many supporters of the idea of the *conviction intime*, however, Van Rappard stressed that this feeling needed to be based on a rational weighing of the evidence and that the judge should follow (non-legal) rules based on experience. Van Rappard also contrasted the system based on the internal conviction with the evidentiary system of the *ancien régime*. He stated that in earlier times one worked with an almost mathematical division of the evidence and that when less than a full proof existed people were convicted to an extraordinary punishment. Now it had been rightfully acknowledged that the truth in criminal cases is indivisible and that the judge cannot convict on partial certainty.[29]

Van Rappard concluded that the proposed negative evidentiary rules could not offer any real guarantees against judicial arbitrariness and that they still left everything to the internal conviction of the judge. Instead of negative evidentiary rules, he argued that guarantees against arbitrary decisions should be found in the publicity of the trial, the greatest possibility for the accused to defend himself and a larger number of judges entrusted with the decision.[30] In a second work, commenting on the concept criminal procedural code, Van Rappard summarily explained why he was against a jury system. Most importantly, he deemed that it was impossible to separate the question of fact from

---

27 W.L.F.C. van Rappard, *Aanmerkingen op het ontwerp van een Wetboek op het Strafregt I*, pp. 46–54.
28 Ibidem, pp. 54–57.
29 Ibidem, pp. 57–63. Importantly, Van Rappard argued that while some rules could more easily be made regarding the question whether someone had factually committed a certain deed, it was, nevertheless, entirely impossible to create rules on the question if the fact was imputable. He stated that whether the accused had the necessary criminal state of mind could only be deduced from the circumstances but could not be captured in rules.
30 Ibidem, pp. 64–65.

the question of law and he argued that lay persons did not have the necessary juridical knowledge to decide on the guilt of the accused. Furthermore, jurors could be led to acquit obviously guilty persons simply because they considered the punishment too harsh and were more easily convinced by the sophisms and rhetoric of the lawyers. Lastly, Van Rappard also criticized the idea that the publicity and orality of the procedure were only compatible with a jury system. He remarked that many authors had mistakenly attributed the advantages of a public, oral trial to the jury system, while they could be applied just as well to a system based on professional judges.[31]

Den Tex, a professor of law in Amsterdam, reacted in strong terms against the clamour for a jury system coming from the southern provinces. He criticized the constant use of pompous rhetoric and stated that in the northern provinces the people did not feel the enchantment of words such as *liberté politique*, *civilisation* and *progrès de lumière*. Den Tex intentionally used these French words ironically in an otherwise Dutch article and projected the northern provinces as more down-to-earth. He stated that civil liberty and the freedom of the press were valued just as much in the north but, in contrast to the south, people were not swept away by idealistic rhetoric devoid of content. In the north they trusted sound laws and the ability of capable men. Den Tex was clearly very irritated by the claim, which he perceived to be the coming from the southern provinces, that those who were against a jury system did not value civil liberty sufficiently and were not caught up with the progress of civilized people.[32]

Essentially, Den Tex declared that he was against the jury system because he did not see a stronger guarantee in lay jurors than in professional judges appointed for life. He lauded the tradition of impartial and outstanding judges in the Dutch Republic and clearly had trust in the professional magistrates. Furthermore, he did not believe that common sense sufficed to answer the question of fact but deemed that legal training and experience were necessary. Den Tex presented two further reasons why he was against the jury system. Firstly, he considered jurors to be too lenient. To substantiate this claim he presented a large number of cases drawn from the French magazine *Gazette des Tribunaux* where jurors appeared to have acquitted guilty persons seemingly out of compassion with the accused. The second reason why he was against a jury system in the Netherlands, was that it was foreign to Dutch customs,

---

31 W.L.F.C. van Rappard, *Het ontwerp van een Wetboek van Strafvordering, op zich zelf en in vergelijking met de bestaande Fransche wetgeving II*, pp. 3–12.
32 C.A. Den Tex, "Is de instelling van gezworenen, in strafzaken, voor Nederland wenschelijk?", pp. 287–293.

institutions and traditions. He was willing to concede that a jury system might be useful in England, and perhaps in France, where it had been working for many years, but argued that it was very difficult to introduce this foreign institution in the Netherlands.[33]

At the end of his article Den Tex again reacted against several claims accompanying the appeal for a jury system which he perceived as unjustified. He disagreed strongly with those who appeared to presume that all the recent advances in the criminal procedural law, such as the publicity and orality of the procedure, were inextricably tied to a jury system. He stated that he was in favour of the publicity and the orality of the trial but that these innovations worked just as well with professional judges. In this context, Den Tex also remarked that he considered 'judging on the internal conviction' one of the advances of recent times. Almost in passing by and without any further argumentation, he stated that he considered it impossible to create a sound legal theory of evidence where in the end everything did no come down to the internal conviction of the judge. Although he did not state it explicitly, Den Tex appeared to be in favour of a system based on the internal conviction of professional judges without any legal evidentiary rules.[34]

9.2.1.2.2 *The Proponents of Professional Judges Combined with a Negative System of Legal Proofs*

The preference of Van Hamelsveld, Van Rappard and Den Tex for professional judges unbound by evidentiary rules was as yet still the opinion of a minority. The commonly held opinion at this time in the northern provinces was in favour of a negative system of legal proofs in combination with professional judges, as was proposed in the design for the new concept criminal codes. This view was defended in 1827 in treatises by Weiland, Asser, and Donker Curtius. The last two authors argued in favour of a negative system of legal proofs and against the jury system. Weiland, on the other hand, focused predominantly on presenting a theoretical justification for the necessity of negative evidentiary rules in general without giving a clear pronunciation for or against a jury system.

Donker Curtius, a relatively 'liberal' parliamentarian, fulminated against the existing French regulation which referred everything to the inner feeling of the judge or jurors and presumed a certain 'instinct' for the truth. He remarked that the French reformers had drawn an over-exaggerated conclusion by arguing from the fact that no perfect positive legal system of proofs could be

---

33 Ibidem, pp. 295–346.
34 Ibidem, pp. 338–341.

created to the idea that, therefore, everything had to be left solely to the internal conviction. Donker Curtius argued that everything depended on the grounds and reasons for the conviction and that referring merely to an inner feeling denied this fact. Because everything depended on the grounds, he deemed it possible and necessary to make certain legal rules which prescribed at least a minimum evidentiary standard which needed to be present for a conviction. Nevertheless, he also acknowledged that it was impossible to positively prescribe when sufficient evidence existed and that in the end the internal conviction was always necessary. He, therefore, stated that a middle ground needed to be sought between on the one hand the extreme of the French system and on the other hand the extreme of the systems which positively prescribed when sufficient evidence existed.[35]

Asser, who worked for the Ministry of Justice and cooperated on the designs of the new criminal codes, completely agreed with Donker Curtius regarding the criminal law of evidence and spoke in strongly condemnatory words of the French legislation which left everything to the 'moral conviction'. He stated that if one wanted to give a definition of arbitrariness, one would not be far from the truth if one cited Article 342 of the *Code d'Instruction Criminelle* (containing the instruction for jurors). He remarked that the greatest error of the French legislator lay in the fact that it presumed that mere common sense was sufficient to judge on the question of fact and that no rules could be created to guide the conviction. Even if one wanted a jury system, he claimed, evidentiary rules could and should still be created. He disagreed with those who claimed that a jury system was incompatible with evidentiary rules and mentioned the example of England where many evidentiary rules existed. Asser concluded that the legislator should create minimum evidentiary requirements for a conviction while at the same time the moral conviction of the judge should always be required.[36]

By far the theoretically most sophisticated and elaborate argumentation in favour of a negative system of legal proofs came from Weiland, a versatile lawyer from Rotterdam who also published a satirical magazine and had a strong interest in philosophy. He was especially inspired by Feuerbach, Mittermaier and Jarke, and reacted in his treatise against the ideas of the Prussian report.[37]

---

35 W.B. Donker Curtius, *Iets over de theorie der en het bewijs der misdrijven*, pp. 89–107. Donker Curtius was also firmly against a jury system, but presented his argumentation only in the parliamentary debates which are the subject of the following section.

36 C. Asser, *Vlugtige beschouwingen van eenige voorname beginselen des strafregts*, pp. 109–130.

37 On Feuerbach, Mittermaier and Jarcke see Sections 3.1. and 3.2. of Chapter five.

Weiland began by observing that the question whether an accused is innocent or guilty of a certain crime always contained factual as well as juridical elements which could not be entirely separated. He disagreed with the Prussian report that lay persons have sufficient juridical knowledge to make this decision simply because they know in general what is forbidden and what, for example, a theft or a murder is. In the criminal legislation there are many subtle differences between the various crimes, their gradations and aggravating circumstances and, for example, the level of criminal intent. While civilians in everyday life only needed to have a 'passive' knowledge of what not to do, judges had to be able to actively apply the criminal law in all its complexity. For this reason, Weiland argued, the argument was invalid that all citizens have sufficient knowledge of the laws to judge on the question of fact. 'Active' juridical expertise was required to correctly evaluate whether the accused was guilty and what he was guilty of, while the people merely needed to know passively what not to do.[38]

Subsequently, Weiland continued to criticize what he considered to be the most important presuppositions behind the Prussian report and the French idea of the *conviction intime*. Their main presumption was that it was impossible to predetermine in general rules when sufficient proof existed and that the only criterion for historical truth, therefore, lay in the 'subjective conviction' of the judge or jurors. Underlying the presumption that no evidentiary rules were possible, was the idea that all rules are either too broad or too narrow and can never do justice to the complexity of the individual case, and that no absolute certainty could be acquired but only a high level of probability. Weiland first criticized the argument derived from the juxtaposition of mathematical certainty (where absolute certainty was attainable) with historical certainty (where only a high level of probability was attainable). Simply because no absolute *a priori* rules could be developed for historical matters as for mathematical matters did not, according to Weiland, mean that no objective criteria could be formulated at all. In short, from the difference between mathematical and historical certainty, it could never be deduced that all possible knowledge concerning historical matters should depend solely on a subjective conviction.[39]

After the rejection of the conclusions drawn from the abovementioned juxtaposition, Weiland continued to consider what the 'truth' was which was

---

38   J.A. Weiland, *Bijdragen tot de wetenschap der Strafregtspleging*, pp. 1–27.
39   Ibidem, pp. 28–34.

required in criminal cases. Weiland agreed with the idea of the Prussian report that truth lies in the correspondence of the belief a person has with the relevant object (i.e. historical event). However, crucially, the Prussian report did not give a criterion according to which we could assess whether our belief actually corresponded with the object. Instead, the report stated that all truth that could be acquired concerning historical matters lay in the internal conviction of the person judging. With this idea, Weiland fundamentally disagreed. He also blamed the Prussian report and the French reformers for giving as a sole guarantee for the veracity of the internal conviction the presumption of an 'instinct' for the truth and the argument that common sense sufficed. The main mistake that the Prussian report made was that it presumed that the internal conviction – the 'subjective thinking that something is true' – is already sufficient while they did not look at the *grounds* or the *reasons* which underlay the conviction and of which the conviction was only the result. In line with Jarke, Weiland argued that everything depended on the strength of the grounds which determined the value of someone's conviction.[40]

Concerning historical matters and knowledge derived from experience, we cannot have any absolute certainty whether our belief corresponds to the object. There is no possibility of formulating *a priori* rules for these matters because, unlike with mathematical certainty, we can never have full knowledge of the object. Weiland stated that any knowledge we have regarding historical matters or matters of experience can only be *approximative*: "It may be true that knowledge gained through experience cannot provide absolute certainty; but is also true that the certainty which it provides contains different steps or degrees".[41] Weiland argued that general rules could be formulated regarding knowledge which we have acquired in matters of experience, and that these rules can and should guide our decision-making. Furthermore, the knowledge acquired through experience which one person has was necessarily very small in comparison to the knowledge based on experience which existed in society as a whole. The advantage of evidentiary laws was that they could provide rules which were based on the accumulative experience of society as a whole. By comparing the grounds underlying someone's conviction with these rules, Weiland argued, the judge could acquire the largest possible certainty of not making an erroneous judgement. It is this comparison of the grounds with the more general negative evidentiary rules which elevated the subjective conviction

---

40 Ibidem, pp. 35–43 and 130–131.
41 Ibidem, pp. 46–47.

to a more objective validity, in as far as this was possible concerning matters of experience.[42]

In his conclusion Weiland explained why the rules should not be left to a scientific theory of evidence but should be laid down in binding laws. His main reason was that it provided a guarantee against judicial arbitrariness because it would at least be impossible for the judge to ground his decision on reasons which directly contradicted the minimum requirements of the legal rules. A second advantage lay in the fact that the legislator could work from a more elevated standpoint and could create the rules with more composure and precision than the criminal judge working from the individual case. Thus, Weiland presented his theoretical argumentation for the necessity of negative evidentiary rules. Although he did not deem it possible to positively prescribe when sufficient evidence existed in the individual case, it was at least desirable to prescribe what grounds were generally insufficient. Like virtually all authors in the Netherlands who defended the necessity of evidentiary rules, Weiland did not give a more concrete presentation of what rules he thought should be laid down in the criminal legislation. He merely argued in principal for their usefulness.[43]

Finally, it is important to note that Weiland did not argue against a jury system in general, but against the idea of the Prussian report that evidentiary rules were useless and that everything should, therefore, depend solely on the subjective internal conviction. In his view the English version of a jury system had clearly shown that a jury system could be combined with a system of evidentiary rules. He, for this reason, criticized the dichotomy which existed in the contemporary German discussion where it was assumed that a jury system and evidentiary rules were mutually exclusive. This was not the case and it was only derived from the wrongful understanding of the French revolutionaries of how the jury system should work.[44] Lastly, Weiland also presented an argumentation

---

42   Ibidem, pp. 44–63.
43   Ibidem, pp. 64–82.
44   Weiland also gave a long summary of the conclusions of Feuerbach in his work *Öffentlichkeit und Mundlichkeit*, which showed that (negative) evidentiary rules could be combined with a jury system. In a footnote he, nevertheless, blamed Feuerbach for having contributed to the confusion and wrong dichotomy in the German discussion through his earlier work *Betrachtungen über das Geschwornen-Gericht*. In his argumentation against the jury system Feuerbach, who at this time still had too little knowledge of the English jury system, generalized too strongly from the French version of the jury system and appeared to argue that a jury system was principally incompatible with evidentiary rules. See J.A. Weiland, *Bijdragen tot de wetenschap der Strafregtspleging*, pp. 78–117.

against extraordinary punishments and for the necessity of an absolute distinction between the verdicts of guilty and not-guilty in his last chapter.[45]

9.2.1.2.3 Proponents of a Jury System

In addition to the influential work of Meyer there were only a few publications in the northern provinces which pleaded for the restoration of a jury system. There was, first of all, in 1824 one short statement in favour of a jury system from Van Hogendorp who had been one of the key figures in the creation of the Kingdom of the Netherlands and who was the main author of the constitution of 1815. After disagreements between Van Hogendorp and King William I he had eventually become one of the most critical members of parliament. He published his critical observations on how the government functioned in large volumes which focused predominantly on the economic policy of the kingdom. In one volume Van Hogendorp stated that the opinions still seemed to be divided on the subject of the jury system. However, for him experience was a deciding factor and he remarked that the experience in England and the Prussian territories seemed to speak in favour of the jury system. Furthermore, Van Hogendorp was in favour of a jury system because he thought it could make the people more acquainted with the laws and more interested in public affairs. The largest obstacle Van Hogendorp saw, was that the jury system was foreign, complex and unknown. This could, nevertheless, be overcome after a few years of experience with the institution.[46]

---

45 Ibidem, pp. 78–140. A last work which was partly in favour of a negative system of legal proofs, was a commentary on the concept criminal procedural code by J.J. Uijtwerf Sterling, F.A. van Hall, J. van Hall and C.A. Den Tex. The first two were lawyers and the latter two were professors of law, all from Amsterdam. In their discussion of the criminal law of evidence they declared that they were all against a jury system, and for their argumentation they referred to the article by Den Tex which has been described earlier in this section. Regarding the necessity of legal evidentiary rules, it was stated that the authors were divided on this subject. Even though it was not specified which of the authors were for or against evidentiary rules, from his earlier article it is apparent that Den Tex was one of the authors who argued in favour of a free evaluation of the evidence. The authors only differed of opinion on the question whether the evidentiary theory should be left to the legal science or whether it was useful to put some minimum evidentiary rules in the criminal legislation. It was stated in the treatise that the authors did agree on the fact that in any case almost everything unavoidably needed to be left to the internal conviction of the judge. These points of view were not substantiated by any further argumentation. See J.J. Uijtwerf Sterling, F.A. van Hall, C.A. Den Tex and J. van Hall, *Aanmerkingen op het ontwerp van het Wetboek van Strafvordering*, pp. 416–427.

46 G.K. van Hogendorp, *Bijdragen tot de Huishouding van Staat in het Koningrijk der Nederlanden*, vol. 8, pp. 75–76. Although the argumentation was short, the fact that Van Hogendorp made a statement in favour of the jury system was significant in itself. During the later

In the period from 1826 until 1830 there were also two important 'liberal' magazines which pleaded for the introduction of a jury system: *De Weegschaal* and *De Bijenkorf*. Two articles were published anonymously in *De Weegschaal* in 1827. Judging by the difference in style, depth of juridical knowledge and focus in argumentation they were written by two different authors. Although it is unknown who wrote the articles for this magazine, most contributions came from the journalist d'Engelbronner. He edited the magazine and determined its political direction. *De Weegschaal* was one of the most government-critical magazines in the northern provinces, for which d'Engelbronner had at one time even been given a prison sentence and a public whipping.[47]

The first article in *De Weegschaal* was brief and quite superficially argued in favour of a jury system for the reason that it offered greater guarantees for the accused. It presumed without any further argumentation that the question of fact and the question of law could be separated. The article remarked that it creates a too great concentration of power when the decisions on the guilt of the accused and on the punishment are combined in the hands of the criminal judge. In the article it was stated, furthermore, that only the people had the right to decide on the question of fact and that a greater impartiality could be expected from lay jurors than from professional judges.[48] In this article the juridical-technical arguments were bypassed completely and the argumentation was predominantly of a political-constitutional nature.

The second article consisted of a critical evaluation of the work by Donker Curtius (who had pleaded for a negative system of legal proofs). The author was in favour of a jury system which he called 'that invaluable palladium of civil liberty'. He was convinced that it offered strong guarantees against judicial arbitrariness when the decision on the question of fact was separated from the decision on the question of law. The author, nevertheless, focused first and foremost on arguing that evidentiary rules were useless in general and that he even preferred professional judges to decide after their freely formed internal conviction. He stated that it was entirely impossible to prescribe the value of different forms of evidence and that the recent past had shown that these rules could be missed without negative consequences. He deplored the many unjust convictions which had occurred under the use of artificial divisions of evidence

---

parliamentary debates, when the constitutionality of the jury system was discussed, the fact that the principal author of the constitution was in favour of its restoration was used as an argument for the jury system. On Van Hogendorp see N. van Sas, *De metamorfose van Nederland*, pp. 424–427.

47   J. van Zanten, *Schielijk, Winzucht, Zwaarhoofd en Bedaard. Politieke discussie en oppositievorming 1813–1840*, pp. 109–123.

48   *De weegschaal*, 1827, "Iets over de gezworenen, of de jury", pp. 287–290.

in quarter, half and full proofs. Furthermore, he argued that the idea of a negative system of legal proofs was a *contradictio in termini*. How and when an internal conviction should develop could not, in his opinion, be prescribed in evidentiary rules. Not even in negative rules.[49]

The magazine *De Bijenkorf* was also in favour of a jury system. It was created in 1828 and formed the most liberal and progressive magazine in the northern provinces. The authors of the magazine proclaimed to follow the ideas of, among others, Royer-Collard and Guizot, and pleaded for an array of constitutional reforms such as the introduction of ministerial responsibility and freedom of the press.[50] Although the magazine was published anonymously, Van Zanten states that several young jurists were behind the magazine while Meyer most likely played a role in the background. In an article in 1829 there was an explicit call for the restoration of the jury system.[51]

9.2.1.2.4 *Conclusion*

There are several important conclusions which can be drawn from the discussion in the literature in the northern provinces between 1813 and 1830. First of all, it is remarkable how quickly the idea gained ground that legal evidentiary rules were either useless or could only have a negative role to play because in the end the evaluation still needed to be left to the internal conviction of the judge. Between 1795 and 1813 the idea of completely abolishing the evidentiary rules had not even been contemplated and there was a general consensus that at least some negative evidentiary rules should bind the decision of the judge. Although a large majority of the authors in the northern provinces were against a jury system, the theoretical criticisms of the French reformers and the Prussian report concerning the usefulness and plausibility of evidentiary rules seeped

---

49   *De weegschaal*, 1827, "Het ontwerp van het strafwetboek voor de *Nederlanden*, en het *Iets van den heer Mr. W.B. Donker Curtius*, over dit onderwerp, kort en bescheiden overwogen", pp. 549–596.
50   N.C.F. van Sas, "Het politiek klimaat in Noord-Nederland tijdens de crisis van het Verenigd Koninkrijk, 1828–1830", pp. 105–113.
51   J. van Zanten, *Schielijk, Winzucht, Zwaarhoofd en Bedaard. Politieke discussie en oppositievorming 1813–1840*, pp. 218–224 and 265–266. Another author who stated that he was in favour of a jury system was J.H. Sassen, a lawyer from 's-Hertogenbosch. He published an anonymous letter in 1829 in which he evaluated the concept criminal procedural code. Sassen found that too much of the repressive Napoleonic criminal procedural system had been retained and that the design offered too little guarantees for civil liberty. In this letter he noted in passing by that he regretted the fact that there was no jury system, which he considered 'the only guarantee and palladium of all civil liberties'. He did not present any further arguments in favour of a jury system. See J.H. Sassen, *Brieven over het ontwerp van wetboek van Straf-vordering*, pp. 1–5.

into the Dutch discussion within a short time span. In particular the argumentation by Meyer and the Prussian committee spread the ideas of the French reformers and these were accepted to a relatively large extent. Nevertheless, an important part of the Dutch authors thought that Meyer and the Prussian committee went too far in their criticisms and that at least some evidentiary rules could and should be made to negatively bind the judge. Furthermore, they did not accept the idea of an almost 'instinctively' formed *conviction intime* and that common sense sufficed to judge on the question of fact. Instead, the emphasis was placed on the fact that experience and juridical knowledge were necessary, and that the internal conviction needed to be the result of a rational analysis of the evidence.

A second conclusion that can be drawn, is that there were important differences between the discussion in the juridical literature in the northern provinces and the contemporary debate in Germany. Even though there was a large influence from the German discussion – in particular of the Prussian committee, Feuerbach, Jarcke and Mittermaier –, the highly dichotomized and dogmatic discussion in the German territories was rejected in the northern provinces. While in the German territories the discussion was dominated for a long time by the idea that the free evaluation of the evidence and the public, oral trial were necessarily tied up with a jury system (which was juxtaposed with professional judges who had to be bound by a system of legal proofs), this dichotomous view was not accepted in the northern provinces. Most authors in the northern provinces were strongly in favour of a public, oral trial with a public prosecutor, but rejected a jury system and explicitly stated that there was no reason why these procedural innovations could not function with a system based on professional judges. One obvious reason which most likely contributed to the acceptance of these innovations was the fact that, unlike a large part of the German states, the northern provinces had concrete experience with these changes because the *Code d'Instruction Criminelle* had remained in force.[52] In the Netherlands the actual practice in this period was that professional judges freely evaluated the evidence after a public and oral trial, which showed that these reforms were in fact compatibel with a system based on professional judges. A second reason lay in the fact that in the northern provinces a more 'pragmatic' approach dominated the discussion.

The difference between the German discussion and the discussion in the northern provinces was, furthermore, intimately connected with the level of

---

52   Within the German territories this effect was visible as well. The Prussian Rhine provinces and the other provinces who had been under French control were more strongly in favour of a public, oral trial with a public prosecutor than other parts of Germany.

trust in the professional magistrates. In Germany the remaining secret, inquisitorial procedure had created a strong sense of distrust among a large group of authors which radicalized their demand for a complete overhaul of the existing criminal procedural law, and consequently, for a jury system (as had been the case in Revolutionary France). In the northern provinces, on the other hand, there was a high level of trust in the professional judges, at least among those who published on the subject (who were almost all professional jurists themselves). In the less dichotomized discussion in the northern provinces it was easier for most authors to be in favour of innovations such as the public, oral trial, while still rejecting the jury system. Within the context of the kingdom of the Netherlands as a whole, however, there was a more similar schism and dichotomy between the southern and the northern provinces as could be seen within the German territories. As will be discussed in the following subsection, in the southern provinces a strong distrust of the professional judges had grown and even important innovations such as the publicity and orality of the trial would not placate many of the liberals here. They overwhelmingly called for a jury system.

9.2.2   The Discussion in the Southern Netherlands 1814–1830

The first few years after the creation of the United Kingdom almost no publication appeared which reflected on the criminal law of evidence or the jury system in the southern provinces. In 1819 and 1820 the interest in the jury system was ignited in the southern provinces by the fact that an intense discussion started in France over the question whether press offences should be brought under the jurisdiction of the courts of assizes with a jury system. After the fall of Napoleon, the jury system had remained in place in France but because most press offences were misdemeanours they fell under the jurisdiction of professional judges in the correctional courts. Influential French liberal writers such as Constant published a number of treatises and articles pleading for a jury trial in press offences. They argued that this would increase the freedom of the press which they considered of vital importance because they saw the political journalists as the watchdogs of the constitutional monarchy.[53] Furthermore, they stressed that a jury would consist of citizens who were better acquainted with public opinion and were, therefore, in a better position to judge press offences than professional judges. When the French liberals acquired a

---

53   On the importance of the freedom of the press and the role of the jury system in the ideas of Constant see, for example, B. Fontana, *Benjamin Constant and the post-revolutionary mind*, pp. 81–97.

greater representation in parliament in 1819 they managed to create a new law which brought the press offences under the jurisdiction of jury courts.[54]

The intense discussions about the jury system and its role in press offences in France created a greater interest on this subject in the southern provinces. It was a significant fact that the interest in the southern provinces in the jury system was aroused by a debate taking place within the highly politicized context in France. Here the focus of the discussion did not lie on the technical-juridical aspects of the role of the jury system. The question, for example, whether jurors were suited to decide on the question of fact did not play a prominent role. The emphasis lay on the political-constitutional aspect. Especially on the role of the jury in guaranteeing the greatest possible freedom of the press and the central role that the freedom of the press played in a constitutional monarchy to combat arbitrariness and despotism from the government. The discussion about the jury system in the southern provinces, therefore, did not emerge in a largely academic atmosphere as had occurred in the north, but was taken up predominantly by politicians and journalists.[55]

The politicians and journalists in the southern provinces were inspired by the French liberal writers and popularized their ideas among a larger public in the southern provinces. The desire for the introduction of a jury system was normally not dealt with in isolation but was part and parcel of a broader package of political reforms. These reforms included a greater freedom of speech and of religion, more openness and accountability from the government and, among other things, the introduction of ministerial responsibility which would strengthen the role of parliament. Until around 1826, the opposition against the regime of William I in the southern provinces was still relatively mild and the call for the introduction of a jury system came predominantly from a select group of liberal political journalists. This situation changed, however, between 1826 and 1830. As the opposition grew stronger and the criticisms from both the liberal and Catholic side sharpened, the demand for a jury system became

---

54   B. Delbecke, "<<Le fruit du terroir?>>. The Debate on Trial by Jury in the United Kingdom of the Netherlands (1814-1830)", pp. 97-100. Even after the promulgation of this new law, the question whether press offences should be tried by jury courts remained an important point of debate in France in the 1820s. In reaction to the assassination of the Duke of Berry in 1822 the French government clamped down on acts of political criticism and again made professional magistrates competent to judge on press offences in a decree on 25 March. This ensured that the question of trying press offences by a jury system remained an important point of discussion in France and also of enduring interest in the southern provinces.

55   Ibidem, p. 100.

more prominent and gained a larger popular support. In this more hostile climate the government reacted with increasing repression which led to an escalating dialectic of protest and repression. Under the policy of the Minister of Justice Van Maanen, journalists who criticized the government too strongly were given severe prison sentences, while consequently the clamour for reforms became louder.[56] In the opinion of the southern liberals, the absolutist behaviour of the government and the harsh repressions of the freedom of the press clearly showed the validity of their ideas and the necessity of better guarantees for the freedom of the press. The ideas of authors such as Constant and Guizot seemed to apply perfectly to their situation within the Kingdom of the Netherlands.

One of the first to demand the introduction of the jury system was Van der Straeten in 1819, in a very government-critical publication. In his treatise he pleaded for the introduction of the jury system and ministerial responsibility. He argued that a jury system was advantageous for the judges as well as for the accused. It was advantageous for the judges, because in the possible situation where they were pressured by the government to convict someone they deemed innocent, they would be saved from any embarrassment or risk for their position as they were not responsible for the judgment. Although Van der Straeten presented no arguments for this claim, it is obvious from his treatise that he deemed that jurors would be far more impartial and independent than professional judges. Significantly, the main object against which his distrust was directed was not the king himself, but 'ministers and powerful men' who might seek to influence the judges: "En un mot, le jury est le rampart inexpugnable de l'innocent; car il le met à l'abri de la tyrannie des ministres et des attaques de l'homme puissant, injuste et oppresseur".[57] Van der Straeten acquired a martyr-status in the southern provinces after he was sentenced to a two year imprisonment for his publications. When he later suddenly died in 1823 after his release from prison, people spoke of an *assasinat juridique*.[58]

Particularly between 1826 and 1830 the opposition in the southern provinces became fiercer and the call for the introduction of a jury system louder. This was partly due to a new generation of young, liberal lawyers who joined the editorial boards of influential political newspapers such as the *Courrier des Pays-Bas, Le Politique* and *Courrier de la Meuse*. The new generation had grown up in an upper class urban milieu which was at the time strongly orientated

---

56   B. Delbecke, *De lange schaduw van de grondwetgever*, pp. 28–38.
57   F. van der Straeten, *De l'Etat actuel du Royaume et des moyens de l'améliorer,* 1819 vol. 2, pp. 18–32.
58   B. Delbecke, *De lange schaduw van de grondwetgever*, pp. 24–25.

towards the political discussions taking place in France. The young intellectuals were versed and educated at the universities of Gent, Louvain and Liège where a strong interest had grown in the liberal constitutional ideals coming from France. The influence this education had on an enthusiastic young generation can, for example, be seen in the recollections of the liberal Nothomb, who had studied in Liège: "L'indépendance des pouvoirs, la responsabilité ministérielle, les avantages du jury, les effets de la presse libre ... furent enseignés dans la chaire professionnelle, au pied de laquelle se pressait une jeunesse électrisée peu à peu par ce genre d'instruction".[59] The students were not only educated in the liberal constitutional ideas but also met in café's and societies discussing these ideas, creating an important network of friendships. This laid the foundation for a generation of young lawyers and journalists who would play a central role during the Belgian revolution and who would often occupy the most important governmental positions in the new Belgian state after 1830.[60]

Another young critical journalist educated at the university of Liège was Tielemans, who would play an important role during the Belgian revolution. In 1827 he published a sharp anonymous critique of the regulation of press offences in the concept criminal code. He particularly criticized the broad and vague formulations of press offences which potentially criminalized any publication that did not offer 'due respect' to government officials. In his introduction Tielemans explained why he deemed that the freedom of the press was of crucial importance in establishing civil liberty and in attaching the people to their nation and their government. Although he did not explicitly argue for a jury system, a remark in his introduction makes it clear that he deemed the constitutionally guaranteed independence of the judiciary a farce as long as the procedure was secret and there was no jury system: "Nos tribunaux sont indépendants, mais l'instruction des affaires, et l'audition de témoins sont secretes; de jury, point. Enfin, nous avons une foule d'autres droits précieux, dont

---

59   Ibidem, p. 47.
60   Ibidem, pp. 45–49. Delbecke remarks that it is hard to overestimate the influence of the French liberal writers on this generation of Belgian liberals. The influence of the French liberals can be clearly seen in the program of political reforms for which the Belgian liberals pleaded, and in the fact that they frequently cited Rémusat, Royer-Collard, Guizot, Chateaubriand and above all Constant as sources of authority. Revealing of this influence is, for example, a remark cited by Delbecke in the *Courrier des Pays-Bas* in 1829, stating that in the southern provinces for every ten liberals there were at least nine liberals *à la Benjamin Constant*.

l'exercice pourrait nous familiariser avec la liberté. Mais le peuple est l'objet, plutôt que le ressort du gouvernement".[61]

In the late 1820s, the *Courrier des Pays-Bas* became the leading journal of the liberal opposition in the southern provinces and attracted many young intellectuals who later played a prominent role during the revolution. One of the most influential journalists and editor of the *Courrier des Pays-Bas* was De Potter. An important moment in the escalation of the conflict between the government and the southern opposition occurred when De Potter anonymously published a highly critical open letter to the king in the *Courrier des Pays-Bas* on 8 November 1828. The immediate cause for the open letter was the conviction to prison sentences of Ducpétiaux, Jottrand and Claes who had too strongly criticized Van Maanen. De Potter stated in strong wordings that the Dutch government was failing because there was no jury system, no freedom of the press, no ministerial responsibility, no independent judiciary, an overbearing taxation and a badly functioning administration. On 15 November De Potter publicly acknowledged that he had written the open letter and was arrested. During the trial on 20 December 1828 before the court of assizes of Brabant, he defiantly held a long speech in which he repeated his main points of criticism. When he was convicted to a severe fine and a prison sentence the attendant people started to shout and stampede in protest, while later a crowd gathered before the courthouse which scanted "Long live De Potter! Down with Van Maanen!".[62]

The criticisms which De Potter presented and the criminal procedure which was conducted against him were representative of the growing tensions between the government and the opposition in the southern provinces. Far from scaring the political journalists into silence, the high-profile criminal procedures against journalists such as De Potter worked as catalysts which inflamed further opposition. Not long after the conviction of De Potter, the resilience of the political journalists was visible in, for example, an article in the *Courrier des Pays-Bas* on 7 January 1829 where a list of grievances was presented under the heading 'what the people want'. The article declared:

> Les garanties que la nation réclame maintenant avec force comme juste, sages et indispensable sont: la liberté de la presse ; l'émancipation de

---

[61] J-F. Tielemans, *Projet du Code Pénal, du Royaume des Pays-Bas. Délits de la presse*, pp. 5–26. See also B. Delbecke, *De lange schaduw van de grondwetgever*, pp. 32–33. Very telling for his approach was the motto which Tielemans presented on the first page of his publication: "Toute loi, qui ne suppose pas l'homme bon et le magistrat méchant, est une mauvaise loi".

[62] B. Delbecke, *De lange schaduw van de grondwetgever*, pp. 34–36.

l'enseignement public; le jury; une bonne organisation judiciaire; une code pénal et une code d'instruction criminelle, plus doux, plus humains, moins dangereux pour la vie, l'honneur, la fortune et la liberté des citoyens ... elle demande le jury parce qu'alors les conspirations facties sont impossibles, les prétendus crimes politique jugés par ceux qui peut le mieux les apprécier.[63]

The opposition in the southern provinces was strengthened when the Catholics decided to join forces with the liberals from around 1827 onwards. This cooperation became known as the 'monstrous alliance' because until then liberals and Catholics had normally opposed each other. The increased willingness of the Catholic side to work together with the liberals was influenced by the ideas of the French liberal priest De Lamennais who argued that an extensive protection of civil liberties was the best instrument to support the restoration of a truly Catholic society. In this vein the Catholics in the southern provinces now also started to support the introduction of a jury system. Throughout the period of 1814 until 1830 there had been persecutions of Catholic priests for their criticisms of the government. It was realized that a panel of jurors in the southern provinces, made up predominantly of Catholics, would not be so hasty in convicting Catholic officials. The jury system was embraced by the Catholic side as an effective instrument to preserve their freedom of speech.[64] The turnaround from the Catholic side can be seen clearly in a number of articles devoted to the jury system in 1827 in *Le Catholique des Pays-bas*, one of the leading Catholic journals in the southern provinces. The journal presented a description of the historical development of the jury system in three separate articles and described the institution in highly positive terms as a safeguard of civil liberty.[65]

The broad support for the program of political reform which authors such as De Potter presented also became visible in the presentation of hundreds of

---

63 Courrier des Pays-Bas, January 7, 1829. See also B. Delbecke, "<<Le fruit du terroir?>>. The Debate on Trial by Jury in the United Kingdom of the Netherlands (1814–1831)", pp. 107–108. De Potter himself was not scared into submission either and continued to publish highly critical articles from his prison cell in December 1829. This led to another criminal procedure against him in 1830 which again attracted nationwide attention. De Potter and his 'conspirators' Tielemans and De Nève were convicted to respectively eight, seven and five years of banishment from the United Kingdom of the Netherlands this time. See B. Delbecke, *De lange schaduw van de grondwetgever*, pp. 41–42.
64 B. Delbecke, "<<Le fruit du terroir?>>. The Debate on Trial by Jury in the United Kingdom of the Netherlands (1814–1831)", p. 108.
65 Le Catholique des Pays-Bas, July 18 1827, July 19 1827 and July 26 1827.

petitions to the lower house of parliament from the southern provinces between November 1828 and May 1829, similar to the *cahiers de doléances* which had been presented before the French Revolution. The most important demands were freedom of education, freedom of the press, restoration of the jury trial and the independence of the judiciary. Of the total number of petitions a hundred and sixty-three petitions explicitly called for the restoration of the jury system. Such a massive movement of protest and extensive use of the right to petition had not occurred in the Netherlands until this time. As a reaction to the petitions the government hastened to present a new design for a law regulating press offences on 22 December 1828. Although the law was approved by parliament, it remained very strict in its punishments and vague in the description of the offences. The law was, therefore, received with strong criticism in the south and quickly became known as the *loi du mutisme*. The opposition from the south proved so strong that the government saw itself forced to present a more lenient proposal which was approved on 16 May in 1829.[66]

9.2.2.1 Conclusion

The examples of authors from the southern provinces declaring themselves in favour of the introduction of a jury system to increase the impartiality of the courts and to enlarge the freedom of the press which have been discussed in this subsection, can be multiplied manifold. Delbecke accurately points out the difference between the publications in the northern and the southern provinces when he remarks that: "the comments seem to have been less well developed than in the North, [but] their frequency was much higher".[67] Although the number of publications in favour of a jury system was far higher, from a juridical-technical point of view, the argumentation was less well developed. Most often the publications from the southern provinces which advocated a jury system did not engage with the juridical-technical arguments against this institution which could typically be found in publications from authors of the northern provinces. They normally did not, for example, give a more elaborate argumentation to defend the idea that the question of fact and of law could be separated. The articles also did not present a deeper argumentation against the usefulness of evidentiary rules. In as far as these difficult

---

66   B. Delbecke, *De lange schaduw van de grondwetgever*, pp. 35–37. The demand for political reforms was, furthermore, supported by the *associations constitutionelles* which emerged in 1829 and 1830. See A. Smits, *1830, Scheuring in de Nederlanden*, pp. 56–58.
67   B. Delbecke, "<<Le fruit du terroir?>>. The Debate on Trial by Jury in the United Kingdom of the Netherlands (1814–1831)", p. 107.

points were touched upon, the ideas on these matters of the French revolutionaries and, for example, Meyer were followed.

In the publications from the southern provinces it is often stated more as a matter of fact that common sense suffices to judge on the question of fact and that it is impossible to create useful evidentiary rules. It is not surprising that these matters were given relatively little attention in the southern provinces because most of the publications consisted of rather short articles in newspapers and were intended for a broad public. Furthermore, and perhaps more importantly, the difficulties attached to the jury system were considered of minor significance in comparison to the far more important objectives of a greater freedom of the press and a more impartial judgement in criminal cases. Most authors from the southern provinces approached the subject of the jury system and of the criminal law of evidence from an entirely different perspective and with different priorities than authors from the northern provinces.

A key element underlying these different approaches lay in the fact that in the north there was a high level of trust in the professional judiciary while this was not the case in the southern provinces. In the publications from the southern provinces a constant and prominent concern can be found with the lack of independence of the judiciary and the perception of an overbearing control of 'the ministers'. Although he is often not directly mentioned, it is clear that most authors were thinking of the Minister of Justice Van Maanen who came to be regarded in the southern provinces as the quintessential despotic bogeyman. This concern with the lack of independence of the judiciary and a too strong power of the ministers was largely absent in the writings of juridical authors from the northern provinces, just as in the publications from the southern provinces the aspect of the juridical-technical arguments was largely absent.

Summarizing, in the southern provinces the question of the jury system and of the criminal law of evidence was placed firmly within the framework of a set of political-constitutional reforms, while in the north the subject was approached predominantly from a juridical-technical point of view. The consequence was that two largely different discourses developed which engaged only to a limited extent with the argumentation coming from either side. This relative lack of engagement is visible in the juridical treatises and newspaper articles discussed in this section and was to a certain extent also visible in the parliamentarian debates on the jury question in 1829, which is dealt with in the following section.

The two different approaches to the question of the jury system also formed part of a broader difference in 'political culture' between the northern and southern provinces at the time. Van Zanten stresses that there was a weariness in the northern provinces after 1814 about more divisive partisanship and political-constitutional experimentations. After 1814 there was a strong tendency to emphasize unity and harmoniously working together under the paternal governance of the king. There was a taboo on criticizing the government too harshly and too openly. The term 'public opinion' acquired a rather different connotation in the northern provinces than in the southern provinces at this time. The voicing of one's opinion was, of course, allowed but it was expected that this needed to happen in a constructive and harmonious way. The creation of an actual opposition against the policy of the government and the sowing of divisiveness was considered highly undesirable.[68]

The situation was different in the southern provinces where, under influence of the French liberal authors, a critical public opinion came to be seen as a necessary corrective against the power of the government, especially through a highly critical press which functioned as a political watchdog. The difference between the northern and the southern provinces, in this respect, can be seen in the fact that the severe prosecutions of political journalists did not lead to the strong sense of outrage in the northern provinces as it had done in southern provinces. The differences in political culture should, however, not be over exaggerated. There were groups in the northern provinces as well who sympathized with what were considered 'liberal' ideas, and who shared a large part of the political-constitutional desiderata of the southern provinces (such as ministerial responsibility and more openness by the government). Especially in the second half of the 1820s these groups became more vocal and the tone of the debate in the northern provinces as well became more critical.[69]

A good example of this was formed by the magazine *De Bijenkorf* from the northern provinces which argued in favour of ministerial responsibility and the introduction of a jury system, and explicitly advocated a closer cooperation between 'liberal' elements in the northern and southern provinces.[70] Nevertheless, although the differences should not be over exaggerated, there was a noticeably different idea of the role of public opinion and how the freedom of the press should be exercised.

---

[68] J. van Zanten, *Schielijk, Winzucht, Zwaarhoofd en Bedaard. Politieke discussie en oppositievorming 1813–1840*, pp. 48–52 and 105–114.

[69] In the northern provinces a new generation of young 'liberals' came to the fore in the second half of the 1820s who were dissatisfied with the existing political-constitutional system. See J. van Zanten, *Schielijk, Winzucht, Zwaarhoofd en Bedaard. Politieke discussie en oppositievorming 1813–1840*, pp. 217–234.

[70] N.C.F. van Sas, "Het politiek klimaat in Noord-Nederland tijdens de crisis van het Verenigd Koninkrijk, 1828–1830", pp. 103–113.

9.3 The Attempts to Create New Substantive and Procedural Criminal Codes 1813–1830

Soon after the liberation of the northern provinces from the Napoleonic regime it was decided that new 'national' codifications had to be made. This was prescribed in Article 100 of the constitution which was promulgated on 30 March 1814. On 18 April 1814 the king appointed a committee to create new codifications of the civil, criminal and commercial law and for the judicial organisation. Farjon, Byleveld, Van den Burgh and Philipse were the members of the committee entrusted with creating new civil and criminal procedural codes and a law on the judicial organisation. Within this group van den Burgh was responsible for the criminal procedural law. Philipse was appointed together with Kemper to create a code for the substantive criminal law. Already on 17 January 1815 the committee presented complete designs for the substantive and procedural criminal law.[71] The committee was able to present new concept codes so quickly because they consisted essentially of reworked versions of the designs of the substantive and procedural criminal law created in 1809 with only contained relatively minor modifications. For the criminal procedural law this would, for example, mean that the distinction between the ordinary and the extraordinary procedure would be reintroduced and that the publicity of the trial would remain severely restricted.[72]

Furthermore, in the design of 1815 the criminal law of evidence was again part of the substantive criminal code, in line with the criminal code of 1809. For the largest part it copied the regulation of the negative system of legal proofs which could be found in the twenty-ninth title of the criminal code of 1809. In the design of 1815 this now formed the seventh title of the first book (which contained the general part of the substantive criminal code). Apart from some new rules concerning witness testimony, the regulation of the different forms of evidence remained entirely the same.[73] One difference between the design of 1809 and 1815 was that the design of 1815 contained a new Article which stated more explicitly that no form of evidence could be sufficient unless the

---

[71] J.C. Voorduin, *Geschiedenis en beginselen der Nederlandsche wetboeken, Deel I algemeen deel*, pp. 1–26. The committee also presented a design for the commercial law, the judicial organisation and the civil procedural law, while only the substantive civil law had proven to be so complex that more time was required.

[72] J.C. Voorduin, *Geschiedenis en beginselen der Nederlandsche wetboeken, Deel VI, Wetboek van Strafvordering, 1ᵉ deel*, pp. III–IX.

[73] The concept code of 1815 can be found in *Algemeen Rijksarchief* (Den Haag), Archief Kemper-Cras, 2.21.098, nr. 33.

judge was entirely convinced that the accused was guilty. This article did not constitute a break with the design of 1809 but merely formed a more precise formulation of the fact that the internal conviction of the judge was required to convict someone.[74]

Summarizing, with the proposals of 1815 the committee intended to largely discard the existing French legislation and return almost completely to the codes of the substantive and procedural criminal law of 1809. The situation changed, however, after the unification of the southern and northern provinces. On 5 September 1815 the king instituted a committee of three representatives from the southern provinces with the task of evaluating the designs of the substantive and procedural criminal law. The representatives were Kersmaker, Willems and Calmyn, who were all judges in the high court of Brussels. On 29 November 1815 this committee presented a critical report. Above all the committee argued against the secret procedure and in favour of a public, oral trial. The committee stated that in the southern provinces a whole generation had grown up with the French legislation and had learned to appreciate several important advantages which this legislation had provided, in particular the public, oral trial. It becomes clear from the report that the committee preferred a reform of the French procedural legislation over a code based on the old Dutch criminal law. The committee, however, delivered almost no critique of the chapter regulating the criminal law of evidence. Significantly, the committee from the southern provinces did not criticize the principle of the proposed negative system of proofs and did not call for the restoration of a jury system.[75]

As a consequence of the critical report, new committees were formed which needed to rework the concept criminal codes taking into account the earlier criticisms of the committee from the southern provinces. The new committee responsible for the code of substantive criminal law consisted of Lammens, Kemper, Raoux and Membrède, who were also responsible for reforming the substantive civil code. They eventually revised the substantive criminal code

---

74 J.C. Voorduin, *Geschiedenis en beginselen der Nederlandsche wetboeken, Deel VI, Wetboek van Strafvordering, 2ᵉ deel*, pp. 614–615. Another new Article dictated that every form of evidence could be disproven by counterevidence. This article was also not intended as a substantive deviation from the design of 1809, but only formed an additional clarification.

75 The report can be found in *Algemeen Rijksarchief* (Den Haag), Archief Kemper-Cras, 2.21.098, nr. 34.

between 13 November and 29 December in 1826, after which the concept code was sent to parliament for discussion on 23 April 1827.[76]

The new committee for the reform of the criminal procedural code was appointed on 21 November 1816. It consisted of Kemper, Van Gennep, Philipse and Farjon. They presented their first new design on 6 February 1819. This design made only few concessions to the criticisms of the committee of the southern provinces and was again essentially the same as the design of 1809. The design was, for this reason, never presented to the Dutch parliament for approval. It was clear that the attachment to the French criminal procedural law was too strong and that there would be too much resistance against the idea of returning to the old procedural law of the Dutch Republic. A new committee was then formed with the task of reforming the *Code d'Instruction Criminelle* and to combine it with the useful procedural institutions of the old Dutch law. The new concept criminal procedural code created by this committee was presented for discussion in parliament on 23 October 1828 and strongly resembled the French procedural code.[77]

9.3.1 *The Parliamentarian Discussion on the Substantive Criminal Code 1827–1828*

The concept code of substantive criminal law was discussed in parliament between October 1827 and March 1828. The title regulating the criminal law of evidence in the design of 1815 – which was almost the same as that of the criminal code of 1809 – had remained virtually unchanged in the concept code offered to parliament in 1827. Nevertheless, there appear to have been doubts on the side of the government whether the criminal law of evidence should be regulated in the substantive criminal code or in the procedural code. In a special memorandum accompanying the concept code the government asked thirty-four questions to parliament of which the second question was whether the criminal law of evidence should be part of the procedural or the substantive code. The question whether it was desirable at all to regulate the criminal law of evidence in a negative system of legal proofs was not asked, this appears to have been presupposed by the government.[78]

---

76 F. Steven, "La codification penale en Belgique. Heritage Français et debats Neerlandais (1781–1867)", pp. 296–297.
77 J.C. Voorduin, *Geschiedenis en beginselen der Nederlandsche wetboeken, Deel VI, Wetboek van Strafvordering, 1ᵉ deel*, pp. IV–XII and J. de bosch Kemper, *Wetboek van Strafvordering, naar deszelfs beginselen ontwikkeld, deel 1*, pp. CXLI–CXLII.
78 J.J.F. Noordziek, *Geschiedenis der beraadslagingen gevoerd in de tweede kamer der Staten-Generaal over het ontwerp Wetboek van Strafregt van 1827*, pp. 1–28.

The parliamentarians were generally divided in seven sections in which they evaluated the legislative proposals. They presented their criticisms as a section and mentioned how many parliamentarians within the group were for or against a certain proposal. In response to the question of the government, a majority of the sections in parliament declared that the substantive criminal code should only describe the various crimes and their punishments and that the criminal law of evidence should, therefore, not be part of the substantive but of the procedural code. There was, nevertheless, also a significant number of parliamentarians who preferred to retain the title in the substantive criminal code. The latter group argued that the substantive criminal law should regulate what elements constituted a crime and for this reason should also contain the evidentiary rules.[79]

In reaction to the parliamentarian majority who wanted to transplant the criminal law of evidence to the procedural code, the government at first responded negatively. In a memorandum on 25 February 1828, the Minister of Justice stated that he considered the place of the title in either the substantive or procedural code of minor importance. In foreign codes examples of both systems could be found. Despite its minor importance, the government preferred to retain the title in the substantive criminal code because the civil law of evidence was also regulated in the substantive civil law and this would, therefore, be more consistent.[80] In March 1828, however, the government decided to follow the opinion of the majority in parliament and transplanted the regulation of the criminal law of evidence to the criminal procedural code. The most important reason for this change of heart lay in the fact that it had become clear to the government that there was too much resistance against the substantive criminal code – predominantly because of the way it regulated press offenses – and that it was not going to be accepted. Thus, the government retracted their concept substantive criminal code and at the same placed the title regulating the criminal law of evidence in the concept criminal procedural code.[81]

In the period between October 1827 and March 1828 the merits of the proposed negative system of legal proofs remained almost entirely undiscussed.

---

79   Ibidem, pp. 1–28. 58–59, 99, 112, 140,154–155.
80   Ibidem, pp. 163–168.
81   J.C. Voorduin, *Geschiedenis en beginselen der Nederlandsche wetboeken, Deel VI, Wetboek van Strafvordering, 2ᵉ deel*, pp. 617–621.

Most parliamentarians did not want to discuss this topic until the title was placed in the criminal procedural code. Only a very brief discussion was held on the question whether convictions should be allowed on the basis of indicia. Several sections declared that they were against convictions on the basis of mere indicia or suspicions and several declared that they were in favour of this option. Only the parliamentarians Donker Curtius and De Secus presented, separate, more elaborate notes on whether they deemed that convictions should be possible on the basis of indicia. Donker Curtius stated that he agreed with the proposed negative system of legal proofs, but that he wanted an explicit prohibition of convicting on the basis of one indicium alone. He argued that indicia could only suffice when they were supported by another form of evidence. De Secus, who was in favour of allowing convictions on indicia, remarked that in many criminal cases indicia were the only form of evidence available and indispensable for an effective repression of crimes. Furthermore, the direct forms of evidence such as witness testimony could often be more uncertain than a combination of indicia.[82]

The government reacted in a memorandum and stated that it agreed with De Secus. If it was not possible to convict on the basis of strong and mutually supporting indicia then many crimes would go unpunished. Furthermore, the government observed that there seemed to be some confusion among the parliamentarians who thought that the proposed legislation allowed convictions on simple presumptions or suspicions. The government then stated that the legislation did not allow convictions on a mere 'moral conviction', but that the indicia needed to be correctly proven themselves and should not be seen as simple presumptions. As becomes clear from the concept code, the phrase 'correctly proven' meant that indicia could not be proven by indicia themselves but had to be proven by, for example, the testimony of two witnesses.[83] This explanation by the government, that convictions were not possible on mere suspicions, appears to have worked reassuringly on the parliamentarians. The interest in the subject subsided and was not raised against during the later parliamentarian discussions.

---

82   J.J.F. Noordziek, *Geschiedenis der beraadslagingen gevoerd in de tweede kamer der Staten-Generaal over het ontwerp Wetboek van Strafregt van 1827*, pp. 2–26, 53–55, 90, 108, 133,150 and 161.

83   J.C. Voorduin, *Geschiedenis en beginselen der Nederlandsche wetboeken, Deel VI, Wetboek van Strafvordering, 2ᵉ deel*, pp. 656–662.

9.3.2 *The Discussion on the Desirability of a Jury System 1828–1830*

After the discussion on the correct place for the criminal law of evidence, title seven of the general part of the substantive criminal code became title twenty of the concept criminal procedural code. The title in the concept procedural code of 1828 contained several slight changes in formulation and a number of explanatory Articles were removed, but it remained essentially the same as the title in the concept substantive criminal code of 1827. The concept procedural code was discussed in two parliamentarian terms between October 1828 and March 1830. During the first term, between October 1828 and March 1829, the title itself attracted only relatively minor criticisms. However, very importantly, several sections declared that they wanted to have a plenary debate on the question whether a jury system should be introduced. On 16 March 1829 Reyphins, the president of the lower house, accepted the proposal to have such a debate. After some further deliberations, three questions were formulated which would be discussed during this debate. The first question was: shall a jury system be introduced for criminal cases in the provincial courts and other criminal courts. The second question was: shall a jury system be introduced for press offences. The last question was whether a *jury d'accusation* should be introduced next to a *jury de jugement*.[84] As explained in Chapter four, the accusation jury made the preliminary decision whether the evidence was sufficiently strong to proceed to a trial before the criminal tribunal. It was an extra safety valve to prevent unjustified prosecutions.

In light of the popular demand for a jury system in the southern provinces, the debate on the jury system was a highly politicized discussion. The parliamentary debate lasted three days starting on 9 April 1829 and ending on 11 April. Schooneveld, from the northern provinces, was the first to speak, and opened with the remark that he found it difficult to debate the proposed questions because they were posed abstractly without any concrete proposal of how the jury system should function. Was it, for example, intended that the English or French model would be followed, or was it the intention to create something completely new. He then stated that although the jury system is normally described as the most liberal institution and the essence of a representative government, he himself deemed good professional judges a far more liberal institution and a better safeguard for the citizens than a jury system.[85]

---

84   Ibidem, pp. 319 and 492–507.
85   J.J.F. Noordziek, *Geschiedenis der beraadslagingen gevoerd in de tweede kamer der Staten-Generaal over het ontwerp Wetboek van Strafvordering en het vraagstuk der jury 1828–1829*, deel I, pp. 36.

Schooneveld stated that he thought that the two most important objections against a system of professional judges were that they could be influenced by the government and that the risk existed that criminal judges could become too harsh due to continually judging criminal cases. The first problem, he thought was largely abetted by guarantees for an independent judiciary in the constitution. Judges were appointed for life and they were chosen on the proposition of the provincial or national representative institutions. These constitutional guarantees made the judges largely independent of the administrative power. Furthermore, one had to remember that a perfect system did not exist and that jurors could also be influenced. Concerning the second objection, Schooneveld remarked that a first remedy against this possible effect lay in the fact that judges were appointed to decide in criminal as well as civil cases to make sure that they were not hardened by judging criminal cases alone. Secondly, the concept ordinance created a public trial and a large room for the accused to defend himself which introduced further guarantees. Lastly, even if one judge might be too harsh in his judgement, in every case at least five out of seven judges were needed to declare someone guilty, and there was a possibility of cassation. The combination of these guarantees were, according to Schooneveld, more than sufficient to take away the possible objections against professional judges.[86]

The main reason why Schooneveld was against the jury system, however, was that he did not believe that the question of fact could be separated from the question of law. When jurors were asked if the accused was guilty of a crime, they did not only decide whether a certain fact had taken place but they also had to decide on the culpability of the accused. This question, he stated, was so difficult that it could only be answered after years of training and a profound understanding of the principles of the criminal law and the workings of the human psyche. Not only the difficult question of the imputation would have to be entrusted to lay jurors, but also the juridical qualification of the facts. Schooneveld did not think that lay persons could adequately perform these tasks, not even if the criminal laws were clear and simple. Furthermore, because lay jurors did not have the necessary experience or knowledge they would be too dependent on the president of the court who could influence them through his questions and summaries of the discussions. In this way it would often be one judge who had a decisive influence in the criminal cases.[87] Schooneveld, like many authors from the northern provinces, therefore, followed the idea of Feuerbach that the questions of law and of fact could

---

86 Ibidem, pp. 7–9.
87 Ibidem, pp. 9–15.

not be separated, while the proponents of a jury deemed that this was possible. It was one the most important arguments that was frequently presented by the opponents of a jury system to show that legal training was necessary to decide in criminal cases and that lay jurors were not qualified for this task.

In his conclusion Schooneveld stated that the jury system could be analysed from a juridical and from a constitutional perspective. He had already shown that from a juridical perspective professional judges were preferable. He then continued to explain that he was also not convinced that the jury system was desirable in the Netherlands from a constitutional perspective. Reacting against the idea that a jury system would create a greater unity in the public spirit and would bring the northern and the southern provinces closer together he stated: "je crois au contraire que, puisque tout jury ne s'exerce que dans des localités restreintes, cette institution formerait plutôt un esprit de parti dangereux".[88] The differences in religion and local customs could have a dangerous effect on the impartiality of jurors, while on the other hand professional judges were in his view better suited to strictly and impartially follow the law. Schooneveld also argued that a jury system ran against the spirit and the letter of the constitution. In line with the treatise of Van der Meer Mohr, he stated that it was not in accordance with the spirit of the constitution because the creators of the constitution had not intended to introduce a jury system and never even spoke about the institution. Secondly, Article 186 of the constitution stated that the members of provincial courts would be appointed for life. Since obviously jurors would have to judge in criminal cases and would not be appointed for life, they could not be part of the provincial courts.[89]

The second speaker was De Secus from the southern provinces who was in favour of a *jury d'accusation* for press offences and political crimes. For normal crimes he deemed that the jury was dispensable. With murder and theft, for example, the immorality of the act and the definition of the crime was more straightforward and the judge or jurors would merely have to decide whether the facts were proven. In case of political crimes and press offences, however, the definitions of the crimes were necessarily very vague and malleable. This was especially dangerous because those responsible for repressing these crimes were also often the ones against whom the press offences or

---

88 Ibidem, p. 16.
89 Ibidem, pp. 15–22. In the end Schooneveld remarked that he would not mind to temporarily institute a jury system for press offences, because this would show all the proponents that the jury system was far less liberal and ideal as they seemed to think. He was also of the opinion that the freedom of the press to criticize the government should be large, but that he did not believe that the calls for the jury system in the newspapers was representative for what the majority of the people in the Netherlands wanted.

political crimes were directed. A *jury d'accusation* would form a bulwark against unjustified prosecutions of journalists and citizens who had merely criticized or protested against acts of the government in a rightful manner. Finally, De Secus deemed that a jury system was compatible with the constitution, because the installation of a jury system was not explicitly prohibited. The creators of the constitution had never discussed the matter of the jury system and could, therefore, also not have intended to prohibit it.[90]

The third speech came from Donker Curtius, from the northern provinces. His aim was to show that professional judges, appointed for life and bound by a negative system of evidentiary rules, offered better guarantees for the accused than a jury system. He pointed out that the three most important arguments in favour of a jury system were their supposed greater impartiality, that a larger number of people would decide on the question of fact and that it would increase the public spirit of citizens. Concerning the first argument, Donker Curtius stated that it was wrong to presuppose that the essence of impartiality lay in the disinterestedness of jurors because they only judged one time and had no hope of gaining the favour of the government. Instead, he deemed that true impartiality lay in the sense of duty of a man that he needed to be as objective as possible and be guided only by the force of the evidence. He should not allow himself to be swept away by religious or political prejudices or the rhetoric of lawyers. This kind of impartiality was far more likely to be found among professional judges than among lay jurors chosen at random. Furthermore, the impartiality of the professional judges could be strengthened significantly through the publicity of the trial which he strongly favoured.[91] With this conception of impartiality Donker Curtius stood diametrically opposed to the idea of impartiality and disinterestedness of the proponents of a jury system.

Regarding the second argument, Donker Curtius noted first of all that there was no inherent reason why the number or jurors would have to be larger than the number of judges, and that the number of judges could be increased to, for example, eight or twelve. The true reason, however, why he was against the jury system and why he found that a larger number of jurors made no difference, was that he deemed it a grave error to suppose that the questions of fact and of law could be separated and that common sense sufficed to answer the question

---

90   Ibidem, pp. 23–30.
91   Ibidem, pp. 33–41. True impartiality, Donker Curtius stated "tire sa source la plus pure et la plus solide d'un sentiment intime du devoir de l'homme appelé à se prononcer sur l'innocence ou sur la culpabilité; il faut qu'il ne se laisse entraîner ni par l'animosité, ni par l'impulsion instantanée d'affection ou d'aversion". See p. 38.

of fact. When jurors were asked whether someone was guilty of a certain crime they necessarily had to qualify the facts in the juridical terminology. They had to interpret and correctly understand this terminology. For this, juridical knowledge and training were indispensable. Most importantly, Donker Curtius was horrified by the idea that the judgement on the guilt of the accused should depend on a mere sentiment, an intimate conviction for which no reasons could be given. In this he essentially reacted against the French conception of the *conviction intime*:

> Vraiment, Nobles et Puissants Seigneurs, je ne sais ce dont je dois m'étonner le plus, du paradoxe et des erreurs que me paraît contenir cette proposition, ou de l'influence qu'elle a exercée sur des esprits d'ailleurs éclairés; car d'abord, je n'admets nullement que le jugement d'un fait ne peut reposer que sur un sentiment intime de conviction, dont on ne peut se rendre compte ... Et d'abord qu'est-ce que la conviction et quelle doit-être sa base ? Certes elle n'est pas comme une foi aveugle chez la plupart des hommes, descendant d'en haut et naissant comme par inspiration, sans être soumise à la raison; non! ayant pour objet, non pas des choses invisibles et spirituelles, mais des faits matériels, elle est soumise à la raison, à l'intelligence, aux connaissances acquises, au jugement de comparaison et d'application et surtout à l'expérience.[92]

Donker Curtius argued that not every internal conviction was equally valid and that the conviction of a trained judge who had to account for his decision was far more reliable than that of a lay juror. He continued to explain, just as in his published treatise, that evidentiary rules which negatively bound the judge could and should be created. He acknowledged that it was impossible to create an encompassing system of rules which positively determined when sufficient evidence existed for a conviction. In the end much inevitably needed to be left to the discretion of the judge and he should never be forced to convict when he was not morally convinced. Nevertheless, like Weiland, he deemed that the proponents of a jury system had drawn far too radical and untenable conclusions from the difficulty of establishing evidentiary rules and the fact that it was impossible to attain mathematical or absolute certainty in criminal cases. He argued that despite these difficulties the conclusion could not be drawn that no evidentiary rules could be established at all and that the only possible

---

92   Ibidem, p. 51.

measure of deciding on the question of fact was, therefore, an internal conviction of which no rational account could be given.[93]

On the third argument, Donker Curtius stated that he attached great value to strengthening the public spirit of the people. He considered a good education, a large freedom of the press and, for example, more openness in the affairs of the state useful measures to this end. Although he acknowledged that jury duty could further enliven the sense of public duty of the people, he deemed that this good effect was in no way equal to the disadvantages connected to a jury system. Lastly, Donker Curtius explained why he was also against a jury system for press offences. In essence he reversed the argument of De Secus that because of the vague definitions of press offences jurors should decide on these matters. Donker Curtius stated that precisely because of the difficulty of terms such as *calomnie*, *injure* and *provocation punnisable*, a profound juridical knowledge was necessary to apply them correctly and to know the boundaries of criminal responsibility. This could not be expected of lay persons.[94]

The Parliamentarian Boelens, from the northern provinces, devoted his speech predominantly to giving an exposé of the historical development of the jury system. He explained that the jury system had emerged in the late Middle Ages and was at that time an adequate improvement on the old system of ordeals. However, Boelens argued that the jury system was at present not a sign of progress, as many supporters of the institution seemed to think, but in fact a relatively backward institution which was not compatible with the state of progress that the Netherlands had achieved. He, furthermore, deemed the jury system a highly dangerous institution because jurors could decide to convict on the basis of a mere feeling of being convinced. This could be based on nothing more than a suspicion or the bad reputation of the accused. He strongly preferred professional judges 'of whose intelligence and high moral standard the general opinion is convinced'.[95]

Van de Kasteele, from the northern provinces, declared that he entirely agreed with Schooneveld and Donker Curtius. His speech was interesting

---

93   Ibidem, pp. 51–58. Donker Curtius also gave an explanation for what he saw as the origins of this exaggerated idea which was repeated so often by the proponents of a jury system. He saw it as a consequence of the French Revolution: "C'est que sorti du gouffre des révolutions, ayant en abomination des institutions judiciaires antécédentes, justement réprouvées, préférant l'arbitraire du jury aux abominations et à l'arbitraire de ses tribunaux révolutionnaires et de ses malheureux antécédents, *il s'est jeté dans un extrême opposé*".
94   Ibidem, pp. 60–66.
95   Ibidem, pp. 94–102.

because he also expressed the view that the old system of legal proofs was an incongruent relic of the past. He remarked that at least some negative evidentiary rules were necessary and beneficial but then added: "It is not that I want to return to the old scholastic theory of full, half and quarter-proofs or agree with this idea; but I believe that some rules can be made, as has been done in the concept procedural code".[96] Van de Kasteele stated that he was above all against the jury system in press offences and political crimes because this would mean that these crimes would often go unpunished. The opinion of the people would too easily side with rebellious troublemakers who criticized the government without impunity. He remarked that some might accuse him of belonging to unenlightened times for this opinion. However, he stated that he had more faith in a Hugo de Groot or a Simon van Slingelandt than in the opinion of all those 'new publicists' with their beautifully sounding but in the end hollow rhetoric.[97] Van de Kasteele, in short, was rather conservative and strong in his condemnatory statements of those 'southern publicists' who were in his opinion only sowing division with their misplaced rhetoric of 'liberal' and 'enlightened' principles.

A quite exceptional parliamentarian was Luzac, a young liberal from the northern provinces who out spoke in favour of a jury system. He stated that he deemed that there were two important reasons why there was so much resistance against the jury system in the northern provinces. First of all, they were still prejudiced against this institution because it had been imposed by the Napoleonic regime. Secondly, they considered the institution too one-sidedly from the juridical perspective and did not sufficiently recognize the usefulness of the institution from a political-constitutional point of view. In the opinion of Luzac it was necessary that in a representative system of government, as existed in the Netherlands, the citizens should participate in every branch of the government. Within the judicial branch this could best be achieved through a jury system. For a more elaborate argumentation on this point he referred to the work of Meyer. Another political advantage which Luzac expected of a jury system was that it would increase the public spirit of the citizens and enhance the unity in the Netherlands. This he considered especially useful because at the moment most citizens were driven too strongly by egotism and were turned inwards to the affairs of their private families, while they had little interest in public affairs and neglected their duties as citizens.[98]

---

96 Ibidem, p. 104.
97 Ibidem, pp. 102–110.
98 Ibidem, pp. 110–132. Luzac also refuted the argument that a jury system was incompatible with the national character of the Dutch. Quite the contrary, he stated, the dutiful and

The main reasons why Luzac was in favour of a jury system, therefore, were of a political-constitutional nature. Nevertheless, he was also in favour of a jury system from a more juridical-technical point of view. Remarkably, considering the many parliamentarians who were in favour of a negative system of legal proofs, he stated that almost no one doubted anymore that it was impossible for the legislator to create useful evidentiary rules and that the internal conviction could not be bound by these rules. This fact was proven by the concept procedural code itself, he argued, where only rules were made to guide the judge but none to force his internal conviction. Reasoning from the impossibility of evidentiary rules, Luzac argued that lay persons were more suited than professional judges to decide on the question of fact. Professional judges supposedly became too severe and prejudiced through their constant judging of criminals. Furthermore, the jurors could just as well decide on the question of fact using their common sense and they were even more capable because they could better understand the customs and manner of speaking of the accused than the judge from his elevated standpoint. Lastly, it is clear that Luzac expected a greater impartiality from lay jurors and that he deemed that many of the northern parliamentarians had a too naïve image of the influence which could be exerted on professional judges by the government.[99]

A fervent speech in favour of the jury system was subsequently given by De Broukere, an influential representative of the young liberal generation from the southern provinces. He was by far the most outspoken advocate of a jury system in parliament. De Brouckere first elaborately argued that a jury system was not explicitly forbidden in the constitution and that no decision on this subject had been made. A jury system was, therefore, not incompatible with the constitution. Then he stated that the questions of fact and law could and should be separated and argued that lay jurors were better predisposed to answer the question of fact:

> Mais on décline l'aptitude du jury à l'appréciation du fait, on pose des règles à la conviction. La conviction ne peut être le résultat d'une évaluation factice, elle ne se compose pas d'éléments déterminés ; *c'est un sentiment, une impression morale qu'on ne peut pas plus tarifer que la conscience.* Un de nos collègues a prétendu qu'elle était soumise à la raison, à l'intelligence, à l'expérience, aux connaissance acquises; il a sans doute voulu dire que la conviction d'un homme qui réunit ces qualités était préférable à celle

---

impartial character of the Dutch made them especially suited for fulfilling this function as the period between 1811 and 1813 had shown. See pp. 143–152.
99   Ibidem, pp. 134–141.

> d'un idiot, et à cet égard je partage son opinion. Qu'il me soit cependant permis de définir les mots. L'expérience que je désire n'est pas l'habitude de condamner; les connaissances ne sont pas des études en jurisprudence … Ce que je demande, c'est l'expérience du monde et la connaissance pratique de l'homme … Lors même que la question est compliquée, l'expérience du jury est préférable à celle du magistrat.[100]

De Brouckere, in short, denied the usefulness of evidentiary rules and described the necessary internal conviction as an intimate feeling which could not be tied to rules and could not be rationally reconstructed. Later he repeated unequivocally "La conviction, je le répète, ne peut se motiver, ne peut être sujette à l'appel".[101] Besides the idea that everything in the end needed to depend on an internal conviction which could not be tied to rules, he argued that lay jurors were better suited to judge on the question of fact than professional judges who had acquired a habit of finding criminals everywhere and who were estranged from ordinary life. The most important underlying idea, however, was that De Brouckere deemed the jury system necessary to ensure an impartial and independent judgement. Impartial of the influence of the government and the *esprit de corps* which made them prejudiced against any form of criticism. He stated that the combined power of judging on the questions of fact and of law made the professional judges too powerful and that this would inevitably lead to arbitrariness.[102]

De Brouckere was supported by De Gerlache, a parliamentarian from the southern provinces who also played a prominent role during the Belgian revolution. He placed the desirability of the jury system firmly within the context of a broader set of political-constitutional reforms: "J'ai voulu justifier d'avoir avancé précédemment que tout se tient dans un système constitutionnel: inviolabilité royale et responsabilité ministérielle, liberté de la presse et jury".[103] He deemed a jury system necessary as a safeguard of civil liberty and argued that it would enliven the public spirit. He frankly acknowledged that he had paid little attention to the juridical-technical aspect. Nevertheless, he remarked that he did not see the impossibility of jurors to follow evidentiary rules as problematic because jurors were more than capable enough to decide on the question of fact without them: "Tant mieux, peut-être! Guidés par la droite et

---

100   Ibidem, pp. 200–201.
101   Ibidem, p. 204.
102   Ibidem, pp. 193–206.
103   Ibidem, p. 220.

simple raison, ils ignoreront l'art de déraisonner savamment, subtilement, infailliblement ... Mais lorsqu'il ne s'agit que d'apprécier la vérité d'un fait, scrupuleusement, en conscience, sans prévention, sans esprit de corps, tout homme honnête et éclairé peut être juge".[104]

After three days of discussion the votes were cast on 13 April 1829. On the first question, whether a jury system should be instituted for criminal cases, 67 parliamentarians voted no and 30 voted yes. Regarding the question whether a jury system should be instituted for press offences, 56 voted no and 41 yes. Lastly, on the question if a *jury d'accusation* should be created, 64 voted no and 33 yes. On all three questions a majority rejected the institution of a jury system. Most support could be found for the creation of a jury system for press offences. However, if we distinguish between the northern and the southern provinces, a clear divergence becomes visible. In the northern provinces 45 parliamentarians voted no on all three questions and only one person, Luzac, voted yes on all questions. In the southern provinces a majority of 29 against 22 voted yes on the first questions, a majority of 40 against 11 voted yes on the second question and a majority of 32 against 19 voted yes on the third question. In the southern provinces there was, therefore, a majority in a favour of a jury system in general, and an overwhelming majority in favour of a jury system for press offences.[105]

9.3.3 *Problematic Aspects of the Negative System of Legal Proofs*
So far in this chapter attention has mainly been paid to the discussion about the principal question whether a jury system, a negative system of legal proofs or a system based on the free evaluation of the evidence by professional judges should be introduced. The reason for this emphasis lies in the fact that the discussion in the juridical literature and in parliament focused predominantly on this principal question. The proponents of a negative system in the juridical literature, for example, virtually never elaborated on how the negative system of legal proofs should be given shape. In parliament as well, the most intense

---

104 222–243. Similar to the argumentation of De Brouckere and De Gerlache was the speech delivered by Le Hon. He developed largely the same arguments and insisted strongly on the idea that no juridical knowledge or expertise were necessary to decide on the question of fact. After citing, among others, Meyer and Rossy, Le Hon concluded: "chacun son metier. Le jurisconsulte doit développer et appliquer le droit; l'homme du monde, l'homme d'affaires doit connaître des faits et des intentions, car l'expérience lui fournit pour cela toutes les données nécessaires".

105 G. Bossers, *"Welk eene Natie, die de jurij gekend heeft, en ze weder heeft afschaft!"*, pp. 110–113.

discussion took place on the principal question whether a jury system should be introduced at all.

Nevertheless, even though the focus in the discussions lay predominantly on the question which evidentiary system should be introduced, in the parliamentarian debates attention was also paid to the question how the negative system of legal proofs should actually be regulated. In these debates four important, problematic subjects can be discerned which attracted discussion between 1827 and 1830, and which would be of a particular significance for the negative system of legal proofs after the promulgation of the new criminal procedural code in 1838. The first subject regarded the question whether convictions should be possible on the basis of indicia and how they needed to be regulated. The second question was what the value should be of the testimony of reproachable witnesses. The third question was whether the judge had to motivate his verdict and to what extent. The fourth question, which attracted less discussion, was whether the accused had a right to remain silent or if he had an obligation to answer questions. Before these four questions will be discussed, a general overview is given of what the negative system of legal proofs looked like in the substantive and procedural codes between 1827 and 1830.

9.3.3.1 The Negative System of Legal Proofs in the Criminal Procedural Code of 1828–1830

In the various designs for substantive and procedural criminal codes between 1814 and 1830 there was always a chapter which regulated the negative system of legal proofs in a largely identical manner as the chapter in the criminal ordinance for the Kingdom of Holland of 1809. Very little changed in this period in the idea of how the negative system of legal proofs should be given shape. In a memorandum accompanying the revised criminal procedural code in October 1829, the government explained what they saw as the most important elements of the negative system of legal proofs. The government remarked that while there was no doubt that it was impossible to give a positive prescription of when sufficient evidence existed for a conviction, it was certainly possible and useful to prescribe certain negative evidentiary rules. According to the memorandum the negative system of legal proofs contained two elements. Firstly, the guilt of the accused could only be proven in a juridical sense through the forms of evidence which had been acknowledged in the criminal procedural code and when the minimum evidentiary standards were met. Secondly, an accused could not be convicted unless the judge was morally convinced that he was guilty. With this regulation, the legislator stated, it was attempted to make sure that judges had to follow duly considered rules, and that they could not simply decide on the basis of a mere feeling that someone was guilty.[106]

The negative system of legal proofs prescribed that solely the following forms of evidence could be used: witness testimony, written documents, indicia and the confession. The minimum rules beheld that the judge could not convict on the basis of the testimony of one witness or on the basis of the confession of the accused alone. There needed to be other circumstances or forms of evidence which confirmed the witness testimony or the confession before the minimum requirement was met. It seems that one indicium was also insufficient for a conviction because the legislation normally spoke in the plural of 'indicia'.[107] Another restriction on the use of indicia was that indicia could not be proven by indicia themselves. The combination of different forms of evidence to form a sufficient proof was allowed. The testimony of one witness and one indicium could, for example, sufficiently proof the guilt of the accused. Apart from the legally prescribed forms of evidence and the minimum evidentiary standards, the judge was free in the evaluation of the strength of the evidence. Van Rappard was, therefore, right when he stated that the negative system of legal proofs proposed in the concept criminal ordinance left a very large room for judicial discretion.[108] Many authors would later comment in a similar manner that the judicial discretion was so large that the negative system of legal proofs almost amounted to a system based on the free evaluation of the evidence.

9.3.3.2 The Question of Indicia

As has been described above, a short discussion had already taken place on the subject of indicia in the period between October 1827 and March 1828, when the criminal law of evidence was still regulated in the substantive criminal code. Several sections of parliament expressed doubts whether convictions should be possible on the basis of indicia alone and several declared that they

---

106 J.J.F. Noordziek, *Geschiedenis der beraadslagingen gevoerd in de tweede kamer der Staten-Generaal over het ontwerp Wetboek van Strafvordering 1829–1830*, pp. 209–210.

107 De Bosch Kemper in his handbook on the criminal procedural ordinance of 1838, however, argued that one indicium could be sufficient for a conviction (although this would rarely be the case). See J. De Bosch Kemper, *Het Wetboek van Strafvordering. Deel III*, pp. 590–592.

108 W.L.F.C. van Rappard, *Aanmerkingen op het ontwerp van een Wetboek op het Strafregt I*, pp. 46–54. Especially when the Dutch regulation is compared to the more complex regulations of indicia that could be found in the Bavarian and Austrian criminal legislations of the early nineteenth century.

were in favour of this possibility. Only the parliamentarians Donker Curtius and De Secus presented separate, more elaborate notes on whether they deemed that convictions should be possible on the basis of indicia. De Secus argued that convictions should be possible on the basis of indicia because otherwise many crimes would have to go unpunished, and he also remarked that 'direct' forms of evidence were often more uncertain than indicia.[109] The government reacted in a memorandum and stated that it agreed with De Secus. If it was not possible to convict on the basis of strong and mutually supporting indicia then many crimes would go unpunished. Furthermore, the government observed that there seemed to be some confusion among the parliamentarians who thought that the proposed legislation allowed convictions on simple presumptions or suspicions. The government then stated that the legislation did not allow convictions on a mere 'moral conviction', but that the indicia needed to be correctly proven themselves and should not be confused with simple suspicions.[110]

The explanation offered by the government that convictions were not possible on mere suspicions appears to have worked reassuringly on the parliamentarians. The interest in the subject subsided and in the subsequent parliamentarian discussions between 1828 and 1830 there was no further principal discussion on the question whether convictions should be possible on the basis of indicia alone. The government did make a further remark on this subject in the memorandum accompanying the revised criminal procedural code in October 1829. Here the government stated that it was beyond doubt that indicia could form a complete and sufficient proof to convict an accused. Nevertheless, the government acknowledged that there was a certain inherent danger in indicia. Their guarantee against this supposed uncertainty of indicia was that every indicium had to be proven 'in the normal way' and that indicia could, therefore, not be proven by indicia.[111] It was prescribed in the criminal procedural ordinance that indicia could be proven solely through the following instruments: witness testimony, written documents, the personal inspection or survey by the judge and through the judicial or extra-judicial confession of the accused.

---

109   J.J.F. Noordziek, *Geschiedenis der beraadslagingen gevoerd in de tweede kamer der Staten-Generaal over het ontwerp Wetboek van Strafregt van 1827*, pp. 2–26, 53–55, 90, 108, 133,150 and 161.
110   J.C. Voorduin, *Geschiedenis en beginselen der Nederlandsche wetboeken, Deel VI, Wetboek van Strafvordering, 2ᵉ deel*, pp. 656–662.
111   J.J.F. Noordziek, *Geschiedenis der beraadslagingen gevoerd in de tweede kamer der Staten-Generaal over het ontwerp Wetboek van Strafvordering 1829–1830*, pp. 212–213.

The rule that indicia could not be proven by indicia was not a substantively new idea, because the same prescription could be found in the criminal ordinance of 1809 and in the subsequent concept codes. Nevertheless, it was now prescribed more explicitly in the criminal procedural code and this was pointed out by the government in the memorandum. This evidentiary rule formed an important limitation on the discretion of the judge which would become one of the most problematic aspects of the criminal law of evidence in the period after 1838. Effectively it meant that judges could not draw further conclusions from conclusions they had already drawn on the basis of certain proven circumstances. This entailed that the judge had to be very careful in his verdict and could not show his entire process of reasoning, because this could be seen as proving indicia by indicia. Every logical step taken by the judge could be seen as drawing a conclusion from a conclusion that was already drawn from certain proven circumstances.

The important and problematic rule that indicia could not be proven by indicia attracted virtually no discussion in parliament. After the explanation of the government that convictions were not allowed on the basis of mere suspicions and that convictions based on indicia were necessary because otherwise many crimes would have to go unpunished, the possibility of allowing convictions based on indicia appears to have been accepted without discussion.[112] It can be concluded that there was still a certain distrust against indicia and an uneasiness with the large judicial discretion that it entailed. This distrust inspired the rule that indicia could not be proven by indicia. It is, nevertheless, surprising how little discussion the highly important subject of indicia attracted in parliament and how easily the possibility was accepted that the accused could be convicted on the basis of indicia alone. This stood in a sharp contrast to the intense discussions in the German territories surrounding the use of indicia. As was described in Chapter five, in the German discussion the possibility of convictions on the basis of indicia was seen as highly problematical (and as virtually introducing the free evaluation of evidence) and many attempts were made to prescribe in minimum rules when there were sufficient indicia for a conviction. In the Dutch legislation the decision was left largely to the discretion of the judge.

9.3.3.3   The Regulation of Reproachable Witnesses
A difficult question, which led to some discussion in parliament, was what the evidentiary value of 'reproachable' witnesses should be. In the old system of

---

112   J.C. Voorduin, *Geschiedenis en beginselen der Nederlandsche wetboeken, Deel VI, Wetboek van Strafvordering, 2ᵉ deel*, pp. 655–668.

legal proofs there was a system of rules which dictated when witnesses were reproachable and could, therefore, not give a legally valid testimony. A full proof could only be created by the testimony of two or more irreproachable eyewitnesses. The negative system of legal proofs in the concept criminal procedural codes contained several categories of witnesses (remnants from the old system of legal proofs) which were not allowed to give a legally valid, irreproachable testimony. The categories in the concept codes included, for example, close relatives of the accused, fellow suspects, children below the age of fifteen, people who were mentally insane and people who had undergone a dishonouring punishment. These persons could not be heard under oath and could not give a normal witness testimony.[113]

The government was faced with a dilemma. On the one hand these categories of persons were excluded from giving a fully valid testimony because they were seen as being generally too unreliable. On the other hand, however, the government also did not want to exclude the use of these sources of information which could often be crucial in uncovering crimes (for example, through the testimony of children or convicted criminals). Faced with this dilemma the government tried to formulate an intermediary solution in which the reproachable witnesses could not give a legally valid testimony but in which the judge could still hear them and use their information. Thus, the government, for example, proposed the following ambiguous formulation in the concept criminal procedural code of 1829:

> Dans les cas où la loi permet d'entendre des personnes inhabiles à rendre témoignage, leurs déclarations ne pourront être considérées que comme *renseignements*. Le juge *ne pourra ajouter foi* à ce que ces témoins inhabiles déclareront avoir entendu, vu ou éprouvé, lors même qu'ils allégueraient leur raison de science; mais leurs déclarations ne pourront servir qu'à mener à la connaissance et sur la trace de faits, qui peuvent être prouvés par les moyens ordinaires.[114]

The government, in short, proposed that the judge could only use the testimony of reproachable witnesses as clarifying information (*renseignements*) and he could not 'give full credence' to what they had declared. The information could be used to uncover certain facts which could then be proven by

---

113   J.C. Voorduin, *Geschiedenis en beginselen der Nederlandsche wetboeken, Deel VI, Wetboek van Strafvordering, 2ᵉ deel*, pp. 668–672.
114   J.J.F. Noordziek, *Geschiedenis der beraadslagingen gevoerd in de tweede kamer der Staten-Generaal over het ontwerp Wetboek van Strafvordering 1829–1830*, p.183.

legally valid forms of evidence. In the memorandum attached to the concept criminal procedural code of 1829, the government stated that this rule formed a cornerstone of the negative system of legal proofs. The government explained that they explicitly forbade the judge to entirely believe the testimony of reproachable witnesses. This was necessary because otherwise there would be no difference between the value of reproachable and irreproachable witnesses. If this distinction was not made the judge could just as well use the testimony of the reproachable witness to form his conviction. They intended to prevent this possibility by stating that the judge could only use the testimony as information to uncover the crime.[115]

Unsurprisingly, this view of the government led to some criticisms in the parliamentarian discussion and also later in the juridical literature after 1838. It was argued, first of all, that if the judge could hear these reproachable witnesses it was unavoidable that they would shape his conviction and could even be decisive in creating this conviction. Simply stating that the judge could hear the reproachable witnesses but could not give (full) credence to them, could not prevent this effect. Secondly, it was remarked that the idea was incorrect that the reproachable witnesses could be used by the judge to give information which could then be used to investigate and uncover the crime. This was the case during the preliminary investigation but not in the stage of the main trial. Van Reenen was one of the parliamentarians who expressed these criticisms most clearly in a separate memorandum and argued that the reproachable witnesses should have the evidentiary status of an indicium.[116]

Despite the criticisms, the Article was left largely unchanged in the following concept criminal procedural codes. Only one change was made in the final version which formed part of the criminal code of 1838. Instead of prescribing that the testimony of reproachable witnesses could be used to provide information which could then be proven in the ordinary way, it now read that the information could be 'corroborated by other circumstances'.[117] The precise evidentiary status of the testimony of a reproachable witness thus remained highly ambiguous. The Article, nevertheless, formed an important limitation on the

---

115   J.C. Voorduin, *Geschiedenis en beginselen der Nederlandsche wetboeken, Deel VI, Wetboek van Strafvordering, 2ᵉ deel*, pp. 668–673.
116   Ibidem, pp. 673–683.
117   De Bosch Kemper rightfully remarked that to allow the judge to use the testimony of reproachable eyewitnesses as evidence created an inconsistency with Article 428 which exhaustively described which forms of evidence could be used. Article 428 prescribed that only witness testimony, written documents, indicia and the confession could be used as evidence, but did not mention the testimony of reproachable witnesses. See J. De Bosch Kemper, *Het Wetboek van Strafvordering. Deel III*, pp. 596–600.

freedom of the judge to evaluate the evidence. He could hear the reproachable witnesses to gather clarifying information, but he could not ground his conviction (solely) on the testimony of reproachable witnesses. If, for example, the judge only had the testimony of two or three children under the age of fifteen and no other sources of evidence, he could not ground his conviction on their testimony. The rather vague prescription was that the judge needed to have at least some other circumstances which confirmed the testimony of the reproachable witnesses. In the period after 1838 this article would become one the most criticized aspects of the negative system of legal proofs.

9.3.3.4 The Motivation of the Verdict

Closely connected to the question how the criminal law of evidence should be given shape, was the question if and to what extent the judge needed to motivate his verdict. Under the French *Code d'Instruction Criminelle*, the jurors did not have to motivate why they were convinced of the guilt of the accused. It was generally deemed impossible for jurors to rationally reconstruct why they were convinced. Furthermore, the decision on the question of fact by the jurors was final because there was no possibility of appeal. After the jury system had been abolished in the Netherlands, the Articles of the *Code d'Instruction Criminelle* which regulated the motivation of the verdict remained the same. This meant that between 1813 and 1838 the criminal judges in the Netherlands were not obligated to motivate in their verdict why they were convinced of the guilt of the accused. In accordance with Article 172 of the constitution, the verdict only needed to contain a description of the crime for which the accused was convicted. The verdicts of the criminal courts between 1813 and 1838, for this reason, merely described the facts which had been proven but contained virtually no motivation why or how the guilt of the accused was proven.[118]

The first concept criminal procedural code of 1828 did not attempt to change this situation and contained no further obligation for the judge to motivate why he was convinced of the guilt of the accused. This only changed after several parliamentarians argued for the introduction of such an obligation. The government took over this recommendation in the altered concept criminal procedural code of 1829. The obligation was now expressed in the criminal procedural code that the judge had to describe the crime and the facts which had been proven, and it needed to be 'substantiated by the relevant grounds'. How extensive this obligation to 'mention the grounds' was intended by the government, nevertheless, remained uncertain because the government did

---

118   W.H.B. Dreissen, *Bewijsmotivering in Strafzaken*, pp. 38–40.

not explain what they meant with this obligation. It is not clear whether the government intended that the criminal judge would have to motivate substantively why he was convinced of the guilt of the accused or if he only needed to mention the forms of evidence which had led him to this conviction (so that it would be possible to see whether he had followed the rules of the negative system of legal proofs).[119] This was a question which became an important point of discussion in the period after the criminal procedural code came into force in 1838, and will be dealt with further in the following chapter.

9.3.3.5 The Right to Remain Silent

In the previous chapter it has been described that between 1795 and 1813 the Dutch reformers thought that it should be forbidden to use physical torments to extract a confession, but that it was also thought that the accused had an obligation to answer questions. To this end the concept criminal procedural ordinances of 1799 and 1809 proposed to grant the judge certain disciplinary measures to remind the accused of his 'obligation to answer questions'. Similarly, in many German states in the first half of the nineteenth century, the judge could use disciplinary *Ungehorsamstrafe* to pressure the accused to answer questions. The use of disciplinary measures by the judge to force the accused to answer questions did not exist under the Napoleonic *Code d'Instruction Criminelle* of 1808 and was, therefore, not allowed between 1811 and 1838 when this code remained in force. Nevertheless, although it was no longer deemed acceptable that the judge could force the accused to answer questions, the accused also did not have a positively acknowledged 'right to remain silent'. At least morally, it was deemed that the accused had an obligation to answer questions and to cooperate, to a certain extent, with the judge.

The situation remained largely the same under the criminal procedural code of 1838. Little attention was paid to this subject during the legislative discussions, but it becomes clear from Article 199 of the procedural code that it was still deemed that the accused had at least a moral obligation to answer questions. This article stated that the court had to proceed with the trial when the accused refused to answer questions, after the president of the court had made clear to the accused that he had an obligation to answer. However, no sanctions existed to force the accused to answer questions, and Article 201 makes clear that the legal counsel of the accused could continue to present the defense of the accused even if he remained silent. Although it was held that the accused should answer questions, de facto he was free to remain

---

119   J.C. Voorduin, *Geschiedenis en beginselen der Nederlandsche wetboeken, Deel VI, Wetboek van Strafvordering, 2ᵉ deel*, pp. 124–129.

silent. In short, at this time the idea did not prevail that the accused had a right to remain silent nor that, for example, a caution should be given of this right before interrogations. This right would only find recognition in the criminal procedural code of 1926, when there was a new concern with strengthening the defensive rights of the accused.[120]

9.4 The Consequences of the Belgian Separation from the Netherlands

During the last round of discussions between October 1829 and March 1830 the parliamentarians offered virtually no fundamental criticisms anymore on the proposed negative system of legal proofs. Title twenty of the concept criminal procedural code, regulating the criminal law of evidence, was approved during the session of 22 March 1830. Eighty votes were cast in favour of the title and five were cast against it by members from the southern provinces.[121] The concept criminal procedural code as a whole was approved on 31 March 1830. The proposed negative system of legal proofs was, therefore, accepted in parliament. However, even though the criminal procedural code was approved, due to the Belgian revolution it never acquired force of law in the southern provinces.

After independence had been proclaimed on 4 October 1830, work quickly started on a new constitution for Belgium. A Constituent Assembly was elected and started its work on 10 November 1830. Within three months the Constituent Assembly approved a new constitution for Belgium on 7 February 1831. Unsurprisingly, there was a strong consensus in the Constituent Assembly on the desirability of the reintroduction of a jury system. Article 98 of the new constitution, which stated that there shall be a jury system for all crimes, including political and press offences, was approved in the Constituent Assembly by an overwhelming majority. The creation of a *jury d'accusation* was rejected by the Constituent Assembly.[122] Subsequently, on 19 July 1831, the Belgian legislator approved an ordinance which annulled the Dutch decree of 1814 that abolished the jury system. The French regulation of the jury system in the

---

120 On the legislative discussion concerning Article 199 of the criminal procedural code, see J.C. Voorduin, *Geschiedenis en beginselen der Nederlandsche wetboeken, Deel VI, Wetboek van Strafvordering, 2ᵉ deel*, pp. 104–107, and J. De Bosch Kemper, *Het Wetboek van Strafvordering. Deel II*, pp. 133–145 and 519–523.

121 J.J.F. Noordziek, *Geschiedenis der beraadslagingen gevoerd in de tweede kamer der Staten-Generaal over het ontwerp Wetboek van Strafvordering 1829–1830*, p. 140.

122 B. Delbecke, *De lange schaduw van de grondwetgever*, pp. 63–67 and 90–98.

criminal procedural code was thereby reinstated and the jury system started its work again in Belgium from 1 October 1831 onwards.[123]

In the northern provinces the approved criminal procedural ordinance of 1830 also did not directly acquire force of law. The coming into force of this procedural ordinance was postponed because of the revolutionary situation. After it became clear that the separation would most likely be permanent it was decided on 24 February 1831 that a last revision would take place of the criminal procedural ordinance. The parliamentarian sessions on the revised criminal procedural ordinance were held in April 1836 and, after the ordinance was approved, it was promulgated on 24 April 1836. The new criminal procedural code acquired force of law on 1 October 1838. In the revision of the concept criminal procedural ordinance, following the separation of Belgium, no significant changes were made to the title regulating the criminal law of evidence and it was approved virtually without discussion.[124] Thus the negative system of legal proofs acquired force of law from 1 October 1838 onwards.

9.5 Conclusion

The period between 1813 and 1830 saw a significant transformation in the discussion surrounding the criminal law of evidence in comparison to the period between 1795 and 1813. In the period between 1795 and 1813 there had already arisen increased doubts about the system of legal proofs and the tenability of the idea that only the confession or the testimony of two eyewitnesses could create a 'full proof'. Under influence of the changed epistemological ideas, it can be seen that people such as Cras, Van der Keessel and Aansorgh argued that moral certainty was necessary for a conviction and that this could be created just as well by other forms of evidence such as indicia. They, furthermore, placed a new emphasis on the internal conviction of the person judging and explicitly made the conviction of the judge a constitutive requirement for a conviction. Nevertheless, this did not lead them to reject the possibility or usefulness of evidentiary rules. The whole effort in this period lay on reconciling the demand of moral certainty with evidentiary rules. In, for example, the criminal code of

---

[123] G. Bossers, "Welk eene Natie, die de jurij gekend heeft, en ze weder heeft afschaft!", pp. 123–126.

[124] J.C. Voorduin, Geschiedenis en beginselen der Nederlandsche Wetboeken, Deel VI, Wetboek van Strafvordering, 1ᵉ deel, pp. XXVII–XXXX and J.C. Voorduin, Geschiedenis en beginselen der Nederlandsche wetboeken, Deel VI, Wetboek van Strafvordering, 2ᵉ deel, pp. 614–685.

1809 the evidentiary rules were intended in a negative manner as minimum standards next to the requirement of the internal conviction. In this attempt at reconciling the requirement of moral certainty with a system of evidentiary rules, the Dutch largely followed the ideas of authors such as Filangieri.

In the period between 1795 and 1813 the more 'radical' ideas of the French reformers were virtually unknown and remained undiscussed in the Netherlands. The idea that evidentiary rules were logically untenable and that they should be completely abolished, or that the only criterion for the truth should be the subjective conviction of the person judging, were not even seriously contemplated in the Netherlands in this period. The political-constitutional ideas which supported the adoption of a jury system were also still largely absent from the discussion in the Netherlands before 1813. This changed entirely in the period after 1813. Through the acquaintance with the French procedural legislation and, among others, the Prussian report and the work of Meyer, the Dutch jurists now became familiar with the ideas underlying the abolition of the system of legal proofs and the introduction of a jury system in France. These ideas broadened and deepened the discussion which took place in the United Kingdom of the Netherlands between 1813 and 1830. The jurists in the Netherlands were no longer focused solely on reconciling the demand of moral certainty with (negative) evidentiary rules but now saw themselves forced to react to the French ideas and explain why evidentiary rules were desirable at all and why they did not want to relinquish everything to the conviction of the judge or lay jurors.

Influenced by the ideas of the French reformers, essentially two sides developed in the discussion in the period between 1813 and 1830. On the one hand there were those in favour of a negative system of legal proofs with professional judges and on the other hand there were those in favour of the freedom of evaluation of the evidence by lay jurors. These two sides were divided largely along the lines of the northern and the southern provinces, although there were also proponents of a jury system in the northern provinces and proponents of a negative system of legal proofs in the southern provinces.

Besides these two main sides that dominated the discussion, there were also a few authors such as Van Rappard and Van Hamelsveld who already argued for the free evaluation of evidence by professional judges. In their complete rejection of evidentiary rules they appear to have been inspired by the ideas of the French reformers and Meyer, although it is difficult to be certain as these authors did not present a very developed argumentation for their position. They stated more as matter of fact that evidentiary rules were useless and that everything in any case depended on the conviction of the judge. Instead of explaining why evidentiary rules were useless, these authors focused more on arguing why they were against a jury system and why they deemed that professional judges could better evaluate the evidence. However, the idea to let professional judges freely evaluate the evidence was still a minority opinion between 1813 and 1830. It was, for example, also never seriously contemplated in the legislative attempts to reform the criminal law of evidence between 1813 and 1830.

In this chapter it has, furthermore, been described that there was an important difference of approach to the criminal law of evidence between the northern and the southern provinces. The discussion in the northern provinces was dominated by professional jurists who focused on the juridical-technical aspects. They strongly reacted against the epistemological claim of the French reformers that evidentiary rules were entirely useless and that the 'subjective' *conviction intime* was the best criterion for the truth in criminal cases. Similar to German authors such as Jarcke and Mittermaier, they argued that a reasoned conviction was necessary and that this conviction could and should be tied to certain minimum evidentiary standards that would form a guarantee against light-hearted convictions. Furthermore, they argued against the idea that the question of fact and the question of law could be separated and that lay jurors were more capable of deciding on the guilt of the accused than professional judges. The discussion in the southern provinces, on the other hand, was dominated by journalists and young jurists who often had little professional experience. They largely ignored the juridical-technical aspects and put a strong emphasis on the political-constitutional arguments in favour of a jury system (which were given far less attention in the northern provinces).

The clearest and most elaborate expression of the ideas that divided both sides could be seen in the parliamentarian discussion in April 1829. Here the arguments and ideas were expressed which led the northern provinces to adopt a negative system of legal proofs and the southern provinces to reintroduce the jury system after 1830. In the parliamentarian discussion there were several points of contention which divided the proponents and opponents of the jury system. One important point which was touched upon by almost all the speakers, was the question whether a jury system was compatible with the constitution. Essentially, the discussion on this point was quite simple. The makers of the constitution had not addressed this issue and had not explicitly decided for or against a jury system. The formulation of the relevant Articles on the judicial branch in the constitution only addressed the courts staffed with professional judges but did not explicitly prohibit a jury system. The proponents of a jury system interpreted the silence of the constitution to mean that the possibility of creating a jury system was left open for the future, while the opponents argued that the spirit and the formulations of the constitution were against its establishment. This issue remained unresolved but was taken very seriously by the parliamentarians. A large part of the speeches was often devoted to this aspect and it was used especially by the northern parliamentarians as an important argument against the creation of a jury system.

Nevertheless, even those who deemed a jury system unconstitutional continued to give an evaluation of the merits of the institution itself. As was visible in the juridical literature, the parliamentarians from the northern provinces approached the subject predominantly from a juridical-technical point of view while the representatives from the southern provinces placed a great emphasis on the political-constitutional aspects. The underlying difference between these two sides can be reduced to a large extent to the level of trust that the parliamentarians had in the professional judges. The proponents of a jury system distrusted the professional judges, especially concerning press and political offenses and, therefore, focused on the political-constitutional perspective. They saw a guarantee of impartiality in the judgement by lay persons as opposed to professional magistrates who in their eyes could be influenced too easily by the government. For this reason they downgraded the importance of the technical-juridical aspect and even argued that lay persons were in fact better suited to decide on the question of fact. To substantiate the latter claim they used the same arguments which could be found in the work of Meyer and in the Prussian report. They denied that evidentiary rules were possible or useful and argued that the internal conviction was a 'feeling' which could not be rationally reconstructed or bound by evidentiary rules. Additionally, they stated that lay persons were more capable to decide on the question of fact because they had a better practical understanding of everyday life and were not hardened or blinded by the constant judging of criminal cases. Another frequently used argument was that the creation of the jury system would contribute to the public spirit of the people.

The opponents of a jury system reasoned in an opposite manner. They trusted the professional magistrates and frequently praised the impartiality and high moral standards of the judges in the Netherlands. They sought the guarantees for an impartial judgment in different institutions. Almost uniformly they argued that more than sufficient guarantees for impartiality existed when the trial was public, when there was a large freedom of defence for the accused and when the judge was bound by negative evidentiary rules. Some also stated that the judge should motivate his verdict, although this point as yet attracted relatively little attention. The focus of the opponents lay on the juridical-technical aspects and from this perspective they deemed that the jury system offered far less guarantees for the accused. As was stated before, a central argument of the opponents of a jury system was that they deemed that the questions of fact and law could not be separated and that juridical knowledge and training was necessary to decide on the guilt of the accused. They, furthermore, feared that the institution of a jury system would mean that jurors would decide merely on the basis of their subjective *conviction intime*. This, they argued, contained a far greater risk of arbitrary decisions.

Virtually all the parliamentarians who were against a jury system appeared to agree with Donker Curtius that negative evidentiary rules were possible and necessary, and that lay jurors could not be expected to adequately apply these rules. Different from the juridical literature, however, was that there were almost no parliamentarians who argued for professional judges unbound by evidentiary rules. This option was, therefore, not seriously discussed during the parliamentarian debates on the concept criminal procedural code. As will be described in the next chapter, after the separation of Belgium from the Netherlands the discussion regarding the criminal law of evidence would again significantly change. Inspired by the developments in the German juridical literature, there now emerged a large group of authors who explicitly argued for the introduction of the free evaluation of the evidence by professional judges. From the 1840s onwards, the discussion in the Netherlands would be dominated by those in favour of a negative system of legal proofs and those in favour of the free evaluation of the evidence by professional judges, while only a small minority still pleaded for the introduction of a jury system.

Finally, there was one last interesting aspect of the discussions between the proponents and opponents of a jury system in the period between 1813 and 1830 which has to be noted here. There was a clear tendency visible to place the discussion on the jury system within a wider framework surrounding the ideas of what was 'liberal' and what was 'progressive'. The proponents of a jury system consistently remarked that the most advanced nations – England, the United States and France – had embraced the jury system as a cornerstone of their civil liberty. They presented it as an undisputable fact that the jury system was a liberal institution and a clear sign of progress. Typical in this respect was, for example, the following sarcastic remark by the parliamentarian Le Hon: "rejeter le jury, c'est mettre, pour ainsi dire, en question s'il est préférable d'être civilisé comme l'Espagne, le Portugal et les autres

Etats despotique du jour, que d'être barbare à la manière de l'Angleterre, de l'Amérique et de la France".[125]

Almost all the parliamentarians from the northern provinces felt the need to react to the, in their eyes unjustified, allegation that they did not appreciate civil liberty sufficiently and were not caught up with the progress of civilized nations. Conversely, they tried to claim the concepts of 'liberal' and 'progressive' for their own ideas and to show that the jury system was actually a rather backward institution. Several parliamentarians remarked that the jury system was developed in the late Middle Ages to replace the then existing ordeals. They argued that while it may have been good at the time for the English, this did not mean that it was good for the far more developed society of the Netherlands in the nineteenth century. They, furthermore, remarked that the reason that the English still held the jury system in such high esteem lay in the fact that they were strongly attached to their traditions but that it could not be explained by the inherent usefulness of the institution. Typically, several parliamentarians used the following quotation of Bentham to argue that not all Englishmen were blind to the backwardness and the downsides of the jury system: "Le jury est un institution admirable dans les temps barbares, mais indigne d'un siècle de lumières".[126]

Combined with the rhetoric which aimed to show that the jury system was not a sign of progress, there was also a tendency among the authors and parliamentarians from the northern provinces to attempt to reclaim the concept 'liberal'. Many parliamentarians remarked that they were just as keen on protecting civil liberty as those who accused them of backwardness and despotism, but that they just did not believe that the jury system was the right way to protect civil liberty. It is in this context that they often presented their package of procedural guarantees as the best way to protect civil liberty and to show that they were the real 'liberals'. There was, in short, clearly a rhetorical battle going on between the opponents and proponents of a jury system which included a constant fencing with the terms liberal and progressive. In this

---

125   J.J.F. Noordziek, *Geschiedenis der beraadslagingen gevoerd in de tweede kamer der Staten-Generaal over het ontwerp Wetboek van Strafvordering en het vraagstuk der jury 1828–1829*, deel I, p. 228.

126   Ibidem, pp. 10, 94–102 and 109. The parliamentarian Boelens even devoted the largest part of his speech to demonstrating that the jury system was a relatively backward institution and not at all a sign of progress. The same quote of Bentham was also used by Den Tex in his article in a similar manner as by the parliamentarians.

discourse the proponents of the jury system – especially the journalists from the southern provinces – were continuously on the offensive and accused their opponents of backwardness, while the parliamentarians and the authors from the northern provinces felt a need to defend themselves and to show that they were in fact liberal and progressive. As will be shown in the following chapter, this sharp rhetorical dimension between the proponents and opponents of a jury system largely disappeared after the separation of Belgium from the Netherlands.

CHAPTER 10

The Criminal Law of Evidence in the Netherlands between 1838 and 1870

10.1 Introduction

After the separation of Belgium from the United Kingdom of the Netherlands and the coming into force of the new criminal procedural code in 1838, the discussion regarding the criminal law of evidence changed. The separation of Belgium from the Netherlands meant that there was no longer a large and vocal group which pleaded for the introduction of a jury system. Furthermore, the newly established negative system of legal proofs came into force which now needed to be interpreted and worked with in practice. These changes entailed a shift in focus of the discussion. The intense discussion on the question whether a jury system should be introduced quickly subsided after the separation of Belgium from the Netherlands. Instead, the focus at first turned on explaining the new negative system of legal proofs, and quite soon on the question whether the free evaluation of the evidence by professional judges was not preferable to the existing negative system of legal proofs.

The discussion about the criminal law of evidence in the period of 1838 until 1870 can be divided into two phases. In Section two the first phase, which lasted from 1838 until the end of the 1850s, will be discussed. The second phase, which consisted of the 1860s, is discussed in Section three. In the first phase, especially during the 1840s, most publications regarding the criminal law of evidence consisted of handbooks and articles which sought to explain and reflect on the new negative system of legal proofs. They evaluated the jurisprudence of the Supreme Court and critically analysed how the system of legal proofs functioned. In this period sharp criticisms can already be seen of the negative system of legal proofs and a significant number of authors pleaded for the introduction of the free evaluation of the evidence in combination with professional judges.

The discussion evolved further and became more intense in the 1860s. The direct cause for the intensification of the discussion lay in the fact that the Dutch government had created a new concept criminal procedural code in 1861 which would abolish the negative system of legal proofs and replace it with a system based on the free evaluation of the evidence in combination with professional judges. By this time it appears that a majority of the authors in the Netherlands deemed that the negative system of legal proofs did not function properly and that a system based on the free evaluation of the evidence was preferable. Those who wanted to abolish the negative system of legal proofs argued that it did not offer any real guarantees and that the evidentiary rules could not do justice to the complexities of the individual case. They also often referred to the German discussion which had grown increasingly in favour of the free evaluation of the evidence. The concept criminal procedural code of 1861 was eventually not approved by parliament and the interest in reforming the criminal law of evidence again subsided for a long time. Nevertheless, even though the negative system of legal proofs remained in force, a very large group had grown decidedly in favour of either a completely free evaluation of the evidence by professional judges or an even more minimalistic negative system of legal proofs. Finally, in the fourth section of this chapter a short description will be given of the changes in the criminal law of evidence which occurred after the 1870s.

10.2 The Discussion on the Criminal Law of Evidence between 1838 and 1860

From 1 October 1838 onwards, the new criminal procedural code went into force. The criminal procedure remained to a very large extent the same as it had been in the *Code d'Instruction Criminelle* of 1808. There were, nevertheless, a number of important changes in the code of 1838 to which the juridical practice had to accommodate itself. First of all, the main trial was again made entirely public as it had been in the original French code. The second important change was that criminal judges were now bound by a negative system of legal proofs and that they had to 'motivate' their verdicts. These changes raised the question how the negative system of legal proofs should be understood and to what extent a criminal judge had to motivate his verdict. A number of handbooks and articles were published between 1838 and 1860 which attempted to answer these questions and which reflected critically on the negative system of legal proofs. In this section first the general reflections on the new negative system of legal proofs will be described and then a separate subsection is devoted to the reflections on the question how the criminal verdicts should be motivated.

10.2.1 *Reflections on the Negative System of Legal Proofs*
The two most influential authors on the criminal procedural law between 1838 and 1860 were De Bosch Kemper, who worked as a public prosecutor, and De Pinto who worked as a lawyer. Both published a juridical handbook and several

articles on the new criminal procedural code. The handbook of De Bosch Kemper consisted of three volumes published between 1838 and 1840. In the first volume he presented a concise history of the criminal procedural law in the Netherlands since the time of the Germanic tribes, and in the third volume he also gave a specific overview of the historical development of the criminal law of evidence. De Bosch Kemper used an extensive array of sources and was particularly influenced by the German discussion. In his analysis of the criminal law of evidence he started by contrasting two opposed views. He observed that on one side there were those who deemed that historical truth lay in the subjective conviction alone and who wanted to leave everything to the freely formed moral conviction, and on the other side there were those who saw the truth as something entirely objective which could be regulated in general *a priori* rules. As examples of the first view he mentioned advocates of the French jury system and cited Bourguignon and Constant. As examples of the latter point of view, he mentioned Carmigniani and Rosshirt. De Bosch Kemper continued to remark that most jurists, nevertheless, deemed that a middle road needed to be found between these two points of view through the creation of a negative system of legal proofs. As representatives of this view he mentioned Mittermaier and Weiland.[1]

At this time De Bosch Kemper appeared to agree with the middle road and was very close in his views to Mittermaier who he cited very often and approvingly. Regarding the juridical certainty necessary for a conviction he stated that no absolute or mathematical certainty was attainable, but only a high degree of probability. As an elucidation of this criterion de Bosch Kemper gave, among others, the following quotation of the German author Weber:

> In Vergleichung mit dieser absoluten Gewissheit ist dann freilich jene empirische und insbesondere die historische Gewissheit, der wir uns im Leben doch auch öfters überlassen müssen häufig nur ein unter den gegebenen Umständen nicht weiter zu steigernder *hoher Grad von Wahrscheinlichkeit*. Es wird dadurch die Möglichkeit des Gegenteils nicht ausgeschlossen, aber doch so weit in die Ferne gestellt, dass wir uns nach dem gewöhnlichen erfahrungsmäßigen Lauf der Dinge bei dem Fürwahr halten beruhigen können.[2]

---

[1] J. De Bosch Kemper, *Het Wetboek van Strafvordering. Deel III*, pp. 478–490.
[2] Ibidem, pp. 502–507.

De Bosch Kemper, furthermore, agreed with Mittermaier and Jarke who argued that the strength of the evidence lay in the grounds supporting the conviction, and not in the subjective conviction itself which was merely the result of these grounds. The grounds adhere to certain general rules of experience which could form the basis of a system of evidentiary rules. At this time De Bosch Kemper still supported the idea that these rules should not only create a scientific theory of evidence, but that it was possible and useful for the legislator to prescribe them in legal rules. Nevertheless, he deemed that these general rules should only guide the judge in a negative manner, because in the end the question of the strength of the evidence always necessarily depended on the concrete evaluation by the judge.[3]

Concerning indicia, De Bosch Kemper praised Mittermaier for having convincingly demonstrated that there was no principal difference between indicia and the so-called direct forms of evidence. Witness testimony and the confession did not prove the crime 'directly' because just as with indicia the judge still had to draw probable conclusions from the testimony. The judge still needed to evaluate whether the testimony or the confession was trustworthy and whether they sufficiently proved the guilt of the accused. De Bosch Kemper stated that all these forms of evidence, therefore, worked in essentially the same manner. On the basis of the fact that indicia created the same form of certainty as other forms of evidence, De Bosch Kemper principally disagreed with the rule of the criminal procedural code of 1838 that indicia could not be proven by indicia. He deemed that this rule came forth out of an old mistaken presupposition regarding the uncertainty of indicia, but that this distinction could not be justified.[4]

As in the German territories, there was another argument against the system of legal proofs which became more important from the 1830s onwards. This argument had its foundation in the greater emphasis that was placed on the need to prove the precise level of criminal intent of the accused and to modify the punishment accordingly. De Bosch Kemper was a good example of an author who argued that the system of legal proofs was particularly inadequate to deal with the subjective side of the crime (i.e. the subjective *Tatbestände*). He stated that a more free evaluation of the evidence and

---

[3] Ibidem, pp. 506–518 and 523–529. As a definition of the required conviction De Bosch Kemper put forth the formulation of Mittermaier: "Einen Zustand aber, in welchen unser Fürwahrhalten auf völlig befriedigenden Gründen beruht, deren wir uns bewusst sind, nennen wir Ueberzeugung".

[4] Ibidem, pp. 564–590.

especially a free use of indicia was necessary for the judge to be able to infer the criminal intent of the accused from the proven circumstances.[5] De Bosch Kemper, in this respect, quoted the influential French jurist Rauter who stated unequivocally that the use of indicia was necessary to prove the criminal intent: "Certains éléments de la culpabilité, par exemple l'intention criminelle, ne peuvent être prouvés directement, mais le peuvent seulement d'une manière indirecte".[6]

Although De Bosch Kemper criticized the rule that indicia could not be proven by indicia, he still appeared to generally support the negative system of legal proofs in his juridical handbooks published in 1838–1840. His opinion, however, had changed significantly after almost ten years of practical experience with the new criminal procedural code. In 1847 he published an article in which he presented a highly critical evaluation of the criminal procedural code. Concerning the criminal law of evidence, he now unequivocally stated that he regarded the negative evidentiary rules as useless and in some situations even damaging. He stated that almost unavoidably the evidentiary rules were incomplete and superficial 'guiding rules' which were normally already followed by professional judges in any case. The evidentiary rules could only have a real effect if they were prescribed in a far more encompassing and restrictive manner, but then the system would become too rigid which was even more undesirable. Furthermore, he stated, that the juridical practice had shown that the evidentiary rules had given cause to unnecessary acquittals and had prevented the criminal judge from openly declaring the grounds which had actually convinced him. Instead the judges only took care to formulate their verdicts in such a manner that they would not be liable to cassation. For all these reasons, he deemed that the negative system of legal proofs should be abolished and that this subject should be left to legal science. De Bosch Kemper had, in short, after ten years of practical experience become in favour of a system based on the free evaluation of evidence by professional judges.[7]

---

5 This argument is in line with the emphasis that Pihlajamäki placed on the increased importance of the 'subjectivisation' of the substantive criminal law for the development of the criminal law of evidence. H. Pihlajamäki, *Evidence, Crime, and the legal profession*, pp. 128–129.
6 J. De Bosch Kemper, *Het Wetboek van Strafvordering. Deel III*, pp. 496–498.
7 J. de Bosch Kemper, *Het Wetboek van Strafvordering aan ervaring en wetenschap getoetst. Deel I*, pp. 73–74 and *Het Wetboek van Strafvordering aan ervaring en wetenschap getoetst. Deel II*, pp. 70–75. De Bosch Kemper was not in favour of a jury system. To support the possibility of combining professional judges with a free evaluation of the evidence he also mentioned the example of the recent Prussian legislation of 1846.

Unlike De Bosch Kemper, De Pinto was from the start very critical of the negative system of legal proofs. His first publication on this subject was an article in 1843. He stated that he deemed evidentiary rules useless because in the end everything still depended on the conviction of the judge. This was especially the case when convictions were allowed on the basis of indicia. He argued that allowing convictions on the basis of indicia was in general incompatible with an actual system of legal proofs, because the judge would then have so much room that he could virtually always convict someone and find the suitable indicia to support this conviction. Nevertheless, De Pinto also deemed the use of indicia indispensable for an effective criminal procedural law. He stated that one was, therefore, forced to choose either an ineffective criminal procedural system where convictions were only possible on the basis of witness testimony and the confession, or a system of legal proofs which in practice still left everything to the conviction of the judge. Supporting this claim, he stated that an experience of five years with the new procedural system had shown him that the introduction of the negative evidentiary rules had indeed changed nothing besides the fact that there were some new formalities. Finally, De Pinto remarked that he preferred the introduction of a jury system. He did not, however, provide any further argumentation for this preference.[8]

In his juridical handbook, published in 1848, De Pinto repeated and extended his criticisms of the negative system of legal proofs. Unlike in his article where he mostly stressed the uselessness of evidentiary rules, De Pinto now also argued that they had significant practical downsides. One such downside was that there was a tendency to convict when judges had sufficient evidence according to the negative evidentiary rules, instead of searching for the substantive truth. Furthermore, although the situations were rare, the negative rules prohibited convictions in some cases in which there could be no doubt of the guilt of the accused, for example, when the evidence consisted of the testimony of a large number of children or convicted criminals (who were reproachable witnesses). Another downside was the fact that the evidentiary rules were often used by lawyers to unnecessarily complicate cases and appeal for cassation which was costly and extended the procedures. De Pinto again concluded that the evidentiary rules should be abolished and that he preferred a jury system.[9]

---

8 A. de Pinto, "Iets over het bewijs door aanwijzingen in strafzaken", pp. 171–175.
9 A. de Pinto, *Handleiding tot het Wetboek van Strafvordering. Deel II*, pp. 568–584. De Pinto also commented that the old system of extraordinary punishment had been an unjustifiable practice. There should only be the possibility to either find someone guilty or innocent: 'tertium no datur'.

Besides the works by De Pinto and De Bosch Kemper, an annotated version of the criminal procedural code appeared by Schüller, and a juridical handbook on the criminal procedural law by Lipman.[10] Except for some explanatory remarks and references to rulings by the supreme court, these works contained no deeper reflections on the way the criminal law of evidence was regulated. Only Lipman made some general observations in which it can be seen that he thought that the judicial discretion was so large in the Dutch criminal law of evidence that there was almost no difference between the negative system of legal proofs and the free evaluation of the evidence which had existed between 1813 and 1838. Interestingly, Lipman also made the remark that the existing evidentiary system differed immensely from the situation before the nineteenth century in the Netherlands where 'half and quarter-proofs' were used.[11]

In the 1850s almost no work appeared which reflected on the criminal law of evidence. One important exception was an article published in 1854 by Gratama. He strongly condemned the existing negative system of legal proofs and pleaded for the introduction of the free evaluation of the evidence. His first argument against the existing system was that sixteen years of experience had shown him that the evidentiary rules were useless at best and harmful at worst. He deemed that the legislator had felt the need to create the evidentiary rules under the misguided fear that letting judges decide after their *conviction intime* created the possibility that they would decide light-heartedly on the basis of some mere subjective feeling. However, Gratama asked, when had the situation existed that the judges in the Netherlands did not carefully evaluate the evidence? The experience between 1813 and 1838 had shown the opposite. The Dutch judges were educated in the theory of evidence and applied these ideas in any case. The very generally formulated negative rules which still left almost everything to the conviction of the judge had not changed this situation in the

---

10   C.L. Schüller, *Wetboek van Strafvordering, met aantekeningen*.
11   S.P. Lipman, *Wetboek van Strafvordering, vergeleken met het Romeinsche en Fransche regt*, pp. 210–216. Finally, a very unusual work in this period was published in 1845 by J.H. van der Schaaff. In this work he compared the criminal procedure before 1795, when he already practised as a jurist, with the existing procedure. He did not think that the modern criminal procedural law was an improvement and even lamented the abolition of judicial torture. He illustrated his point of view by extensively discussing a case of arson in which the accused was wrongly acquitted, while under the old procedural law the possibility would have existed to torture the accused. This was a highly singular point of view and there have been no other publications after 1813 which still defended the use of judicial torture. See J.H. van der Schaaff, *Proeve van onderzoek over het verschil tusschen den voormalige en hedendaagschen vorm van procederen*.

sense that it had made the judges more careful in their evaluation. If anything, it might have made the judges complacent and convict more easily as soon as they had sufficient evidence according to the evidentiary rules.[12]

A second important reason why Gratama was against the negative system of proofs, was that he deemed it to be incompatible with the centrality of the internal conviction and the principle of orality engrained in the existing procedure. The whole point of the orality of the procedure had been that the judge could see and hear the accused, the witnesses and other forms of evidence so that they could work directly on his conscience. The smallest details such as a stammering voice could have a crucial role in the creation of the conviction of the judge. However, the judge could not use these kinds of circumstances if they did not stem from a legally allowed source of evidence. Gratama argued that it was not the number of witnesses or indicia per se which determined their strength in an oral procedure, but the total impression of the presented evidence. The evidentiary rules might have suited a written procedure where the judge had no direct impression of the evidence presented to him, but they did not suit an oral procedure where everything depended on the internal conviction of the judge.

Lastly, Gratama argued that the idea behind a system of legal proofs was wrong in principle. As the attempt at a negative system of legal proofs in the criminal procedural code had shown, it was not possible to predetermine for the endless variety of possible circumstances whether sufficient evidence existed in the individual case. This needed to be left to the concrete evaluation of the judge. He stated that in particular the matter of indicia clearly showed that this could not be regulated in legal rules but should be left to the field of legal science. Gratama also offered the insightful criticism that it was a mistake of the legislator to mention indicia as a *source* of evidence in the code of 1838. The nature of indicia was that first certain facts needed to be proven from actual sources of evidence, after which the judge could then draw probable conclusions from these facts concerning the crime and the accused. The conclusions which were drawn by the judge from certain circumstantial facts – which were proven by other sources of evidence – constituted the indicia. The indicia existed only by grace of the conclusions that the judge had drawn from a source of evidence and were, therefore, not a *source* of evidence themselves. For example, the witness testimony or written documents which proved certain circumstances were in fact the sources of evidence and not the indicia because

---

12   M.S. Gratama, "Eenige bedenkingen omtrent de voorschriften van ons Wetboek van Strafvordering aangaande het bewijs der misdrijven", pp. 213–222.

they were only the conclusions drawn from these proven circumstances. In theory a judge could draw conclusions about the guilt of the accused from any proven fact, while a different judge might see no indicia in these facts at all. Gratama deemed that allowing convictions on indicia – which was indispensable for an effectively functioning criminal justice system – meant that everything principally depended on the reasoning and the conviction of the judge. He concluded, finally, that the criminal law of evidence should be left to the prudence of the judge and to the *doctrina juris*.[13]

10.2.2   *The Motivation of the Verdict*

The question how the verdict had to be motivated was a matter of crucial importance for how the negative system of legal proofs would function in practice. Because the legislator had been vague on this point, it was a question which needed to be answered by the Supreme Court. Since 1811, severe crimes in the Netherlands were tried by the courts of assizes and the sole possibility of appeal was to the Supreme Court. The Supreme Court did not judge on the question whether the facts were correctly established by the courts of assizes but only on the question whether the law was applied correctly. This stemmed from the French system in which the judgment on the question of fact by the jury was definitive and the court of cassation could only decide on questions of law. Between 1813 and 1838, when there were no evidentiary rules and the judges decided after their *conviction intime*, the decision on the guilt of the accused and the strength of the evidence by the courts of assizes could not be a ground for cassation. Like the judgment by jurors, the internal conviction of the judges in the courts of assizes was final. This situation changed with the introduction of the negative evidentiary rules and the obligation for the courts of assizes to motivate their verdict in 1838. The Supreme Court was still not allowed to scrutinize whether the evidence was sufficient for a conviction because this was a question of fact and left to the discretion of the judges in the courts of assize. However, the Supreme Court could now quash a conviction if it became apparent from the verdict that the negative evidentiary rules had been violated. The Supreme Court had, therefore, become the institution which could interpret the negative evidentiary rules and scrutinize whether the courts of assizes correctly applied them.

The case law of the Supreme Court established the guiding interpretation of how the negative evidentiary rules and the obligation to motivate the verdict should be understood. Naturally, the courts of assizes knew that if they did not abide by this interpretation their verdict would be quashed. The only way the

---

13   Ibidem, pp. 218–230.

Supreme Court could see whether the negative evidentiary rules were correctly applied was through the motivation of the verdict by the court of assizes, which made the motivation of the verdict of central importance for the question how the negative system of legal proofs functioned. Article 211 of the criminal procedural code stated that the verdict needed to contain, among other things, the relevant crime, the proven facts and the grounds on which the conviction was based. The very general formulation of 'containing the grounds' could be interpreted in a narrow or in a broad sense. The most important question after 1838 was whether it was, for example, necessary that the judges explained which different grounds they had for their conviction and what the relative weight of these grounds was, or whether the obligation to state the grounds for the decision should be understood in a more narrow sense.

Very soon after the new criminal procedural code came into force, it became clear that the Supreme Court opted for a relatively narrow interpretation. The Supreme Court deemed that the obligation to state the grounds had to be interpreted in light of the negative system of legal proofs. The Supreme Court stated in a case in 1838 that the demand to motivate the verdict meant that "from the mentioning of the grounds it had to become apparent that the evidentiary rules had not been neglected, so that the accused could find in them a guarantee against arbitrary convictions, based solely on an internal conviction".[14] Stating the grounds, in other words, was interpreted to mean that the judge had to mention the sources of evidence which formed the basis of his conviction (which needed to conform to the standards of the negative evidentiary rules). The criminal judge was not required to explain why he deemed certain testimony or indicia convincing or what their relative weight was for the formation of his internal conviction. As was prescribed in the evidentiary rules in the criminal procedural code, this was left to the discretion of the judge.[15]

---

14   W.H.B. Dreissen, *Bewijsmotivering in strafzaken*, pp. 41–42.
15   Advocate-General G.A.G. van Maanen agreed with this interpretation by the Supreme Court in his conclusion to the case (one task of the Advocate-General was – and still is – to write conclusions regarding individual cases for the Supreme Court, in which the Advocate-General give his view on how the relevant question of law should be answered). He stated that it was not only practically impossible for the judge to explain of every fact or source of evidence why he deemed it convincing, but that it was also useless because it was not the task of the Supreme Court to scrutinize the evaluation of the strength of the evidence by the lower courts. This conclusion has been printed in G.A.G. van Maanen, "Beweegredenen bij de Vonnissen op te geven. De feiten, derzelver qualificatie, en de schuld der beklaagden te onderscheiden", *Nederlandsche Jaarboeken voor regtsgeleerdheid en Wetgeving 1839*, pp. 68–83.

The Supreme Court did not demand a substantive motivation of why the judge was convinced because it deemed that it was not its role to quash decisions of the lower courts on the basis that their assessment of the facts had been incorrect. Concerning its own role as the court of cassation, the Supreme Court remarked in a case in 1839:

> To the aspects which need to be evaluated by the court of cassation does belong the scrutiny of the *legality* of the forms of evidence which formed the basis of the juridical conviction, but this scrutiny must not extend itself to a substantive evaluation of the forms of evidence ... or to the question if they can be deemed sufficiently strong to constitute a juridical conviction.[16]

The Supreme Court, therefore, only required that the verdict showed that the sources of evidence which were used met the standards of the negative evidentiary rules. The verdict, for example, had to show that the conviction was not based on the testimony of only one witness or that indicia were proven by other indicia. Otherwise the verdict could be quashed. Nevertheless, the Supreme Court made it clear that it would not scrutinize whether the evidence was sufficiently strong for a conviction.

10.2.2.1 The Discussion on the Motivation of the Verdict in the Juridical Literature

The narrow interpretation of the obligation to motivate the verdict by the Supreme Court was supported in the juridical literature. Historically there had never been a situation in the Netherlands in which the criminal judge was obligated to motivate substantively why he was convinced of the guilt of the accused. Before 1813, under the extraordinary procedure, the judges were not required to state the grounds for the conviction of the accused at all, and between 1813 and 1838 the judge was only obligated to mention the facts which had been proven (and the article of the criminal procedural code on the basis of which the accused was convicted). The judge did not have to mention the substantive grounds for his conviction. During the first half of the nineteenth century many authors in general appeared to believe that it was almost impossible for the judge to explain precisely why he was convinced of the guilt of the accused. This applied especially to the supporters of a jury system but also to many

---

16   W.H.B. Dreissen, *Bewijsmotivering in strafzaken*, p. 42.

authors in favour of (negative) evidentiary rules.[17] Although several authors mentioned the obligation to motivate the verdict as a guarantee against arbitrary decisions, it is likely that they only intended this obligation in a very restricted sense. The demand to motivate the verdict in this period should, therefore, not be confused with the currently existing and more far-reaching obligation for the criminal judge to substantively motivate – at least to an important extent – why he is convinced that an accused is guilty. This obligation only developed from the early twentieth century onwards.[18]

An even more restricted interpretation of Article 211 than that given by the Supreme Court, was defended in an article by Van Heusden. Van Heusden stated that although the words 'contain the grounds' could be interpreted in a broad or narrow sense, the history of the Article showed that it should be understood narrowly. He stated that, first of all, it had to be kept in mind that the legislator had taken the *Code d'Instruction Criminelle* as the basis for the criminal procedural code. For the French courts of assizes it was prescribed that their judgement needed to 'contient les motifs' while for the lower criminal courts it was also prescribed that 'tout jugement définitif de condamnation sera motivé'. With this formulation the French legislator meant merely that the facts should be described in the verdict for which the accused was convicted. Van Heusden argued that because the words 'contain the grounds' were a literal translation of the French prescriptions, and because between 1813 and 1838 the criminal judges in the Netherlands only had to mention the facts which were proven, Article 211 should be interpreted as meaning exactly the same unless the legislator had expressly stated that it should be interpreted more broadly. After an encompassing description of the history of the parliamentarian debates on this article, Van Heusden concluded that the government had nowhere expressed a clear desire that the words 'contain the grounds' were meant to change anything in the existing practice of motivating the verdicts. The criminal judge was, therefore, in his view not obligated to mention the sources of evidence on the basis of which he had formed his conviction, but merely to describe the facts which were proven and their juridical qualification.[19]

---

17   On the prevailing idea in the contemporary German discussion that it was impossible to substantively motivate why one was convinced, see Section three of Chapter five.

18   Importantly, the Dutch authors who advocated the obligation to motivate the verdict, normally only mentioned it as a guarantee but did not explain more specifically to what extent they wanted the criminal judges to motivate their verdicts. It is, therefore, difficult to assess how they envisioned this obligation.

19   C.J. van Heusden, "Bijdrage tot beantwoording van de vraag: moeten, volgens het tegenwoordig regt in Nederland, de strafvonnissen anders, dan onder de hier te Lande vóór 1

As described above, the Supreme Court did interpret Article 211 in connection with the negative evidentiary rules and deemed that the criminal judge was obligated to express the sources of evidence on which the conviction was built. De Bosch Kemper agreed with this interpretation. He argued that the verdict should contain everything on the basis of which the Supreme Court could see whether the evidentiary rules were correctly applied, while it was unnecessary to motivate the aspects which were left to the discretion of the judge. In the view of De Bosch Kemper, the judge did not have to motivate his perception of the strength or trustworthiness of the witness testimonies and indicia, because this was left to his discretion. The motivation of the verdict was intended solely as a guarantee that the lower court had judged *lawfully*, not that it had judged correctly on the facts. De Bosch Kemper also remarked that it was in most cases impossible to express entirely why and through what means the judge had become internally convinced. This was not the kind of motivation that the legislator intended.[20]

De Pinto, like De Bosch Kemper, explained the obligation to motivate the verdict in light of the negative evidentiary rules.[21] In his article of 1843 he presented an important additional reason why he wanted the Supreme Court to judge only on the legality of the decision from lower courts and refrain from scrutinizing their evaluation of the strength of the evidence. The reason was that the Supreme Court solely received written documents and did not directly hear the witnesses or the accused. De Pinto considered it a breach of the principle of orality and, therefore, very dangerous if the Supreme Court would itself decide on the strength of the evidence on the basis of written documents alone.[22] Gratama repeated this argument in his article. He stated that the

---

October 1838 bestaand hebbende Wetten, worden gemotiveerd?", pp. 17–52. Van Heusden also rejected the idea that the introduction of a negative system of legal proofs influenced the way the verdict needed to be motivated. He argued that the obligation to abide by the negative evidentiary rules and the requirement to motivate the verdict were two separate obligations for the judge, and that the legislator had not made an explicit connection in which he had made clear that the judge had to make apparent in the motivation that he had abided by the negative evidentiary rules. Finally, it is important to note that Van Heusden did stress that he defended this interpretation not because he personally deemed it desirable per se that the verdicts were motivated less extensively, but that he only attempted to give a correct interpretation on the basis of what the legislator had presumably meant with Article 211.

20 J. De Bosch Kemper, *Het Wetboek van Strafvordering. Deel II*, pp. 573–579.
21 A. de Pinto, *Handleiding tot het Wetboek van Strafvordering. Deel II*, pp. 359–373.
22 A. de Pinto, "Iets over het bewijs door aanwijzingen in strafzaken", pp. 181–182.

Supreme Court was installed for the purpose of creating unity in the application of the law, it should not function as a higher court on the question of fact.[23]

The interpretation of Article 211 by the Supreme Court had important repercussions for the judicial practice. From 1838 onwards it was required that the verdicts contained all the sources of evidence on which the conviction was based. A consequence was that now the testimonies of witnesses and of the accused had to be presented in the verdict. If the court had inferred indicia from witness testimony or, for example, from written documents, it needed to describe these indicia. However, if it became clear from the verdict that from one indicium a further indicium was deduced the verdict could be quashed. The verdict could also be quashed if it became clear that the judge had deemed the crime or aspects of the crime proven by a source of evidence which was not mentioned in Article 428 (i.e. witness testimony, the confession, written documents or indicia). The most problematic point in the new situation was the correct use of indicia. A result of the rule that indicia could not be proven by indicia was that the criminal judges became very careful to avoid describing their entire process of reasoning and how they arrived at conclusions, because even when they had made completely valid deductions from indicia their verdicts could be quashed. The description of every further step in the process of reasoning by the judge could be seen as proving indicia by indicia. The result was that verdicts which were substantively very well motivated were often also the most liable to be quashed by the Supreme Court.[24]

Summarizing, because the obligation to motivate the verdict was linked to the negative evidentiary rules, the courts developed the practice of writing very formalistic verdicts which abided by the evidentiary rules. Although this formalistic practice was not strongly criticized at first, in the course of the second half of the nineteenth century and the early twentieth century it was increasingly regarded as unsatisfactory. A first point of criticism was that the existing practice led to many futile and costly appeals to the Supreme Court. Secondly, it was deemed undesirable that the judges only motivated their decisions in such a formally correct manner that their verdicts could not be quashed, while they did not explain substantively why they were actually convinced. It was increasingly argued that the real guarantee against arbitrariness should be found in the substantive motivation of the verdict which could be

---

23   M.S. Gratama, "Eenige bedenkingen omtrent de voorschriften van ons Wetboek van Strafvordering aangaande het bewijs der misdrijven", pp. 222–230.
24   W.B. Dreissen, *De bewijsmotivering in strafzaken*, pp. 38–44.

scrutinized in appeal and in cassation, and that this should replace the existing formalistic motivations that offered no insight in the reasoning of the criminal judges. These criticisms eventually led to the adoption of the obligation to better substantively motivate the verdict in the new criminal procedural code of 1926.[25]

10.3 The Discussion Regarding the Abolition of the Negative System of Legal Proofs in the 1860s

In the juridical literature between 1838 and 1860 it can already be seen that most of the authors who wrote on the criminal law of evidence were highly critical of the negative system of legal proofs and pleaded for its abolition. This had, however, not yet led to a legislative discussion on the option to abolish it. In the 1860s this discussion took place for the first time in the Netherlands. In 1861 the Dutch government intended to create an important reform of the judicial organization in a new concept law. This reform of the judicial organization also necessitated a reform of the criminal procedural law. The government proposed a revision of the criminal procedural code in 1861, presented to parliament for the first time on 8 November 1863, in which the negative system of legal proofs would be abolished. This proposal led, first of all, to a discussion on this matter by several governmental institutions; most of them appeared to be in favour of the proposal. The proposal also ignited a discussion in the juridical literature in which a majority of the authors were in favour of the proposal by the government. These two discussions will be described in the following two subsections.

10.3.1 *The View of the Governmental Institutions on the Abolition of the Evidentiary Rules*

The design for a new criminal procedural code was created and published under the supervision of Godefroi, the Minister of Justice between 1860 and 1863. It was presented to parliament for the first time on 10 November 1863 under his successor Olivier. The proposal was accompanied by an explanatory memorandum from the government and by reports on the concept procedural code from the Council of State, the Supreme Court and a parliamentarian committee. In the design there was no longer an enumeration of the sources of evidence which were allowed, and there were no longer articles which described

---

25   Ibidem, pp. 42–53.

minimum requirements for a conviction. The decision on the guilt of the accused was left entirely to the freely formed internal conviction of the judge.

The explanatory memorandum accompanying the concept procedural code stated that the government considered it superfluous to give an elaborate argumentation for the abolition of the negative system of legal proofs. According to the government, the sheer endless literature on this subject had led to a more general recognition of the harmfulness of evidentiary rules which hindered the judge in his decision. Concerning the discussion in the German literature, the government referred to an oversight given by the Austrian writer Herbst in his *Einleitung in das Oesterreichische Strafprocessrecht*. As far as the Dutch literature was concerned the memorandum referred to De Bosch Kemper and De Pinto, and for France to 'the excellent work of Hélie'. As a further significant example of the supposed general consensus regarding the uselessness of evidentiary rules, the government enumerated the German states that had recently introduced the free evaluation of the evidence, ranging from Oldenburg and Saxony to Prussia. It becomes clear from the memorandum that those responsible for the concept criminal procedural code were well aware of the contemporary development of the discussion on the criminal law of evidence in the German territories. The mention that was made of the German authors and of German states which had abolished the evidentiary rules, shows the important influence that the German discussion had on the Netherlands.[26]

More specifically the government argued that unavoidably all systems of evidentiary rules had the problem that they were either formulated so narrowly that many crimes would have to go unpunished, or so broadly that they merely formed a general advice which still left almost everything to the internal conviction of the judge. The memorandum stated that the latter was the case with the existing negative system of rules. From this the government concluded that while no real benefits were to be expected, there were clear downsides to the evidentiary rules. First, the danger existed that judges would not sufficiently investigate the substantive truth and contend themselves with a formal truth (meaning that they might acquire the habit of simply convicting when they had reached the minimum requirements expressed in the law). Secondly, the government stated that everyone who has had experience with the prosecution of crimes knew at least one example of a criminal case where the judges were convinced of the guilt of the accused on very good grounds, but could not convict because the minimum evidentiary requirements were not met. Lastly, the government remarked that it did not believe that the criminal

---

26   Tweede Kamerstukken, 1863, p. 734.

judges did not already automatically follow the general rules of logic and experience which had been developed in legal science and which had been laid down in the negative system of legal proofs. The legal sanctioning of these rules was unnecessary because it did not make the criminal judges more careful or circumspect in their evaluation of the evidence.[27]

In short, the government concluded that no benefits could be expected from legal evidentiary rules while there were clear downsides. The memorandum also explained that the obligation to motivate the verdict would remain the same. The criminal judges would, therefore, still have to mention what sources of evidence formed the basis of their conviction but their verdicts could no longer be quashed when they, for example, had proven indicia by indicia. The government did not agree with those who stated that the obligation to motivate the verdict was only compatible with a system of evidentiary rules. Instead, it argued that the obligation to motivate the verdict would strengthen the trust of the people in the fact that criminal judges did not base their judgement on thin air. Furthermore, the obligation to motivate the verdict improved the possibility of appeal and of cassation, because then the higher courts could better scrutinize the soundness of the verdict of the lower courts.[28]

The Council of State, an institution which provided advice on new legislation, stated in its report that it entirely supported the argumentation presented by the government for abolishing the negative system of legal proofs. The Council of State observed that the number of supporters of a system of evidentiary rules appeared to have diminished on a daily basis in recent times and that it had been abolished in most of the modern European legislations. Furthermore, the Council of State remarked that, to its knowledge, no author had yet objected to the proposal of the government and that it expected no real opposition against it. Finally, the Council of State stated that it wanted to supplement the argumentation of the government with two important additional arguments. Firstly, the system of legal proofs had given rise to many unjustified appeals to the Supreme Court in which it was attempted to seduce the court to actually judge on the question of fact. Secondly, the evidentiary rules had created the undesirable consequence that criminal judges who most extensively motivated their verdicts were the most liable to have their verdicts quashed.

---

27   Ibidem, pp. 734–735.
28   Ibidem, pp. 735–736.

This the Council deemed two important additional arguments for the abolition of the negative system of legal proofs.[29]

The members of the Supreme Court were more divided in their advice on the concept criminal procedural code. The Supreme Court stated that a majority of the court did not agree with the proposal to abolish the evidentiary rules. The minority that did support the proposition mentioned as an argument that the experience between 1813 and 1838 had shown that criminal judges were no less careful in their judgements when there were no evidentiary rules. The majority, however, stated that they considered evidentiary rules a useful guarantee against light-hearted convictions, and that the downsides attached to the system of legal proofs did not outweigh this benefit. Furthermore, the majority felt that the obligation to motivate the verdict was not a sufficient guarantee and that it would be less efficacious once the evidentiary rules were abolished because the judge was then allowed to be convinced by anything. The majority of the Supreme Court did not present a further substantive argumentation of why it supported a system of evidentiary rules. They did acknowledge that there were many defects in the existing system of rules and that a thorough revision was necessary.[30]

The last evaluation by a governmental institution came from a committee of parliamentarians which had to present a preliminary advice on the concept criminal procedural code. The report first stated that a minority of the committee did not agree with the proposal to abolish the evidentiary rules and that they missed a sufficient guarantee against light-hearted and arbitrary convictions. After all, the judge could now form his internal conviction on the basis of almost anything, even on mere suspicions or information that he had acquired outside of the procedure itself. The minority acknowledged that it is true that most judges would still diligently do their job, but the evidentiary rules formed a guarantee against precisely those judges who were too easily convinced. The minority also remarked that the complaints about the negative system of legal proofs were caused by the fact that the Dutch legislation was deficient and needed to be improved. They did not agree with the report of the government which stated that the idea of a system of evidentiary rules

---

29 Ibidem, pp. 792–793 and 799. Interestingly, at a later point in its report, the Council of State remarked about the Article which regulated the motivation of the verdict that it deemed that motivating the verdict did not really belong in a system without evidentiary rules but that the obligation needed to be retained because it was also required by Article 172 of the constitution. Here again the scepticism is visible of the possibility or usefulness of the obligation to substantively motivate the verdict.

30 Ibidem, pp. 827–828.

was flawed in principle. A last commentary from the minority was that if the government wanted a system based purely on the intimate conviction, they deemed that it was useless to still demand the motivation of the verdict.[31]

The majority of the parliamentarian committee, nonetheless, agreed with the proposal to abolish the evidentiary rules and supported the argumentation of the government. The majority criticized the opponents in the committee by stating that it was not the intention of the government to introduce the French idea of the *conviction intime*. The majority, like the government, pleaded for a reasoned conviction based on sufficient grounds and in accordance with the general rules of experience which are used to ascertain historical truth. For this reason, the majority stated that, if anything, the obligation to motivate the verdict would need to be strengthened and extended. They argued that the verdict had to express the sources of evidence and the reasons which had led to the conviction of the accused. The most important downside of the evidentiary rules was that they bound the judge to unnatural, formalistic categories which forced him to evaluate the evidence in a certain way. For example, they forbade him to use the testimony of a witness *de auditu* (hearsay evidence) even though this testimony might have been crucial in the formation of the conviction of the judge. These limitations needed to be taken away and the judge should be left free to research the substantive truth as best he could. However, with this freedom came responsibility and the criminal judge should, therefore, be obligated to present the reasons for his conviction. In conclusion, the majority deemed that the judges should decide freely on the basis of a reasoned conviction and not on the basis of the French idea of the *conviction intime*.[32]

Even though a majority of the governmental institutions and the parliamentarian committee were in favour of the introduction of the free evaluation of the evidence, the revised criminal procedural code was in the end not accepted. The revised criminal procedural code was submitted six times to parliament between 1863 and 1870 (because legislative proposals needed to be reintroduced every parliamentary year if they were not accepted), but it was never approved. The reason appears to have been that the revision of the criminal procedural law was part and parcel of an intended reform of the judicial organization and in the end no consensus could be reached on the proposed reform of the judicial organization. On 23 June 1870 parliament voted against the

---

31   Ibidem, pp. 1810–1811.
32   Ibidem, p. 1811.

proposed reform of the judicial organization and all the reform laws which accompanied this proposal (including the proposed revision of the criminal procedural law).[33]

Summarizing, there seems to have been a majority in favour of the introduction of the free evaluation of the evidence in 1863, but the revised criminal procedural code was in the end not accepted predominantly because no consensus could be reached on the broader reform of the judicial organization. Conversely, however, it can also be concluded that there was apparently not a strongly felt need to introduce the free evaluation of the evidence because no new separate legislative proposal was made after 1870 to introduce the free evaluation of the evidence. This meant that the negative system of legal proofs continued to function unchanged until the revision of the criminal procedural law in 1926.

10.3.2 *The Juridical Literature in the 1860s*

The proposal by the government to abolish the negative system of legal proofs reinvigorated the interest in the criminal law of evidence in the 1860s and led to a number of publications on this subject. All publications in this period were in favour of abolishing the negative system of legal proofs, except for the works of Jongstra. A first article was published in 1862 by De Pinto who gave a short evaluation of the reforms proposed in the concept criminal procedural code. In general he was very positive about the intended reforms and particularly applauded the strengthening of the defensive rights of the accused during the preliminary investigation. He also supported the abolition of the evidentiary rules, using the same argumentation that he had presented in his earlier works.[34]

Another article which supported the abolition of evidentiary rules was published in 1866 by De Jong van Beek en Donk. De Jong van Beek en Donk reacted against the argument of the proponents of a negative system of legal proofs that a system of evidentiary rules had existed in all the great legal systems in history and that it was, therefore, a dangerous innovation to abolish them. Against this argument he stated that especially when it concerns the criminal law, the fact that an institution had a long history certainly did not automatically plead for its inherent wisdom or usefulness. In fact, the older the criminal

---

33   A.A. de Pinto, *Handleiding van het Wetboek van Strafvordering. Tweede herziene deel* (1882), pp. 7–10.
34   A. de Pinto, "Het Ontwerp-Wetboek van Strafvordering", pp. 19–26.

institution was the more absurd it often seemed to be. Here he mentioned the example of ordeals, trial by combat and judicial torture. Furthermore, the existing guarantees of the publicity of the trial, the independence of the judges and the more humane character of the modern criminal procedure made it less necessary to bind the judge to evidentiary rules as it had been in the past. In short, although he deemed an understanding of the historical development of the criminal law of evidence of great importance, De Jong van Beek en Donk did not agree with the argument that the long existence of an institution necessarily pleaded in its favour.[35]

A more thorough analysis of the criminal law of evidence came from Stuffken and B. De Bosch Kemper (not to be mistaken with his father J. de Bosch Kemper who has been discussed above). They both wrote their doctoral thesis on the subject. Stuffken was especially elaborate and devoted his thesis in 1866 to the history of the criminal law of evidence. In his historical analysis Stuffken started by briefly describing the development of the system of legal proofs and the great undermining impact that the thinkers of the enlightenment had had on it. He mentioned in particular the influence of Beccaria, Filangieri and the French revolutionaries. The largest part of his historical analysis, however, focused on describing the development of the discussion on the criminal law of evidence in the German territories and the Netherlands in the nineteenth century. In this analysis he explained that at the beginning of the nineteenth century a system of evidentiary rules was still considered an absolute necessity. It was not even considered as a possibility to abolish the evidentiary rules. The thread throughout his narrative was that in the course of the nineteenth century there had been a growing realization that the idea of a system of evidentiary rules was in itself flawed, because in the end everything necessarily depended on the subjective evaluation by the judge. Stuffken then mentioned several authors and examples of the recent changes in the legislation of the German states to support his claim that there had grown a clear consensus on the uselessness of evidentiary rules. He acknowledged that there were still many supporters of a negative system of legal proofs, but deemed that this idea was continuously losing support.[36]

In the final chapter Stuffken presented his own opinion and argued that it was right that the idea of a system of legal proofs was increasingly losing

---

35 J. de Jong van Beek en Donk, "Eenige historische beschouwingen over de leer van het bewijs in strafzaken", pp. 339–356.
36 N.G. Stuffken, *Het wettelijk bewijs in strafzaken*, pp. 1–76.

support. Stuffken agreed that the judge had to follow general rules of logic and of experience. Nevertheless, he argued against the reasoning of authors such as Weiland that it was useful to lay down these rules in legislation. He stated that such rules were only true in general and represented a 'probable theory'. It was impossible, however, to predetermine for the concrete case with any level of accuracy when sufficient proof existed. All the most important questions such as the trustworthiness of the evidence and how the different forms of evidence related to each other could not be predetermined in general rules. He remarked that in this sense the negative theory of proof was based on the same flawed principle as the positive theory. The evidentiary rules only distracted from the search for the substantive truth in criminal cases, which should be the highest goal in a criminal procedure. In conclusion, Stuffken stated that it was wrong to presume – as many had done in the past – that judging on the internal conviction meant judging on some shady, intuitive feeling of which no account could be given. This was based on a misinterpretation of the French idea of the *conviction intime* and applied neither to professional judges nor to jurors. He also deemed it possible and useful for the judge to motivate his verdict. Of course, Stuffken remarked, the judge could never explain in minute detail how his internal conviction had been formed but he could at least motivate his verdict to such an extent that any presumption of arbitrariness would be dissipated. Stuffken, therefore, argued that the obligation to motivate the verdict should remain intact if the evidentiary rules were to be abolished.[37]

In 1865, B. de Bosch Kemper devoted his doctoral thesis to a comparative legal analysis of the contemporary developments in the criminal procedural law. De Bosch Kemper was unequivocally against either positive or negative evidentiary rules. He deemed that evidentiary rules could never determine what probative force evidence should have in the concrete case. The testimony of one witness under oath, for example, never had the same probative value in two different cases. A negative system of legal proofs was less harmful than a

---

37 Ibidem, pp. 77–87. Stuffken was particularly inspired by Hélie and Mittermaier and cited them often to substantiate his point of view. To underline his idea that general evidentiary rules could not describe when sufficient proof existed in the concrete case, he gave the following important quote of Mittermaier: "Der Gesetzgeber darf es nicht wagen, dasjenige was im gewöhnlichen Laufe der Begebenheiten die Erfahrung als regelmäßig an die Hand gibt, zu einer gesetzlichen Regel für alle Fälle zu erheben, weil jeder scheinbar geringfügige Nebenumstand die Anwendung der Regel modifiziert, und so die Richter durch die allgemeine Regel irregeleitet werden".

positive one, but it still prevented the judge from convicting in certain situations when he was entirely convinced on good grounds. This was harmful because the purpose of convicting those guilty of a crime was just as important as preventing convictions of innocent accused persons. De Bosch Kemper was in favour of a free evaluation of the evidence based on similar reasons as his father. He also argued that the obligation to motivate the verdict needed to be retained if the evidentiary rules were abolished. The function of the motivation would, nevertheless, have to change. It should no longer focus on demonstrating that the evidentiary rules had been correctly applied but it should form a substantive motivation of why the judge was convinced (which could then be evaluated in appeal by a higher court). Like Stuffken, however, De Bosch Kemper warned that one should not have to high expectations of this motivation and that it is, to a certain extent, impossible to precisely articulate why someone is convinced.[38]

10.3.2.1 Modderman and Jongstra

The most profound and elaborate contributions to the discussion in the 1860s came from Modderman and Jongstra who both published a book on the criminal law of evidence in 1867. They submitted their works as the answer to a price question from the Provincial Society for Arts and Sciences of Utrecht. The question was whether a system of evidentiary rules or the free evaluation of the evidence was preferable. The works of Modderman and Jongstra are of special interest because they both contain the most encompassing and 'state of the art' argumentation for and against the system of legal proofs in the 1860s. In this respect, they were exemplary of the two main sides of the discussion in the Netherlands in this period. Modderman argued for the free evaluation of the evidence and Jongstra for a negative system of legal proofs. The work of Modderman was rewarded with the gold medal.

Modderman, a professor of law in Groningen, wrote his treatise under the appropriate motto of Disraeli that "we put too much faith in systems, and look too little to men". His work consisted of three parts. The first part contained theoretical reflections on the purpose of the criminal law of evidence and on which kind of certainty had to be obtained in criminal cases. The second part contained a description of the historical development of the criminal law of evidence and the third part his arguments against evidentiary rules. In the first part Modderman stated that the certainty required in criminal cases was a historical or 'empirical truth', which consisted of a very high degree of probability

---

38 B. de Bosch Kemper, *De strafvordering in hare hoofdtrekken beschouwd*, pp. 182–226.

that could, however, never amount to absolute certainty. It would always be approximative. He aligned himself with authors such as Mittermaier and Jarcke and argued that not just any conviction was sufficient but that what really mattered were the grounds for the conviction. Nevertheless, Modderman remarked, the ultimate foundation in the end always had to be the subjective conviction of the judge.[39]

In his conception of the certainty required in criminal cases it is, furthermore, significant that Modderman very strongly rejected the idea that this certainty could be divided in arithmetic units. This he deemed a central flaw of the old system of legal proofs which used 'quarter, half and full proofs' and correspondingly used different punishments depending on the strength of the evidence. Modderman not only criticized the old system of legal proofs but also the more recent attempts to reduce the different degrees of probability into numbers. As an example he mentioned Bentham who had proposed the idea of dividing the credibility of witnesses in numbers ranging between 10, 100 and 1000. Later he also mentioned Condorcet and Laplace. These arithmetic attempts Modderman considered a hopeless effort.[40]

After an extensive description of the historical development of the criminal law of evidence from Roman times to the present – based predominantly on the historical research of German authors –, Modderman returned to the question of the desirability of legal evidentiary rules. He emphasized that the question needed to be understood correctly. The question was not whether a general theory of evidence, based on logic and experience, was possible and desirable, but only if these rules should be laid down in the law. He stressed the need of having a clear understanding of the question, because for the longest time in the nineteenth century the debate had been dominated by a misguided dichotomy. Namely the dichotomy that one had to choose either the free

---

39   E.A.J. Modderman, *De wetenschappelijke bewijsleer in Strafzaken*, pp. 10–45.
40   Ibidem, pp. 46–79 and 136. In his theoretical part Modderman agreed with Mittermaier that there was no principal difference between direct and indirect forms of evidence and that "*es überall nur eine Kette* von *Vermuthungen* ist, worauf wir unsere Ueberzeugung bauen". Similar to Gratama, Modderman also came to the important conclusion that indicia were mistakenly treated as a *source* of evidence in the criminal procedural code.

He remarked that a general confusion existed in the criminal procedural code between the sources of evidence and the grounds they produce. Sources of evidence are the medium through which certain facts or grounds are transmitted to the judge. The testimony of witnesses or the accused are, for example, a source of evidence which can prove different facts or circumstances which themselves form the grounds for the decision. Categorizing indicia under the sources of evidence, as the criminal procedural code did, was therefore eminently wrong, because the indicia were just conclusions drawn from other evidentiary sources.

evaluation of the evidence in which the decision was based on a *conviction intime* (that was supposedly arbitrary and based on no rules), or professional judges who rationally applied evidentiary rules. Modderman stated that the origins of this flawed dichotomy lay, first of all, with the French revolutionaries who presented the internal conviction too strongly as based on an intuitive, unreasoned, feeling of the truth in opposition to the old system of legal proofs. This was the first exaggeration. The second exaggeration, which created the dichotomy, was the reaction against this view by German and Dutch authors who presented the question as if one could only choose between the subjective *conviction intime* proposed by the French, or a rational system based on evidentiary rules. Modderman stated that, nevertheless, this dichotomy had been largely superseded in the last two decades through the more correct understanding that the free evaluation of the evidence did not necessarily mean that judges would arbitrarily have to decide on the basis of a subjective intuition or feeling. He stated that most German and Dutch authors now acknowledged that the abolition of evidentiary rules did not mean that professional judges would no longer rationally weigh the evidence and follow general rules of logic and experience. The result of this more correct understanding was, according to Modderman, visible in the literature and the fact that many German and Italian legislations had accepted the free evaluation of the evidence in the last two decades.[41]

Modderman felt the need to emphasize this 'correct' understanding of the question, because many advocates of a negative system of legal proofs were still arguing within the parameters of this flawed dichotomy. As an example, he mentioned the minority of the parliamentarian committee who were against the free evaluation of the evidence. Modderman quoted this minority which stated that it feared that if the evidentiary rules were abolished the professional judges could decide on the basis of some feeling or mere suspicions and that they deemed that the "theory of the moral conviction was more compatible with a jury system".[42] Against this view Modderman made it clear that he, as well as most recent advocates of the free evaluation of the evidence, did not propose to let the judges decide after some arbitrary *conviction intime*. He stated that it should be presupposed that professional judges had to follow general rules of logic and experience, and that they could and should give account of

---

41   Ibidem, pp. 80–262. In his historical description, Modderman also strongly criticized the old practice of extraordinary punishments. He stated that it was one of the most absurd and unjustifiable practices that the intensity of the punishment was moderated after the strength of the evidence. Modderman correctly observed that the use of extraordinary punishments and judicial torture were the result of the too strict system of legal proofs.

42   Ibidem, pp. 164–165.

their internal conviction through the motivation of the verdict. The only real point of dispute should be whether it was useful to lay down the theory of evidence in legal rules or whether it should be left to legal science and the own responsibility of the judge.[43]

In his argumentation against a negative system of legal proofs, Modderman used largely the same arguments as De Bosch Kemper, Meyer and Stuffken. He relied heavily on the recent German literature and often quoted Mittermaier, Köstlin, Endemann, Schwarze and Hélie. The central tenet of his argumentation was that legal evidentiary rules were useless and harmful because the high probability required in a criminal case was something which could not be predetermined in general rules. No two crimes were alike and it was foolish to try to capture the endless variety of circumstances in abstract rules which could never do justice to the complexity of the individual case. The most difficult aspects of the evaluation of the evidence, such as the trustworthiness of witnesses and whether the accused had the required criminal intent, were all questions which could not be regulated satisfactorily in evidentiary rules. The goal of a criminal procedure should be to find the substantive truth in the individual case and this was hindered by evidentiary rules which forced the judge to look for a formal truth that met the minimum evidentiary requirements. The evidentiary rules could only be justified if they provided a real guarantee against arbitrary decisions. However, Modderman deemed that the judicial practice of the last decades had decisively shown that this was not the case. Many attempts had been made to create a system of useful negative evidentiary rules but all attempts had suffered from the same defects. They were either formulated so restrictively – for example, by not allowing convictions on indicia – that many crimes would have to go unpunished, or they were formulated so broadly that the judge was still left almost entirely free in his evaluation. Both options were harmful and hindered the search for the substantive truth in the individual case, which should be the highest goal in the criminal procedural law.[44]

---

43 Ibidem, pp. 165–263.
44 Ibidem, pp. 157–300. Modderman also stated that he was against the introduction of a jury system in the Netherlands. He argued that the desire in other countries for a jury system had been driven predominantly by a distrust in the professional judges, but he argued that no such desire existed in the Netherlands because the judges were trusted. He was, furthermore, against a jury system because he deemed that the question of fact could not be separated from the question of law and that lay jurors lacked the technical capacity to decide on the technical-juridical aspects.

Like De Bosch Kemper, furthermore, Modderman emphasized that a system of legal evidentiary rules was particularly inadequate to deal with the subjective side of the crime. Apart from Rauter and Helié, Modderman deemed that it was especially the German author Köstlin who had shown that the subjective side of the crime could not be regulated in evidentiary rules. He approvingly cited Köstlin on this subject: "die Hauptsache, die Seele der Handlung, die Schuld hat kein Zeuge gesehen, kann der Richter nicht sehen und kein Papier kann sie enthalten".[45] The degree of criminal intent could only be inferred indirectly by the judge from the proven 'external' circumstances of the case.

In the last part of his work Modderman explained that the 'illusory guarantee' offered by the negative system of legal proofs was not necessary, because there were other, better guarantees against arbitrary convictions. One of the most important guarantees was the publicity of the trial which made it possible to monitor the judges. A second, crucial, guarantee lay in the obligation of the judge to motivate his verdict and the possibility of appeal and cassation. Modderman strongly disagreed with those authors who stated that the obligation to motivate the verdict was useless when there were no legal evidentiary rules because then there were, supposedly, no rules anymore on the basis of which the judge could be held accountable. On the contrary, Modderman argued, the criminal judge would still have to abide by the general rules of logic and experience and his argumentation could be scrutinized in appeal. In any normal affair, whenever someone expresses an opinion, we ask for the grounds for his opinion and we appreciate his opinion according to the rules of logic and experience. Why would this be any different when it concerns the internal conviction of a criminal judge? He deemed that the obligation to motivate the verdict was even more useful without evidentiary rules, because under the current circumstances the judges merely attempted to show that they had adhered to the formalities of the law. Modderman, in short, thought it was possible and desirable to create a more extensive obligation to substantively motivate the verdict when the evidentiary rules were abolished.[46]

Jongstra, who worked as a lawyer and later became a member of parliament, won the second price with his contribution in which he defended a negative system of legal proofs.[47] Although the work of Jongstra was just as extensive as that of Modderman, it was on many points more superficial in its

---

45 Ibidem, pp. 23–38.
46 Ibidem, pp. 263–300.
47 Jongstra had also already published an article defending a negative system of legal proofs in 1863. This article essentially formed a summary version of his later treatise and is, therefore, not treated separately. See A.F. Jongstra, "Over wettelijke bewijsregelen", pp. 577–614.

argumentation. Jongstra started with refuting the, in his view, most important arguments against a negative system of legal proofs. The first argument he rebutted was the idea that it was impossible to create evidentiary rules for the endless variety of circumstances of the concrete case and that almost everything was inevitably left to the discretion of the judge. He discussed this argument by analysing how it was defended in the memorandum by Von Savigny. Jongstra remarked that the argument concerning the difficulty to create general rules for these complex situations proved too much, if it was concluded that therefore no useful rules could be made at all. In all the areas of the law general rules were made which regulated complex situations. In the application of all laws a large room was unavoidably left to the discretion of the judge. The argument proved too much, according to Jongstra, because it would mean that all laws should be abolished. If it was, on the other hand, acknowledged that it was possible and useful to create general rules for complex situations, then why should this not be possible for the criminal law of evidence?[48]

The criticism that a negative evidentiary system would prevent the judge from doing justice to the concrete circumstances of the case was, in the view of Jongstra, also unjustified. He observed that many authors who argued against a negative system of legal proof appeared to be confusing it with a positive system of legal proof which predetermined when sufficient evidence existed for a conviction. The negative theory, however, acknowledged that in the end the decision necessarily depended on the concrete evaluation of the evidence by the judge and his internal conviction. It merely forbade the judge to take heed of certain sources of evidence which experience had shown to be generally unreliable and it forbade the judge to convict when a certain minimum evidentiary standard had not been met. This formed an important guarantee against light-hearted convictions while it at the same time allowed the judge to do justice to the concrete circumstances of the case.[49]

After the refutation of these two critiques, Jongstra presented his arguments in favour of a negative system of legal proofs. He first gave a historical description of the criminal law of evidence and concluded that in the last twenty-five centuries every major legal system had contained evidentiary rules which

---

48 A.F. Jongstra, *Over wettelijke bewijsregelen*, pp. 15–30.
49 Ibidem, pp. 52–62 and 72–102. Modderman later replied that this argument was rather superficial because it ignored that there was a fundamental difference between the subject of the normative legal rules which could be found in, for example, the substantive criminal law and civil law, and the rules regarding the criminal law of evidence which focused on whether historical facts had taken place. See W. Modderman, "Over wettelijke bewijsregelen. Dupliek aan Mr. A.F. Jongstra", pp. 541–543.

confined the decision of the judge. In all this time, until the French Revolution, no one had considered to leave everything to the subjective conviction of the judge or jurors. Jongstra then continued to show that the French Revolutionary reforms had been built on a bad understanding of how the English jury system functioned and that they were an exaggerated reaction against the then existing abuses in the French criminal procedural law. The French revolutionary reformers misguidedly thought that the oral procedure was incompatible with evidentiary rules and they never duly considered the possibility of a negative system of evidentiary rules. They, furthermore, confused the function of the mind with that of the conscience or instinct from which their conception of the *conviction intime* was born. The French reforms, and the later German reforms of 1848, were the product of passion, haste and incompetence. In conclusion, Jongstra remarked, the experience of twenty-five centuries had always regarded a system of evidentiary rules as useful and necessary while only recently an aberration had emerged under revolutionary circumstances. History was, therefore, decidedly on the side of a system of evidentiary rules.[50]

As far as the advantages of a negative system of legal proofs were concerned, Jongstra largely followed the argumentation and ideas of authors such as Donker Curtius and Weiland. He remarked that the legislator worked from a more elevated standpoint than the criminal judge and that the sum of the knowledge of those who created the criminal legislation was far greater than that of the individual criminal judge. The legislator was not influenced by a specific criminal case in front of him but could, from his elevated standpoint, more objectively determine what the evidentiary rules should be. The downside of leaving the rules to legal science was, furthermore, that in legal science every idea was principally under discussion which left too much uncertainty for legal practice. Prescribing the evidentiary rules in the law provided certainty and created a guarantee against arbitrary decisions. Jongstra acknowledged that many judges might also evaluate the evidence prudently without a system of legal proofs, but the legislation would protect especially against judges who might be too careless. Finally, Jongstra observed that a negative system of evidentiary rules strengthened the role of the motivation of the verdict because it created criteria on the basis of which the motivation could be

---

50   Ibidem, pp. 105–178. Jongstra, furthermore, remarked that a large majority of the most prominent jurists had been in favour of a negative system of evidentiary rules, including Feuerbach, Filangieri, Zachariae and Mittermaier. Remarkably, he also mentioned Beccaria and Köstlin (who had both argued strongly against the possibility of evidentiary rules) and neglected to mention that Mittermaier had clearly changed his mind on the usefulness of negative evidentiary rules since the late 1840s.

scrutinized. If the rules were abolished the usefulness of the motivation of the verdict would severely diminish.[51]

10.4 Changes in the Criminal Law of Evidence after 1870

Even though a legislative proposal had been made to introduce the free evaluation of the evidence in the concept revised criminal procedural code of 1863, it was eventually not accepted by parliament and thus the negative system of legal proofs continued to function unchanged. After the reinvigorated discussion in the 1860s, the interest in the criminal law of evidence again subsided for some time. It was momentarily reawakened in the early 1880s when the creation of a new substantive criminal code made it necessary that the criminal procedural code would be revised as well. Knowing that the criminal procedural code would be revised, in 1882 the Dutch Association of Jurists (*Nederlandsche Juristenvereniging*) decided to organize a discussion on the question whether the negative system of legal proofs should be replaced with the free evaluation of the evidence. In this discussion the same spectrum of ideas could be seen as that which existed in the 1860s. Some jurists were in favour of a jury system, but the main discussion was again between those in favour of a negative system of legal proofs and those in favour of the free evaluation of the evidence by professional judges.

In anticipation of the plenary discussion of the Dutch Association of Jurists in 1882, two preliminary advices were written by Willemeunier and Tripels, and one article was published by Pols. Tripels argued for a jury system, Pols for a negative system of legal proofs and Willemeunier for the free evaluation of the evidence by professional judges.[52] During the plenary discussion these three authors and Van Hamel and Levy were the ones who spoke most often. Van Hamel, Levy and Willemeunier followed the argumentation set out by

---

51 Ibidem, pp. 179–223 and A.F. Jongstra, "Over wettelijke bewijsregelen", pp. 610–614. A year after the price question Jongstra and Modderman also reacted in separate articles to the publications of each other. The articles predominantly formed a repetition of the ideas presented in their monographies and contained virtually no new arguments. See A.F. Jongstra, "Overwettelijke bewijsregelen. Repliek aan Mr. W. Modderman", pp. 5–26 and W. Modderman, "Overwettelijke bewijsregelen. Dupliek aan Mr. A.F. Jongstra", pp. 505–544.

52 C.M.J. Willeumier, "Is wijziging van de regelen over het bewijs in strafzaken wenschelijk? Zoo ja, in hoever moet het wettelijk bewijs worden behouden?", pp. 100–141, G. Tripels, "Is wijziging van de regelen over het bewijs in strafzaken wenschelijk? Zoo ja, in hoever moet het wettelijke bewijs worden behouden?", pp. 142–166, and M.S. Pols, "De wettelijke bewijsleer in strafzaken", pp. 333–389.

Modderman and often quoted him. Pols, on the other hand, expressed largely the same ideas as Jongstra but also remarked that he deemed that the existing negative system of legal proofs was in need of serious reform. After the discussion a vote was held on the question whether the negative system of legal proofs should be abolished and replaced with the free evaluation of evidence by professional judges. Thirty-six members voted in favour of its abolition and twenty-four for its preservation. The vote of the Dutch Association of Jurists forms an important indication that there was at this time a relative balance among professional jurists. Even though the majority was in favour of the free evaluation of the evidence, a very significant minority was still in favour of a negative system of legal proofs. Nonetheless, when the criminal procedural law was revised in 1886, the question of reforming the criminal law of evidence was not raised by the legislator. Only relatively minor reforms were made to the criminal procedural code.[53]

Significant reforms to the criminal law of evidence were finally achieved in the new criminal procedural code of 1926. A committee under the heading of Ort created a first design in 1913 which proposed to abolish the rules containing minimum evidentiary standards. The design did contain an Article which enumerated the admissible sources of evidence (the testimony of witnesses, the confession, reports by expert witnesses, written documents and the own observation of the judge), but the judge would be entirely free in the evaluation of the evidence. An enhanced obligation to motivate the verdict was prescribed for the situations where formerly the minimum standards had applied (such as the possibility to convict on the basis of one witness or the mere confession of the accused). Through the exhaustive description of the possible sources of evidence the committee wanted to exclude certain sources which were deemed untrustworthy by their very nature, such as the *testimonium de auditu* (i.e. hearsay evidence) and the testimony of fellow suspects. In 1913 the committee presented their design to the Council of State for advice. In its advice the Council of State remarked that it was in favour of retaining the minimum evidentiary standards. Subsequently, a majority of the relevant Parliamentarian committees also made clear that they were in favour of retaining at least some minimum evidentiary standards. For this reason the committee under the leadership of Ort saw itself forced to reintroduce some evidentiary minimum standards in the new design.[54]

---

53   W.H.B. Dreissen, *Bewijsmotivering in strafzaken*, pp. 24–27.

54   Ibidem, pp. 29–37.

Even though the minimum evidentiary standards were reinstated, two very important changes were achieved in the new criminal procedural code of 1926. First of all, there was by now a large consensus in the committee and in parliament that indicia were not a source of evidence but only the inferences drawn from facts proven by other sources of evidence. Indicia were, therefore, left out of the Article which enumerated the admissible sources of evidence. This also implied that the rule was abolished that indicia could not be proven by indicia. The abolition of this rule constituted a significant extension of the freedom of evaluation of the judge and also had important consequences for the motivation of the verdict. The rule that forbade proving indicia by indicia had made the motivation of the verdicts often very unclear and formalistic because the judges were afraid to show their complete process of reasoning. The criminal procedural code of 1926 replaced this old rule with the obligation for the judge to better describe the 'facts and circumstances' which had led him to the conclusion that the accused was guilty. Summarizing, instead of the rule that indicia could not be proven by indicia the judge was now required to better motivate why he was convinced of the guilt of the accused. The removal of indicia from the sources of evidence also meant the removal of a significant remnant of the old system of legal proofs.[55]

The second important change was that the judge could now ground his conviction on the testimony of reproachable witnesses which were formerly deemed to be too unreliable (such as children under the age of fifteen or convicted criminals). Under the vague prescriptions of the legislation of 1838 their testimony could only be used to 'inform' the judge but he could not ground his conviction on them. In 1926 this prohibition was replaced by an enhanced obligation to motivate why the judge had deemed the testimony of this kind of witnesses reliable in the concrete case. The most important changes of the criminal procedural code of 1926 were, therefore, that it removed two of the most criticized impediments of the old negative system of legal proofs: the prohibition to prove indicia by indicia and the rule that several categories of reproachable witnesses could not be used to support the conviction. The goal of the legislative committee was precisely to replace these impediments by the obligation to give a better substantive motivation of the verdict. The committee wanted to break with the old formalistic form way that the verdicts were

---

55   Ibidem, pp. 34–37. An interesting terminological move away from the old centrality of the confession could also be seen in the criminal procedural ordinance of 1926. Where earlier procedural codes had always mentioned 'the confession' as one of the sources of evidence, the code of 1926 only spoke generally of the 'testimony or declarations of the accused'.

motivated, which was only aimed at not being liable for cassation. Instead, they wanted to replace this practice with a motivation in which 'the logical thought process' underlying the verdict was made explicit.[56]

Summarizing, the most important reform in the criminal procedural code of 1926 was that it placed a stronger emphasis on the substantive motivation of why the judge was convinced and that it removed two central obstacles of the old negative system of legal proofs. The ideas underlying this reform were not new but had essentially already been formed in the first decades after the creation of the criminal procedural code of 1838. While in the 1860s a clear momentum existed for a complete abolition of the negative system of legal proofs, in the early twentieth century the pendulum seems to have swung more in favour of the retention of at least some minimum evidentiary standards. The criminal procedural code of 1926 can, in this light, be seen as a compromise. Some minimum standards were retained while two of the most criticized restrictions of the former negative system of legal proofs were removed. At the same time the criminal procedural code now placed a far greater emphasis on the substantive motivation of the verdict.

Essentially only two important minimum evidentiary standards were retained in the criminal procedural code of 1926. It was forbidden for the judge to convict on the basis of the testimony of one witness alone or on the basis of a bare confession without any other form of evidence. Soon after the promulgation of the procedural code of 1926, however, even the effect of these rules was restricted to a bare minimum through a very restrictive interpretation by the Supreme Court. The Supreme Court interpreted these rules in such a manner that only the indictment as a whole could not be proven by one witness or the bare confession, while, for example, the most important parts of the indictment could be proven by these forms of evidence on their own. Furthermore, the Supreme Court allowed that the smallest possible other source of information which confirmed the testimony of the witness or the confession of the accused could be used to 'complete' the evidence. The restrictive interpretation by the Supreme Court of the few minimum evidentiary standards that remained after 1926, meant that the Dutch criminal law of evidence had in fact very closely approximated a system based on the completely free evaluation of the evidence.[57]

---

56   Ibidem, pp. 44–54.
57   Ibidem, pp. 55–101. Another important development occurred in the infamous *de-auditu* case in 1926. Shortly after the promulgation of the criminal procedural code the Supreme Court decided in this case that hearsay testimony was admissible. The Supreme Court decided that it was, for example, even allowed for a police officer to describe in a written statement what another original witness had declared to have seen. Even though the

10.4.1 *The Right to Remain Silent*

It has been described in the previous chapter that during the creation of the criminal procedural code of 1838 the presupposition was still that the accused had a moral obligation to answer questions, which found its expression in Article 199 of the criminal procedural code. During the late nineteenth and the early twentieth centuries a change of opinion occurred regarding this subject. The creators of the criminal procedural code of 1926 generally deemed that a new balance needed to be created between the side of the prosecution and the defensive side, and that the defensive rights of the accused – particularly during the preliminary investigation – should be further strengthened. Inspired by the English procedural model, they wanted to create what they called a 'moderately accusatorial procedure', in which the accused was more an autonomous party to the procedure than an object of investigation. To this end a positive right to remain silent was established in Article 29 of the criminal procedural code, which also contained the obligation for the police and the investigatory judge to give a caution to the suspect before his interrogation that he was not obligated to answer any questions. Thus in Article 29 of the criminal procedural code finally the 'modern' positive right the remain silent was accepted.[58]

10.5 Conclusion

In this chapter the Dutch discussion, between 1838 and 1870, has been described. The most striking change in comparison to the period between 1815 and 1838, is the fact that the discussion was far more 'depoliticized'. There was

---

criminal procedural code of 1926 appears to have presumed that the testimony of witnesses needed to be presented directly and orally during the trial, the case law of the Supreme Court made it possible to use the testimony of the original witnesses through hearsay testimony in the form of a written statement. The effect of the case law of the Supreme Court was that far less emphasis was placed on the importance of the immediate oral presentation of witness testimony. Instead the main trial now functioned far more to scrutinize the testimony that had been acquired earlier in the preliminary investigation through the filter of written statements by, among others, police officers and the public prosecutor.

58 L. Stevens, *Het nemo-teneturbeginsel in strafzaken*, pp. 42–55, and E. Myjer, *Van duimschroef naar bloedproef*, pp. 12–15. As Stevens has made clear, the positive right to remain silent and the introduction of the caution were contentious proposals and many members of the legislative committee had strong reservations regarding Article 29. In the more repressive 1930s this led to new renewed discussion on this subject, and in 1934 it was decided to abolish the caution and to retain the right to remain silent. Only in 1974 was the caution reintroduced in the Dutch criminal procedural legislation.

no longer a vocal group, such as the liberals from the southern provinces, who demanded the introduction of a jury system in newspapers, pamphlets and petitions on the basis of predominantly political-constitutional grounds. Instead, between 1838 and 1870 the discussion was held by professional jurists in juridical handbooks and juridical journals. Among the Dutch jurists in this period there was clearly a large trust in the professional magistrates. Although there remained some proponents of a jury system, the two main sides of the discussion in this period were formed by those who desired a negative system of legal proofs and those who desired the free evaluation of the evidence by professional judges.

While there had been some authors between 1815 and 1830, such as Van Hamelsveld and Rappard, who were in favour of professional judges with the free evaluation of the evidence, this had been a minority opinion and these authors offered relatively little argumentation for their position. They often simply remarked that the system of legal proofs was logically untenable and that the existing situation of professional judges who freely evaluated the evidence appeared to be working fine. Between 1838 and 1870, on the other hand, a majority of the publications were in favour of the free evaluation of the evidence and the authors now offered a far more elaborate argumentation in favour of this position. Authors such as De Bosch Kemper, Stuffken and Modderman were not particularly original in their position, but predominantly followed the argumentation that was developed in the German literature in this period. They constantly referred to, among others, Jarcke, Mittermaier, Von Savigny, Weber and Köstlin to argue that the system of legal proofs offered no real guarantees and that it only formed a nuisance in the attempt to establish the substantive truth. Furthermore, they followed the opinion of German authors that the abolition of the legal evidentiary rules did not mean that the judge would then simply have to decide on the basis of some unreasoned subjective conviction. He would still have to rationally weigh the evidence and follow the general rules of logic and experience. These rules should, however, be developed in legal science and should not be inflexibly prescribed in the criminal legislation.

The importance of the German example can also be seen in the motivation of the legislative proposal of the government to abolish the negative system of legal proof in 1863. Explicitly referring to the recent developments in the legislation in the German states and the German literature, the government argued that a consensus had emerged that the system of legal proofs was useless and that it should be abolished. A momentum appeared to exist at this time to introduce the completely free evaluation of the evidence by professional judges. Nevertheless, due to a general failure of the attempt to reform the judicial organisation, the new concept criminal procedural code was never accepted. The fact that the free evaluation of the evidence was not introduced in the period after the 1870s, was also due to the circumstance that a significant part of the jurist remained in favour of at least some minimum evidentiary standards. These jurists did see some useful safeguards in the negative rules to prevent light-hearted convictions. This cautious approach was also the reason that in the revision of the criminal procedural code of 1926 some negative evidentiary rules were retained. By now, however, the already minimalistic negative system of legal proofs was hollowed out to a shell of its former self. The negative system of legal proofs had become even less restrictive, because the rule that indicia could not be proven by indicia was removed and the judge was allowed to convict even on the basis of formerly reproachable witnesses. What remained was an almost completely free evaluation of the evidence.

CHAPTER 11

Conclusion

11.1   Introduction

The purpose of this study has been to write a legal history of the reform of the criminal law of evidence in the Netherlands, France and Germany between 1750 and 1870, with a particular focus on the ideas underlying these reforms. The emphasis has, for this reason, been placed on the theoretical reflections on the criminal law of evidence in the juridical literature and on the legislative level. This period saw the transition from the system of legal proofs, embedded in a secret, predominantly written, inquisitorial procedure, to the free evaluation of the evidence, by either judges or jurors, within in a public and oral trial. This transition was accompanied by a significant change in the decision types that were available to the criminal judge. Under the old system of legal proofs a scale of decision types existed which depended on the strength of the evidence, while between 1750 and 1870 a far more absolute distinction was made between the possibilities of pronouncing the accused 'guilty' or 'not-guilty'. Furthermore, the forms of punishment changed. During the *ancien régime* the emphasis lay on exemplary punishments which consisted of severe corporal and capital punishments that were executed in public. In the period between 1750 and 1870, however, corporal and capital punishments were used less and less, and instead imprisonment became the most important form of punishment.

In Chapter two a general description has been given of the most important characteristics of the system of legal proofs and it has been attempted to explain to what extent it differed from the free evaluation of the evidence that emerged between 1750 and 1870. It has been argued that this contrast should not be drawn too sharply. There exist many exaggerations regarding the rigidity of the system of legal proofs which generally derived from the polemical misrepresentations of this system by the reform-minded authors of the eighteenth and nineteenth centuries. In fact, much was left to the discretion of the judge under the system of legal proofs. As, for example, Lepsius has argued, it was never the case that the judge was seen as an automaton who had to mechanically apply the evidentiary rules. Many aspects, such as the question whether the confession and the testimony of witnesses were reliable and whether they sufficiently proved the crime, were explicitly left to the evaluation of the judge.[1] Furthermore, there were conflicting tendencies within the

---

1   S. Lepsius, *Der Richter und die Zeugen*, pp. 126–137.

system of legal proofs and there were significant differences of opinion among the authors concerning the strictness of the system of legal proofs. Some authors, for example, argued for a less rigid system and wanted to allow the judge to convict on the basis of undoubtable indicia while others argued that indicia could never create a full proof.

The distinction between the system of legal proofs and the principle of the free evaluation of the evidence that emerged between 1750 and 1870 should, therefore, not be seen as an absolute distinction between a very rigid, formalistic system where the judge had little discretion and a system where the judge became completely free in the evaluation of the evidence. The differences between these two 'systems' were, in many respects, more fluid. There are, nevertheless, certain significant qualitative differences between the large judicial discretion which existed under the system of legal proofs and the free evaluation of the evidence that was introduced in the eighteenth and nineteenth centuries. First of all, as will be further discussed in Section three, the free evaluation of the evidence in the eighteenth and nineteenth centuries was embedded in a strongly altered procedural and penological context. Secondly, the free evaluation of the evidence was influenced by, among other things, changed epistemological and political-constitutional ideas.[2] Between 1750 and 1870 the possibility and usefulness of legal evidentiary rules was explicitly rejected and instead the internal conviction of the judge or jurors was presented as the central criterion for the question whether sufficient evidence existed to convict someone. This situation differed in an essential manner from the system of legal proofs where the focus lay overwhelmingly on the formulation of objective criteria which predetermined when a judge could pronounce a severe corporal or capital punishment.

11.2 The Theoretical Framework

The central research question has been why the system of legal proofs – which had functioned for almost six centuries in continental Europe – was replaced

---

2 As Nobili remarked, the mere change in the underlying epistemological ideas already meant that the free evaluation of the evidence was understood in a different way: "[es gibt] einen weiterer Faktor für die Einführung des neuen Maßstabes der ‚inneren Überzeugung"; er begründet zugleich dessen Selbständigkeit gegenüber allen früheren Systemen freier Beweiswürdigung. Gemeint ist die Übertragung der wissenschaftlichen und philosophischen Erkenntnisse des 18. Jahrhunderts, vor allem der induktive-experimentellen Methode, in den Bereich richterliche Erkenntnis". See M. Nobili, *Die freie richterliche Überzeugungsbildung*, p. 73.

in a relatively short period of time by a system based on the (largely) free evaluation of the evidence. This study has aimed to show that this reform of the criminal procedural law and the criminal law of evidence was, to an important extent, inspired by a change in the underlying epistemological and political-constitutional ideas. Obviously, the changes in the epistemological and the political-constitutional discourses were not the only factors which influenced the transition from the system of legal proofs to the free evaluation of the evidence, and accordingly the claim in this study has not been that the reform of the criminal law of evidence can be explained solely from this perspective. The development of the 'modern' criminal justice system between 1750 and 1870 was also influenced by, among other things, socio-economic changes, theological changes, penological changes and changes in sensibility. A good example of the latter is the fact that there was an increased sensitivity to physical suffering. In particular Spierenburg has shown that there was a growing antipathy in the seventeenth, eighteenth and nineteenth centuries against gruesome physical punishments. This increased sensitivity inspired a reform of the kinds of punishment that were used and, for example, also made the use of judicial torture less acceptable. Furthermore, this change in punishments was tied to the emergence of stronger, centralized states and their internal pacification. Spierenburg has argued that it was only in the eighteenth and nineteenth centuries that the power of the state had become so firmly established that it no longer needed to display its monopoly on violence in 'spectacles of suffering'.[3]

Although there are, therefore, different perspectives from which the reform of the criminal procedural law and the criminal law of evidence can be understood, it has been the contention of this study that the changed political-constitutional and epistemological ideas were two important factors which help explain this transformation. In the way that the reform-minded jurists expressed themselves in the juridical literature and in the legislative debates, the epistemological and political-constitutional ideas were consistently a prominent factor. Regarding the epistemological ideas, virtually all the jurists in the period between 1750 and 1870 showed a marked preoccupation with the need to explain what kind of certainty was required in criminal cases and

---

[3] P. Spierenburg, *The spectacle of suffering*, pp. 66–67 and 200–207. Similarly, it can be argued that, for example, the changed political-constitutional discourse was itself the ideological expression of broader socio-economic changes. It is possible to argue that the rise of the middle classes and dissatisfaction with their limited political rights constituted one of the most important forces underlying the French revolutionary reforms. In particular the strong distrust in the professional magistrates (the *noblesse de robe*) can be ascribed to the important conflict that existed between the rising middle classes and the vested authorities.

frequently referred to the more general philosophical discussion to legitimize what they were doing. Many explicit citations were, for example, given in the juridical treatises of authors such as Locke and Bayle which illustrate the connection with the broader philosophical discussions about knowledge and certainty.

In a similar manner the political-constitutional ideas had a prominent influence on the juridical discussions. For example, many authors in the second half of the eighteenth century argued that it was against natural law to use judicial torture to force someone to contribute to his conviction. Another example is that the discussion in the first half of the nineteenth century was strongly dominated by the demand of the political liberals for a jury system which was seen as the palladium of civil liberty. The demand for a jury system was almost never posed in isolation but consistently formed part of a broader set of constitutional reforms such as the introduction of ministerial responsibility and freedom of the press.

11.2.1   *The Epistemological Ideas*

This study has attempted to show that the changed epistemological discourse had an important impact on the criminal law of evidence and that it essentially furnished two closely related criticisms which undermined the system of legal proofs. Firstly, it made the distinction between the so-called direct and indirect forms of evidence seem untenable. Secondly, from the new probabilistic conception it appeared impossible to determine *a priori* when sufficiently strong evidence existed for a conviction in the concrete case.

Concerning the first critique, a central idea within the system of legal proofs was that normally only the confession or the testimony of two irreproachable eyewitness could create a full proof. It was thought that they proved the crime 'directly' and provided a different and higher kind of certainty than circumstantial forms of evidence. From the new probabilistic conception, however, it was argued that the various forms of evidence could merely provide differing degrees of probability which depended on the circumstances of the case, but that they were not qualitatively different from each other. It was recognized that even the confession and witness testimony did not prove the crime directly and that the judge still had to make a chain of probable inferences regarding the question whether, for example, the testimony was reliable and whether the testimony actually sufficiently proved the crime. The Prussian-Rhenish committee is a good example of a committee that explicitly came to the conclusion that there was no essential difference between direct and indirect forms of evidence, because everything in the end consisted of a chain of probable inferences. In his *Lehre vom Beweise* Mittermaier similarly remarked:

Es ist ein Irrtum zu glauben, dass die Beweismittel, durch welche wir den natürlichen Beweis begründen zu können meinen, Augenschein, Geständnis oder Zeugnis, nur auf der sinnlichen Erwiderung beruhen und für uns nun dadurch überzeugend werden, dass wir dem Zeugnisse unsrer Sinne trauen. Es ist überall nur eine Kette von Vermutungen, worauf wir unsere Überzeugung bauen.[4]

These examples are particularly important because they had a significant influence in the Netherlands and the German territories. As has been show in Chapters five and ten, many German and Dutch authors explicitly followed Mittermaier and the Prussian-Rhenish committee on this point. De Bosch Kemper, for example, praised Mittermaier for having convincingly demonstrated that there was no principal difference between indicia and the so-called direct forms of evidence, and that indicia could create the same level of certainty. He stated that all these forms of evidence worked in essentially the same manner. On the basis of the fact that indicia created the same kind of certainty as other forms of evidence, De Bosch Kemper also argued that the judge should be allowed to freely convict on the basis of indicia and called for the abolition of the rule that indicia could not be proven by indicia. He deemed that this rule in the Dutch criminal procedural code of 1838 arose from an old mistaken presupposition regarding the uncertainty of indicia, but that this distinction could not be logically justified.[5]

The changed epistemological ideas, therefore, undermined one of the most important divisions within the system of legal proofs and led to the general acceptance of the idea that circumstantial forms of evidence could suffice for a conviction. The more general recognition between 1750 and 1870 of the possibility to convict on the basis of indicia had an important impact on the system of legal proofs, because it was virtually impossible to regulate the endless variety of indicia and the strength that they could have in the individual case. Especially in the German literature it can be seen that the possibility to convict on the basis of indicia was almost equated with the free evaluation of the evidence because of the impossibility to regulate indicia satisfactorily.[6]

---

4 C.J.A. Mittermaier, *Lehre vom Beweise*, pp. 402–403.
5 J. De Bosch Kemper, *Het Wetboek van Strafvordering. Deel III*, pp. 564–590.
6 However, it has to be kept in mind here that within the system of legal proofs there had also been authors who made a less sharp distinction between indicia and the so-called direct forms of evidence, and who argued that convictions should principally be possible on the basis of indicia. A good example hereof was the Dutch author Matthaeus. Nevertheless, this remained a minority opinion and most authors adhered to the view that indicia provided a

As explained in Chapter two, however, the epistemological change was most likely not the only factor which influenced the increased acceptance of the possibility to convict on the basis of indicia. It is probable that underlying theological changes also had an impact on this development. In line with the work of Whitman it has been stressed that there was a certain moral anxiety involved in deciding criminal cases, particularly regarding those cases that could lead to a severe corporal or capital punishment. The system of legal proofs on the continent and the jury system in England at least partially functioned to shift the responsibility for the decision away from the judges. It appeared to be the abstract rules of the law instead of the judge himself which convicted the accused.[7] Apart from epistemological considerations, this moral anxiety of judging in capital cases may also have had an important impact on the reluctance to convict on the basis of indicia. While with witnesses testimony and the confession the moral responsibility for the conviction appeared to lie primarily on the witnesses and the accused who provided the evidence, indicia were dependent on conclusions drawn by the judge and the moral responsibility for drawing the right conclusions rested on his shoulders. It is not unlikely that with a more secularized approach to the criminal procedure in the eighteenth and nineteenth centuries and a decreased use of capital punishments, this moral anxiety lessened and made it easier to decide on the basis of indicia

The second critique, which was closely connected to the first one, consisted of the fact that from the new probabilistic conception it seemed impossible to determine *a priori* when sufficiently strong evidence existed to convict someone in the concrete case. There was no reason anymore to assume that only the confession or the testimony of at least two eyewitnesses created a full proof while other forms of evidence automatically could not. The question whether there was a sufficiently high probability for a conviction depended on the concrete circumstances of the case and how the different kinds of evidence related to each other. The attempt to predetermine in general rules when sufficient evidence existed in the concrete case had become incomprehensible

---

lesser kind of certainty. This slowly but fundamentally changed between 1750 and 1870. In this period, it became generally accepted that indicia did not principally differ from other forms of evidence and it was explicitly allowed in France, Germany and the Netherlands to ground a conviction on indicia as long as the judge was convinced (although in the Netherlands the last inhibition on the use of indicia was only removed in the criminal procedural code of 1926).

7   J.Q. Whitman, *The origins of reasonable doubt*, pp. 93–123.

and untenable for authors ranging from Voltaire, Beccaria, Dupaty and Servan to Von Savigny, Möhl, Stuffken and Modderman. A good example of the rejection of the possibility to prescribe in general rules when there was sufficient evidence forms the following observation of Brissot de Warville:

> Une découverte utile pour le genre humain, et qui épargnerait bien des atrocités judiciaires aux tribunaux, ferait l'art de fixer le degré de certitude de chaque preuve, d'en faire une échelle invariable: mais ce thermomètre judiciaire est une chimère aussi impraticable que l'impraticable paix de l'abbé de Saint-Pierre. Le nombre des crimes est si considérable, les circonstances qui les accompagnent peuvent produire tant de milliards de combinaisons différentes, qu'il est impossible d'estimer le degré de certitude que peut donner la réunion de ces circonstances, même dans des cas donnés. Ne cherchons donc point l'art d'estimer les preuves. C'est la pierre philosophale de la jurisprudence criminelle. Il est impossible de les réduire à un genre déterminé, d'établir des règles fixes et certain pour distinguer une preuve complète d'une incomplète, les indices vraisemblables des incertains. Le flambeau de la raison, le calcul du moraliste, la voix de l'humanité, sont les seuls guides que le juge doit suivre dans ce labyrinthe ténébreuses.[8]

Instead of evidentiary rules, most authors now argued that only a high probability of guilt was required and that the question whether this high probability existed in the concrete case unavoidably had to be left to the free evaluation and the conviction of the judge. As Padoa-Schioppa so accurately summarized, a new attitude towards the law of evidence emerged in which moral certainty was deemed sufficient to convict someone, and "A son tour, la certitude morale résulte du degré de 'probabilité' qu'un fait donné présente aux yeux du juge: donc, c'est l'attitude du juge par rapport aux preuves qui devient fondamentale dans la notion moderne de certitude morale".[9] It has been shown throughout this study that with the rejection of evidentiary rules, the conviction of the judge became the central hinge on which the sufficiency of proof was based within the criminal law of evidence.[10]

---

8   J-P. Brissot de Warville, *Théorie des loix criminelles, Tome II*, pp. 85–88 and 156.
9   A. Padoa-Schioppa, "Sur la conscience du juge dans le ius commune Européen", pp. 122–123.
10 In the Netherlands this transition could, for example, be seen in concept criminal procedural code of 1804 and the criminal code of 1809, which for the first time explicitly made

Two conceptions then emerged of how this conviction should be understood. In their attempt to argue that lay jurors were more suited to decide in criminal cases than professional judges, the French revolutionaries presented their idea of the *conviction intime* predominantly as a subjective and even intuitive conviction. In the nineteenth century, the German and Dutch authors who opposed a jury system, argued against this conception and stated that a reasoned conviction was necessary based on a more objective high degree of probability. However, as has been observed in Chapter three, the distinction between the so-called *conviction intime* and *conviction raisonnée* should not be drawn too sharply. Modderman correctly remarked that, to an extent, this distinction was the result of a polemical exaggeration from two sides. The first exaggeration consisted of the fact that the French revolutionaries and French authors presented the internal conviction too strongly as based on an intuitive, unreasoned, feeling of the truth. They did so in order to justify that no legal training was necessary to correctly evaluate the evidence and that lay jurors could just as well decide on the evidentiary question as professional judges. The second exaggeration, which created the dichotomy, was the reaction against this view by, among others, German and Dutch authors who presented the question as if one could only choose between the unreasoned subjective *conviction intime* proposed by the French revolutionaries, or a system based on evidentiary rules in which the judge rationally weighed the evidence.[11]

It is in any case difficult to ascertain to what extent the French revolutionaries actually had an 'irrational' and subjective interpretation of the *conviction intime*. There were some conflicting tendencies in the expressions of the French revolutionaries on this subject and the jury instruction, for example, also prescribed the jurors to ask themselves what impression the evidence had made on their 'reason'. Nevertheless, although it is difficult to determine to what extent the revolutionaries endorsed an 'irrational' understanding of the internal conviction, it can be stated that they placed a relatively strong emphasis on the intuitive and subjective nature of the conviction. This accent of the French revolutionaries becomes particularly clear when it is contrasted with the rhetoric of many Dutch and German authors who argued that it is not primarily the conviction that matters but the grounds supporting this conviction

---

the conviction of the judge a requirement to convict someone. The same applied to the negative systems of legal proof that developed in the German states in the first half of the nineteenth century.

11   E.A.J. Modderman, *De wetenschappelijke bewijsleer in Strafzaken*, pp. 10–45.

and that the judge should give account of his conviction in the motivation of the verdict. The German and Dutch authors, however, also acknowledged that it was not possible to entirely justify and rationally reconstruct why someone was convinced. This can, for example, be seen in the work of the Dutch author Stuffken who was in favor of a *conviction raisonnée* but who at the same time remarked that the judge could never explain in minute detail how his internal conviction had been formed. Even though a judge could never precisely explain why he was convinced, Stuffken deemed that he could at least motivate his verdict to such an extent that any presumption of arbitrariness would be dissipated.[12]

In conclusion, there was at least a significant difference in emphasis between the rhetoric of the French revolutionaries and that of the supporters of the *conviction raisonnée*. It has to be kept in mind, however, that there was also an element of polemical exaggeration in this contrast. It is most likely better to understand the distinction as one of degrees only. On the one hand, proponents of the 'reasoned' conviction placed a strong emphasis on the importance of the grounds underlying the conviction but also acknowledged that the conviction in the end depended on the evaluation of the person judging and, therefore, always contained a subjective element. On the other hand, there were only few who would defend the extreme variant that a conviction was sufficient which was based entirely on a subjective and unreasoned feeling. Even the French revolutionaries most likely desired that the jurors would carefully scrutinize and weigh the evidence that was presented to them. However, in their rhetoric they did not emphasize this point and instead argued that the mere existence of a *conviction intime* among a majority of the lay jurors offered sufficient certainty to convict someone.

11.2.2   *The Political-constitutional Discourse*

Similar to the epistemological ideas, the changed political-constitutional ideas played a prominent role in the legislative discussions and in virtually all juridical treatises between 1750 and 1870. The political-constitutional discourse had an impact which was closely connected to that of the epistemological discourse, but it was also different because the political-constitutional discourse was preoccupied with a different question. While the epistemological discourse dealt with the kind of certainty that was necessary for a conviction, the political-constitutional discourse focused on how the state should relate to its citizens in criminal cases and what powers it could legitimately exercise over

---

12   N.G. Stuffken, *Het wettelijk bewijs in strafzaken*, pp. 77–87.

someone accused of a crime. In short, the developments in the political-constitutional ideas led to a different view on how the criminal procedural law should be regulated and how the state could proceed against an accused.

From the perspective of the changed natural law and social contract theories it was unacceptable that an accused could be tortured and forced to contribute to his own conviction without an adequate right to defend himself. Moreover, a new emphasis was placed on the idea that an accused should be presumed innocent and that the state could only take away its protection of a citizen when the guilt of that citizen had been fully and legally established. It has been shown on many occasions in this study that the idea that it was against natural law to force someone to contribute to his own demise, was used as an important argument to abolish judicial torture and to extend the defensive rights of the accused. A good example of this combination could be seen in the Dutch author De Witt, who argued in his treatise of 1778 that judicial torture was contrary to natural law and that instead the accused should be allowed to use his natural right to freely defend himself.[13]

The focus on natural or civil rights was enabled by the idea of the social contract as the legitimation of state authority, which envisioned society as a group of individual contractors who would always retain certain fundamental individual rights after the creation of the social contract. The existing inquisitorial procedure, the use of judicial torture and the use of extraordinary punishments seemed incompatible with these premises. The changes in the political-constitutional discourse, thereby, made the procedural practice, of which the system of legal proofs was a central part, seem illegitimate. The changed political-constitutional ideas influenced and necessitated a reform of the criminal law of evidence precisely because the system of legal proofs was so tightly interwoven with the secret, inquisitorial procedure that focused on extracting a confession from the accused.

However, as was explained in Chapter three, it has to be kept in mind that the ideas which underpinned the *nemo tenetur* principle and the procedural changes did not remain unchanged in the long period of the eighteenth and nineteenth centuries. While during the second half of the eighteenth century there was a strong focus on the idea that it was against natural law to force someone to contribute to his own conviction, in the nineteenth century natural law theories became far less prominent and the *nemo tenetur* principle was no longer primarily based on natural law. Instead, the legacy of the natural law

---

13   C. de Witt, *Bedenkingen over het aanhoudend gebruik van de pijnbank*, pp. 1–48.

and social contract theories was that they had led to a general rethinking of the relationship between the state and its citizens which strongly influenced the liberal political tradition of the nineteenth century. In an altered form the political liberals of the nineteenth century continued on the natural law and social contract theorists' ideas and argued that there were certain fundamental civil rights that the state should not infringe. In this liberal tradition many of the criticisms of the excesses of the inquisitorial procedure of the second half of the eighteenth century were internalized and used to define the proper limits of how the state could legitimately proceed in criminal cases.

Apart from its influence on the reform of the criminal procedure, the changed political-constitutional discourse also provided strong arguments in favor of the introduction of a jury system which functioned as a crucial catalyst in the transition from the system of legal proofs to a system based on the free evaluation of the evidence. In particular two important arguments in favor of a jury system were derived from the changed political-constitutional discourse. First, it was argued that a jury system constituted an expression of the sovereignty of the people in the judicial branch. This argument was, for example, eloquently expressed by Servan. He stated that a conviction should not depend on the moral certainty of one or two men because nobody would have been foolish enough in the 'original contract' to let his life and honor depend on the decision of a single judge. Society alone had the right to punish someone when it was offended by a crime, and to have this right society had to declare herself whether someone was guilty or to have its representatives make this decision: "Tel est donc le contrat originaire sur les peines entre chaque homme et tous les autres; je consens d'être puni par tous, quand tous jugerount que j'ai nui à tous, et que je suis coupable".[14] In this way Servan argued that it was only justified to convict an accused when a large number of his peers (who represented society) had acquired the moral certainty that he was guilty.

Secondly, the idea was derived from the changed political-constitutional discourse that a separation of powers should be created within the criminal procedure to prevent a too strong concentration of powers. The importance of

---

14   J.M.A. Servan, *Réflexions sur quelques point de nos loix*, pp. 136–139. Other important arguments in favor of the jury system were used as well. For example, proponents of a jury system argued that it would enliven the public spirit of the people and that jurors were more capable to decide on the question of fact because they stood closer to the experiences of everyday life. Furthermore, because they only judged once they would not form a habit of seeing criminals everywhere as a result of the continuous judging of criminals. On the use of these arguments in the United Kingdom of the Netherlands between 1815 and 1830, see Chapter nine.

CONCLUSION

this idea for the introduction of the jury system was particularly apparent among the French revolutionaries. They explicitly sought to create a separation of functions within the criminal procedure to prevent the concentration of too much power in the criminal judge alone. The role of the public prosecutor was more clearly distinguished and separated from that of the judge, while the accused acquired the role of defending himself for which he was granted far stronger defensive rights and the use of legal counsel. However, most importantly for the criminal law of evidence, a division of functions was also created on the level of the judgement itself by separating the question of fact from the question of law. In the ideal of the French revolutionaries the criminal judge would only have to mechanically apply the law, excluding any room for judicial arbitrariness. The jurors would decide on the question of fact and then the judge merely had to apply the punishment that was strictly prescribed by the law.[15]

Finally, it has been shown that a central motive underlying the political-constitutional discourse was the distrust against professional magistrates and the government. In France, the Netherlands and in the German states, this distrust was often exacerbated by juridical scandals which seemed to prove that the criminal judges abused their powers. The question whether there was trust or distrust in the professional judges determined to an important extent whether there was a desire for a jury system. This could be seen most clearly in the Kingdom of the Netherlands between 1815 and 1830. In the southern provinces the central government and the professional magistrates were distrusted, and concomitantly there was a strong desire for the introduction of a jury system. Conversely, in the northern provinces there was trust in the professional

---

15 Nevertheless, the French idea that a clear separation could be made between the question of fact and the question of law also did not go unchallenged in the nineteenth century. In the chapters on Germany and the Netherlands it could be seen that especially the idea that a clear separation could be made between the question of law and the question of fact attracted a lot of criticism from the opponents of a jury system. A first rejection of this idea could be found in Feuerbach's *Betrachtungen über das Geschworenengericht* (1812), and he was followed by many authors. They argued that the question of 'guilty or not-guilty' was essentially a mixed question. The jury was always asked whether they deemed a fact proven but this fact fell under a certain legal description. The jury, therefore, not only had to decide whether the facts were true but also whether these facts fitted into the terms of the criminal law. This meant that the jury decided on the veracity of the facts but at the same time they had to interpret the meaning of juridical terms. Accordingly, the opponents of a jury system argued that juridical knowledge and training was necessary to decide whether someone should be convicted of a crime, because the question of fact and the question of law could not be separated. They deemed that lay jurors did not have the necessary skills and that, therefore, professional judges were preferable.

judges and here the jurists and politicians were overwhelmingly against the introduction of a jury system.

In conclusion, the introduction of a jury system functioned as a highly important catalyst in the transition from the system of legal proofs to the free evaluation of the evidence because most reformers agreed that lay jurors could not apply a complex system of evidentiary rules. This could be seen well among the French revolutionaries who deemed that a jury system was entirely incompatible with a system of evidentiary rules. Nevertheless, although it was an important catalyst, the introduction of a jury system was certainly not the only reason for the introduction of the free evaluation of the evidence. Between 1750 and 1870 the epistemological changes had provided important arguments to abolish the system of legal proofs and to introduce the free evaluation of the evidence by either professional judges or lay jurors. In the German states and the Netherlands, for example, in the nineteenth century the conclusion was also increasingly drawn by authors who were against a jury system that professional judges should freely evaluate the evidence because the system of legal proofs was logically untenable. It was, therefore, the combination of the epistemological and the political-constitutional changes which underlay the introduction of the free evaluation of the evidence.

11.3 The Connection with the Criminal Justice System as a Whole

Throughout this work it has become apparent that the development of the criminal law of evidence cannot be treated in isolation from the changes in the procedural law, the substantive criminal law and the forms of punishments that were used. Between 1750 and 1870 virtually every aspect of the criminal justice system underwent profound changes and these changes were closely intertwined. The connection between the reform of the criminal law of evidence and the procedural context has been stressed on many occasions in this study. The introduction of the free evaluation of the evidence was almost always suggested in concomitance with the creation of a public, oral trial with stronger defensive rights for the accused and later also with the obligation for the judge to substantively motivate the verdict. The change in the criminal law of evidence, therefore, formed part and parcel of the transition from the inquisitorial procedure, which was strongly focused on acquiring the confession of the accused, to a more adversarial trial in which the accused could better defend himself.

For many authors the free evaluation of the evidence was acceptable only if new guarantees would be created for the accused within the procedural framework. The procedural reforms between 1750 and 1870 were, furthermore, directed at the creation of a different role for the judge than he had had under the *ancien régime*. This goal is very well visible among the French revolutionary reformers and among the Dutch and German reform-minded authors in the nineteenth century. Essentially, they tried to break up the large and discretionary powers of the inquisitorial judge who was expected to perform the threefold function of public prosecutor, judge and protector of the rights of the accused. This concern could be seen, first of all, among the French revolutionaries who tried to separate the roles of the public prosecutor, the defense of the accused and that of the judgement on the question of fact and on the question of law. Inspired by their distrust of the professional magistrates, the revolutionaries went very far in their attempt to create a differentiation between these functions. Within this framework the revolutionaries attempted to limit the power of the judge to the automatic application of the law as a 'bouche de la loi'.

The overstrained enlightenment ideal of the judge as an automaton without any discretion was soon relaxed in the nineteenth century, but the thought that it was useful to create a better separation of functions within the criminal trial remained widely shared.[16] This can, for example, be seen among the German reform-minded authors of the first half of the nineteenth century who wanted to break up the 'threefold role' of the inquisitorial judge. A significant shift of focus occurred among the German authors who were not in favor of a jury system but who did argue for a clear separation of functions within the criminal trial. They did not follow the ideal of the French revolutionaries that the separation of functions served to take away all judicial discretion. Instead, they argued that by making the trial more adversarial, the differentiation of functions would serve primarily to make sure that the judge could be more impartial, which would improve the possibility to establish the truth.[17] Although it was also deemed just that the accused should have the right to use legal counsel and to freely defend himself, the German authors at the same

---

[16] In some places, such as the Dutch Republic, where there was a relatively large trust in the judges, the enlightenment idea was never truly accepted that the judge should be turned into an 'automaton'. As is described in Chapter seven, many Dutch authors reacted against this idea of Beccaria and Montesquieu, and remarked that it was an unrealistic and undesirable idea. They argued that some judicial discretion was always necessary and useful to apply the law to the individual case.

[17] The German authors also argued that it would be improper in a public trial that the judge would seem to be acting as a public prosecutor, and not as an impartial judge. This would harm the trust in the judges.

time developed an important 'psychological' argument for the clear separation of functions. They argued that this separation was necessary for the judge to be impartial, while the idea of letting the judge perform a threefold role in fact put him in an impossible psychological predicament. This recognition is very well visible in the following remark Zachariae made in 1846: "Dem Inquirenten aber zuzumuten, bald auf die, bald auf die andere Seite zu springen und mit beiden Waffen resp. gegen sich selbst zu fechten, zugleich aber auch als Kampfrichter den Streit zu leiten, ist an sich eine Absurdität".[18]

Especially in connection with the changed perception of the role of the criminal judge, it can be seen that the reform of the criminal law of evidence formed part of a complete overhaul of the early modern criminal justice system. In the period between 1750 and 1870, the guarantees against a too rigorous and unjust criminal procedure were sought in very different institutions than the ones that existed under the *ancien régime*. In the old criminal procedure, most of the safeguards of the criminal procedure were centred around the person of the judge who had to be diligent, respect the solemnities of the law and abide by what were considered the virtues of a good, Christian judge.[19] Authors such as Jousse and Muyart de Vouglans, who represented the old approach, did not understand the criticisms of the reform-minded authors against the 'arbitrary' powers of the criminal judge, because they believed that these arbitrary powers were useful for the judge to have a certain flexibility in practice. In this way the criminal judge could show clemency to the accused and even help him. They thought that the criticisms of the reform-minded authors were largely incomprehensible and unjustified, because they presumed a benevolent judge who scrupulously followed the rules and the formalities of the existing criminal procedure. They did not see great risks in the secret inquisitorial procedure and the large powers of the judge and argued that

---

18   H.A. Zachariae, *Die Gebrechen und die Reform des deutschen Strafverfahrens*, p. 146. On the important changes in the perception of the function of the criminal judge in the eighteenth and nineteenth centuries, see also in particular W. Küper, *Die Richteridee der Strafprozessordnung und ihre geschichtlichen Grundlagen*.

19   As Monti and the recent historiography in general have observed, the early modern authors primarily sought the guarantees to protect innocent suspects in elaborating the duties of the judge: "L'historiographie la plus récente a d'ailleurs bien remarqué la tendance des criminalistes – au premier rang desquels Jousse – à concentrer leur attention sur les obligations et les devoirs des juges, dont l'accomplissement était considéré comme la meilleure garantie des droits de la défense". With the great distrust in the professional judges of the late eighteenth and early nineteenth centuries, however, this approach became untenable and the guarantees were sought in different institutions. See A. Monti, "Le rôle et les pouvoirs du juge dans l'œuvre de Daniel Jousse", pp. 40–65.

these powers were necessary for an effective and flexible criminal procedural system.

The generally strong distrust in the professional judges among the reform-minded authors in the period between 1750 and 1870 made this judge-centred approach unacceptable and inspired the search for a different constellation of guarantees. Instead of the focus on the 'moral' responsibilities of how a good Christian judge should operate, the function of judging was now approached predominantly from a political-constitutional perspective. The central question became how to limit abuses of judicial power by institutional restrictions that would prevent this possibility in the first place.[20] As can be seen with the French revolutionaries and the Dutch and German reform-minded authors, the institutional guarantees were sought in a jury system, binding the judge to an encompassing codification, a clear differentiation of functions within the criminal procedure that limited the power of the inquisitorial judge, the publicity of the trial and in a strengthening of the defensive rights of the accused. Natural law and social contract theories were crucial in how the new approach took shape in this period. From these ideas important arguments were, for example, derived that the accused had a (natural) right to defend himself and that he had to be considered innocent until his guilt had been fully established.

Not only was the criminal law of evidence intertwined with the criminal procedural law, but also with a change in penology and a change in the substantive criminal law. The connection between the criminal law of evidence and the possible forms of punishments was of particular importance, because the system of legal proofs had always been closely tied to a scale of different decision types which depended on the strength of the evidence. Concerning penology as well, the period between 1750 and 1870 witnessed the search for new institutional guarantees and the perception of the role of the criminal judge changed. As was stressed in Chapter one, it is important to keep in mind that the old criminal procedure was not necessarily more severe or cruel towards the accused and that there are many exaggerations on this point. The exemplary capital and severe corporal punishments were only intended for particularly heinous crimes and when it was possible to arrive at a full proof. However, the early modern criminal procedure had important ways to

---

20   The question was also strongly perceived in light of the political significance of the judges and how they could be used to suppress political opponents. The guarantees that, for example, the French revolutionaries and the German liberals hoped to find in the jury system were directed against the potential political oppression which the professional criminal judges enabled. This perspective to a large extent determined how they approached the function of judging (in criminal cases) in general.

circumvent the potential rigidity of the system of legal proofs and the severe punishments that were 'legally' prescribed. The large discretionary powers of the judge in the application of the punishment were not seen as particularly problematic under the *ancien régime*, because it was deemed that they gave the judge the necessary freedom to moderate the punishment to the specific circumstances of the case and the strength of the evidence. This gave him the possibility to be lenient and to show clemency.

The situation changed significantly between 1750 and 1870. The large judicial discretion in the application of punishments was no longer considered unproblematic and an attempt was made to regulate their application more strictly and more uniformly. As, for example, Foucault has stressed, the irregular terrorism of the old criminal justice system with its multiplicity of courts, competing jurisdictions and innumerable loopholes, appeared to the reformers as at once over-severe and ineffective. Instead they demanded a more rational and certain system of justice. They wanted neither excess nor leniency but a certainty and comprehensiveness of application which would operate 'down to the finest grain of the social body'. In short, the reformers sought to create a more effective deterrent and at the same time to limit the arbitrary powers of the criminal judge.[21]

The ideal for many of the enlightened reformers was that the punishments should be clearly and rigidly prescribed in a criminal codification so that the citizens could know exactly what punishment would apply to what sort of crime. Presuming a rationally calculating citizen, they argued that the punishments should not be cruel but merely so severe that they outweighed the potential benefits of the crime. Reformers such as Beccaria stressed time and again that the threat of a lenient but certain punishment was far more efficacious than the threat of a severe but uncertain punishment.[22] The codification of the (more lenient) punishments, therefore, served three purposes. The strictly prescribed punishments would work better as a deterrent, they would be more humane, and at the same time they would limit the arbitrary powers of the judge. This new nexus around which the modern penology was built, made the large discretionary powers of the judge in the determination of the

---

21 M. Foucault, *Discipline and Punish*, p. 80, and D. Garland, *Punishment and modern society*, pp. 141–142.

22 It is also in this respect that many of the reform-minded authors argued that the possibility for the king to use the royal pardon and annul punishments, should be abolished. This arbitrary power of the king undermined the deterrence of the criminal sanctions. On Beccaria's argumentation for certain but more lenient punishments and against the royal pardon, see J.M. Michiels, *Cesare Beccaria. Over misdaden en straffen*, pp. 101–136.

punishment and in applying extraordinary punishments seem undesirable. Concerning penology as well, the enlightenment, therefore, brought with it a significant change in the perception of the role of the judge.

As explained in Chapter two, the strict requirements of a full proof had always only applied to the possibility to convict someone to a severe corporal or capital punishment while the judge had a far larger discretion in pronouncing a less severe, extraordinary punishment. Because of the close connection between the system of legal proofs and the possible forms of punishments, the change in penology between roughly 1750 and 1870 had an important impact on the criminal law of evidence. The decreasing use of severe corporal and capital punishments must have made the free evaluation of the evidence far more acceptable in this period since a more free evaluation of the evidence had always been acceptable for less severe punishments. Vice versa, the acceptance of the free evaluation of the evidence may have made it less desirable to maintain severe corporal and capital punishments. There was clearly a confluence between the developments in the criminal law of evidence and in penology which mutually reinforced each other. Both changes were part and parcel of the complete and complex reform of the criminal justice system between 1750 and 1870.

Although the developments in the criminal law of evidence and penology were obviously closely intertwined, it seems unlikely that the change in either of these spheres was simply a consequence of the other. It is, to an important extent, for this reason that the thesis of Langbein has been rejected that the emergence of the free evaluation of the evidence was merely a change in practice which was the result of an extension of the use of extraordinary punishments – where the judge already had a large judicial discretion –, and a decreased use of severe corporal and capital punishments. Although the change in penology was important, the thesis of Langbein is a too monocausal explanation of the complex reforms within the criminal procedural law and the criminal law of evidence between 1750 and 1870. There were also clear 'autonomous' developments in both spheres. Regarding the criminal law of evidence, the reforms were, for example, also influenced by the changed epistemological and political-constitutional ideas which had little to do with the change in penology.

Finally, there were two important connections between the criminal law of evidence and the developments in the substantive criminal law. First of all, especially from the 1820s onwards, a new emphasis was placed in the substantive criminal law on the need to moderate the punishment to the precise level of the moral 'imputability' of the crime. Consequently, it became far more important for the criminal judge to precisely prove the criminal intent of the accused. With the decreased possibility in the nineteenth century to force a confession from the accused, it became especially apparent that the criminal intent could only be inferred indirectly from the circumstances of the case. Many authors, such as Rauter, Köstlin and De Bosch Kemper, argued that a free evaluation of the evidence was especially necessary to determine the criminal intent of the accused and that it was impossible to regulate this aspect satisfactorily in evidentiary rules. While the necessity to prove the criminal intent was used as an argument for the free evaluation of the evidence, conversely, the free evaluation of the evidence was an essential prerequisite for the judge to be able to moderate the punishment to the criminal intent of the accused. As Pihlajamäki stated: "Without the freedom of judgment ... the sophisticated categories of guilt provided by the latter [the substantive criminal law] would have been impossible to put into practice".[23]

The second important connection between the criminal law of evidence and the substantive criminal law lay in the encompassing codification of the criminal law and the new centrality of the legality principle. Before the end of the eighteenth century the specific crimes were often defined relatively broadly and there was a multiplicity of overlapping and sometimes competing sources which the judge could use. Furthermore, he was not yet as strictly bound by a specific indictment of a public prosecutor. This changed with the codification process and the acceptance of the legality principle. The fact that the crimes were now explicitly and exclusively defined by the law and that the judge became bound by these terms through the indictment of the public prosecutor, meant that the criminal judge had to interpret the description of the crime and see if these specific terms (*Tatbestände*) were proven. In other words, because the judge was bound by the exact definition of the crime in the substantive criminal codification and by the terms of the indictment, he always had to interpret the precise wordings of the legal definition and see whether the proven facts fell under these terms. The legal definition of the crime became, far more strictly than before, the prism through which the judge had to perceive the facts.

11.4 A Comparison between the Netherlands, France and Germany

Even though similar ideas underlay the transition from the system of legal proofs to the free evaluation of the evidence in France, Germany and the

---

[23] H. Pihlajamäki, *Evidence, Crime, and the legal profession*, p. 256.

Netherlands, there were at the same time significant differences in chronology and in the way that this development manifested itself in these regions. In France the reforms took place earlier and in a far more radical fashion than in the Netherlands and the German territories. The French reformers of the second half of the eighteenth century were at the forefront of the transition from the system of legal proofs to the free evaluation of the evidence, and their reforms subsequently had a profound impact on the reform discussions in the rest of continental Europe in the nineteenth century. The relatively gradual development in the Netherlands showed more similarities to the development in the German territories than in France, but also some important differences.

In the intellectual ferment of the French enlightenment, the reform of the criminal justice system became one of the most hotly discussed topics. Many of the famous *philosophes*, from Voltaire and Diderot to Condorcet, devoted substantial attention to the topic. What set the French intellectuals apart from their Dutch and German contemporaries, was the fact that they were far more willing to break with established authorities and that they had a particular optimism regarding the possibility to reform existing governmental structures and practices on the basis of their supposedly more 'rational' and 'humane' philosophical ideas. To have a certain disregard for established authorities and customs was even fashionable. It was in this context that the French reform-minded authors were the first to argue for a complete overhaul of the criminal procedural law and the criminal law of evidence.

The French authors were more radical and thorough in their approach to the reform of the criminal justice system than their German and Dutch contemporaries. In contrast to the latter, during the second half of the eighteenth century the French authors were also highly interested in the English procedural system. Starting with Montesquieu, the French authors who wanted to criticize the defects in the existing political and judicial structure looked at the English system for possible solutions. For several of the 'defects' of the inquisitorial procedure the English system appeared to offer useful remedies. For example, the French authors deemed that the defensive rights of the accused were far better protected in the English procedure and they praised the English procedural system for the fact that it had no need for judicial torture. Furthermore the jury system and the public trial appeared to be useful remedies against judicial arbitrariness. It is a significant fact that the English model shaped the direction of the French reform ideals to such a strong extent, and it is difficult to imagine that the reforms would have gone (entirely) the same way without the 'Anglomania' of the French authors in the second half of the eighteenth century. This was different from the Netherlands and the German territories where reforms were only sough incrementally within the existing procedural system.

Apart from the fact that the French reformers looked at the English system as an example, there was another factor that decisively shaped the French reforms. This was the fact that the most important reforms were achieved between 1789 and 1791 under a revolutionary and 'idealistic' atmosphere which acquired a logic of its own. As has been described in Chapter four, there was a strong anti-aristocratic sentiment in the Constitutional Assembly and the introduction of the jury system was seen as an important instrument to break the power of the *noblesse de robe*. Among men such as Duport and Thouret, the idea prevailed that the trial had to be public and that the evidentiary rules should be completely abolished, because otherwise a jury system could not function properly and the door would be left open for a return to the old system.[24] Under these revolutionary circumstances, and in their attempt to force a complete rupture with the old system, the revolutionaries exaggerated their praise of the capabilities of ordinary, upright citizens who judged almost instinctively by their *conviction intime*. As Ranouil has observed, there was also a clear 'Rousseauistic' tendency among these reformers who exalted the honest, simple and uncorrupted way that lay jurors would judge in contrast to the way that professional judges decided on the basis of complex legal rules.[25]

The regulation of the criminal procedural law in 1791 can, furthermore, be described as very 'liberal' and as strongly directed at the protection of the defensive rights of the accused. In the period after 1795 the political climate in France became more conservative and repressive, and the supposedly too liberal and idealistic spirit of the Constituent Assembly was criticized. Particularly under Napoleon, reforms were made which enhanced the repressive and inquisitorial nature of the criminal procedure. For example, the accusation jury was abolished and, most importantly, the preliminary investigation was again made secret. These reforms, which culminated in the *Code d'Instruction*

---

24 The remark of Robespierre that discarding the civil jury meant "aider à la renaissance de cet esprit aristocratique qui se montre chaque jour avec l'assurance qu'il avait perdue depuis plusieurs mois" was typical of the political significance that was attached to the introduction of a jury system was. See A. Padoa-Schioppa, "La giuria all'Assemblea Costituente francese", pp. 91–102.

25 Typical of this exaltation of the jury system was the following comment of Duport: "Les jurés, sont une institution primitive qui sent encore les bois dont elle est sortie et qui respire fortement la nature et l'instinct. On n'en parle qu'avec enthousiasme, on ne l'aime qu'avec passion ... Ce qui plaît dans l'établissement des jurés, c'est que tout s'y décide par la droiture et la bonne foi, simplicité bien préférable à cet amas inutile et funeste de subtilités et formes que l'on a jusqu'à ce jour appelé justice". See P.C. Ranouil, "L'intime Conviction", pp. 90–94.

Criminelle of 1808, to a significant extent determined the contours of the French criminal procedure in the nineteenth century.

Importantly, however, during the nineteenth century the abolition of the system of legal proofs and the introduction of the free evaluation of the evidence were never seriously questioned anymore in France. Even though there were important discussions in the nineteenth century on the question whether lay jurors or professional judges were preferable, the free evaluation of the evidence had become firmly established. The opponents of the jury trial in the nineteenth century, furthermore, did not manage to abolish the institution because it proved to be too popular as an achievement of the revolution. Many liberals continued to see it as a palladium of civil liberty. Although the jury trial was not abolished in the nineteenth century, it did become significantly less important through the process of 'correctionalization'. This meant that effectively, for an increasing number of crimes, it were the professional judges in the correctional tribunals who freely evaluated the evidence.

There were important differences in the development of the criminal law of evidence between, on the one hand, France and, on the other hand, the German territories and the Netherlands. In France the introduction of the free evaluation of the evidence occurred far earlier, more abruptly and it was closely tied to the introduction of the jury system. Another significant factor in the French discussion of the second half of the eighteenth century was that it was dominated by the *philosophes* who were often not practicing jurists and who had little experience with the criminal procedural law. They had more of an outsider perspective and from this position delivered a strong ideological critique on the criminal justice system. In the Netherlands and the German territories, the development was generally far more gradual and for the largest part the discussion about the criminal law of evidence was dominated by professional jurists. In this more gradual development, the free evaluation of the evidence and the public, oral trial eventually became dissociated from the jury system, and were defended as useful reforms in their own right (with either professional judges or lay jurors).

In the German territories and the Netherlands, the discussion on the criminal law of evidence remained relatively moderate during the second half of the eighteenth century. In this period the discussion mainly focused on the question whether judicial torture should be abolished, and whether the possibility for the judge to convict on the basis of indicia should be extended. A complete reform of the criminal procedural law and, for example, the abolition of the system of legal proofs was not yet considered. Nevertheless, an important gradual change is visible in the discussion in the German territories and the Netherlands in this period which paved the way for more significant reforms.

Firstly, many authors in this period started to argue on the basis of the changed political-constitutional ideas that the defensive rights of the accused should be strengthened and that judicial torture was unjust because, among other things, it forced the accused to contribute to his own demise. Furthermore, a probabilistic conception of the certainty required in criminal cases was adopted by many jurists and the tenability of the system of legal proofs was, albeit cautiously, criticized. This can be seen well in the work of Globig and Huster who argued that there was no essential difference between witness testimony, the confession and indicia because they all created different degrees of probability dependent on the circumstances of the case.[26]

In the late eighteenth and early nineteenth centuries, the Netherlands went further in its reforms than the German states. In the period between 1795 and 1813 reforms were achieved in the Netherlands that were still unacceptable in (large parts of) the German territories. After the abolition of judicial torture in 1798, a provisional ordinance was created which extended the possibility to convict someone in the extraordinary procedure on the basis of witness testimony and indicia, while at the same the defensive rights of the accused were significantly strengthened. The accused was, for example, allowed the right to use legal counsel in the extraordinary procedure, at least, when he had not confessed. Subsequently in the concept ordinance of 1804 and in the substantive criminal ordinance of 1809, an essentially negative system of legal proofs was already adopted. The internal conviction of the judge became a central requirement to convict someone and the evidentiary rules were reformulated as minimum standards. Moreover, it was now legislatively acknowledged that indicia could create the same kind of certainty as other forms of evidence, and the judge was explicitly allowed to convict on the basis of indicia (with the limitation that he could not 'prove indicia by indicia').

For most German states these reforms went too far and would only become accepted in the course of the first decades of the nineteenth century. While many German states abolished judicial torture, they remained particularly unwilling to allow judges to convict on the basis of indicia and, instead, preferred to extend the use of extraordinary punishments or 'security measures'. This difference between the Netherlands and the German states can, at least partially, be explained by two factors. Firstly, there was more of a revolutionary atmosphere in the Netherlands between 1795 and 1813 than in most German states, and there was a clear willingness to codify and reform the criminal justice system. Furthermore, with the creation of a unified state there was now a legislative platform on the basis of which a national codification could be

---

26   A.M. Ignor, *Geschichte Strafprozess*, pp. 167–167.

made. Secondly, the Germans by and large followed and remained attached to a more rigid variant of the system of legal proofs as it was prescribed in the *Constitutio Criminalis Carolina* of 1532. The *Carolina* explicitly forbade convictions to the ordinary punishment on the basis of indicia and remained an influential source of legislation well into the nineteenth century. In general, it can be stated that the German authors had a more conservative and dogmatic approach to the criminal law of evidence in the late eighteenth and early nineteenth centuries than most Dutch authors.

In the period between 1813 and 1848 the reform discussion changed significantly in the Netherlands and in the German territories. In this period the real intellectual confrontation occurred with the French reform ideals. In contrast to the Netherlands, a more dogmatic and dichotomous discussion developed in the German territories in this period. In the German territories roughly two sides emerged which dominated the discussion in this period. On the one hand, the liberals wholeheartedly supported the French reform-ideals and pleaded for the introduction of a public, oral trial with a jury system. These liberals were often politicians or journalists, but not practicing jurists. On the other hand, within the more technical-juridical discussion most authors followed Feuerbach and rejected the French idea of the jury system and the supposedly irrational conception of the *conviction intime*. These authors had become proponents of a negative system of legal proofs. A dichotomized discussion ensued in the German territories in which the dominant view was that there was a qualitative difference in the way that lay jurors and professional judges evaluated the evidence. Jurors supposedly decided on the basis of their *Totaleindruck* or *conviction intime* in a manner which could not be rationally reconstructed, while judges as trained jurists reasoned in an analytical way where they individualized the different forms of evidence and fitted them into general evidentiary categories.

Subsequently, a breakthrough occurred in 1848, when under revolutionary circumstances the liberals gained a decisive momentum and most German governments conceded to introduce a public, oral trial with a jury system, following the French example. These reforms were clearly inspired by the political-constitutional ideals of the liberals. Even though the free evaluation of the evidence was, therefore, introduced in most German states in concomitance with a jury system, at the same time, on the basis of more epistemological considerations, a large part of the German authors came to the conclusion that the free evaluation of the evidence by professional judges was in any case preferable to a negative system of legal proofs. Authors such as Möhl, Foelix and Von Savigny stated that it was impossible to predetermine the value of the different forms of evidence for the concrete case. They argued, furthermore, that the negative system of legal proofs did not offer any real guarantees because in the end everything was still left to the evaluation of the judge. Instead they thought that the development of a theory of evidence should be left to the juridical science. Furthermore, between roughly 1840 and 1870, the dichotomized view which held that jurors and professional judges decided in a different manner on the evidentiary question, definitively broke down. Through this long and complex development the conclusion was reached in the German territories that lay jurors and professional judges evaluated the evidence in an essentially similar manner, and that – whichever option was chosen – they both should decide on the basis of their freely formed conviction.

The discussion in the Netherlands between 1813 and 1870 in many respects followed and strongly resembled the discussion in the German territories, but in some ways also differed from it. A first important difference derived from the political tensions within the United Kingdom of the Netherlands between 1815 and 1830. The similarity to the German discussion was that in both regions there was a majority among the professional jurists who argued for a negative system of legal proofs, while there was at the same time a vocal group of liberals who pleaded for the introduction of a jury system in accordance with the French model (predominantly on the basis of political-constitutional motives). The difference between the two regions consisted of the fact that in the Netherlands a great majority of the liberals who pleaded for the introduction of a jury system came from the southern provinces, and that the call for a jury system became part of the more general political conflict between the southern and the northern provinces. There were only few liberal supporters of the jury system in the northern provinces and here the discussion was dominated by professional jurists who were against a jury system. A factor underlying the lack of enthusiasm for the introduction of a jury system in the northern provinces was that there was a large trust in the professional judges. Because there was no large group of liberal supporters of a jury system in the northern provinces, the call for the introduction of a jury system almost completely disappeared after the separation of Belgium from the Kingdom of the Netherlands in 1830. This differed significantly from the situation in the German territories where a large group of liberals remained in favor of a jury system and where the jury system was introduced in many states.

A second important difference between the discussion in the Netherlands and the German territories, was that the discussion among the professional jurists in the Netherlands was less conservative and less dogmatic. This could, for example, be seen in the fact that it was accepted sooner and more easily that convictions should be possible on the basis of indicia. The Dutch discussion also did not have the same strong dichotomous idea – which characterized the

German discussion – that the public, oral trial was only compatible with a jury system, while supposedly a written, non-public trial was better suited to professional judges. Many of the Dutch jurists, such as Donker Curtius and Van Hamelsveld, were against a jury system but were at the same time strongly in favour of a public, oral trial. This was undoubtedly also stimulated by the fact that between 1813 and 1838 the Dutch had experience with professional judges who decided on the basis of their freely formed internal conviction in a (partially) public, oral trial. Lastly, the more pragmatic approach of the Dutch jurists can be seen in the fact that at a relatively early stage, several authors pleaded for the free evaluation of the evidence by professional judges on the basis of the argument that it appeared to work fine in practice. Van Rappard, Van Hamelsveld and Den Tex, for example, saw no problem in the situation which existed between 1815 and 1830 when the professional judges freely evaluated the evidence.

Although there were, therefore, some important differences between the development of the Dutch and the German discussion on the criminal law of evidence, the Dutch authors closely followed the development of the German discussion and the ideas of authors such as Feuerbach, Jarcke, Mittermaier and Köstlin had a large influence in the Netherlands. This influence can be seen particularly well in the period between roughly 1840 and 1870 when the German authors developed a thorough argumentation in favor of the free evaluation of the evidence and reached the conclusion that the formation of a theory of evidence should be left to legal science. Most Dutch authors followed these conclusions and the Dutch government even referred to this development in their legislative proposal in 1863 to argue that the system of legal proofs had been definitively superseded.

In conclusion, there were important similarities and several significant differences between the development of the criminal law of evidence in France, Germany and the Netherlands. The transition from the system of legal proofs to the free evaluation of the evidence occurred far earlier and under revolutionary circumstances in France, which was particularly inspired by the English procedural model. The development in the Netherlands and the German territories was shaped, to an important extent, by the French reform ideals but occurred far more gradually. Although the Dutch and German development resembled each other more, there were also important differences between these two regions. The Dutch discussion was more pragmatic and, unlike in Germany and France, the free evaluation of the evidence was never completely introduced in the Netherlands. Some negative evidentiary rules were retained even in the Dutch criminal procedural code of 1926. However, despite the significant differences, a common thread throughout the development of the criminal law of evidence in these three regions was that they were inspired by similar changes in the underlying political-constitutional and epistemological ideas.

11.5 Developments in the Late Nineteenth and Twentieth Centuries

In this study a particular emphasis has been placed on the changes in the criminal justice system between 1750 and 1870. Less attention has been paid to the important continuities with the old inquisitorial procedure. It has also been argued that these changes were crucial for the creation of the 'modern' criminal (procedural) law. It is, however, important to further qualify this statement. After all, the development of the criminal law (of evidence) did not stop after 1870. Nevertheless, three developments occurred in the criminal procedural law and the criminal law of evidence in the period between 1750 and 1870 of which it can be said that they laid the foundation for the 'modern' criminal procedure. These developments have, for the most part, continued to characterize the contemporary criminal procedure, although further significant changes have, of course, occurred.

First of all, the modern criminal trial in France, Germany and the Netherlands is characterized by the fact that the judge is (almost) entirely free in the evaluation of the evidence and that his internal conviction is a central prerequisite to convict someone. This is a significant departure from the system of legal proofs under the old criminal procedural law. Secondly, the accused acquired far better defensive rights and the right to be represented by legal counsel. Moreover, the accused has acquired a right to remain silent and has to be presumed innocent until his guilt has been fully proven. Third and lastly, the trial has been made public and a clearer differentiation of functions has been created between the role of the public prosecutor, the judge and the defense. Of these three important changes it can truly be said that they form a significant departure from the old criminal procedure, and that they continue to characterize the 'modern' criminal procedure.

11.5.1 *Continuities and Changes in the Criminal Procedural Law*
In this study the focus lay on describing and understanding the changes in the criminal procedural law between 1750 and 1870. Nevertheless, it is important to note that there were also significant continuities and tensions within the criminal procedural law that have continued to this day.[27] A first important

---

27 On the relation between the continuities and the changes in the continental criminal procedural in the nineteenth and twentieth centuries, see also P. Marchetti, *Testis Contra Se*, pp. 274–290.

continuity lies in the way the preliminary investigation was conducted in the period between 1750 and 1870. Most of the reform principles that have been described, such as the publicity and orality of the trial and the right of the accused to use legal counsel, applied predominantly to the main trial while the accused remained far more an object of investigation during the preliminary investigation. Therefore, the way the preliminary investigation was conducted between 1750 and 1870 remained similar to how it was conducted under the *ancien régime*.[28]

Apart from the continuities in the preliminary investigation, there are certain structural features which have continued to characterize the way the criminal procedure is conducted in continental European countries. These structural features become particularly apparent from a comparison with the criminal procedural law in common-law countries. Although the trial in continental Europe undoubtedly became more adversarial between 1750 and 1870, there were still significant differences with the adversarial procedure in common-law countries. In common-law countries the judge remained more passive while cross-examination became the most important procedural tool to scrutinize the evidence. The trial is here conceived as a battle between the public prosecutor and the defendant.[29] By contrast, in continental European countries the judge is far more active and he is expected to investigate what actually happened. Furthermore, although the public prosecutor in continental European countries is expected to present the indictment and the incriminating evidence, he is not seen as a 'party' to the trial. He has an obligation to

---

28 It has been described in Chapter four that the French revolutionaries had at first created a largely public preliminary investigation in which the accused already enjoyed more defensive rights. This situation was strongly criticized after 1791 and particularly under Napoleon a return was made to the way the preliminary investigation was conducted under the ordinance of 1670. In general, it can be argued, as Damaška has done, that compared to the Anglo-American trial the principle of the publicity and orality of the trial plays a far less central role in continental European countries. Even though in theory the judge is only supposed to decide on the basis of the evidence that has been presented at the public trial, the trial in fact revolves to a large extent around a verification of the records of the preliminary investigation. Damaška remarks that the European trial essentially appears to be an audit of work done before and that normally there are very few unforeseen developments during the trial (in contrast to the Anglo-American trial). In this comparison the important 'inquisitorial' continuities of the continental criminal trial become particularly apparent and it shows that the reforms principles of the publicity and orality of the trial have a relatively limited meaning in the continental criminal procedure. See M. Damaška, *Faces of Justice and State Authority*, pp. 47–53.

29 On the modern adversarial trial in common law countries and the differences with the continental European tradition, see J. Langbein, *The Origins of Adversary Trial*, pp. 253–330.

impartially investigate the substantive truth and to present the incriminating evidence as well as the evidence that is in favour of the accused. These features of the criminal procedure are clearly a legacy of the long-standing inquisitorial tradition in continental Europe.[30]

It is, furthermore, important to observe that the development of the criminal procedural law from roughly the late eighteenth century until the present day should not be conceived as a linear development from a very inquisitorial, repressive procedure to a more adversarial and 'humane' procedure in which the defensive rights of the accused were increasingly strengthened. There appear to have been continuing fluctuations in the development of the criminal procedural law which are, at least partially, dependent on a more general increase or decrease of the repressiveness of the climate. For example, during the first years of the French revolution there was a very liberal atmosphere and a strong focus on strengthening the rights of the accused.[31] Shortly afterwards, however, under Napoleon there was again a more repressive 'law and order' climate under which many of the liberal reforms were undone. Similarly, in the twentieth century there was a very repressive climate in the 1930s and 1940s – especially, but not exclusively, in the totalitarian states –, while there was again a far more liberal climate in the 1960s and the 1970s during which the defensive rights of the accused were again significantly strengthened.

Although there is, therefore, an important influence of the general repressiveness of a period on the development of the criminal procedural law, this does not mean that there have not been certain structural long-term changes. It has been shown throughout this study that such changes in the criminal procedural law did occur between 1750 and 1870 which have remained in force to this day. While structural changes have occurred, since the late eighteenth century an important feature of the reforms of the criminal procedural law has also been the continuous and conscious search to find a right balance

---

30 On the continued differences between the continental European legal tradition and the common law tradition, and on the limited usefulness of the general distinction between the adversarial and the inquisitorial trial, see generally M. Damaška, *Faces of Justice and State Authority*.

31 As Foucault has argued, however, it is wrong to assume that the reform-minded authors of the second half of the eighteenth century and the French revolutionaries were only driven by a concern for the rights of the accused and to 'humanize' the criminal law. In fact they were also strongly concerned with the creation of a more effective criminal justice system. The reform-minded authors did not aim merely to punish less and more humanely, but also to punish differently and 'better'. This dual effort can, for example, be seen very well in the work of Beccaria who argued that a more certain and less severe punishment was far more efficacious to prevent crimes. See M. Foucault, *Discipline and Punish*, pp. 73–90.

between the advantages of the more inquisitorial procedure and the advantages of the more adversarial procedure. Furthermore, as Helié aptly remarked, the discussions about the criminal procedural law are characterized by a constant balancing act between the social interests of effectively punishing crimes and the interest of protecting the (defensive) rights and tranquillity of the citizens:

> Deux intérêts, également puissants, également sacrés, veulent être à la fois protégés: l'intérêt général de la société qui veut la justice et prompte répression des délits; l'intérêt des accusés qui est bien aussi un intérêt social et qui exige une complète garantie de droit de la cité et des droits de la défense. De là l'un des problèmes les plus difficiles que la législation ait à résoudre.[32]

11.5.2 *Further Changes in the Criminal Law of Evidence*

The standout further change in the late nineteenth and early twentieth centuries, which probably affected the criminal law of evidence most strongly, was the rise of the forensic sciences. Next to the classical juridical approach of the nineteenth century, a sociological, psychological and bio-anthropological perspective was applied to analyze 'the criminal'. The ideas and claims of empirical scientists had a significant impact on the criminal law of evidence. It led to a changed and more complex understanding of criminal behavior, new investigative instruments and an increased importance of the testimony of expert witnesses. It is a development that has been given little attention in this study, because it largely occurred after the 1870s. Before the 1870s, authors predominantly focused on the question whether the free evaluation of the evidence should be introduced at all and whether lay jurors or professional judges were preferable to decide on the evidentiary question. The forensic sciences were not yet as important in the discussion before the 1870s. Furthermore, the question of the judicial autonomy in the evaluation of the evidence in relation to the testimony of expert witnesses was still of relatively little concern.

In Chapter three it has been observed that even though in theory it was increasingly recognized between 1750 and 1870 that indicia could provide the same kind of certainty as other forms of evidence, during the largest part of the nineteenth century oral testimony remained the central and most highly valued form of evidence that was used in the criminal trial. At the same time there was still a lingering distrust against indicia. Only with the rise of forensic sciences during

---

[32] F. Helié, *Traité de l'instruction criminelle, tome I*, p. 4.

the last decades of the nineteenth century and the first half of the twentieth century, did indicia become a far more highly valued form of evidence. The new methods of investigation that were developed in this period – such as the study of fingerprints, footprints and the use of the polygraph – and the 'scientific aura' of these methods, made the use of circumstantial forms of evidence and the testimony of expert witnesses far more important. Furthermore, while indicia appeared increasingly reliable because of the connection with the forensic sciences, new psychological insights during this period made the testimony of witnesses and the accused seem to be more unreliable than had long been thought. In many respects indicia and expert testimonies started to be seen as a more certain form of evidence than the confession or the testimony of witnesses. In light of the long-term history of the criminal law of evidence, this constituted a radical reversal.[33]

The 1870s can, for this reason, be seen as a useful ending point before the start of the 'second great development' in the modern criminal law of evidence. A good example of the culmination and the conclusion of the first change is the treatise of Modderman in 1867. Modderman gave the most up-to-date and extensive argumentation for the free evaluation of the evidence and against the usefulness of legal evidentiary rules. In many ways he gave a description of how the judge should evaluate the evidence and how he should present his motivation which has lost none of its relevance today. However, the treatise of Modderman is also characterized by a conspicuous absence of a concern with the forensic sciences and how the judge should relate to the reports of expert witnesses. These questions had simply not yet become an issue before the 1870s.

The precise significance of the rise of the forensic sciences for the further development of the criminal law of evidence is a question that has not been answered in this study, and which requires further research. One observation that can be made, however, is that the emergence of the free evaluation of the evidence, to a certain extent, paved the way for a more important role of the forensic sciences and the scientific analysis of circumstantial forms of evidence. It negated the importance of the distinction between one the hand indicia and, on the other hand, the confession and witness testimony, and thereby principally cleared the way for the judge to ground his decision on any form of evidence.

Furthermore, the adoption of a probabilistic conception of the certainty required in criminal cases in the eighteenth and nineteenth centuries made the

---

33 F. Chauvaud, "Le Sacre de la preuve indiciale. De la preuve orale à la preuve scientifique (XIXe-milieu du XXe siècle)", pp. 221–239.

criminal law of evidence fundamentally open to insights from other scientific fields.[34] The 'juridical certainty' that prevailed in the system of legal proofs was relatively closed to claims from other scientific fields. It had been predominantly the confession or the testimony of multiple irreproachable eyewitnesses which constituted a sufficient juridical certainty. This changed in the period between 1750 and 1870 with a far more open probabilistic conception of the required certainty. Foucault was, therefore, right to remark that with the abolition of the system of legal proofs, jurists had largely lost their monopoly on what constituted sufficient certainty for a conviction:

> Henceforth, penal practice was to be subject to a common rule of truth, or rather to a complex rule in which heterogeneous elements of scientific demonstration, the evidence of the senses and common sense come together to form the judge's 'deep-seated conviction'. Although penal practice preserves the forms that guarantee its equity, it may now be opened up to all manner of truths, provided they are evident, well founded, acceptable to all. The legal ritual in itself no longer generates a divided truth. It is resituated in the field of reference of common proofs. With the multiplicity of scientific discourses, a difficult, infinite relation was then forged that penal justice is still unable to control. The master of justice is no longer the master of its truth.[35]

Finally, although the claims within the forensic sciences have raised important questions about how the judge should evaluate the evidence and to what extent he is bound by the conclusions of expert witnesses, the overarching evidentiary system has remained essentially the same. The judge still has to freely evaluate the evidence and his conviction still is one of the central requirements to convict someone. In this sense, it can be stated that although the rise of the forensic sciences has had a significant impact on the forms of evidence that are used, it has not fundamentally changed the principle of the free evaluation of the evidence.

---

34   If the system of legal proofs had remained in place and the judge could only convict an accused on the basis of a confession or the testimony of two eyewitnesses it would have been hard if not impossible for the forensic sciences to play a significant role within this system.
35   M. Foucault, *Discipline and Punish*, pp. 96–98.

Bibliography

Archival Sources and Literature until 1870

Aansorgh, S., *Eenige bijdrage tot de wijsgeerige rechtskunde. Bestaande in eene proeve over de rechterlijke overtuiging betrekkelijk misdaden*. Utrecht, 1800.

Algemeene Manier van Procedeeren in civiele en crimineele zaaken. The Hague, 1799.

Aller, K. van, *Generaale reguleren, en definitien van beschreeve Romeynsche rechten ... Mitsgaders eene nauwkeurige verhandeling van de Pynbank*, second edition. Dordrecht, 1729.

Amalry, J.S., *Beschouwinge der crimineele zaaken*. Amsterdam, 1777.

Anonymous, "Iets over de gezworenen, of de jury", *De weegschaal*, 1827, pp. 273–291.

Anonymous, "Het ontwerp van het strafwetboek voor de *Nederlanden*, en het *Iets* van den heer Mr. *W.B. Donker Curtius*, over dit onderwerp, kort en bescheiden overwogen", *De weegschaal*, 1827, pp. 549–596.

Archives Parlementaires de 1787 à 1860 : recueil complet des débats législatifs et politique des Chambres françaises. Première série, 1787 à 1799, Tome XXII, Gallica.bnf.fr.

Asser, C., *Vlugtige beschouwingen van eenige voorname beginselen des strafregts in verband met het ontwerp des lijfstraffelijks wetboeks*. Amsterdam, 1827.

Barels, J.M., *Crimineele advysen, door verscheide voornaeme Nederlandsche Rechtsgeleerden over gewichtige gevallen*. Amsterdam 1778.

Bergasse, N., *Discours sur l'humanité des juges dans l'administration de la justice criminelle*. 1787.

Bort, P., *Alle de wercken van Mr. Pieter Bort, advocaet voor de respective Hoven van Justitie in Hollandt, begrepen in ses Tractaeten*, second edition. Leiden, 1702.

Bosch Kemper, B. de, *De strafvordering in hare hoofdtrekken beschouwd*. Amsterdam, 1865.

Bosch Kemper, J. de, *Wetboek van Strafvordering naar deszelfs beginselen ontwikkeld, en in verband gebragt met de algemeene regtsgeleerdheid met een bijvoegsel bevattende formulieren en voorbeelden der ambtsverrigtingen van regter-commissarissen, officieren van justitie, griffiers, hulpofficieren, enz.*, three volumes. Amsterdam, 1838–1840.

Bosch Kemper, J. de, "Het Wetboek van Strafvordering aan ervaring en wetenschap getoetst, two parts", *Nederlandsche Jaarboeken voor Regtsgeleerdheid en Wetgeving*, vol. 9, 1847.

Boucher d'Argis, M., *Observations sur les loix criminelles de France*. Brussel, 1781.

Brissot de Warville, J-P., *Théorie des loix criminelles, deux tomes*. Utrecht, 1781.

Bruneau, A., *Observations et maximes sure les matières criminelle*. 1716.

Calkoen, H., *Verhandeling over het voorkomen en straffen der misdaaden*. Amsterdam, 1780.

Calkoen, H., *Twee gevangenen tegen de aanklacht van Mr. Reinier Willem Tadama, procureur der gemeente van Amsterdam, hen beschuldigende van het vervalschen of doen vervalschen van drie recepissen, verdeedigd*. Amsterdam, 1801.

Courrier des Pays-Bas, January 7, 1829.

Dagverhaal der handelingen van de nationaale vergadering representeerenden het volk van Nederland en van de Constitueerende Vergadering representeerende het Bataafsche Volk. The Hague, 1796–1798.

Damhouder, J. de, *Practycke in criminele saken*. Rotterdam, 1660.

Deiman, A.J., *De zaak der beleedigde gerechtigheid voldongen voor de vierschaar van het kundig en onzijdig publiek*. Amsterdam, 1801.

Delolme, J.L., *Constitution de l'Angleterre*. Amsterdam, 1774.

Den Tex, C.A., "Is de instelling van gezworenen, in strafzaken, voor Nederland wenschelijk?", *Bijdragen tot Regtsgeleerdheid en Wetgeving*, vol. 4, 1829, pp. 287–353.

Donker Curtius, W.B., *Iets over de theorie der en het bewijs der misdrijven, naar aanleiding van het ontwerp van het strafwetboek voor de Nederlanden*. Utrecht, 1827.

Dupaty, Ch.M., *Mémoire justificatif pour trois hommes condamnés à la Roue*. Paris, 1786.

Dupaty, Ch.M., *Lettres sur la procédure criminelle de la France*. Paris, 1788.

Elben, O., *Die Entbindung von der Instanz vom dogmengeschichtlichen und allgemein rechtlichen Standpunkt aus erörtert. Ein Beitrag zur Geschichte und Gesetzgebung des deutschen Strafverfahrens*. Tübingen, 1846.

Feuerbach, P.J.A., *Lehrbuch des gemeinen in Deutschland Geltenden Peinlichen Rechts*. Giessen, 1801, P.J.A.

Feuerbach, P.J.A., *Betrachtungen über das Geschworenengericht*. Landshut, 1813.

Feuerbach, P.J.A., *Betrachtungen über die Öffentlichtkeit und Mundlichkeit der Gerechtigkeitspflege, 2 vol*. Giessen, 1821–1825.

Filangieri, G., *La scienza della legislazione*. Napels, 1780–1785.

Globig, H.E., and Huster, J.G., *Abhandlung von der Criminal-Gesetzgebung*. Zürich, 1783.

Gmelin, C.G., *Grundsätze der Gesetzgebung über Verbrechen und Strafen*. Leipzig, 1786.

Gneist, R. von, *Die Bildung der Geschworenengerichten in Deutschland*. Berlin, 1849.

Gratama, M.S., "Eenige bedenkingen omtrent de voorschriften van ons Wetboek van Strafvordering aangaande het bewijs der misdrijven", *Opmerkingen en mededeelingen betreffende het Nederlandsche regt*, 1854, pp. 213–241.

Hall, M.C. van, and Hamelsveld, W.Y. van, *Harmen Alfkens of eene wijsgeerige en rechskundige bijdrage tot de geschiedenis van het lijfstraffelijk recht*. Amsterdam, 1798.

Hamelsveld, W.Y. van, "Zoude de wederinvoering der jurij, bij de nieuwe wetgeving van lijfstraffelijke regtspleging voor ons te noodzakelijk en te wenschen zijn?", in *Bijdragen tot het lijfstraffelijk regt*. Amsterdam, 1817.

Hasselt, J.J. van, *Onderricht over het houden van krygsraad in de Guarnisoenen van den Staat der Vereenigde Nederlanden*. Arnhem, 1777.

Hautefort, Ch. de, *Aanmerkingen over een werkje genaamd verhandeling over de misdaaden en der zelver Straffen*. Utrecht, 1769.

Heemskerk, J. van, *Batavische Arcadia, fourth edition*. Amsterdam, 1662.

Hélie, F., *Traité de l'instruction criminelle: ou théorie du Code d'instruction criminelle*. Paris, 1865–1866.

Heusden, C.J. van, *Merkwaardige voorbeelden uit de hedendaagsche lijfstraffelijke regtspleging*. Breda, 1822.

Heusden, C.J. van, "Bijdrage tot beantwoording van de vraag: moeten, volgens het tegenwoordig regt in Nederland, de strafvonnissen anders, dan onder de hier te Lande vóór 1 October 1838 bestaand hebbende Wetten, worden gemotiveerd?", *Nederlandsche Jaarboeken voor Regtsgeleerdheid en Wetgeving*, vol. 2, 1840, pp. 17–56.

Hogendorp, G.K. van, *Bijdragen tot de Huishouding van Staat in het Koningrijk der Nederlanden, volume 8*. The Hague, 1823.

Houten, B.A. van, *Rechtsgeleerd advis, in de zaaken van Mr. Reinier Willem Tadama*. Amsterdam, 1801.

Huber, U., *Heedendaegse Rechtsgeleertheyt soo elders, als in Friesland gebruikelijk*. Leeuwarden, 1686.

Jarcke, C.E., "Bemerkungen über die Lehre vom unvollständigen Beweise, vornehmlich in Beziehung auf die außerordentlichen Strafen", *Neues Archiv des Criminalrechts*, Vol. 8, 1825, pp. 97–144.

Joncktijs, D., *De pynbank wedersproken en bematigt*. Rotterdam, 1651.

Jong van Beek en Donk, J. de, "Eenige historische beschouwingen over de leer van het bewijs in strafzaken", *Nieuwe Bijdragen voor de Regtsgeleerdheid en Wetgeving*, 1866, pp. 339–356.

Jongstra, A.F., "Over wettelijke bewijsregelen". Heerenveen, 1868.

Jongstra, A.F., "Overwettelijke bewijsregelen. Repliek aan Mr. W. Modderman", *Nieuwe Bijdragen voor de Regtsgeleerdheid en Wetgeving*, 1868, pp. 5–26.

Jousse, D., *Traité de la justice criminelle de France*. Paris, 1771.

Kamerstukken, Tweede, 1863, pp. 734–828 and 1810–1811.

Kemper, J.M., *Crimineel Wetboek voor het Koningrijk Holland met eene Inleiding en Aanmerkingen*. Amsterdam, 1809.

Kleinschrod, G.A., *Bemerkungen über den Entwurf eines peinlichen Gesetzbuches für die Kurpfalzbaierischen Staaten*. München, 1802.

Kleyn, B., *Vrymoedige gedachten over den plicht een's rechters in crimineele zaaken*. Arnhem, 1798.

Köstlin, S.R., *Der Wendepunkt des deutschen Strafverfahrens im 19. Jahrhundert*, Tübingen, 1849.

Köstlin, S.R. *Das Geschworenengericht, für Nichtjuristen dargestellt*. Tübingen, 1849.

Le Catholique des Pays-Bas, July 18, 19 and 26, 1827.

Leeuwen, S. van, *Rooms-Hollands-Recht, waar in de Roomse Wetten, met het huydendaagse Neerlands Regt over een gebragt werden.* Leiden, 1664.
Leeuwen, S. van, *Manier van procedeeren in civile en crimineele saaken.* Leiden, 1666.
Leeuwen, S. van, *Costumen, Keuren, ende Ordonnantien, van het Baljuschape ende Lande van Rijnland.* Leiden, 1667.
Letrosne, M., *Vues sur la justice criminelle.* Paris, 1777.
Lievens Kersteman, F., *Academie der jonge Practisyns, of Beredeneerde Consideratien over de Theorie en de Practycq in Zaaken van Regtspleeging.* The Hague, 1765.
Lievens Kersteman, F., *Hollands Rechtsgeleerd Woordenboek.* Amsterdam, 1768.
Lievens Kersteman, F., *Aanhangzel tot het Hollandsch rechtsgeleerd woorden-boek.* Amsterdam, 1772.
Linden, J. van der, *Verhandeling over de judicieele practijcq of form van procedeeren voor de Hoven van Justitie in Holland gebruikelijk. Two volumes.* Leiden, 1794-1798.
Linden, J. van der, *Regtsgeleerd, practicaal, en koopmans handboek ten dienste van regters, practizijns, kooplieden en allen die een algemeen overzicht van regtskennis verlangen.* Amsterdam, 1806.
Lipman, S.P., *Wetboek van Strafvordering, vergeleken met het Romeinsche en Fransche regt.* Amsterdam, 1842.
Maanen, G.A.G. van, "Beweegredenen bij de Vonnissen op te geven. De feiten, derzelver qualificatie, en de schuld der beklaagden te onderscheiden", *Nederlandsche Jaarboeken voor regtsgeleerdheid en Wetgeving* 1839, pp. 68-83.
Marat, J-P., *Plan de la législation en matière criminelle.* Paris, 1780.
Marck, F.A. van der, *Schets over de rechten van den mensch, het algemeen kerkenstaat-en volkerenrecht, ten dienste der burgery ontworpen.* Groningen, 1798.
Meer Mohr, J.C. van der, *Bedenkingen over het grondwettige, nuttige en noodzakelijke der jury in Nederland.* Rotterdam, 1823.
Meerman, J., *Eenige berichten omtrent Groot-Brittannien en Ierland.* The Hague, 1787.
Meister, G.J.F., *Practische Bermerkungen aus dem Criminal- und Civilrechte; erster Teil.* Göttingen, 1791.
Meulen, J. van der, *Ordonnantie ende instructie op de stijl ende maniere van procederen voor den hove van Utrecht.* Utrecht, 1706.
Meyer, J.D., *Esprit, origine et progress des institutions judiciaires des principaux pays de l'Europe. Tom. I–VI.* Amsterdam, 1819-1823.
Mittermaier, C.J.A.,, *Handbuch des peinlichen Prozesses. Two volumes.* Heidelberg, 1810-1812.
Mittermaier, C.J.A. *Die Lehre vom Beweise im deutschen Strafprozesse nach der Fortbildung durch Gerichtsgebrach und deutsche Gesetsbücher in Vergleichung mit den Ansichten des englischen und französischen Strafverfahrens,* Darmstadt, 1834.
Modderman, W., *De wetenschappelijke bewijsleer in Strafzaken.* Utrecht, 1867.

Modderman, W., "Over wettelijke bewijsregelen. Dupliek aan Mr. A.F. Jongstra", *Nieuwe Bijdragen voor de regtsgeleerdheid en wetgeving*, 1868, pp. 505-544.

Möhl, A., "Über das Urtheilen rechtsgelehrter Richter ohne gesetzliche Beweistheorie", *Zeitschrift für Deutsches Strafverfahren*, 1842, pp. 277-309.

Möhl, A., "Über die Wertlosigkeit einer gesetzliche Beweistheorie", *Zeitschrift für Deutsches Strafverfahren*, 1844, pp. 184-203.

Nani, T., *Degl'indizi e dell'uso de' medesimi per conoscere i delitti*. Milan, 1834.

Nieuwe Nederlandsche Jaerboeken. Mai, 1778.

Nicolas, A., *Si la torture est un moyen sur a vérifier les crimes secrets*. Amsterdam, 1682.

Ortloff, H., "Beweisregeln und Entscheidungsgründe im Strafprozesse", in: *Goltdammers Archiv*, 1860, pp. 461-477 and 591-608.

Pinto, A. de, "Iets over het bewijs door aanwijzingen in strafzaken", *Themis*, 1843, pp. 171-189.

Pinto, A. de, *Handleiding tot het Wetboek van Strafvordering*. The Hague, 1848.

Pinto, A.A. de, *Handleiding van het Wetboek van Strafvordering*. Zwolle, 1882.

Placaat. Vryheid, Gelykheid ... in naame van de provisioneele Vertegenwoordigers van het vrye Volk van Gelderland. September 9 1795. Arnhem, 1795.

Précis des discussions, et des deliberations du Conseil d'Etat sur le Code Criminel. Amsterdam, 1810.

Pufendorf, S., *Le droit de la nature et des gens ... traduit du Latin ... par Jean Barbeyrac*. Amsterdam, 1706.

Pols, M.S., "De wettelijke bewijsleer in strafzaken", *Themis: regtskundig tijdschrift*, 1882, pp. 333-389.

Rappard, W.L.F.C. van, *Aanmerkingen op het ontwerp van een Wetboek op het Strafregt voor het Koningrijk der Nederlanden*. Nijmegen, 1827.

Rappard, W.L.F.C. van, *Het ontwerp van een Wetboek van Strafvordering, op zich zelf en in vergelijking met de bestaande Fransche wetgeving*. Zutphen, 1828.

Reglement en ordonnantie op de crimineele justitie en den styl van procedeeren in Crimineele Zaaken voor den geregte van 's Hertogenbosch 1794.

Reinar, J.N., *Nemesis Rationalis, of redenkundig vertoog over het crimineele recht uit het natuur-recht afgeleid en volgens het Civile recht voorgesteld*. The Hague, 1778.

Rousseau, J-J., *Du contrat social ; ou principes du droit politique*. Amsterdam, 1762.

Sassen, J.H., *Brieven over het ontwerp van wetboek van Straf-vordering, voor het Koningrijk der Nederlanden*. Amsterdam, 1829.

Savigny, F. von, "Ueber Schwurgerichte und Beweistheorie im Strafprozesse", *Goltdammers Archiv*, 1858, pp. 469-491.

Schaaff, J.H. van der, *Proeve van onderzoek over het verschil tusschen den voormalige en hedendaagschen vorm van procederen; met betrekking tot de leer van het bewijs der misdrijven*. Amsterdam, 1845.

Schall, J.E.F., *Nalezing op, en beoordeling van het werk van den Marquis Beccaria, over de misdaden en derzelver straffen*. Nijmegen, 1789.

Schomaker, J., *Selecta Consilia et Responsa Juris. Volume four*. Zutphen, 1752.

Schorer, W., *Vertoog over de ongerymdheid van het samenstel onzer hedendaagsche regtsgeleerdheid en praktyk*. Middelburg, 1777.

Schorer, W., *De jonge practisyn ontmaskerd*. Middelburg, 1777.

Schuessler, R., "Probability in Medieval and Renaissance Philosophy", *The Stanford Encyclopedia of Philosophy*, (Winter 2016 Edition). URL: <https://plato.stanford.edu/archives/win2016/entries/probability-medieval-renaissance/>.

Schüller, C.L., *Wetboek van Strafvordering, met aantekeningen*. Utrecht, 1843.

Servan, M., *Discours sur l'administration de la justice criminelle*. Genève, 1767.

Servan, M., *Réflexions sur quelques points de nos loix à l'occasion d'un événement important*. Genève, 1781.

Sonnenfels, J., *Verhandeling over het afschaffen der Pynbank*. Translated by Pieter van Cleef. The Hague, 1776.

Spiegel, L.P. van der, *Gedagten over het samenstel onzer hedendaagsche burgerlyke regtsgeleerdheid*. Goes, 1777.

Stadsrecht van Zwolle, en reglement voor het edel schoutengerichte. Zwolle, 1794.

Straeten, F. van der, *De l'Etat actuel du Royaume et des moyens de l'améliorer*. Brussels, 1819.

Stuffken, N.G., *Het wettelijk bewijs in strafzaken*. Leiden, 1866.

Swinderen, Th. van, *Schoolboek der Strafwetten van Ons Vaderland*. Groningen, 1810.

Tielemans, J-F., *Projet du Code Pénal, du Royaume des Pays-Bas. Délits de la presse*. Brussels, 1827.

Tydeman, H.W., and Meyer, J.D., *Briefwisseling van eenige regtsgeleerden, over de aanstaande Nederlandsche Wetgeving*. Leiden, 1819.

Uijtwerf Sterling, J.J., Hall, F.A. van, Den Tex, C.A., and Hall J. van, *Aanmerkingen op het ontwerp van het Wetboek van Strafvordering, voor het Koningrijk der Nederlanden*. Amsterdam, 1829.

Vermeil, F-M., *Essai sur les réformes à faire dans notre législation criminelle*. Paris, 1781.

Verzameling van Reglementen, Instructien, en Dispositien, gestatueert door zijne doorlugtigste hoogheid W.C.H. Friso ... voor de Provincie van Stadt en Lande. Groningen, 1761.

Vitringa, L.J., *De eer der Hollandsche natie, en van hare wetgevers, rechters, en rechtsgeleerden, met eene zeedige, dog naar den aard der beledigingen geschikte vrymoedigheid verdedigd*. The Hague, 1777.

Vitringa, L.J., *De valschelijk ontmaskerde jonge practizyn*. The Hague, 1777.

Voltaire, *Commentaire sur le livre des délits et des peines*. 1766.

Voorda, B., *De Crimineele Ordonnantien*. Leiden, 1792.

Voorduin, J.C., *Geschiedenis en beginselen der Nederlandsche wetboeken, Deel 1 algemeen deel*. Utrecht, 1837.
Voorduin, J.C., *Geschiedenis en beginselen der Nederlandsche wetboeken, Deel VI, Wetboek van Strafvordering*. Utrecht, 1839.
Vouglans, M. de, *Les loix criminelles de France, dans leur ordre naturel*. Paris, 1781.
Weiland, J.A., *Bijdragen tot de wetenschap der Strafregtspleging*. Delft, 1826.
Wetboek op de regterlijke instellingen en regtspleging in het koningrijk Holland. The Hague, 1809.
Witt, D. de, *Bedenkingen over het aanhoudend gebruik van de pijnbank, in de Nederlanden*. Dordrecht, 1778.
Wittichius, J., *Redevoering over de onbillykheid en de onnutheid der pynigingen*. Leiden, 1736.
Zachariae, H.A., *Die Gebrechen und die Reform des deutschen Strafverfahrens, dargestellt auf der Basis einer consequenten Entwicklung des inquisitorischen und accusatorischen Prinzips*. Göttingen, 1846.

Literature Published after 1870

Alessi Palazzolo, G., *Prova legale e pena: la crisi del sistema tra Evo medio e moderna*. Napels: Jovene, 1979.
Andrews, R.M., *Law, Magistracy, and Crime in Old Regime Paris, 1735–1789. Vol 1, The System of Criminal Justice*. Cambridge: Cambridge University Press.
Astaing, A., "Le refus du dogmatisme et du pyrrhonisme : la preuve pénale dans *le traité de la justice criminelle de France* (1771)", in : *Daniel Jousse. Un juriste au temps des Lumières (1704–1781)*. Limoges: Presses Universitaires de Limoges, 2007.
Bartlett, R., *Trial by fire and water: the medieval judicial ordeal*. Oxford: Clarendon Press, 1986.
Beattie, J.M., *Crime and the Courts in England 1660–1800*. Oxford: Clarendon Press, 1986.
Beattie, J.M., "Scales of Justice: Defense Counsel and the English Criminal Trial in the Eighteenth and Nineteenth Centuries", *Law and History Review*, 1991, vol. 9, pp. 221–267.
Beinart, B., and Warmelo, P. van, *Dionysius Godefredus van der Keessel. Lectures on Books 47 and 48 of the Digest, setting out the criminal law as applied in the courts of Holland (based on Cornelis van Eck) and on the new criminal code, 1809, 6 volumes*. Cape Town: Juta, 1969–1981.
Berenson, E., *The Trial of Madame Caillaux*. Berkeley: University of California Press, 1992.
Berger, E., *La justice pénale sous la Révolution. Les enjeux d'un modèle judiciaire libéral*. Rennes : Presses Universitaires de Rennes, 2008.

Berman, H.J., *Law and Revolution*. Cambridge, Ma: Harvard University Press, 1983.

Binsbergen, W.C., *Algemeen Karakter van het Crimineel Wetboek voor het Koninkrijk Holland*. Utrecht: De Vroede, 1949.

Binsbergen, W.C. van, *Poenaal Panorama; strafrechtshistorische verkenningen*. Zwolle: Tjeenk Willink, 1986.

Blockmans, W.P., "Vete, partijstrijd en staatsmacht. Een vergelijking (met de nadruk op Vlaanderen)", in: *Bloedwraak, partijstrijd en pacificatie in laat-middeleeuws Holland*. Hilversum: Verloren, 1990.

Blusch, C., *Das Bayerische Strafverfahrensrecht von 1813: die Reform des bayerischen Strafverfahrensrechts am Anfang des 19. Jahrhunderts unter Paul Johann Anselm von Feuerbachs Mitwirkung*. Frankfurt am Main: P. Lang, 1997.

Bosch, A.G., "Het Openbaar Ministerie in de periode van 1811–1838", in *Twee eeuwen Openbaar Ministerie*. Den Haag: Sdu Uitgevers, 2011.

Bosch, J.W., "Quelques remarques sur la sécularisation du droit pénal au XVIIIe siècle en Belgique et aux Pays-Bas", *Tijdschrift voor Rechtsgeschiedenis*, 1969, vol 37, pp. 557–569.

Bosch, J.W., "Aantekeningen over de inhoud der Hollandse Hervormingsplannen van de criminele ordonnantiën van 1570 in de 18de eeuw, deel I", *Tijdschrift voor Strafrecht*, 1956, vol. 65, pp. 197–212.

Bosch, J.W., "Aantekeningen over de inhoud der Hollandse Hervormingsplannen van de criminele ordonnantiën van 1570 in de 18de eeuw, deel II", *Tijdschrift voor Strafrecht*, 1956, vol. 65, pp. 290–308.

Bosch, J.W., "Aantekeningen over de inhoud der Hollandse Hervormingsplannen van de criminele ordonnantiën van 1570 in de 18de eeuw, deel III", *Tijdschrift voor Strafrecht*, 1957, vol. 66, pp. 267–288.

Bosch, J.W., "Aantekeningen over de inhoud der Hollandse Hervormingsplannen van de criminele ordonnantiën van 1570 in de 18de eeuw, deel IV", *Tijdschrift voor Strafrecht*, 1958, vol. 67, pp. 179–198.

Boomgaard, J.A.E., *Misdaad en Straf in Amsterdam. Een onderzoek naar de strafrechtspleging van de Amsterdamse schepenbank 1490–1552*. Zwolle: Waanders, 1992.

Bossers, G.F.M., *Welk eene natie die de jurij gehad heeft, en ze weder afschaft! De jury in de Nederlandse rechtspraktijk, 1811–1813*. Delft: Eburon, 1987.

Bossers, G., "Een ontwerp *manier van procederen in criminele zaken* uit 1798", in *Verslagen en mededelingen nieuwe reeks, deel 9*. Bussum: Kemink, 1997.

Boulet-Sautel, M., "La Preuve dans la France Coutumière", in *La Preuve, Moyen Age et Temps Modernes*, Brussel: Eds. de La Librairie encyclopédique, 1963–1965, pp. 275–325.

Boven, M.W. van, *De rechterlijke instellingen ter discussie: de geschiedenis van de wetgeving op de rechterlijke organisatie in de periode 1795–1811*. Nijmegen: Gerard Noodt Instituut, 1990.

Boven, M.W. van, "Een blijvend domein van juristen. De rechtspraak vóór en na de Bataafse omwenteling van 1795", in: *De Bataafse omwenteling en het recht: acta van het rechtshistorische colloquium over de betekenis van de Bataafse Revolutie (1795) voor de rechtsontwikkeling in Nederland*. Nijmegen: Gerard Noodt Instituut, 1997.

Braun, P., "Turgot et la réforme de la procédure pénale", in *Turgot, économiste et administrateur*. Paris : PUF, 1982.

Broers, E.J.M.F.C., *Geschiedenis van het straf- en schadevergoedingsrecht: een inleiding*. Apeldoorn: Maklu, 2012.

Byrne, E.F., *Probability and Opinion: a study in the medieval presuppositions of post-medieval theories of probability*. The Hague: Martinus Nijhoff, 1968.

Caenegem, R.C. van, *Geschiedenis van het strafprocesrecht in Vlaanderen van de XIe tot de XIVe eeuw*. Brussel: Paleis der Academiën, 1956.

Caenegem, R.C. van, "La Preuve dans l'Ancien droit Belge, des origines à la fin du XVIII siècle", in : *La Preuve, Moyen Age et Temps Modernes*. Brussel: Ed. de La Librairie encyclopédique, 1963–1965, pp. 375–430.

Caenegem, R.C. van, "La Peine dans les anciens Pays-Bas", in *La Peine, deuxième partie: Europe avant le XVIIIe siècle*. Brussel: De Boeck-Wesmael, 1991.

Caenegem, R.C. van, *Legal History: A European Perspective*. Londen: The Hambledon Press, 1991.

Carbasse, J-M., *Histoire du droit pénal et de la justice criminelle*. Paris : Presse Universitaire de France, 2006.

Carbasse, J-M., Depambour-Tarride, L., ed., *La conscience du juge dans la tradition juridique européenne*. Paris: Presse Universitaire de France, 1999.

Chauvaud, F., "Le Sacre de la preuve indiciale. De la preuve orale à la preuve scientifique (XIXe-milieu du XXe siècle)", in : *La Preuve en Justice. De l'Antiquité à nos jours*. Rennes: Presses Universitaires de Rennes, 2003.

Cogrossi, C., "La criminalistica italiana del XVIII secolo sulla 'certezza morale' antesignana dei libero convincimento del giudice", in *Rivista di Storia del diritto italiano*, 2000, pp. 121–235.

Cogrossi, C., "Alle origini del libero convincimento del giudice. La morale certezza in Tommaso Briganti trattatista del primo settecento", in: *Amicitiae pignus: studi in ricordo di Adriano Cavanna*. Milan: Giuffré, 2003.

Cogrossi, C., *La formazione della probabilità e del concetto die "certezza" giudiziale nei giuristi-filosofi europei fra il XVII e il XVIII secolo*. Milan: Narcissus Self Publishing, 2012.

Cowdry, H.E.J., "The Peace and Truce of God in the Eleventh Century", *Past and Present: a Journal of historical Studies,* 1970, vol. 46, pp. 42–67.

Crijns, J.H., "Een kroniek van de strafrechtelijke waarheidsvinding", in: *De waarde van waarheid. Opstellen over waarheid en waarheidsvinding in het* strafrecht. Den Haag: Boom Juridische Uitgevers, 2008.

Damaška, M., "The Quest for Due Process in the Age of Inquisitio", *The American Journal of Comparative Law*, 2012, vol. 60, pp. 919–954.

Damaška, M., *Faces of Justice and State Authority: a Comparative Approach to the Legal Process*. New Haven: Yale University Press, 1986.

Damaška, M., "Book reviews. The Death of Legal Torture", *Yale Law Journal*, 1987, pp. 860–884.

Darwall, S., "The foundations of morality: virtue, law and obligation", in: Rutherford, D., *The Cambridge Companion to Early Modern Philosophy*. Cambridge: Cambridge University Press, 2006.

Daston, L., *Classical Probability in the Enlightenment*. Princeton: Princeton University Press, 1988.

Daston, L. and Stolleis, M., *Natural Law and Laws of Nature in Early Modern*. Farnham: Ashgate, 2008.

Dautricourt, P., *La criminalité et la répression au parlement de Flandre au XVIIIe siècle, 1721–1790*. Lille : G. Sautai, 1912.

Decock, W., "The Judge's Conscience and the Protection of the Criminal Defendant: Moral Safeguards against Judicial Arbitrariness", in: *From the Judge's Conscience to the Legality Principle*. Berlin: Duncker & Humblot, 2013.

Delbecke, B., *De lange schaduw van de grondwetgever perswetgeving en persmisdrijven in België (1831–1914)*. Gent: Academia Press, 2012.

Delbecke, B., "<<Le fruit du terroir?>>. The Debate on Trial by Jury in the United Kingdom of the Netherlands (1814–1831)", in: *Popular justice in Europe (18th–19th centuries)*. Berlin: Dunker und Humblot, 2014.

Diederiks, H.A., Roodenburg, H.W., ed., *Misdaad, zoen en straf. Aspekten van de middeleeuwse strafrechtsgeschiedenis in de Nederlanden*. Hilversum: Verloren, 1991.

Donovan, J.M., *Juries and the Transformation of Criminal Justice in France in the Nineteenth and Twentieth Centuries*. Chapel Hill: The University of North Carolina Press, 2010.

Dreissen, W.H.B., *Bewijsmotivering in Strafzaken*. Den Haag: Boom Juridische Uitgevers, 2007.

Dubelaar, M.J., "Nullius in verba: waarheidsvinding en getuigenverklaringen in het strafproces", in: *Het procesrecht en de waarheidsvinding*. Den Haag: Boom Juridische Uitgevers, 2001.

Dupont, G., "Les temps des compositions. Pratiques judiciaires à Bruges et à Gand du XIVe au XVIe siècle", in: *Amender, Sanctionner et punir*. Leuven : Presses Universitaire de Louvain, 2012.

Dupont, L., *Beginselen van behoorlijke strafrechtsbedeling: bijdrage tot het grondslagenonderzoek van het strafrecht*. Antwerpen: Kluwer, 1979.

Durand, B., "Arbitraire du juge et droit de la torture: l'exemple du Conseil souverain de Roussillon, 1660–1790", *Recueil de mémoires et travaux publié par la Société d'histoire du droit et des institutions des ancien pays de droit écrit*, 1979, vol. 10, pp. 141–179.

Egmond, F., "Fragmentatie, rechtsverscheidenheid en rechtsongelijkheid in de Noordelijke Nederlanden tijdens de zeventiende en achttiende eeuw", in: *Nieuw licht op oude justitie: misdaad en straf ten tijde van de Republiek*. Muiderberg: Coutinho, 1989.

Esmein, A., *Histoire de la procédure criminelle en France et spécialement de la procédure inquisitoire depuis le XIII siècle jusqu'à nos jours*. Paris: Larose et Forcel, 1882.

Faber, S., *Strafrechtspleging en criminaliteit te Amsterdam, 1680–1811. De nieuwe menslievendheid*. Arnhem: Gouda Quint, 1983.

Faber, S., "Straffen in Nederland sedert 1811", in: *Het Franse Nederland: de inlijving 1810–1813: de juridische en bestuurlijke gevolgen van de 'Réunion' met Frankrijk*. Hilversum: Verloren, 2012.

Feldhausen, P., *Zur Geschichte des Strafprozessrechtes in Frankreich von der Revolution bis zum Erlass des 'Code d'instruction criminelle' (1789 bis 1808)*. Bonn: publisher unknown, 1966.

Fiorelli, P., *La tortura giudiziaria nel diritto commune*. Milaan: Giuffrè, 1953–1954.

Fontana, B., *Benjamin Constant and the post-revolutionary mind*. New Haven: Yale University Press, 1991.

Foriers, P., "La Conception de la Preuve dans l'École de Droit Naturel", in : *La Preuve. Deuxième partie, Moyen Age et Temps Modernes*. Brussels : Librairie Encyclopédique, 1965.

Forsyth, M., "Hobbes contractarianism. A comparative analysis", in: *The social contract from Hobbes to Rawls*. London: Routledge, 1994.

Foucault, M., *Discipline and punish: the birth if the prison*. London: Penguin Books, 1975.

Foucault, M., *Archeology of Knowledge*. London: Routledge, 1989.

Fraher, R.M., "The theoretical Justification for the new Criminal Law of the High Middle Ages: 'Rei Puclica interest, ne crimina remaneant impunita'", *University of Illinois Law Review*, 1984, vol. 3, pp. 577–595.

Fraher, R.M., "Preventing Crime in the High Middle Ages: The Medieval Lawyers' search for Deterrence", in: *Popes, Teachers and Canon Law in the Middle Ages*. Ithaca: Cornell University Press, 1989.

Fraher, R.M., "Conviction According to Conscience: The Medieval Jurists' Debate Concerning Judicial Discretion and the Law of Proof", *Law and History Review*, 1989, vol. 7, pp. 23–88.

Fraher, R.M., "IV Lateran's revolution in criminal procedure: the birth of *Inquisitio*, the end of ordeals, and Innocent III's vision of ecclesiastical politics" in: *Studia in honorem eminentissimi cardinalis A.M. Stickler*. Rome: LAS, 1992, pp. 97–111.

Garland, D., *Punishment and modern society: a study in social theory*. Chicago: University of Chicago Press, 1990.

Gaudemet, J., "Les ordalies au moyen âge: doctrine, législation et pratique canoniques", in : *La Preuve, Moyen Age et Temps Modernes*. Brussel: Ed. de La Librairie encyclopédique, 1963–1965.

Geary, P.J., "Vivre en conflit dans une France sans état: typologie des mécanismes de règlement des conflits (1050–1200)", *Annales : économies, sociétés, civilisations*, 1986, vol 41, pp. 1107–1133.

Glaser, J., *Beiträge zur Lehre vom Beweis im Strafprozess*. Leipzig: Dunker und Humblot, 1883.

Goetz, H-W., "Die Gottesfriedensbewegung im Licht neuerer Forschungen", in: *Landfrieden Anspruch und Wirklichkeit*. Paderborn: Buschmann, 2002.

Gou, L. de, *Het plan van constitutie van 1796*. Den Haag: Martinus Nijhoff, 1975.

Gou, L. de, *Het plan van constitutie van 1797*. Den Haag: Martinus Nijhoff, 1985.

Green, T.A., *Verdict According to Conscience: perspectives on the English criminal trial jury, 1200–1800*. Chicago: University of Chicago Press, 1985.

Haakonssen, K., *Natural Law and Moral Philosophy, from Grotius to the Scottish Enlightenment*. New York: Cambridge University Press, 1996.

Haastert, J. van, "Beschouwingen bij de criminele vonnissen van de schepenbank van de stad Breda uit de jaren 1626 tot 1795", *Jaarboek van de Geschied en Oudheidkundige kring van Stad en Land van Breda "De Oranjeboom"*, 1976, pp. 62–119.

Hacking, I., *The Emergence of Probability*. Cambridge: Cambridge University Press, 1975.

Halpérin J-L., "Continuité et rupture dans l'évolution de la procédure pénale en France de 1795 à 1810", in: *Révolutions et justice pénale en Europe : modèles français et traditions nationales, 1780–1830*. Paris : L'Harmmatan, 1999.

Hattum, W.F. van, *Non bis in idem: de ontwikkeling van een beginsel*. Nijmegen: Wolf Legal Publishers, 2012.

Heijnsbergen, P. van, *De pijnbank in de Nederlanden*. Groningen: Noordhoff, 1925.

Helmholz, R.H., "Origins of the privilege against self-incrimination: the role of the European *ius commune*", *New York University Law Review*, 1990, pp. 962–990.

Helmholz, R.H. ed., *The Privilege against Self-Incriminaton: its Origins and Development*. Chicago: University of Chicago Press, 1997.

Henschel, J.F., *Die Strafverteidigung im Inquisitionsprozess des 18. und im Anklageprozess des 19. Jahrhunderts*. München: Schön, 1972.

Hertz, E., *Voltaire und die französische Strafrechtspflege im 18. Jahrhundert. Ein Beitrag zur Geschichte des Aufklärungszeitalters*. Stuttgart: Enke, 1887.

Hewett, M.L., *On crimes. A commentary on books XLVII and XLVIII of the digest by Antonius Matthaeus volume IV*. Cape Town: Juta, 1996.

Hildebrand, K., *Het reglement reformatoir in de stad en lande in de praktijk*. Groningen: Wolters, 1932.

Hofmann, H., "Zur Lehre vom Naturzustand in der Rechtsphilosophie", in: *Rechtsphilosophie der Aufklärung: Symposium Wolfenbüttel 1981*. Berlin: De Gruyter, 1982.

Holzhauer, H., "Zum Strafgedanken in frühen Mittelalter", *Beitrage zur Rechtsgeschichte*, 2000, pp. 112–126.

Hostettler, J., *The Criminal Jury Old and New: jury power from early times to the present day*. Winchester: Waterside, 2004.
Hunt, L., *Inventing Human Rights: a history*. New York: Norton, 2007.
Huussen, A.H., "Jurisprudentie en bureaucratie: het Hof van Friesland en zijn criminele rechtspraak in de achttiende eeuw", *BMGM*, 1978, vol. 93, pp. 241–298.
Huussen, A.H., *Veroordeeld in Friesland. Criminaliteitsbestrijding in de eeuw der verlichting*. Leeuwarden: Hedeby Publishing, 1994.
Hyams, P., "Trials by Ordeal: The Key to Proof in the Early Common Law", in: *On the Laws and Customs of England: Essays in Honour of Samuel E. Thorne*. Chapel Hill : University of North Carolina Press, 1981.
Ignatieff, M., *A Just Measure of Pain: The Penitentiary in the Industrial Revolution, 1750–1870*. New York: Pantheon Books, 1978.
Ignor, A.M., *Geschichte des Strafprozess in Deutschland: 1532–1846: von der Carolina Karls v. bis zu den Reformen des Vormärz*. Paderborn: Schöningh, 2002.
Isenmann, M., *Legalität und Herrschaftskontrolle (1200–1600). Eine vergleichende Studie zum Syndikatsprozess: Florenz, Kastilien und Valencia*. Frankfurt am Main: Vittorio Klostermann, 2010.
Israel, J.I., *Democratic enlightenment: philosophy, revolution and human rights 1750–1790*. New York: Oxford University Press, 2011.
Jansen, C.J.H., "H.C. Cras (1739–1820), hoogleraar en natuurrechtsgeleerde in hart en nieren", in: *Athenaeum Ilustre: Elf studies over de Amsterdamse Doorluchtige School 1632–1877*. Amsterdam: Amsterdam University Press, 1997.
Jerouschek, G., "Busse, Strafe und Ehre im frühen Mittelalter", in *Karl von Amira zum Gedächtnis*. Frankfurt am Main: Peter Lang GmbH, 1999.
Jerouscheck, G., "Die Herausbildung des peinlichen Inquisitionsprozess im Spätmittelalter und in der frühen Neuzeit", *Zeitschrift für die gesamte Strafrechtswissenschaft*, 1992, vol. 104, pp. 328–360.
Kamphuis, H.A., *Stad en Lande tijdens de Bataafse Republiek*. Assen: Koninklijke van Gorcum, 2005.
Kavka, G.S., "Hobbes War of all against All", *Ethics*, 1983, no. 2, 291–310.
Kennedy, E., *A cultural history of the French Revolution*. New Haven: Yale University Press, 1989.
Kéry, L., *Gottesfurcht und irdische Strafe; Der Beitrag des mittelalterlichen Kirchenrechts zur Entstehung des öffentlichen Strafrecht*. Cologne: Böhlau Verlag, 2006.
Kleinheyer, G. von, "Zur Rolle des Geständnisses im Strafverfahren des späten Mittelalters und der frühen Neuzeit", in: *Beitrage zur Rechtsgeschichte: Gedächtnisschrift für Hermann Conrad*. Paderborn: Schöningh, 1979.
Klementowski, M.L., "Die Entstehung der Grundsätze der Strafrechtlichen Verantwortlichkeit und der öffentlichen Strafe im Deutschen Reich bis zum 14. Jahrhundert",

Zeitschrift der Savigny-Stiftung für Rechtsgeschichte, Germanistische Abteilung, 1996, vol. 113, pp. 217-246.

Kluit, M.E., *Cornelis Felix van Maanen: tot het herstel der onafhankelijkheid: 9 december 1769-6 december 1813*. Groningen: Wolters, 1953.

Knapp, N., *Die Ungehorssamstrafe in der Strafprozesspraxis des frühen 19. Jahrhunderts*. Berlin: Dunker und Humblot, 2011.

Krieter, H., *Historische Entwicklung des "Prinzips der freien Beweiswürdigung" im Strafprozess*. Hildesheim: Borgmeyer Verlag, 1926.

Küper, W., *Die Richteridee der Strafprozessordnung und ihre geschichtlichen Grundlagen*. Berlin: De Gruyter, 1967.

Laingui, A., en Lebigre, A., *Histoire du droit pénal II. La procédure criminelle*. Parijs: Cujas, 1979.

Laingui, A., en Lebigre, A., *Histoire du droit pénal I. Le droit pénal*. Parijs: Cujas, 1979.

Landau, P., "Schwurgerichte und Schöffengerichte in Deutschland im 19. Jahrhundert bis 1870", in: *The Trial Jury in England, France, Germany 1700-1900*. Berlin: Dunkler & Humblot, 1987.

Landsberg, E., *Die Gutachten der Rheinischen Immediat-Justiz-Kommission und der Kampf um die Rheinische Rechts- und Gerichtsverfassung 1814-1819*. Bonn: Droste Verlag, 1914.

Langbein, J., *Torture and the law of proof: Europe and England in the ancient régime*. Chicago: Chicago University Press, 1977.

Langbein, J.H., "The criminal trial before the lawyers", *The University of Chicago Law Review*, 1978, vol. 45, pp. 263-316.

Langbein, J., *The Origins of Adversary Trial*. Oxford: Oxford University Press, 2005.

Lent, L. van, *Externe openbaarheid in het strafproces*. Den Haag: Boom Juridische Uitgevers, 2008.

Leeuwen, H. van, *The Problem of Certainty in English Thought: 1630-1690*. The Hague: Nijhoff, 1970.

Lepsius, S., *Der Richter und die Zeugen. Eine Untersuchung anhand des Tractatus testimoniorum des Bartolus von Sassoferrato*. Frankfurt am Main: Vittorio Klostermann, 2003.

Lepsius, S., *Von Zweifeln zur Überzeugung. Der Zeugenbeweis im gelehrten Recht ausgehend von der Abhandlung des Bartolus von Sassoferrato*. Frankfurt am Main: Vittorio Klostermann, 2003.

Lessnoff, M., *Social Contract*. Atlantic Highlands: Humanities Press International: 1986.

Lévy, J-P., "La preuve dans les droits savants au moyen âge", in: *La Preuve, Moyen Age et Temps Modernes,* Brussel: Ed. de La Librairie encyclopédique, 1963-1965, pp. 137-165.

Lévy, J-P., *La hiérarchie des preuves dans le droit savant du Moyen-Age depuis la renaissance du droit romain jusqu'à la fin du XIVe siècle*. Paris : Librairie du Recueil Sirey, 1939.

Lieber, N., *Schöffengericht und Trial by Jury: eine rechtsvergleichende Untersuchung zur Entstehung, gegenwärtigen Praxis und möglichen Zukunft zweier Modelle der Laienbeteiligung an Strafverfahren in Europa*. Berlin: Dunker und Humblot, 2010.

Luhmann, N., *Ausdifferenzierung des Rechts. Beiträge zur Rechtssoziologie und Rechtstheorie*. Frankfurt am Main: Suhrkamp Verlag, 1981.

Luhmann, N., *A sociological theory of law*. London: Routledge, 1985.

Maestro, M., *Cesare Beccaria and the Origins of Penal Reform*. Philadelphia: Temple University Press, 1973.

Marchetti, P., *Testis Contra Se. L'imputato come fonte di prova nel processo penale dell'eta moderna*. Milan: Giuffré, 1994.

Martinage, R., *Punir le crime. La répression judiciaire depuis le code pénal*. Paris : Villeneuve d'Asq, 1989.

Martinage, R., *Geschiedenis van het strafrecht in Europa*. Nijmegen: Ars Aequi Libri, 2002.

Mauss, D., *Die "Lügenstrafe" nach Abschaffung der Folter ab 1740*. Marburg: Philips-Universität zu Marburg, 1974.

Mayali, L., "The concept of discretionary punishment in medieval jurisprudence", in: *Studia in honorem eminentissimi cardinalis Alphonsi M. Stickler*. Rome: LAS, 1992.

McAuley, F., "Canon Law and the End of the Ordeal", *Oxford Journal of Legal Studies*, 2006, vol. 26, issue 3, pp. 473–513.

Meccarelli, M., *Arbitrium. Un aspetto sistematico degli ordinamenti giuridici in età di diritto comune*. Milaan: Giuffré, 1998.

Mer, L-B., "La procédure criminelle au XVIIIe siècle: l'enseignement des archives bretonnes", *Revue Historique*, 1985, pp. 9–42.

Michels, K., *Der Indizienbeweis in Übergang vom Inquisitionsprozess zum reformierten Strafverfahren*. Tübingen: Universität Tübingen, 2000.

Michiels, J.M., *Cesare Beccaria. Over misdaden en straffen*. Antwerpen: Kluwer, 1982.

Moglen, E., "The Privilege in British North America: The Colonial Period to the Fifth Amendment", in: *The Privilege against Self-Incrimination: its Origins and Development*. Chicago: University of Chicago Press, 1997.

Monballyu, J., "Het onderscheid tussen de civiele en de criminele en de ordinaire en de extraordinaire strafrechtspleging in het Vlaamse recht van de 16e eeuw", in: *Misdaad zoen en straf: aspecten van de middeleeuwse strafrechtsgeschiedenis in de Nederlanden*. Hilversum: Verloren, 1991.

Monballyu, J., *Filips Wielant verzameld werk I. Corte instructie in materie criminele*. Brussel: Paleis der Academiën, 1995.

Monballyu, J., *Zes eeuwen strafrecht. De geschiedenis van het Belgische strafrecht (1400–2000)*. Leuven: Acco, 2006.

Monté Verloren, P. de, *Geschiedenis van de wetenschap van het strafrecht en strafprocesrecht in de noordelijke Nederlanden voor de codificatie*. Amsterdam: N.V. Noord-Hollandsche Uitgevers, 1942.

Monti, A., "Le rôle et les pouvoirs du juge dans l'œuvre de Daniel Jousse", in: *Daniel Jousse. Un juriste au temps des Lumières (1704–1781)*. Limoges: Presses Universitaires de Limoges, 2007.

Moore, R.I., *The Formation of a Persecuting Society. Power and Deviance in Western Europe, 950–1250*. Oxford: Basil Blackwell, 1987.

Moorman van Kappen, O., "Uitwendige schets der wordingsgeschiedenis van het ontwerp-Lijfstraffelijk Wetboek 1804", in: *Samenwinninge. Tien opstellen over rechtsgeschiedenis geschreven ter gelegenheid van het tienjarig bestaan van het Interuniversitair Instituut Nederlands Centrum voor Rechtshistorische Documentatie*. Zwolle: Tjeenk Willink, 1977.

Moorman van Kappen, O., "Bijdrage tot de codificatiegeschiedenis van ons strafrecht rond het begin van de negentiende eeuw: het ontwerp-lijfstraffelijk wetboek van 1804", *BMGN*, 1978, vol. 93, pp. 299–323.

Moorman van Kappen, O., *De ontwerpen Lijfstraffelijk wetboek 1801 en 1804. Two volumes*. Zutphen: De Walburg Pers, 1982.

Moorman van Kappen, O., "Het Crimineel Wetboek voor het Koningrijk Holland van 1809 in het licht van zijn wordingsgeschiedenis", in: *Nederland in Franse schaduw: recht en bestuur in het Koninkrijk Holland (1806–1810)*. Hilversum: Verloren, 2006.

Mortel, H. van de, *Criminaliteit, rechtspleging en straf in het Hollandse drostambt Heusden*. Tilburg: Stichting Zuidelijk Historisch Contact, 2005.

Müller, M., *Misdaad en straf in een Hollandse stad: Haarlem, 1245–1615*. Hilversum: Verloren, 2017.

Myjer, E., *Van duimschroef naar bloedproef. Beschouwingen over de regel dat niemand gedwongen mag worden zichzelf te belasten*. Deventer: Kluwer, 1978.

Nicholas, D.M., "Crime and punishment in fourteenth-century Ghent", *Revue belge de Philosophie et d'Histoire*, 1970, pp. 289–334.

Nijboer, J.F., "Legaliteit en het strafrechtelijke bewijsrecht; uitholling van het wettelijk bewijsstelsel in strafzaken?", *Ars Aequi*, 2004, vol. 53, pp. 492–503.

Nijboer, J.F., *Strafrechtelijk bewijsrecht*. Nijmegen: Ars Aequi Libri, 2011.

Nobili, M., *Die freie richterliche Überzeugungsbildung: Reformdiskussion und Gesetzgebung in Italien, Frankreich, und Deutschland seit dem Ausgang des 18. Jahrhundert*. Baden-Baden: Nomos, 2001.

Noordziek, J.J.F., *Geschiedenis der beraadslagingen gevoerd in de tweede kamer der Staten-Generaal over het ontwerp Wetboek van Strafregt van 1827*. Den Haag: Nijhoff, 1883

Noordziek, J.J.F., *Geschiedenis der beraadslagingen gevoerd in de tweede kamer der Staten-Generaal over het ontwerp Wetboek van Strafvordering en het vraagstuk der jury 1828–1829*. Two volumes. Den Haag: Nijhoff, 1888.

Nörr, K.W., *Zur Stellung des Richters im gelehrten Prozess der Frühzeit: Iudex secundum allegata non secundum conscientiam iudicat*. München: C.H. Beck's Verlag, 1967.

Oddens, J., *Pioniers in Schaduwbeeld. Het eerste parlement van Nederland 1796–1798*. Nijmegen: Vantilt, 2012.

Overdijk, D.A.J., *De gewoonte is de beste uitleg van de wet. Een onderzoek naar de invloed van het Hof van Gelre en Zutphen op de rechtspleging in criminele zaken in het Kwartier van Nijmegen in de zeventiende en achttiende eeuw*. Nijmegen: Gerard Noodt Instituut, 1999.

Padoa-Schioppa, A., "I Philosophes e la giuria penale", in: *The Trial Jury in England, France, Germany 1700–1900*. Berlin: Dunkler & Humblot, 1987.

Padoa-Schioppa, A.,"Sur la conscience du juge dans le ius commune européen", in: *La conscience du juge dans la tradition juridique européenne*. Paris: Presse Universitaire de France, 1999, pp. 95–129.

Pasnau, R., "Medieval social epistemology: *Scientia* for mere mortals", *Episteme*, 2010, vol. 7, issue 1, pp. 23–41

Pasnau, R., "Science and Certainty", in: *Cambridge History of Medieval Philosophy*. Cambridge: Cambridge University Press, pp. 357–368.

Pihlajamaki, H., *Evidence, Crime and the Legal Profession. The Emergence of the Free Evaluation of the Evidence in Finnish Nineteenth-Century Criminal Procedure*. Lund : Institutet för rättshistorisk forskning, 1997.

Popkin, R., *The History of Scepticism. From Savonarola to Bayle*. Oxford: Oxford University Press, 2003.

Porteau-Bitker, A., en Talazac-Laurent, A., "La Renommée dans le Droit Pénal Laïque du XIIIe au XVe Siècle", *Médiévales*, 1993, vol. 24, pp. 67–80.

Ranouil, P.C., "L'intime Conviction", in: *Les destinées du jury criminelle*. Hellemmes : Hester, 1990.

Riskin, J., *Science in the age of sensibility. The sentimental empiricists of the French enlightenment*. Chicago: University of Chicago Press, 2002.

Rogall, K., *Der Beschuldigte als Beweismittel gegen sich selbst. Ein Beitrag zur Geltung des Satzes "Nemo tenetur seipsum prodere" im Strafprozess*. Berlin: Duncker und Humblot, 1977.

Rosendaal, J., *De Nederlandse Revolutie. Vrijheid, volk en vaderland 1783–1799*. Nijmegen: Vantilt, 2005.

Rosoni, I., *Quae singula non prosunt collecta iuvant: la teoria della prove indiziaria nell'età medievale e moderna*. Milan: Giuffre, 1995.

Ruller, S., "Franse strafwetgeving in Nederland", in: *Bijdragen tot de rechtsgeschiedenis van de negentiende eeuw: studiedag 1993*. Arnhem: Gouda Quint, 1994.

Ruller, S. van, and Faber, S., *Afdoening van strafzaken in Nederland sinds 1813: ontwikkelingen in wetgeving, beleid en praktijk*. Amsterdam: VU Uitgeverij, 1995.

Rutjes, M., *Door gelijkheid gegrepen: democratie, burgerschap en staat in Nederland 1795-1801*. Nijmegen: Vantilt, 2012.

Rutland, R.A., *The Birth of the Bill of Rights 1776-1791*. Chapel Hill: The University of North Carolina Press, 1962.

Sabadell da Silva, A.L., *Tormenta juris permissione. Folter und Strafverfahren auf der iberischen Halbinsel: dargestellt am Beispiel Kastiliens und Kataloniens (16.-18. Jahrhundert)*. Berlin: Dunker und Humblot, 2002.

Sas, N. van, "Het politiek klimaat in Noord-Nederland tijdens de crisis van het Verenigd Koninkrijk, 1828-1830", in *Colloquium over de geschiedenis van de Belgisch-Nederlandse betrekkingen tusen 1815 en 1945*. Gent: Erasmus, 1982.

Sas, N. van, *De metamorfose van Nederland: van oude orde naar moderniteit, 1750-1900*. Amsterdam: Amsterdam University Press, 2004.

Scattola, M., "Before and after natural law. Models of Natural Law in Ancient and Modern Times", in: Hochstrasser, T.J., and Schröder, P., *Early Modern Natural Law Theories – Context and Strategies in the Early Enlightenment*. Deventer: Kluwer Academic Publishers, 2003.

Schlosser, H., Sprandel R., en Willoweit, D., ed., *Herrschaftliches Strafen seit dem Hochmittelalter*. Cologne: Böhlau Verlag, 2002.

Schlosser, H., *Neuere europäische Rechtsgeschichte: Privat- und Strafrecht vom Mittelalter bis zur Moderne*. München: Beck Verlag, 2012.

Schmidt, E., *Einführung in die Geschichte der deutschen Strafrechtspflege*. Göttingen: Vandenhoeck & Ruprecht, 1965.

Schmidt, S., *Die Abhandlung von der Criminal-Gesetzgebung von Hans Ernst von Globig und Johann Georg Huster*. Berlin: Dunker und Humblot, 1990.

Schmoeckel, M., *Humanität und Staatsraison: die Abschaffung der Folter in Europa und die Entwicklung des gemeinen Strafprozess- und Beweisrechts seit dem hohen Mittelalter*. Cologne: Böhlau, 2000.

Schnapper, B., "Les Peines Arbitraires du XIIIe au XVIIIe Siècle (Doctrines Savantes et usages Français)", *Tijdschrift voor Rechtsgeschiedens*, 1973, vol. 41, pp. 237-277 and 1974, vol. 42, pp. 42-81.

Schnapper, B., "Testes Inhabiles. Les Témoins Reprochables dans L'ancien Droit Pénal", *Tijdschrift voor Rechtsgeschiedens*, 1965, vol. 33, issue 4, pp. 576-616.

Schnapper, B., "Le jury français aux XIX et XXème siècles", in: *The Trial Jury in England, France, Germany 1700-1900*. Berlin: Dunkler & Humblot, 1987.

Schnapper, B., "La diffusion en France des nouvelles conceptions pénales dans la dernière décennie de l'ancien régime", in: *Voies nouvelles en histoire du droit : la justice, la famille, la répression pénale (XVIème–XXème siècles)*. Paris : Presses Universitaires de France, 1991.

Schrader, W.H., "Naturrecht und Selbsterhaltung: Spinoza und Hobbes", *Zeitschrift für philosophische Forschung*, 1977, vol. 31, pp. 574–583.

Schwinge, E., *Der Kampf um die Schwurgerichte bis zur Frankfurter Nationalversammlung*. Breslau: Schletter, 1926.

Shapiro, B.J., *Probability and Certainty in Seventeenth-century England. A study of the relationships between Natural Science, Religion, History, Law and Literature*. Princeton: Princeton University Press, 1983.

Shapiro, B.J., "'To a Moral Certainty': Theories of Knowledge and Anglo-American Juries 1600–1850", *Hastings Law Journal*, 1986, vol. 38, pp. 153–193.

Shapiro, B., *"Beyond reasonable doubt" and "probable cause". Historical perspectives on the Anglo-American Law of Evidence*. Berkeley: University of California Press, 1991.

Shapiro, I., *The Evolution of Rights in Liberal Theory*. Cambridge: Cambridge University Press, 1986.

Shoemaker, K.B., "Criminal Procedure in Medieval European Law. A Comparison Between English and Roman-Canonical Developments after the IV Laterean Council", in *Zeitschrift der Savigny-Stiftung für Rechtsgeschichte, kanonistische Abteilung*, 1999, vol. 116, pp. 174–202.

Smidt, J.Th., and Huussen, A.H., *Bronnen van de Nederlandse codificatie sinds 1798 I*. Utrecht: Kemink, 1968.

Smith, H.E., "The Modern Privilege: Its Nineteenth-Century Origins", in: *The Privilege against Self-Incrimination: its Origins and Development*. Chicago: University of Chicago Press, 1997.

Smits, A., *1830. Scheuring in de Nederlanden*. Brugge: Uitgeverij Wiek Op, 1950.

Spierenburg, P., *The spectacle of suffering: executions and the evolution of repression: from a preindustrial metropolis to the European experience*. Cambridge: Cambridge University Press, 1984.

Stern, L.I., "Public Fame in the Fifteenth Century", *The American Journal of Legal History*, 2000, vol. 44, pp. 198–222.

Stevens, L., *Het nemo-teneturbeginsel in strafzaken: van zwijgrecht naar containerbegrip*. Nijmegen: Wolf Legal Publishers, 2005.

Stichweh, R., "Zur Subjektivierung der Entscheidungsfindung im Deutschen Strafprozess des 19. Jahrhunderts", in: *Subjektivierung des justiziellen Beweisverfahrens: Beiträge zum Zeugenbeweis in Europa und den USA (18.–20. Jahrhundert)*. Frankfurt am Main: Vittorio Klostermann, 1994.

Tierney, B., *The Idea Of Natural Right. Studies on Natural Rights, Natural Law, and Church Law, 1150–1625*. Atlanta: Scholars Press, 1997.

Thäle, B., *Die Verdachtsstrafe in der kriminalwissenschaftlichen Literatur des 18. und 19. Jahrhunderts*. Frankfurt Am Main: P. Lang, 1993.

Thuijs, F., *Op zoek naar de ware Jaco: Jacob Frederik Muller, alias Jaco (1690–1718), zijn criminele wereld, zijn berechting en de mythe na zijn dood*. Hilversum: Verloren, 2008.

Tripels, G., "Is wijziging van de regelen over het bewijs in strafzaken wenschelijk? Zoo ja, in hoever moet het wettelijke bewijs worden behouden?", *Handelingen der Nederlandsche Juristen-vereeniging*, 1882, pp. 142–166.

Trusen, W., "Der Inquisitionsprozess. Seine historischen Grundlagen und frühen Formen", *Zeitschrift der Savigny-Stiftung für Rechtsgeschichte* 1988, vol. 77, pp. 168–230.

Tuck, R., "The 'modern' theory of natural law", in: *The languages of political theory in early-modern Europe*. Cambridge: Cambridge University Press, 1987.

Tully, J., *An approach to political philosophy: Locke in context*. Cambridge: Cambridge University Press, 1993.

Ulrich, D., "La répression en Bourgogne au XVIIIe siècle", *Revue historique de droit Français et étranger*, 1972, vol. 50, pp. 398–437.

Vallerani, M., *Medieval public justice*. Washington D.C.: Catholic University of America Press, 2012.

Veen, T.J., and Kop, P.C., *Zestig juristen: bijdragen tot een beeld van de geschiedenis der Nederlandse Rechtswetenschap*. Zwolle: Tjeenk Willink, 1987.

Vielfaure, P., *L'évolution du droit pénal sous la monarchie du juillet. Entre exigences politiques et interrogations de société*. Aix-en-Provence : Presses universitaires d'Aix-Marseilles, 2001.

Vrugt, M. van de, *De criminele ordonnantiën van 1570: enkele beschouwingen over de eerste strafrechtcodificatie in de Nederlanden*. Zutphen: De Walburg Pers, 1978.

Wadle, E., "Zur Delegitimierung der Fehde", in: *Herrschaftliches Strafen seit dem Hochmittelalter*. Cologne: Böhlau Verlag, 2002.

Warmelo, P. van, "Van der Keessel en Beccaria", *Tijdschrift voor Rechtsgeschiedenis*, 1967, vol. 35, pp. 573–583.

Weel, A.J. van, "De strafvonnissen van de Haagse Vierschaar in de periode 1700–1811", *Jaarboek die Haghe*, 1984, pp. 135–189.

Westerman, P.C., *The disintegration of natural law theory*. Leiden: Brill, 1998.

Wettstein, E.J., *Der Öffentlichkeitsgrundsatz im Strafprozess*. Zürich: Schulthess, 1966.

Willeumier, C.M.J., "Is wijziging van de regelen over het bewijs in strafzaken wenschelijk? Zoo ja, in hoever moet het wettelijk bewijs worden behouden?", *Handelingen der Nederlandsche Juristen-vereeniging*, 1882, pp. 100–141.

Willoweit, D., ed., *Die Entstehung des öffentlichen Strafrechts*. Cologne: Böhlau Verlag, 1999.

Witt, J.F., "Making the Fifth: The Constitutionalization of American Self-Incrimination doctrine 1791–1903", *Texas Law Review* 825 (1999), pp. 825–922.

Whitman, J.Q., *The origins of reasonable doubt: theological roots of the criminal trial.* New Haven: Yale University Press, 2008.

Wohlers, W., *Entstehung und Funktion der Staatsanwaltschaft: ein Beitrag zu den rechtshistorischen und strukturellen Grundlagen des reformierten Strafverfahrens.* Berlin: Dunker und Humblot, 1994.

Zanten, J. van, *Schielijk, Winzucht, Zwaarhoofd en Bedaard. Politieke discussie en oppositievorming 1813–1840.* Amsterdam: Wereldbibliotheek, 2004.

Subject Index

Absolutio ab instantia 54, 153–155, 273–275, 358–360
Accusatorial procedure 30–31, 36–37, 229
Arbitrium 67, 260, 267, 274–275
Aristotelian philosophy 10, 41, 88–95
Austria 183, 191–192, 237

Bavaria 183, 191–193, 234–236, 241

Cahiers de doléances 145
Calas-affaire 86, 127, 153
Code d'instruction criminelle 119, 162–168, 343, 380–381
Confession 43–45, 269–273, 354
Conservatives 119, 171–173, 269–270
Consilia 265
Constitutio Criminalis Carolina 181–182, 263–264
Conviction intime 109–113, 152–158, 402, 431, 471, 477, 496
Conviction raissonnée 113–115, 209–213, 471, 477, 496
Criminal Ordinances of 1570 249–255

Epistemological discourse 88–115, 492–497
Extraordinary punishments 53–54, 153–155, 187–189, 232–233, 273–275, 358–360

Forensic sciences 108, 518–520
Fourth Lateran Council 30–31
Freedom of the press 171–172, 226–227, 411–421
Friesland 250, 258, 284

Groningen 319–321, 335

Holland 256–258, 262, 269–270, 322–324, 368

Indicia 46–49, 183–188, 223–224, 354–357, 365, 438–440, 484–485
Inquisitorial procedure 31–36, 81, 229

Judicial torture 52–53, 79–81, 122–124, 183–190, 259–266, 290–297, 337–340

Jury system 83–88, 146–153, 205–207, 234–237, 332–336, 409–436

Liberals 119, 171–179, 205–207, 410–421, 450–451

Ministerial responsibility 411–421
Moral certainty 99–104
Motivation of the verdict 218–221, 443–444, 461–467, 479, 484–485

Natural law 67–70, 295–301
Negative system of legal proofs 1, 196–216, 404–409, 436–444, 454–461
Nemo tenetur-principle 77–83, 233–234, 444–445, 486

Ordeals 27–34

Penology 6–8, 13–14, 58–61, 504–506
Peace- and truce of God movement 34–35
Political-constitutional discourse 67–87, 497–501
Presumption of innocence 76–79, 145, 233

Rheinischen Immediat-Justiz-Kommission 201–205, 390–392, 399
Prussia 190–192, 218–220, 236

Schepenen 279
Schöffengerichten 240–242
Schout 279
Social reputation 49–50, 251, 275
Social contract theories 70–74, 297–303
Spinhuis 281
System of legal proofs 38–42, 120–122, 181–183, 247–278

Totaleindruck 203–204

Utrecht 257–258

Witch trials 291
Witness testimony 45–46, 354–355, 440–443

Author Index

Aansorgh 370–371
Alessi Palazzolo 57
Amalry 302–304
Asser 405

Bartlett 32
Beattie 79
Beccaria 102, 129–130, 141, 170, 289, 298–304, 308, 370, 473, 505
Bergasse 132
Berger 161–162
Bort 257, 262, 270
Bossers 3, 380–387
Boven, Van 378–380
Brissot de Warville 132–134

Caenegem, Van 35, 50
Calkoen 307–313, 371–373
Carpzov 181–182, 249
Cras 351–358
Condorcet 138

Damaška 58, 515–518
Damhouder, De 249–252
Daston 94
Delolme 130
De Bosch Kemper 455–457, 465
De Brouckere 112, 434–435
De Pinto 458–459, 465, 472
De Secus 426, 429–430
Den Tex 403–404
Donker Curtius 404–405, 426, 430–431
Donovan 171–174
Dreissen 3, 443, 462–463
Dupaty 136–138
Duport 110, 147–151

Elout 351–358, 363
Eisenhart 187–188

Faber 59, 279
Feuerbach 189, 197–201, 226
Fraher 32
Filangieri 104, 352–355
Foucault 42, 520
Frederick the Great 190–191

Gandinus 48
Garland 13
Glaser 204
Globig and Huster 102–103, 184–185
Gmelin 182
Gneist, Von 222
Graevius 291–292
Grotius 69

Hacking 94–96
Hamelsveld, Van 399
Hegel 206–207
Hobbes 70–71

Ignor 5, 182, 243

Jarcke 209–210
Jongstra 475–481
Jousse 142–143
Justi, Von 195

Kant 73–74
Keessel, Van der 261–264, 313–316, 376–377
Kleinschrod 185–186
Köstlin 221–222
Kuhn 5
Küper 213–215

Lepsius 56
Lévy 43–44
Leyser 182
Locke 71, 88–89
Luzac 433
Landau 240–241
Langbein 8–9, 55–62
Leeuwen, Van 257, 262, 269
Lepsius 56
Lévy 88–89, 401
Louis Napoleon 362–367

Maanen, Van 366, 415–420
Marat 131–132
Matthaeus 264, 275–278
Meer Mohr, Van der 397–398
Meister the younger 185
Meulen, Van der 257–258

Meyer 112, 391–398
Michels 187, 191, 215
Mittermaier 189, 210–213, 234
Modderman 113–114, 475–481
Möhl 217–218, 229
Monballyu 252–256
Montesquieu 84, 126, 156, 289, 352
Muyart de Vouglans 141–142

Napoleon 165–167
Nothomb 416

Ortloff 240
Overdijk 258, 283

Padoa-Schioppa 106, 139
Pasnau 90–91
Pihlajamäki 9, 15, 60, 221–222
Planck 240
Popkin 94
Potter, De 417–418
Pufendorf 71–72

Rappard, Van 401–403
Reinar 300–301
Robespierre 148–154
Rosoni 57
Rousseau 72–73, 129

Savigny, Von 113, 218–221, 480
Schmidt 35
Schmoeckel 57, 65, 77, 290
Schnapper 46, 125–126, 141
Schomaker 265
Servan 130, 134–136
Shapiro 92–94
Soden 195
Sonnenfels 301–302
Stichweh 107, 210

Thouret 111, 151–152
Thuijs 271
Tronchet 148–153
Turgot 138

Vallerani 50, 37–38
Vezin 188–189
Vielfaure 170
Vives 290
Voltaire 127–128, 184
Voorda 317–319

Weiland 405–409
Wielant 249–253
Witt, De 301–302
Wittichius 296

Printed in the United States
By Bookmasters